THE RISE OF THOMAS CROMWELL

THE RISE OF
THOMAS
CROMWELL

POWER AND POLITICS IN THE REIGN
OF HENRY VIII

MICHAEL EVERETT

YALE UNIVERSITY PRESS
NEW HAVEN AND LONDON

For information about this and other Yale University Press publications, please contact:

U.S. Office: sales.press@yale.edu   www.yalebooks.com
Europe Office: sales@yaleup.co.uk   www.yalebooks.co.uk

Typeset in Adobe Caslon Pro by IDSUK (DataConnection) Ltd
Printed in Great Britain by TJ International Ltd, Padstow, Cornwall

Library of Congress Control Number: 2015932999

ISBN 978-0-300-20742-2

A catalogue record for this book is available from the British Library.

10 9 8 7 6 5 4 3 2 1

CONTENTS

ILLUSTRATIONS

NOTE ON CITATIONS, TRANSCRIPTIONS
AND DATES

IN ORDER TO PRESERVE something of the flavour of the sixteenth century for the reader, I have elected not to modernise the English of the original documents consulted. In quotations from manuscripts, therefore, all spelling, punctuation and capitalisation are generally as they appear in the original, although abbreviations have been silently expanded. For convenience, however, I have converted Roman numerals to Arabic numerals when transcribing currency.

The folio references to SP1 and SP2 in The National Archives, Public Record Office refer to the printed folio number on each page. Information contained in any parentheses after a manuscript reference refers to a printed volume in which the manuscript is calendared or transcribed in full.

All dates are in the old style but the year has been taken as beginning on 1 January.

PREFACE

THOMAS CROMWELL HAS BECOME rather fashionable in recent years, thanks in no small part to the novels of Hilary Mantel. Yet my interest in Cromwell started well before he became the subject of popular attention. I first encountered him when, as a sixth-former, I read the works of the late Sir Geoffrey Elton. It was Elton's powerful and articulate arguments that first captured my interest in the reign of Henry VIII, and in Thomas Cromwell in particular. In a string of great works, including *The Tudor Revolution in Government* (1953), *England under the Tudors* (1955) and *Reform and Reformation* (1977), Cromwell was portrayed as a man of incredible vision during a revolutionary decade in English history. It was only when I came to study history at university, and started to scrutinise the sources for myself, that I began to doubt Elton's portrayal of Cromwell as the most remarkable figure of the sixteenth century. An undergraduate dissertation on the minister confirmed my impression that the sources would not support the weight of interpretation that Elton had often placed on them; and it was to my great regret that I found Cromwell to have been a very different man from the one presented in Elton's writings. When I later decided that I would like to do a PhD, and spoke to my potential supervisor, George Bernard, it was he who suggested that I return to Cromwell as a topic. At first I was somewhat hesitant. There was certainly no shortage of works on Cromwell, and I wondered whether I would be able to contribute much to such a well-trodden area. It was only when I followed my supervisor's advice, and started working my way through *Letters and Papers of the Reign of Henry VIII*, that I began to realise that no one had quite got to the bottom of Cromwell's early work for Henry, or satisfactorily explained how the son of a Putney brewer rose to become the most powerful man in England after the king. Such an intriguing question surely deserved a proper answer.

When I first began to contemplate writing a study of Cromwell's early political career, a biographical approach seemed a fitting way to attempt it. Such an approach, I reasoned, would allow a variety of themes to be examined concurrently, thereby helping to avoid the (to my mind) one-dimensional studies of Cromwell that have sometimes emerged when writers have focused on a single aspect of his career. Elton himself, of course, famously never wrote a biography of Cromwell. This was mainly due to Elton's hostility to biography as an acceptable form of history. As he once put it,

> The limits of one man's life rarely have any meaning in the interpreta-
> tion of history ... However influential he may have been, no individual
> has ever dominated his age to the point where it becomes sensible to
> write its history purely around him.[1]

But Elton's refusal to write a biography specifically of Cromwell also owed something to his belief that Cromwell himself was not 'biographable' because the historical record is so silent on the first thirty years of his life.[2] To a considerable extent, I am actually inclined to agree with Elton on both points. Although in recent years there has been a reclaiming of biography by academic scholars, many of the qualities that make a good biography do not necessarily make good history.[3] History, it is often argued, is about 'much more than the lives of individuals; it is about the study of political, social, economic and intellectual movements that are much more than the sum of those involved in them'.[4] Of course, history should also involve placing the lives of ministers and statesmen in context, 'so that a distinctive political culture may be interpreted through the study of one individual'.[5] But a biography must give considerable attention to its subject's personal life, private relationships and leisure activities. This is essential in presenting a well-rounded picture of a person, yet it is not always clear what, if any, historical significance these things might carry.

When studying the political environment of the late medieval and early modern period, however, a time when the nature of court politics often conflated the public and the private, a biographical *approach* can prove more rewarding. If this is conducted thematically, but within a broad chronological framework, a study of an individual's public activities can be placed alongside a study of their relevant personal and private concerns. This complements the political structures of the early sixteenth century, while also ensuring that a more analytical reconstruction of an individual's life and career is given. In short, by adopting a methodology which embraces the culture in which Cromwell's early political career developed, a much more accurate reflection of the minister can be drawn.

In regard to Elton's second, specific objection – that Cromwell himself is not 'biographable' – I have greater sympathy, although not quite for the reason which Elton gave. While it is true that there is little evidence for Cromwell's earliest life, there is actually a good deal of evidence for his activities during the 1520s. Very few historians have given this period of Cromwell's life much consideration. Yet this surely needs exploring if a proper assessment of his career during the 1530s is to be made. A far more challenging problem facing a biographer of Cromwell is the lack of evidence which sheds light specifically on his inner life and character. Quite remarkably, although over 350 of Cromwell's own letters have survived, these reveal frustratingly little of what he was really like as a person, and fail to offer much that could provide a basis for psychological insights.[6] Consequently, Cromwell's personality must be inferred from his actions and work, which, as Elton once noted, is not the most satisfactory way of understanding anyone's psychology.[7]

Ironically, however, perhaps the greatest impediment to a worthy biography of Cromwell is not the lack of sources but rather the abundance of them. There are hundreds – possibly thousands – of surviving letters which were sent to him during the 1530s; and I have serious doubt as to whether a single volume could do justice to such a rich archive. Any attempt at reconstructing Cromwell's ministry during that decade would therefore need to be either highly selective or extremely cursory. It was partly for that reason that I felt a sharper focus on Cromwell's early career and rise to power would be fruitful, as it would enable areas of seemingly mundane work, which could not have been considered in a study of his entire career, to be examined in much greater detail. I should perhaps point out here that although this book could certainly fit into a two-volume study of Cromwell, it is not envisaged as such. It was and is intended to stand alone.

In writing this book I have incurred a good deal of debts which I am now pleased to recognise. First, I would like to thank the Arts and Humanities

Research Council and the University of Southampton for generously awarding me a three-year scholarship which enabled me to undertake the research on which this book is based. Second, I wish to thank the staff at the many archives that I have had the pleasure of visiting, especially The National Archives, the British Library, Westminster Abbey Muniments and the Worshipful Company of Drapers. I am also grateful to his Grace the Duke of Devonshire for allowing me to consult the Bolton Abbey Manuscript. A particular word of thanks similarly needs to go to Janet Dickinson, whose course on the Henrician Reformation I took while an undergraduate at Southampton, and who encouraged me a good deal more in my early historical endeavours than I suspect she realises. Paul Cavill, the external examiner of my thesis, offered many helpful comments on an earlier version of this book, and has continued to remain encouraging of my efforts. Martin Heale, Mark Stoyle and Joan Tumblety also kindly read and commented on various chapters of this book, while Philip Ward and Mary Robertson were both good enough to share their own views on Cromwell with me. I am also grateful to Robert Baldock, Candida Brazil, Tami Halliday and Rachael Lonsdale at Yale University Press for putting this book through the press, and for guiding a first-time author through the publishing process.

Without doubt, however, my greatest intellectual debt goes to George Bernard. It was he who first suggested that I return to Cromwell as a topic, and he has remained a constant source of sound support and sage advice ever since. More importantly, his ever-questioning approach to the history of the sixteenth century – never accepting anything on orthodoxy alone – has been truly inspirational. He has read and commented on every draft of this book, and it is immeasurably better thanks to his advice, thoughts and encouragement.

A final, heartfelt note of thanks naturally goes to my family. My parents have been a tremendous source of support and encouragement throughout my life, while my wife Clarissa has had the patience and understanding to put up with someone absorbed in the reign of Henry VIII. No doubt she is relieved that this book is finally finished. It is dedicated in loving gratitude to her.

INTRODUCTION

THIS BOOK IS A study of Thomas Cromwell's early political career, specifically, his rise to power. Although it adopts a biographical approach, in the sense that it examines a man's early life and public career, it is not a full biography. Instead, it considers Cromwell's greatly neglected life and activities before he entered Henry VIII's service, then focuses on his political career under the king during the early 1530s, and ends with his appointment as the king's secretary in April 1534. By examining all of Cromwell's activities during these years, and not only those which supposedly prefigure his later life and work, this book offers a reinterpretation, not only of Cromwell himself, but also of the nature of politics at the Henrician court.

Who was Thomas Cromwell?

Thomas Cromwell (*c*.1485–1540) was the son of a Putney blacksmith and brewer who rose to become Henry VIII's chief minister throughout much of the 1530s. During that momentous decade Cromwell played a key role at the heart of government, amassing a considerable collection of offices and positions. Having acquired legal expertise in his early life and working as Cardinal Wolsey's legal fixer in the mid-1520s, Cromwell entered the king's service in 1530. By April 1532 he had been made master of the king's jewels, and this was soon followed by his appointments as keeper or clerk of the hanaper in July 1532; chancellor of the exchequer in April 1533; and finally principal secretary in April 1534.[1] Following this meteoric rise, which is the subject of this book, Cromwell then became master of the rolls in October 1534;[2] vicegerent in spirituals in early 1535;[3] lord privy seal in July 1536;[4] and earl of Essex and great chamberlain in April 1540.[5] For almost ten years, therefore, Cromwell was at the centre of some of the most significant events in English history. He helped steer through the legislative changes which enabled the break with Rome, masterminded the dissolution of the monasteries and oversaw the union between England and Wales. Cromwell's ministry also witnessed the implementation of parish registers in 1538, ensuring for the first time that all births, marriages and deaths in England and Wales were recorded. He was similarly instrumental in the production of the Bible in English, a notable cultural landmark, as well as a religious one. As one historian has put it, Thomas Cromwell was a royal minister 'who cut a deeper mark on the history of England than have many of her monarchs'.[6] His spectacular political career was then followed by an equally spectacular fall. In mid-1540, quite suddenly and without warning, Cromwell was arrested and charged with treason. He was beheaded on Tower Hill on 28 July.

Unsurprisingly, given the role that he occupied in such a formative decade, Cromwell has already received considerable attention from historians. Yet what is striking about many existing studies is that all too often one particular aspect of Cromwell's life or career is emphasised, and then used to interpret or explain everything else. The earliest, and in recent years most influential, interpretation of Cromwell was the one put forward by the Elizabethan historian and martyrologist John Foxe. In his *Acts and Monuments*, first published in 1563, Cromwell was the 'valiaunt Souldier and captayne of Christe' who, driven by his zeal to 'set forwarde the truthe of the Gospel', sought 'all meanes and wayes to beate down false Religion and to aduaunce the true'.[7] Foxe's Cromwell was a figure entirely motivated by his religious faith: 'His whole life was nothing els, but a continuall care and trauaile how to aduaunce & further the right knowledge of the Gospell, and reforme the house of God'.[8] It was an attitude that continued to find advocates among some late sixteenth-, seventeenth- and eighteenth-century writers. Raphael Holinshed also thought Cromwell 'a fauorer to the gospell, and an enimie to the pride of prelates'.[9] Gilbert Burnet, in his *History of the Reformation*, similarly argued that Cromwell 'did promote the Reformation very vigorously' and was 'certain he was a Lutheran'.[10] Other writers, however, were becoming less certain of Cromwell's religious affiliation. Jeremy Collier, writing at the beginning of the eighteenth century, readily acknowledged that 'Cromwell was no papist at his death: but then, it is pretty plain, he was no Protestant neither'.[11]

'Whig' historians of the nineteenth century, eager to emphasise English constitutional progress, had a curious attitude towards Cromwell. On the one hand the methods he employed, which were seen as ruthless and destructive, were despised; but on the other, there was a grudging admiration for the necessity of the political and religious changes that he helped bring about. J. A. Froude, for instance, believed that Cromwell had been 'the most despotic minister who had ever governed England', with a 'long list of solemn tragedies . . . upon his memory'.[12] And yet,

> He had taken upon himself a task beyond the ordinary strength of man . . . He pursued an object, the excellence of which, as his mind saw it, transcended all other considerations – the freedom of England and the destruction of idolatry: and those who from any motive, noble or base, pious or impious, crossed his path, he crushed, and passed on over their bodies.[13]

Arthur Galton was another who argued that as 'a minister of destruction Cromwell is almost without an equal in history'. When, however, the causes and results of this destruction were examined 'we see how wise and necessary his policy was'.[14] The Reverend James Ellis was even more fulsome in his praise, claiming that Cromwell had been 'a patient, practical, far-seeing statesman'.[15]

> The fact that here in England the changes that rent other nations into antagonistic sections were comparatively peaceful is largely due to his genius . . . undoubtedly he sometimes stooped to crooked methods of policy. But there is so much lacking to enable us to judge adequately of his policy, that it is wise to believe that did we know the secret forces that acted behind and around him we might perhaps forgive if we could not justify what we now deplore.[16]

By the early twentieth century the majority of historians had come to see Cromwell as an entirely secular figure. In 1902 R. B. Merriman put forward what has proven to be another resilient interpretation of Cromwell, that of a Machiavellian schemer. Merriman claimed that Cromwell possessed an 'utter lack of emotion' in everything he did, and totally disregarded the 'justness or morality of any action'.[17] It was such characteristics that enabled him 'to tick off in his memoranda the lives of human beings, as if they were items in an account'.[18] Merriman's Cromwell was corrupt, greedy and materialistic, with no concern for religion: 'Catholicism and Protestantism passed over his head; he was not touched by either of them'.[19] It was a view shared by many of Merriman's contemporaries. A. D. Innes claimed Cromwell to have been 'the most passionless figure' in English history, who cared 'not a straw' for any religious dispute of the time.[20] Peter Wilding was another who argued that for Cromwell 'God . . . was just a good idea; his prophet was Machiavelli; his bible was *The Prince*. He was in fact as near to being an atheist as any man has ever been.'[21] In a similar vein, A. F. Pollard, the foremost Tudor historian for much of the early twentieth century, saw little to commend Cromwell. Pollard claimed Henry VIII to be the leading figure of his reign, and argued that Cromwell did little more than enable the king's march towards despotism.[22]

These interpretations, despite the occasional dissenting voice, remained the overwhelming view of Cromwell for almost fifty years.[23] In 1948, however, this orthodoxy began to be challenged, and Cromwell once again came to be seen in a more favourable light. In that year Geoffrey Elton completed a study of Cromwell's administrative work in government, and would soon go on to argue that Cromwell was the architect of a 'revolution' in the way that government was structured, as well as being the man who laid the foundations of a 'modern' nation-state in England. Elton's most influential work, *The Tudor Revolution in Government*, appeared in 1953, building on the findings of his doctoral research. In it he argued that Cromwell deliberately replaced the existing medieval household system of government with the beginnings of a 'modern' structure of bureaucratic departments.[24] Central to this revolution was a reorganised and reconfigured Privy Council, which Elton claimed was given a permanent and fixed membership by Cromwell in the mid-1530s, and overall control of all other government departments. This thesis generated considerable debate among historians. A lengthy argument played out on the pages of *Past and Present* between Elton, Gerald Harriss, Penry Williams and J. P Cooper,[25] while some of Elton's own students also sought to reassess the novelty of the administrative changes he professed.[26] Nevertheless, Elton defended and continued to expand his interpretation of Cromwell throughout his academic career, arguing that the minister was not only an innovative political reformer, but also a social, economic and religious one.[27]

But Elton's Cromwell was as singularly driven as Foxe's Protestant hero. Cromwell's purpose, according to Elton, was 'to remake and renew the body politic of England'.[28] He was no despotic or Machiavellian politician, but rather 'England's first parliamentary statesman', utilising statute law as the weapon of this transformation.[29] Cromwell was not erecting a tyranny, but instead a polity governed by a partnership between king and parliament.[30] Moreover, 'Cromwell, not Henry, was really the government'.[31] The king had 'an unoriginal and unproductive mind';[32] it was Cromwell who 'instigated and in part accomplished a major and enduring transformation in virtually every aspect of the nation's public life'.[33] While many later historians have since challenged or modified Elton's 'revolution' in government thesis, his assertion that Cromwell was the innovative force and dominant partner in the relationship between king and minster has become the standard view held by the majority of historians ever since.

And yet, while Cromwell continues to feature heavily in narratives of the 1530s, only a handful of historians have examined him as an individual since Elton. Mary Robertson wrote a PhD thesis on Cromwell's household, as well as articles on his landed estates and management of the localities.[34] Philip Ward has also written a detailed doctoral thesis on Cromwell's work for Cardinal Wolsey, which goes some way towards redressing the imbalanced focus on Cromwell in the 1530s.[35] Yet there has been nothing resembling a serious academic book on Cromwell since the short biographies by Neville Williams and B. W. Beckingsale, published in 1975 and 1978 respectively.[36] Neither of these historians substantially questioned Elton's views. Nor did they consult many original documents, instead relying almost exclusively on the calendared (and sometimes inaccurate) summaries of the State Papers given in *Letters and Papers of the Reign of Henry VIII*. More recently, however, the success of Hilary Mantel's novels, *Wolf Hall* and *Bring Up the Bodies*, has rekindled wider interest in Cromwell.[37] This has resulted in several new biographies, including Robert Hutchinson's *Thomas Cromwell: The Rise and Fall of Henry VIII's Most Notorious Minister*, which again reinstates Cromwell rather one-dimensionally as a sinister and unscrupulous politician.[38] Although such books often offer accessible accounts, they are largely – if not exclusively – based on printed sources, and offer little in the way of fresh interpretations.

Indeed, the most significant scholarly interpretation of Cromwell since Elton came as far back as 1959. In that year A. G. Dickens published *Thomas Cromwell and the English Reformation*, which resurrected Foxe's Protestant hero, and again argued that Cromwell had been one of the principal guiding forces of the Reformation during the 1530s.[39] This has been followed in more recent years by the emergence of a considerable consensus among historians, who now tend to agree that Cromwell was indeed a committed and driven evangelical.[40] Even Elton, who in his earlier work had dismissed claims that Cromwell was a Protestant as 'demonstrably wrong',[41] modified his view, and later presented him as a religious reformer.[42] This revival of Cromwell as a committed Protestant neatly fitted with the interpretation of factional struggles at the Henrician Court, which has proved equally popular among many more recent historians. For David Starkey, Cromwell was 'a supreme master of the bloody game of faction politics' and leader of an evangelical group at court.[43] John Guy also saw Cromwell as an increasingly important member of the reformist faction battling for control in 1532.[44] Proponents of the factional interpretation of Tudor politics usually present Cromwell as having pushed the king towards an ever more Protestant religious policy. Susan Brigden typifies this approach when arguing that Cromwell 'insistently led the king towards reform in religion more radical than the king could countenance'.[45] Guy also believed Cromwell to have been 'the driving force behind the Reformation in the 1530s' and that he 'steered the Reformation beyond the point the king decided was expedient'.[46] Other historians have argued that Cromwell took risks promoting and protecting religious radicals in England and Calais,[47] while the entry for Cromwell in the *Oxford Dictionary of National Biography* states that he possessed 'genuine evangelical convictions' and 'persistently encouraged Henry to consider evangelical reforms'.[48]

Previous historians have therefore interpreted Thomas Cromwell in a variety of seemingly conflicting forms – as an evangelical reformer, as a Machiavellian politician, as an administrative and constitutional genius, or as a prominent player in factional politics. More often than not, proponents of each of these views have seen the one they favour as key to an understanding of Cromwell; and in doing so they often leave a narrow, almost one-dimensional interpretation of the minister. The approach adopted for this study is, in part, an attempt to offer a more rounded picture.

Reassessing Cromwell's Rise

Despite the considerable attention that Cromwell has received from historians, surprisingly few have been interested in his early life and career. The chief area of historical interest has always been Cromwell in the 1530s, and the majority of historians have tended to concentrate on the years beyond

1534. This is certainly understandable. The 1530s was one of the most revolutionary periods in English history, and many of its most formative events – the dissolution of the monasteries, wider religious change, possibly a 'revolution' in government – all of which Cromwell was closely involved with, occurred during the second half of that decade. Nevertheless, Cromwell was probably in his mid-forties when he entered Henry VIII's service. The fact that there has been little serious investigation into his background, activities and experiences for what was the vast majority of Cromwell's life remains surprising. Existing books on Cromwell treat the years before 1534, and certainly before 1530, as little more than a prelude to his ministry and years of ascendancy. This book adopts a different approach, ending in 1534 with Cromwell's appointment as the king's secretary. This is because Cromwell's early life and career have their own intrinsic value and are worthy of study in their own right. In particular, looking closely at the years 1531–1534 enables a reappraisal of much of the seemingly mundane material surrounding Cromwell and his work that scholars have passed over as insignificant. Doing so not only transforms our understanding of his early career, particularly the manner of his rise, but it also prompts us to rethink assumptions about his later years.

Previous accounts of Cromwell's rise to power, in keeping with interpretations of him more generally, have usually placed tremendous significance on one particular aspect of his work: Henry VIII's break with Rome.[49] By contrast, the numerous other tasks that occupied Cromwell during the years 1531–1534 have been largely neglected. True, in his earliest work, Elton did emphasise the importance of Cromwell's wider administrative hack-work when briefly discussing how he became a prominent councillor.[50] But above all, Elton saw Cromwell as 'the man behind' the break with Rome, and believed that his revolutionary ideas about sovereignty had enabled it.[51] According to Elton, this was crucial in Cromwell's securing the king's confidence and emerging as Henry VIII's chief minister.[52] Subsequent historians, keen to emphasise Cromwell's religious convictions, have presented him as the leader of a reformist group that championed the ideas of 'empire' underpinning the break with Rome, thereby enabling Cromwell's triumph over alleged rivals on the council.[53] Most recently, Hilary Mantel's *Wolf Hall*, a well-received fictional account of Cromwell's rise, has also focused heavily on his role in the Anglo-papal schism.[54]

Yet these interpretations are perplexing. After all, there is little evidence that Cromwell was notably involved with the king's 'great matter' until

1532 – almost a year and a half after he had entered Henry VIII's service. His work on the Anglo-papal schism therefore does not provide a satisfactory explanation of his meteoric rise. Just what was it that Cromwell was doing, presumably brilliantly, during these years, and what qualities did he possess that enabled him to rise so quickly? Rather than emphasising factional battles and political machinations, as many previous works have, this book insists upon the importance of the mundane, and seeks to show how the routine royal business that Cromwell transacted established him in Henry VIII's favour.

One of the earliest tasks that Cromwell undertook for the king, for instance, was the conveyance work connected with the expansion of a number of royal residences and parks. This work has never been examined before, yet a central thesis here is that it was crucial in the unfolding of Cromwell's political career, while also explaining how he became involved with the Crown's finances. Management of the king's interests in relation to the English Church was another responsibility that Cromwell quickly acquired in the early 1530s. Existing consideration of Cromwell and the Church, however, has usually focused on the high politics of the period: the break with Rome; the dissolution of the monasteries; and Cromwell's responsibility for the doctrinal changes of the decade. Instead, this book focuses on Cromwell's earlier involvement with the more routine aspects of the Church, such as administration, finance and, perhaps most interestingly, monastic elections. Similarly, Cromwell's activities connected to English government might seem to be another well-trodden aspect of sixteenth-century history. Again, however, a focus on his earlier, quotidian responsibilities sheds new light on the administrative system during the period, while also offering an intriguing new perspective of Cromwell as an administrative reformer. In short, a full examination of Cromwell's early career, looking at all his work for the king between his entry into the royal service and his appointment as principal secretary in April 1534, offers a very different picture to the traditional account of how Cromwell became Henry VIII's chief minister, while also questioning the conventional, if rival, views of his character.

A reassessment of Cromwell's early career also allows us to consider broader themes. While many historians share in the assumption that the break with Rome was crucial in Cromwell's emergence as the king's chief minister, there has been less agreement on the exact nature of Cromwell's power. Elton, for example, although unwavering in his belief that Cromwell secured Henry VIII's confidence via his ability to deliver the king's divorce, very much saw Cromwell's authority more generally as being founded on institutions and bureaucracy. According to Elton, Cromwell deliberately sought offices and positions in a variety of administrative departments, ensuring that he had influence and command over virtually every area of government.[55] This view was subsequently challenged. Starkey has argued that while Cromwell's power was certainly institutionalised, 'the institution it depended on was not the bureaucracy or Council but the court'.[56] Cromwell's power, therefore, lay in his control of its people and personnel.[57] This is a view implicitly shared by other historians who see Cromwell's rise as being made possible through his mastery of court factions.

These interpretations neatly encapsulate a much broader debate about the nature of politics and government during this period. Elton's view on Cromwell reflected his belief that formal institutions – the council, parliament, judicial courts and financial departments of state – as well as the 'bureaucrats' who ran them, were vital to unlocking the policy-making process during the sixteenth century. Gradually, however, this theory of government came to be questioned, with later historians disputing whether the political process could be understood so narrowly through such formal structures. Starkey's disagreement with Elton rested on his belief that the court, and in particular, the Privy Chamber (a set of private apartments at court where the king was waited on by close servants), was the most significant arena in policy making.[58] George Bernard has highlighted that the nobility continued to remain powerful during this period, both politically and militarily.[59] Guy has also stressed the importance of considering wider political culture, and a growing number of scholars have highlighted the importance of understanding the informal structures of power, such as the patronage networks, local affinities and even the role played by women in politics.[60] As one historian has put it, these approaches

> have constructed a more socially derived understanding of Tudor politics . . . one that identifies social networks and clienteles as central to the process of governance and, as a result, identifies the court as the centre of politics, rather than the privy council.[61]

Undoubtedly, these broader approaches to the political history of this period have provided a much fuller and more comprehensive picture of the political process, and greatly enhance historical understanding.

But perhaps the pendulum has swung too far in that direction. Administrative history has become rather unfashionable in recent years, but even routine administrative work, the type that occupied much of Cromwell's labours during the years 1531–1534, can be political.[62] The debate between Elton, Starkey and others surrounding court and council all too often assumes that politics and administration were separate and distinct spheres. Yet many of the seemingly trite or routine decisions taken by royal ministers such as Cromwell were inherently political. Which tasks to prioritise in order to ensure that government runs smoothly and efficiently, whom to reward with a grant of office, how to respond to rumours of dissent – decisions such as these do not preclude a certain ideological commitment. Moreover, was the court really the fulcrum of Henrician politics? To be sure, much policy was discussed and decided away from the council, and by people who were not sworn councillors, but was it necessary to be a player at court in order to thrive during this period? A key argument which will be advanced in this book is that the pathways to power were more diverse than is generally recognised. Consideration of court factions, by contrast, is given less attention – not because they did not exist, but because there is little evidence that they played a notable part in Cromwell's rise and early career.

Sources

Cromwell's private papers, confiscated on his fall in 1540 and fortuitously preserved, form the overall basis of this study. This work is therefore the first book on Cromwell in over thirty years to be based on extensive archival research, rather than relying almost exclusively on the printed summaries of the State Papers given in *Letters and Papers, Foreign and Domestic, of the Reign of Henry VIII (LP)*. Although *Letters and Papers* remains an indispensable tool for historians, and provided the starting point for this research, the comprehensive recourse to the originals adopted here has frequently enriched, and sometimes corrected, the calendar's summaries of Cromwell's papers. The insights that can be drawn from this make a sharper focus on Cromwell's rise worthwhile in its own right. It has also highlighted some important redating of many of Cromwell's papers.[63] As the editors of *Letters and Papers* rightly noted, 'Cromwell's correspondence . . . includes a vast number of letters on mere private matters of no political significance, and their chronology is consequently far more dubious and uncertain'.[64]

When arranging this correspondence in the bound volumes of the State Papers now held in The National Archives, Public Record Office, Kew, the editors were often forced to make arbitrary decisions when assigning a year to many of these papers. While this was understandably necessary, it has given Cromwell's correspondence (and the State Papers more generally) a structure that is not always chronologically accurate. Anyone using either the calendar or the State Papers needs to bear this in mind at all times. That being said, the research undertaken for this book would not have been possible without *Letters and Papers*. And having relied so much on this calendar as a starting point, I am paying the editors a compliment.

Because the State Papers themselves underpin this study, someone seeking to find fault with it might point out that the type of sources a historian relies upon often determines the picture drawn. To put it another way, if administrative documents are used heavily when examining a person's life, one is highly likely to find that person to be an administrator. There is little that can be done to avoid relying on Cromwell's voluminous papers. It is important to keep this conscientiously in mind, therefore, when using them. Of course, it is entirely conceivable that additional material on Cromwell might exist in non-governmental archives; and during the three years of research that underpins this book, every effort was made to uncover some. Frustratingly, results were often disappointing. Consideration is therefore given here to wider contemporary views of Cromwell, such as those expressed by the rebels involved with the Pilgrimage of Grace or those offered in the act of attainder condemning him, which fall outside the chronological framework of this study. Doing so, I hope, reduces the likelihood that Cromwell's papers have been allowed unduly to dictate the picture offered of him.

Finally, it should also be recognised that the survival of Cromwell's considerable correspondence, set against the lack of such correspondence for a comparable figure, may have left historians with a disproportionate impression of his influence more generally: one that sees him active everywhere and doing everything. It is important to remember that Cromwell was one actor in a fluid political system, and this book seeks to present him as such. Where possible, therefore, an attempt has been made to locate Cromwell's work alongside that of other royal ministers. It is hoped that this has enabled a more balanced appraisal of his influence during these years to be drawn.

CHAPTER ONE

LONDON LAWYER AND MERCHANT

FEW HISTORIANS HAVE SHOWN much interest in going beyond establishing a very basic sketch of Thomas Cromwell's life before he entered Henry VIII's service.[1] Admittedly, such reluctance has been partially conditioned by the dearth of surviving sources. For much of Cromwell's youth, little more can be known than that which can be pieced together from the later accounts of several of his contemporaries or near contemporaries. The State Papers are also largely silent on Cromwell until about 1520. But after that date, when Cromwell was established as a lawyer and merchant living in London, the evidence for his activities becomes much more abundant. Overlooking these years misses a whole series of activities that were significant steps in Cromwell's rise to power. Equally important, to neglect this period is to obscure aspects of Cromwell's life that are particularly pertinent if he is to be understood in a more accurate light. It has long been recognised that a background in law was an increasing feature of many Crown servants during this period.[2] Since the mid-fifteenth century, common lawyers had gradually been replacing clerics in the great departments of state, and the impact that this had on the Crown's ability to interpret its rights in law, thereby strengthening royal government, is well known.[3] But just how typical was Cromwell as a lawyer who would carve out a position for himself at the centre of power? And how did his careers in both the legal and mercantile professions shape his outlook and beliefs? Exploring Cromwell's early life and pre-ministerial careers is crucial, not only to explain the trajectory of his rise, but also to place him within a broader context of legally minded Crown servants.

Early Years

A problem faced by any historian or biographer of Thomas Cromwell is that there is very little evidence for his earliest life. It is not even clear, for example, exactly when Cromwell was born, although 1485 is the date usually given. More certain is that he was born in Putney, a parish which then comprised some 1,239 acres, and which formed part of the manor of Wimbledon.[4] Situated on the north-east bank of the River Thames, four miles from Hyde Park Corner, Putney was already something of a 'commuter belt' for London. A ferry had existed there since at least the Norman Conquest, and most travel to and from the capital was by boat. Because of this, Putney had become a notable wool depot, with merchants from London coming up the river to purchase wool for sale aboard.[5] Its proximity to the capital also perhaps explains why several notable sixteenth-century statesmen can be linked to it. Besides Cromwell, the parish was also the birthplace of Nicholas West, bishop of Ely, who until his death in 1533 was prominent under Henry VIII. More significant, perhaps, were the efforts of two royal ministers who both built up considerable land holdings there: Cromwell himself would secure Wimbledon Manor from Henry VIII in 1536 as part of the landed endowment which accompanied his elevation to baron;[6] and William Cecil would later acquire the same manor from the Crown in the 1560s.[7]

Cromwell's family had been settled in Putney since around 1461, and his father, Walter, was a blacksmith, cloth-shearer and 'berebruer' there.[8] Walter Cromwell was evidently something of an unruly man, appearing in the court rolls for the manor of Wimbledon over ninety times, often for various offences. On forty-six occasions he was fined sixpence for breaking the assize of ale, that is, for selling freshly brewed beer before it was tasted and passed fit for drinking by the parish ale-taster.[9] In 1477 Walter had also been fined 20d for assaulting and drawing blood from one William Mitchell, while in 1513 he had also 'falsely and fraudulently erased the evidences and terriers of the lord, in divers particulars, to the disturbance and disinheritance of the lord and his tenants'.[10] Despite such misdemeanours, Walter Cromwell was a man of reasonable prosperity. By 1480 he held two virgates of land in Putney, and to this was added a further six virgates of copyhold land (about 90 acres) granted to him by Archbishop Morton, the lord of Wimbledon Manor, in 1500.[11] In 1495 and 1496 Walter was also elected as constable of Putney.[12]

Much less is known about Cromwell's mother. She was the aunt of a man called Nicholas Glossop, of Wirksworth in Derbyshire, and probably married Walter Cromwell around 1474.[13] Together they would have three surviving children. Katherine, the eldest, would marry a Welshman named Morgan Williams, who was a member of a prominent family in Putney. Their other daughter, Elizabeth, married a sheep farmer by the name of Wellyfed.[14] Thomas was their only surviving son, and he would later tell the Imperial ambassador (somewhat improbably) that his mother had been fifty-two years old when he was born.[15] Two further members of the Cromwell family are also worth mentioning briefly. An uncle of Cromwell would become a cook to the archbishop of Canterbury, William Warham, while Cromwell's cousin, Robert, would become vicar of Battersea, and served for a time as Cardinal Wolsey's head of works.[16]

It seems likely that Cromwell was somewhat troublesome during his earliest life. When describing the minister in 1535, the Imperial ambassador Eustace Chapuys claimed that he had been 'an ill conditioned scapegrace' in his youth,[17] and this is corroborated by Cromwell himself, who would later tell Archbishop Cranmer that he had been a 'ruffine . . . in hys young dayes'.[18] The Italian novelist Matteo Bandello suggested that Cromwell had quarrelled with his father, and that it was this that prompted him to leave England.[19] Chapuys, by contrast, claimed instead that Cromwell was 'thrown in prison' for 'some offence' and was 'obliged afterwards to leave the country'.[20]

Irrespective of exactly why Cromwell chose to leave England, it is clear that he did indeed spend time on the Continent during the 1500s. He can be placed in Italy on several occasions. A somewhat dubious claim by Bandello is that Cromwell served as a mercenary with the French at the Battle of Garigliano, carrying a pike.[21] If true, this would place him in Italy as early as December 1503. Following the battle, he allegedly encountered the merchant and banker Francesco Frescobaldi in Florence. Frescobaldi offered Cromwell hospitality, and provided him with sixteen gold ducats to aid his return to England.[22]

Nevertheless, Cromwell was back in Italy in 1514. On 29 May he gave evidence at the papal Rota in a longstanding tithe dispute between the abbot of Stratford Langthorne and William Shragger, the vicar of West Ham.[23] It has been suggested that while doing so Cromwell was part of Cardinal Bainbridge's entourage at Rome.[24] The abbot on whose behalf Cromwell gave evidence was certainly supported by Bainbridge, and in June

1514 'Thomas Cromwell of London diocese' is recorded as having stayed at an English hospice in Rome where several of Bainbridge's men lodged, and which was also under the cardinal's protection.[25] Nonetheless the only study of Bainbridge's *familia* in Rome fails to list Cromwell;[26] and it seems much more likely that in 1514 he was there merely as a witness.

John Foxe records another visit to Rome, during which Cromwell encountered the pope while on a mission to renew a set of papal indulgences for the town of Boston, Lincolnshire.[27] These indulgences had a long history dating back to 1401, and were renewed vigorously by the guild, who were proud of them and no doubt keen to maintain their lucrative potential.[28] That they employed Cromwell for this purpose suggests that they were confident in his abilities. Evidently, their trust was well placed. According to Foxe, 'hauyng knowledge how the popes holy touth greatly delited in new fangled straunge delicates and dayntie dishes', Cromwell prepared certain 'fine dishes of gelly', and, with the help of three musicians singing pleasant songs, he waited for the pope to return from a hunting expedition. Marvelling at the strange sight and sounds, the pope stopped to sample the dishes that Cromwell had prepared. Liking them 'so well', the pontiff renewed the town's pardons there and then.[29] Foxe suggested that this event occurred in 1510 but the Boston Guild's records, which confirm the overall veracity of the story, reveal that Cromwell was in Italy on its behalf in 1517 and 1518.[30]

In addition to these adventures in Italy, Cromwell also spent time among the English merchants at Antwerp during the 1510s. Foxe claimed that Cromwell worked as a 'Clerke or Secretary' for them for a time, while a Chancery petition refers to Cromwell's presence 'at the towne of Andewarpe' in the company of several merchants 'abought the vth yere' of Henry VIII's reign, i.e. 1513–1514.[31] George Elyot, a Calais mercer, also reminded Cromwell of the 'love & trew hart that [I] have gowtt vnto you sense the syngsson martt at medelborow' in 1512, suggesting that Cromwell had been there.[32] These fragmented details are the only pieces of evidence for Cromwell's early life. It is difficult to know just what to make of them or what inferences can be convincingly drawn. Perhaps all one can say is that Cromwell was plainly well travelled in his younger days, had sharpened his business skills and probably acquired his ability to speak Latin, French and Italian during his time abroad.

At some point during his early life Cromwell returned to England and married Elizabeth Wykys, the daughter of a wealthy fuller. Chapuys suggests that Cromwell may then have spent some time serving his father-in-law.[33] If so, this might explain how Cromwell soon established his own mercantile interests, which he also supplemented with a growing legal practice. In keeping with the elusive nature of Cromwell's earliest life, however, it is unclear exactly when he established these careers. That he was recorded as being 'of London diocese' when he stayed at the English hospice in Rome in 1514 certainly suggests that by that date he had settled in London. On the basis of the approximate age of Cromwell's son, Gregory (1516–1561), it has been suggested that his marriage to Elizabeth must have occurred before 1516.[34] Cromwell's account book, which records various debts owed to him (although, frustratingly, not the business owed for) also begins in 1518, and therefore points to a more settled existence and occupation by that point.[35]

Nevertheless, the first dateable evidence for Cromwell's legal activities is not found until 1520. Earlier examples of his legal work have been given by historians, but these merely indicate the problem in dating much of Cromwell's correspondence. The editors of *Letters and Papers*, for instance, placed a document relating to the ownership of Whitingham Manor, Buckinghamshire, bearing an endorsement by Cromwell, in 1512, making this both his earliest appearance in the State Papers and the earliest example of his legal work.[36] The problem is that there is no indication when this document was drawn up; nor is it apparent why the editors ascribed it to 1512. It may well be of later date, and can hardly be taken as conclusive proof of Cromwell's legal work in that year. Similarly, a case before the Court of Requests and a Chancery petition corrected by Cromwell have also been taken as evidence of his early legal activities.[37] The matter before the Court of Requests, however, is not connected to Cromwell at all (and in any case dates to 1530), while the Chancery petition, although relating to a crime committed in 1516, offers nothing on when the litigation itself had been commenced.[38] It was not unusual for litigation to be initiated several years after an alleged crime took place. Any proposed date for this petition is therefore conjectural.

It is not until 1520 that a legal dispute involving Cromwell can be dated with any certainty. In that year he can be shown working for the prioress of Cheshunt, Hertfordshire, in a case that initially came before the consistory court of the bishop of London, but which was eventually appealed to Rome.[39] There can be little doubt, however, that Cromwell was present in England and operating in a legal and mercantile capacity before that date.

After all, it seems unlikely that he could have learned the peculiarities of English common law while abroad in Rome and Flanders, so he must surely have been present before then to acquire the necessary legal knowledge to enable him to work as a lawyer. On this point it might be significant that a document turned up during the course of the research for this book provides a piece of previously unknown information about Cromwell's early life, with potential implications for his legal career. This is a writ to the sheriffs of London, dated 23 January 1516, instructing them to certify all that they have pertaining to matters sued before them against Thomas Cromwell. The sheriffs, William Bayly and Henry Warley (their names date the document to Henry VIII's reign), then replied that before the arrival of this writ Cromwell had been arrested in the city and imprisoned in their custody by virtue of a certain plea sued against him by Alice Reynold, widow, for a debt of £4.[40] What could be significant is that Cromwell is described as 'gentleman' in these documents. This was a designation which members of the legal profession used very often, although obviously not all gentlemen were lawyers.[41] The attribution of the term 'gentleman' to Cromwell in this context could be taken to imply that by 1516 he was a member of the legal profession, and possibly studying at an Inn of Court or Chancery. Unfortunately, it is by no means convincing proof, and given that these years of Cromwell's life are so poorly documented, all that can be safely said is that by 1520 he was married, settled in England, and had established himself at the heart of London's legal and mercantile communities. It is to his work and activities in both these professions that this chapter must now turn.

London Lawyer

When Cromwell finally entered the king's service in 1530, he belonged to the professional group from which an increasing number of Crown servants had been drawn since the fifteenth century: the common lawyers. Men like Thomas Lovell, Richard Empson, Edmund Dudley, Thomas More and Thomas Audeley, to mention only a few, were all royal servants with a background in this profession. Legal training was a common and useful quality for a royal minister. But just how typical was Cromwell, as a lawyer who would eventually enter the royal service?

Sixteenth-century England was a highly litigious society, and the law influenced or touched virtually every aspect of people's lives. Because of its

'universal relevance', many people practised law in a variety of environments.[42] There were men, usually formally trained, who worked and pleaded
in the principal courts of King's Bench, Common Pleas, Exchequer and
Chancery at Westminster. The common lawyers who populated these
institutions had normally studied at one of the Inns of Court or Chancery,
where they undertook the study of writs, readings and debating, all of
which characterised life in the Inns during the sixteenth century.[43]

But the number of lawyers who practised in the Westminster courts was
relatively small, perhaps as low as 400.[44] There were also people throughout
the realm who worked and operated in provincial, town, manorial and
ecclesiastical courts. Those working in these environments also had some
grounding in the law, yet comprised a more diverse group of legal practitioners. They might include stewards, bailiffs, court-holders, town clerks
and scriveners, among others. Some of these men, like their senior counterparts at Westminster, might have obtained a formal legal education at an
Inn before returning to their localities. Others were instead self-taught, and
had never attended an Inn.[45] The Cheshire gentleman Humphrey Newton
was one man who possessed no proper legal training but still built up a
respectable practice providing counsel and arbitration in Cheshire, as well
as holding several manorial courts as steward.[46] Similarly, John Smalbroke
of Yardly, Worcestershire, was a weaver, yeoman, 'hostrekeper', 'rentgaderer',
under-bailiff and receiver, while John Boleler, gentleman, was town clerk of
Coventry, clerk of the peace and clerk of the Crown in Worcestershire.[47]
These men were engaged in legal work and offices throughout the country,
yet possessed varying degrees of legal expertise.

All this makes defining a 'typical' sixteenth-century lawyer exceedingly
difficult. Indeed, some have even questioned whether it is possible to talk
of a single legal profession at all during this period, given the diversity of
work that was undertaken and the wide range of people who undertook
it.[48] More convincing, however, is the suggestion that this heterogeneous
group of legal men can be broadly described as working within one profession. At the most basic level, all practitioners were required to operate
within the same common law framework. Those who had attended an Inn
had also received a structured education that helped to impose the
uniformity befitting a profession.[49] But individuals who spent the majority
of their time practising and earning a living from the law, irrespective of
whether they were Westminster-based attorneys or self-taught men operating in the provinces, also surely warrant the term 'professional lawyer'.[50]

As Eric Ives has argued, while there was undoubtedly considerable differ-ence between 'provisional court-keepers and stewards, and the judges and barristers at Westminster . . . it is impossible to draw a distinction between the two groups; they differed in degree, not in kind'.[51]

But if the legal profession was diverse, the type of lawyers who entered the Crown's service during this period were less so. The vast majority of those who served Henry VII and Henry VIII were drawn from the upper branches of the legal profession, that is, those who had studied at an Inn and who had been called to the bar. Sir Thomas Lovell (c.1449–1524), prominent for a time under both kings, had studied at Lincoln's Inn from 1464, where he became autumn reader in 1475.[52] Thomas Audeley was admitted to Inner Temple in 1510, serving as autumn reader there until 1526, before being appointed speaker of the House of Commons in 1529.[53] Christopher Hales studied at Gray's Inn, where he was an ancient in 1516 and autumn reader in 1524. He was appointed solicitor-general in August 1525, and would become attorney general in June 1529.[54] Similarly, Thomas More studied at New Inn before gaining admittance to Lincoln's Inn two years later in 1496. He would remain there until he was called to the bar, and was speaker of the House of Commons during the parliament of 1523.[55]

Thomas Cromwell, by contrast, did not emerge from quite the same legal circles as these men. During his own private career in the 1520s, Cromwell never reached the upper echelons of the sixteenth-century legal world. There is no evidence, either among his private papers or in the records of the courts themselves, that he pleaded in the principal common law courts of King's Bench or Common Pleas.[56] He did not hold one of the legal profession's senior positions, such as a serjeant-at-law, a judge, an apprentice-at-law or even a clerk in one of the central courts. Nor, signifi-cantly, does he appear to have studied at an Inn. It is true that Cromwell did become a member of Gray's Inn in 1524,[57] but this did not necessarily mean that he had studied there. Membership of an Inn was more an indi-cation of professional status, and 'as a warrant for claiming the vague quali-fication "learned in law"'.[58] It is possible, of course, that Cromwell attended one of the lesser notarial or conveyancing schools about which we know so little.[59] But it is far more likely that Cromwell was self-taught, perhaps obtaining his legal knowledge through service to another lawyer, which was by no means an unusual route into the legal profession.[60] In several impor-tant respects, therefore, he does stand out from many lawyers who entered the royal service during this period. He had no formal legal training, had never held a senior position within the profession and was not active in quite the same areas as many of these common lawyers were. This carries an important implication for Cromwell's later political activities in the 1530s. While he undoubtedly had an excellent grasp of the law, it seems reasonable to question whether he comprehended some of the more detailed matters of substantive law and jurisprudence to quite the same extent as did more senior members of the legal profession. Indeed, on several matters in the early 1530s Cromwell was to seek the advice of men – like Thomas Audeley – who had occupied much more prominent legal positions in the 1520s. This suggests that Cromwell, while certainly highly competent in the law, did not have a first-rate legal training, and deferred on certain matters to the opinions of others. Such a conclusion immediately casts doubt on the likelihood that Cromwell was, as Elton once claimed, a revolutionary political theorist, who was in many respects well ahead of his time.

Unlike many of the lawyers who joined the king's service during this period, Cromwell made his living as a lawyer practising 'below the bar', in what has been broadly described as the 'lower branches' of the legal profession.[61] This is perhaps a little misleading, as Cromwell, who was already acquainted with Hales, Audeley and Sir William Paulet by the 1520s, was well connected in senior circles. Nonetheless, the term most befitting of Cromwell's legal work is probably 'solicitor', provided the word is understood rather loosely as denoting somebody who 'solicited' and handled the legal affairs of someone else, rather than specifying a distinct and identifiable group within the profession.[62] Solicitors were gradually emerging throughout the sixteenth century to cope with the increasing demand of legal work. Although it was normally the serjeants-at-law, apprentices and attorneys who pleaded on behalf of litigants in the Westminster courts, the total number of these men was not high.[63] The increase in the business of both Chancery and Star Chamber,[64] combined with the fact that the number of attorneys actually allowed to plead in these courts was restricted,[65] meant that cases or disputes which did not hinge on difficult matters of substantive law could be handled by competent men who, while not always formally trained, still had a sound grasp of legal technicalities. The work undertaken by these men was naturally very similar to that of attorneys. They were often the first practitioners to meet someone with a grievance; they might provide advice as to whether the prospective plaintiff had a case; and, if so, they would offer counsel on the best course of action and perhaps prepare a petition.

Requests among Cromwell's correspondence show that he was often approached for advice and counsel in this manner. In April 1529, for example, Hugh Shaw and John Copley, both of the Guild of Our Lady in Boston, wrote thanking him for his 'good councel labours and payne' already taken in legal matters, and requested that he

> be [a] good maister vnto this berar oure neyghburs and what tyme that ye doo here there mater and causes that ye wyll gyve them your best advice and councell theryn and which wey is best and moost esist [easiest] in the law for them whether it be bithe commune law or bi supplicacion for thei be but poore men.[66]

Sir William Gascoigne was another who asked Cromwell to help the bearer of his letter 'in suche matters as he hathe to do in the lawe & to be of hys councell'.[67] Cromwell can even be shown providing a client with legal advice. Writing to Sir Thomas Boleyn, Viscount Rochford, in late 1527, Cromwell recounted how he had been approached by Rochford's sister Alice, daughter of Sir William Boleyn and second wife to Sir Robert Clere (c.1452–1531).[68] Cromwell was to 'be of counsayll' to Clere in a dispute between him and Elizabeth Fyneux, wife of the deceased chief justice of King's Bench. After examining the matter, Cromwell's opinion was that Clere was 'vtterlye without Remedye by course of the common lawe', and he advised Rochford to move the lord chancellor 'to graunt a wryt of Iniunctyon', preventing the execution of the writ of extent Elizabeth had obtained against him, as well as ensuring that

> no wryttes of liberata goo out of the Chauncerye [vntyll] suche time [as] the hole matyer tochyng the premysses may dulye and accordyng to conscyence be harde and examyned.[69]

Cromwell's comments reveal that he provided Rochford with legal advice, and the most effective way of implementing it, but they offer no indication that he acted or appeared in Chancery on Clere's behalf, or in any way other than providing him – via Rochford – with counsel.[70]

Soliciting this sort of legal work occupied much of Cromwell's labours during the 1520s. The courts he was engaged with were therefore the prerogative courts of Chancery and Star Chamber. These had emerged in the late fourteenth and fifteenth centuries respectively, as a result of the inflexible and often sclerotic nature of the existing common law courts.[71] Chancery was presided over by the lord chancellor, while Star Chamber was officiated by members of the King's Council, but which had come into its own under Cardinal Wolsey.[72] Much of the business of these courts overlapped, and 'no very precise division between the two jurisdictions can be made'.[73] Both dealt predominantly with disputes concerning land, although Chancery was concerned mainly with civil cases, while Star Chamber tended to handle more criminal or political matters which the King's Council had retained.[74] To initiate litigation in either of these courts it was necessary to submit a petition written in English, drawn up by a lawyer. When doing so, the lawyer would sometimes sign the petition in the bottom right-hand corner. A Chancery petition on behalf of John Palsgrave, prebendary of St Paul's Cathedral, was signed in such a manner by Cromwell, confirming that he had prepared it.[75] His signature also appears on three other Chancery bills of complaint, all relating to land and property disputes, while another petition survives unsigned but written wholly in Cromwell's hand.[76] His private papers connect him to further cases before Chancery when the formal records of the court alone provide no indication of his involvement. Reynold Lytylprow, from Norwich, had told a man to 'reteyn' Cromwell on 'hys cownsell' regarding a matter to be heard in Chancery or Star Chamber,[77] while an undated draft of a Chancery bill in Cromwell's hand similarly requested that a writ of certiorari (a writ from Chancery which ordered an inferior court to present the records of a case before it) be issued to prevent action taken by 'on[e] [Thomas] Twyn of London barboure'.[78]

Alongside this Chancery work, Cromwell prepared similar bills for Star Chamber. In September 1529, a priest from Guernsey told Cromwell that he had 'bisynes ... in my lord cardinalles court ... In the whiche bysnes your gud word and advyse may do me moche ease ... let me haue your lavfull ayde & aduyse in hyt'.[79] Similarly, a Star Chamber petition was amended by Cromwell and later readdressed to Wolsey in Chancery.[80] It also seems that Cromwell was active on behalf of Thomas Kenett in a case before Star Chamber concerning the ownership of certain lands in Brabourne, Kent.[81] Another draft petition in his hand also requested that Wolsey 'graunt the kinges lettres of Pryuie seale to be dyrectyd vnto ... Jahn Roper commandyng her ... to appere before your grace ... in the Star Chamber'.[82] A letter from William Popley of Bristol even asked Cromwell to act as an attorney 'before the Kinges Counsaill', presumably when sitting in Star Chamber, and requested that he procure a commission from that body enabling a case to be heard by the mayor and commonalty of Bristol. Popley promised to repay Cromwell 6d for the necessary seals.[83]

Reconstructing a handful of the cases before Chancery and Star Chamber in which Cromwell was involved can offer us a glimpse of his legal skills and abilities as a lawyer. In October 1525, for example, Cromwell had begun to work on a dispute for Lawrence Giles, a Calais chandler, and his brother-in-law Richard Rutter. According to a draft petition in Cromwell's hand, about twenty-seven years before one John Rutter of Calais had sold a variety of merchandise to another merchant, Cornelius Peterson, for which payment was never fully met.[84] John Rutter subsequently died, and the obligation eventually passed to Richard Rutter and Lawrence Giles. Cromwell became involved in October 1525, when Giles requested his assistance in the dispute with Peterson's widow, Gertrude.[85] Cromwell's advice was to petition Wolsey in Chancery and request a writ of subpoena, forcing her to appear before the court.[86] On 9 December, however, Cromwell was informed of a problem. The woman's name 'was wrong in the subpena for her ryght name ys Gertvde Cornelys'. Because of this 'she regardys thys same subpena nothing at all by cawsse here name was sett wrong in the wrytyng'.[87] What is interesting is that Giles's original letter to Cromwell requesting his help was written on 31 October, meaning that Cromwell's efficiency in handling the matter was notable. In the space of just over a month he had drawn up a bill, albeit with an alleged error, sent it to Chancery, and obtained a subpoena, which was dispatched to Calais. And despite the problem with the subpoena, the case did eventually go before that court. Giles wrote again on 9 January (although the year is not specified), remarking that a friend had shown him 'that my mater was made an ynd [end] of howbeit he could not shewe me to what poynt it was brought'. He therefore asked Cromwell to inform him of the outcome.[88]

Another Chancery case with which Cromwell was involved reinforces the impression that he was an efficient and highly competent legal operator. This was a dispute between Richard Chaufer, a Calais merchant, and William Blount, Lord Mountjoy, in late 1522. Chaufer was trying to reclaim debts from Mountjoy as executor of the will of Henry Kebell, alderman. Cromwell had been active on Chaufer's behalf for some time, even giving evidence before the bishop of London, who had tried to settle the matter.[89] Whether as a result of a failed settlement on the bishop's part,

Cromwell's advice or perhaps on his own initiative, Chaufer was soon seeking another remedy. First he tried a commission in Calais; then he took action in Chancery. The latter option appears to have been the course Cromwell advised. On 22 September Chaufer wrote to Cromwell thanking him for his 'good advyse and counsell', but telling him that he had decided not to follow it: 'sir your advyse I doo not refute but For the shortyst And most expedyton to be had I wyll Furst have a commysshon with a penaltye as greate as ye canne gett it'.[90] A bill that Cromwell had devised (perhaps for Chancery) was also enclosed, and which Chaufer had amended, to enable Cromwell 'to gett me the said commysshon ... and send me the same to Callaiz'.[91] Chaufer was

> determyned Furst to perceive what this comysshon shall doo... And if it wyll not helpe I wyll haue accyon vpon his goodes At Callaiz / And if he Remove it ... then I wyll haue a writte in the Chauncery Against my lord & sewe hym to the most extreme.

Wolsey was petitioned for two commissions to be held at Calais, the second requested at the failure of the first.[92] Revealingly, once again, the speed and efficiency with which Cromwell obtained these commissions – the second commission being dated 21 October, less than one month after Chaufer's initial request – are striking.[93] Both commissions must have failed, however, because the matter apparently went before Chancery, just as Cromwell had originally advised.[94]

Of similar interest is a dispute before Star Chamber in 1529 between two mercers, John Ap Powell and William Clay.[95] A robbery had occurred on 8 October 1526, in which Clay and others had broken into Ap Powell's shop and stolen over £2,400 worth of cloth and merchandise.[96] Cromwell was active on behalf of Ap Powell, and, in the months following the robbery, he had begun to sue a 'certen bill of ryott ... before the kinges highnes and the honourable lordes of your most honorable Counsayle in your Stare Chambre aganst the seid Cley'.[97] The claim of a riot was a common legal fiction, which Cromwell used to enable the case to be heard in Star Chamber rather than in the less effective common law courts. But Clay attempted to prevent this. His replication, which claimed that Cromwell's bill was 'insufficiannt in the lawe' and not 'determynable' in Star Chamber, was customary.[98] More ingenious was his persuading Thomas Hine, a man to whom Ap Powell was already in debt, to sue him before the sheriffs in

London with a view to having him imprisoned.[99] Cromwell's response illustrates not only his quick thinking but also his ability to solve problems. To counter Hinde's actions, Cromwell petitioned Wolsey in Chancery to grant a writ of certiorari ordering the mayor and sheriffs to explain the cause of Ap Powell's arrest.[100] This presumably worked, because Wolsey ordered a commission to investigate and arbitrate the original dispute in June 1527.[101] Although the commissioners do not appear to have acted until October 1529, probably because Clay fled to Antwerp to evade his various troubles,[102] they gave their final conclusion – that Clay owed Ap Powell £800 – on 29 November 1529.[103]

Arbitration and compromise, as attempted in the case between Clay and Ap Powell, was a popular way of settling legal disputes in the sixteenth century, owing to the speed with which an agreement could be made, and its relative cost.[104] Many lawyers therefore spent time engaged in this sort of work. In the first book of *Utopia*, Thomas More had commented on his own legal activities: 'I am constantly engaged in legal business, either pleading or hearing, either giving an award as an arbiter or deciding a case as a judge'.[105] It comes as no surprise, then, that Cromwell's legal career also saw him act as an arbitrator in many disputes during the 1520s.[106] Along with Roger Chameley, Cromwell arbitrated and settled a dispute in April 1527 between the merchants Richard Paten and John Balevalt, and drafted the final determination for this.[107] A dispute between John Creke, another London merchant, and Ralph Dodmer, was also settled by Cromwell, and his determination offers a glimpse of what the process of arbitration might involve.[108] First, both parties had agreed to 'abyde obey and fulfill the awarde arbytrement ordenunce and Fynall judgement of . . . Thomas Crumwell as sole arbytratour'.[109] Cromwell then called both men before him and examined 'the bookes accompttes, lettres, [and] wrytynges . . . brought and layed bifore me'. Arbitration, which was often employed when some right lay with both parties, 'had to offer a degree of satisfaction on both sides'.[110] In this award Cromwell deemed that Dodmer should pay Creke £110 for his expenses,[111] while Creke was instructed to deliver a number of bills to Dodmer whereby several merchants were under obligations owing to him.[112] It is worth noting here that for any dispute to be settled in this manner it was necessary for each party to agree on arbitration as a method of settlement, and on who should arbitrate. That Cromwell frequently acted as an arbitrator during the 1520s is therefore a testimony to his legal skills and reputation. The implication is that Thomas Cromwell was perceived to be a man of fair and sound legal judgement.

Alongside this Chancery, Star Chamber and arbitrational activity, Cromwell also undertook a variety of fairly low-level legal work, which reinforces the suggestion that he was not a formally trained lawyer. He acted as a draftsman on many legal documents during these years, including the Chancery petitions and arbitrational awards already mentioned, as well as leases on properties and land conveyances.[113] This type of scribal work 'was not usually high-powered, and was generally undertaken by the lower ranks of the legal profession'.[114] In 1525 Cromwell was also appointed to the clerkship of Salisbury by Cardinal Wolsey.[115] Duties performed by town clerks varied enormously, and exactly what this particular office entailed is unclear.[116] Generally, though, town clerks were expected to 'translate and read to the community any communications from Westminster', as well as being 'well-versed in the law and able to argue effectively when disputes arose'.[117] Those with some legal knowledge were naturally well suited to these roles. In this instance, however, the office was little more than a sinecure, as Cromwell was discharged of his duties by a deputy, but pocketed a yearly fee of £4, with an additional 13s 4d for the clerk's livery.[118]

In 1528 Cromwell was also appointed by Cardinal Wolsey as chief steward of the manor of Tottenham, Middlesex, a position that came with a fee of £6 13s 4d per annum.[119] The steward of a manor was responsible for holding the manorial court. He was both the judge of matters before that court and the secretary or clerk who was responsible for maintaining the court's records.[120] A chief steward was usually found only on the largest estates and had the responsibility for an entire receivership.[121] The necessity that chief stewards possess sound legal knowledge had again resulted in lawyers being preferred for such positions. The records of the manor of Tottenham show that Cromwell presided over the five manorial courts held during his stewardship, before being replaced by William Paulet, another lawyer and a royal servant, in 1530.[122]

Those who employed Cromwell on legal matters during these years largely reflected his geographical surroundings and connections. As late as September 1522, Cromwell was occupying a residence in Fenchurch Street close to the Halls of the Ironmongers and Bricklayers.[123] By September 1523 he was living in a house in Throgmorton Street next to a community of Augustinian friars, and this remained his principal residence until his execution in 1540.[124] Both properties were at the heart of the City of London, and Cromwell's legal clients reflected the mercantile and professional communities from which he emerged and among whom he continued to live. A number of the cases mentioned above involve merchants.[125] These connections also enabled him to obtain legal work from foreign merchants trading in London, including Perpoynt Deovanture, merchant of the Hanse, for whom Cromwell drafted a licence enabling him to pass into France unhindered in 1523.[126] Cromwell worked for a group of French merchants in London, amending their replication in matters which had resulted in the seizing of their 'goodes weres & marchaundises'.[127] He also prepared a draft petition on behalf of a Florentine merchant John Corce,[128] as well as licences for a blacksmith and a London grocer.[129]

Cromwell's legal clients, however, were by no means narrowly confined to London. Although based in Westminster, the courts of Chancery and Star Chamber heard cases from all over the country, and Cromwell's clients reflected this. Members of the Guild of St Mary, Boston, Lincolnshire, used Cromwell in a legal capacity in 1529.[130] The guild's account book also records two payments to Cromwell for his work on their behalf in Rome in 1517 and 1518.[131] Cromwell also worked for merchants from Calais,[132] while in May 1525 he drew up a lease on the manor of Tanghall near York, between Robert Shorton, prebendary of Fridaythorpe, in York Cathedral, and the mayor and commonalty of York.[133] Reynold Lytylprow, from Norwich, made use of his legal skills on at least two occasions,[134] and judging by the letters of William Popley, of Bristol, Cromwell was not only active on his behalf regarding legal matters, but also for other men in and around Bristol.[135] Legal clients elsewhere came from Guernsey, Hertfordshire and Suffolk.[136] Not all of this business could have been conducted via the post, so Cromwell must have spent a good deal of time in the saddle. This was a lifestyle typical of many lawyers, who were often required to travel to meet clients regarding suits. In fact, lawyers travelled so frequently during this period that there was a good possibility that their deaths might come while they were away on business.[137] Many made the practical provision in their wills, as did Cromwell himself, that they should be buried 'where it shall please god to ordeyn me to die'.[138]

Alongside his legal work on behalf of laymen, Cromwell also worked for several members of the clergy during these years. The abbot of St Mary's, York, wrote to him sometime in the late 1520s, requesting that he help with the 'fortherance of my chart[er] sealyng whiche ye wor of concell of as of all other my causes'.[139] Cromwell's account book, which lists various bills, debts and obligations owed to him between December 1518 and February

1529, also records a number of clergy who owed him money.[140] In most cases only the name of the debtor and the sum owed are listed, making it difficult to establish the nature of the business that Cromwell was owed for.[141] One clergyman listed, however, John Palsgrave, made use of Cromwell's legal skills on at least three occasions. A petition was drafted by Cromwell on Palsgrave's behalf to recover debts on his parsonage of Ashfordby, Leicestershire,[142] and Cromwell also devised an agreement between Palsgrave and Richard Pynson for the printing of 750 copies of 'one boke namyd lez le clarissimaunt'.[143] On a third occasion Palsgrave promised to pay Cromwell £7 6s 8d if he obtained a papal bull enabling him to unite the benefice of Alderton, Suffolk, with his prebend of Portpool in St Paul's Cathedral.[144] It will also be recalled that Cromwell was working on behalf of the prioress of Cheshunt in 1520. This matter concerned a tithe dispute. What is interesting is that the case was initially before the bishop of London's consistory court, before then being appealed to the archbishop's prerogative court of Canterbury, and then finally to the papal curia in Rome.[145] Presumably Cromwell was active on the prioress's behalf right from the very beginning (and he was still working for her in 1524, with the matter unresolved).[146] If so, this, and Palsgrave's papal bull request, suggest that Cromwell was competent enough to deal with matters before both lay and ecclesiastical courts, as well as courts outside the borders of England.

Wolsey's Service

Because of the skills which they possessed, many lawyers were retained in the service of members of the nobility and gentry, who might require legal counsel or assistance with the administration of their lands and estates. The lawyer Thomas Kebell (c.1439–1500) was retained by Sir Charles Somerset, illegitimate son of Henry Beaufort, duke of Somerset, for 26s 8d a year from 1489, as well as by several urban corporations in parts of the Midlands.[147] The account book of Edward IV's queen, Elizabeth Woodville, similarly reveals that she retained attorneys in both King's Bench and Common Pleas.[148] While there is no indication that Cromwell himself was ever retained formally by deed, his legal skills did eventually attract the attention of Henry VIII's first chief minister, Thomas Wolsey, and Cromwell entered the cardinal's service. Exactly when this occurred has been the subject of much dispute. Elton argued for an early date, claiming that Cromwell was a member of Wolsey's household by 1516, and of his council by 1519.[149] In support of this he offered two pieces of evidence. The first was the account book for the Boston Guild of St Mary's, in which both Cromwell and Wolsey are mentioned. Although this connects both men to the guild, at no point does the account book link or associate the two men to each other.[150] The other piece of evidence was an undated petition addressed to Cromwell as 'oone of the lorde Cardynalles honerable Councell', which concerned the theft of 30 gallons of 'blaktyn' in 1519. It has already been noted, however, that legal disputes were often initiated several years after an offence had occurred. In this case, the petition's phrasing of the value of blacktin stolen – 'wich at that tyme was worth' – suggests just that.[151]

Beyond these highly questionable pieces of evidence, there is a telling dearth of sources to support the notion that Cromwell was working for Wolsey as early as 1516. Several sources seem actually to contradict it. Two draft documents survive, probably dating to *c.*1523, granting power of attorney and the right to collect debts to a number of men, including Cromwell, on behalf of the Hanse merchant Perpoynt Deovanture.[152] In both of these, one Robert Carter is listed as a member of Wolsey's household, while Cromwell is merely referred to as 'Thomas Crumwell de London Gentilman'. This surely suggests that he was not yet part of Wolsey's entourage. What is clear, however, is that Wolsey and Cromwell were familiar with each other from about 1520 onwards. Cromwell's legal career naturally brought him into contact with the lord chancellor, and their paths also crossed in several private suits. In each of these, though, Cromwell was working not for Wolsey but for the other party.[153]

Merriman, Dickens, Robertson and Ward all, for slightly differing reasons, correctly identified 1524 as the year of Cromwell's entry into the cardinal's service.[154] Merriman suggested that Cromwell's entry may have come through the patronage of his cousin, Robert Cromwell, vicar of Battersea, or perhaps through Cromwell's work for the marquis of Dorset.[155] Both are highly conjectural. Cromwell's links with Dorset, in particular, are based on two inconclusive and undated letters.[156] Nevertheless, Merriman identified 1524 as the decisive year on the grounds that Cromwell helped draft an indenture for the sale of Kexby, a Yorkshire manor, in which Wolsey was the purchaser.[157] There are hints, however, that Cromwell might have been working for the seller, John Aleyn.[158] More reasonable was Dickens's suggestion that Cromwell's parliamentary speech in 1523, which opposed Henry VIII's campaigns in France, could not have been made by someone in Wolsey's employment. He also therefore accepted 1524–1525 as the date of Cromwell's entry.[159] Robertson concurred with this, accepting the evidence given by Merriman, but also mentioned further material suggesting Cromwell was active on Wolsey's behalf at this time.[160] This consisted of an annuity grant to Richard Clement, bearing an endorsement by Cromwell on the back, placed in 1524 by the editors of *Letters and Papers*.[161] The year the grant was made is missing, however, and Cromwell's endorsement does not appear to be connected to it, suggesting that it was added later. Nevertheless, Philip Ward has convincingly demonstrated that 1524 was indeed the crucial year, although he dismissed much of the evidence offered by earlier historians.[162] He argued that Cromwell's skill in drafting various conveyances on behalf of Thomas Hennage, a member of Wolsey's household, provided Cromwell with a patron through whom he obtained formal work in the service of the cardinal.[163] While disagreement therefore remains over the method of Cromwell's entry into Wolsey's service, it is plain that the transition itself did occur in 1524. There is simply no dateable evidence to support an earlier date, while in that year there are the first signs that Cromwell was working for Wolsey in minor legal matters.[164] Moreover, in 1524 Wolsey was about to embark on a project which would require the legal skills that Cromwell possessed in abundance.

Between 1524 and 1529 Cardinal Wolsey secured papal and royal approval for the suppression of some twenty-nine religious houses in England for the establishment of a college at Oxford and a grammar school in his native town of Ipswich.[165] The purpose of these institutions was to extend humanist education in England, as well as to be a permanent and lasting memorial to Wolsey. The Augustinian monastery of St Frideswide, Oxford, was dissolved to make way for the college built there.[166] Over the next year a further twenty-one monasteries were suppressed, and their lands and revenues diverted for the establishment and upkeep of Cardinal College, Oxford.[167] Barely three years later, the Augustinian monastery of St Peter and St Paul was suppressed for the site of the second college in Ipswich.[168] Thomas Cromwell was involved throughout the entire process of the establishment of these foundations. The chronicler Edward Hall rightly described Cromwell as Wolsey's 'chefe doer . . . in the suppression of abbeis',[169] while John Foxe also recollected that when

> certeine small Monasteries and Priories, in diuers places of the Realme,
> were by the sayd Cardinall suppressed, and the landes seased to the

Cardinalls handes. The doyng wherof was committed to the charge of Thomas Cromwell ... [who] shewed hym selfe verye forward, and industrious ... in the handlyng therof.[170]

What has received less recognition, however, is that Cromwell's work on Wolsey's colleges was actually the key to the beginnings of his own future political career.[171] Not only was this work responsible for Cromwell's progression in Wolsey's service but, as the next chapter will show, his knowledge of the cardinal's colleges would unintentionally lead to his entry into the king's service in 1530. For these reasons, the nature of the work that Cromwell undertook for Wolsey merits some attention.

Cromwell's earliest involvement with Wolsey's colleges concerned surveying the lands, possessions and properties of many of the houses intended for dissolution. On 4 January 1525 Cromwell was named, along with Sir William Gascoigne and William Burbank, as part of a commission to survey the monasteries – of Tickford, Buckinghamshire; Ravenstone, Buckinghamshire; Canwell, Staffordshire; Sandwell, Staffordshire; Poughley, Berkshire; Medmenham, Buckinghamshire; Wallingford, Berkshire; and Finchbrooke, Cambridgeshire – which had been marked for suppression, and which were intended for the creation and endowment of Cardinal College, Oxford.[172] Less than three years later he would also survey lands connected to the college at Ipswich. William Capon, the dean there, informed Wolsey how Cromwell and John Smith, Wolsey's auditor, 'haue takyn greate paynes in surveyeng the Landis' of St Peter's, Felixstowe, Bromehill and Rumburgh, and had made 'very good bookes' detailing the lands and rents connected to these.[173] Cromwell's skills as a surveyor and his eye for detail were readily acknowledged. Capon believed that both Cromwell and Smith had 'a very excellent cast in surveyeng of Landes Insomoche they woll not loose oon peny bilongyng thervnto'.[174] An indication of exactly what this surveying work entailed is neatly illustrated by a set of instructions prepared by Cromwell's office for another of Wolsey's surveyors, William Fryer. He was instructed to discover

whether the manour of huddon be a manor and how manye Free tennaunttes it hathe and whether they kepe any courtis and whether they haue eny Lawe Daye or Lete And also to knowe / how manye Acres of pasture / howe many Acres of meadow / howe many Acres of wede / howe manye Acres of hethe / howe many Acres of more / and what rent / and the value by the yere of the hoole about all charges / And whether it haue eny patronage or parsonage.[175]

Once the monasteries identified for closure had been surveyed, valued and their lands accounted for in this way it was necessary to suppress the houses themselves. To dissolve an entire religious community was a considerable undertaking, and required not only a papal bull, but also the founder or patron's consent, and that of the community itself.[176] In reality, however, the combination of papal and royal approval for Wolsey's project made the surrenders something of a foregone conclusion.[177] Teams of men travelled across England to receive and witness these surrenders formally. Cromwell was frequently among them. He was present at Dodnash, Suffolk, and Snape, Suffolk, on 1 February 1525, for example, and received their surrenders alongside John Alen and Anthony Hussey, both notaries public. On 9 and 10 February he was among a different group of men who received the surrenders of Blackmore and Stanesgate in Essex.[178]

Once a house had been surrendered it was necessary to hold inquiries to determine its ownership. When determining ownership to land or property that might 'escheat', or fall to the Crown, it was necessary to have a jury empanelled in the respective county to ensure that the king's title to it was established through due legal process (this was known as finding an 'office').[179] Ownership of obsolete religious houses followed a similar pattern, and this was usually found in favour of the descendants of the monastery's original founder, or the Crown if this was unknown. Several of the religious houses that Wolsey intended for his college projects regarded the king as their founder anyway, and therefore posed no problem. Once they had surrendered, an 'office' was found for the king, and the house and its land could then be formally transferred into Wolsey's possession. But as some of the houses Wolsey suppressed had founders other than the king, Wolsey's men ensured that the inquests returned verdicts of 'unknown', so that ownership still reverted to the Crown, which again then transferred it to Wolsey.[180] Cromwell's private papers confirm that he managed many of the escheator inquests held for these purposes. In one letter from 1528, Cromwell told Wolsey that he had 'founde offices ... of the saide late monasterye of Wallinsforde and of all the londes and tenementtes belonging to the same',[181] while among the costs listed in one of his account books for 'Paymentes made and issued by Thomas Crumwell in and abowtes the affares and busynes of my lord his grace and his college' were various payments to county escheators and under-sheriffs in Suffolk, Oxfordshire, Berkshire, Buckinghamshire and Essex.[182] The verdicts of juries relating to such inquests were also returned by Cromwell to Chancery.[183]

Cromwell also played a role in drafting the deeds required to establish Wolsey's colleges formally. Drafts of letters patent for the licence to found the college at Oxford, as well as drafts of licences granting the suppressed monasteries to be used for the college's establishment and revenue, bear Cromwell's hand.[184] Responsibilities for the preparation of such documents then increased as Cromwell rose in Wolsey's services. He 'surueyed amended and refourmed' various letters patent from the king granting lands,[185] and in September 1528 he wrote to Wolsey on the progress of the Ipswich foundation, informing him that 'I haue caused suche billes as be allredie signed to passe the pryuy signet and pryuate Seale, and shall nowe put to writing the letteres patenttes for the brode Seale', which would enable further lands to be bequeathed to the college there.[186] Legal technicalities and problems with grants of land were similarly reported to Cromwell for rectification.[187]

The financial side of Wolsey's college project was yet another area of Cromwell's concern. One of his accounts includes payments for 'wages and rewardes youen and paide' to the late abbots, priors and monks of suppressed houses.[188] Essentially, Cromwell was pensioning these men off to ensure that they left their monasteries quickly and quietly. In addition, he also personally renegotiated and settled rents for various lands which now belonged to the colleges.[189] William Capon, for instance, referred to certain 'half yeres Rentes . . . receyued bifore my comyng of the tenantes By master Cromwell' in a letter to Wolsey.[190] At some point in the late 1520s, Cromwell was then appointed receiver-general of the Oxford college lands.[191] This effectively meant that he was responsible for managing the collecting of rent from all of its lands – a responsibility that would continue during his early years under the king. Payments made by Cromwell to John Higdon, dean and paymaster of the works at Cardinal College, Oxford, also suggest that he may have had some oversight regarding the building works themselves.[192] Cromwell would certainly remark to Stephen Gardiner, who was also then in Wolsey's service, how he had 'incouraged the workemen and labourers' to resume work after an overflow of the Thames had destroyed the work at Lesnes, Kent.[193] Apparently not even the smallest tasks connected to the erection of Wolsey's colleges evaded him. On one occasion Cromwell even brought 'coopes vestementes aulter clothes plate & other thinges' to the Ipswich college, while also taking moche payne & Labour not only in surveyeng your graces stuff hether caryed sawfely, But also in prepayring & ordering off hanginges Benchis with all other necessaries to the furniture of our hall whiche ys now well trymmed & ordered thrugh his good diligence and helpe.[194]

Although Cromwell's work for Wolsey would contribute to the unfolding of his future political career, it is also of interest here because it helps cast him in a somewhat different light to that in which he is usually held. It was noted earlier that historians have often interpreted Cromwell in a variety of seemingly conflicting forms. But one aspect of his life which has hitherto received curiously little attention is his legal career. First and foremost, however, Cromwell was a lawyer, and his work for Wolsey shows that actually he was something of a stickler for procedure and due legal process. In a letter to Thomas Arundell in 1528, Cromwell included instructions for Wolsey, emphasising in great detail that the cardinal

maye not in any wise procede to therrection of his saide colledge in Gipswiche, bifore the xxi Daye of Julye next coming, for asmuche as thoffices in the Chauncerie shall not expire, vnto the full accomplishment of iii monethes, vntill the saide xxi Daye, nor his grace cannot haue the Syte and circuyte of the late Monastori of Saynct Peter suppressed, vpon the whiche saide colledge muste be erected by thordres of the lawe of this londe bifore the saide xxi Daye.[195]

Evidently, Cromwell believed in the binding nature of the law and the legitimacy that it provided. Also of note are Cromwell's instructions to William Holgill, one of Wolsey's men, who was sent to Yorkshire to take possession of the rectory of Rudby, which had been obtained to provide further financial endowment for the college at Oxford.[196] Holgill was told to search the 'euydence towching thaduowson of the patronage of Rudby, and to se whether it be aduowson appendaunte, that is to saye, apperteynyng to a manour or to an Acre of londe'. He was also told that the deed of 'ffeoffement' must be read at the parsonage at the door of the church and on the acre of land, and 'to take at the leste xxx or xl witnesses, calling therto asmany yonge children as ye may'.[197] Cromwell's attention to detail is striking: there was to be no corner-cutting here. Holgill was instructed to carry out all the correct procedures to ensure that due legal process was followed. The intriguing instruction that young children should be used as witnesses was not 'a kindly trait in Cromwell's character'.[198] Instead, the use of children in this way was a method that ensured there were witnesses who would probably live for some time, and who would be able to testify to the purchase if required.[199]

The abiding image that the painter Hans Holbein has left of Cromwell is, in the words of one unsympathetic biographer, that of a 'corpulent' royal official who spent most of his time 'poring over voluminous paper work'.[200] Holbein's portrait of Cromwell is considered in Chapter Six but the image of Cromwell as an administrator and bureaucrat has often been compounded by historical scholarship, which has usually considered him as a Westminster or court-based official. Cromwell's work on Wolsey's collegiate foundations offers another perspective, and reveals that he could also be a man of energy and action. The monastic houses which Wolsey's project had targeted for dissolution were scattered across the country. Cromwell was frequently required to ride considerable distances to attend to business at any one of these sites. One of Cromwell's accounts records costs of £9 5s 8d 'for the saide Thomas riding abouttes the fynding thoffices of the late monasterye of Dauentrie in the counties of Northampton Leyc [sic] and Rutland withe v horses by the space of xviij Dayes'.[201] Another shows that between 21 May and 20 June he rode across Essex and Suffolk, viewing monastic lands, taking possession of, and holding courts at, Dodnash, Wix, Horkesley, Tiptree, Stansgate, Thoby and Blackmore.[202] The travel required for such work was evidently gruelling. Cromwell's accounts for this latter trip reveal that one of the men who accompanied him was paid 46s 8d 'for ii horses that he killed and tyred', which hints at the intensity of the travel Cromwell's group was subjected to.[203] Perhaps most strikingly, out of all the men involved in Wolsey's suppressions, Cromwell alone made 'a determined attempt' to be present at the suppression of seventeen houses conducted in as many days in 1525.[204] This involved dividing his time between the two separate parties conducting these suppressions, criss-crossing the south-east of England in order to do so, and covering a total of approximately 685 miles in the process. Such onerous work not only required physical fitness and good horsemanship, two qualities not usually associated with Thomas Cromwell, but also a determination to go above and beyond that which was required, perhaps in the hope that his efforts would not go unnoticed.[205]

If impressing Wolsey was Cromwell's intent, then it appears to have worked. Having joined the cardinal's service in 1524, and proving his abilities by competently managing a variety of legal and administrative matters connected to the colleges, Cromwell rose in Wolsey's esteem. Letters addressed to Cromwell in 1526 as 'oon of my lorde cardynalles counsaill' reveal that by that date he had been appointed to Wolsey's private council – a position of considerable respect.[206] And certainly, by the end of the 1520s, Cromwell had become a senior figure in Wolsey's administration. Yet Cromwell's work for the cardinal was entirely concerned with Wolsey's private affairs; he was not engaged in government business until he entered the king's service in 1530. Nonetheless, Wolsey did make use of Cromwell's legal skills on matters away from the collegiate foundations. In 1528, Cromwell corrected a draft indenture renegotiating and reaffirming the cardinal's ecclesiastical authority with the town of Beverley in the diocese of York.[207] He acted as a trustee on Wolsey's behalf during his purchase and subsequent sale of the manor of Baddisworth, Yorkshire, in 1529.[208] Cromwell even managed the inquests into the lands of the deceased Sir William Compton for Wolsey in 1528–1529,[209] and his 1527 involvement in settling the disputed wardship of Thomas Stanley, son and heir of Edward Lord Monteagle, may also have been connected to the cardinal.[210]

Yet despite his progression in Wolsey's service, Cromwell did not abandon his private legal work during the late 1520s. On the contrary, his private practice benefited because many associated with Wolsey employed Cromwell on their own personal matters. William Capon, dean of Cardinal College, Ipswich, requested that Cromwell provide him with his 'good counseill eyed & helpe how to come by my money whiche the priest of Southampton owith vnto me', and desired Cromwell to 'put the sayd priest in sayte [suit] in my name'.[211] John Keall, another priest connected with the Oxford college, had reminded Cromwell of the need to 'gett owt' certain indentures required at Oxford, before adding that 'I haue a matter of myn own that ye shall haue as moche mony for yf ye bring hyt to passe'.[212] The wife of Thomas Hennage, a member of Wolsey's entourage, also requested that Cromwell 'make a deide off feffment for me off the landes my husband purchysid in lyncoln schere'.[213] This request was probably connected with Hennage's purchase of the manor of Reston, Lincolnshire. Cromwell had drawn up a draft indenture of this purchase, and corrected several others, in February 1525.[214] Evidently, then, service under Wolsey not only brought Cromwell personal advancement but it also enabled his private legal career to flourish.

Mercantile Interests, Wealth and Standing

Alongside his legal career and work for Wolsey during the 1520s, Cromwell also operated as a London merchant. Although it might be thought that his background in this profession was far less significant to the unfolding of his later political career than his work as a lawyer, several of the earliest jobs which Cromwell would do for Henry VIII certainly benefited from his background in trade. Among the tasks that Cromwell undertook during his first three years in the royal service, one saw him obtaining fabrics for the king and the duke of Norfolk,[215] while another saw him providing clothing for royal minstrels and arranging the patterns on the king's collars.[216] In 1533 Cromwell also managed the sale of the king's wines.[217] A background and connections in the mercantile trade would clearly assist in such diverse responsibilities; indeed, this probably explains why Cromwell was given them in the first place.

Cromwell's mercantile activities initially concerned the cloth trade, and the origins of this surely stemmed from his time abroad among merchants in Antwerp. It will also be recalled that Cromwell had married the daughter of a wealthy fuller in the 1510s, and he probably used this connection to establish his own mercantile interests. Certainly Cromwell's correspondence for the 1520s contains a number of letters attesting to these activities. Thomas Twesell, for example, enquired whether Cromwell had 'dressed my cloith' and asked for him to 'send me word what ye payed for [the] dying of my cloith'.[218] Another who wrote was John Robinson, from Boston, Lincolnshire, thanking Cromwell for 'my clothe for yt ys verely well done'.[219] Of course, because of the nature of Cromwell's legal work, for which written evidence survives, there is far more evidence relating to his career as a lawyer than to that as a merchant. Nonetheless Cromwell operated in his legal and mercantile capacities simultaneously, and several clients made use of him in both lines of work. The merchant John Ap Powell, when writing to inform Cromwell on the progress of his legal suit in June 1527, also thanked him for 'the deleuery of the ij balis of chamlets', a type of fabric originally made from camel hair.[220] Another man, William Cowper, requested 'a pece of lynyn clothe to make schetys of' and 'a gown clothe to make me a schort rydyng gown'. He also asked for counsel in a legal matter, for Cromwell's help in obtaining a benefice for his brother, for 'A nodyr' plaster for his knee, and for Cromwell to 'speke to master byrd the marchaunt for a but of Romenay [wine]'.[221] John Robinson's letter thanking

Cromwell for his cloth similarly hints that Cromwell was engaged on a legal matter for him, as well as helping with the printing of four thousand letters and briefs.[222]

Cromwell was well connected and entirely at home within the London mercantile communities. When Richard Cave wanted to establish his son in England, thinking him 'verry meet for a marchand', he approached Thomas Cromwell for help.[223] Cromwell's circle of friends included such men as merchant adventurer Stephen Vaughan, the merchants John Creke and 'Master Woodall' and the Luccan merchant Anthony Bonvisi.[224] Another merchant with whom Cromwell was acquainted was Joachim Hochsteter, from Augsburg, who was described to Cardinal Wolsey as being of 'oon of the gretteste and Rycheste cvmpaygne of merchantes' in those parts, a great importer of wheat to London, and a man of 'soche a power' and with such friends that 'yf your grace wolld haue eny thynge done here in thes partyes or in any other I know nott soche a man ... to brynge your pvrpose a bowte'.[225] At some point in the 1520s Hochsteter hired a horse from Cromwell, but promptly returned it, complaining about the animal's fitness and ability to work.[226] In July 1528, at Hochsteter's request, Cromwell aided his servant in a case before the mayor's court in London.[227] Curiously, Cromwell was then involved in a legal dispute against Hochsteter only months later, and appears to have been acting on behalf of Richard Gresham, an equally well-connected merchant, and the very man who had lauded Hochsteter to Wolsey in the letter cited above.[228]

Although Cromwell's mercantile activities primarily concerned the cloth trade, he also dabbled in other commodities when there was a profit to be made. The term 'man of business' is therefore a succinct description of his interests during the 1520s. Moneylending was one such activity.[229] A letter from John Williamson, Cromwell's servant and brother-in-law, reveals that he provided a fishmonger named Turnball with a 'barrell of Salmon' for 30s.[230] In February 1528 Cromwell supplied 'metall towardes the making of a greate bell', weighing 5,388 lb, to John White of Reading.[231] William Capon, the dean of Wolsey's college at Ipswich, also thanked Cromwell 'for the Labours & paynes ye haue takyn for me in [the] makyng of my ryng',[232] while Sir William Gascoigne similarly thanked him 'for the payn ye toke for my wyne'.[233] Foreign trade was yet another area of interest. A friend in Flanders was instructed to inform Cromwell 'what thinges myght be laden vnto these parties out of Englonde to take proffit by'. The friend was Stephen Vaughan, who advised Cromwell that if it were 'your pleasure to sende any maner of grayne out of Englonde vnto thise parties yow shulde no doubte take therby right good aduantage ... [of] the pryses of all maner of graynes' in Flanders.[234] Vaughan had previously told Cromwell that 'if youe wold healpe to get alycence for chese, I could get bothe yow and me muche money'.[235]

Like other members of the legal and mercantile professions, Cromwell also invested in land during these years.[236] A letter from Harry Wykys, Cromwell's brother-in-law, refers to one among several early unsuccessful efforts by Cromwell to obtain land.[237] During the late 1520s, however, perhaps owing to the increasing prosperity that working for Wolsey brought, Cromwell was more fortunate. Thomas Whalley told Cromwell in February 1527 how 'Thomas Perkyns & I haue made sale of iiij akers of vnderwod in youre woodes of Tyckthornies',[238] while in October 1527 Cromwell purchased the manor of Tolshunt Darcy, Essex, for £3,200.[239] This was followed in July 1529 by the purchase of the manors of Sutton at Hone and Temple Dartford, Kent, from Sir John Gage, vice chamberlain of the household, for 500 marks.[240] Cromwell then sold this on to Sir Brian Tuke the following March for a quick profit.[241] A grant dating to February 1531 similarly refers to a lease Cromwell shared with Sir Humphrey Bowland on the rectory of Gingemargaret, Essex, which the pair had taken out in March 1528.[242] An indenture agreed 'in the 22nd yere' of Henry VIII's reign also suggests that Cromwell leased the parsonage of Melbourne, Derbyshire, from John Kite, bishop of Carlisle.[243] These modest purchases, however, were the only successful land acquisitions that Cromwell made during these years. His investment in land was therefore actually quite small during the 1520s, particularly when compared with other members of the legal profession. Thomas Kebell, for instance, had built up considerable estates amounting to over 3,000 acres in Leicestershire thanks to his own lucrative legal career.[244] Perhaps Cromwell's mercantile activities required ready cash, making it unwise for him to invest too heavily in land at this point.

How wealthy did Cromwell become through these various careers, activities and investments during the 1520s? Calculating a typical lawyer's income during this period is almost impossible, as this varied enormously depending on the lawyer and his work. Thomas More's income in the year 1517 was estimated to be around £400, while Thomas Kebell was worth almost £800.[245] It is perhaps easier to offer an indication of the sort of fees a lawyer might command. A fairly standard charge in London for a legal consultation was 3s 4d, but fees in the provinces were often much higher.[246] Once litigation was under way there were also fees for the production of documents and searches, as well as payment for any argument before the bench. Merchants might also make considerable sums, and several of the richest merchants certainly rivalled the wealth of many lawyers. References among Cromwell's papers offer hints at his own costs and expenses for both these lines of work. Two subpoenas 'ayenst goodwyn' were recorded as costing Cromwell 5s, while a 'pece of chamlet' cost him 11s.[247] He also paid 45s 4d to the servants of 'the lorde chief justeces of the commen plees . . . for writing and ingrossing writtes of couenaunttes' relating to Wolsey's colleges,[248] while 'certayn searches and copies out of the chauncerie commen pleas and excheqre [*sic*]' for similar purposes cost 45s.[249] Other costs associated with Cromwell's legal work for Wolsey included over £16 for twenty-four days' work taking possession and holding courts at several monasteries, and money for 'vellon [vellum, i.e. parchment] bought for thingrosing of certain lettres of Attourney for my lords colledge and trymyng the same withe laces of silke'.[250]

Perhaps a better indication of Cromwell's wealth and prosperity at this time is given by the fourth assessment of the subsidy granted by the parliament of 1523, which took place on 20 March 1527 and assessed Cromwell as part of Wolsey's household. The highest-worth individual among the members of the household was Richard Warren, who was evaluated at £300; Cromwell, by contrast, was valued 'in goodes' at £50.[251] In the same assessment Sir Thomas More was assessed in lands and fees at £340 as part of the king's household.[252]

Cromwell's will, drawn up by Thomas Wriothesley in July 1529 and amended sometime after September 1532 by Cromwell himself, probably offers the best indication of his disposable wealth by the end of the 1520s.[253] Cromwell's three children by his wife, Elizabeth, had over £600 bequeathed to them in this.[254] Gregory, the only one of the children who would survive their father, was to get £400 (later revised to £666 13s 4d), and a further £100 (later £200) when he turned twenty-four. Cromwell's two daughters, Anne and Grace, both of whom presumably died between the 1529 drafting of the will and the subsequent revisions, were to get 100 marks each and £40 towards their 'fynding' in marriage.[255] Other family members were to receive smaller sums, which amounted collectively to well over £240 (many received more in the subsequent revision). Cromwell's servants would also have collectively received over £60 had he died in 1529. Although by no means a complete picture of his wealth at this point, Cromwell's will indicates that he was in a comfortable financial position by the end of the 1520s.

Cromwell was once accused of a 'notorious accessibility to bribes' during the 1520s, particularly in relation to his work for Wolsey.[256] How far can corruption and venality account for his wealth by this point? It is certainly interesting that in October 1526, Thomas Strangways, Wolsey's controller, was bound in recognisance not to commit 'any boddelye hurte vnto ... Thomas Cromwell or his servuantes'.[257] It suggests that even in the 1520s Cromwell aroused hostility. There are also hints that he was capable of acting rather unscrupulously. Christopher Burgh, parson of Spenythorn, York, brought a suit against Cromwell in Star Chamber, accusing him of extorting £20 from him on 16 May 1528.[258] A letter from Edward Fetyplace similarly hints at financial duplicity. He recalled the 'promyse' that Cromwell made him at the suppression of Poughley during the establishment of Wolsey's colleges

not onely for the seid parsonage bot also for the seid lease ... perteynyng to the seid monastery / Apon whice promise I delyuered you 40s thinking to haue founde your worde & ded one And sithe that tyme it hathe pleased you to graunte the seid lease vnto a noder man.[259]

During Wolsey's suppressions Cromwell also extracted an annual fee of 26s 8d from the priory of Shulbred, Sussex, on 10 March 1525.[260] The priory had given this to ensure that 'they maye ... dwell att rest with owte trowbill & contynue styll yn ther howse'.[261] The brethren there were evidently unaware that the monastic houses intended for dissolution had already been identified and that theirs was not among them.[262] Cromwell clearly capitalised on the uncertainty surrounding Wolsey's suppressions, although it was another man, one Richard Bedon, who had suggested this action to him, and who prompted the priory to grant this fee.[263] Given that Cromwell was accused of bribery and corruption on his fall in 1540, allegations of venality must receive greater consideration in later chapters examining his career in the 1530s.[264] Nevertheless, the evidence suggests that in the 1520s Cromwell was certainly capable of acting dishonestly for his own financial gain.

Although Cromwell would not become a major political figure until he had entered the king's service in late 1530, by the end of the 1520s he had undoubtedly risen to a position very close to the fringes of the serious political class. A legal career naturally enabled people to increase their position in sixteenth-century society, but it was Cromwell's work for Wolsey that placed him in a position of recognised influence, albeit over the cardinal's private affairs. The merchant Edward Baxter, writing in 1529, provides the most unequivocal illustration of this. Baxter told Cromwell that he had two sons and hoped 'too purveye fore one of theym sume goode spiritual lyvinge'. He added that

> As I vnderstand ye be in good Favors withe mye lordes grace whoo haithe gyfte and collacione of menye goode promotions / I inteerelie desire you too be soo goode mastere too me as too provyde me of sume substanciall promotione fore one of mye saide sonnes at mye lorde cardinalles graces hand.[265]

Baxter was by no means alone in his belief that Cromwell was a man with influence in the right places. The priest John Gray, on hearing that Wolsey might obtain the priories of Tickford and Ravenstone, Buckinghamshire, for Cardinal College, Oxford, requested that Cromwell 'helpe me that I may contynue and enioye the Ferme of Tykford ... And also that ye woll helpe me to haue the other said pryory likewise in Ferme.'[266] Similarly, when Roger Richardson, mint master of Wolsey's coin at Durham, died in 1528, Cromwell received a letter petitioning him to persuade Wolsey to appoint Richardson's son, John, permanently to his father's former position.[267] Cromwell was apparently successful in this, as John did indeed succeed his father.[268]

Yet perhaps the most interesting point in relation to Cromwell's position and standing during these years relates to the people with whom he was already involved, albeit very much as a subordinate, before he made the transition into the king's service. Cromwell's book of debts and obligations ranging from 1518 to 1529 reveals that he had already had contact with a number of prominent figures.[269] Henry Percy, sixth earl of Northumberland, was listed for a number of obligations starting from 15 January 1527.[270] The marquis of Dorset is another who appears several times;[271] so too is 'my lorde George graye', who is recorded owing four different obligations.[272] It will also be recalled that Sir Thomas Boleyn had made use of Cromwell's legal skills in 1527. In the same year Cromwell was involved in settling the disputed wardship of Thomas Stanley, Lord Monteagle, which brought him into contact with Thomas, Lord Darcy and Sir John Hussey.[273] Sir Edward Guildford, lord warden of the Cinque Ports and a close friend of Henry VIII, was also acquainted with Cromwell during these years,[274] as was the earl of

Westmoreland.[275] Cromwell's friendship with Sir John Gage, Henry VIII's vice chamberlain, similarly stemmed from the late 1520s.[276] Cromwell was therefore already acquainted with, working for and operating among a number of prominent people well before he entered the royal service. Although he was 'unfamiliar' with the royal court before 1530,[277] it is clear that Cromwell was already handling the affairs of some of its notable figures. This experience can only have enhanced his ability to manage and work alongside such people during his career under Henry VIII.

Cromwell and Parliament

So far, this chapter has been concerned with Cromwell's private career during the 1520s. To conclude it, some of the more public activities Cromwell was engaged with will be examined, in particular, his career in parliament. There are certainly indications throughout the 1520s that Cromwell already possessed the ambition to advance himself in more 'public' roles. In December 1523 he sat on the London wardmote inquest for Broadstreet ward.[278] Wardmotes were held to ensure the smooth running of London's wards, and examined breaches of city regulations, as well as making sure streets, properties and pavements were safe and clean.[279] As late as September 1522 Cromwell was living in Fenchurch Street, in Langborne ward, yet the wardmote he sat on in December 1523 was for Broadstreet, where his newly acquired house at the Austin Friars was located. He must have established himself quickly to obtain a position on its inquest, hinting at a desire for advancement. In 1524 he would also act as a subsidy commissioner for the hundred of Osultone, Middlesex.[280] Commissioners were often appointed 'from the leading men in the shires and boroughs'.[281] It was their job to select local assessors, explain the rates of payment and assessment to them and produce a list of taxes in response to their assessments.[282] Perhaps most indicative of Cromwell's desire for advancement, however, is that he obtained a seat in both parliaments called during this decade. In 1523 he sat for an unknown constituency, and may have delivered a speech opposing Henry VIII's campaigns in France.[283] In 1529 he sat for the borough of Taunton, Somerset.[284]

Bold claims have been made about Cromwell's regard for parliament. Elton believed he entered it in 1529 determined 'to make a career',[285] and that his entry 'appears to be the first definite step in his rise to power'.[286] He also felt that Cromwell's commitment to parliament went beyond that of his legal contemporaries, that he alone realised the potential of statute law in erecting a unified nation-state and that Cromwell 'well deserves the name of England's first parliamentary statesman'.[287] It is certainly true that Cromwell's intentions on securing a seat in 1529 were an attempt to strengthen his position following the fall of his existing master, Thomas Wolsey. George Cavendish, the cardinal's usher and earliest biographer, recollected how, fearing for his own prosperity, Cromwell decided 'to ride to London and so to the court / where I wyll other make or marre or I come agayn'. On his return, Cavendish discovered that Cromwell had been made a burgess in the parliament, and had 'put ... his foote where he trusted shortly to be better regardyd'.[288]

But whether Cromwell entered parliament with the specific intent of securing the king as his new master, as Elton thought, seems doubtful.[289] Cromwell was no stranger to parliament, having sat there in 1523. Nor did he deliberately abandon Wolsey's service for the king's, as the next chapter will show. Driven by the opportunities it offered for patronage, lawyers had been sitting in parliament in increasing numbers since the fifteenth century.[290] Cromwell's actions were therefore typical of his legal contemporaries, and the most likely explanation is that Cromwell sought a seat in 1529 to help stabilise his own position following Wolsey's fall.

What of Elton's wider claims? Cromwell left so little by way of motive or reason for his actions that it is difficult to pronounce on his attitudes or beliefs. Many of Elton's conclusions regarding Cromwell, which have since become almost unshakeable Tudor orthodoxies, are in fact entirely conjectural. Cromwell did, however, make one comment that is revealing of his attitude towards parliament. On 17 August 1523 Cromwell wrote to his merchant friend John Creke about his experiences in the parliament of 1523 in which he sat. Cromwell wrote:

> ye shall vnderstonde that by long tyme I amongist other haue Indured a parlyament which contenwid by the space of xvij hole wekes wher as we communyd of warre pease Stryffe contencyon debatte murmure grudge Riches pouerte penwrye trowth falshode Justyce equyte discayte oppres- cyon magnanymyte actyuyte Force attempraunce Treason murder Felonye consyli[ation] and also how a commune welth might be edif- fyed and a[lso] contenewid within our Realme howbeyt in conclusyon we haue d[one] as our predecessors haue bene wont to doo that ys to say as well as we myght and lefte wher we began.[291]

For many historians working in the late nineteenth and early twentieth centuries, Cromwell's apparent disdain for parliament expressed in this letter confirmed their belief that he was an oppressive and despotic minister.[292] Elton, by contrast, in an interpretation which became the prevailing orthodoxy,[293] argued that Cromwell's use of parliament in the 1530s undermines such a conclusion, and dismissed these comments as humorous remarks that should not to be taken too seriously.[294] Neither view is entirely convincing.

Instead, what Cromwell's complaint to Creke suggests is that he regarded parliament as being rather ineffective. It is worth considering why this might have been so. Parliament sat at the apex of the common law system, and Cromwell's background as a lawyer furnished him, like many lawyers, with a belief in the supremacy of statute law. But as this chapter has also shown, Cromwell simultaneously operated as a merchant in the 1520s. Might his mercantile background have also shaped his attitude towards parliament? When examining the institution, many historians have focused on the Crown's relationship with it, and the legislation passed with regards to official government sponsorship. Yet many of London's professional circles had a vested interest in parliament because it controlled their trade and regulated their privileges.[295] Private bills were frequently introduced on behalf of a variety of groups. But many of these either never became acts or, if they did, took a number of sessions, sometimes even a number of parliaments, before they did so. Helen Miller, for example, has shown that London's professional circles had a highly active parliamentary programme, but during the early parliaments of Henry VIII's reign they were often unsuccessful in getting legislation passed that would be beneficial to their trades.[296] Cromwell, who sat in both the 1523 and 1529 parliaments, would not only have witnessed the failure of a variety of bills, but may even have seen some fail in which he himself, as a merchant, had a vested interest.

This suggestion is in fact supported by some of Cromwell's own activities in the 1520s. Even before he became a royal servant, Cromwell was drafting bills for parliament. Unsurprisingly, this was often on behalf of the merchant and professional circles that he lived among. It was during the 1523 parliament, for instance, that Cromwell amended and corrected a bill on behalf of the Glaziers' Company designed to curb the influence of foreign glaziers who, so the bill alleged, were harming the interests of the king's subjects.[297] This does not appear on the statute books, and presumably failed in parliament. Another bill Cromwell drafted in 1523 was on behalf of the abbot of St Mary's of the Holme, Cumberland, on the Scottish border.[298] This requested that the monastery be permanently discharged from the payment and collection of all subsidies, taxes and payments to the Crown, on the grounds of persistent attacks and robberies by the Scots. Again, this bill presumably failed: a later draft suggests that Cromwell placed a similar petition on behalf of the abbot before the King's Council.[299] In the first session of the 'Reformation' parliament, Cromwell was also among five men who endorsed a bill on behalf of the Mercers' Company designed to halt protections.[300] Given that Cromwell endorsed the bill, it would be surprising if he did not wish to see it passed. Though once again, the bill does not appear to have come into law.

The success rate of the legislation that Cromwell drafted during the 1520s is therefore unimpressive. Under such circumstances, it is not difficult to see why he might have regarded parliament as being rather ineffective and little more than a talking shop. Of course, this is not to claim that Cromwell did not regard parliament highly. But given that, since the fifteenth century, there had been 'no doubt that legislative supremacy lay in the High Court of parliament', perhaps Cromwell's extensive use of it during the 1530s was driven less by a desire to establish the beginnings of constitutional monarchy and more by one to ensure that the radical changes brought about were seen to be as legitimate – and enforceable – as possible.[301] What is perhaps more significant, at least in terms of Cromwell's later political career, is that by the end of the 1520s he had already had practice of drafting legislation, a task he would soon employ skilfully in the service of the king. Moreover, given that roughly half of the Members in each new parliament during this period were novices, and that Cromwell himself had been an MP in two parliaments, he was actually something of a parliamentary veteran.[302] This experience would prove invaluable for any royal minister required to manage parliament on the Crown's behalf.

Conclusion

Until now, the full extent of Cromwell's life in the 1520s has never been specifically examined. Yet here it has been possible to establish what Cromwell was doing during these years with a reasonable degree of accuracy. All the evidence suggests that Cromwell was a prosperous, and fairly typical, lawyer and merchant, whose work and activities were similar to those of many men engaged in the legal profession during the early sixteenth century. While he was not a formally trained lawyer, the work Cromwell undertook for suitors in Chancery and Star Chamber – arbitrating disputes, drafting land conveyances and taking on all manner of minor legal tasks – reflected the work carried out by many men in the middle and lower branches of the legal profession during this period. Cromwell was also already a man of striking efficiency and organisational ability. These were two qualities that would prove crucial for handling the routine work of government, much of which 'took place under legal forms and demanded some facility in law'.[303] Perhaps most importantly, however, Cromwell's skills as a lawyer had enabled him to enter Cardinal Wolsey's service. Having then proved himself by managing all sorts of complicated legal and administrative matters connected to Wolsey's private affairs – notably his colleges at Oxford and Ipswich – Cromwell rose in Wolsey's esteem. By the end of the 1520s, Thomas Cromwell was one of the cardinal's most trusted servants.

The next chapter discusses how Cromwell, quite unintentionally, would leave Wolsey's service and begin to work for Henry VIII himself. What is significant here is the recognition that when he finally entered the king's service, Cromwell was following in the footsteps of other lawyers, including Richard Empson, Edmund Dudley, Thomas More and Thomas Audeley. Although he did not emerge from quite the same branch of the legal profession as this group, Cromwell was still broadly reflective of a much wider movement of legal-minded men into the Crown's service. It is well recognised that the shared legal background of many royal servants naturally created a 'common outlook' among them. This was broadly in favour of utilising statute law, parliament and the common law courts to expand the Crown's powers.[304] It is against this common outlook, therefore, that Cromwell's own actions in the 1530s are better judged and understood. Although Elton claimed that Cromwell's regard for parliament and his commitment to its use went beyond that of other lawyers, the likes of Edmund Dudley and Christopher St German were already voicing the necessity of curbing the role of the Church and extending royal power well before Cromwell's ministerial career in the 1530s.[305] Cromwell's later use of parliament, his involvement in the assault on the Church in the 1530s and his willingness to help extend royal authority over it, are therefore best understood as part of this wider attitude among his near-legal contemporaries. Placed within his proper legal context, Elton's revolutionary political and constitutional theorist evaporates.

Yet despite the implications of Cromwell's early life for understanding his later political career under the king, it is worth concluding this chapter by emphasising the significance of his pre-ministerial years regardless of later events. Even if Cromwell had not progressed into Henry VIII's service or gone on to play such a prominent part in the radical changes of the 1530s, his earlier life and careers would still be interesting, and worthy of study, in their own right. By 1530, Thomas Cromwell was a prosperous London lawyer and merchant. He was already a man of some wealth and standing, and was acquainted with, working for and operating among a number of prominent figures. His early life therefore provides an instructive case history of an early sixteenth-century man on the rise, demonstrating that sheer ability could overcome (up to a point) extremely humble origins.

CHAPTER TWO

ENTRY INTO THE KING'S SERVICE, 1529–1530

CROMWELL'S CAREER AS A lawyer and merchant gradually came to an end following his entry into the king's service in 1530. This was made possible thanks to the position that Cromwell found himself in following the fall of his existing master, Cardinal Thomas Wolsey. Between Wolsey's fall in the autumn of 1529 and his death in November the following year, Cromwell was called upon to solicit the cardinal's affairs at court. It was this opportunity and proximity to the centre of power that first enabled Cromwell to make an impression there. Yet although these events have been discussed before, some of the commonly held assumptions surrounding Cromwell's entry into the king's service certainly bear scrutiny.[1] Three of the earliest accounts that describe these events all placed enormous weight on Cromwell's growing contact with Henry VIII during 1530, yet neglect the other relationships that Cromwell relied on for survival and prosperity. While access to the monarch was important for a career in the royal service, Cromwell's earliest success at court was far more dependent on the favour, connections and work he undertook for other prominent figures than it was on the nascent relationship between king and minister. A somewhat different account of how Cromwell became Henry's man was offered by Elton almost sixty years ago. He portrayed Cromwell as being 'intent on power' from the very beginning, and determined to go 'as high as possible' in his search for a new master.[2] In this chapter, however, it is argued that Cromwell's entry into the royal service was unexpected, unintended and wholly dependent on fortune and circumstance.[3]

Wolsey's Fall

It is not entirely clear when Henry VIII came to the momentous decision that his marriage to Catherine of Aragon was invalid in the eyes of God. But when he did, it was Cardinal Wolsey, his leading minister for almost fifteen years, who was given the unenviable task of trying to obtain a divorce. The king had convinced himself that to have married his brother's widow was contrary to divine law, as proscribed in Leviticus 18:16 and 20:21.[4] In addition to this plague on his conscience, Henry had also fallen in love with Anne Boleyn, and therefore looked to Wolsey to secure the annulment of his first marriage so that he might marry Anne. The earliest known attempt by the English, and Wolsey in particular, to resolve the king's 'great matter' was a secret legatine court, held at Westminster in May 1527.[5] This was intended to pronounce on the validity of the king's marriage to Catherine, and was presided over by the cardinal. Little detail is known regarding who else was in attendance or exactly what was discussed. In any case, on 31 May the court was adjourned with no verdict reached. Following this, in the summer of 1527, Wolsey unsuccessfully attempted to have himself elected as papal deputy, hoping to secure what Henry most wanted through this.[6] Though unbeknown to Wolsey, the king himself had also secretly sent his secretary, William Knight, on an ill-considered mission to obtain a dispensation from the pope that would enable Henry to remarry.[7] Although a dispensation was eventually obtained, it only allowed Henry to remarry if his first marriage was proved to be invalid. Moreover, in clumsily trying to secure this dispensation, the king had made manifest to his Holiness his desire to marry Anne Boleyn, which rather compromised his moral position.[8]

Then, in February 1528, Henry and Wolsey sent Edward Foxe and Stephen Gardiner on a diplomatic mission to Rome. What Wolsey now sought from the pope was a decretal commission, empowering him to act as judge and pronounce on the king's marriage to Catherine domestically.[9] Fox and Gardiner worked tirelessly to persuade the pope to grant this, and Clement VII did eventually agree to a secret decretal commission for Wolsey and Cardinal Campeggio to examine the matter and decide the validity of the royal marriage without appeal.[10] Campeggio arrived in England in October 1528, but had been instructed by the pope to play for time. He therefore set about trying to reconcile Henry to Catherine. Wolsey's and Henry's chances of success were then further hampered when the queen produced a papal brief that had permitted her marriage to Henry in the first place. This brief, which was different from the one that the English lawyers had been working with, technically invalidated the decretal commission, and Wolsey was back to square one. Further attempts were made to obtain another commission, but the diplomatic context was such that the pope was now much less willing to cooperate.[11] Wolsey pushed on regardless, and he and Campeggio held a second legatine trial at Blackfriars in May 1529.[12] Although Catherine challenged the court's authority and appealed to the pope, the trial continued. Arguments were heard for and against both sides, including an impassioned speech in favour of the queen by Bishop John Fisher.[13] Then, on 23 July, Campeggio adjourned the court, which would never meet again. Wolsey's chances of success were slipping away.

Throughout 1529 Wolsey's relationship with the king had been gradually deteriorating, as Henry lost confidence in his minister's ability to secure his divorce. By the end of July Wolsey was no longer in charge of government business.[14] He also met ambassadors less regularly, and had become increasingly isolated from Henry, who ignored several of his requests for a meeting.[15] When the king finally agreed to meet the cardinal in mid-September, as Campeggio was about to take his leave from England, the Imperial ambassador, Eustace Chapuys, claimed that Wolsey had 'been long asking permission to re-appear at Court', but had only now 'obtained it through Campeggio's influence'.[16] It is true that, to everyone's surprise, Henry greeted Wolsey warmly at that meeting;[17] nevertheless, the appearance was deceptive, and this would be the last time the two men would meet. What is more, rumours had been circulating for some time about the uncertainty of Wolsey's position. On 1 September Chapuys noted in a dispatch that 'it is generally and almost publicly stated that the affairs of the cardinal are getting worse and worse every day'.[18] The French ambassador also claimed that Wolsey had been 'betrayed' by his own men at court, while Florentius Volusensus, writing to Cromwell, referred to the 'painful rumours' surrounding Wolsey.[19] Another of the cardinal's agents, Thomas Alvard, also sought to reassure Cromwell that the reports against their master were marvellously false. Nonetheless, he still urged Cromwell to uncover the culprits.[20]

Wolsey's downfall did not, however, come until October. Historians have long debated exactly how and why Wolsey was toppled. Many have pointed to the role of those supposedly hostile to Wolsey at court, suggesting that they now sensed their opportunity to turn the king's disillusionment with the cardinal into outright hostility.[21] Others have claimed that it was

the king himself who destroyed Wolsey, and dismiss the role of an aristo-
cratic or Boleyn faction.[22] The simple truth, however, is that Wolsey had
failed to deliver the king his divorce, and Henry was now willing to turn on
a man who had loyally served him for over fifteen years. On 9 October
charges were brought against Wolsey in King's Bench. Specifically, he was
accused of having 'procured bulls from Clement VII to make himself
Legate', contrary to the fourteenth-century statute of praemunire.[23] On
17 October Wolsey had ceased to be lord chancellor, having resigned the
Great Seal.[24] By 22 October the cardinal had accepted his guilt of praemunire in an indenture with the king, and his possessions were forfeit to the
Crown.[25] He was then ordered to relocate from York Place at Westminster
to his house at Esher, near Hampton Court.

On Wolsey's fall in October 1529 there was nothing inevitable, or even
likely, about Thomas Cromwell's entry into Henry VIII's services. Indeed,
there was a real concern shared by Cromwell and his associates that he
might be ruined along with his fallen master. Stephen Vaughan wrote to
Cromwell on 30 October, anxiously enquiring as to how Cromwell was
fairing following 'this sodeyn ouerthrow' of the cardinal. Vaughan's remark
that 'yow ar more hated for your maisters sake then for any thing whiche I
thinke yow haue wrongfully done' makes it clear that Vaughan saw
Cromwell's involvement with Wolsey as threatening.[26] This concern probably reflected a wider belief at the time. Recollecting Cromwell's rise in
1539, Reginald Pole remembered that 'a rumor everywhere circulated' on
Wolsey's fall that Cromwell was imprisoned because of his work for the
cardinal.[27] Although there is no evidence to support Pole's claim, Cromwell
was certainly fearful that his service to Wolsey might have consequences
for his own prosperity. In late 1529 he tearfully lamented to George
Cavendish, Wolsey's gentleman-usher and earliest biographer, that he was
'lyke to losse all that I haue travelled for all the dayes of my lyfe ... I ame
in disdayn with most men / for my master's sake and suerly without Iust
cause / howbeit an yll name oons gotten wyll not lightly be put a way'.[28]

Cromwell's fearful reaction is understandable, but even discounting
hindsight it is difficult to see that he was in any immediate danger.
Cromwell's work for Wolsey had been confined to the cardinal's private
affairs; it is hard to imagine that he aroused hostility, or was a principal
concern, for Wolsey's enemies at court. The animosity towards Cromwell
which Vaughan referred to most likely stemmed from the landed gentry
and clergy with whom Cromwell had come into contact while suppressing

monasteries for Wolsey. Certainly Thomas Rush, writing on college business in December, told Cromwell of 'the manyfold talys and lyes and slaun-
derouse wordes [that] hath bene spokyn of me & you in these parties'.[29]
More importantly, Cromwell was not dependent on Wolsey for his own
security or income. He continued to work on college matters in late 1529,
while his private legal practice also occupied him.[30] In December, for
instance, Cromwell took part in an arbitrational award between two
London grocers, and during the final months of 1529 he continued his
involvement in a longstanding dispute between the merchants Oliver
Leder and Richard Reynolds.[31] Perhaps most significantly, however, there
is no evidence that any of Wolsey's servants suffered directly as a result of
his fate (interestingly, the same can be said for Cromwell's own servants on
his fall in 1540). Instead, Ralph Sadler reported to Cromwell on 1 November
how 'dyuers of my lorde his seruauntes . . . [have] ben elect and sworne the
king his seruantes'.[32]

Unlike many of Wolsey's men, Cromwell did not enter the king's service
in 1529, nor is there evidence of any direct contact between the king and
Cromwell at this point. In fact, between Wolsey's fall and his death in
November 1530, there is no indication that Cromwell contemplated abandoning Wolsey, or that he ever deliberately sought to exchange the cardinal's service for that of the king. This loyalty shown to Wolsey by Cromwell
is often held, by contemporaries and historians alike, as being one of
Cromwell's most positive attributes. In the months following his fall,
Wolsey referred to Cromwell as 'Myn onely ayder in thys myn intolerable
anxiete And heuynes',[33] 'My onely refugy And ayde',[34] and 'Myn only
comfort'.[35] He also acknowledged to Cromwell that 'without yow I can do
no thyng'.[36] Throughout Wolsey's disgrace, Cromwell was busy soliciting
members of court on the cardinal's behalf, defending him in parliament,[37]
drafting letters to the king for Wolsey,[38] and even handling the more
mundane task of accommodating the cardinal's requests for quails and
seeds.[39] Cromwell may also have been involved in the initial, short-lived
attempts by Wolsey to mount a defence against the charges of praemunire
brought against him.[40] In one letter from 1530 Cromwell would allege that
he had spent over £1,000 on Wolsey's affairs.[41]

Yet Cromwell was plainly aware that the cardinal's predicament might
impact upon his own. Why, then, did he not abandon Wolsey as others
appear to have done? Three likely reasons emerge. First, the cynically minded
should not discount that a genuine bond had emerged between the two

men. Cromwell had worked closely with Wolsey since 1524, and when Cromwell was granted a coat of arms in 1533 he proudly incorporated part of Wolsey's former arms in it.[42] Another possible reason for Cromwell's loyalty to Wolsey is that Cromwell knew that people respected servants who stuck by disgraced figures: an assiduously cultivated reputation for loyalty might have made him more attractive to a future patron. But perhaps a third, and far stronger, factor for Cromwell's loyalty in 1529 and 1530 was that it was by no means certain that Wolsey was in fact finished. The cardinal's decision to submit to charges of praemunire in 1529 had meant that his goods were forfeit, but his life was safe.[43] And the months following his fall were full of political wrangling and plea-bargaining. Many at the royal court were genuinely expecting Wolsey to stage a comeback. As early as 27 October 1529, the French ambassador had reported that he thought it possible that Wolsey might regain his authority.[44] Chapuys also noted that in February 1530 the duke of Norfolk feared Wolsey's revival,[45] while Cavendish too believed that many of Wolsey's enemies were fearful of a revival in his fortunes.[46] Much of this uncertainty was fuelled by the king himself. From the very beginning Henry had done much to foster in Wolsey a hope that all was not lost. A pardon was granted to him, following negotiations, on 10 February 1530,[47] and Henry sent the cardinal gifts on several occasions as a sign of his good will.[48] When Wolsey became sick in December 1529, Henry had even sent his own doctors to attend him.[49] Perhaps, as Peter Gwyn has suggested, Henry was surreptitiously leaving open the possibility of using the cardinal as a means to threaten papal power in his quest for a divorce.[50] By not totally destroying Wolsey, Henry kept several options open, including the possibility of recalling the cardinal, and using his diplomatic expertise to engineer an alliance against the papacy, or perhaps even further disgracing him in order to put greater pressure on Rome. In such an uncertain environment, Cromwell may well have calculated that it might not be worth his while to sever links with Wolsey too soon. It would prove to be a significant decision, and one which unexpectedly presented Cromwell with the opportunity to begin his own career under the king.

A Meeting with the King?

Three of the earliest commentators on Cromwell's entry into the king's service all placed great significance on a momentous first meeting between Henry VIII and his future chief minister. Eustace Chapuys, writing in 1535, reported how, following the cardinal's fall, Cromwell had been threatened by Sir John Wallop. In an attempt to secure protection, Cromwell managed to procure an audience with the king, whom he

> addressed in such flattering terms and eloquent language – promising to make him the richest King in the world – that the King at once took him into his service, and made him councillor, though his appointment was kept secret for more than four months.[51]

A similar account was given by Reginald Pole in his *Apologia ad Carolum Quintum Caesarem*, written in 1539.[52] Pole hated Cromwell, for Cromwell was closely involved in the execution of Pole's brother, Lord Montague, and condemned his mother, the countess of Salisbury, for treason during the later 1530s.[53] According to Pole's account, Cromwell was the 'messenger of Satan' and disciple of Machiavelli, who approached the king and suggested a break with Rome as the resolution to Henry's sought-after divorce from Catherine of Aragon.[54] The martyrologist John Foxe, writing several decades later, also described a meeting between the two men, whereby Cromwell made

> manifest vnto his highness, how his princely authoritie was abused within his owne realme, by the Pope and hys Clergie, who beyng sworne vnto hym, were afterward dispensed from the same, and sworne a new vnto the Pope, so that he was but halfe a king, & they but halfe his subiectes.

According to Foxe, Cromwell also told Henry that he might 'accumulate to him selfe great riches', if he followed his advice and asserted his authority over his clergy.[55]

Yet despite the general similarities between these accounts, there is reason to doubt their overall veracity as reliable sources on the beginnings of Cromwell's royal career. Modern historians have convincingly demonstrated that Cromwell was not the man responsible for the 'intellectual origins' of the break with Rome. Henry VIII was already aware of the possibility of breaking with Rome and acting independently to secure his divorce from Catherine of Aragon; he did not require Thomas Cromwell to suggest this to him.[56] This virtually extinguishes the possibility that there was one significant meeting between Henry and Cromwell during which Cromwell presented a plan that would lead to schism and royal supremacy. Equally significant are the issues with the accounts themselves. By his own admission, Pole was not present at the meeting he referred to, and heard of it later from someone else.[57] Chapuys must also have heard his account second hand, as it is unlikely that he would have been present at a private meeting between Cromwell and the king. Neither, of course, could Foxe have been present. Nevertheless, the fact that three independent accounts exist, all of which are broadly similar, does suggest that there was a contemporary belief that it was Cromwell's direct contact with the king that enabled him to secure royal favour.

Elton, writing in the 1950s, was rightly dismissive of these three sources as reliable accounts of Cromwell's entry into the royal service (although he would later come broadly to accept them).[58] Instead, he offered a far more plausible alternative for the beginnings of Cromwell's career under Henry, well supported by Cavendish and evidence in the State Papers. Elton demonstrated that there was not one single meeting between the two men, but rather a series of meetings that enabled Cromwell to make a good impression on the king while he was soliciting Wolsey's affairs.[59] Like earlier commentators, therefore, Elton's interpretation still hinged considerably on Cromwell's contact and proximity to the king. But while Elton was certainly correct to conclude that access to the king was an integral step in Cromwell's entry into the royal service, he somewhat overstated the extent of Cromwell's relations with Henry VIII at that time. More importantly, he also failed sufficiently to acknowledge Cromwell's dependence on other patrons and contacts at court. To illustrate this, the chronology of Cromwell's entry into Henry's service needs re-examining.

Although the accounts of Pole, Chapuys and Foxe offer little by way of dating on exactly when Cromwell became Henry's man, the chronicler Edward Hall recollected that at the time of Wolsey's procession northwards following his disgrace 'diuers of his servauntes departed from him to the kynges seruice, and in especiall Thomas Crumwel one of his chief counsayle'.[60] If Hall's information was correct, this would date Cromwell's entry into Henry's services to around April 1530. Elton, however, argued that the transition occurred earlier than this, in January 1530,[61] noting a letter sent to Cromwell on 6 February in which Reynold Lytylprow of Norwich wrote, 'I do here that yow be the Kynges sarvand & In hys heye Favor'.[62] Although the editors of Letters and Papers had placed this in 1531, Elton suggested that Lytylprow's subsequent remark – 'also I here saye that

my lorde Cardenall ys ded wyche I thynke ys not trewe' – meant that the
letter required redating. As Wolsey had died on 29 November 1530, Elton
believed that two months was an unrealistic length of time for such news
to reach Norwich. He therefore reassigned the letter to 1530, linking
Lytylprow's rumour to Wolsey's illness in January 1530.[63]

But while this redating seems correct, it remains unlikely that Cromwell
was in Henry's service as early as January 1530. The salient fact is that there
is little evidence attesting to any work done for Henry by Cromwell at this
time, a point Elton was forced to concede.[64] True, a letter on the king's
behalf to the people of Ripon was placed in 1530 in *Letters and Papers*, and
thought to have been written by Cromwell.[65] Elton rightly pointed out,
however, that this letter is not written in Cromwell's hand, and there is no
reason to attribute it to him.[66] A more reasonable conclusion to draw is that
Cromwell's initial encounter with the king had occurred at the beginning
of 1530, during the period when he solicited Wolsey's affairs, but Cromwell
was not yet working for him. This is certainly supported by Cavendish,
who recalled how Wolsey had first instructed Cromwell to meet and negotiate with Henry on his behalf at Candlemas (2 February): 'my lord ... so
contynued still at Assher vntill Candyllmas ... Than commaunded he
master Cromwell beyng with hyme to make sewt to the kynges magestie
that he might remove thence to some other place, ffor he was wery of that
howsse at Assher.'[67] It seems likely, then, that just as Lytylprow's comments
on Wolsey's death were based on rumour, so too were his remarks about
Cromwell being the king's servant. Cromwell probably first encountered
the king around this time, but Lytylprow's remarks that 'yow be the Kynges
sarvand & In hys heye favor' are likely to be a sincere misinterpretation of
Cromwell's role as Wolsey's 'go-between'.

Nevertheless, what is clear is that Cromwell continued to enjoy access
to the king while he solicited Wolsey's affairs at court. On 17 May, for
instance, Cromwell warned the cardinal how 'His Grace [Henry] shewed
me how it is come to his knowlege that your Grace should haue certein
words of him and other Noblemen vnto my Lord of Norfolk'.[68] In an
undated letter to Wolsey, Cromwell also referred to 'being in communyca-
cyon' with the king.[69] On 12 July he similarly hinted at this when reporting
decisions made by the king on the fate of the cardinal's colleges.[70] Cavendish,
too, gives the impression of repeated contact during these months.[71]
Crucially, however, it was not until mid-1530 that Cromwell would begin
to be noticed by Henry. On 1 June Sir John Russell reported to Cromwell

that 'After your departure from the kyng his grace hadd very good comvnycac[i]ion of you'.[72] Not only does this reveal that Cromwell's access to Henry continued but, significantly, it suggests that Cromwell was only now beginning to make a favourable impression. What is lacking here is an acknowledgement of the role that other patrons played in fostering this.

From the outset of Wolsey's fall, Cromwell was far closer to certain figures at court than Elton would allow. In December 1529, for instance, Wolsey himself was urging Cromwell to work through prominent people to help improve his position. Wolsey instructed Cromwell that Stephen Gardiner, now the king's secretary, was 'to be laburyd And my lordes of Northfolke and Suffolk [who] knowyth honor and what ys convenyent to be done with the Kynges honor'.[73] Cromwell was in contact with Sir William Fitzwilliam, treasurer of the household, and Sir Thomas More, the new lord chancellor.[74] He also appears to have made use of his own contacts at court in order to facilitate both his and the cardinal's affairs there. Letters from Cromwell's servant Ralph Sadler reveal that in the initial months following the cardinal's fall, Cromwell had been in contact with Sir John Gage, vice chamberlain of the royal household, and that he continued to remain so.[75] Sadler wrote to his master at some point before February 1530, informing him how

> I repaired vnto the courte And there according to your commaunde-
> ment resorted to master viz chamberleyn desiring to knowe of him
> suche newes as he had concerning my lorde his affayres who answered
> me that of trewth he knew nothing more then he dyd at your last being
> with him.[76]

This contact and dealing with Gage in 1529–1530 was possible thanks to an existing friendship between Gage and Cromwell. The two men had known each other since at least 1528, when debts from Gage are recorded as being owed to Cromwell.[77] Cromwell had also purchased land from Gage in 1529, while Gage had left certain fabrics at Cromwell's 'howsse' to be made into vestments.[78] That the two men shared a genuine and long-standing friendship is evident from Sir William Fitzwilliam's later remarks to Cromwell, regarding 'the *olde fryndeship* that hath been between the said master vicechamberlayne and you'.[79] For Cromwell, this friendship was evidently a fruitful one. In April 1530 Gage wrote to inform him of 'shoche sayengeys as I have harde of the maner of my lord cardenallys departheynge towardeys the northe'. He warned Cromwell that 'ytt hathe byn reportheydde in the corthe that he [Wolsey] rodde in ... somteuss [sumptuous] fascheone [fashion]', and Gage advised that Wolsey exercise caution.[80] His final remarks to Cromwell – 'I truste to see you here thys ester holy days' – also points to their ongoing contact.

Yet Gage did not merely help Cromwell with the cardinal's affairs; Cromwell also made use of this friendship to strengthen his own position in 1529. It will be recalled that Cromwell endeavoured to re-enter parliament following Wolsey's fall. To do this, he relied heavily on the support and friendship of Gage and others. A letter from Sadler to Cromwell on 1 November 1529 illustrates how Cromwell intended to obtain a seat.[81] Sadler reported that he had spoken 'with Master Gage and according to your commaundement moved him to speke vnto my lorde of Norffolk for the burgeses Rowme of the parlyament on your behalf'. Gage had done this 'lyke a faythfull Frende', and Norfolk spoke with the king before reporting that 'his highnes was veray well contented ye [Cromwell] should be a Burges'. Royal approval was therefore sought, perhaps because Cromwell felt tainted by his association with Wolsey, but neither the king nor Norfolk provided a seat. Having received subsequent instructions from Cromwell, Sadler then spoke with Thomas Rush, another of Cromwell's friends, to see whether Cromwell might sit for the borough of Orford, Suffolk.[82] If this failed, Sadler assured Cromwell, he would speak with Wolsey's former man, William Paulet, and 'requiere him to name you ... one of the Burgeses of one of my lordes townes of his busshopriche of wynchester'. It was through this latter connection that Cromwell finally secured his seat, for in 1529 he sat for the borough of Taunton, Somerset, a possession of the see of Winchester.[83] But it is Cromwell's and Sadler's actions that are of more interest. Cromwell was not only relying on his friendship with Gage in order to facilitate his affairs but also on his friendships with Rush and Paulet. Both of these men had been in Wolsey's service, thereby explaining Cromwell's acquaintance with them. Of far greater significance was Cromwell's dependence on the duke of Norfolk. He was content to speak favourably to Henry on Cromwell's behalf, and not only was the king's approval obtained but Sadler was also instructed that Cromwell should follow Norfolk's direction once in parliament: 'order your self in the saide Rowme according to suche instructions as the saide Duke of Norff[olk] shall gyue you from the king'.[84]

Elton, when discussing these events, was quick to play down Cromwell's reliance on Norfolk. He sought to present Cromwell's entry into parliament as the product of his own ambition and ability: 'while the king's approval was sought for Cromwell's entry into parliament, neither the king nor Norfolk had anything to do with the provision of a seat. There was no question of official patronage.' He also argued that Cromwell was 'determined to enter parliament whether or not the king proved gracious'.[85] But while it does seem that neither Norfolk nor Henry was expected to provide a seat, Sadler's letter does make it clear that royal approval was requested before Cromwell made significant preparation to obtain one. Sadler's letter suggests that Cromwell sent him to move Gage and Norfolk first, and later sent further instructions: 'a litle *before* the receipte of your letter ... I spake with Master Gage and according to your commaundment'.[86] True, Sadler's letter also reveals that he had spoken with Rush while he was at court, but it is by no means clear whether they discussed provision for a seat. On the contrary, Sadler's remarks to Cromwell, that 'if I then had knowen your pleasure I could now haue sent you answere of the same', do rather suggest that Cromwell's subsequent letter containing further information was sent after Sadler's visit. Sadler's other comment – 'I will then according to your ferther commaundment' speak with Paulet – also confirms that the idea of approaching Paulet was a subsequent instruction. Sensibly, then, Cromwell was determined to ensure that he had royal approval first, before procuring a seat. He used his proximity to Gage and the support of Norfolk to obtain this.[87]

The idea that Cromwell relied on Norfolk's favour for both Wolsey's affairs and his own survival throughout these months can be more widely supported. Cromwell's position as Wolsey's 'go-between' necessitated contact with Norfolk, who, following Wolsey's disgrace, had become Henry's chief councillor.[88] Wolsey himself had urged Cromwell to speak with Norfolk,[89] while the cardinal's remarks that he had not received Cromwell's letter informing him 'of the coming hyther of the duke of Norfolke' also suggest that Cromwell had enough access to the duke to know of his movements and intent.[90] William Capon revealed that Cromwell had informed him 'how the duke of Norfolke shulde send to me a wrytyng to be sealed', again hinting that the two men had met.[91] Cavendish also reported frequent contact, recollecting how Cromwell had 'dayly accesse' to Norfolk during these months.[92] When the duke visited Wolsey at Esher, Wolsey even thanked him 'for your noble hart & gentill nature whiche ye haue shewed me behynd my bakke / as my seruaunt Thomas Cromwell hathe made report vnto me'.[93] Again, this implies that Cromwell was close enough to Norfolk to know what was going on. That Cromwell relied on the duke's favour – or, at the very least, his indifference – in order to survive at court during 1529 and 1530 is understandable. Indeed, it is hard to see how he could have operated at court, or have entered Henry VIII's services, had Norfolk been hostile to him. If the duke wanted to prevent or destroy Cromwell at this point, he surely could have.

Yet Cromwell's proximity to Wolsey also meant that he himself became a useful man for courtiers to know. In his attempts to secure a favourable pardon and improve his general situation, Wolsey had bestowed fees and rewards on those whose support he sought. Following advice from Cromwell and Gardiner, Wolsey informed Cromwell how he had instructed Gardiner to enlarge the fees he had granted to the courtiers Henry Norris, Sir John Russell, William, Lord Sandys and Sir Henry Guildford. Wolsey added that he would make these bequests 'with all myn herte And more as ye shul thynke expedyent', suggesting that Cromwell's advice was also something the cardinal was prepared to follow.[94] Small wonder, then, that when the king began to distribute fees and rewards from the cardinal's former lands of Winchester and St Albans, Cromwell was the man who many approached to help secure the requisite patents from Wolsey.

Wolsey's goods and temporal possessions had been forfeited to the Crown on 22 October 1529 through his acknowledgement of praemunire.[95] Under the terms of the pardon finally granted in February 1530, Wolsey was allowed to keep the archbishopric of York and was given a pension of £6,374, 3s 7½d per annum, but had formally surrendered the spiritualities and possessions of the lucrative see of Winchester and the abbey of St Albans.[96] Why, then, were patents required from the cardinal to grant annuities and fees from possessions already forfeited to the Crown? As Cavendish recollected, those who had been granted these rewards by the king feared that their patents 'cowld not be good but duryng my lordes lyfe / for as myche as the kyng had no lenger estate or title therin / whiche came to hyme be reason of my lordes attendure in the premunire'.[97] In short, there was concern about the validity of the king's claim to these lands, which had not yet been established through the correct legal process. Those granted annuities therefore felt it wise to ensure that they had a patent from Wolsey to legitimise the grants for term of life. To bring this about, 'there was non other mean but to make sewte to master Cromwell to atteyn ther confirmacion / at my lordes handes / whome they thought myght best / opteyn the same'.[98]

That Cavendish was correct to ascribe Cromwell a prominent role in securing these patents is evident from a number of letters sent to Cromwell over the summer of 1530. Writing from Winchester, probably in early July, William Paulet reminded Cromwell to 'haue in your remembraunce my lord of Norf[olk]es patent & my lord of Rochefordes [George Boleyn] patent master controllers [Sir Henry Guildford] & oders that I may haue them to Winchester bifore Tuwsday next'.[99] On 17 July Paulet received a box from Cromwell containing patents for Rochford, Guildford and Norris, but added that he had yet to receive the duke of Norfolk's patent and Sir William Fitzwilliam's.[100] Of equal note are the letters sent to Cromwell from Sir John Russell and the lord chamberlain, William Lord Sandys. Russell wrote to Cromwell on 1 June, informing him that the king had decided to grant Sandys 100 marks per annum out of the lordship of Farnham, one of Wolsey's former possessions as bishop of Winchester. Russell's instructions to Cromwell are worth quoting in detail:

> Syr yt hath pleasyd the Kyng to gyve my lord chamberlayne a hundred markes by the yere owt of the lordship off Fernham duryng his lyff / And *he* knowing greate famylyaryte and also you my speciall ffrende / desyryd me to wryte vnto you / that yt wold please you to make *hym* owt a pattent of the same / *he* to be keper of the castell ther ... And also *he* desyryd you to sendes hym the Forme of a letter how the *kyng* shuld wryte to my lord cardenall for his consent ... & for his signe and seale praying you that you wold send yt to my Lorde Chamberlayne as shortly as you can.[101]

Elton mistakenly believed Henry himself had instructed Russell to write to Cromwell requesting that he make out the patent.[102] It is clear from the wording of this letter that it was Sandys who had asked Russell to do this, not the king.[103] Nevertheless, Cromwell carried out the request with characteristic efficiency.[104] Four days later Russell revealed that 'you haue sent hym all suche thinges as I wrott vnto you for'.[105] Not only had Cromwell handled this matter speedily, but Russell's remarks following his further request, that Cromwell write to Wolsey on Sandys behalf, are also revealing. In doing this, Russell remarked, Cromwell would not only do Russell great pleasure, but he would 'also bynd hym [Sandys] to be yours to the best of his power'. Sandys, too, returned his engrossed patent to Cromwell on 4 June so that Cromwell could send it to Wolsey to be signed.[106] In doing this, Sandys added, 'you shall mynister vnto me singular pleasur ... I woll not faile to endevour my self [to you] at all tymes herafter to the best of my power'. In carrying out such requests Cromwell was gaining some useful friends.

Devising and obtaining these patents occupied Cromwell from June to September 1530.[107] According to Cavendish, who was well placed to witness all of this, the goodwill and friendship that Cromwell received from handling these patents helped facilitate – though did not cause – Cromwell's transition into the royal service:

> for his paynnes therin susteyned / they promysed euery man not oonly worthely to reward hyme but also to shewe hyme suche pleasures as shold at all tymes lye in ther seuerall powers ... in processe of tyme he served all ther tornes so that they had ther purposes / And he ther good wylles / thus roose hys name & frendly acceptaunce with all men / the fame of his honestie & wisedome sounded so in the kynges eares that by reason of his accesse to the kyng he perceyved to be in hyme no lesse wysdome than ffame had made of hyme report.[108]

What is striking here is that Cavendish makes it plain that Cromwell's gradual impression on the king depended as much on the favour and good-will of others as it did on the king himself. His wording suggests that those about the king spoke favourably of Cromwell before Henry himself had any significant contact.

Wolsey's Colleges

The turning point for Cromwell came as a result of the inquests held throughout the summer of 1530 to establish the king's legal right to Wolsey's college lands.[109] Since the cardinal's fall there had been uncertainty and concern among Wolsey and his associates over the fate of these institutions. Wolsey himself remained highly active on the fate of his colleges following his fall, and wrote to many influential figures in an attempt to gain their support in protecting his foundations.[110] On 9 November 1529, the dean of Cardinal College, Ipswich, anxiously wrote to Cromwell asking whether he should 'sue to the Kynges grace in the cawses of our collage'.[111] In late November he then ominously informed Cromwell that the king's commissioners had been to Ipswich to take an inventory of the college's possessions.[112] Thomas Rush also wrote to Cromwell on 29 December, reporting that 'Master Audeley ... said to me that he thought the kinges grace wold take all the monasteryes suppressyd by reason of the atteynour of my lord Cardinall ... & that his grace laufully might sett all the fermes belongyng to the said monasteries at his pleasur'.[113]

Uncertainty persisted throughout the early months of 1530. William Tresham wrote to Wolsey in May and reported the rumour that Henry would 'take yn iii lordshipes that lyeth nye to ho[n]sdon & recompense the owners partly with ypiswiche partly with owr [Oxford] college londes'.[114] Yet it seems that firm decisions were not made until late June or early July. William Capon reported to Wolsey on 9 July that he had been to London and retained the best counsel he could find to examine the legal position of the colleges. These opinions were not favourable. Those he consulted did not believe 'that the Lawe will bere vs in our cawses concernyng your graces collage by reason that your grace was kome in the premuniere by fore the er[e]cion of your sayd collage'. Capon added that 'the same ys so found by the Kynges Lerned Counseill'.[115] In other words, because Wolsey had confessed to the charges of praemunire, all monastic lands granted to Wolsey for his college project by the king 'reverted in to theyr Fyrst nature', that is, they would escheat (revert through forfeiture) to the Crown.[116] The dean of Cardinal College, Oxford, reported similar opinions on the legal position of Wolsey's Oxford establishment.[117] On 12 July Cromwell himself then broke the news to Wolsey that 'touching your Colleges, the King is determined to dissolve them'. His subsequent remark – 'whether his Highnes, after the dissolution of them meane to revive them againe and founde them in his owne name, I know not' – hints, however, that uncertainty remained over precisely what would become of them.[118] Perhaps the king himself had not yet decided.

In his letter to Wolsey concerning the colleges, Cromwell had also revealed how 'new offices shall be found of all the Lands belonging to them newly to intitle his Highnes which be already drawne for this purpose'.[119] William Capon similarly reported that 'the Counseill haue made bookes to fynd offices' of all the college premises.[120] The finding of offices, it will be recalled, referred to the inquests needed to establish the king's legal title to these lands. Although the lands reverted to the king on Wolsey's acknowledgement of praemunire, due legal process still required the king's right to be re-established before an escheator. An inquest or 'office' was therefore again required in each of the counties in which Wolsey possessed lands that escheated to the king. As Sir William Weston, prior of the hospital of St John of Jerusalem, noted on 12 July, once the king had made the decision to take possession of the cardinal's colleges, Cromwell himself was the obvious choice for the king to turn to for advice and information on them. Weston wrote to Cromwell:

I vnderstonde commyssioners shalbe assigned to sett and Inquyre of all
suche londes as be appropriate and annexed to senct Friswides Colledge
in Oxforde and *by cause no man knoweth the perfect truyth how euery thing
is past therein so well as ye doo* the king hath put his faithfull trust and
confidence in yow that euery thing may appere according to right and
the true meanyng.[121]

Cromwell's first work for the king was therefore connected with the
Crown's attempts to appropriate Wolsey's collegiate foundations, although
evidence relating to his involvement in this is frustratingly thin. Weston's
letter alludes to it; so too does a letter from Thomas Donnington, thanking
Cromwell for ensuring that the prebend of Wetwang, Yorkshire, formerly
part of the Oxford college's landed endowments, might be reunited to the
church of York.[122] A letter from John Pladon also beseeched Cromwell 'to
haue me in remembrance of the matter that I did sue vnto your maistership
as concernyng thoffice of clerk of the landes of my lord Cardinalles coledge
in Ipwiche', which hints that Cromwell was still involved with those lands,
even though they were now forfeit to the king.[123] Perhaps most crucially,
Philip Ward also identified that the names of commissioners listed on two
draft bills partially written by Cromwell, which recorded the receipt of
'comyssions letters and indentures' from the king's attorney general to
them,[124] were the very same men listed on the patent rolls as the commissioners for the inquests into Wolsey's lands.[125] The commissions, letters
and indentures they received were surely those authorising them to hold
inquests into these lands. In case any doubt remains, Cavendish also
confirmed that Cromwell's first task as a royal servant was connected with
the attempts to appropriate these lands. He recalled how, during Wolsey's
disgrace, 'master Cromwell executed his office the whiche he had ouer the
londes of the colleges so Iustly and exactly that he was had in great estima-
cion'. He also emphasised Cromwell's 'great occasion of accesse to the kyng
for the disposicion of dyuers londes *wherof he had the order & gouer-
naunce* / by means wherof and by his witty demeanor / he grewe contynu-
ally in to the kynges favor'.[126] It was Cromwell's competent handling of the
arrangements for these lands, then, that convinced the king that his
courtiers and councillors who had spoken favourably of him had been
correct in their assessment. As Cavendish recollected, 'His Majesty
perceived that there was in him no less wisdom than fame had reported of
him, forasmuch as he had the government and receipt of those lands'.[127]

Cromwell, then, joined the king's service sometime after mid-1530, somewhat later than Elton and others have suggested, and he was initially recruited in order to deal with the legal transfer of Wolsey's college lands. Although he continued to act on Wolsey's behalf until the cardinal's death on 29 November 1530,[128] Cromwell's work for the Crown evidently continued. At some point in November 1530, Cromwell began a correspondence with Stephen Vaughan in an attempt to secure William Tyndale's pen for the royal cause.[129] On 30 December Cromwell then received £13 6s 8d from the Privy Purse, which he paid to a Florentine sculptor on 7 January 1531, for work done on the king's tomb.[130] Finally, a letter from a priest, dated 10 January 1531, in which Cromwell was addressed as one 'of the kinges . . . Counsaill', reveals that he had become a member of that body, probably in December 1530.[131] Similar appellations continued throughout early 1531 and beyond.[132] Thomas Cromwell was now a royal minister.

Conclusion

Rather than being 'intent on power', as Elton sought to portray him, Cromwell's entry into the king's service in mid-1530 was unintended, and occurred more by chance than by any deliberate effort. His undoubted talents had come to the king's attention as he solicited Wolsey's affairs at court, but Cromwell was then recruited by Henry for a very specific purpose: to manage the inquests into Wolsey's confiscated college lands. Yet although the contact between the king and his future minister was important, Cromwell also relied considerably on other figures during these crucial months, notably Gage, Norfolk, Russell, Sandys, Paulet and Rush. A focus on king and minister can lead to a one-dimensional interpretation of Cromwell's rise, which fails to acknowledge the role that friends, acquaintances and patrons played in his advancement. By elucidating these relationships, a fuller, more rounded picture emerges, which places Cromwell's contact with Henry in a more multi-dimensional light. Cromwell clearly enjoyed some access to the king as he worked on Wolsey's affairs, and later Henry's own, but this access was fairly limited. Cromwell had made an impression – enough to enter the royal service – but the paucity of evidence attesting to his work for Henry during the final months of 1530 suggests that Cromwell's proximity to the king was still not especially great. As the next chapter will show, this would remain the case during the early months of 1531.

CHAPTER THREE

THE CROWN LANDS AND KING'S WORKS

ALTHOUGH CROMWELL HAD JOINED the King's Council during the final weeks of 1530, becoming a council member did not in itself unlock a wealth of new responsibilities for him. In many respects, being a councillor during this period was more a status than it was a job with defined duties. True, there were several tasks that Cromwell undertook throughout 1531, such as receiving and handling petitions or attending to the council's judicial matters, which did reflect the specific responsibilities of a councillor.[1] But there was no sudden eruption of 'government' work for Cromwell on joining this body. The matters he was engaged with during the early months of 1531 were the same as those he had been doing since entering the king's service in 1530. The earliest and most significant of these was Cromwell's responsibility for various Crown lands. Matters connected to these dominated Cromwell's first year as a royal councillor, and continued to occupy him well beyond this. When discussing Cromwell's rise and early ministerial career, historians have usually focused on his role in Henry VIII's break with Rome, and have passed over any wider work as insignificant. Yet it was Cromwell's management of various Crown lands that was probably the greatest single contributing factor in explaining his rise. It demonstrated the legal and administrative skills he had acquired during his early career, and it helps to explain how he became one of the Crown's principal financial agents. In order to illustrate just how integral this work was to the unfolding of Cromwell's ministerial career, it is necessary to begin by examining his position throughout 1531.

Cromwell's Position and Influence in 1531

For most of 1531 Cromwell was occupied far more with the private concerns of the Crown, most notably the management of royal lands, than he was with administrative work that affected the governance of the realm. Although Elton once claimed that Cromwell was already accumulating government work in order to establish himself at the centre of power, many details cited in support of an early date for Cromwell's prominent role in national government have been misinterpreted. I. D. Thornley suggested that in early 1531 Cromwell was involved with the initial attempts to amend the law of treason. An aborted draft of what would eventually become a new treason act, which was probably prepared during the initial weeks of that year, contains corrections in a hand which Thornley thought belonged to Cromwell.[2] Examination of the draft, however, reveals that the handwriting on it is not Cromwell's but that of Thomas Audeley, another lawyer also in the royal service at that time.[3] A request from the mayor and corporation of Salisbury to Cromwell asking for fresh gaol deliveries was also placed in 1531 by the editors of *Letters and Papers*.[4] This was dated 6 April, and taken by Elton as an early example of Cromwell conducting official legal business on behalf of the Crown.[5] There is no reason, however, that the petition must be of 1531; it may well be of a later date, and cannot be taken as convincing proof of Cromwell's work at that time.[6] Similarly, a petition entitled the 'Cawsse of the Vexacion of Roger Dycker prysoner', reported a rumour that in 1531 'Abovthe the Fest off Sayntt John the Baptyste [25 June] ... one Master Cromwell pennyd sertayn matters in the parllmentte howse the whiche no man agayn sayd'.[7] For Elton, this was proof that Cromwell was 'already a recognised leader and promoter of government policy'.[8] Yet the 'Vexacion' is perplexing. Parliament was prorogued at the end of March and did not reconvene until January 1532.[9] Equally significant is that there is simply no evidence of Cromwell acting as parliamentary draftsman for the king before the end of 1531, at which time his hand can be found on a treason draft with enactments prepared for the following February.[10] In all likelihood, the 'Vexacion' was written well after the events it concerned itself with, and the remark about Cromwell a contorted chronological recollection of his 'official' work from the third session in 1532. It will be recalled that when seeking approval for a seat in 1529, Cromwell had been instructed to work under Norfolk's direction in parliament.[11] This situation had probably not altered by the closing of the second session in early 1531. Cromwell was surely active in parliament then, but supporting, rather than drafting, government bills, and lobbying and cajoling on behalf of the Crown.

Cromwell's administrative responsibilities did not begin to broaden until about September. It will be shown that this was the result of the skills that Cromwell exhibited over the Crown lands, which naturally led to the accumulation of wider jobs of similar nature, more than anything deliberate on Cromwell's part. Financial matters, aside from those discussed below, were limited during 1531.[12] The editors of *Letters and Papers* did place letters to Cromwell indicating his oversight of the surveying and collecting of revenues from the lands of the vacant bishopric of Coventry and Lichfield in 1531, but a later chapter, which discusses these in detail, reveals these actually belong to 1532.[13] Several undated financial papers annotated by Cromwell were also placed in 1531, but date to later years.[14] In September, however, Cromwell did receive 'Instuctions youen by the kinges highness vnto his trustie Counsailor Thomas Crumwell to be declared ... to his lerned counsaill and indelayedlie to be put in execucyon this terme of Saynt Michaell'.[15] Nonetheless, these are of greater use as an indicator of the council's workload rather than Cromwell's. While he certainly handled many instructions himself, several were for 'Master Attourney', and other council members surely dealt with some. A letter from Nicholas Carew, master of the horse – if it dates to 1531 – reveals that he and Cromwell were authorised to swear commissioners for the sewers in September.[16] During the final weeks of 1531 Cromwell also began to play a greater role in the management of parliament, a subject we shall return to in a later chapter.[17]

Cromwell's position at the end of his first full year in the royal service is neatly illustrated by the observations of the Venetian ambassador. On 10 November 1531, when describing the composition of the King's Council, he included Cromwell seventh in a list of eight councillors, suggesting that by then Cromwell had risen to a position on the council's 'inner ring'.[18] The council's leading figures, however, remained: Thomas Howard, third duke of Norfolk; Charles Brandon, duke of Suffolk; Stephen Gardiner, bishop of Winchester and secretary to the king; and Thomas Boleyn, earl of Wiltshire. The Venetian ambassador saw fit to describe Norfolk in detail. He noted that 'His Majesty makes use of him in all negotiations more than any other person', adding that since Wolsey's death Norfolk's 'authority and supremacy have increased, and every employment devolves to him'.[19]

Two letters from John Longland, bishop of Lincoln, are also illuminating on this point. Writing in early January 1532, Longland reported an encounter with a man whom he suspected of misdemeanours.[20] The matter was forwarded to the council, but Longland, despite being in correspondence with Cromwell around this time,[21] addressed his letter to 'my lorde of norfolke, And in his absence, to my honourable good lord of Wilteschire'.[22] This suggests that it was Norfolk whom Longland perceived to be the council's leading figure. He enclosed his findings and informed the duke, 'I shall kepe hym saffe ... tyll I knowe frome you, other the kyng his plesur or yours'.[23]

It was Cromwell, however, who finally handled this matter. Two days later Longland remarked to Cromwell that 'I wrotte and sent [my findings] vnto my said lord of Norfolke, *whiche wrytinges his lordeshipe sent vnto you by my seruaunt*'.[24] The duke had received Longland's letter, and, seeing that it concerned a routine judicial matter, decided to delegate it. That Cromwell was specifically chosen for this seems doubtful. Longland's initial letter addressed to Norfolk was readdressed, 'To maister Threesourer [Sir William Fitzwilliam] Maister Controller [Sir Henry Guilford] and to Maister Cromewell or to any of them'.[25] Whether Cromwell seized the opportunity to undertake this work ahead of the other two men, or, more prosaically, he was merely the first of the three whom Longland's servant encountered is impossible to determine, and there is an evident danger of circular argument. The significance is that this episode illustrates that at the beginning of 1532 Cromwell, along with the likes of Sir William Fitzwilliam and Sir Henry Guildford, was seen as one of the council's workhorses.

A further indication that Cromwell was not yet a leading figure on the council is that he still found time to operate in a private business and legal capacity during 1531. A number of undated letters showing Cromwell engaged in such matters have been placed in that year (and later) in *Letters and Papers*. Although most of these probably belong to the 1520s, several can be dated to 1531.[26] On 10 January Sir John Barkar, addressing Cromwell as 'one of the Kinges most gracious Counsaill', asked for his 'goode helpe and futheraunce' regarding a matter of private debt in which Barkar was bound concerning Wolsey.[27] In March Sir James Worsley asked for Cromwell's 'indifferent ayde and aduyce' concerning a longstanding legal suit surrounding the attempted poisoning of Worsley's wife in February 1528.[28] Other suitors continued to seek Cromwell's legal skills in 1531.[29] Moneylending also continued, as did his mercantile interests.[30] Throughout his time in Flanders, for example, Stephen Vaughan repeatedly informed Cromwell of the difficulties he was experiencing in trying to sell Cromwell's spermaceti, a type of wax used in candles and ointments. In

January 1531 Vaughan was telling Cromwell that he could not sell the spermaceti because 'it is in maner nothing worthe'. By February of the following year, Vaughan remarked to Cromwell that trying to sell it 'putteth me to more payne then any thingeuer I had to sell in all my lyfe'.[31]

Of course, being a member of the King's Council naturally conferred a measure of status and influence on the holder of such a position. It is therefore not surprising that Cromwell's correspondence contains many letters attesting to this in 1531. Given that in January he was 'newly come to the fauor of the kyng', there are fewer examples of such requests during the initial months of that year.[32] From about April onwards, requests for favours begin to hint at a more widely perceived influence. Nevertheless, neither the requests nor the language used to make them suggest these were anything other than the type of appeals surely received by every councillor or prominent figure at court.[33] Similarly, a number of documents suggesting that Cromwell had considerable influence over ecclesiastical patronage were placed in 1531 by the editors of *Letters and Papers*. These have been erroneously dated, and will later be shown to belong to 1532 or 1533.[34] The examples of Cromwell's influence over church appointments that ostensibly do belong to 1531 fail to indicate that he was yet anything other than a royal servant close to the centre of power.[35]

Although the nature of the relationship between Cromwell and Henry VIII is a question we will return to throughout the remaining chapters of this book, some general conclusions about Cromwell's influence with the king in 1531 are of obvious interest here. Several letters received by Cromwell requested or thanked him for moving Henry on particular matters. In April 1531, for instance, Cuthbert Marshall, archdeacon of Nottingham, thanked Cromwell for 'laboring to the Kinges highnes' that he should not be exempt from the pardon granted to the York convocation for the English clergy's praemunire offences.[36] Similarly, Henry Sadler wrote in July that his wife had told him Cromwell would 'gett the warrant signed by the Kynges grace' so that William Holgill, master of the savoy, would take Sadler's account sooner.[37] Wolsey's former comptroller, Thomas Strangways, also asked that Cromwell move the king to finish the Hospital of Jesus Christ at Branforth,[38] while James Layburn requested that Cromwell 'speke one wourd to the kynges grace' for a pardon for his brother.[39] Such requests not only point to Cromwell's constant access to Henry, but also suggest that he enjoyed a degree of influence. Whether this went beyond that of other courtiers or councillors is of course difficult to determine. Some of Cromwell's own correspondence, however, can offer us some hints.

There is very little in Cromwell's correspondence for 1531 that suggests he was notably close to Henry VIII. One letter written in Cromwell's hand on behalf of the king was placed in 1531 in *Letters and Papers*; to whom the letter was addressed is unclear, but it requested the recipient to 'move the Frenche kynge . . . for the preferment of on[e] Frere Thomas beryer' so that he 'may be now elect to be gardyan of the grey freers in parys'.[40] The letter is not dated, and while 1531 cannot be ruled out, it seems unlikely that Cromwell acted in a secretarial capacity in that year. Stephen Gardiner was Henry's secretary from July 1529 until April 1534, at which point Cromwell formally replaced him.[41] The correspondence between Cromwell and Gardiner in June 1531 suggests that the latter was closer to Henry at this point.[42] Cromwell did, however, act in a secretarial capacity while Gardiner was in France between January and March 1532, and while Gardiner was in exile following the Supplication of the Ordinaries.[43] Perhaps this letter dates to that period. Whatever the case, the matter referred to in this letter was anything but 'high' policy.

Perhaps more revealing of Cromwell's position is a letter sent to him from the abbot of St Mary's, York, in July 1531. The abbot informed Cromwell that he was sending a falcon and two tassels to be 'presentid to the kynges most graciouse highnesse'. What is of interest is that the abbot asked for Cromwell's 'councell who ye thynk best to present theme for me'.[44] That he did not instinctively request Cromwell to present them seems significant. It suggests that he believed that there were others closer to Henry at this point better suited to this purpose. That he asked for Cromwell's advice also shows he did not think that Cromwell would feel irritated that the abbot thought he was insufficiently close to the king to make the presentation.

It will also be recalled that, since November 1530, Cromwell had been at the centre of attempts to persuade the religious reformer William Tyndale to return to England and write in support of Henry VIII's 'great matter'. This continued throughout the first half of 1531, and Cromwell's associate, Stephen Vaughan, was the man in Flanders meeting Tyndale to facilitate this. The attempts themselves need not concern us.[45] Yet a couple of points surrounding this episode are illuminating. First, it must be emphasised that the efforts to obtain Tyndale's assistance should not be viewed one-dimensionally, as king and minister working closely together. Vaughan's correspondence with

Cromwell alluded somewhat cryptically to the involvement of 'Master Treasourer' in several letters, while in one he referred to 'certeyn lettres directed to me from Master Fitzwillyam' containing instructions sent in January 1531.[46] Evidently, Cromwell was not the only royal servant corresponding with Vaughan on this matter.[47] Equally significant is that, while Vaughan was in constant contact with Cromwell, it was the king himself who was controlling these attempts, and who was kept well informed. A letter to Henry on 26 January makes it plain that Cromwell was acting under Henry's direction. Vaughan remarked how 'your magestie commaunded me to lerne, and practise in these parties, and therof taduertise youe, from tyme to tyme, as the case shulde requyre'.[48] Vaughan was sceptical that Tyndale could be persuaded to return, telling Cromwell privately on 26 January that 'It is vnlikely to gett Tyndall into Englond, when he Dayly hereth so many thinges from thense which scarethe hym'.[49] Nonetheless, in April Vaughan sent Tyndale's *Answer* to Thomas More's *A Dialogue Concerning Heresies*. Cromwell's reply to Vaughan in May then cautioned that '*his highness nothing liked the sayd boke beyng fyllyd with Scedycyous Slaunderous lyes and Fantastycall oppynyon ... The kinges highness therfor* hathe commaunded me expressely to wryte vnto you *to aduertyse you that is* [sic] *pleasure ys* that ye should desiste and leve any ferther to persuade or attempte *the sayde tyndalle to Com into this realme*.'[50] All this suggests that the direction of this policy was being dictated by the king rather than Cromwell. Sensibly, Vaughan's attempts to persuade Tyndale to return ceased after this.[51]

By the end of 1531, then, Cromwell had risen to a prominent but by no means leading position on the King's Council, handling much of that body's routine work. Nevertheless, his administrative responsibilities connected to this did not begin until well into the second half of 1531. This cannot therefore explain his rise to that position, nor does it explain why he was entrusted with these administrative tasks in the first place. The key to this, and to Cromwell's rise generally throughout 1531, lay in his management of various Crown lands. It is to such activity that this chapter must now turn.

The Crown Lands, 1531–1534

The fate of Wolsey's college lands not only provided Cromwell with the means of entry into the king's service but continued to occupy him during his early years as a royal minister. The lands belonging to the Ipswich college had been forfeited to the Crown in September 1530. Most were then redistributed the following year.[52] The college at Oxford was similarly forfeited, but was allowed to continue, stripped of most of its endowments. It was formally refounded in July 1532 as King Henry VIII's College, before becoming Christ Church in 1546.[53] Aside from the dealings with Tyndale discussed above, the only evidence of Cromwell's work for the king during the initial months of 1531 concerned the collection of rents from lands formerly belonging to Wolsey's colleges. Although Cromwell was not formally re-appointed as receiver-general for these until January 1532,[54] annotations in his hand can be found in the book of arrearages due at Michaelmas (29 September) 1530 for the Oxford lands, indicating that he had continued to oversee the administration of unpaid rents.[55] In addition, on 2 February 1531 Cromwell's servant William Laurence told him, 'I haue byne accourdyng to your commaundment in Cambrigesheare Northfolk and Suffolke for ... the rearages'.[56] In April Laurence wrote again asking Cromwell to 'asserteyn me whan ... I shall cum after the renttes be gathreid and make payment to your mastershipp', confirming that Cromwell was already receiving money on behalf of the Crown.[57] Other agents also wrote to Cromwell on the collecting of rents in early 1531.[58] On 5 April Henry Hargryppe reported the difficulties he was experiencing in gathering and receiving the rents from the lands of a suppressed priory.[59] Several letters from John Knight to Cromwell, written in March and April and placed in 1533 in *Letters and Papers*, also date to 1531.[60] These concerned lands connected with the manor of Raunston, or Ravenstone, Buckinghamshire, acquired by Cromwell and others to provide income for Cardinal College, Oxford, in the late 1520s, and now belonging to the king.[61] In March Knight wanted to know 'whether the kynges grace shall haue the rent of Raunston at owr Lady day next' or whether this should go to the previous owner, Sir George Throckmorton.[62] In mid-April, having received Cromwell's response, Knight informed the king's tenants at Raunston to pay the rent to him next May Day.[63]

Cromwell was also occupied during early 1531 with the redistribution of former college lands, many of which were sold or given by the king as rewards or patronage. John Smith, Wolsey's former auditor, acquired the manor of Blackmore, Essex, in February.[64] Cromwell was probably involved with this grant, as a copy of Smith's bill was in Cromwell's possession.[65] Similarly, in March, Nicholas Hurelton, clerk of the green cloth, was granted a lease on the manor of Bawdewyn's, Kent.[66] A draft of the grant for this contains an endorsement by Cromwell.[67] Further grants were then made in April. The duke of Norfolk received the site of the monastery of Felixstowe, Suffolk, along with a number of manors belonging to it there.[68] A draft of this patent is partially corrected by Cromwell.[69] Sir John Gage was similarly granted a number of former lands belonging to the college at Ipswich, while Robert Downes received licences to alienate certain lands of Rumburgh, Suffolk, and Dodnash, Suffolk.[70] Although no draft patents survive for either of these, jottings in Cromwell's hand confirm he was involved with Downes's grant.[71] In April William Laurence informed Cromwell of his findings concerning the 'valor' of 'the wood called the lunt that master alford shulde haue'.[72] This presumably comprised part of the Ipswich lands that Alvard was granted in August 1531. The draft of this is also in Cromwell's hand.[73]

That Cromwell was the Crown's principal agent in these redistributions is further attested by his influence over them from a surprisingly early date. In January Lord Morley wrote to him regarding a canon who had been granted 'the Farme of Bromefelde' by the prior and convent of Christchurch, London. He had since been 'wrongffully vexyd' by Wolsey's former auditor, John Smith, who laboured for the same farm.[74] Evidently Morley believed Cromwell was the man to approach on this matter, and asked him to 'be goode master onto hym aswell towchyng hys lese as also yff ony bylles of complaynte be put vp'. William Laurence told Cromwell in April that if Thomas Alvard were allowed to purchase certain lands then he would be 'much beholdyng to your mastershipp'; he also referred to 'the medows ye grawntt me'.[75] John Knight, receiver at Ravenstone, Buckinghamshire, similarly mentioned that Cromwell 'grauntid to me your especiall favour for the hauyng of Westhaddon'.[76] Each of these comments hints that Cromwell had some say over the arrangement of the lands. In February Richard Wharton had also warned a priest who received tithes from certain college lands to avoid Cromwell's 'farther dysplesur', and to follow his commandment over payments due to the king.[77] Other farmers were similarly reluctant to pay their rents without direct instruction from Cromwell.[78] All this suggests that he was, and continued to be, a man with considerable authority over these lands.

Serious redistribution of former college lands did not begin, however, until mid-1531, when the Crown began negotiations for a complex and continuing series of land exchanges. It has been noted that, following the fall of Wolsey, Henry VIII 'suddenly took up building as a passion', and having acquired many of the cardinal's former residences, the king set about transforming these into magnificent royal palaces.[79] What has largely escaped recognition is that Cromwell was one of the royal ministers who co-ordinated the exchanges of land that enabled the Crown to expand and transform these buildings. An indenture made on 16 May 1531 records that Waltham Abbey, Essex, had agreed to grant the manor of Stansted, Essex, to the king in return for the late priory of Blackmore, Essex, previously endowed to Wolsey's Oxford college. Thomas Cromwell, alongside Sir William Paulet, Sir John Daunce, Christopher Hales and Baldwin Mallet, was listed as one of those who would receive the eventual grant on behalf of the king.[80] Similarly, a draft copy of articles 'concludyd and aggrede the 30th day of Maij' 1531, between William Weston, prior of St John's of Jerusalem, London, and four of the king's councillors, is corrected in places by Cromwell.[81] This concerned an exchange between the king and the convent by which Henry would receive the manor of Hampton Court, Middlesex, along with its surrounding lands, a messuage (dwelling house) in Chancery Lane and a prebend in Salisbury Cathedral. In return, the priory received the lands of the late monastery of Stanesgate, Essex, which had also previously belonged to Cardinal College, Oxford.

The Crown's precise intention for each of these lands is not entirely clear given their geographic spread. It seems likely, however, that the acquisition of Hampton Court was to ensure that the king held it permanently before embarking on major rebuilding work there. Wolsey had been granted a ninety-nine-year lease on the manor of Hampton Court in 1514 from the priory of St John's of Jerusalem.[82] Presumably, when Wolsey had gifted the manor to the king at some unknown date in the mid-1520s, the lease was transferred to Henry. The efforts of Cromwell and others in 1531 were therefore designed to ensure that the Crown held Hampton Court in full before beginning to transform it.

The councillors who conducted the Hampton Court negotiations were not named in the draft,[83] but they were surely the four men listed as receiving the formal grant resulting from these negotiations on 5 June on behalf of the king.[84] Once again, these were Paulet, Hales, Mallet and Cromwell. As the king's attorney and solicitor general respectively, Hales and Mallet were not only the Crown's principal prosecutors but also two of its chief legal advisers.[85] Paulet was surveyor-general of the king's lands and master of the wards, which explains his inclusion in a matter of land exchange.[86] But why was Thomas Cromwell involved? The answer, aside from his obvious legal and administrative talents, was surely that these exchanges involved former college lands. The Crown would naturally require that any lands exchanged were of similar value, and that the deal was beneficial to the king. Cromwell was the obvious man to ensure this, given his unrivalled knowledge of these.[87] Nevertheless, he was more than just an adviser; his involvement was clearly considerable. Both the draft of the articles of agreement with St John's and a draft of the grant itself are corrected by him, revealing that he oversaw some of the legal drafting.[88] Three of Cromwell's own men, Ralph Sadler, Hugh Whalley and William Brabazon, were also used to deliver up possession, which further suggests that Cromwell was a – if not the – principal agent on behalf of the Crown.[89]

On 5 September 1531 a series of agreements was reached for further exchanges in which Cromwell continued to play a considerable part. A draft agreement between the king and the charterhouse of Sheen, Surrey, is heavily amended by Cromwell.[90] According to this, the king would receive 'the manours and lordships of lewesham and Estgrenewich and all other *woodes vnderwoodes waters ffysshynges aduousons thayr and all other thayr heredytanementtes* . . . apperteynyng to the said manours or Lordshippes'.[91] In return, the charterhouse received the late priory of Bradwell, Buckinghamshire, and a number of other lands, all of which had belonged to Wolsey's Oxford college.[92] Although the terms of the agreement were merely described as being 'devised by the lerned Counsaill of our said Souereigne lord', Cromwell was again one of the Crown's leading agents in this exchange.[93] Not only did he heavily amend the draft indenture, but he also managed wider details connected with it. William Wogan, for instance, received a letter from Cromwell in August enquiring 'wetherre I be mynded to leve my interest of my Ferme off Bradwell', one of the tenements shortly granted to Sheen.[94]

Several other exchanges were drawn up on the same day. Robert Catton, abbot of St Albans, consented that the king should have the abbey lands of the More, Hertfordshire, Asshelesse and Bachewortte, in return for the late monastery and lands of Pré, Herefordshire.[95] Eton College, Berkshire, agreed to exchange the house of St James-in-the-Field, along with over 185 acres between Charing Cross and Aye Hill, for lands in Kent.[96] John Islip, abbot of St Peter's, Westminster, also agreed to an exchange on a messuage called Pete Caleys in King's Street, Westminster, in return for the site of the late monastery of Poughley, Berkshire.[97] As was the case with all of these exchanges, including the earlier ones with St John's and Sheen, the grants for these were not ratified until December, and were confirmed by acts of parliament in January 1532.[98] Two further exchanges were also in negotiation, and were finally made on 1 November before then being formalised in December.

Waltham Abbey finalised its grant to the king of the manor of Stansted Abbot, along with other lands in Stansted, Hertfordshire, and Roydon, Essex; it was recompensed with the lands of Blackmore Priory, Essex, in January 1532. Christ's College, Cambridge, also consented to the king having the manor of Roydon, in return for Bromehill Priory, Norfolk, another of Wolsey's former lands; it would also receive this officially in January.[99]

Given that many of these agreements were entered into on the same day, was Cromwell involved with all of them? The exchange with St Albans concerned former college lands, and Cromwell's 'clerk' William Candisshe witnessed the convent's grant for this in November.[100] Another two of Cromwell's men, Ralph Sadler and William Brabazon, were used to deliver up possession in the exchange with Eton.[101] Both grants made in November by Waltham Abbey and Christ's College, Cambridge, were also witnessed by Sadler.[102] J. D. Alsop similarly discovered an uncalandered draft of the Waltham Abbey exchange, with amendments in Cromwell's hand.[103] These included the addition of others – Sir Robert Norwich, chief justice of the Common Pleas; William Paulet; Thomas Audeley, in his capacity as a serjeant-at-law; and Baldwin Mallet – alongside the existing names of Cromwell and Christopher Hales, as those who would receive the grant on behalf of the king.[104] From this Alsop rightly deduced that 'Cromwell was in control of the entire negotiation'.[105] How he was involved with the exchange with St Peter's, Westminster, is less clear. Former college lands did form part of the exchange, and a draft of this listed Cromwell and Hales among those who would receive the grant.[106] But both their names have then been replaced with those of Richard Lister, Robert Norwich and William Paulet on the formal grant for this in December.[107] Evidently, a number of the Crown's legal servants were involved in these exchanges, which is not surprising given the considerable estates that were changing hands. Cromwell, if not involved in every single aspect, was clearly one of the Crown's principal agents in this process.

The Crown's intention for the lands acquired through the exchanges made in September 1531 is not always immediately apparent. The House at St James's (later St James's Palace) was transformed into a 'magnyffycent and goodlye' house, and endowed with considerable park land.[108] Other lands were later used to endow Anne Boleyn or kept as royal residences and hunting estates.[109] Taken collectively, however, all of these exchanges may have formed part of a wider attempt by the Crown to expand the king's estates and increase the money received from royal lands. The Crown's ordinary revenues had long been derived from its hereditary royal estates, and since the beginning of Henry VII's reign, the Crown had taken every opportunity to extend these territorial possessions and pursue its feudal holdings.[110] It is interesting that a memorandum directed to the general surveyors (auditors in charge of the administration of royal castles and Crown estates), which probably dates to 1532, instructed them to investigate and certify the values of a wide range of royal lands for the 'profitt' of the king's 'most Roiall estate'.[111] These instructions hint that the Crown was indeed continuing to take broader steps to review and increase the money it received from its lands. Perhaps such efforts owed something to the increased presence of lawyers in the royal service. Certainly many of those involved in the exchanges of 1531 had legal backgrounds; and Cromwell, Audeley and Paulet would continue to work together to defend and protect the king's rights to lands that fell to the Crown through escheat and forfeiture. In 1532, for instance, Cromwell and Audeley were hard at work defending the king's rights to the lands of the deceased Sir William Spencer, after it was reported that the king was being defrauded.[112] There are strong indications here that the Crown was seeking to maximise its revenues by exploiting its estates and royal demesne more widely.

Extending the Crown's landed estates may well have been a wider ambition during this period, yet much of the land that Cromwell helped acquire in and around Westminster was secured to enable the construction of the king's new palace of Whitehall. Wolsey's surrendered residence of York Place provided the basis for this, and work had begun by early 1531.[113] But while the king would acquire over 185 acres of land around Westminster and Charing Cross through the exchange with Eton College and St Peter's, Westminster, a number of smaller properties and surrounding lands were also required to enable the construction and expansion of Whitehall.[114] The Milanese ambassador noted in April how the king

> comes often to Westminster, having designed new lodgings there, and a park adjoining York House, which belonged to the late Cardinal Wolsey. The Plan is on so large a scale that many hundreds of houses will be levelled, well nigh all of which belong to great personages.[115]

The Imperial ambassador, Eustace Chapuys, similarly reported in May how Henry was 'having a great park made in front of the house which once belonged to the Cardinal'. For this purpose, he added, 'a number of houses have been pulled down to the great damage and discomfort of the proprietors without there having yet been any question of indemnifying them for their losses'.[116]

But Chapuys was somewhat mistaken. The Crown had been making preparations to recompense many of the inhabitants whose properties were required in King's Street, Westminster. In early 1531 the lands and properties that were required had been surveyed and valued.[117] In May, two commissioners were then dispatched to negotiate purchases for the lands and leases. One of the commissioners was John Islip, abbot of Westminster, from whom many of the tenants held their existing leases; the other was Cromwell himself. An account of the 'sommes' paid to obtain these leases reveals that most of the agreements were concluded by Cromwell and Islip by 18 May 1531, although amendments in Cromwell's hand suggest a few agreements and payments were made later.[118] Overall, this account reveals that Cromwell paid out over £1,129 purchasing these leases on the king's behalf, while personally negotiating the terms of at least twenty-six indentures for them.[119]

Out of all the Crown's legal agents involved with the larger exchanges of college lands, only Cromwell had been involved with these earlier, smaller purchases in King's Street. This underlines the important point that Cromwell was overseeing the entire series of transactions. Whether this was intended from the start is unclear. Given his experience managing Wolsey's suppressions, Cromwell was a fitting choice to acquire the properties in King's Street. His first-hand experience of the topography gained when doing so would then naturally have made him a useful agent when the Crown began negotiations for the required lands around Charing Cross possessed by Eton. But his knowledge of the college lands was surely the greater reason for his involvement with the later, larger exchanges. Whatever the case, crucially, Cromwell's role in both the large and smaller land acquisitions in 1531 helps to elucidate much of what he well was doing during this initial year in Henry's service. Although most of the indentures concerning the lands in King's Street were concluded on 18 May, their negotiation must have occupied Cromwell before this. (They also continued to occupy him for some time after.)[120] Similarly, the agreements made for the larger exchanges represented weeks – if not months – of work. The initial agreement for the Waltham Abbey lands, for example, was concluded on 16 May 1531, but the grant was not made until 1 November, and was finally formalised in December. The abbey then had to wait until January to receive lands in exchange.[121] The negotiations and legal process were evidently lengthy; Cromwell's involvement explains why there is little evidence of him undertaking government work until well into the second half of 1531.

Alongside these exchanges, Cromwell continued to handle matters connected with the lands of Wolsey's former Oxford college. Having stripped this foundation of much of its landed revenue, the Crown was periodically required to grant the 'King's college at Oxford' money during 1531 and early 1532, before its formal re-establishment provided it with a more permanent income. Given his association with the institution and his continuing role supervising the collecting of rents, it is unsurprising that Cromwell was the Crown's agent for this. In April 1531, for instance, the king granted the half-year's rents and profits from several lands, including the late monasteries of St Frideswide, Oxfordshire; Littlemore, Oxfordshire; Canwell, Staffordshire; Daventry, Northamptonshire; and Wallingford, Berkshire, to the college.[122] A draft of the grant for this was amended by Cromwell.[123] His general management of these lands also persisted. On 28 June Cromwell wrote to a chantry priest at Lamburon, accusing him of 'the witholdyng of certain londis whyche ... shuldbe long to the monastery of Walyngford', a former college endowment.[124] The later remarks of the bishop of Lincoln to Cromwell in October 1532 are also interesting. He referred to the King's College at Oxford, 'whiche is nott yet perfyted ne stabylished in ther lyveleode *the ordre wherof is in your handes*'.[125] The canons at Oxford would similarly refer to Cromwell's 'grett care for thestablishement' of the King's College in June 1533.[126] In July of that year Cromwell would also be certified 'of the state of this the kings college which *ye so sincerely fauour & sette forward to your grette paynes*',[127] while in February 1534 the canons at Oxford complained to Cromwell of the difficulties they were experiencing receiving the money recently assigned to them. What is interesting is that they remarked that 'considering that youre mastership / next of all men vnder the kyng his highness haue most beneficially hitherto stande and helpen this house / we further most instantly desire you to be so for vs Amediatour vnto the kynges mageste', not only for their arrears but also 'for the establisshement of this his grace honourable College'.[128] Such remarks not only indicate that Cromwell managed the college lands in 1531, but also that he continued to handle its affairs well beyond this.[129]

Such responsibilities towards various Crown lands naturally ensured that Cromwell accumulated wider work of a similar nature. On 4 December 1531 Rhys ap Gruffyd was executed for treason. According to Chapuys, he was executed for failing to inform the king of an alleged plan by the Scots and the Welsh to conquer England, although he had clearly been a problem for the Crown for some time.[130] Ap Gruffyd was a member of a prominent Welsh family, and possessed considerable estates, notably in Carmarthenshire.[131] A letter from the king to the sheriffs of London authorising his execution referred them to the king's 'welbelouyd Counsaillours' Christopher Hales and Thomas Cromwell, 'who shall declare vnto you our ferther pleasure in that behalf'.[132] Cromwell's involvement is interesting; he may well have been one of the king's councillors whom the chief justice referred to in his account of the trial, as providing evidence to indict ap Gruffyd.[133] Given that the account did not name these councillors, however, this is speculative. What cannot be doubted is Cromwell's involvement supervising the inquests into the lands held by ap Gruffyd, which fell to the king by reason of attainder. In late 1531 he amended a set of instructions for the king's commissioners.[134] They were ordered to go into Wales 'where any of the Castells Mannors Lordshipes Landes tenements and offices of Rice ap Griffith ... do lye', examine all auditors, surveyors and stewards connected with these lands, and obtain their rental and manorial accounts. They were also empowered to enter these lands and make surveys of the various goods, and 'cause offycys' to be found before the county escheators.

The earliest surviving draft of the instructions given to the commissioners offers a fascinating opportunity to see Cromwell at work. They have been prepared in the hand of a clerk, presumably his own, and are heavily amended by Cromwell. The clauses, while coherent in themselves, are in no logical order, which gives the impression that they were initially dictated, probably by Cromwell himself. Once drawn up they were amended by him, with two further clauses added entirely in his own hand. Most amendments are fairly minor, but some indicate that Cromwell sharpened several instructions, while expanding others. He amended a clause, for instance, telling the commissioners to have an auditor sworn by adding a further instruction to produce a 'vew' of the various lands and properties, while also providing the commissioners with a specified time frame for their enquiries, which was lacking in the original draft.[135] It also seems that on reviewing the instructions Cromwell began to give them a more logical structure. He added a letter next to each clause, in the following order: A; A; d; b; c; E; F; g; h; and J (i). This was surely an attempt to rearrange the instructions – an inference confirmed by a later draft where the clauses are indeed reordered alphabetically in accordance with the letter ascribed to each.[136]

The commissioners who would look into the ap Gruffyd lands were not named in the earlier draft, but their names have been added by Cromwell in the later version.[137] They were: Thomas Jones, a gentleman usher of the King's Chamber;[138] Moris ap Harrye, another man with connections to the royal household;[139] and two of Cromwell's men, John Smith and William Brabazon.[140] Cromwell's use of his own men, in this instance alongside servants of the king, is a recurring feature in the tasks he undertook during these early years. Many of his own servants had been used in the land exchanges in 1531, having cut their teeth working for Cromwell on Wolsey's college projects in the 1520s.[141] In late 1532 Cromwell would also oversee the grants of lands used to endower Anne Boleyn as marchioness of Pembroke.[142] Smith and Brabazon, both of whom had worked alongside Cromwell in the 1520s and on the ap Gruffyd lands for the king,[143] were again used to take possession of her newly acquired lands in North and South Wales in early 1533.[144] Operating in this fashion enabled Cromwell to delegate – and therefore maximise – work to men he knew well and trusted implicitly. It also ensured that he maintained a greater degree of control over such work by giving it to those in his own service.

Cromwell oversaw the entire operation of enquiries into ap Gruffyd's lands. A list of the Welshman's lordships, presumably those which the commissioners were to investigate, is written in Cromwell's hand.[145] More indicative still is the fact that the commissioners' findings were returned to him and remained in his possession.[146] The revenues from these attainted lands were also paid to him. William Brabazon's 'computus', or account, of the revenues of a number of ap Gruffyd's castles and demesnes from 29 September 1530 to 29 September 1531, records that the revenues would be paid to Thomas Cromwell.[147] Cromwell's accounts for 22 November 1532 to 11 March 1533 also record the receipt of £139 7s 3d from several of ap Gruffyd's other lands.[148]

That Cromwell received these revenues is crucially significant because it helps to explain how he became a 'minister of finance'.[149] The earliest offices that Cromwell held under the king – master of the king's jewels, clerk of the hanaper and chancellor of the exchequer – were all financial offices.[150] When Elton discussed these positions over sixty years ago, his explanation of how and why Cromwell obtained them was less than satisfactory; he claimed that Cromwell deliberately 'snapped up every financial office of some standing that happened to fall vacant'.[151] Yet it is unclear whether the king appointed Cromwell or whether he himself asked for each office. Elton stated confidently that 'the chances are that the initiative came from him [Cromwell]';[152] and he argued that Cromwell deliberately sought to accumulate these offices to ensure that he had authority and power over virtually every area of government.[153] It is certainly true that lobbying for offices was a common occurrence, and it is reasonable to suppose that Cromwell did show interest in obtaining formal positions, not least for their financial benefits. But central government during this period was not, as Elton claimed, 'sufficiently organized to compel a man to seek specific offices if he wished to exercise minute and precise influence on its workings'.[154] Nor was there a position or office to which a man could aspire that would ensure he became all-powerful under the king. The office of secretary, with its almost daily access to the king's person, might seem the most desirable position for somebody who wanted to achieve this. Yet even here the office alone was not enough. Wolsey was Henry VIII's chief minister for almost fifteen years, yet never held the position of secretary. Thomas More and Stephen Gardiner both held it, yet neither became Henry's factotum.[155] What was surely more important in determining Cromwell's earliest acquisition of office is that he had already been acting vigorously and substantially in a financial capacity before he obtained the Jewel House in April 1532. This makes it far easier to understand why his initial positions under the king were financial ones.

The college lands provide the clearest indication that Cromwell was handling what were now Crown revenues from an early date. It will be remembered that he had continued to receive and oversee the collection of rents associated with these since their forfeiture to the Crown; and this continued throughout 1531 and beyond. On 18 July 1531 Cromwell received his first royal warrant, which noted that 'ye haue receyved to our vse certain Somes of money of the Rentes and Revenues of the Landes sumtyme apperteignyng vnto the college ... Late called the Cardinall College'. It authorised him to pay £100 for wages of the scholars there.[156] A warrant to Sir John Daunce, John Hales and Thomas Tamworth in December reveals that Cromwell paid 1,400 marks into the king's Privy Coffers, one thousand of which were from college rents collected at Michaelmas.[157] On 3 January 1532 Cromwell received £266 13s 4d of 'the residue for the reuenues issues and proffites of the londes belonging to the college in oxford'.[158] On 9 January Cromwell was then formally made receiver-general of those lands,[159] and in early February William Percy told him he had sent £10 for rents, addressing Cromwell as 'generall receyuer of the kynges graces landes nowe in his graces handes by Atteynder'.[160] On 17 January Cromwell had also paid £200 to Thomas Hennage 'due of the issues reuenues and profittes' of the Oxford and Ipswich lands.[161] In March he then received £26 19s 4d from the duke of Norfolk, for two years annuity on lands belonging to the suppressed priory of Felixstowe, Suffolk.[162] In the same month he also received £100 from the college lands of Oxford and Ipswich.[163]

Admittedly, not all the revenues that Cromwell handled before his appointment as master of the king's jewels were connected with land. Of the £500 he paid into the Privy Coffers on 25 February 1532, only £33 6s 8d was from the residue of rents for college lands.[164] By contrast, £300 was in part-recompense for the bishop of Bath and Wells's fine for escaped prisoners; £140 was in part-payment of the revenues of the archbishop of York; and £26 13s 4d was for a fine made with a prisoner. But Cromwell's earliest financial responsibilities had been almost exclusively associated with land, the sole exception being his modest receipt of £13 6s 8d from the Privy Purse, which he paid towards work on the king's tomb in January 1531.[165] It will be remembered that from May 1531 Cromwell was paying money for the purchase of land and leases in Westminster. In December, as noted, he then managed the inquests into the extent and value of ap Gruffyd's lands, with the revenues again being paid to him. His reliable handling of these revenues would explain why he began to receive wider sums on behalf of the Crown. When the existing incumbent of the Jewel House, Robert Amadas, died in early 1532, Cromwell was an obvious choice to succeed him, given the relative insignificance of the office and Cromwell's financial skills and experience. Whether, once in this office, Cromwell deliberately expanded its influence, as argued by Elton, will be considered in a later chapter.

During his initial year in the king's service, then, Cromwell had been heavily occupied with responsibilities connected with various Crown lands. Although he would accumulate wider tasks from late 1531 onwards, these matters continued to be among his foremost concerns between 1532 and 1534. An undated document in Cromwell's hand, headed 'Thinges done by the kynges highness sythyn I came to his seruyce', contains a list of thirty-three tasks that Cromwell managed during these early years.[166] It shows the wide range of jobs that Cromwell was involved with, although it demon-strably does not list everything. (Modern scholars might be struck by the absence of anything connected with the Royal Supremacy.) What seems significant is that, of the thirty-three jobs listed, nineteen of them concern land acquisitions, and a further four concern building works associated with this. The list therefore succinctly illustrates the extent to which the Crown's landed affairs dominated Cromwell's early career under the king.

Just one example of Cromwell's ongoing preoccupation with the Crown's landed interests during these years was the series of further land acquisitions and exchanges that he continued to oversee. During 1532, for example, he concluded a string of land exchanges with Christ's College, Cambridge.[167] Later in that year he would acquire a number of smaller lands and properties in Calais, to enable the king to repair and expand the town's defences.[168] Throughout 1532, 1533 and 1534, Cromwell also assisted with the Crown's procurement of various parks and manors in Essex. This commenced in February 1532 when Cromwell bought Giles Heron's house, called Alderbroke, in Wanstead, Essex, on behalf of the king, with the assistance of Christopher Hales and Baldwin Mallet.[169] Negotiations for this had begun in late 1531, and Cromwell personally visited these lands, making 'a vew' of them,[170] before they were subsequently enclosed in the park at Eltham.[171] It was probably in late 1532 that Cromwell also began negotiations for an exchange with Robert Fuller, abbot of Waltham Abbey, for the manors of Coppydhall and Netyswell.[172] On 31 December Fuller wrote to Cromwell to inform him that he had assembled the convent for sealing the deeds relating to the exchange, but questioning whether it would consent. He therefore asked Cromwell 'to take the payn to cum over and speke with them in the Kynges behalf as your polytyk wisdom shall thynke best'.[173] Whether Cromwell did so is unknown, but the king did eventually acquire these lands.[174] Memoranda in Cromwell's hand also reveal that he was identifying further lands to be granted in exchange for these from mid-1533.[175]

The articles of agreement with Waltham specified that in return for its lands the abbey would receive 'lands which the king will purchase from Humphrey Browne'.[176] Cromwell had already begun negotiation with Browne for this in 1532,[177] but his direct involvement was temporarily cut short when he accompanied the king to Calais for his meeting with Francis I in October. From Calais, however, Cromwell co-ordinated further negotiations via Christopher Hales, the attorney general. Hales, it will be recalled, had been involved with many of the exchanges already discussed,[178] and he and Cromwell were in fact good friends.[179] Hales worked in conjunction with Cromwell in order to facilitate these negotiations. He reported on 17 October that he had spoken with a number of people, including Humphrey Browne, about several land exchanges. Hales told Cromwell that Browne was not willing to sell his land, but instead wanted an exchange of similar value.[180] Cromwell then sent further instructions from Calais, and Hales replied on 23 October, telling him, 'I intend to comen with master Browne after such sort as ye write'. He also confirmed that he and Richard Riche had concluded negotiations with 'master mannock' for the manor of 'chyngford'.[181] On 26 October Cromwell was then told that Hales and Riche 'be at a Full point with [Thomas] Roberttes the Audytor' for his lands beside Coppydhall, having promised him £220 for them.[182] Although all this might seem mundane, it is nonetheless important. The survival of Cromwell's considerable correspondence often gives the misleading impression that the minister was almost single-handedly dealing with Henry VIII's affairs during these years. These letters show that Cromwell co-ordinated work with others.

Not surprisingly, Cromwell worked effectively with other royal servants on many landed matters during these years. From May 1532, for example, Thomas Audeley, William Paulet and Cromwell were busy working to defend the king's right to title to the lands of the deceased Sir William Spencer.[183] These two men had worked with Cromwell on several of the earlier exchanges in 1531, and Paulet, in particular, was a royal minister whose name frequently appears alongside Cromwell's in connection with royal lands. Perhaps this explains why Cromwell was mistakenly described as being master of the king's wards in several letters during these years.[184] Cromwell never held this position, but Paulet did.[185] Certainly, all the available evidence for the years 1531–1534 points to a cordial working relationship between Cromwell and Paulet.[186] In one letter to Cromwell, Paulet referred to 'moche Frindship ... bitwene you and me',[187] while both men were jointly appointed masters of the king's woods, probably in early 1533, and worked together in this.[188] Letters and surveys concerning the king's woods were addressed to them both, while warrants for the sale of woodland were also issued in both their names.[189] Evidently, Paulet was just as active as Cromwell in fulfilling his responsibilities in this office. The only letter from Paulet to Cromwell relating to their joint responsibilities, in which Paulet told Cromwell 'I haue sent you new lettres to signe *wherewith I troble you often*', supports this conclusion.[190]

One final land exchange in which Cromwell was involved during his early years as a royal minister is of interest here. In February 1532 Cromwell had informed Henry, Lord Scrope of Bolton that the king wanted to have his 'maner of Pisshoo with the comodites of the sayme to be Annexede to his honour of hunsdone'.[191] Negotiations for this were ongoing, and the lands were not acquired by the Crown until 1534.[192] Cromwell again managed the exchange, and did so alongside other familiar legal agents, including Hales, Riche and one John Chauncey.[193] Of greater interest, however, is that these negotiations cast further light on the relationship between Cromwell and Henry VIII. Scrope told Cromwell in May 1532 that he was prepared to exchange his land, rather than sell it, and for this 'his grace hade commaundet youe to enserche for other Londes for my recompence'.[194] Cromwell's role was therefore understood well enough at the time. He was to carry out much of the detailed work identifying lands of similar value for the exchange. In January 1533 Scrope sent him 'the trewe valew' of the Pissho lands to aid Cromwell in this,[195] and a list headed 'Maneres londes and tenements within the countie of York to be gevyn by the kynges highness to John lord Scrope in recompense For the manor of Pisho' was probably one of the fruits of Cromwell's labours.[196] But while Cromwell had a formative role in identifying lands for exchange, it was the king who made the final decision on exactly what would be given. At the foot of the list is the telling comment, 'Any of thes landes by what parcelles yt *will please the kynges grace to appoint* so that Amount to the valew of Pisho'.[197] Scrope's comment to Cromwell regarding the 'great payne' he had taken 'laboryng the kyngis highnes for an awnswer to be had off exchaynge off suche landes as it pleased the Kyngis highnes that I shuld haue in recompence' also underlines the fact that it was Henry who had the final say, not Cromwell.[198]

Of course, this is not to suggest that Cromwell did not possess influence over the exchange. In a practical sense he exerted a formative one. After all, it was he who identified and selected the lands from which the king was to choose; and it would be reasonable to assume that his opinion was sought on precisely which lands should be given for a favourable deal. Intriguingly, there are even hints that Cromwell was prepared to act unscrupulously for personal gain when doing this. In several letters Scrope made cryptic remarks to Cromwell, probably alluding to some form of bribe, regarding 'suche promesse as my servaunt did mak[e] secretly vnto you (yff the promyssis goy [*sic*] forwarde) I haue commaundet hym to performe'.[199] This was to ensure that Scrope might keep 'the Reedhouses and the lordschipe' belonging to Pissho as part of his recompense. What this 'promesse' entailed is unclear, but it seems Cromwell was receptive. He told Scrope 'as to the rede howsys with the other thinges mouyd to me by this berer your seruaunt I wyll vndowtydlye doo my best'.[200] Frustratingly, Henry, Lord Scrope died in 1533, and further details on this are lacking. Negotiations over Pissho were concluded with his son John, who was eventually forced to settle for money rather than land.[201]

Nevertheless, it is clear that the Crown's landed interests were an area over which Cromwell had a very real influence with regards to the king. Letters of thanks testify that Cromwell often had success in moving Henry to grant lands and bestow offices connected to estates. In one such instance, Nicholas Poyntz reminded Cromwell that

> where the kinges grace gaue to one Thomas ap gwillyams the keping of mykelwod chase in gloucester shir during his graces pleasur / afterwardes by your (as yet ondeserued) goodness and at your only desire / yt pleasid . . . his highnes to gyue me the same office for terme of my life.[202]

Of greater significance are the attempts by Sir John Russell to move Henry on the paling of More Park, Hertfordshire, in April and May 1532. Paling is a process in which trees are turned into fencing material, and Russell reported that men had broken down the existing 'pailes' (fences) at the More and made 'highe wais through the parke'.[203] Henry had acquired the More as part of his exchange with St Albans in late 1531 and Russell had become custodian and keeper of the parks there.[204] He had written to Cromwell several times about their ruinous state. In one letter, he told Cromwell, 'I moved the kynges highness dyuerse tymes ... toching the pailyng of the More park and showed his grace what fowle lanes and wais wer goyng to the More'. Henry had agreed 'it should be pailyd shortely' but Russell had received no money or authorisation to do this yet.[205] Russell continued to write to Cromwell on this matter, which is unsurprising given the response he received from Thomas Heritage, who had also been in conversation with the king on Russell's behalf.[206] He told Russell, 'I cowld Gette no Graunte of money ne othor answare' from the king, because

> I cowld nott cause hym [to] loke apon your letter but seyd he *wold Furste haue master Cromwell and me to gether* . . . Seconderely he mervelyd what hathe be done with the Revenyv[e]ws of the more syne the lord cardenall was depossyd to the whyche I showyd hym ... that master harvye Receuyd hyt ... and master cade as Receuor or surveyor / where vnto *he seyd he Gaue but lytle credence vnto he myght here master Cromewell and me to gether.*[207]

Heritage also told the king of the 'Ruynes of the parke pall [pale]' and that the workmen would not labour without pay, to which the king agreed they should be, 'bute Furste he woll here master Cromwell speke'.[208] What is striking here is just how insistent Henry was on hearing from Cromwell before he made a decision. It serves to underline that the Crown lands were an area over which Cromwell had a very real influence. Henry was the decision maker, but he used advice and information provided by trusted ministers. He relied in this instance on Cromwell because of his detailed knowledge of these lands. Cromwell had managed the original exchange that acquired the More, and Russell's remarks indicate that he was familiar with its financial arrangements since then.[209] What is more, Russell's repeated request, that Cromwell 'solycite his highenes effectuously' for the paling of the park, emphasises that he felt Cromwell could achieve this.[210] And sure enough, where Russell and Heritage themselves had failed, Cromwell succeeded. On 15 May Russell told Cromwell that 'my wyff brought me £40 which she Receyuyd of you for the payling of the more park And also that I shuld receyue of your seruaunt Candisshe A nother some of money of the Reuenuez of the more for the same'.[211]

Many of the requests for patronage that Cromwell received over the years 1531–1534 were connected with Crown lands. These again underline both the extent of his involvement, and the wider influence towards them that Cromwell was perceived to have. Numerous letters were written to Cromwell with the intent of obtaining his help in regards to land. Most would be tedious to describe here, but some are worthy of particular note because they offer glimpses into the extent of this influence. Unsurprisingly, given his long-standing involvement, Cromwell was often approached on matters concerning Wolsey's former college lands.[212] In December 1531, for instance, Anthony Cave, receiver at the late priory of Tickford, Buckinghamshire, asked that Cromwell 'continewe your good Remembraunce & jentilnes to me concernyng this hows of tickfford'. Cave complained that his lease on Tickford was of small value and 'of lesse proffyt with owtte your good helpe'.[213] Whether Cromwell aided him is unclear, but in early 1534 he was still active on Cave's behalf, requesting and obtaining a new 'graunte of a lease to Antony Cave concernyng the Farme of Tykeford' from the canons at Oxford.[214]

Members of the nobility, upper gentry and courtiers also looked to Cromwell as a figure capable of assisting them with matters concerning land.[215] Henry, earl of Essex, wanted Cromwell to get him a licence from the king enabling him to enter certain lands, as well as obtaining 'A writte to fynde an office' in others formerly held by the deceased Lord Berners in May 1533.[216] Lord Leonard Gray similarly asked Cromwell to 'remembre me for my land wiche the king hath geven me thorowe your good helpe' in one letter.[217] In another he asked him to assist his sister, who was trying to obtain certain lands in Ireland.[218] Sir Edward Guildford, master of the armoury and lord warden of the Cinque Ports, wanted Cromwell to obtain the king's signature and warrants for the paling of Leeds Castle, Kent.[219] John, Lord Dudley requested that Cromwell 'move the kynges highness that it may be his pleasure to take in to his hands and possession' Dudley's lordship of Segeley, Kent, and discharge him of his debts.[220] Even Thomas Audeley, recently promoted to keeper of the Great Seal, looked to Cromwell when requesting favours regarding land. In October 1532, for example, Audeley wanted to be made keeper of the house and park of Southwell, recently granted to Anne Boleyn.[221] The fact that Audeley, himself no mean figure at court, asked Cromwell to assist him with this request indicates that by late 1532 Cromwell was close to the summit of court patronage.

Of course, not all of Cromwell's requests concerning landed patronage were successful. In March 1532 Cromwell had written to Dr John London, warden of New College, Oxford, for a 'Farme callyd Alton in Wilschyer' for a friend.[222] In this London was forced to disappoint because one John Benger already held an existing lease. He did, however, offer Cromwell 'a nother farme within 4 myles of yt callyd strertt', which Cromwell accepted, before selling the lease on for £10.[223] A similar response was given by Richard Wenman in September 1532, when he responded to Cromwell's request that 'I showlde make labor to master Dene of the kynges college in Oxford / to be Frendly vnto ... John hygges for the Farme of the parsoneg of wytney'. He was unable to do this, having already laboured the dean to grant Edward Wilmot a lease for three years.[224] The abbot of Cockersand wrote in October 1532 over Cromwell's request for the advancement of Sir James Layburn to lands belonging to the monastery there. He again refused, on the grounds of a previous agreement.[225] Thomas, Lord Lawarr also begged Cromwell's remembrance 'tochyng certyn land that off right I owght to have', and sought a loan from the king to aid him in this.[226] A subsequent letter reveals that, despite Cromwell's attempts, 'the kynges highness is nott mynded to geve nether lend me nothyng'.[227] A letter from the bishop of London, also from 1533, reveals yet another unsuccessful attempt by Cromwell, this time when trying to obtain a farm for William Tyndale's brother.[228] In many respects, these failed attempts at dispensing patronage are as significant as those in which Cromwell succeeded. This is because the voluminous survival of letters requesting his support or asking for favours often leaves a distorted impression that Cromwell was the only figure approached in such a way. Common sense should dictate that this cannot have been the case, but it is all too easy to lose sight of this when lacking the correspondence of another royal minister for comparison. Such examples illustrate that, no matter how powerful or influential Cromwell became, he was by no means always successful in soliciting patronage; nor was he the only minister approached to acquire it.

The King's Works, 1532–1534

Given that many of the lands Cromwell helped acquire for the Crown during 1531 were used for the construction of certain royal residences, it is perhaps not surprising that he soon obtained additional responsibilities connected with the building works themselves. It might be thought that this began around the time that Cromwell was purchasing land and property for the creation of Whitehall. Certainly, in May 1531 Cromwell had amended a draft indenture through which Sir John Gage agreed to deliver timber to Thomas Heritage and Thomas Alvard.[229] He had also corrected a draft document authorising Alvard and Heritage 'as pryncipalle survey-ours of our works at our new manour besides Westminster' to retain carpenters, masons and other craftsmen for these works.[230] But this, at most, suggests that Cromwell may have been involved with the negotiations for these indentures. The account books of payments made in 1531 for the works at Westminster do not mention Cromwell.[231] In 1531 his involvement was therefore limited to that of a negotiator and legal draftsman.

By 1532, having demonstrated his administrative talents and competence managing many of the Crown's landed acquisitions, this had changed. In a letter to the abbot of Bury St Edmund's, Cromwell himself referred to 'I and and [sic] other hauyng charge aswell of the Kynges buldynges at his Towre of london as also at westminster'.[232] These two projects were among the largest works that Henry VIII undertook during the 1530s. The work required at the Tower comprised 'a general repair of the whole circuit of walls and towers',[233] and much of this was undertaken between June 1532 and early 1533, under Cromwell's supervision.[234] The construction of Whitehall at Westminster had begun by early 1531, and would eventually see the emergence of 'a sprawling palace' covering over 23 acres. Hampton

Court, by way of contrast, covered a mere 6 acres.[235] During the years in focus here (1531–1534), most of the western side of Whitehall Palace was erected, containing the 'Tennysplays cokffyghtes and [a] wallyd in . . . park ther with a somptyo[u]s wall', which Cromwell referred to as being built in his list of 'Thinges done by the Kynges highness sythyn I came to his seruyse'.[236] In this memorandum he also referred to 'his highness' having 'newlye byldyd Hampton cowrt', the building of a 'magnyffycent and goodlye howse' at St James-in-the-Field, and the king newly edifying 'a gret parte of the wallys of Caleys'.[237] With the possible exception of Hampton Court, Cromwell was involved with all of these building works in varying capacities. He also oversaw minor works at Lesnes, Kent.

The first dateable evidence of Cromwell's direct involvement with the king's works is an indenture between Cromwell and James Nedeham, master carpenter, dated 11 June 1532. It employed Nedeham to 'buyelde and sett vp oon substanciall house' on the north side of the west end of St Thomas's Tower, at the Tower of London, and to edify the Tower itself.[238] Cromwell not only made this indenture, but articles of agreement partially in his hand show that he negotiated its terms on the king's behalf.[239] Evidently, then, Cromwell was the royal minister charged with the detailed implementation of the work required at the Tower. His involvement in securing some of the requisite building materials for these works confirms this.[240] Cromwell was similarly required to ensure that there were sufficient craftsmen available for the works at both the Tower and Westminster. Writing to the abbot of Bury in 1532, he remarked how the 'lakke of masons carpenters and other woorkmen' had 'compellyd' him 'to sende in to all the plases of this Realme For prouysyon of the same'; and he reprimanded the abbot for having retained workmen who should have been released to serve on the king's works.[241]

As Cromwell's letter to the abbot of Bury makes plain, he was by no means single-handedly overseeing the royal building projects during these years. Much of the day-to-day 'on-site' management of the works at Westminster continued to be handled by Thomas Alvard and Thomas Heritage, the principal surveyors who had been occupied with the construction of Whitehall since its commencement in 1531. Both of these men were already acquainted with Cromwell, having also been in Wolsey's service.[242] Alvard and Cromwell were particularly close friends.[243] While Cromwell was in Calais in late 1532, Alvard sent him several letters on the progress of work at Westminster, suggesting that he and Heritage were now working under Cromwell's direction.[244] Similarly, at the Tower on-site management was handled primarily by James Nedeham, who had previously worked for Wolsey, and probably knew Cromwell through this.[245] In addition to Nedeham, Cromwell employed one of his own servants, John Whalley, to manage the works there and act as paymaster.[246] Whalley kept Cromwell informed on progress, telling him in October 1532 that 'within three wekes our works at the tower shalbe at agoode poynt'.[247] It is interesting to note that all of these men – Whalley, Nedeham, Alvard and Heritage – were simultaneously working for Cromwell on his own private building works at his house in London.[248]

Undoubtedly, Cromwell's most important task relating to the works at the Tower and at Westminster was securing and distributing the money required for them. On 23 June 1532 Cromwell paid £2,000 of the king's money to Alvard for work at Westminster.[249] Further evidence among Cromwell's papers reveals that he paid another £2,000 to him in March 1533,[250] and £1,000 sometime between 29 September 1532 and 28 June 1533.[251] Initially Cromwell was not monopolising the payments for the Westminster works. Alvard himself had previously paid out over £8,700 for this between April 1531 and April 1532 – a larger amount than Cromwell supplied over a similar period from June 1532.[252] Moreover, Alvard's account, which technically terminates on 21 April, reveals that a further payment of over £5,883 was made by him from 22 April onwards, for 'seueralle pays made for the seid buyldinges vppon a newe yere'. This coincides with the period during which Cromwell began supplying revenue, but appears distinct from it.[253] On 2 July 1532 Alvard also received £2,000 'to be employed aboutes his graces buyeldinges at Westm[inster]' from the Privy Purse.[254] Once Cromwell became involved, however, and the money supplied by Alvard had been used up, Cromwell was the sole distributor of money. Similarly, at the Tower, Cromwell supplied Whalley with £1,200 for the works there between 1532 and early 1534.[255] An undated memorandum, placed in 1532, also refers to another £2,736 7s 5d 'delyuerid' to Whalley.[256] This was probably also provided by Cromwell, although it may date to a later year.[257] Nevertheless, given that the estimated cost of the repairs at the Tower was £3,593, it seems reasonable to suppose that Cromwell was the sole supplier of money for this.[258]

The expenditure and cost of the king's works was similarly monitored by Cromwell. Thomas Alvard's account as paymaster at Westminster from 7 May 1531 to 21 April 1532 was audited by William Candisshe, one of Cromwell's men.[259] H. M. Colvin has also suggested that two accounts from the Tower, one specifying payments made between June and September 1532, were drawn up by Whalley for Cromwell.[260] This seems likely, given that among Cromwell's papers was 'a vew of John Whalles accompt for the recept of money to be imployd about the Kynges buyldinges in the tower of London'.[261] Perhaps most interestingly of all, Cromwell himself also became concerned with the general cost of the king's enormous building programme during these years. One of his remembrances 'touching the byldinges' noted 'what a gret charge it is to [his] highness to contenew his byldinges in so many placys at oons'. It also noted that 'yf his grace woolde spare For on[e] yere how much proffytable yt woold be to hym'.[262] These memoranda neatly illustrate whose initiative building was; that Henry did not relent on the scale of his building during these years suggests that Cromwell's advice had little impact.

The transformation of Hampton Court was another project embarked on by Henry VIII during the 1530s. Serious modifications to the manor were begun in 1533, and continued intermittently until 1539.[263] Cromwell referred to the king's work at Hampton Court in his memorandum listing 'Thinges done by the Kynges highness sythyn I came to his seruyse', but this provides the only hint that he may have been involved with this between the years 1532 and 1534.[264] This memorandum also referred to the king having 'purchasyd Saynt Jamys in the Felde and all the grownd wher of the new parke of Westminster ys now made', as well as the building of a substantial house there.[265] The chronicler Hall similarly noted how 'the Kyng purchased all the medowes about saynt Iames ... and there made a fayre mansion and a parke, & buylded many costly and commodious houses for great pleasure'.[266] St James-in-the-Field, it will be recalled, was one of the properties Cromwell had helped acquire in 1531.[267] Again, however, evidence of his direct involvement with the works themselves is thin. Nevertheless, Cromwell did continue to acquire land for the park surrounding it.[268]

Drainage work required at former college lands was a further example of Cromwell's concerns over royal works. The abbey of Lesnes, near Erith, Kent, had been one of the first monastic houses suppressed by Wolsey for the establishment of his Oxford college. It was now in the hands of the Crown, and efforts were overseen by Cromwell to prepare and parcel these lands. Its proximity to the River Thames, however, meant that Lesnes was vulnerable to flooding. Edward Boughton told Cromwell in July 1533 that the king's works there would be 'greatly hyndryd' because a levy for the upkeep of the flood defences remained 'vnpayde'.[269] He was also informed that the labourers making ditches for drainage remained unpaid and 'wolle leve worke'. Boughton was concerned that

> it shalbe harde to haue diches made in con[v]enyent tyme to drye the grownde afore winter / whiche may cause . . . the Kynges grace & other owners . . . [to] lose the proffyte of the marshe an other yere . . . it wolbe so wete in wynter that it shall not be able the marches to be sowne or pasturyd [sic].[270]

Cromwell paid £5 to Richard Swyfte of Erith to make ditches at Lesnes for this purpose.[271] There were also memoranda among his remembrances for the marshes at Lesnes to be measured and allotted, a response to another of Boughton's requests.[272] Once again, then, Cromwell can be shown dealing with problems and requests with speed and efficiency. Though in this particular instance, previous experience also stood him in good stead. He had already made payments towards the levy at Lesnes on the cardinal's behalf in 1526,[273] and the flooding of Wolsey's works there was a problem he had dealt with personally in January 1529.[274]

　　Can Cromwell's responsibilities towards the king's works shed any further light on the relationship between king and minister? Between 1532 and 1534 Cromwell oversaw the arrangements for the fortification at Calais. He had helped acquire a number of tenements there for this purpose during the king's visit in late 1532,[275] and the lands that Sir Robert Wingfield had 'draynyd & dyched' in Calais were also surveyed by fifteen commissioners, including the dukes of Norfolk and Suffolk, along with Cromwell himself, to ensure that they caused no impediment to the intended fortifications. A draft list of the commissioners for this, along with their instructions, was drawn up by Cromwell.[276] A later version of the same list also contains minor corrections by him.[277] Nevertheless, Henry VIII himself took considerable interest in this project. During the visit in 1532, Henry had viewed the existing defences and produced 'A Devyse made by the kings highenes . . . for the fortification of the saide towne'.[278] Whether these particular plans were implemented in 1532–1534 seems doubtful.[279] What they illustrate is that the king was actively involved with royal works. It would be more realistic, therefore, to see Cromwell and Henry working with one another on these fortifications than to imagine king or minister as being individually responsible. It is surely revealing, for instance, that when Lord Lisle, deputy at Calais, sent updates on the progress of the works, letters were dispatched to both Henry and Cromwell respectively.[280] The king was informed by Lisle that 'I haue caused to be tacken downe bechaumps towre and Deublyn tower', and was then asked to give 'commaundment to your vice tresorar here to leve suche a some of money' for the rebuilding of these 'according vnto the bill which your graces surveyour here hathe ... sent vnto master Cromewell'.[281] The following day, Cromwell himself was asked to

> haue in remembraunce that commission may be gevin vnto master vice-treseryer here from the kynges majestie to leve suche money as shalbe nedefull and requysit to the building & repayring of suche works as ar ... now in hande / as by the bill of parcelles that master surveyour / sendithe you it shall more / plainly appere.[282]

Cromwell was sent the bill of money required because he was now firmly established as the figure who handled much of the detail of government administration on the king's behalf. But Lisle also kept the king well informed: Henry was updated on the work; he was told that Cromwell knew the necessary financial requirements; and he was looked to for authorisation of the final decision. All this very much suggests that Lisle expected the two men to discuss and work with one another on this matter. As we shall see, this would prove to be a recurring feature in the correspondence of king and minister during these years.

Conclusion

No previous attempt has been made to examine Cromwell's duties towards the Crown's lands and king's works, yet much of his early responsibilities under the king concerned these, and they go some way towards explaining Cromwell's rise. At the beginning of 1531 Cromwell was 'newly come to the fauor of the kyng';[283] but by its end he was a member of the council's inner circle. That was a remarkable increase in status, during a year in which there is little evidence of Cromwell handling work obviously associated with government or the king's 'great matter'. By contrast, the work he undertook towards the Crown's lands was considerable, and would continue to occupy him throughout the years 1532–1534 and beyond. Yet all this has failed to attract attention. Why? In part, no doubt, it is because Cromwell's responsibilities towards both the Crown lands and king's works were diverse, and the relevant evidence fragmented and difficult to reconstruct. But it is also surely due to historians' tendency to focus on the 'high' politics of these years, often to the detriment of the more routine aspects of administrative work that Cromwell undertook. Yet it was precisely this work that enabled Cromwell, day in, day out, to demonstrate the legal, administrative and financial skills that were so helpful to Henry VIII. His competence and efficiency then naturally brought him wider responsibilities as he rose in the king's favour.

CHAPTER FOUR

CROMWELL AND THE ENGLISH CHURCH

THE LATE MEDIEVAL ENGLISH Church has rightly been described as a 'monarchical church'.[1] Although monarchs swore at each coronation to uphold and protect the Church's rights and jurisdiction, where the interests of Church and State collided – 'as over benefices as property and the Church's temporal wealth as a source of taxation – the Church largely bowed to the Crown's demands'.[2] Monarchs also enjoyed considerable ecclesiastical patronage. The Crown could appointment priests to numerous church livings in their own gift, while monarchs also possessed the 'regalian right' to take over episcopal lands, seek revenues from these and exercise the bishop's patronage during an episcopal vacancy.[3] The appointment of bishops was another area where the Crown enjoyed de facto control. Strictly speaking, the papacy maintained its right to appoint to bishoprics through papal provisions. But in practice, a 'working compromise' had existed since the reign of Edward III which usually ensured the appointment of the preferred royal choice.[4] Under Henry VII, and during the early years of Henry VIII, royal involvement in Church affairs was extended further still. Ecclesiastical resources were exploited, certain rights previously enjoyed by the Church, such as benefit of clergy (which prevented priests from punishment in secular courts), were curtailed and the king's powers over Church appointments were vigorously pursued.[5] It would be wrong, of course, to suggest from all this that Church and State were locked in constant struggle during the medieval period. For the most part, co-operation, rather than conflict, characterised the relationship between kings and their clergy. Nor should it be thought that the break with Rome in the 1530s was in any way an inevitable outcome of these tensions. But what is crucial to recognise is that long before the Reformation English kings exerted considerable practical direction over the Church. The management and enforcement of this influence were therefore important aspects of royal government.

Almost from the very beginning of his career as a royal servant, Cromwell was handling various ecclesiastical matters on the king's behalf. Yet because historians have been interested in Cromwell's role in the religious changes of the later 1530s, his earlier involvement with the Church has been overlooked. This chapter therefore explores Cromwell's responsibilities towards some of the more quotidian aspects of the English Church, such as administration, finance and monastic appointments, between 1532 and 1534. It offers a glimpse into how the Crown controlled the Church on the very eve and beginning of the Reformation, while also shedding light more specifically on Cromwell, his religious convictions and the claims that he promoted and protected religious radicals.

Church Administration and Finance

Before we look at exactly what Cromwell was doing in relation to the Church between 1532 and 1534, it is perhaps worth offering some initial thoughts on how and why Cromwell became involved with the Crown's ecclesiastical interests in the first place. Evidence of how the Crown managed the more routine aspects of the Church during the late medieval period is often frustratingly lacking. But the overall picture – that leading churchmen, who were simultaneously royal servants, were relied upon – is clear enough. Certainly during the 1520s Wolsey had effectively run the English Church on Henry VIII's behalf; and it has even been suggested that the acquisition of Wolsey's first legatine commission in 1518 may have been partially driven by a desire to strengthen Henry's and Wolsey's mastery over the Church.[6] Cromwell, of course, was not a member of the clergy, and it is therefore more difficult to explain why he became involved in this sort of work. Once again, his earlier life and pre-ministerial career are instructive here. It would not be unreasonable to claim that when Cromwell entered the king's service in late 1530, he already possessed a thorough knowledge of the English Church. Wolsey's college projects had given him over four years' experience in and around monastic communities, and he had even had some involvement in the administration and financial arrangements of Wolsey's bishopric of Durham.[7] Such familiarity with the institutional workings of the English Church would naturally have made him a useful figure for the king to entrust with certain ecclesiastical matters. Whether Cromwell also deliberately sought out this type of work is a question to which we shall return.

The earliest ecclesiastical work that Cromwell performed on behalf of the king was connected with the administrative and financial details surrounding the appointment of new bishops. In September 1531 the king granted two of the most significant sees formerly held by Cardinal Wolsey.[8] Edward Lee, a former royal chaplain, was nominated to the archbishopric of York, while Stephen Gardiner, the king's secretary, would become bishop of Winchester.[9] During the vacancy of any bishopric, the estates of that see would pass to the king, who received the profits from its temporalities during the interim. In order to have this temporal wealth reinstated, the new bishop-elect had to swear an oath renouncing anything he had received from Rome that could be prejudicial to the king's authority, and pay a fine calculated from the taxable income of his new see. The restitutions of temporalities for York and Winchester were granted at the end of November,[10] and Cromwell was the royal agent who handled and received these fines on the king's behalf from early 1532. The work was of course routine, but it required Cromwell to be a constant mediator between the prelates and Henry. On 14 February Lee thanked Cromwell for his 'paynes taken for me in knowing the kynges pleasur' concerning his fine, and asked that 'by your good mediation' the king might be content to grant Lee favourable terms for its payment.[11] Henry had in fact already agreed to this in principle, so it was left to Cromwell to remind him of it before implementing his response.[12] Gardiner, too, was in correspondence with Cromwell over his fine, and he wrote in June 1532 that he had been notified by William Paulet 'howe it wer expedient for me to be at a point with the kings highness for my temporalties'.[13] He also reminded Cromwell that 'at my last communicacion with youe in that matier I remitted al to the kinges pleasur *an executor wherof ye be in that behaulf*'.[14] What is revealing here is that both Gardiner and Lee recognised Cromwell as the king's executor – that is, the person carrying out his requests. Evidently, they also believed it possible for Cromwell to obtain favourable terms for the repayment of their debts. Gardiner requested that Cromwell 'doo for me as ye maye doo for your frend and procure such an end as I may be able to perfourme', while Lee had given Cromwell specific details which he wanted him to include in his pardon.[15] Cromwell was therefore not merely handling these payments but was already thought capable of moving Henry VIII on them.

During the early months of 1532, Cromwell quickly established himself as the minister who managed the king's ecclesiastical revenues. Alongside the negotiation for the restitution of temporalities, he also oversaw the inquests and collection of revenues owed to the king for vacant bishoprics. During such a vacancy it was necessary to appoint persons to administer the estates on the king's behalf and account for these before the general surveyors.[16] Dr William Strangways, Wolsey's former vicar-general at Durham, had been appointed receiver-general of the king's possessions there and in York, following the cardinal's death. He wrote to Cromwell in February 1532, asking that 'I may bee dyscharged of such money as I have had forth of the temporaltiese' of Durham.[17] He also sent Cromwell his accounts of the revenues from York for auditing,[18] while £140 of these arrears was paid to Cromwell on 24 February 1532.[19] Richard Strete, archdeacon of Salop, had also been appointed receiver-general of the bishopric of Coventry and Lichfield following the death of Bishop Geoffrey Blythe.[20] By March 1532 Strete was working in conjunction with Cromwell, sending him rents and accounts throughout 1532 and 1533.[21] One of Cromwell's own accounts shows that he received a total of £612 18s 1d from Strete between 22 November 1532 and 11 March 1533.[22]

Several historians have suggested that this concentration of church revenues that was starting to come into Cromwell's hands reflects an attempt to exert and exploit royal authority over the Church.[23] The handling of the Coventry and Lichfield revenues provides an interesting case in point. Several of the estates pertaining to this see were located in Cheshire, and Richard Strete told Cromwell's associate Rowland Lee that on his arrival there in March 1532 'the exchetur [escheator] of chesshire had settyn apon an office apon the deithe of the late bisshop / and therapon intendith to gedre and receyue all the rentes within the said chesshire'.[24] During the thirteenth and fourteenth centuries it had often been common for the local escheator to handle the temporalities of vacant bishoprics on the Crown's behalf, and this occasionally continued during the early sixteenth century.[25] Strete, however, was refusing to co-operate with the escheator until 'I know master Cromewell mynd & pleasur [sic]'.[26] In April 1532 Cromwell responded, telling Strete:

> ye shall receyue the kings commission and warraunte yeuyng *you* auctoryte to Suruey the londes of the bisshopriche of Couentre and Lichfeld and to receyue the rentes and profites of the same to the kings vse / And

also ye shall receyue his gracious lettres directed to the Eschetour of the
Countie palentyne of Chester vppon the sight wherof I doubte not but
he will not onelie surcease to medle any ferther with the receipt of any
rentes there but also in case he haue receyued any / will repay the same
vnto your hands.[27]

The half-year rents, Cromwell concluded, should then be sent up to
London before 24 June. Was this an illustration of Cromwell seeking to
impose personal control over the collection of ecclesiastical revenues in
order to exert royal authority over the Church? Perhaps, but it might
equally have been an attempt to maximise Crown revenues. Strete had
reported his concern as being that 'if thay shall receyue those lands I
thynke the kyng shuld have but small advauntage ther / if the chambreleyn
ther accompt I suppose he wyll accompt but after the old rent / and
that wylbe loose to the kyng'.[28] As much as anything, therefore, Cromwell's
personal control was an attempt to ensure that the maximum amounts
were collected.

Nevertheless, it is certainly clear that Cromwell was keen to receive and
manage the king's ecclesiastical revenues himself. When Thomas
Skeffington, bishop of Bangor, died in late 1533, Cromwell made a note to
'wrytt to Sir Charles Bowkley for the reue[news] of the bisshoprych of
Banger',[29] and to send letters to the bishop's executors, and to William
Glynn, the vicar-general.[30] Glynn came to London in February 1534,
having made a book for Cromwell detailing the temporalities of Bangor
and the names of those who received them.[31] Similarly, John Hornyold,
receiver of the bishopric of Worcester, wrote to Cromwell in June 1533
wishing to know 'your pleasure & mynde yf ye woll I shul paye my
money to your hands to the kynges vse of the Revenos of the Bishopryshe
of worcestor or noo'.[32] He was told to 'come vppe' to Cromwell in
London with his 'accompte' and all the revenues that he had received
from the bishopric.[33]

More telling is Cromwell's handling of the vacant bishopric of Ely. The
bishop, Nicholas West, had died on 28 April 1533; but it was not until
October that Cromwell sent out letters in the king's name, instructing the
monastery there not to 'medle with the receipt or gathering' of the revenues
of the see because the king had appointed collectors to receive the temporalities on the Crown's behalf.[34] The prior objected to this, telling Cromwell
that the monastery possessed patents and grants authorising receipt of the

temporalities, and that it should 'nott thus be discharged for leveing And gathering the kynges duetys but by curse and ordyr of the kynges high curte of escheter [*sic*] wher the monastery of Ely doth stande charged to Answer And pay the kynges duety'.[35] Evidently this did not satisfy Cromwell, as one of his memoranda reveals that he intended 'A nother letter to be sent eftesones to the prior of Ely not to medle with the ... reuenues of the Bisshopriche'.[36] He also sent his own clerk, William Candisshe, to Ely, armed with letters from the king, to 'exercise and occupie the offices of Auditor and Receptor'.[37] Given the wider assaults on the Church's independence during the early years of this decade, it is hard not to see such actions as a further effort to assert royal authority. But, again, it may also have been an attempt to ensure that the Crown extracted the maximum revenues available by preventing local fraud. The chapter at Ely had indeed received the revenues for temporalities at earlier points in Henry VIII's reign,[38] but the sums they paid at three previous vacancies separated by over a century had been consistently the same.[39] By using agents under his direct control, Cromwell could be sure that the Crown was exacting its full entitlements. And there does seem to have been a contemporary recognition of his ability to increase these revenues. When, for instance, Richard Lister noted that certain revenues from vacant temporalities would be paid to the king, he remarked to Cromwell that 'with your policy' these would amount to 'more than the kyng had in a hundredth yeres byfore'.[40]

Two of Cromwell's accounts detailing the money he received on the king's behalf record further sums connected to temporalities which were paid to him during these years. One account, running from 25 September 1532 to 28 June 1533, records over £76 received from restitution of temporalities for several monastic houses.[41] Another account overlaps the first, but records separate receipts from other religious houses amounting to £135.[42] Money received for 'Vacations of Bysshopriches and Abbeyes' on this second account also records £612 from Richard Strete for Coventry and Lichfield, £666 13s 4d for the monastery at Westminster and £1,100 from the executors of the late archbishop of Canterbury, William Warham, who died in August 1532.[43] Throughout the late fifteenth and early sixteenth centuries, revenues arising from vacant bishoprics and fines for temporalities appear to have been paid into the Chamber.[44] In the years immediately preceding Cromwell's ascendancy at least some of them were paid into the Privy Coffers.[45] From early 1532, however, Cromwell began handling these revenues, and following his appointment as master of the king's jewels in April of that year, they were not only paid to him, but were mostly held by him. Whether Cromwell's appropriation of these monies had been his deliberate intention is difficult to say. But what can be said is that his ability to receive them reflected the flexibility of the financial system at that time. The account into which such revenues were paid was probably far more arbitrary than many historians of government administration have allowed. Cromwell's assumption of them was also a reflection of his protean talents, and of the king's need to have a capable minister tending to the day-to-day issues arising from their collection in order to maximise profits. On this point it is interesting to note that when one of the Crown's receivers in the localities reported numerous problems during the vacancy of the bishopric of Worcester in 1533, including tenants unwilling to pay rents and a steward holding unauthorised courts, it is not difficult to see why it might be necessary to have a central figure managing this on the king's behalf.[46] Strikingly, the receiver believed 'that worschipfull man master Cromwell' should be moved, so that 'he of his goodenes & grete wisedome who haue high experiaunce in souche thynges may Redrese all the premysses'.[47]

Another ecclesiastical revenue handled by Cromwell during these years comprised the fines paid to the Crown by individual members of the clergy. Charles Booth, bishop of Hereford, gave £266 13s 4d of the 1,000-marks fine he had agreed to pay the king for 'the certefieng of an vntrew certificate of non Bigamye' to Cromwell on 3 January 1532.[48] Cromwell received a further £200 from Booth sometime between November 1532 and March 1533.[49] John Clerk, bishop of Bath and Wells, and John Longland, bishop of Lincoln, were also both forced to pay fines in 1531–1532 for the escape of prisoners at the bishops' gaols. Clerk was fined £700, of which he paid £200 to Cromwell on 25 February 1532,[50] followed by another instalment of £133 6s 8d between November and March 1533.[51] Although these fines were entirely conventional, Cromwell certainly received others that were less so. In early 1531 both provinces of the English Church were pressured into paying a combined sum of £118,840 to the king in return for a pardon for offences committed against the statutes of provisors and praemunire.[52] These fourteenth-century statutes, which had been enforced sporadically since their inception, declared it illegal to appeal to a court outside the realm in matters which were perceived to fall under the king's jurisdiction.[53] Implicit in any charge of praemunire was a direct challenge to papal power and an assertion of the king's supremacy within his own realm.[54] The imposition of this enormous fine was therefore the clearest indication that the Crown was seeking to impose its authority over the Church. The sum itself was specified to be paid to the treasurer of the Chamber,[55] but Cromwell's accounts reveal that he received £242 2s 3½d from the executors of Archbishop Warham, listed as 'Mony graunted By the Spiritualtie at the last convocation'.[56] Presumably this was part of the praemunire fine owed by Warham, and Cromwell received this because he was overseeing the administrative details of the vacant see following the bishop's death.[57]

Not only was Cromwell involved in receiving payments resulting from the formal pardon of the clergy in early 1531, but he also dealt with clergy who had been fined as individuals for other offences against praemunire.[58] The praemunire manoeuvres began in July 1530, when fifteen clerics and one lay proctor were charged with praemunire. Thomas Skeffington, bishop of Bangor, was one of the accused. He had to pay a fine of £333 6s 8d to the king.[59] Four hundred marks of this were received by Cromwell and delivered to members of the Privy Chamber on 11 December 1531.[60] The remaining 100 marks were paid to Cromwell sometime in May 1532 before being transferred into the king's coffers on 27 May.[61] But in the summer of 1531, after the whole English clergy had felt sufficiently threatened to purchase a pardon, a further eight clerics who had been specifically excluded from the general pardon granted were individually charged with praemunire offences and required to pay separate fines.[62] Two of the clerics fined in July 1531 – John Alen, archbishop of Dublin, and Peter Ligham, dean of the Arches – were in correspondence with Cromwell over their fines. Alen thanked Cromwell in March 1532 for 'suche labors & paynes as yow ... right lovynglie hath taken to bryng my (second) great praemunire to a conclusion'.[63] This was in response to a pardon granted on 7 February, which was negotiated by Cromwell.[64] The archbishop was to pay £1,466 13s 4d to the king. Of this, £200 was given to Cromwell on 10 February 1532, before being paid into the Privy Coffers,[65] and another £200 was paid to him between November 1532 and March 1533.[66] By contrast, Peter Ligham's pardon was granted in June 1532 in return for a fine of £132 6s 8d.[67] Cromwell received 100 marks for this, which he paid into the Privy Coffers in June;[68] again, the remainder was paid to him sometime between November 1532 and March 1533.[69]

Cromwell was not, however, the sole collector of these individual fines. Robert Fuller, abbot of Waltham and prior of St Bartholomew's, Smithfield, one of the original clergy charged in 1530, paid £200 towards his fine to Sir William Fitzwilliam, treasurer of the household, who then paid it into the Privy Coffers.[70] Thomas Alvard also received £800 of Archbishop Alen's fine.[71] What is important to acknowledge, therefore, is Cromwell's role as an executor of royal policy. He was one of several ministers handling the implementation and administration of the details connected with the praemunire manoeuvres; as Chapter Seven will show, he was not involved in the formulation of this policy itself. What is more, his role as an executor of policy was clearly recognised at the time. The abbot of Furness wrote to Cromwell in March 1532 about the difficulties he was experiencing in collecting money for the second instalment, and asked that Cromwell write to a recalcitrant farmer commanding him to pay the assessment levied on his church.[72] Similarly the abbot of St Werburg's, Chester, sent updates to him on the progress of the collection of the king's subsidy there.[73] Clearly, Cromwell was perceived to be a key figure overseeing these administrative and financial matters.

Cromwell was also involved in what might be loosely termed church 'jurisdictional' matters during these years. In August 1532 Thomas Bedyll wrote requesting that Cromwell return 'the book conteynyng the som of the priuilegies of the churche of cauntrebury', which hints that Cromwell had had some interest in this. Bedyll wanted it back 'to see what priuilegies the said church hath that the prior and chapter conuent may cal a conuocation of the prouince'.[74] The archbishopric of Canterbury was vacant following the death of Warham, and during such a vacancy the priory of Christ Church, Canterbury, possessed the right to exercise jurisdiction in the archiepiscopal see, and preside over the southern convocation.[75] The prior there informed Cromwell, however, that he wished to be excused from presiding on the grounds of lacking the 'experience and qualitees necessary'. That he wrote to Cromwell suggests he expected him to be dealing with this issue, and he asked that 'I may knowe the kynges gracious pleasure to what Bysshop of Any dioces of this province of cauntebury I shall make my commission to be president of the same Convocacion and me self to be Absent'.[76] Cromwell did indeed handle the matter, and instructed the prior to have a commission sealed 'levyng in the same a voyde place for the name of hym that it shall please the kynges highness to nomynatte or appoint to be president of the conuocacion'.[77]

Henry VIII's break with Rome also raised immediate jurisdictional questions given to Cromwell's attention. In September 1533 John Salcot, alias Capon, the abbot of Hyde, was nominated to the see of Bangor.[78] On the nomination of a bishop it was customary for the pope then to grant a papal bull confirming the appointment. This was usually something of a formality, but as Salcot reported to Cromwell, 'the poopys hollynes wyll in noo wysse grawnte me the bulles Accordynge to the tenor off my supplycacyon to hym made', thereby preventing his consecration as bishop.[79] The pope's stance was in retaliation for Henry VIII's split with the papacy, ostensibly confirmed by the act of appeals, which had been drafted by Cromwell and passed only months earlier. Yet, for all historians' claims about the act of appeals as the declaration of a novel concept of sovereignty, it is often overlooked that the act itself was designed for a very specific purpose.[80] Technically, it did not prevent every appeal from going outside the realm of England, merely several specific ones – those concerned with all 'Causes of Matrimony and Divorces, rightes of Tithes Oblacions, and Obvencions'.[81] This was, of course, designed to ensure that the king's 'great matter' could be settled domestically, without Catherine of Aragon's valid appeal for assistance to the pope or any other foreign prince. Although new jurisdictional procedures regarding appeals had been designed by Cromwell, the act itself made no mention of the appointment of bishops.[82] It is therefore worth emphasising the English hypocrisy of disputing papal power yet still seeking bulls from Rome for Salcot's installation, including one enabling him to hold the abbey of Hyde *in commendam*, both as late as October 1533.[83] The pope's response must surely have been anticipated, and on his refusal Salcot told Cromwell, 'I cane goo noo further in thys matter tylle I knowe yowr cowncelle'.[84] In the absence of the pope's bull of confirmation it was decided, perhaps unsurprisingly, that the archbishop of Canterbury could confirm and consecrate English bishops, and Salcot was consecrated in April by Cranmer, along with Rowland Lee at Chester and Thomas Goodrich at Ely.[85] It should also be noted here just how ill thought out much of the detail surrounding the break with Rome really was.

Other ecclesiastical matters over which Cromwell was consulted between 1532 and 1534 included the protection of rights for monastic houses, and disciplinary matters concerning pluralities.[86] In November 1533 he was also engaged in mediating a jurisdictional dispute between Edward Lee, archbishop of York, and William Knight, archdeacon of Richmond.[87] Of interest here are Lee's remarks to Cromwell that 'I shalbe as glad to come to a raysonable and charitable communication in this controuersie betwene tharchdieacon and me as the kinges highnes by you wolde haue me'. He told Cromwell that if all else failed he would be content to have himself and the lord chancellor make an end in the matter.[88] This perhaps raises a question about Cromwell's authority over such affairs, which was certainly a concern at the time, as letters on a separate issue from the nuns of Stratford-at-Bow, Middlesex, illustrate. The nuns were having problems with their prioress, and had written to Cromwell wishing to have her removed.[89] The chancellor of the bishop of London, however, 'rebewked' them for approaching Cromwell, saying 'we had goten a temporall man to [be] ower ordinary'.[90] An ordinary was someone (usually an archbishop or bishop) with immediate right to jurisdiction in ecclesiastical matters within a diocese, including over laymen. Because Cromwell was not in holy orders, the chancellor clearly felt that there should be limits to the extent of his involvement with the nuns. Why was it, then, that Cromwell was able to involve himself with these ecclesiastical affairs, some of which – as with the case at the priory of Stratford – prompted objections? The answer, surely, is that Henry VIII allowed Cromwell to take on these responsibilities. Archbishop Lee's letter concerning his dispute with the archdeacon makes it clear that the king wanted the dispute resolved and was prepared to have Cromwell see to this. It has been argued by Gwyn that during the 1520s Henry VIII used Wolsey to control and manage the English Church on his behalf.[91] There are tentative hints here that the same may have been true of Cromwell in the early 1530s. This is a suggestion that certainly finds greater credence from Cromwell's involvement with religious houses.

Cromwell and the Monasteries

On the eve of the Reformation there were almost nine hundred religious houses in England.[92] Each of these required a head, and whenever a head died or relinquished office – perhaps owing to infirmity – it was necessary to fill the vacancy through an election. Religious orders had their own procedures for this. Held in the chapterhouse on a specified date, monastic elections were conducted by one of three methods.[93] The first was the *via Spiritus sancti*, the unanimous declaration of the whole convent, moved by the Holy Spirit. The second, *per viam scrutinii*, was by individual voting; and the third, known as *electio per compromissum*, involved the choice of a selected number, sometimes even one person, who elected in the name of the community. The Crown had long had a considerable interest in this process. Many reform-minded kings, and their councillors, saw monastic heads as crucial to the wellbeing of religious houses and were concerned that good heads be appointed. The Crown also had a part to play in the actual procedure of many elections. Whenever an abbot died, it was necessary to inform the founder of the monastery, or his or her descendant, and seek permission to proceed to an election. Many of the smaller, and almost all of the greater, monasteries regarded the Crown as their founder or patron, and a royal *congé d'élire*, or leave to elect, was therefore required before any election could take place. The Crown also took possession of the revenues of the vacant office, and appointed officials to administer this on its behalf. Only once a new head had been elected, and the sovereign had given the royal assent to this, were the new abbot's temporalities then granted to him.

There was, in short, considerable business for royal officials to attend to. Much of this was of course routine, but royal interference in monastic elections had also been steadily increasing. As one historian has observed,

> royal intervention in monastic elections (common in twelfth- and thirteenth-century England) was unusual throughout the later Middle Ages, but increased markedly during the second half of Henry VII's reign. Government involvement in elections intensified during the rule of his son and by the 1530s was relatively widespread.[94]

Exactly what prompted this increase is unclear. It may have reflected 'Erasmian' doubts about the quality of monasteries, the need for reform, and a belief that this could best be advanced by effective abbots. But it is also difficult not to see it as a further illustration of the Crown seeking to exercise its perceived prerogative over the Church. For our purposes, however, what is important to recognise is that if royal interference in monastic elections increased, then so too did the work associated with it. But who handled this, specifically? Bishops undoubtedly played a part in the oversight of religious houses within their diocese. Following any election, the bishop of the diocese was required to examine the legal documents drawn up by notaries in the chapterhouse, and scrutinise the formal process of the election. Royal ministers and Crown servants also played some part in elections that required the king's approval, although evidence for this is often frustratingly thin. Cardinal Wolsey certainly attended to much of the work associated with monastic appointments during the 1520s. Between

1518 and 1529 he was closely involved with at least twenty elections, eighteen of which were 'compromitted', or decided, personally by him as cardinal legate.[95] What is striking, however, is that this royal interference continued under Cromwell, who was of course a layman, and may even have intensified. Judging by the number of *congés d'élire* requested between December 1530 and April 1534, there were at least twenty-three monastic heads appointed at religious houses under royal patronage during this period. Of the six elections between December 1530 and March 1532, none appears to have involved him.[96] But between April 1532 and April 1534, a further seventeen heads were elected, and, with the exception of one,[97] Cromwell can be shown to have been involved in some form with every single appointment. His correspondence also links him with the resignation or replacement of heads at four additional monasteries, as well as with the promotion of several priors. Such striking numbers can leave no doubt that Crown interference continued during these years, and that from 1532 Cromwell was managing the king's interests in religious houses.

Cromwell's first dateable involvement in a monastic election on the king's behalf came in May 1532.[98] William Bolton, prior of St Bartholomew's, Smithfield, had died in April,[99] and Robert Fuller, abbot of Waltham Abbey, had emerged as the likely candidate to replace him. On 22 May he wrote to Cromwell, asking him to 'contynewe your most herty goodnes to the ende and fynisshynge of this matter for the house of seynt bartilmews'.[100] His remarks suggest that Cromwell was handling his election, and Fuller was indeed made prior of St Bartholomew's in July.[101] Thereafter, a number of Cromwell's remembrances demonstrate that he handled most of the administrative details surrounding monastic appointments between 1532 and 1534. Among the notes he regularly made of things he had to attend to is one reminding himself to obtain 'a conge de lyre for thurgarton' in 1534, and 'for the signyng of the restytucyons of Burton' in 1533.[102] Cromwell's receipt of various revenues from vacant houses also provides some indication of his involvement at a handful of monasteries where wider evidence is sometimes lacking. In May 1532 a *congé d'élire* was granted to the monastery of St James, Northampton, followed by the royal assent to the election of John Dasset as abbot there in June.[103] That Cromwell dealt with the administrative details for this appointment is suggested by the fact that the entry for 'a Fyne made with the Abbott of Saynt Jamys in northampton for the Restytucyon of his temporalties' was written in Cromwell's hand on a list of fines owed to the king.[104] Whether

Cromwell himself received this sum is unclear, but he certainly received the money for the new prior of Huntingdon's temporalities in July.[105] Cromwell also received £666 13s 4d of the revenues from St Peter's, Westminster, following the death of the abbot there.[106] Another of his memoranda similarly lists money owed from the new abbots of Westminster, Malmesbury, Colchester, Burton and Athelney for their temporalities.[107] Cromwell can again be linked with each of these elections, even if in some cases he was merely dealing with the routine work associated with them. At St John's Colchester, Essex, for example, a *congé d'élire* was requested in May 1533, and by 10 June Thomas Marshall had been elected abbot at St John's.[108] He wrote to say that he had sealed four obligations Cromwell had asked for, concerning 'the pa[y]ment of too hunderith poundes to the kyngges vse'. Marshall had sent this to Cromwell, 'trustyng now of your especiall favor to haue the resatucion [*sic*] of my temporaltes'.[109]

Once Cromwell began overseeing the Crown's monastic affairs, he was very likely to acquire considerable influence over the appointment of heads. When, for instance, Thomas Charde, the prior at Montacute, Somerset, resigned in July 1532,[110] Cromwell was perceived to be the figure worth approaching on the matter of a successor. Sir John Fitzjames, chief justice of the King's Bench, had done just that, and wrote on 4 August to thank Cromwell, having heard 'that the mater at montagew hathe taken gode effect accordyng to my suyte', while assuring him that the bearer would 'performe suche promyse as hathe ben made'.[111] Fitzjames's man, Robert Shirbourne, had been installed at Montacute in late July, and Fitzjames requested that Cromwell 'gett hym the kyngges Royall Assent with Restitucion of his temporalties', again showing that Cromwell handled the administrative details of this appointment. Shirbourne received his temporalities on 29 August,[112] and Cromwell was thanked by Fitzjames 'for your kynd & substancyall dealyng for the prior off mountegewe' in early September.[113]

What happened over the vacancy at Malmesbury, Wiltshire, in mid-1533, offers further insight into Cromwell's influence over elections, while also providing an illustration of a monastery attempting to resist royal interference. The abbot of Malmesbury died in May 1533, and Cromwell had sent a 'compendivs letrre' on 13 May requiring the prior there to send somebody 'to sertyffy vp the dethe of … the abbot vnto the kynges hyghtnys'.[114] Evidently, a formal notification was required before a *congé d'élire* could be issued, and it is again interesting that Cromwell was attending to such administrative formalities, and that he took care to follow the correct legal process.[115] To undertake the election at Malmesbury, in June Cromwell sent his ecclesiastical agent, Rowland Lee, to conduct an election by 'compromisse'.[116]

An election by 'compromisse', it will be recalled, was one in which the authority to choose the abbot was delegated to a person or persons who elected in the name of the monastic community. Two candidates had emerged for the position of abbot at Malmesbury. One was the monastery's 'cosyner' (or cofferer?), Dan Walter Bristow.[117] The other was Robert Frampton, the chamberlain of the monastery. Although Cromwell wished to see Frampton elected,[118] other figures at court, notably Thomas Audeley, supported Bristow.[119] Lee had therefore been dispatched to ensure that Cromwell's man was elected, but shortly after his arrival, those at the monastery of 'the cosynneres party' had told him 'thay whold not consent' to an election compromitted to him 'for soo myche as thay hade the kynges licens grantyd to thame for thyre fre eleccion'.[120] Lee told Cromwell that they wanted to proceed 'per modum scrutinii', that is, by individual voting, and he felt that if they 'myght a getten the congy delyre In to thayre handes' they would have 'mayd thayre eleccion at thayre owne mynde and soo a frustratyd and deludyd' Cromwell's expectations by electing the cosyner.[121] Unable to resolve this impasse, Lee postponed the election until 17 July,[122] and continued to try to conclude matters at the monastery but to no avail.[123]

On 5 July, following news of the monastery's resistance, Sir Edward Baynton, steward of the abbey, had also begun negotiation with the monks at Malmesbury on the king's behalf. He reported to the king that he had declared to the convent that Henry 'was not as yet holy and effectually determynyd in on[e] man' as abbot. As a result of this the king was told that the monks there 'were contentyd to put iiii in compromission to youre highness ... of the which iiii the chamberer to be on[e] / and your hignes to chose and nominate soche on[e] as god shall put in your most gracious mynde'.[124] Cromwell was informed by Lee on 12 July of Baynton's agreement and compromise with the monks, and that a response from the king was expected within two or three days. The meaning behind Lee's subsequent remark, that 'after thys tydynges it whas foly for me to doo eny ferther ... for trust of contrary commandment to me wiche boundes not to the kynges honer' is unclear, but requires comment.[125] In some circles this might be taken as proof that Cromwell had been acting independently, without the king's approval or knowledge. Alternatively, if this remark is taken at face value, Lee was merely waiting to hear the king's response in case his instructions had changed. The latter scenario appears far more plausible. After all, Lee's belief that if the monks at Malmesbury went 'vnpunnisseyd' for their refusals 'lett neuer the kynges grace trust to have suche spede for his perogatiffe in monasteries' certainly suggests that he believed he was following the king's instructions, rather than Cromwell's own.[126]

Lee's remark about the king's prerogative towards monasteries hints that the Crown was actively concerned with enforcing any perceived rights over these institutions. The extent of activity at the royal court, with different groups working to secure the election of a desired candidate, is also conspicuous. Although Cromwell wanted the monastery's chamberlain elected, the lord chancellor, Thomas Audeley, supported Bristow. Cromwell and Audeley are usually thought of as being close, possibly even part of the same court faction, yet here is an example of each pushing for a different candidate. Evidently court alignments were far more multi-dimensional than the simplistic model of conservative versus reformist that is sometimes given, and the tactics Cromwell employed to circumvent them are worthy of brief comment. In order to help 'sat[i]sfy' Cromwell's 'purpoce' and ensure that Frampton was elected, Lee had sent him a copy of the abbot of Gloucester's visitation at Malmesbury from 1527, which detailed Bristow's 'dissolute lyffe'. He told Cromwell that those things 'oppenyd to my lorde chanceler and other his frendes by your good police and wysdome shall soo stope thayre mothes and and [sic] mynde'.[127] The abbot's visitation, however, also implicated the chamberlain's 'frendes' at Malmesbury, and therefore reflected badly on him as a candidate. Lee had 'mayd a crosse' next to this information in the visitation so that Cromwell could conceal it.[128]

Finally, the king's activity in this election is also worth noting. Cromwell had initially secured Henry's support for Robert Frampton, but the king later allowed Sir Edward Baynton to negotiate with the monastery – possibly without Cromwell's awareness – when Lee's efforts encountered resistance from the convent. This may suggest that the king was not greatly concerned with who was appointed at Malmesbury (provided his authority was acknowledged), but had been, and evidently still was, open to persuasion. The next abbot at Malmesbury was, after all, a relatively minor issue, while the dispersal of patronage was a useful tool through which Henry was happy – and probably expected – to reward his courtiers by appointing their nominees. Although Cromwell may have been successful in persuading the king to appoint Robert Frampton, both Cromwell and Lee still felt it necessary to make preparations to dissuade Audeley and others from acting in support of Bristow. This certainly implies that they believed Henry might be persuaded to support a different candidate. On 17 July, however, following the monastery's submission to the king, Lee finally reported to Cromwell that 'I have browght the mater of eleccion at malmsbury ... in too myne arbitrament'.[129] The royal assent for the election of Cromwell's candidate, Robert Frampton, as abbot was given on 22 July 1533.[130]

Cromwell's ability to influence who was appointed in monastic elections, and Henry's frequent willingness to accept this provided his own interests were served, is similarly indicated in the election at Muchelney, Somerset, in September 1532. The abbot there, John Sherborne, had resigned in June.[131] Why he had to do so is unclear, but letters from both Henry and Cromwell had commanded his resignation.[132] Cromwell was then lobbied hard to secure the appointment of one Dan Thomas Inde to succeed Sherborne, and there are even hints that he was offered, and probably accepted, a form of bribe for this. Henry Thornton, acting on Inde's behalf, had certainly made some sort of unscrupulous deal with Cromwell. In one letter he cryptically assured Cromwell that 'on my fayth & pour honestie ther shale be no cryater [creature] levyng know what is or shale be done betwe[en] your mastershipe & me consernyng mechelnes'.[133] Nevertheless, other parties were lobbying for other candidates. Thornton told Cromwell that the convent at Muchelney by 'gret polacie & craftie menys' were set against Inde, and were working to have the bishop of Bath and Wells appoint a monk from Glastonbury as abbot. The canons at the cathedral church were also set against him, but Thornton told Cromwell he cared 'nat gretlye ... becawse I ... well remembre your assured discret worddes'.[134] Cromwell indeed confirmed on 20 July 1532 that 'ther hathe bene moche busynes at the Courte / made by the Frendes of the sayd convent', but he reassured Thornton that Rowland Lee would shortly be at Muchelney and 'ye shall know more who I trust at his Repayre'.[135]

On Lee's arrival in August, rival parties were still lobbying for another candidate.[136] Moreover, questions had been raised as to whether Dan Thomas Inde was of sufficient canonical age (i.e., twenty-four) to be elected abbot, and Thornton told Cromwell that his age would be 'proved' by one hundred people 'bessyddes those xiiii names that I send your mastership'.[137] Money, however, continued to be the motivating factor, and Thornton was concerned by the 'gret labore ... mayde' by others 'with more largger offers then I am prevye vnto'. While continuing to assure Cromwell of Inde's credentials, he therefore thought it prudent to promise him that 'any offer that hathe or shale be mayde / above that your mastership & I wase agreid vppon for the kynges profyt or otherwise at your commandment / dan thomas shale be so good that way as the best with owt fayle'.[138] This guarantee was enough to secure Thornton his man, and Inde became abbot in September, receiving his temporalities in October.[139] It is worth emphasising that to secure his choice Thornton had been required to make financial promises to both the king and Cromwell. The king's money was of course customary, and Cromwell no doubt ensured that the successful candidate paid the highest fine. But the separate promise to Cromwell also confirms that he himself was thought highly capable of securing a particular outcome.

Cromwell's influence over monastic appointments is further evident in many of the requests he received during these years. On 14 June 1533 Sir William Courtenay requested Cromwell's favour towards the abbot-elect of Athelney, 'nott only for the kynges hyghnes Riall assent Butt also for the Resitucions of his temporaltes'.[140] A letter sent by Rowland Lee on 17 June shows that Cromwell was obliging. Lee reported that he had 'fynisseyd the eleccion at Athelney and thayre was electyd the steward of stawystoke acordyng to master cawrteney[es] desire as your pleasure whas'.[141] In April 1534 the marquis of Exeter wrote to Cromwell believing the election for a new prioress at Witney, Hampshire, 'is compromitted into your handes'. He wished to see his wife's kinswoman appointed there.[142] In February 1533 the bishop of Exeter told Cromwell he would ensure that 'your beides man Thomas wanswurthe' would be installed as prior at Bodmin, Cornwall.[143] Similarly, in October Cromwell requested the election of Thomas Hammond as sub-prior of the Austin Friars in London.[144] The prior of St Gregory's, Canterbury, also attributed his promotion there to Cromwell, while Christopher Hales asked him to favour a monk at Sherborne, Dorset, to succeeed as abbot if the existing head died.[145] All this not only points to Cromwell's further involvement in monastic elections, but it also confirms that his influence was considerable and widely perceived.

This is not to suggest, however, that Cromwell was always successful in securing his choice of head. For one thing, other courtiers might seek to persuade the king to appoint one of their recommendations. When Thomas Skeffington, bishop of Bangor and abbot of Beaulieu, died in August 1533, 'myche labore' was made for 'his rome'.[146] On that occasion, Sir William Fitzwilliam, treasurer of the household, successfully secured the king's support for the abbot of Waverley to succeed at Beaulieu.[147] In March 1534

Cromwell was also written to by the prioress of Wilton, Wiltshire, who complained that 'we stond & haue done long for lack of an heed yn grett Inquyetnes', following the death of Isabel Jordayne.[148] Richard Lister, chief baron of the Exchequer, wrote to Cromwell on this vacancy, probably in early 1534. He wanted Cecile Lambert to succeed as abbess there, and offered Cromwell the incentive of £100, and the promise of the steward-ship of that house, with a fee of £10, if Cromwell advanced her to the king.[149] A number of Cromwell's notes reminded him to 'speak with the king for the abbess of Wilton',[150] emphasising that the real decision, as well as the formal act of nominating, lay with Henry VIII. It is interesting that the abbess appointed at Wilton in April 1534 was Cecelia Bodenham, not Lister's (and perhaps Cromwell's) choice of Cecile Lambert.[151]

Resistance from monasteries themselves could inhibit success at influ-encing elections for both Cromwell and the Crown. The abbey of Croxton, Leicestershire, rejected Cromwell's request on behalf of their founder not to proceed with their election, although the convent were anxious to placate him, 'having regarde and reuerence to your mastership ... whose favour ayde and assistens we desire gretly'.[152] Cromwell's efforts to have John Fulwell appointed abbot of Burton-on-Trent, Staffordshire, were also thwarted by the monks there. They would consent to an election 'compro-mitted' to Rowland Lee and Richard Strete only if one of their own was guaranteed to be elected.[153] Cromwell's original candidate therefore lost out, and William Edis, a prior at Burton, was elected as abbot on 30 July.[154] Similarly, Cromwell managed the replacement of the head at Tewkesbury Abbey, Gloucestershire,[155] and dispatched John Tregonwell and Thomas Bagarde to obtain an election by 'compromisse' for the king. These agents reported that it had been 'noysed amonges the Bretherne' that the king intended to appoint a 'strainger' as abbot, and the two men 'cowld non oderwyse obteigne the said compromys ... by any [of] our pollycie' other than by promising the convent that one of their own would be appointed by the king.[156] The monastery's objections provide a reminder that deci-sions by the Crown were often made in response to local realities.

Nevertheless, despite the limits to the influence of Cromwell and the Crown, it would not be unreasonable to claim that by 1534 the minister had established something of a mastery over the affairs of religious houses. This is quite remarkable when one considers that Cromwell himself was a layman. It is also something that has not been recognised before; yet, crucially, it predates Cromwell's appointment as Henry VIII's vicegerent in spirituals in 1535, and perhaps goes some way towards explaining why it was Cromwell, and not a leading churchman such as Cranmer, who was appointed to that newly created position in the first place. With later events in mind, it is also worth noting that, because many monastic heads were now increasingly owing their positions to Cromwell's support and patronage, they may have become vulnerable to future requests. It is just possible that this compromised many foundations in the long term, making the ease with which many of the larger houses agreed to 'voluntary' surrenders between 1538 and 1540 that bit easier to understand.[157]

Yet Cromwell's growing influence over religious houses was certainly not some premeditated scheme. Despite assumptions still common in popular culture, Cromwell was not inherently hostile to monasticism. The bishop of Chichester, when writing to Cromwell in 1532, remarked on the 'good opynion and report ... I haue of you from the tyme I knewe that by your prudent counsel and charitable words the prorye of hardham (the which was decreyde to be suppressed) standith and prosperithe'.[158] This was probably a reference to a house intended for dissolution under Wolsey's scheme in the 1520s, but it does hint that Cromwell may have acted to save a monastery at some point, and certainly did not take every available opportunity to suppress one. Moreover, in his will of 1529 Cromwell had stipulated that the five orders of friars in London should receive bequests on his death, and this was not removed when the will was amended sometime after September 1532.[159] While it certainly seems reasonable to suppose that Cromwell was keen to manage the Crown's monastic affairs from 1532 onwards, this probably owed a good deal more to his taste for this type of work than to religious conviction or desire to remake the commonwealth. Another hugely motivating factor was, of course, money. The fees that candidates were prepared to pay to Cromwell were considerable, as the appointment at Muchelney neatly shows. Individual gifts or one-off payments were often given to secure his goodwill or patronage. Many religious houses were also prepared to grant Cromwell an annuity, or annual fee, to ensure his continuing favour. At least twenty-three such annuities were granted to him from monastic houses between 1532 and June 1534.[160] Robert Fuller, the hopeful candidate for the vacancy at St Bartholomew's, Smithfield, for example, not only reminded Cromwell of the 'liberall mocyons [motions]' promised him as 'reward' for his 'labors takyn' over his election 'but also such yerely remembrances'.[161] The latter was a £20 annuity, which Fuller and the convent granted him on 20 September 1532.[162] Cromwell's purchase of the manor of Canonbury from the convent on 23 September, presumably on favourable terms, may also have formed part of his reward.[163] It barely needs saying that such financial incentives made this sort of work highly attractive.

But there was another, more intriguing explanation for Cromwell's involvement in monastic affairs during these years: Cromwell became involved with this sort of work because Henry VIII wanted him to, or at least was willing to allow him to. The king's actions in response to the need for a new abbot at Beaulieu, Hampshire, in 1533 are revealing here. It will be recalled that Sir William Fitzwilliam had successfully secured Henry's support for the abbot of Waverley to succeed at Beaulieu.[164] What is interesting, however, is that it was not Fitzwilliam but Cromwell to whom the king then looked to implement the installation. After informing Cromwell of his success with the king, Fitzwilliam added that Henry 'willed me to write vnto you / that ye shall put his grace in remembraunce at his cumyng to London that he maye speke with you in that behalf / and take an ordre in the same saying that the said Abbot shuld haue it'.[165] The king's instructions seem highly significant, and suggest that Cromwell was involved in monastic elections very much because Henry wanted him to be. It should not be forgotten that much of the work that Cromwell did – such as obtaining a *congé d'élire* or restoring the temporalities to a newly elected abbot – involved largely routine tasks that simply needed to be done, particularly if the king was keen on emphasising his authority over the monasteries. During the 1520s Wolsey had attended to much of this, but now Henry had found an equally capable servant to whom he could delegate. Cromwell's experience in monastic affairs through working for the cardinal, as well as his ability to devise solutions to thorny issues, no doubt also made him the ideal candidate. Sir John Fitzjames acknowledged as much when writing to Cromwell in September 1532 over the monastery of Bruton, Somerset. Fitzjames was seeking Cromwell's favour to ensure a 'kynd neybour' was appointed there to replace the resigning abbot. He reported, however, that 'Sir Andrewe lutterell and his anncestors' were founders at Bruton, and 'off them the howss[e] hathe hade long & meny tyme a licence to goo to ther eleccion'.[166] Nevertheless, Fitzjames was confident that 'whan tyme schall cume the kyngges fauorable letter with *other your policie schall do moche yn the matter*'.[167] Cromwell not only 'moued the kinges hignes concerning thelection of the Abbote of Bruton', securing Henry's consent for Fitzjames' nominee, but he also told Fitzjames that 'your lordship ... should stay the saide election vntill the kinges title might be tried'.[168] In short, Cromwell had devised an inquest to be held before the local escheators to test the validity of the founder's claim, with the intent of seeking to establish a legally binding title for the king.[169] The outcome of this is unclear but it provides a neat illustration of Cromwell working to ensure the Crown might extend its authority over monasteries still further. It is not difficult to see why Henry was content to let Cromwell do this.

Although the Crown's increasing interference in monastic elections reflected a much broader desire to influence and control the English Church, it is possible that royal involvement in the appointment of monastic heads was also driven by a wish to see the best monks appointed. After all, the quality of abbots was vital to the condition of religious houses, and several of those promoted by the Crown after 1495 had enjoyed strong academic careers.[170] Are there any indications, then, that Cromwell, when managing the king's monastic interests, was concerned with the quality of heads or with the wellbeing of the monasteries themselves? Cromwell was involved in the resignation of Richard Pexall, abbot of St Mary's, Leicestershire, at the end of 1533.[171] The abbey there had performed poorly in several visitations, and Pexall, in particular, was presented in a bad light by the injunctions that followed the visitation of John Longland, bishop of Lincoln, in the 1520s.[172] Efforts to remove the abbot were not attempted, however, until the summer of 1532,[173] and by August Cromwell was also ostensibly of the opinion that Pexall should be removed.[174] Negotiations for his resignation were not settled by Cromwell until the very end of 1533, and John Bourchier was then elected abbot there in February 1534.[175] He was evidently a better leader. Pexall had left the monastery 'a thousand pound in debt', but by 1538 Bourchier had reduced this to £411 10s.[176]

Yet all was not what it seemed. Cromwell was in direct correspondence with Pexall throughout, and their correspondence suggests that Cromwell's favour could be bought. In July 1532, when Bishop Longland was campaigning to remove the abbot, Pexall told Cromwell, 'I haue been enformed it shulde be your pleasurr that I shulde sende fourty poundes to your maistership by the whiche you myght soner stey myn aduersite & troble whiche is deyly wroght agence me for myn office'.[177] He enclosed this sum, and a short while later he sent Cromwell 'a copull of . . . geldinges', adding that he wanted nothing more 'but that I may continue my lyffe in quietnes'.[178] In July 1533 the abbot thanked Cromwell 'for yowre laburs to the kynges highness in my behalf', and concluded by requesting Cromwell's 'fauors towards me & by yowre wysedom make some meyne to the kynges

hyghnes to be gudde & gracious lord to me ... & the pore monastery'.[179]
Evidently, Cromwell was unconcerned enough about the abbot's conduct
to act in his favour – provided the price was right.[180] Moreover, when the
abbot's position became untenable, Cromwell ensured that he was granted
a pardon and a sizeable pension.[181] This amounted to £100 per annum, and
Cromwell instructed the new abbot there to seal the indenture confirming
this quickly.[182] Cromwell was also responsive to Pexall's requests to appoint
his late canon, Thomas Deydyk, as prior at the monastery of Thurgarton,
York, in early 1534.[183] Deydyk was elected there in April after the convent
had 'compromytt the hoill matter to the kynges highnes'.[184] Cromwell was
clearly prepared to sweeten the blow for Pexall.

There is, however, some evidence that Cromwell did make attempts to
remove allegedly poor abbots. Two letters from Margaret, marchioness of
Dorset, reveal that Cromwell instigated the removal of Edmund Emery
from the monastery of Tilty, Essex, in late 1532. In one letter, dated
17 October, she referred to Cromwell's pains

> taken for me and specially nowe of late concernyng the reformacion of
> this pore house of Tyltey which if ye had not of your goodness proudyed
> the remedy which this day is fully executed by my lord abbott of Towre
> hill thabbott of coksal and master watkyns ... [who are] desposyng our
> olde vnthrifty abbot and chosen anewe oone.[185]

In another the marchioness claimed that 'iff yow hadde not put to your
louyng hande' the monastery at Tilty would have been 'vtterly destroyed and
confunded'.[186] Similarly, if the findings of royal commissioners in the north
are to be believed, the removal of Edward Kirkby, the abbot of Rievaulx, at
the end of 1533 may also have been partially due to 'hys abhomynable
living'; although it might be more realistic to attribute his removal to the
letter he had written 'to the slaundare of the kinges heygnes' and refusal to
follow the royal command.[187] Cromwell sent a letter to the abbots of
Fountains and Byland on 8 November 1533 reprimanding them for not
having yet 'indevored youreselfes to thaccomplishemente' of the king's
commandment for the election of a new abbot at Rievaulx.[188] This was
enough to ensure Rowland Blyton, abbot of Rufford, was installed there on
6 December.[189]

Cromwell can likewise be shown taking disciplinary action when
reports of wrongdoing at monasteries were reported to him. In August

1532 Gawyne Boradalle, a monk of Holmcultram, Cumberland, was placed in the custody of the abbot of Byland on Cromwell's orders because he had been accused of poisoning the recently appointed abbot there.[190] The conflicting reports make it difficult to ascertain the veracity of the charges,[191] but Cromwell evidently took them seriously enough to have the monk held for some time.[192] Cromwell was also concerned about the abbot of Woburn's intention to depose Henry Saxton, abbot of Vaudey, Lincolnshire, whom Cromwell described as 'my welbeloued Frende' in 1532 or 1533.[193] According to the abbot of Vaudey's letter to Cromwell, the abbot of Woburn wanted to promote his own 'celerer . . . to myn offyce'.[194] Cromwell wrote in his defence, telling Woburn

> he is agood religious man And that his house wiche was in gret debt at the tyme of his promocion is nowe by his good policie reduced to good & welthy state & condicion aswell in catell as in corn furnished with other requisites & necessaries.[195]

Woburn was then instructed to 'loke therupon baryng your good & lawfull favour vnto hym' by Cromwell. He was also told that another monk 'wiche ye know well haith gretely mysordered hymselff' should be instructed to reform so that 'he shall not need to be further reconciled to amend his lyvyng'.[196] Here, then, is an example of Cromwell ordering a bad monk to be reformed by the relevant authority, while also defending someone he believed to be a competent head. The problem is that there may have been a grain of truth in Woburn's misgivings about Saxton. In his reply to Cromwell, Woburn referred to 'manyfolde accusations' proved by himself, and the abbots of Fountains and Pipewell in their visitation. Because Cromwell had written on his behalf, however, these three had been content to persuade the abbot to resign with a pension of £20 per annum, which it was reported he was willing to take.[197] The difficulty lies in ascertaining who was correct about the abbot. The abbot of Woburn was apparently a man of good character, yet his opinions might be suspect, given that it was his brother whom he wanted to succeed at Vaudey.[198] It is interesting that for Cromwell, however, the point worth emphasising in Saxton's favour was that he had competently managed the monastery's finances and reduced its debt. As a layman and an administrator himself, is it possible that Cromwell was judging a 'good head' under broader criteria than those of the religious orders that had conducted the visitation?

Overall, Cromwell's concern for the wellbeing of monastic houses during the years 1532–1534 appears largely unimpressive. While there were certainly occasions when he can be seen to be working to remove an inadequate head or to secure the financial stability of a house, on other occasions his motives appear less reformist, and were probably driven by personal financial gain. Nevertheless, this should not be taken to mean that Cromwell was hostile to monasticism. It is worth reiterating that Cromwell was a secular figure, and therefore perhaps less concerned with the spiritual reform of monasteries than a bishop might be. Nor should we allow ourselves to think that Cromwell wanted, or even envisaged, the later dissolution of the monasteries from 1536. Indeed, a memorandum of Cromwell's, written in January 1536 – less than two months before the act for the suppression of the smaller monasteries passed in parliament – is revealing on this point. This memorandum contained a reminder regarding 'the abhomynacion of religious persones throughout this Realme'. To this, Cromwell had added, 'and a refformacyon to deuysyd there',[199] suggesting that even at the beginning of 1536 a plan for the reform or dissolution of the monasteries had not yet been settled on.[200]

Yet the monasteries were certainly vulnerable. While no one at the beginning of the 1530s could have predicted that by the end of that decade every single religious house would be closed, a serious attempt at monastic reform must have seemed likely. It is true that few houses were guilty of serious abuse, but monasteries generally were no longer performing 'a valuable, spiritual function to the glory of God or for the well-being of the whole of society'.[201] Several leading churchmen had spoken earlier in Henry VIII's reign of the need for monastic reform.[202] In 1518 cardinals Wolsey and Campeggio were also appointed legates for the reformation of monasteries.[203] Wolsey, in particular, held conferences at Westminster to consider visitations and the possibility of a more rigorous application of founders' rules. In 1528 and 1529 he was also granted papal bulls enabling him to suppress certain monasteries and to use their revenues to found new cathedrals and dioceses.[204] These bulls 'hint at the imminence of fundamental reform, thwarted by Wolsey's sudden fall'.[205] New schools and colleges were also being founded or supported from the proceeds of the occasional suppression of decaying houses. Bishop John Fisher closed nunneries in Berkshire and Kent, and diverted their proceeds to St John's College, Cambridge.[206] Wolsey himself also embarked on the much larger suppression of twenty-nine religious houses for the founding of twin colleges at Oxford and Ipswich. Indeed, by the late 1520s there were many who were advocating the suppression of religious houses that no longer fulfilled their purpose and diverting their wealth to perceived better uses.[207] It has been little noted, but the priory of Longleat, Wiltshire, was dissolved by Henry VIII in June 1529 because of the 'decayed state of the said priory'.[208] Two further monasteries were dissolved in the early 1530s, probably for similar reasons. These two closures are of particular interest because they also provide the first instance of Cromwell himself supervising the dissolution of monasteries on the king's behalf.

The suppression of the monastery of Christchurch, Aldgate, London, is familiar to historians of the period, and has been cited as a precursor to later events.[209] The monastery there surrendered to the king on 24 February 1532 because it was overwhelmed by debt.[210] The brethren apparently expected the king to restore the community to prosperity, but, following the receipt of their formal surrender, the decision was made to suppress the house.[211] As a contemporary London chronicler observed:

> in July the kynge put downe the priour of Christchurche in London, all the chanons of the same place the king sent to othar placis of the same relygyon, for be caws the same priour lyvyd vnthriftely & with his vngracious rewle brought the same house in debt, that he was not able to kepe his house and mayntayne it.[212]

Unsurprisingly, given his work for Wolsey, it was Cromwell who oversaw this dissolution for the Crown. A note among his remembrances, 'to devise a commission for Cristis churche', indicates that he was arranging for assessments to be made on the claims of those to whom the monastery was indebted,[213] and several of Cromwell's men compiled the list of lands belonging to the monastery.[214] In a fate that would serve as a preamble to later events, the site of the monastery was eventually granted to a layman, Thomas Audeley.[215]

Although the suppression of Christchurch is well-enough known, the almost simultaneous dissolution of another religious house, the Augustinian priory of Calwich, Staffordshire, has often been overlooked entirely or mistakenly absorbed into the narrative of later events.[216] On 6 April 1532 Richard Strete, who was busy collecting rents for the vacant see of Coventry and Lichfield, reported to Rowland Lee that 'the prior of Calwich is departyd this present lief', leaving only one canon occupant there.[217] Ralph

Longford was patron of the priory, yet Strete reported uncertainty over his rights, and added that because the land was worth 100 marks 'the king shuld putto his power for provision'.[218] The decision to suppress the monastery was taken quickly, and a draft indenture between the king and Ralph Longford, which permitted Henry to dissolve the monastery, was drawn up on 27 April 1532.[219] Cromwell, who was working in conjunction with Lee and Strete concerning the revenues from Coventry and Lichfield, also gained responsibility for this dissolution. On 30 April he sent instructions to Strete, in response to which Strete reported, 'I haue ben at Calwich and takyn an Inventary of the goodes'. A summary of this was sent to Cromwell,[220] who was also in discussions with several men who wanted to purchase the monastery's corn and cattle.[221] On 22 May Strete then sent him 'a draght of an office for Calwich',[222] which did not pass until October,[223] and it was not until the following April that Cromwell was finally told 'The Pr[i]ory of Calwich nowe voide shall rest to the kyng his pleasur be knowen'.[224]

What should be made of these two dissolutions? There is little reason to doubt that the suppression of Calwich was driven by a belief that its revenues could be better spent elsewhere. The priory had been in a poor condition for some time, and with a community of two recorded in a visitation of 1518, it was clearly a small and dwindling house.[225] Moreover, the indenture between Longford and the king enabling its closure states that Henry VIII was 'mynded to suppresse' the house and intended 'the possession and inheritaunce of the same' for some 'oder godly and cheritable vsez and purpose after his graces pleasur & intente'.[226] Following Christchurch's voluntary surrender, a decision had been taken to suppress it too, possibly for a similar purpose. Richard Lyst, a Friar Observant, recalled a rumour that the king intended moving the Observants to Christchurch and to turn their house at Greenwich into a college.[227] Although the king did have Christchurch valued in late 1531,[228] neither dissolution was planned. Instead, both appear opportunistic, with Henry and his counsellors evidently of the opinion that their resources might be put to better use. Cromwell was probably among that number. He certainly had a scholar producing works attacking the possessions of the Church in 1533,[229] and he supported Richard Taverner,[230] who dedicated his translation of Erasmus's epistle 'in laude and prayse of matrymony' to Cromwell.[231] This work called for 'som spedy reformation' and 'specifically anticipates the general assault on religious houses'.[232] Above all, Cromwell's earlier work for Wolsey had probably convinced him that struggling monasteries could be put to better use. This was a view shared by many laymen, and, increasingly, by the king.

The suppressions of Christchurch and Calwich are interesting for a number of further reasons. They were the first monasteries dissolved in England without papal approval, and the secularisation of their wealth was an ominous precursor of later events.[233] Perhaps most significantly, the methods of suppression at both houses cast fresh light on Cromwell's role in the later dissolution. At both Christchurch and Calwich, Cromwell had juries empanelled to find 'offices' in favour of the founder or patron. At Christchurch the Crown was the founder, so the house and its lands legally reverted to the Crown. At Calwich, Ralph Longland was found to be the patron, but he was then persuaded to assent to the dissolution. The crucial point here is that Cromwell followed the established process by which a religious house might be dissolved. At Christchurch, parliament was eventually used in 1534 to ratify the king's title; yet this portentous decision was not made by Cromwell at all, but by Thomas Audeley, after he had doubts over the legitimacy of the grant obtained through the 'offices' which Cromwell had found.[234] Yet despite the use of parliament to settle Christchurch's fate, Cromwell then persisted with his tried-and-tested method for dissolving monasteries well into 1536. During the visitations carried out by royal agents to assess the condition of religious houses in 1535, half a dozen monasteries were suppressed. The process adopted for this again relied on an 'office' being found in favour of the king as patron, and was coordinated by Cromwell.[235] Not only does this reaffirm that Cromwell was not planning or expecting a wholesale suppression in 1536 – why suppress six monasteries individually if a formal measure of wholesale confiscation was intended only weeks later? – but his continued use of escheat as a method for suppression also suggests that he was less radical in his approach to the monasteries than is generally thought. Indeed, an account of the decision-making process behind the suppression act of 1536 actually claims that Cromwell spoke against the use of parliament to dissolve the smaller monasteries because he was fearful of the opposition it might provoke. Cromwell's advice was that dissolution 'should be done by litle & litle *not sodenily by parliament*'.[236] It was the 'rest of the Cowncell', according to one account, who 'agreed it should be done by acte of parliament'. This is consistent with Cromwell's actions during his earlier work dissolving monasteries for both Wolsey and the king. There are strong indications here that in 1536 Cromwell did little more than implement and coordinate a policy largely decided by others.

Ecclesiastical Patronage

From 1532 onwards, Cromwell's increasing involvement with the English Church ensured that he began to acquire tremendous influence over clerical patronage and appointments.[237] As a layman, of course, in theory Cromwell had very little of his own ecclesiastical patronage to distribute, beyond the rights he acquired towards several advowsons (the legal right to present or choose the incumbent of a benefice).[238] Bishops, by contrast, often had a number of important and highly lucrative positions in their gift, including archdeaconries and canonries. It has been calculated, for instance, that in 1524 Wolsey had 380 such livings potentially at his disposal, while William Warham possessed an estimated 135 spiritual livings as archbishop of Canterbury.[239] From 1532 onwards, however, Cromwell's influence over 'indirect patronage' – the ability to persuade others to appoint one's own candidate – became considerable.[240] But to what end did he use this patronage and influence?

First and foremost, Cromwell used it as a reward, obtaining positions, fees or land for a number of his closest servants and family. In January 1534 he requested that the priory of Coventry, Warwickshire, make his servant William Brabazon their receiver, while the prior of Bodmin was asked to give the tithing of fishes at Padstow to another of Cromwell's servants in February.[241] Ralph Sadler was similarly granted an office by Bishop Rowland Lee at Cromwell's instigation,[242] and Cromwell's nephew Richard was given the keepership of Marwell park by Stephen Gardiner, as well as a farm from the abbot of Leicester.[243] Cromwell also went to considerable lengths obtaining ecclesiastical positions for a number of his longstanding friends and acquaintances. In late 1532 he deposed the current incumbent of the benefice of Olderkirke, in the marches of Calais, to obtain it for his friend John Benolt.[244] The following year Cromwell also sought to obtain the vicarage of Sutton-in-Galtres, Yorkshire, for Anthony Middleton, on behalf of Elizabeth Lawson.[245] She was the estranged wife of Cromwell's friend Sir George Lawson, and Cromwell had previously worked for both in a private capacity.[246] Cromwell was highly active on her behalf, writing twice to the prior of Merton on the matter and, on his refusal, he approached the archbishop of York.[247] Archbishop Lee finally consented, telling Cromwell that 'at any ooder mannes requeste the king only except, I wolde not haue done'.[248]

Cromwell also promoted men to ecclesiastical positions in which they might be of use to him. Launcelot Collins correctly attributed Rowland

Lee's promotion to the bishopric of Coventry and Lichfield to Cromwell's instigation in late 1533, and, recognising that Lee was very much Cromwell's prelate, remarked 'I Rakune yow bechope thare yowre selff'.[249] In November 1532 Cromwell also made Thomas Bagarde chancellor of Worcester.[250] Edmund Bonner referred to Bagarde as 'your chaunceler' in a letter to Cromwell, and Bagarde promised to be 'redy' at Cromwell's commandment to 'do yow suche pleasure or seruice as shall lie in me'.[251] A bishop's chancellor had initially been a secretarial position, but by the sixteenth century this office entailed acting as a surrogate judge in the bishop's court or deputising in other non-judicial activities, such as granting licences or dispensations.[252] Bagarde himself reported to Cromwell how 'the people resorte very faste vnto me for the redresse of many maters, and for the due admynistracion of justice'.[253] It was therefore a position that could exert some influence in the localities; and, by appointing his own candidate, Cromwell might do just that. In 1533 he was able to use Bagarde to exert some control over the licensing of preachers. William Hubberdyne, a religious conservative, had gone to Bagarde 'desyryne . . . to haue a licence to preache'. Bagarde assured Cromwell that 'he [will] gett no licence off me as long as hyt schall please godde the kynges grace and your maisterschype'.[254]

Cromwell's growing standing with the king during these years ensured that he was frequently successful at obtaining ecclesiastical patronage for a number of suitors. In June 1532 Anthony Fitzherbert requested a prebend at Lichfield for Nicholas Cotton, which was in the king's gift. Cromwell obtained it for him the following month.[255] Thomas Preston similarly recollected to Cromwell how 'it hathe pleased the kyng . . . By your oonly medyacion and meanes to give vnto me a Lyuyng and yerely pencyon'.[256] Rowland Lee and Richard Strete's request that the latter be made archdeacon of Derby was also carried out.[257] Speed, however, was often of the essence when seeking to obtain a benefice or promotion. When William Clayton died in October 1532, Cromwell was immediately informed by Thomas Bedyll, who listed Clayton's benefices and their values, telling him 'I haue written this vnto you to thentent ye may first enforme the kings grace' before any other suits were made.[258] Yet Cromwell suffered failures as well as gaining successes. Brian Higdon was forced to disappoint Cromwell over his request concerning the office of sub-treasurer of York Minster,[259] while the bishop of Norwich intended to prevent Cromwell's designs for the benefices of 'Romborwho wyssett & Holton' in 1533.[260] Similarly, when Cromwell tried to secure the next advowson of Cottenham for a friend, the bishop of Ely told him that the incumbent had died 'about six dayes Last past ... and I haue given the same benefice to my chauncelor' who was already in posses-sion.[261] Again, the need to move fast to obtain such promotions is evident here; in some instances even pre-emptive action was not enough.

One particular area of church patronage over which Cromwell had little influence was that covering the episcopal appointments made between 1531 and 1534. Of the six nominations made during these years, only Rowland Lee's acquisition of the bishopric of Coventry and Lichfield at the end of 1533 can be attributed to Cromwell.[262] By contrast, the appoint-ments of Stephen Gardiner and Edward Lee to Winchester and York in 1531 were most likely royal decisions. According to Chapuys, Henry did not wait the customary year before appointing them because he wanted two further prelates in parliament who would support him over the divorce.[263] Thomas Cranmer, the new archbishop of Canterbury appointed in 1533, was also very much the king's man.[264] John Salcot, appointed to Bangor in late 1533, and Thomas Goodrich, appointed to Ely around the same time, had also both been highly active on the king's 'great matter', and surely owed their promotions to this.[265] Undoubtedly other courtiers and those about the king had spoken on behalf of these men, but it does seem that episcopal appointments comprised an area that Henry VIII kept closely under his control.[266] Involvement in the king's divorce was the crucial factor in explaining episcopal appointments in the early 1530s.

In fact, the king himself was often highly active in deciding who should be the recipient of much wider ecclesiastical patronage. When the earl of Westmorland had asked Cromwell to be favourable to Lord Conyers in his suit for the benefice of Rudby, Yorkshire, Rowland Lee had told the earl that 'it whas not in you [i.e. Cromwell] to determine in that behalf other-wayes thane might stond with the kynges plesure'.[267] The archbishop of York also expressed a belief that Henry was vigorous at exploiting church patronage. He complained to Cromwell that 'the kingis highness hath had iii promocions of me to gidres syns I gaue anye to anye of my chapleignes'.[268] What is interesting, however, is that Henry and Cromwell often appear to have worked together when dispensing patronage. When Rowland Lee was elected to the bishopric of Coventry and Lichfield, for instance, a number of hopefuls made requests to Cromwell for benefices void as a result of Lee's promotion.[269] Nevertheless, Cromwell reminded himself to 'seke vpp the copye of doctor lees beneffycys now my lorde elect and to move the kyng to gyve them', which underlines the fact that the distribution was discussed with the king, and that the decision ultimately lay with Henry, not his minister.[270] The copy listing Lee's benefices has survived, and it attests to a close working relationship. The names the king specified or consented to have been added in Cromwell's hand next to the vacancies, and this was presumably done in conversation with the king.[271] Certainly, contemporaries were of the opinion that Cromwell discussed appointments with Henry. Both the abbot of St Albans and the prior of Montacute wrote to Cromwell in response to letters they received from the king regarding appointments.[272] That they responded to Cromwell was not because they saw him as the architect of the request, but because they saw him as the king's executor dealing with these matters.

One of the most persistent claims surrounding Cromwell and ecclesiastical patronage is that he used his position to support religious radicals during the 1530s. Arthur Slavin has argued that Cromwell protected such men in Calais, while David Loades has recently claimed that Cromwell 'consistently licensed evangelical preachers to spread the word of reform', and had an extensive patronage network of these men.[273] What has generally been given less consideration is whether Cromwell's support for religious reformers reflected his own religious outlook or the government's need to draw on certain reformist arguments to bolster and defend 'official' policy. William Underwood has suggested, for example, that the 'most convincing conclusion' surrounding Cromwell's support for William Marshall, a lawyer and minor royal official who was translating and publishing certain books, is that Cromwell 'shared the radical [Lutheran] views expressed in Marshall's texts'.[274] Yet it seems significant that the only works by Marshall sponsored by Cromwell were translations of the 'Gift of Constantine', Marsilius of Padua's *Defensor pacis*, and Erasmus's work on the Common Creed.[275] The 'Gift' and the *Defensor pacis* were anti-papal tracts, not Lutheran ones. Unlike many historians, Marshall was under no illusion as to why Cromwell was interested in them. He told Cromwell that, in the 'Gift', 'surely ... there was neuer better boke made & sett, for the defasing of the pope of Rome'.[276] Chapuys, too, was also aware of the anti-papal and official nature of Cromwell's patronage. He reported to Charles V in January 1534 about the 'important treatises now being printed, among which is the one entitled Defensorium pacis ... *against Apostolic authority*'.[277] The king's 'chief purpose in having the said tract written and published' the ambassador added, 'is that he may the better justify himself in the eyes of his people'.[278] Cromwell's propaganda efforts in the early

1530s may therefore have been driven less by his own religious zeal, and more by the practical need of justifying the break with Rome. With such a claim in mind, it is necessary to turn consideration to Cromwell's own religious beliefs.

Cromwell's Religion

It has become highly fashionable to describe Thomas Cromwell as a religious reformer. It was a view first put forward by John Foxe in his *Acts and Monuments*, but in recent years it has found strong support among many modern historians.[279] A. G. Dickens was the first among many to claim that Cromwell and Archbishop Cranmer were leaders of a 'reforming group' at court, and that their theology was 'in a considerable measure Lutheran' (meaning that they believed men achieved salvation through faith in Christ alone).[280] B. W. Beckingsale similarly concluded that Cromwell's earliest interest in the Scriptures soon developed into a 'Lutheran acceptance of the authority of the Bible',[281] while Rory McEntegart, John Schofield and David Loades have also recently claimed that Cromwell was a committed Lutheran.[282] Others have been less specific, but still firmly convinced that Cromwell was a 'crypto-protestant', or an evangelical, perhaps even a sacramentarian (the latter denoting a person who denied the real presence of Christ during the Eucharist).[283] Diarmaid MacCulloch writes that Cromwell was a 'highly motivated evangelical', while Susan Brigden has claimed that he was a member and protector of Protestant 'brethren' in London, and actively supported sacramentarians in Calais.[284] John Guy was reluctant to specify exactly what Cromwell's religious views might have been, noting only that he 'did not deny the real presence in the Eucharist or teach the doctrine of "justification by faith alone"'. Nonetheless, Guy still placed him 'firmly in the "reformed" camp'.[285] Lucy Wooding was similarly judicious in her treatment of Cromwell's religious outlook, but also concluded that the minister had 'evangelical leanings'.[286] Even Elton, who had initially been sceptical of Cromwell's evangelical beliefs, later converted to this growing orthodoxy.[287] Admittedly, there have been a few dissenting voices,[288] but a considerable consensus still prevails that the minister was a deeply committed religious reformer.[289] What is more, many of the historians who interpret Cromwell as a reformer also argue that he was head of a reformist party or faction, who consistently, indeed almost recklessly, manipulated Henry VIII towards reform in religion more radical than the king himself wanted. Rory

McEntegart encapsulates such views in his claim that Cromwell was 'a faction politician for whom religion was a primary motivation; a man who pursued a Protestant alliance with the League [of Schmalkalden] with such unrelenting singlemindedness that in the end it contributed materially to his death'.[290]

There is, however, surprisingly little contemporary evidence on which such judgements on Cromwell's religion are based. Unlike another royal minister, Edmund Dudley, who wrote *The Tree of Commonwealth*, Cromwell did not pen any notable scholarly works which provide glimpses of his religious outlook. Nor does his enormous correspondence contain much on theology or doctrine at all.[291] This, of course, might be because he deemed it politic to keep such views secret: letters could be incriminating. But something of a lack of engagement with theological matters is also evident in Cromwell's actions. Following his appointment as Henry VIII's vicegerent in spirituals in 1535, Cromwell would often preside over convocation.[292] Yet in 1537, when discussions took place on the finer points of doctrine which would culminate in the Bishop's Book, Cromwell failed to contribute or offer any opinion on these matters. Instead, he acted as the chairperson for the debate.[293] Equally, in 1538, when a theological committee was convened to discuss matters of doctrine with Lutheran envoys, Cromwell, despite helping to organise this, played no part in the 'vital doctrinal negotiations' that took place, while in the 'hundreds of folios which the discussions would produce there would not be so much as a scratch from a pen wielded by Cromwell'.[294] Admittedly, the fact that he was a layman who had not studied theology may be pertinent here. Certainly, one historian has suggested that Cromwell might have felt out of his depth in such matters, and has used this to explain his absence from the discussions with the Lutherans.[295] But, then, it is difficult to see how Cromwell could have been the driven religious reformer alleged by so many if he did not hold strong views on doctrine and matters of faith.

The evidence most plausibly supporting the claim that Cromwell was a committed reformer comes very much from the second half of the 1530s. Although this falls outside the chronological framework of this book, given the significance of religious beliefs to the lives of men and women in the sixteenth century, it naturally merits some consideration here. First, however, we should consider whether a sharper focus on Cromwell's early life and career can shed any fresh light on his religious outlook.

Strikingly, the evidence for Cromwell's religious views between 1485 and 1534 largely frustrates the picture of the religious radical commonly given. Cromwell's will from 1529, for instance, suggests that he still held many traditional religious beliefs. In it, he invoked 'our blessed ladie Saynct Mary the vyrgyn and Mother with all the holie companye of heuen to be Medyatours and Intercessours' for his soul.[296] He also specified a priest of 'good lyuyng' should be hired to 'Syng' for his soul,[297] while money was left for the five orders of friars in London to 'pray for my Soule'.[298] Cromwell would later revise the will, but the changes made were prompted by his increasing wealth under the king rather than a religious conversion. The will in its revised form continued to ask the saints to act as mediators for Cromwell's soul, and he even increased payments for his chantry priest from £20 over three years to £46 13s 4d over seven. The amount he left to the orders of friars also rose, from 13s 4d to 20s.[299] Significantly, historians have been unable to define exactly when these alterations were made.[300] References to several properties bequeathed in the revised version, however, confirm that it must have been soon after September 1532.[301] This means that at the end of that year Cromwell still believed in the intercessory power of prayer and in the importance of good works, as well as in the power of saints to act as mediators for men's souls.

Cromwell's correspondence, although containing very little of interest on matters of theology, also frustrates the picture of a religious radical. Writing to Cardinal Wolsey in 1529, Cromwell reported a rumour that Martin Luther had died, adding 'I would he had never bin borne'.[302] In the same year, he told Wolsey that he had discovered a Lutheran sect, from which he had confiscated John Frith's *Revelation of the Antichrist* and Simon Fish's *Supplication for the Beggars*. Describing these as 'pestiferous books', which 'if they be scatired among the common people so destroy the whole obedience and policy of this realm', Cromwell urged Wolsey to put a stop to this doctrine.[303] It is also interesting that inventories of Cromwell's possessions reveal that he continued to possess many traditional religious images during both the 1520s and the 1530s. These included 'ii ymages in lether gylted the one of our ladye the other of saynte christopher' and 'An ymage of saynte Anthony'.[304] There is also an incidental reference to his attending mass, probably in 1532.[305] One intriguing silence among the contemporary evidence is equally worth noting here. The Imperial ambassador, Eustace Chapuys, was often quick to describe Anne Boleyn, Viscount Rochford and Thomas Cranmer as 'Lutherans', a 'habitual catch-all term for anyone of whose religion he disapproved'.[306] It is odd, then, that despite frequent contact with Cromwell, Chapuys appears never to have labelled him in this way.[307]

This has not prevented historians from doing so. Rory McEntegart assumed rather than proved that Cromwell was a Lutheran during the early 1530s. He attributed a shift in English attitudes towards the Lutheran League of Schmalkalden from early 1533 onwards to Cromwell's influence, arguing that Cromwell pursued a 'clandestine religious agenda'; communicating secretly with the German league, and seeking to persuade the king to adopt its reformed doctrine.[308] It is true that in 1533 efforts for an alliance were stepped up with the league. But this was driven by the need to secure continental allies in support of Henry VIII's break with Rome. Cromwell's notes reminding himself to secure passports for English diplomats to go to Germany and his warrants showing that he frequently paid for their meetings abroad are not sufficient proof that he was a leading member of a group of councillors with Protestant sympathies.[309] Nor does Cromwell's use of two of his own men (both evangelical sympathisers, possibly even Lutherans) as diplomats in the earliest efforts prove that Cromwell was pursuing his own independent agenda.[310] As we have seen, Cromwell frequently employed his own men in work for the king, and using those who might be able to converse convincingly with the Protestant League would seem to be a shrewd strategy. A draft memorandum of discussions held by the King's Council regarding the sending of ambassadors 'to practise and conclude with the prynces and potentates of Germany', although heavily amended by Cromwell, also refers these matters to the 'kynges arbytrement' and 'to know when of the kyng'.[311] This very much suggests that Henry was closely involved with the efforts to secure an alliance. Even the most promising evidence in support of Cromwell's Lutheran credentials, which dates to much later years, remains ambiguous at best. In 1540 Lutheran envoys did report a meeting with Cromwell in which they alleged he had said that 'he sees our opinions in matters of the faith'.[312] But this was quickly qualified by Cromwell's remark that 'the world standing now as it does, whatever his lord the king holds, so too will he hold', indicating that, whatever convictions Cromwell had, these were not strong enough to see him disagree with Henry VIII on religious policy. Ultimately, however, it is hard to accept these remarks as anything other than a diplomatic tactic designed to foster closer relations with the envoys.

Nevertheless, if Cromwell was not a Lutheran, it seems likely that he was somewhat anticlerical. The chronicler Edward Hall, a lawyer and member of parliament who knew Cromwell, noted how he 'could not abide the snoffyng pride of some prelates'.[313] An apprehended priest was also warned in 1533 'howe sore that master Crvmwell was ageynst prestes and howe grievously he dydde handle them ... for he is aman withowte any consciens ageynst prestes'.[314] Cromwell's remarks to Wolsey regarding his inability to pay his servants and retainers following his fall in 1529 similarly hint at an anticlerical attitude. Cromwell suggested that the cardinal's chaplains should pay for his servants, for they 'had all the profettes and avuntages at your handes And thes your seruauntes non at all And yet hathe your poor seruauntes taken myche more payn for you in oon day than all your Idell chapleyns hathe don in a yere'.[315] Yet despite this apparent hostility towards the clergy, Cromwell's anticlericalism did not prevent him from being friends with a number of leading churchmen during the 1520s and early 1530s, including Cardinal Wolsey. And there was certainly no prouder prelate than Wolsey.

Cromwell also kept scholars at Oxford and Cambridge during these years. Among these men were Edward Copland, Henry Lockwood, Robert Welles and John Hunt, although, frustratingly, there is no indication of their religious outlooks.[316] Some indication of what they might have studied, however, is hinted at in letters from John Chekyng, who was tutor to Cromwell's son Gregory, as well as to his nephew Christopher Wellyfed and one Nicholas Sadler. In one letter, Chekyng told Cromwell that he had purchased a copy of Erasmus's work, which he expected Cromwell to pay for.[317] Another tutor informed Cromwell how Gregory 'spendith his tyme ... firste, after he hathe herde Masse he taketh a lecture of a Diologe of Erasmus Colloquium, called Pietas puerilis, where inne is described a veray picture of oone the sholde be vertuouselie brought upp'.[318] Interestingly, John Foxe believed that Cromwell had memorised a copy of Erasmus's New Testament by heart during a trip to Rome in the 1510s.[319] Cromwell also appears to have financed William Marshall's printing of Erasmus's Common Creed and the Ten Commandments.[320] All this very much suggests that Cromwell had an interest in the humanist thinking of Erasmus.

At least one of Cromwell's scholars did later go on to exhibit evangelical tendencies. In July 1533 Robert Woodward, warden of All Souls College, Oxford, replied to Cromwell's request that 'Richard Biseley yowr scoler ... be chosen oone of owr number / and felowes of owr colledge', a position to which Biseley was obligingly appointed.[321] Biseley had previously been a scholar at Cardinal College, Oxford, and Cromwell had sustained him there.[322] In 1535 Biseley recalled to Cromwell how

Furste ye appoynted me student in Oxforde in the nue colledg ... afterward, ye promotede me to thefelowshipe of Alsolue Colledge, and now haue preferred me to a Benefice for suere contynuaunce of lerninge so that all my Bringinge vp in studye hathe depended oonlye vn your liberalitie.[323]

Although Biseley also received support from the king, and became a royal chaplain,[324] it was Cromwell who took considerable interest in his career, and Biseley felt his support was 'the deade more of a parent then of a patrone'.[325] It is of interest, then, that later in life Richard Biseley did become a committed Protestant. He was 'pronounced contumacious' under Mary, and fled abroad to Frankfurt, before returning to England during Elizabeth's reign.[326] Yet there is no way of knowing how developed Biseley's beliefs had become by the 1520s and 1530s, and of course whether Cromwell was aware of them.

Historians who have argued that Cromwell was a driven religious reformer have often cited this sort of ecclesiastical patronage, as well as his friendship with several men with radical or reformist views, as evidence that Cromwell must have shared such views.[327] But one should be wary of assuming that acquaintance or friendship implies agreement in all things. Undoubtedly, Cromwell was friendly with many people who held evangelical or radical views between 1520 and 1534. The most striking example of this is probably his friendship with Stephen Vaughan, who had been in Cromwell's service since at least the early 1520s, and was one of his most trusted servants.[328] Cromwell made use of him in his work for Wolsey,[329] and later facilitated Vaughan's entry into the king's service as an agent and diplomat.[330] The correspondence between the two men during these years testifies to a close friendship. Yet there can be no doubt that Vaughan himself was an evangelical, possibly even a Lutheran, and that Cromwell was aware of this.[331] In December 1531 Cromwell even informed Vaughan that he was likely to be accused of Lutheranism, and advised him 'only to applye and endeuoyr ... vnfayuedly to serue the king his magestie'.[332] Is there any indication that Cromwell might have shared his friend's sympathies? Vaughan was certainly obtaining a number of books for Cromwell, including works by Luther, but this was on the king's behalf and concerned the divorce campaign.[333] In fact, Vaughan's letter to Cromwell regarding the charge that he was a Lutheran – which he vehemently denied in the letter – probably provides the most compelling evidence that, during these years, Cromwell was not one.[334] After all, why would Vaughan deny the charge if he thought Cromwell sympathetic to Luther's views?

Miles Coverdale was another of Cromwell's acquaintances during the 1520s.[335] He was a member of humanist circles in London and Cambridge, and possibly also had Lutheran sympathies.[336] At some point before 1528 he wrote to Cromwell, referring to 'the godly communication which your mastyrschype had with me ... in mastyr moorys howse' and to the 'fervent zeall ... yow have to vertu and godly study'. Having begun the 'taste of holy schryptures', Coverdale was in need of books to continue his study, and he looked to Cromwell to supply these.[337] An anonymous writer, most probably John Oliver, master in Chancery, also wrote to Cromwell in the late 1530s referring to 'divers dinners and suppers' at Cromwell's house at the Austin Friars. There he had heard 'such communicacion which were the verie cause of the begynnynge of my conuersion'; and he had gone home to compare Erasmus's translation of the Bible with 'the vulgare which they call Saint Jeromes translacion'.[338] Elton surmised from these comments that as 'early as 1531 or 1532 ... Cromwell was thinking along reformed lines and lines of evangelical theology'.[339]

Cromwell is also thought to have been close to Thomas Cranmer, archbishop of Canterbury from 1533.[340] The two men certainly worked together during the years in focus here.[341] But the same could be said of most of the counsellors involved with the divorce campaign. The archbishop's evangelical beliefs are known well enough, but it is often supposed that Cromwell shared these and worked with Cranmer to further the Reformation.[342] MacCulloch writes that 'the two men valued each other's skills, and recognized how their talents could be complementary in striving for common evangelical goals'.[343] Despite such claims, however, there is little that points to a notably close friendship during the early 1530s. True, Cranmer did sign a letter to Cromwell as 'your awne assured & veray lovynge good frende',[344] but there are noticeably few letters between the two. Indeed, MacCulloch has noted that one 'remarkable feature' of the letter-book containing Cranmer's outgoing correspondence for the years 1533–1535 is that it 'contains hardly a single letter from Cranmer to Cromwell'. Bizarrely, though, he has taken this as a 'clear although topsy-turvy piece of evidence for Cranmer and Cromwell's special relationship', believing that the archbishop must have 'kept a separate file for his letters to his chief ally in politics'.[345] This seems unlikely. Cranmer's letter-book is a transcription of the letters he sent to leading figures, meaning that the originals would obviously lie with the recipients. If there had been a more voluminous correspondence between Cromwell and Cranmer there would surely be a far greater survival of

Cranmer's letters among Cromwell's preserved private papers. A more well-grounded hypothesis might involve questioning whether the two men were quite as close as is commonly thought. Indeed, most of the surviving letters between the two for these years relate to minor matters of patronage.[346] None suggests a notably 'special relationship'.[347] It is unclear if W. Benet's remark to Cromwell that 'yow wul have the advoyson off barnak for your frynd' was a reference to Cranmer, although it seems likely.[348] Cranmer had requested that Cromwell obtain this for John Newman on several occasions, but Cromwell evidently kept him waiting.[349] Cranmer was similarly reluctant to appoint Cromwell's nominee as prior at St Gregory's, Canterbury, despite Cromwell's assurance that the man was of 'good Lernyng and religiouse Lif'.[350] After voicing his objections, however, Cranmer did finally consent.[351] In February 1533 Cromwell also paid the new archbishop-elect a loan of £1,000 from the king,[352] and he was involved in negotiations on Cranmer's behalf to resolve the poor finances of the metropolitan see later in that year.[353] But then, Cromwell had acted as a mediator on similar financial matters for other prelates during these years, including Stephen Gardiner.[354] Throughout both men's early careers under the king, co-operation, rather than a close friendship, is easier to substantiate from their surviving correspondence, and there is little convincing evidence of any shared evangelical sympathies.

In fact, a number of Cromwell's oldest and closest friends held fairly traditional religious beliefs. Cromwell's friendship with Christopher Hales, the attorney general, dated back to at least the 1520s.[355] According to John Foxe, Hales was 'a mighty Papiste, yet bare he such fauour and good lykyng to Cromwell, that hee commended hym to the kyng, as a man most fitte for hys purpose' in 1530.[356] In 1532 Cromwell also went to some lengths to obtain the benefice of Olderkirke, in the marches of Calais, for his friend John Benolt, and even deposed the existing incumbent to secure this.[357] It is intriguing, then, particularly given the claims that Cromwell promoted and protected religious radicals in Calais,[358] that Benolt himself was a religious conservative.[359] John Gostwick, a member of Wolsey's entourage between 1514 and 1529, was another man well acquainted with Cromwell:[360] their association was maintained throughout the 1530s, and they worked closely together following Gostwick's appointment as treasurer of the first fruits.[361] Yet Gostwick was a staunch conservative. He attacked Archbishop Cranmer's heretical preaching in parliament, and was described by John Foxe as 'a man of contrary Religion', meaning he was not an evangelical.[362] Cromwell was also friendly with several conservative clerics. Edmund Bonner had been a chaplain under Wolsey, and he and Cromwell appear to have been close. Cromwell had 'promised' to send Bonner 'the triumphes of petrarche in the ytalion tonge' in 1530, and throughout the cleric's diplomatic sojourn abroad he sent Cromwell gifts, including 'a worcestershire chese' and 'sedes of Rome' for Cromwell to 'sow in your gardyn'.[363] Notes among Cromwell's correspondence reminded him to 'Remembre doctor bonner for sum promocyon' in early 1534, and the cleric himself referred to Cromwell as 'my great patrone' in a letter to the king the previous October.[364] In the later 1530s Bonner became bishop of Hereford, and later London, and according to John Foxe he 'was aduanced only by the Lorde Cromwel'.[365] Although Foxe erroneously believed Bonner to be 'a fauourer of Luthers doctrine', he was in fact 'broadly conservative' and later persecuted evangelicals for heresy under Mary.[366]

Cromwell's acquaintance with Rowland Lee was another that dated to their time working for Wolsey, and there is no doubt that they were firm, and probably close, friends.[367] Cromwell's son Gregory often visited and stayed with Lee,[368] and Henry Dowes, one of Gregory's tutors, felt that Lee treated Gregory as if he 'were his owne naturall sonne'.[369] Lee was another conservative in religion, yet Cromwell obtained several church livings for him between 1532 and 1534. In August 1532 Lee reported that the vicar of St Sepulchre had died, and requested that Cromwell 'contynew your goodnesse towards me for the same if it soo may plesse yow'.[370] Lee was appointed there on 19 August after Cromwell had granted his advowson for this benefice to the king.[371] Lee was also nominated to the bishopric of Coventry and Lichfield at Cromwell's instigation in late 1533.[372] Launcelot Collins remarked to the minister in October that 'I hert say / that ... master doctore lee (by yowr helpe) schalbe bechope off chestore'.[373] It is Stephen Vaughan's response on hearing of Lee's appointment that is particularly interesting. He reprimanded Cromwell in November because

> yow haue lately helpen an erthely beste a molle and an enemy to all godly lernyng ... a papiste an Idolater and a flesshely preste vnto a Busshop of Chester ... who knowethe more of the Busshoppes iniquytie then yow / who knowethe more of theyr tyrannye ... and vntruthe agaynst god prynce and man then yow. And shuld yow helpe in this tyme specially to increace the number of wycked men where there is a lack and so greate a nede of good and vertuous men / Be yow sorye for it ... I am more sorye for this dede done by yow / then for all the thinges that euer I knew yow do.[374]

The letter offers a wonderful illustration of Cromwell's friendship with both Vaughan, an obvious radical, and with Lee, an obvious conservative. Lee's traditional beliefs were clearly not an issue for Cromwell.

The evidence from his early life and career therefore very much suggests that, rather than being a single-minded religious reformer, Cromwell was actually a well-rounded and intellectually curious individual with a wide-ranging circle of friends. His religious beliefs during these years contained several traditional elements, and in many respects Cromwell appears to be the epitome of many of the laymen at the centre of government who seem to have combined a conventional late-medieval faith with a willingness 'to extend royal power over the Church, to exploit the Church's resources . . . and to accept that the clergy needed improving and that the laity, led by the king, had the right to tell them so'.[375] Yet events in Cromwell's subsequent career have tended to overshadow this impression. Although the minister's later political career is beyond the focus of this present study, it seems reasonable to offer some brief thoughts here on the evidence for Cromwell's reformist credentials after 1534.

It is difficult to deny that the most plausible evidence for Cromwell's reformist credentials comes from his later years. Without doubt the most persuasive is his support and patronage for the Bible in English. In his *Acts and Monuments*, John Foxe alleged that Cromwell's 'whole life was nothing els, but a continuall care and trauaile how to aduaunce & further the right knowledge of the Gospell',[376] and there can be no doubt that Cromwell was deeply committed to the idea of a Bible in the vernacular. After aborted attempts to promulgate Miles Coverdale's Bible translation in 1536, the following year Cromwell agreed to Archbishop Cranmer's request that he show a newly translated version of the Bible to the king.[377] Cromwell himself then played a key role in persuading Henry VIII to adopt it, with Cranmer subsequently praising his 'diligence . . . in procuring the king's highness to set forth the said God's word and his gospel'.[378] What is more, in December 1538 Cromwell told the French ambassador that he had contributed £400 towards the Bible's production.[379] Clearly, then, Cromwell was deeply committed to a vernacular Bible. If its production was an exclusively evangelical goal, then this provides the clearest proof that Cromwell was an evangelical – or certainly that he became one. Yet it seems likely that there were many people during the 1530s who clung to fairly traditional religious beliefs but who could also see the benefit of a Bible in the vernacular. A royal proclamation from 1530 had already envisaged the possibility of an English Bible being made generally available one day.[380] Support for this need not necessarily equate with evangelicalism.

Cromwell was also increasingly associated with a number of writers and reformers in the later 1530s. Among these men were Hugh Latimer, Richard Morison, Robert Barnes and Thomas Starkey.[381] As Lehmberg has rightly pointed out, the 'mere list of names is suggestive; although Cromwell's followers were independent thinkers, they were all committed to some variety of religious reform'.[382] A note of caution has already been sounded, however, that Cromwell's support and patronage of such men might be less revealing of his own independent views than at first they appear. After all, the government was often reliant on reformers to produce works justifying the one truly consistent aspect of religious policy during this decade: the defence of the Royal Supremacy. What is sorely needed here, which is beyond the focus and time frame of this book, is a close and nuanced analysis of Cromwell's relations with these men. Although they were reformers, it is by no means certain that Cromwell shared their (often differing) religious views.

Similarly, it is true that many of the rebels involved in the Pilgrimage of Grace in 1536 accused Cromwell of being a heretic,[383] while figures on the Continent included him in a triumvirate, with Cranmer and Audeley, that was 'most friendly to the purer doctrine of the Gospel'.[384] Again, however, this could be less revealing of Cromwell's personal religious outlook than it might seem. Indeed, it may point to little more than Cromwell's support for the break with Rome, the dissolution of the monasteries and the reforms to religious ceremonies and saints' days in the mid-1530s, meaning that he was *perceived* to be an evangelical or crypto-Protestant.

The act of attainder which condemned Cromwell following his fall in 1540 accused him of a variety of crimes, including being a 'detestable herytike' guilty of sacramentarian offences – that is, of denying the real presence of Christ during the Eucharist.[385] On the specific claim that he was a sacramentarian, there is even less evidence than there is for his alleged Lutheran sympathies. Indeed, even religious reformers close to Cromwell denied that he was a sacramentarian. William Gray, for example, who had written *The Fantasie of Idolatrie* for Cromwell, defended him following his death, writing that

> The sacrament of the aulter, that is most hyest
> Crumwell believed it to be the very body of Christ.[386]

Cromwell's attainder alleged that he had licensed heretical preachers and supported the dissemination of banned religious books. He was also accused of treason when he is alleged to have said, on 31 March 1540, that

If the King would turn from it [reform], yet I would not turn; And if the King did turn, and all his people turned, I would fight in the Field in mine own person, with my Sword in my hand, against him and all others.[387]

Yet Cromwell was not permitted to stand trial for his alleged crimes because there was 'no case against him that would have stood up to a moment's judicial scrutiny'.[388] What is more, the attainder which condemned him was probably devised sometime after his arrest, with much of its contents thrown in for good measure to ensure that he was suitably damned. Cromwell's letter to the king, written while he was languishing in the Tower, responded to several of the accusations levelled at him on his arrest. It has been little noted, but the letter does not address the accusation of heresy against Cromwell.[389] There is just a hint here that the initial charges brought against him may have been somewhat different to those contained in his final attainder.

The words spoken by Cromwell before his execution on 28 July, recorded by John Foxe and the chronicler Edward Hall, are frustratingly inconclusive on his religious beliefs. On the scaffold, Cromwell declared:

I die in the Catholicke faithe, not doubting in any article of my faith, no nor doubting in any Sacrament of the Churche. Many hath sclaundered me, and reported that I haue been a bearer, of suche as hath mainteigned euill opinions, which is vntrue.[390]

Cromwell then knelt and said a prayer. Significantly, in this he did not appeal to the Virgin Mary or other intercessors – as he had in his 1529 will – which would seem to indicate that his beliefs concerning the saints had changed. But of course, Henry VIII himself had by this time come to reject the intercession of individual saints, so Cromwell may simply have been following the religious policy he himself had helped to make. He also declared that 'I haue no merites nor good workes, whiche I may alledge before thee'. This could, of course, be read as an acceptance of the Lutheran belief in justification by faith in Christ alone. But then again, it could merely have been a man expressing modesty before his end.[391] In a judicious analysis of Cromwell's religious beliefs, Lehmberg concluded that his final words demonstrate a 'personal conviction that is at once orthodox and reformed'.[392]

During Cromwell's later career, then, there are certainly plausible signs that he might have been a religious reformer. But these are by no means clear-cut, and a detailed analysis of his relations with a variety of churchmen and reformers would be needed before a full assessment could be made. What should be recognised here is that between the years 1485 and 1534 there is little to suggest that Cromwell held evangelical views or that he used his increasing influence to promote or protect religious radicals. Of course, this does not mean that Cromwell could not have become an evangelical later. It is all too easy to forget that men and women were living through the 1530s, a decade of momentous religious upheavel. Times change and people change with them. Cromwell's religious views may well have matured over the decade, particularly given that he was exposed to a variety of religious perspectives in his official position. On this point it is intriguing that the martyrologist John Foxe, who saw Cromwell very much as a Protestant hero, conceded that he was 'not grounded in iudgement of Religion in those hys youthfull dayes', that is, he did not think that Cromwell had always been an evangelical.[393] Nevertheless, the detailed analysis of Cromwell's religious views up to 1534 offered here must surely raise serious doubts as to whether Cromwell was a single-minded religious radical who pursued his own religious agenda in the later 1530s, as is so often alleged.

Conclusion

Having proven his ability by managing various Crown lands, we have seen in this chapter that Cromwell then began accumulating a variety of similar work connected to the administrative and financial affairs of the English Church. Once again, there is little to suggest that Cromwell was notably involved with 'high' policy. Instead, much of the work he was undertaking, particularly in 1532, was simply routine and needed to be done. Cromwell performed such tasks because of his talent and taste for them, and because the king was willing to entrust him with them. Cromwell's competence when dealing with this increasing workload not only then continued to ensure that he became ever more indispensable to the king, but it also meant that by 1534 Cromwell had developed something of a mastery over ecclesiastical affairs. Against this background, Cromwell's position as vice-gerent in spirituals from 1535 is somewhat easier to understand. In many respects, Cromwell's appointment as vicegerent seems a logical consequence of the administrative and fiscal control which he had already assumed over the upper echelons of the clergy and many religious houses.

There is also little between the years 1485 to 1534 in support of the view that Cromwell was a religious reformer. No doubt Cromwell believed that certain elements of the Church were corrupt and in need of reform, and he probably doubted the value of many religious houses (although perhaps not to the extent of wishing to see all of them dissolved). But that does not make him an evangelical. Nor does it mean that he could not later have become one. What it does mean is that the burden of proof lies with those who think that he did.

CHAPTER FIVE

ROYAL GOVERNMENT

FROM LATE 1531 ONWARDS, Cromwell was undertaking a variety of responsibilities that might loosely be termed 'government work'. Among these were his management of parliament, tasks connected with his position on the council and his duties in the various offices he was beginning to accumulate. Cromwell's association with government and administration is of course well known. In 1953 G. R. Elton claimed that the minister was responsible for a revolution in the way that English government was structured, with Cromwell allegedly replacing the existing 'medieval' household system of government with a modern structure of bureaucratic departments.[1] After Cromwell's 'revolution', the work of government supposedly fell to self-regulating departments of state rather than to the king's personal servants or household officers. Central to all of this was a remodelled Privy Council, which Elton claimed was given a permanent membership by Cromwell in the mid-1530s, as well as overall control of all other government departments.[2] This thesis would go on to spark considerable debate, and the question of whether there was a 'revolution' in government during the 1530s has remained one of the most enduring controversies of sixteenth-century history.[3] Yet the concern with the bold concept of revolution, and the search for dramatic change generally, has often come at the expense of the more quotidian aspects of royal government. These can be revealing in themselves because they shed light on the nature and character of the administrative system during this period. This chapter is not therefore intended as yet another critique of Elton's claims of a revolution in government (although inevitably, it does carry some implications for it). Instead, its focus is on Cromwell's earliest work in government before his alleged remodelling of it. Above all, it seeks to show how Cromwell himself worked and operated, and tries to locate this within the framework of the central machinery.

Court and Council, 1531–1534

Cromwell had joined the King's Council during the final weeks of 1530. This body's primary role was to provide the king with advice on any matter that he wished it to discuss, as well as overseeing much of the routine work of government. To manage all of this, the council was comprised of a mixture of leading noblemen, churchmen, household officers and, increasingly, men with a background in the law. In 1531 councillors included: the dukes of Norfolk and Suffolk; Stephen Gardiner, bishop of Winchester; Sir William Fitzwilliam, treasurer of the household; the earl of Shrewsbury; and Cromwell himself.[4] These men would have discussed a wide range of policy matters, both formally and informally, and were particularly involved in the formulation and implementation of foreign policy. The council was also the most important administrative body in the realm, and dealt with matters ranging from rundown dovecotes in Sussex to the sending of ambassadors abroad.[5] Indeed, nothing that happened within the realm appeared to fall outside the council's competence.[6] Yet, despite the wide-ranging business that the council transacted, becoming a councillor did not necessarily mean undertaking government or administrative work. It has already been noted that membership of the council during this period was a status rather than a 'job' with defined responsibilities, and the number of people sworn as councillors was probably high. It is interesting, for instance, that during the early 1530s Cromwell heard several depositions with John Aleyn, a minor councillor and London alderman.[7] Aleyn was rarely required to attend council meetings. His most notable contribution was probably serving on the reduced council that was left to govern the realm during the king's absence in Calais in late 1532. This was made up of a number of minor councillors, including Robert Radcliffe, first earl of Sussex, Thomas, Lord Darcy and Andrew, Lord Windsor, who would also probably not have attended meetings regularly or undertaken council work. In late 1532, however, with more senior figures such as Cromwell absent, these men were required to do so, and were supported by more experienced councillors, including Thomas Audeley and Brian Tuke.[8] The situation in late

1 Thomas Cromwell in
c.1532–1533, attributed to
Hans Holbein the Younger.

2 Cardinal Thomas Wolsey, Henry VIII's
first chief minister. Cromwell entered
Wolsey's service in 1524 and would become
one of the cardinal's most trusted servants.

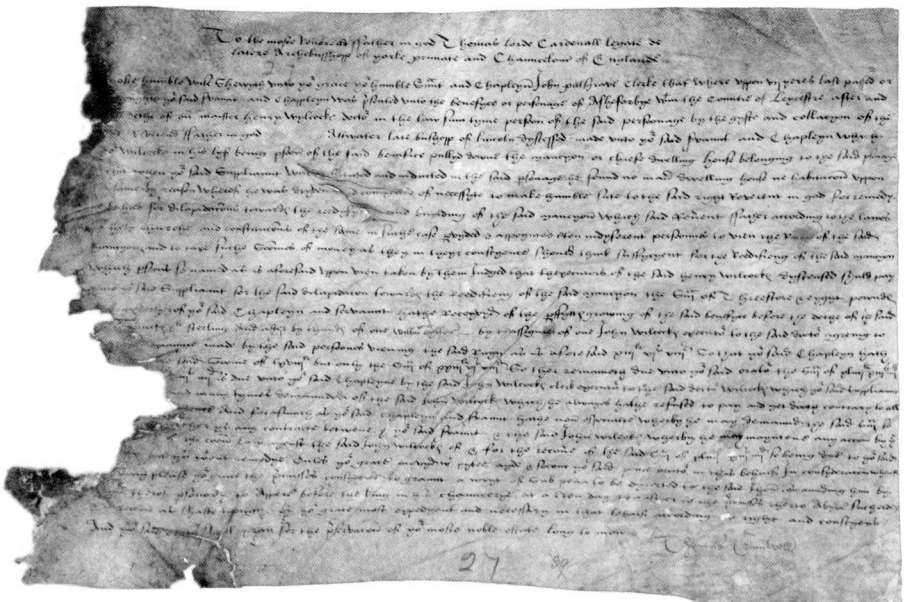

3 A Chancery petition signed by Cromwell. The lawyer who drew up a petition for Chancery would often sign it bottom right.

4 Royal approval of a papal bull authorising the suppression of several monasteries for the establishment of Cardinal College, Ipswich.

5 Wolsey's gateway in College Street, Ipswich. All that remains of the school Wolsey founded there. Cromwell played an important role in helping to found this institution, and its sister college in Oxford (now Christ Church).

6 The opening of the 1523 parliament. Cromwell sat as an MP for an unknown constituency during this parliament.

7 King Henry VIII by an unknown artist.

8 Sir John Gage, a prominent figure at court and a friend of Cromwell's. Gage provided Cromwell with useful support during the months following Wolsey's disgrace.

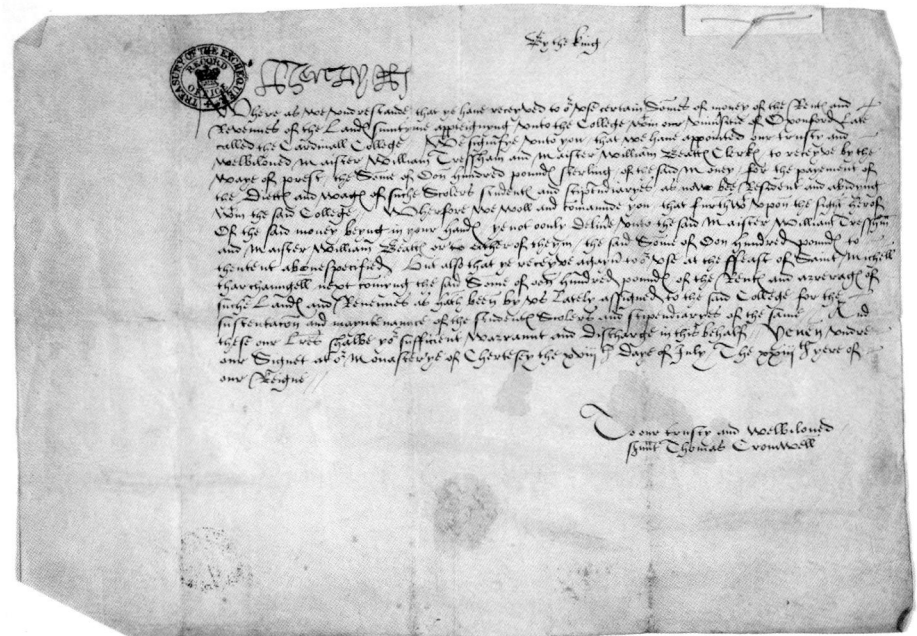

9 Cromwell's first royal warrant, dated 18 July 1531. It notes that Cromwell had received 'certain Somes of money of the Rentes and Revenues' of lands formerly belonging to Cardinal College, Oxford. It authorises him to pay £100 of this as wages for the scholars there.

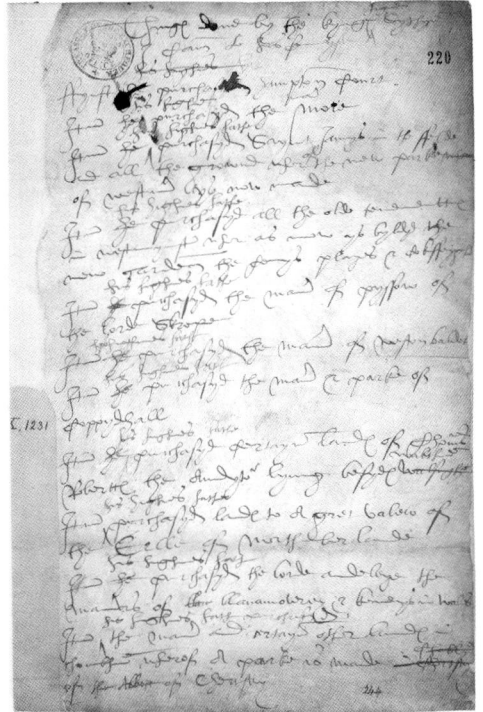

10 Part of a list, written in Cromwell's hand, entitled 'Thinges done by the kynges highnes sythyn I came to his seruyse'. The list illustrates the wide-ranging tasks that Cromwell undertook for Henry VIII during the early 1530s.

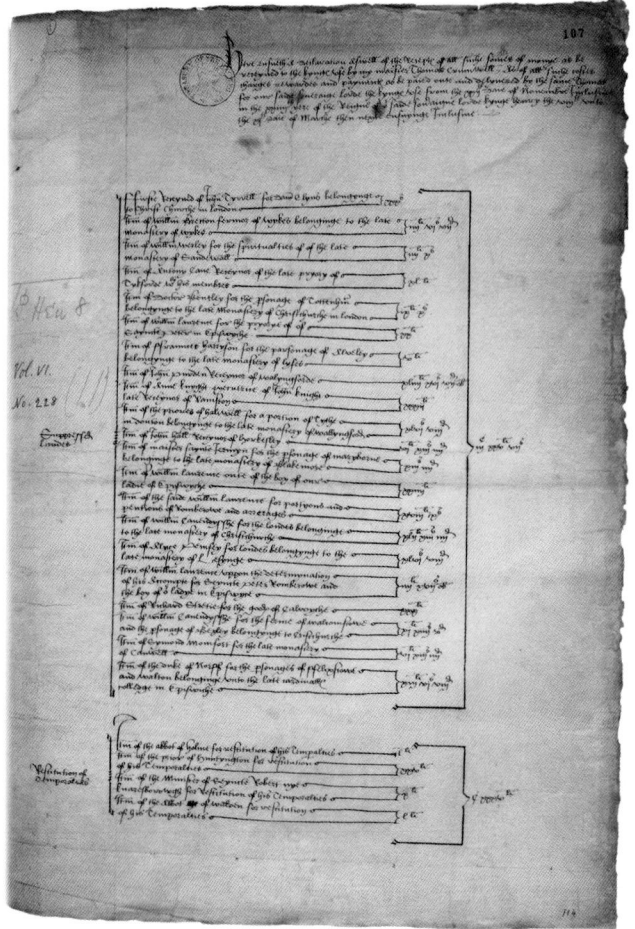

11 Hampton Court, as finished by Henry VIII. Cromwell helped Henry acquire the manor of Hampton Court permanently in 1531. The king then embarked on a major re-building programme there.

12 A page of one of Cromwell's accounts detailing the money he received on the king's behalf between 22 November 1532 and 11 March 1533.

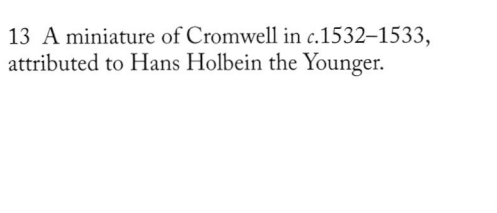

13 A miniature of Cromwell in *c*.1532–1533, attributed to Hans Holbein the Younger.

14 William Paulet by an unknown artist. Paulet and Cromwell worked cooperatively together during the years 1531–1534.

15 Thomas Howard, 3rd duke of Norfolk. Following Wolsey's fall, Norfolk became the king's leading councillor.

16 Sir Brian Tuke, treasurer of the Chamber. Tuke worked with Cromwell on financial matters, and by late 1532 he largely operated under Cromwell's direction.

1532 was nonetheless unusual, and the vast majority of the council's work-load would normally have been undertaken by an inner ring of regular council attenders. These men were among the king's most trusted servants, and it will be recalled that Cromwell had joined this inner group towards the end of 1531, as the Venetian ambassador had recognised.[9]

Much has been written about the King's Council during the 1530s. One of the most contentious debates has been concerned with whether the council was remodelled in the 1530s and given a permanent membership with more formalised procedures. Elton famously claimed that Cromwell had been the architect of this in the mid-1530s.[10] Guy has disagreed with this, and argued that it happened in 1540, perhaps as a result of Cromwell's fall.[11] What is all too often overlooked in this debate is that the council already had a small inner ring of regular attenders with a fairly fixed membership, and had done for over a hundred years. It also had recognised procedures and methods for recording its decisions.[12] While an examination of the structure and composition of the council in the later 1530s is beyond this present study, it does seem probable that whatever may have happened to it during the later 1530s, this was not quite as novel as is sometimes claimed.

Another stimulating debate concerning the council is how far policy making itself can be located within such a formal structure of government, or whether the court, with its patronage networks, clientele and informal channels of power, was the more important arena in the politics of the period. Many historians of the early twentieth century focused heavily on the formal machinery of government when seeking to unlock the political process.[13] Later, Elton would also place a particular emphasis on the council, alongside parliament, as key to understanding this. Over the years, however, such a view has been challenged. David Starkey argued that the court was the most important arena in the political process, and highlighted intimacy – that is, personal contact with the monarch – as having been vital for developing influence and power.[14] Thus, for Starkey, Cromwell's emergence as a leading figure in the early 1530s had depended not on his position on the council but rather on his ability to master the court. Having supposedly inherited, and then taken control of, Wolsey's faction there, Starkey claimed that Cromwell then 'packed' the court more generally with his own supporters and followers.[15] Other historians have essentially followed this interpretation, arguing that Cromwell worked with, and became promi-nent in, an evangelical court faction initially centred on Anne Boleyn.[16]

Tudor historians more generally have also come to view the royal court as the centre of the political process during this period.[17]

Yet, with regards to Cromwell at least, an interpretation that sees him as a leading player at court in the early 1530s is not wholly convincing. Starkey cited little evidence through which to test his claim that Cromwell took control of an alleged faction in the Privy Chamber. Evidence of a 'close relationship' between Cromwell and Anne Boleyn is also surprisingly thin, with barely a single letter surviving between the two from 1529 to 1534.[18] Instead, most of their collaboration during these years appears to have been fairly formal. Cromwell was acting as overseer to the surveying of lands used to endow Anne Boleyn; he also sent the warrant for the delivery of letters patent creating her marchioness of Pembroke, and would help to plan the logistics of her coronation in 1533.[19] It might be objected, of course, that a fairly high standard of proof is being called for here. Just because there is not a letter from Anne to Cromwell (or vice versa) openly illustrating political intrigue, faction or machinations, this does not mean that they did not collaborate.[20] This is true enough, and it is certainly not being claimed that Cromwell and Anne Boleyn were unfamiliar with one another. Anne's position as Henry's queen in all but name ensured that she was an important figure during the early 1530s, and someone with whom Cromwell would be required to get along. But given how entrenched the view that the two figures were close has become, is it not worth pondering on the evidence for this? Perhaps the most vociferous proponent of the view that Cromwell and Anne Boleyn were allies at court has largely relied on evidence from 1534 onwards to support this.[21] The salient point is that there is little that convincingly links Cromwell with any court 'faction' during his early political career. Although there were plainly courtiers whose interests and prosperity encouraged them to work together, Cromwell was not yet obviously one of them. He may have become a leading player at court, but this was the result of his rise, and not the cause of it.

In fact, Cromwell's pathway to power was far less dependent on success at court than is sometimes realised. During his first few years in Henry's services, Cromwell was much more a councillor than he was a courtier. Of course, we should be wary of drawing too great a distinction between administrative government and the royal court during the late medieval period.[22] In a broad sense, 'every councillor was a courtier', and many courtiers were also councillors.[23] Nevertheless, there does seem to have been a distinction, however ill defined, between the type of work performed by men such as Cromwell, Hales and Audeley, and that performed by, say, George Boleyn.[24] Cromwell was certainly not involved in the chivalrous aspects of court life during his early career. What is more, between 1531 and 1534 he was heavily tied to London. Judging by their itineraries, Cromwell often apparently remained in London while Henry and the court were elsewhere.[25] To be sure, Cromwell had men and contacts at court, and no doubt was in attendance there regularly – not least to discuss business with the king. We have also already seen how Cromwell relied on contacts at court to survive during the uncertain months following Wolsey's fall. Nonetheless, Cromwell's ascent was driven by his work for the king. What occupied his early political career was the legal, administrative and financial work of government. Much of this came to depend on his growing position on the council.

What exactly, then, did Cromwell's responsibilities on that body entail? In August 1531 instructions to be executed by the council were given to Cromwell from the king. These offer a glimpse of the considerable business handled by that body. Among these were orders to proceed against a number of clerics suspected of praemunire and to prepare legislation for parliament, including bills for treason and customs on imported wines, as well as an instruction to proceed against the owners of 'galeys and shippes' in Southampton for illegally importing wine.[26] A memorandum prepared for the council by Cromwell himself in 1533 shows that in that year its time was heavily dominated by the break with Rome. Councillors were organising a preaching campaign to defend the abolition of papal authority and preparing a book of articles justifying the king's actions over his 'great matter'.[27] Other instructions concerned the sending of ambassadors abroad, and preparations for the provisions of the royal navy.[28] It is interesting that Cromwell himself implemented many of these directives, as it once again underlines that from late 1531 onwards he was acting as one of the council's workhorses. Of the twenty-eight instructions delivered to the council in 1531, for example, at least eleven were executed by him, either alone or with other councillors. A summary revealing the delegation of the 1533 instructions similarly reveals that the ninth, tenth and eleventh articles – i.e., those concerning the publication of proclamations publicising the appeals act, and the king's new titles – were to be committed to the lord chancellor and 'Master Cromewell'.[29] The thirteenth article – 'to sende exploratours and spies into Scotland' – was committed to Cromwell and the duke of Norfolk.[30] Many of the other articles were also probably overseen by him. For instance, the diminishing and ordering of the princess dowager's household was delegated to the duke of Suffolk, the earl of Sussex, William Paulet and Richard Sampson. Cromwell was kept informed of their progress, and even provided money for the household's re-establishment.[31]

In addition to these administrative and political matters, councillors had judicial responsibilities, and members sat in the court of Star Chamber when formally attending to this. Cromwell himself must have done so, although Guy's belief that he was almost as active in Star Chamber as he was in the council proper is difficult to substantiate.[32] Certainly, in June 1532 he discharged a man from appearing in Star Chamber.[33] Cromwell's remarks to Richard and William Haybourne, that he and the lord chancellor 'will sitt vpon y [sic] the mater in variaunce betwixt Elisabeth Colcoke widowe and you', might also refer to his activity there.[34] Clear-cut evidence that Cromwell regularly attended Star Chamber is lacking; but it can be said that he took an interest in this court, and was keen to add to – and improve – its work. Memoranda suggest that Cromwell was planning an act of parliament enabling murderers in Wales and the Welsh marches to be tried there.[35] More interesting, in light of Star Chamber's later development, is that one of his notes also called for an act to be made enabling the chancellor and two judges to proceed in the court notwithstanding the absence of officials whose attendance was a statutory requirement.[36] This suggests that Cromwell had concerns about the court's efficiency, and provides a foretaste of his later separation of the council in Star Chamber from the Privy Council in the mid-1530s.[37]

Cromwell was also engaged with the quasi-judicial functions of the council itself, that is, those of the executive board. Despite the existence of Star Chamber, people could still submit petitions to the council directly, and its members largely operated in an arbitrational capacity when attending to this.[38] Cromwell and the council were informed that 'one Stephen Mylles schuld vnlawfully take a wey my lady Saluond frome hyr owyn howse a gaynste hyr mynd' in 1532, for instance, and a local inquiry was called with the intent of sending those accused before them early the following year.[39] A considerable number of private petitions were also addressed to Cromwell as 'one of the kynges most honerable councell'.[40] Although these were probably appeals for private intercession, several still urged him to 'call' for and examine people – something the council also did frequently, usually on allegations of treasonous activity or slanderous speech. Thomas Woodhouse and 'on[e] Johnnson' are just two examples of men cited to appear before Cromwell 'and other of the kings grace coun-cell'; there were many others.[41] On occasion it was even necessary to exact some form of obligation to ensure a person would appear when specified. A 'Regestre ... concerny[n]ge the Apperance of certeyne persones ... before the kinge and his counsayll' has survived. This contains a list of all the obligations Cromwell made between July 1532 and February 1533 to ensure that people appeared when called.[42] The depositions of some of those brought before the council were also heard and recorded by Cromwell. In January 1532, for example, he took and wrote the deposition of Peter Alleyn, alongside Sir Henry Guildford, Sir William Fitzwilliam and the earl of Oxford.[43] Somewhat remarkably, Cromwell continued to find time for this type of routine council work throughout his meteoric rise. In August and September 1532 he took further depositions, both alone and with other councillors.[44] Once again, it was Cromwell – by now a senior councillor – who recorded these depositions, despite the fact that he heard some of them alongside several minor councillors, who might have been expected to undertake this work in his place.

Significantly, some of Cromwell's work on the council also casts doubt on the claim that the minister himself was a notably concerned social reformer.[45] In 1531 'unseasonable weather failing' had created a shortage of corn and other victuals. A proclamation issued on 7 September prohibited the export of such produce, and Cromwell was one of those responsible for its enforcement.[46] A 'breeff Regestre of suche specialties ... supposed to be Forfeyte to the kynge for caryeuge oute of corne & other vytayles' was in his possession in 1532. This lists twenty-five instances of forfeited obliga-tions for this that Cromwell had uncovered.[47] One of his accounts similarly records that over £1,580 'forfetted to the kings vse by sondry persones for conueying of corne' was received by him in late 1532.[48] Just before Christmas of that year he had also requested that a scholar produce a short piece of work on the cost of corn.[49] At first sight, all this might seem to be an example of Cromwell's concern for the 'commonweal' or commonwealth. But Penry Williams has noted the 'very detailed supervision' that the council exercised over the grain trade.[50] In particular, it devoted a consider-able amount of its time and energy during periods of poor harvests to making sure that corn was not shipped overseas.[51] It is reasonable, there-fore, to attribute Cromwell's activity over the supply of corn to his position on the council, rather than to any particular personal concern about this problem. The 'Regestre' noted above was produced in response to the king's instructions.[52] Cromwell himself does not appear to have been unduly occupied with agricultural or social issues during these years. True, his activities in parliament, considered shortly, do offer some evidence that he grappled with the problem of enclosure. This, however, is heavily outweighed by the impression gleaned from his memoranda. They are impressively thorough, and a testimony to Cromwell's capacity for work. It is surely revealing, then, that remarkably few are preoccupied with anything resembling social concern or matters affecting the commonweal. Instead, they are mainly focused on high policy or the routine administrative work that Cromwell was engaged with. He does not appear to have been unduly concerned with much else during his early years under the king.

Cromwell's activities on the council offer other indications of his influence and standing during these years. By 1533 Cromwell was one, if not the, leading figure on the King's Council. Drafts survive of an early council schedule prepared by a clerk, which Cromwell has amended; and the final version was produced by Ralph Sadler, Cromwell's clerk.[53] According to Elton, these drafts demonstrated 'Cromwell's complete control of the Council's agenda'.[54] Bernard disputes this, however, arguing, 'A reading more attentive to what the record says would rather suggest that it was the king who was making the decisions and issuing orders on matters clearly of considerable personal concern'.[55] On this subject, Bernard and Elton occupy opposite extremes of a somewhat over-simplified model in which policy was formulated either by the king (in Bernard's case) or the minister (in Elton's). What is beyond doubt is that Henry VIII was informed and actively involved with the council's decisions. The minutes for the meeting in question reveal that it was 'the Kynges Highnes' who appointed the councillors to oversee the newly established households of Catherine of Aragon and Princess Mary, disproving the suggestion that Henry was uninterested or uninvolved with the council's business. But the very purpose of the council was to assist the monarch with the governance of the realm and to rid him of its day-to-day business. That Cromwell was compiling the council's agenda does suggest that he now had considerable influence – even a degree of independent power – over its proceedings. But what the 1533 council agenda suggests in particular is that matters that most closely affected Henry – such as the arrangements surrounding his family – were personally directed by him. Over other areas, particularly those relating to more quotidian aspects of government, Cromwell had much greater freedom and control. In any case, by 1533 Cromwell and

Henry were probably working so closely together that it seems highly likely that Cromwell would have known the king's views or attitude about many issues without having to consult him at every turn.

Parliament, 1531–1534

Alongside his responsibilities as a councillor during these years, Cromwell also sat as MP for Taunton in the so-called Reformation parliament (1529–1536). On obtaining this seat, and during 1530 and most of 1531, Cromwell operated under the direction of the duke of Norfolk, working as one of the Crown's supporters in the Commons. Towards the end of 1531, however, Cromwell had assumed greater responsibility for managing the king's affairs there; and by early 1532 he was drafting much of the government's legislation. It is, of course, well recognised that the Crown's ministers worked to ensure the efficiency and productivity of parliament in dispatching official business.[56] As both an MP and councillor, Cromwell would have been entitled to occupy a special position near the speaker's chair, and would have worked closely with that royal nominee to promote the king's interests personally. Cromwell's name also appears in the journals of the House of Lords, showing that he may have delivered bills from the Commons to the Upper House.[57] Yet detailed information about the management of parliament has often been lacking. It is therefore of some interest that Cromwell's papers can illuminate aspects of this, while offering further glimpses of his own influence over yet another area of royal government.

The Crown was naturally reliant on having sufficient support in parliament to achieve its goals there. The first indication that Cromwell was assisting in the running of parliament is that from December 1531 he had begun receiving requests from members who wished to be excused from attending.[58] Some of these, such as Bishop Fisher of Rochester, writing in February 1534, undoubtedly wanted to be excused for political reasons or matters of conscience relating to the break with Rome.[59] The vast majority probably had more banal motives. Attendance at parliament could prove costly, as John, Lord Latimer claimed when complaining to Cromwell that his continual presence there had proved very 'chargeable' to him.[60] Parliamentary proceedings could also be long and tedious. All of this fuelled absenteeism, which could be a considerable problem if it impeded the efficiency of the Crown's business.[61] Absent members were likely to be a particular issue if those who sought a licence for discharge (or stayed at home regardless) were experienced in the legislative affairs of the Commons. Handling requests to tarry at home, and the problem of absenteeism more generally, must therefore have been an important, yet routine, aspect of Cromwell's management of both Houses.

Another matter closely linked to the smooth running of parliament was ensuring that by-elections were held to fill vacated seats, which had usually been created by the death of a member. This was likely to be an acute problem during the Reformation parliament because it lasted longer than any other parliament in the sixteenth century. Several lists of MPs were in Cromwell's possession, including 'a paper of the names of theme that be ... burgesis in the parlement ho[use]'.[62] These indicate that he took an interest in the composition of the Commons. It is also possible that the cryptic note in one of Cromwell's memoranda, 'to remember the parliament boke', was a reference to the 'book' or register of the clerk of the House of Commons, which contained a roll call of every member.[63] This may also have been in Cromwell's possession. Other papers reveal that Cromwell took care to ensure that the Commons included men who could be relied on to support the king's interests there. A memorandum from 1533 reminded him to attend to 'the new elleccyons of suche burgessys knyghtz and cytyzens as be lakkyng in the parlyament',[64] while a letter from an anonymous man in Huntingdonshire shows that Cromwell had written urging him to 'make ... Frendes in the Countre here to serve the kinges hyghnes ... At this parlyament'.[65] In this instance, Cromwell's efforts were apparently slow. One Thomas Hall of Huntingdon had already been active, canvassing 'all the Frendes that he cowde make', and had become an obstacle to the man whom Cromwell wanted returned in the by-election. Nevertheless, later remarks by Cromwell suggest that on the whole the Crown's servants were effective at ensuring that the king had sufficient support in the Lower House. In 1539 Cromwell would tell Henry VIII that he and the council had ensured that 'your Majestie had never more tractable [a] parlement'.[66]

One or two of Cromwell's papers hint at some of the tactics employed by the Crown to win support in parliament for its objectives. A superficial reading of Stephen Vaughan's comments in 1532, that he had sent Cromwell 'the booke ... I promysed the kynges magestie', might suppose that this was connected with material he was simultaneously sending Cromwell to support Henry VIII's 'great matter'.[67] In fact, Vaughan's book concerned the problems that English merchants faced in Antwerp, and it is revealing that he hoped 'my booke ... might be openly declared in the parliament howse / [so] that the kynges subiectes might be induced to know what detoryment succedethe to the Realme by reason of the contynall haunt to repayre of the merchauntes vnto the marches'.[68] Implicit in these remarks is a suggestion that the government might employ polemical works in parliament to galvanise the Commons into acting. Certainly, a similar tactic was employed during the struggles against the Church in 1532. Early in that year, Cromwell and Henry had the oath that was sworn by bishops to the pope read in the Commons, with the intent of persuading MPs to increase the pressure on the English clergy.[69]

That Cromwell and the Crown felt it necessary to employ such methods is interesting, as it suggests that on many issues the Commons were less pliant than is sometimes assumed. To be sure, much of what went on in the Lower House was controlled by the government, and many of the participants in debates were often acting as spokesmen or advocates for the Crown. The first speaker to raise grievances about the excessive fees charged for probate of testament in ecclesiastical courts, for example, was Sir Henry Guildford, controller of the king's household. He almost certainly did this with the Crown's consent, indicating its endorsement of the debate.[70] Haigh has even suggested that the most significant legislative initiatives depended on the Crown and its supporters for their success.[71] Yet we should be wary of thinking that this meant there was not the opportunity for genuine debate and opposition in sixteenth-century parliaments. Although silence among the sources ensured that for many years historians argued that there was no debate there at all, a careful sifting of the limited evidence available shows that genuine dissent could be, and was, expressed.[72] The first recorded division in parliament (that is, by separating into two sides rather than by acclamation) occurred in 1523, over the wording of a money grant.[73] A division was also required to pass the annates bill in 1532.[74] Nor should we allow ourselves to think, as some have, that debates were carefully orchestrated so that the king could pretend – to his clergy, the pope or perhaps another prince – that he was acting in response to pressure from his subjects.[75] Cromwell's own speech to parliament in 1523, in which he strongly objected to Henry VIII's wars in France, has been interpreted in just such a way. Believing that in 1523 Cromwell was already in Wolsey's service, Guy has suggested that Cromwell delivered this speech as possible cover for a change in the Crown's plans.[76] As we have already seen, Cromwell did not begin working for Wolsey until 1524. Thus, when Cromwell warned the Commons that financing and equipping a great army against

France would 'exhawste and vtterly consume all the cogne [coin] and bolyon withyn this Realme', he was speaking his own mind.[77] The significance of Cromwell's 1523 speech to parliament, therefore, is that it illustrates that debate and opposition in parliament could and did occur.

That there was genuine scope for debate in parliament is not to deny that much of what went on there was tightly controlled. It was, after all, the king who decided when a parliament should be called, and as soon as his objectives were achieved, he could prorogue or dissolve it. From quite an early point in his political career, Cromwell himself was consulted on when this might occur. In December 1531 Christopher Hales requested that Cromwell inform him if parliament should 'holde or be deferred', while at the end of September 1532 he also asked Cromwell 'to let me knowe howe oure parlement shall succede / eyther to be kept at the day prefixed or shalbe proroged'.[78] As remarks by Thomas Audeley make plain, the decision over when to prorogue parliament was taken by the king.[79] Nevertheless, by October 1532 Cromwell was being requested to 'move' Henry on this matter, and on whom the authority to prorogue parliament should be given.[80]

Typically, sixteenth-century parliaments lasted only as long as was needed for the Crown to dispatch its business there. The likelihood that parliament would be needed in the divorce campaign, however, meant that the king was unwilling to dissolve it in the early 1530s. This presented particular issues. Attendance at parliament was not only costly for members, but it also kept them from their own affairs. In March 1532 the Commons were probably expressing concern about the parliament's duration when they requested that it be prorogued so that they 'myght repayre into their countreys', something Henry immediately denied them.[81] Effective management of parliament therefore also involved trying to keep its members as content as possible by not keeping them sitting for too long. This perhaps explains Audeley's remarks to Cromwell in October 1532, that parliament 'must be prorogid' on 4 November.[82] In this instance the king did consent, and the Commons 'right joyusly acceptyd the said prorogacion'.[83]

Yet proroguing parliament created further work. Business in the House still remained unfinished and Cromwell was required to have a list drawn of the bills which had been read but not yet passed, so these could be resumed in the next session.[84] Cromwell's concern for the progress of legislation is understandable, given that he was the one drafting many of the government bills that were introduced. Among the papers in his possession were an 'act that none shall sue to Rome for the Judgement of right of inheritaunce'; 'a bill resiting by what meanes the kyng is disceyued of his custome by reason of brynging in to this Realme silk wrought'; 'a act for Fermes'; 'a byll for Fermes and Fermeholdes'; 'a byll for Tyn works and wasshinges'; bills for the sowing of 'lynsede', 'Flaxsede' and 'hempsede'; 'a byll for consederac[i]ons of derth and vitiall'; 'a byll for the conveyng of clothes owt of this realme'; 'a byll for ... repelling of Atteynders'; 'a byll for the daungers of Fermes'; 'a byll for proteccions'; and a 'byll how the kynges receyuours Ryves and bayliffes do detayne certen offices and reuenues from the kyng'.[85] In addition to these, Cromwell's hand can also be found on a number of draft acts, including one confirming existing statutes on husbandry and another concerning the ports of Plymouth and Dartmouth.[86] What is more difficult to answer is whether Cromwell was the architect of these proposed pieces of legislation. Certainly some of the acts he was involved with, such as the failed bill regulating primer seisins and uses, introduced during the third session of 1532, were strongly in the king's interest and produced under royal instruction.[87] Yet there is good reason to attribute many of these bills, if not solely to Cromwell, then certainly to the council as a whole rather than to the king. It is difficult to imagine that Henry had much concern with the act authorising the destruction of rooks and crows, which Cromwell amended, or the act regulating the import of French wines, a draft of which survives in the hand of one of Cromwell's clerks.[88] There is even a clear instance of Cromwell attempting to persuade the king of the merits of a piece of legislation, which he had most likely produced. In January 1534 Cromwell informed Henry that a bill to limit enclosure, by restricting the number of sheep grazed on enclosed land, had passed the Commons.[89] He added that if this bill

> by the gret wysdom vertuew goodness and zerale [sic] that your highness beryth towards this your Realme might haue good successe and take good effect Amongyst your lords aboue ... I doo coniecture and suppose in my pore simple and vnworthye jugement that your highness shall do the most noble proffytable and most benefycyall thing that euer was done to the commune wealthe of this your Realme ... sythyn br[e]wtyse tyme.[90]

What is striking here is that Henry clearly had little knowledge of this bill and Cromwell was attempting to persuade him to accept it: 'pardon my boldness in this wrytyng to your grace which onlye procedythe for the ... loue I doo bere to your mageste and the common welth'. If this bill had emanated from Cromwell's office, then this provides clear proof that Cromwell did operate with a measure of independence, and initiated his own attempts at reform. At the very least, the episode provides an example of Cromwell attempting to encourage the king to accept legislation that he himself thought beneficial.

Of course, this is not to claim that Cromwell had some preconceived plan to improve the commonwealth. The problem of enclosure was a familiar one, and Cromwell's attempts to tackle it should be seen in the broader context of a long line of efforts by the Crown's ministers.[91] What is more, many of the other bills which Cromwell drafted or corrected were actually produced in response to matters as they arose. The problem of rooks and crows, for instance, had been raised with Cromwell by the abbot of Faversham.[92] A draft bill for the town of Salisbury, which Cromwell corrected, had been requested by the mayor, aldermen and commons of that town.[93] His draft bill for the repair of Dover pier was also produced in response to a petition from the people there to the king.[94] Nevertheless, if Cromwell was not the initiator of every single bill that he drafted or amended, he certainly deserves credit for attempting to remedy the concerns of the king's subjects.

It will be recalled that Elton, in his ceaseless attempt to rehabilitate Cromwell, made bold claims about the extent of the minister's commitment to parliament. Cromwell was supposedly 'the first statesman to understand the potentialities of statute', someone who worked tirelessly to ensure that almost everything done during the 1530s was done using this instrument, and a man who 'well deserves the title of England's first parliamentary statesman'.[95] One of the few comments that Cromwell made regarding legislation does not support these conclusions. In 1535 it became necessary to prevent the export of coin from the realm, and with parliament no longer sitting there was concern about how this could legitimately be done. Writing to the duke of Norfolk, Cromwell informed him that if no existing statute could be found which served this purpose, the lord chief justice and the lord chancellor had told him that the king

> by the aduyse of his Cownsayll myght make proclamacyons and vse all other polecyes at his pleasure aswell in this Case as in Anye other lyke For the avoyding of any suche daungers and that the sayd proclama-cyons and polyces so deuysd by the King & his cownsayll for any such purpose sholde be of as good effect as Any law made by parlyament or otherwyse *which oppy[ny]on I assure your grace I was veray gladde to here.*[96]

Two things are of note. First, Cromwell was concerned to ensure that the most legitimate and legally binding method was employed to enforce government policy; he did not seem concerned that a proclamation might be used to do this instead of a statute.[97] Second, Cromwell was taking advice on the strength of proclamations from Lord Chancellor Audeley, which rather implies that Audeley had a stronger grasp of 'the potentialities of statute' than did Cromwell.

Thomas Audeley was a close ally and associate of Cromwell, whom Audeley himself described as 'oon of my grettest frendes'.[98] Both men had served in the parliament of 1523 and had been members of Wolsey's household during that decade.[99] Like Cromwell, Audeley had been a practising lawyer during his pre-ministerial career, and had occasionally worked with Cromwell on legal matters in the 1520s.[100] Crucially, however, Audeley had received formal legal training. This probably explains why Elton's conjectural claims regarding Cromwell and parliament are far easier to substantiate for Audeley. It was Audeley, for instance, who demonstrably saw an act of parliament as the highest and surest form of law. In October 1532, during the king's absence in Calais, Audeley wrote to Cromwell regarding the concerns of the chief justice, who had enquired whether the king had empowered a lieutenant of the realm so that the 'Lawes and justice shold procede in [his] absens'. Audeley 'secretlie debated' with the king's justices whether the king should have done this. Although the justices 'remayned in some doubtes of their clere resolucion', Audeley decided it was best to keep quiet about the matter with the king due to return soon. Interestingly though, he added to Cromwell that 'incase herafter ther shold happen any doubt of errour in hit / it myght sone be helpen by act of Parliament without difficultie whereunto all they agreed and accorded'.[101] Evidently Audeley, and indeed the broader legal establishment, felt that parliament could be used to rectify any legal discrepancies. A similar conclusion can be drawn from the events following the suppression of the monastery of Christchurch. It will be recalled that, following the monastery's surrender, inquests had been held to determine its ownership. Having replaced Thomas More as lord chancellor, Audeley would become responsible for issuing the letters patent confirming the king's new title of ownership to Christchurch, which had been confirmed by the 'offices' Cromwell had found. Nevertheless, Audeley was uneasy about the legality of Henry's right to Christchurch, and had concerns as to whether a London jury empanelled to return a verdict on the possession of Christchurch would, or could, establish a title in Henry's favour.[102] What is more, two statutes from Henry VI's reign made void all grants or letters patent which were issued before a jury's verdict on the ownership of that land or property was returned to Chancery.[103] It was probably on Audeley's recommendation, therefore, that in March 1534 the king's title to Christchurch was confirmed by an act of parliament, 'as though offyce and offices had been duely founde therof according to the laws of this Realme'.[104] Evidently, it was not merely Cromwell who 'preferred statute to any other form of law-making'.[105]

What all this illustrates is that statute law was well established before Cromwell came to power. Audeley's actions show that both he and the broader legal profession were already of the opinion that statute could be used to remedy any perceived legal discrepancies: it was already seen as the highest, most secure form of law. Other legal-minded people, notably Christopher St German, were also advancing theories of the omnicompetence of statute.[106] The extensive use of parliament during this decade cannot therefore be attributed solely to one man's vision or brilliance. That the 1530s witnessed a watershed in constitutional change is of course beyond doubt. But in many respects, the Crown had little choice but to use parliament, particularly if it wanted the changes it professed to appear as legitimate and enforceable as possible. As the fifteenth-century chief justice Sir John Fortescue argued, the king 'may not rule his peple bi other lawes than such as thai assenten unto'.[107] It is also worth reminding ourselves that it was not parliament, but convocation, which declared Henry VIII supreme head of the Church, and which surrendered the Church's independence. Parliament was then used later – in 1534, when the act of supremacy and the act for the submission of the clergy were passed – to give statutory confirmation to acts of convocation.[108] The insistence on parliamentary sovereignty in the 1530s may actually therefore point to the government being acutely aware of the precarious nature of its position and claims, and shows that it sought ways to strengthen these.[109] After all, Parliament offered the Crown a 'uniquely public context, for the whole realm was supposedly present either in person or by proxy'.[110] Rather than visionary brilliance, then, its extensive use may point to the Crown's insecurity and weakness.

Where does all this leave Cromwell? It certainly diminishes his importance somewhat. But it also carries an invigorating implication. The inference here, surely, is that many of Cromwell's contemporaries were far more interesting people than many historians realised when they imagined Cromwell to be so unique.

Cromwell's Offices

Cromwell held a number of formal offices during his early career under the king. In April 1532 he was made master or treasurer of the king's jewels, and this was soon followed by his appointment as keeper or clerk of the hanaper in July, and chancellor of the exchequer the following April.[111] Cromwell's offices are of interest for a number of reasons. First of all, they have been seen as significant in his rise to power. By pressing these offices 'further than they had been pressed before', Cromwell allegedly used them to establish his own influence and rule as a 'bureaucrat minister'.[112] What is more, Cromwell's work in these positions has been seen as indicative of his approach to government more generally. Cromwell's offices, Elton once wrote, reflect 'the character and extent of his administration'.[113] Yet surprisingly, although many historians have questioned Elton's claims regarding the revolutionary nature of the administrative changes Cromwell would later bring about, no one has looked afresh at Cromwell's early work in these offices since Elton's studies over sixty years ago.[114] A new examination is therefore justifiable. As we shall see, Elton's most significant conclusions regarding Cromwell's activities in these positions do not bear the weight of close scrutiny.

The first three offices that Cromwell held under the king were all connected with financial administration.[115] The master of the king's jewels was a household position, and its holder was responsible for the custody of the king's reserve in plate and jewels. The clerk of the hanaper was a position in Chancery, with the holder overseeing sums paid to the Crown as fees or fines for the letters and writs passed under the Great Seal. Finally, the chancellor of the exchequer was a position confined to the upper Exchequer; its holder had custody of the Exchequer seal and some control over its records.[116] According to Elton, Cromwell deliberately accumulated these positions in order to control Crown finances and to ensure that he had influence over every key area of government.[117] As we have already seen, though, the reality was more prosaic. Each of these offices was held by patent for life, and Cromwell succeeded to each on the death of the previous incumbent. He was therefore unable to cherry-pick these offices; his acquisition of them relied primarily on chance and opportunity. Moreover, as Elton himself conceded, all three offices were minor positions of no great importance.[118] It is therefore difficult to see why Cromwell would even have wanted them, beyond the immediate benefit of profit and prestige.[119]

And yet, still, Elton concluded that Cromwell had acquired these positions for their strategic value:

> Each of these three offices gave Cromwell a definite place in the admin-istration of a financial department ... Such a collection made the detailed control of finance easier ... the offices of the jewel-house, the hanaper, and the chancellorship of the exchequer secured to their holder a more direct and more detailed influence over their affairs than the mere general supervision of a great minister, however powerful, could have given.[120]

Such a view can no longer be sustained. With regard to both the hanaper and the Exchequer, there is little to suggest that Cromwell was notably active there. John Judde, his deputy in the hanaper, certainly kept Cromwell informed on matters, but probably discharged him of most of his duties.[121] Cromwell's papers suggest that he himself did little more than pay the money to the chancellor for his wax in July 1533,[122] receive the £300 surplus his deceased predecessor possessed on his death[123] and negotiate a fine in which he was styled as 'Clerk' in the indenture.[124] In the Exchequer, evidence of his activity is thinner still. Edward Lee, archbishop of York, did write to Cromwell, asking him to use his 'rome of authoritie in the saied exchequier' to obtain a discharge for him from debts owed there, which Cromwell apparently did.[125] He may also have occasionally acted in a judicial capacity there.[126] Nevertheless, none of this suggests that Cromwell was notably active in these positions. Indeed, his lack of activity in these two offices is in stark contrast to his work as master of the king's jewels; in that office, Cromwell's correspondence leaves no doubt that he was actively engaged in the routine responsibilities that came with it. He can be shown delivering plate to the king and to goldsmiths; he sold plate on the king's behalf, oversaw the production of Henry's jewel-encrusted collars and endowed the princess dowager with jewels and plate in 1533.[127] Of far greater signifi-cance is that as master of the king's jewels Cromwell also accumulated wider revenues than those received by any of his immediate predecessors. This led Elton to the conclusion that the Jewel House was transformed by Cromwell into 'one of the leading financial ministries of state'.[128]

What is to be made of such a claim? It is certainly true that Cromwell was increasingly handling the king's revenues. It will be recalled that on entering the king's service he had received money from various Crown

lands; and those responsibilities quickly broadened as he undertook wider
financial negotiations on the Crown's behalf, as well as acting as a financial
mediator between suitors and the king.[129] Cromwell oversaw the settlement
of several outstanding debts relating to Wolsey,[130] and was regularly paying
and receiving wider sums of money on Henry VIII's behalf.[131] Many of
these, such as Cromwell's receipt of church revenues or his responsibilities as
paymaster for the king's works, have already been noted. He also received
the revenues from distraint of knighthood, which the chronicler Edward
Hall recollected as raising 'a greate somme of money to the Kynges vse'.[132]
Money forfeited for the conveying of corn was similarly paid to Cromwell.[133]
He also managed the supply of money for the Anglo-Scottish war in
1532–1533, paid the wages for several ambassadors, received over £95 from
the sale of the king's wines[134] and paid money for the rigging of the king's
ships.[135] What is more, several men and women besought Cromwell to move
the king on financial matters, debts and obligations.[136] His emergence as an
important financial figure was therefore something that was also recognised
by his contemporaries.

Four of Cromwell's accounts survive for this period and neatly illustrate
the considerable sums that he was receiving and paying as master of the
jewels. All four are drafts, and each slightly overlaps another chronologically.[137] The first account runs from 29 September 1532 to 17 December
1532;[138] the second from 22 November 1532 to 11 March 1533;[139] the
third 29 September 1532 to 28 June 1533;[140] and the fourth 2 April 1533
to 2 April 1534.[141] Elton labelled these accounts A, B, C and D respectively,
and for convenience this shorthand is adopted here. A and D are merely
summaries of the total receipt and expenditure by Cromwell, but B and C
offer a much more detailed breakdown of the revenues he was handling.
Among the more unusual payments recorded on these latter two is a sum
for the yeoman of the crossbow's livery coat, the cost of carrying stuff from
the monastery of Christchurch, money for the king's fabrics and £100 for
the wages of men on the king's ships.[142] The total receipt and expenditure
recorded on each account can be summarised as follows:[143]

	Receipt	Expenditure
A	£25,655	£24,606[144]
B	£20,567	£21,240[145]
C	£12,496	£12,332
D	£38,504	£37,232

It was largely on the basis of these impressive figures that Elton argued that the office of master of the jewels became an important treasury under Cromwell. It was a position that enabled him to have the custody and personal control of large sums of money, and which provided him with the independence to finance 'high policy' on his own initiative.[146]

From the two accounts that offer the most detailed breakdown, however, a slightly different picture emerges. Most of the money recorded as being received on accounts B and C came from a single source. Of the money received by Cromwell on account B, £8,000 is recorded as being taken from 'the kynges cofres ... oute of the Towre',[147] while a further £10,991 is recorded as coming from the Tower on account C.[148] This led Elton to believe that most of Cromwell's revenues were derived from a capital reserve transferred into his possession which he used to cover a variety of expenditures.[149] David Starkey concurred with the notion that Cromwell was controlling government expenditure from 1532 onwards, but he drew attention to a document which Elton had overlooked, rightly noting that it 'plays a crucial part in unravelling Cromwell's treasurership'.[150] This was a receipt recording that, on 5 October 1532, £20,000 was delivered out of the Privy Coffers at Greenwich into the hands of Thomas Audeley, Brian Tuke and Cromwell himself, before being 'put ... in a great chest' in the Tower of London.[151] Crucially, however, Starkey failed to realise what this money was actually for, and its real significance was therefore misinterpreted.[152] Although the bill detailing this transfer merely states that this money was 'to be ordered and disposed in such wise as is declared by the kinges warraunt ... delyuered to the saide Thomas Audeley at the making herof', this sum was actually intended for a very specific purpose. In late 1532 a small war was about to erupt on the Scottish border, and the £20,000 was intended to finance the enhanced garrison of 2,500 men at Berwick.[153] There can be little doubt that this was its intended use. The transfer from the coffers to the Tower coincided with the military build-up in the north,[154] while the amount placed there corresponds almost exactly to the £20,084 9s 4d that two of Cromwell's accounts show he paid out to Sir George Lawson, who was acting as treasurer in the north for the conflict.[155] Finally, in case any doubt remains regarding the money's purpose, Cromwell's accounts not only reveal that almost all of the £20,000 'oute of the Towre' was received by him, but the most detailed breakdown of the final five instalments that Cromwell took from there, recorded on account C, gives similar amounts to the final five monthly payments which he sent north for the garrison.[156]

What is significant in all of this is that Cromwell himself did not have personal custody of the £20,000; the key for the money stored in the Tower was in Audeley's possession.[157] What is more, Cromwell's most detailed account (C), closely scrutinised, makes it clear that the second instalment of £10,991 from the Tower was never in Cromwell's possession as a lump sum. Instead, he was arranging for the transfer of small instalments from the Tower, which were sent north on a monthly basis to cover the wages of the garrison.[158] This seems significant because it undermines Elton's and Starkey's belief that Cromwell personally held large sums of capital from the royal coffers, which he controlled with considerable independence.[159] In reality, the money he obtained from this source was used for a very specific purpose – 'disposed in such wise as is declared by the kings warraunt' – and was probably only held by Cromwell in small amounts for a brief period (perhaps less than a day?), before being sent north.[160] With regard to the largest receipts and payments recorded on his accounts, then, Cromwell was less a treasurer and more of a paymaster.

On closer inspection, many of the other larger sums that Cromwell received as master of the jewels appear to have been related to similar transactions. Although in most cases it is impossible to follow the progress of money, the suspicion must be that a great deal of the larger amounts recorded merely passed through Cromwell's hands, rather than being held personally by him as an independent treasurer. It is also likely that, as with the money intended for the Scottish conflict, several of the larger sums recorded came into Cromwell's hands in smaller amounts over a prolonged period, rather than in the impressive totals the accounts record. Although only accounts B and C offer detailed breakdowns, a list of the king's warrants issued to Cromwell survives among his papers, as do several of the warrants themselves.[161] These reveal that many of the larger sums Cromwell received were paid straight into the Privy Coffers. Although very little is known about the Privy Coffers, it is quite clear that it was the largest and most significant royal treasury, and held most of the Crown's reserves. The £533 that Cromwell received on 22 May 1532 was paid into this fund,[162] as was the 100 marks that he received on 27 May from the bishop of Bangor.[163] Another 600 marks owed to the king by Richard Southwell and Peter Ligham was paid into the coffers by Cromwell in June.[164] It was also in that month that he received £2,241 5s 11d from the prior and convent of Westminster on the king's behalf. Of this, £2,000 was immediately redistributed to Thomas Alvard for the works at Westminster, while the residue was again paid into the coffers.[165] Similarly, £2,000 of the £3,304 that Cromwell received from Alvard on account B was given to him on 6 February 1533. Half of this, £1,000, was paid straight into the Privy Coffers, while the other £1,000 was given to Cranmer as a loan at the king's behest.[166] This means that less than half of the £2,100 recorded on account B as being paid into the Privy Coffers came from Alvard; a further £1,100 of the money that Cromwell received was also paid into this, in addition.[167] Account B records another £1,000 paid into the Privy Coffers by Cromwell after 11 March 1533.[168] This should not be mistaken as a duplicate entry for what was yet another sum of £1,000 paid into this reserve on account C,[169] and this was probably the £1,000 that Cromwell paid into the coffers on 11 April.[170] It is also of note that the £1,658 of surplus money on account A is recorded as being 'due' to the king on 17 December, when this early account terminates; all that was left in the custody of William Body, Cromwell's servant, was £595, slightly less than the arrearages brought forward from a previous account that has not survived.[171] Finally, the £4,000 that Cromwell received from Thomas Alvard sometime after 11 March on account B was surely the £4,000 that Cromwell paid to Robert Fowler, vice treasurer of Calais, for the wages of the garrison there.[172] That these two amounts are identical, and are recorded on the same section of the account, suggests that Cromwell may have done nothing more than immediately redistribute this money.

In his discussion of Cromwell's activities in the Jewel House, Elton himself did acknowledge, albeit in a footnote, that Cromwell paid money into the Privy Coffers. Nevertheless, he was quick to play down the significance of this, and argued instead that after Cromwell 'became a treasurer in the full sense he rarely paid money into the coffers'.[173] The previous paragraph suggests this was not the case, and while there are no further surviving accounts of Cromwell's through which to test this claim (or Elton's), the likelihood remains that Cromwell continued to pay many of the larger sums he received into the Privy Coffers. On this point it is worth noting the later arrangements surrounding the Privy Coffers, during the final years of Henry VIII and the early years of Edward VI. Dale Hoak has described the flow of cash through the coffers, noting how royal treasurers and other officials frequently paid money into this fund, which received almost a quarter of a million pounds between 1542 and 1548.[174] Cromwell's actions with respect to the Privy Coffers in 1532–1533 appear similar to these later arrangements.

While it is true, then, that Cromwell was receiving and paying money out on the king's behalf, the money that he personally held or had custody of was less than has previously been realised. The remaining receipts and expenditure recorded on accounts B and C were far smaller than the sums that Cromwell paid into the Privy Coffers or those which he paid out from that source for the war with Scotland. These two expenditures alone account for more than half of the sums recorded on these accounts. By contrast, the other revenues recorded as receipts were even smaller. For instance, the money he received from suppressed lands was £325 on B and a mere £85 on C;[175] that paid out to ambassadors and others for rewards was £935 and £743 respectively.[176] There were also all sorts of smaller miscellaneous payments, which, among others, included: 14s 4d 'for ynke and papyer'; £38 9s 9d to 'Benedicte the kynges Tombemaker'; £55 11s 6d for 'sylkes and velvettes'; and £50 'payde to master speker of the parlament'.[177] It is true that account D reveals that Cromwell kept the larger sum of £1,271 in his possession when that account terminated in April 1534. But this lacks detail on how the total income and expenditure recorded on this account was broken down or whether any of the £37,232 that Cromwell paid out was placed in the Privy Coffers.[178]

Nevertheless, it is important to acknowledge that there were one or two notably large sums recorded on Cromwell's accounts B and C that apparently did remain in his possession. Over £2,200 of the receipts on B came from vacant bishoprics and abbeys (although £1,000 of this was paid into the Privy Coffers); £3,000 was from the receipt 'of suche mony as Late was prested by the kynge'; and £1,366 in obligations owing to the king, which Cromwell had personally settled, was similarly received by him. Account A also lists £1,580 in Cromwell's possession, which had been raised through forfeits for illegally exporting corn.[179] There seems no reason to doubt that Cromwell had custody of these sums, and it was presumably these funds on which he drew to make the various payments recorded on his accounts as expenditure. If the possession of these sums can be described as a 'treasury', it was certainly far smaller than has previously been thought. Moreover, it is difficult to imagine that these revenues would have ensured that Cromwell was independent of all other Crown treasuries when meeting government expenditure, which is what Elton, and later Starkey, believed that the principal purpose of Cromwell's own 'treasury' was.[180]

Illuminating the true nature of Cromwell's financial activities also has implications for broader debates about the condition of royal finances during this period, and the nature of taxation. It has been widely argued that Henry VIII's early continental wars had virtually bankrupted the royal reserves by the late 1520s. Both Cromwell's alleged treasury and the wider attacks on the Church's wealth have been seen as clear attempts at resolving this.[181] Yet Cromwell's financial arrangements surrounding the heightened military activity on the border with Scotland in 1532–1533 suggest a somewhat different picture. During times of war it was customary for parliament to agree to a subsidy to contribute to the defence of the realm. And shortly after Easter 1532, Henry VIII did indeed request a subsidy in parliament to assist with this. Yet the king's request was apparently resisted, and no money was raised to contribute towards the defence of the border in 1532 or 1533.[182] Instead, a retrospective subsidy was granted in 1534 to cover the cost of the conflict.[183] Much has been said about this 1534 grant. Elton thought that this demand, which was made at a time of peace, was exacted to support the ordinary cost of government, and marked an innovative and 'new' approach to taxation devised by Cromwell.[184] What he did not sufficiently recognise was that there had indeed been a conflict between England and Scotland in 1532–1533, and that the retrospective request can be explained by a combination of the cost of that conflict, the likelihood of further trouble in Ireland and the Crown's failure to raise the earlier subsidy. Indeed, the preamble to the act granting the subsidy in 1534 referred specifically to 'the greate somes of moneye & other charges by his Highnes susteyned issued & employed in his last warres ayenst Scotlande' when seeking to justify it.[185] This makes the request for a subsidy far less innovative, and adds weight to G. L. Harriss's argument that there was no change in the nature of taxation under Cromwell.[186]

But if there was no subsidy granted until 1534, then how was the war of 1532–1533 financed? It will be recalled that Cromwell received £18,991 from the £20,000 transferred into the Tower from the Privy Coffers. Starkey, who first drew attention to this transaction, thought that Cromwell received this because 'money was tight, and Cromwell could only run government effectively if his own hand controlled the flow of cash'.[187] As we have seen, however, this money was actually intended to finance the war in the north. And this must mean that, having failed to secure money from parliament, Henry was apparently able to finance the conflict from the Privy Coffers as a last resort. Rather than being short of money, then, the transfer of this sum might actually suggest that the Crown had more money available than many modern scholars have allowed. True, the royal treasury had been enlarged by the recent windfalls of Wolsey's confiscated wealth, and through the £118,840 which the English clergy had agreed to give the king for their praemunire pardon in 1531. But under the terms of this fine, the southern convocation agreed to pay the king £100,000 in yearly instalments (starting on 25 March 1532) of £20,000 over five years.[188] By October 1532 the Crown would only have received the first instalment. If royal finances were in the perilous state commonly assumed, then one might expect this to have been swallowed up by outstanding debt. It is also interesting that the praemunire fine was paid to the treasurer of the Chamber, rather than into the Privy Coffers.[189] Does this mean that it was used to cover routine government expenditure usually met by the Chamber? Similarly, a significant proportion of Wolsey's wealth had already been lavished on the construction of Whitehall and the building works at the Tower of London and Hampton Court.[190] The extent of Henry's spending on buildings and wars throughout the early 1530s does rather suggest that he had more money available than many historians have allowed. At the very least, what all this undoubtedly illustrates is just how difficult it still is to get a sense of the Crown's total income and expenditure.

Nevertheless, if previous historians' arguments surrounding the purpose of Cromwell's 'treasury' and his innovative policy of taxation ultimately fail to convince, the more modest claim that under Cromwell the scope of the Jewel House broadened certainly has merit. Although several of the sums that Cromwell received during these years were the traditional receipts of his various positions,[191] most of the money that Cromwell received or paid out was from or on aspects of government which his immediate predecessor in the Jewel House had not dealt with. What is less clear is whether this accumulation of revenues was deliberate. Elton and Starkey certainly believed that it was, arguing that Cromwell wanted detailed control of Crown finances in order to meet the expenditure of policy he was increasingly directing.[192] Yet Cromwell made no attempt to establish the Jewel House formally, as a key institution of the financial machinery, and this seems significant. Once he was deprived of it in 1540,[193] the master of the jewels reverted to being a minor position.[194] This was in fact typical of the financial system of the period. The Jewel House had previously become an important financial institution during Henry VII's reign, with Sir Henry Wyatt highly active there. It then lapsed into relative obscurity until Cromwell was appointed to it.[195] Cromwell's expansion of this office was not, therefore, a deliberate or a 'bureaucratic' intention. Instead, what all this clearly demonstrates is that much of the financial workings of government depended more on the people behind the offices than on established procedure. It was Cromwell's protean skills and sheer hard work which ensured he amassed more and more responsibilities, while the flexibility and personal nature of government meant that many revenues which had previously gone to another official could just as easily be paid to him.

Cromwell was not, however, single-handedly financing the workings of royal government. Although only a few of his papers have survived, Sir Brian Tuke, treasurer of the Chamber, also continued to play an important role in royal finance. The Chamber had emerged as an important financial position under Henry VII, and continued to be so under his son. Although some of the Chamber's revenues, such as the money received from forfeited lands, were now diverted to Cromwell,[196] Tuke still continued to pay and receive vast sums of money during these years.[197] What is more, his overall revenues still comfortably outstripped those that now went to Cromwell. In the year ending Michaelmas 1530, for instance, Tuke paid out £55,270.[198] Again, this surely prompts doubt over Elton's claim that as master of the jewels Cromwell 'rivalled and in a measure superseded, the treasurer of the chamber'.[199] In fact, Cromwell had little need to transform the Jewel House in this way, because, having quickly established himself as Henry's financial manager, Tuke was operating under Cromwell's direction by late 1532.[200] Tuke and Cromwell's relationship appears to have been one of co-operation, and this once again underlines the informal arrangements which often lay at the heart of effective government.[201] In August 1533 Cromwell instructed Tuke to pay William Gonson £300 for the wages of the men aboard the king's ships.[202] A letter from Gonson to Cromwell confirms that Tuke did so,[203] yet only two months later Cromwell made a note for himself to 'delyuer or cause to be delyuered vnto William Gonson two hundredth poundes . . . not onlie vpon the Riggynge repayringe and newe makynge of our shippes, But also vppon the victuallinge and wages'.[204] A memorandum from 1534 also suggests that Cromwell later paid £1,266 13s 4d to Gonson for similar purposes.[205] Evidently, then, there was no rigid distinction between whether this payment was paid by Tuke or Cromwell. Who paid what, and when, probably depended more on convenience than established procedure. On one occasion Tuke can be shown paying money to goldsmiths for parcels of plate delivered into Cromwell's possession, which the master of the jewels might well have paid himself.[206] Cromwell also paid wages and rewards to the king's ambassadors,[207] yet so too did Tuke,[208] who at times did so under Cromwell's instruction. A letter from Tuke's servant reveals that he had paid the wages for the duke of Norfolk's diplomatic mission abroad at Cromwell's behest.[209] In 1534 Tuke also followed Cromwell's instruction to pay John Hacket, the king's ambassador in the Low Countries, £100 for his arrears there.[210] Perhaps too much emphasis can be placed on the formal procedures of government finance. Did it really matter, as all the money dispersed by Cromwell and Tuke properly belonged to the king, who paid what? Perhaps, as much as anything, it was dependent on who possessed sufficient funds at the required time.

Some aspects of financial administration, however, do appear more formal than others. In a minute drafted by Tuke, headed a 'Remembrance to Master Cromwel', the treasurer revealed himself to be particularly concerned about being properly authorised in his responsibilities in the Chamber. In particular, Tuke told Cromwell that he wanted a more regular audit of his payments and receipts. He also asked Cromwell if he might have more frequent warrants because

> thinges be so grett in receiptes and paymentes as ferre excede any meane mans charge to supporte or beare ... For if I shulde make paymentes by commaundment and afterwarde sue my self for perticuler warant I myzt be vndone in a day lakking any warant when I sue for it And there shulde be no day but I shulde molest the kinges highnes to signe my warantes And I shulde entre in to a common sute for euery mannes money, bring my self in to mystrust whiche of al men shulde not make and sue myn own warantes nor neuer man did in that office or any other.[211]

Tuke's ostensible attitude towards formal authorisation of payments is in stark contrast to Cromwell's own. Notes among his memoranda indicate that Cromwell would often make payments first and then obtain a warrant later. Several reminded him 'to know what thinges that I doo lake warrant for and to cause a warrant to be made therof to be signed', 'to remember the signature of my warrauntes for suche money as I have disbursed of the kinges', to 'cause warrantes to be drawen for suche money as is newly laid owt by me for the king' and 'for my warraunttes to be assigned for all suche money as I haue yssewyd for the kyng sithen the signyng of my last warranttes'.[212] In some instances it is even possible to identify a handful of payments which Cromwell made before having obtained a formal discharge. One remembrance reminded him to obtain 'A warrant for the thowsand markes payd to bonvysxi' in 1533,[213] while the £2,000 he received from Thomas Alvard, half of which Cromwell paid into the Privy Coffers, with the other half going to Cranmer as a loan, was also redistributed before a warrant was obtained.[214] An undated memorandum, which is clearly one of Cromwell's, also refers to there being no warrant yet obtained for the £2,736 7s 5d 'delyuerid' to John Whalley for building works at the Tower.[215] Similarly, during the Anglo-Scottish war, Sir George Lawson wrote to inform Cromwell that he had received £3,000 which Cromwell had sent north for the garrison on 1 February 1533.[216] Cromwell's warrant for this is dated 6 February, meaning that he had again provided this money before having obtained his warrant.[217] All this is further evidence of an administrative system that was at once both formal and informal. Warrants for payments were routinely required, yet the implementation of policy meant that procedures were often adaptable to accommodate practical realities.

What the evidence does not prove is that Cromwell frequently 'paid money on his own initiative and for purposes of which he alone was the judge'.[218] Even despite Henry VIII's reluctance to sign warrants regularly, it is difficult to imagine Cromwell paying out what were often very large sums of money without having at least obtained an oral command or agreement from the king first. Indeed, it was primarily Henry to whom contemporaries looked when decisions were needed regarding money. During the Anglo-Scottish war of 1532–1533, when Cromwell was written to on the question of whether the garrison should receive money for their coats, it was 'the kinges pleasur' which those on the border desired to be informed of.[219] Similarly, when £500 was delivered to William, Lord Dacre, his letter of acknowledgement reveals that this had been done at the 'pleasure of the kinges highnes'.[220] Perhaps most revealingly of all, the impression gleaned from Cromwell's own papers is that the payments he was making were carried out very much with Henry's awareness and approval. In 1533, when the ambassador John Hacket wrote to Cromwell requesting the payment of his arrears,[221] several memoranda reminded Cromwell 'to take hakettes lettres with me to the court' and 'to Remembre master hakkettes dyettes and to make sute to the kyng For the same'.[222] What is striking here is that the king's permission was sought even over a routine payment. It might be better, therefore, to see Cromwell's habit of paying money out before obtaining a warrant as the actions of an efficient administrator – someone who by-passed time-consuming formalities in order to provide money quickly on the king's behalf – rather than as proof that he was an independent policy maker.

Perhaps more significantly, there are strong indications that the practice of obtaining warrants retrospectively, which is so well documented in Cromwell's own correspondence, may have been more prevalent among royal officials than has previously been realised. Despite the reservations Tuke expressed in the letter noted above, he too paid sums of money out on Cromwell's orders before having obtained a warrant.[223] Sir Thomas Audeley was another who employed this practice, albeit on matters other than finance. In July 1533 he asked Cromwell 'to get all my warrauntes assigned which ye haue for my discharge the tymes now ys farr past sythen I dispatched the kynges seales'.[224] Without doubt, the most intriguing examples concern Cardinal Wolsey. There has been no serious attempt to get to grips with Wolsey's control of Crown finances.[225] Elton briefly alluded to the cardinal's 'free control and authority over various treasuries', but the subject still awaits proper examination.[226] Interestingly though, despite Wolsey never having held a formal financial office other than being the king's almoner, there are hints that Wolsey's control of Crown finances may have been even greater than that enjoyed by Cromwell. It is worth noting that one of the charges levelled at Wolsey on his fall in 1529 was that he had authorised payments by his private letters.[227] Some of the cardinal's actions certainly support such a charge. Elton himself noted that a bill signed by the king, ordering money to be paid into the hanaper, was 'amended' by the cardinal, who then ordered that it should be 'payde at the Receipt of the Kinges Eschequier'.[228] In November 1516 £40 was paid to Thomas Magnus, archdeacon of the East Riding, on the authority of a letter from Wolsey.[229] Between 1522 and 1523 several much larger sums, including one of £20,000, were paid to Magnus by Sir Henry Wyatt, treasurer of the Chamber, for military activity in the north. Each of these payments was made in accordance with warrants issued by the cardinal.[230] Another £200 was paid out to John Kite, bishop of Carlisle, on the sole authority of Wolsey's warrant, dated March 1523.[231] Perhaps the most remarkable example of Wolsey's influence over Crown finance, however, is the £1,000 that Edmund Peckham, acting treasurer of the Chamber, paid out in July 1522 on the sole authority of 'my lord legates warrant, *signed with his hand'*.[232] It is worth highlighting here that Elton thought that Wolsey's 'financial government depended on the informal', in stark contrast to the bureaucratic model which would be put in place by Cromwell during the 1530s.[233] In reality, Cromwell's methods of paying money first and obtaining a warrant later appear very similar to the financial methods adopted by Wolsey. Instead of marking a bureaucratic break from medieval government, Cromwell's early ministry appears to have continued with it.

Conclusion

Rather than the innovative administrator described by Elton, then, Thomas Cromwell was merely a highly efficient royal minister. It was this efficiency in dealing with the routine work of government which explains why he was so successful under the king during these years. Henry VIII relied on competent ministers to deal with the quotidian aspects of administration, and Cromwell was plainly happy to perform such tasks quickly and competently. Tremendous energy, sheer hard work and the ability to deal with any issue which arose were also necessary personal attributes. Cromwell evidently possessed these. In particular, his memoranda of things to be done are commendably thorough, and perhaps explain why so few things went wrong in government during these years. These memoranda also illustrate Cromwell's considerable capacity for work. It was qualities such as these that helped him to deal with the increasing amount of work he was amassing, and which, in turn, were gradually ensuring his emergence as the king's new chief minister.

Nevertheless, Cromwell was aided enormously in his capacity to deal with government business by the informal nature of much of its machinery. The flexible character of the financial departments enabled an industrious figure to circumvent some of their more formal proceedings, making the detailed implementation of policy easier. It also meant that Cromwell could receive or pay sums that would previously have been handled by another treasurer, making quick payments possible. Yet Cromwell did not use his official positions to gain control of the Crown's finances, as was suggested by both Elton and Starkey. Instead, Cromwell's amassing of financial work suggests that his influence was personal. It is telling that the sums of money he received as master of the king's jewels were all connected with tasks he was handling himself; he did not divert wider revenues away from other officials into his own hands. Above all, there was not a hint of any innovation or reorganisation of the financial system during the years 1531–1534. Nor is there any sign of a shift from 'medieval' household methods to national bureaucratic ones. Although the revenues received by the Jewel House did increase under Cromwell, the Privy Coffers and the Chamber still remained the most important financial institutions during the early 1530s.

CHAPTER SIX

THE MINISTER AND HIS HOUSEHOLD

ONE OF THE POINTS the Imperial ambassador saw fit to mention when describing Cromwell in 1535 was that 'He lives splendidly', being 'remarkably fond of pomp and ostentation in his household and in building'.[1] Yet surprisingly few historians have sought to examine these facets of Cromwell's life and career. For Elton, and the majority of scholars since, the focus has very much been on the 'public' man and politician.[2] This reflects the approach to the political history of the sixteenth century which Elton advanced more generally: one which placed attention on the men who governed, and the formal institutions and administrative structures which enabled them to do so. In more recent years, however, there has been an increasing recognition of the need to consider more 'informal channels of power', such as the patronage networks, the friendships and affiliations – even the households – of the men and women involved in the political process.[3] Such a focus is particularly pertinent when examining a political system in which the distinction between public and private was by no means rigidly defined. As Barbara Harris puts it, 'the world of kinship, the great household, client/patron relations, and the court conflated concerns that we would label as either personal or political ... much of the distribution of resources and exercise of power took place outside formal institutions'.[4] Steven Gunn has also highlighted the importance of biographical evidence when studying the politics of the Henrician period, noting that 'evidence of the personal affairs and interrelationships of the political actors ... is of particular importance in analysing a political system in which the boundaries of public and private activity were so blurred'.[5] This chapter therefore places Cromwell's private interests alongside his public activities in order to draw a more rounded assessment of his early career and the political environment in which this developed. In particular, the minister's private household is considered, so as to illustrate how Cromwell was assisted in his public role by his private servants. His growing wealth during these years is also examined. Did Cromwell exploit his power for private gain? Finally, can Cromwell's own personality tell us anything about the development or nature of his early political career?

Household and Building Works

Thomas Cromwell's household, like that of any great nobleman or rising courtier, was first and foremost a private institution, designed to serve the minister in his personal needs. A residence was required in which Cromwell could live, rest and sleep, while servants were needed to clean his home, prepare his domestic quarters and cook his meals. Other servants might administer Cromwell's estates or manage his wealth and revenues. Yet despite the household being fundamentally a private institution, perhaps nothing better illustrates how little distinction existed between the public and the private in sixteenth-century politics. In an age that lacked a formal civil service, many of Cromwell's private servants were employed by him on official government business. Moreover, as people increasingly saw Cromwell as a prominent figure who might advance their interests, his household became an important centre of power and patronage in its own right. Not only, then, do the development and expansion of Cromwell's household provide a physical expression of his rise to power, but many of those who served him in a private capacity also played an important part in the success of his early ministry. Before examining these points in greater detail, however, it is useful to begin with an overview of Cromwell's household itself.

'At the heart of every household ... was the same basic unit: the family'; and Cromwell's household was no exception.[6] Although his wife Elizabeth, and their two daughters, Anne and Grace, had probably died by the time Cromwell began to rise under the king, his mother-in-law and sister, along with both their husbands, all lived with him at his London residence during the late 1520s and early 1530s.[7] So, too, when they were not working or studying elsewhere, did Cromwell's son Gregory, and his two nephews, Richard Williams and Christopher Wellyfed. Of Cromwell's family members only Richard Williams need concern us, as it was only he who played any 'public' part in Cromwell's early ministry. He was the son of Cromwell's sister Katherine and her husband Morgan Williams. He had served the marquis of Dorset during the 1520s, and probably entered Cromwell's service following the marquis's death. By the early 1530s he had adopted his uncle's surname, and would later go on to establish the Huntingdonshire branch of the Cromwell family, his great-grandson being Oliver Cromwell.[8] During his uncle's early political career under Henry VIII, Richard would serve as a channel of communication.[9] Other notable work which Richard carried out included examining the servants of a suspected traitor, delivering over £2,000 of the king's money to the borders during the Anglo-Scottish war and conveying Sir Thomas More from the Tower to his trial in 1534.[10] In July 1533 Cromwell attempted to arrange a marriage between his nephew and the daughter-in-law of Sir William Courtenay, a 'kynneswoman to the quenes grace'.[11] This apparently fell through, and Richard Cromwell later married the daughter of a London alderman and lord mayor.[12]

Beyond this family unit, the late medieval and early modern household was chiefly comprised of three types of servant. The domestic staff, which included cooks, stable hands, clerks and accountants, provided the fundamental working core. Next there might be retainers: men who had formally agreed via an indenture to provide military service, usually in exchange for land. By the early sixteenth century, however, these formal feudal ties had largely been replaced by cash fees, while military service had been supplanted by support and attendance at court or in the household itself. A final, third type of household attendee comprised the professional men (like Cromwell himself in Wolsey's household) who worked for, but did not necessarily live with, their master.[13] All of these household members would have been presided over by three principal officers: the steward, the comptroller and the treasurer. The steward was the man responsible for the overall running and management of his master's household. Although there is a reference to Cromwell's 'steward' in November 1532, it is not clear who was occupying this office for him at that point.[14] From 1535 onwards Richard Tomyow was in this position.[15] The next figure, the comptroller, oversaw the household's requisite provisions. Cromwell's brother-in-law and 'trusty seruante' John Williamson acted as his comptroller during the early 1530s, although he was later replaced by Thomas Thacker.[16] Williamson oversaw the first expansion of Cromwell's London residence[17] and had custody of a variety of his private bills, indentures and obligations.[18] The third senior officer was the treasurer, or cofferer, who was responsible for his master's revenues.[19] William Body, one of Cromwell's clerks, appears to have been his principal cofferer during these early years.[20] Certainly many of Cromwell's private revenues were received and handled by Body,[21] although John Williamson himself also received some.[22]

The overall size of Cromwell's household is difficult to determine, as no complete list of his servants survives. A partial list of the gentlemen in Cromwell's service in 1538 numbers 173.[23] Robertson estimated that his household numbered around four hundred men during the 1530s, although during the years in focus here it was undoubtedly smaller.[24] After all, it is difficult to imagine that Cromwell would have needed (or could have afforded) such a large staff in the 1520s. But his staff probably grew quickly once he entered the royal service. Whatever its exact number, as soon as Cromwell was established in the king's favour, the size of his entourage would no longer have been purely designed to meet practical needs. The size and magnificence of a courtier's household were also partially intended to reflect his wealth and power. Something of the awe and immensity of Cardinal Wolsey's household was captured by Cavendish, who noted that 'whan so euer we shall se any more suche Subiectes within thys realme that shall maynteyn any suche estat & howshold [as Wolsey] I ame content he be auaunced above hyme in honour & estymacion'.[25] Quite plainly, then, Cavendish thought Wolsey's position and prestige were reflected by his large entourage.

Cromwell is generally thought to have been far less ostentatious than the cardinal, and his supposedly modest household and building programme are often held in stark contrast to Wolsey's own.[26] It is certainly true that Cromwell's household – even at its height in the later 1530s – was much smaller than the cardinal's. John Stow, admittedly writing later, recalled that Wolsey's household surpassed that of all other subjects of his time, and that the servants who provided daily attendance on the cardinal numbered four hundred.[27] According to Pollard, the total number of Wolsey's household 'was little if at all short of a thousand'.[28] The men in Cromwell's service never matched that number, but this should not be taken to mean that Cromwell did not maintain an impressive entourage, in line with the social elite among whom he could now be counted. The remarks of the Imperial ambassador, noted above, certainly suggest that contemporaries were impressed by Cromwell's household, while Stow himself noted that Cromwell 'kept the like, or greater number' of men in his service as did

William Paulet and Thomas Audeley.[29] He also recalled the scenes at the gates of Cromwell's house:

> I my selfe, in that declining time of charity, haue oft scene at the Lord Cromwels gate in London, more then two hundred persons serued twise euery day with bread, meate and drinke sufficient, for hee obserued that auncient and charitable custome as all prelates, noble men or men of honour and worship his predecessors had done before him.[30]

Such generous hospitality was another way of exhibiting one's position in society: 'to have drink flowing in abundance, to serve up more food than could possibly be eaten, and to feed the poor waiting at the gate with the leftovers was all evidence of power, wealth and glory'.[31] What is more, Cromwell displayed magnificent hospitality and charity from an early point in his political career. Thomas Alvard, writing to commend him on his 'howse kepyng' in November 1532, remarked how 'It is shewed me there is neuer an Englishe man there the kinges grace except That doth kepe and Feaste Englishe men and strangiers as ye doo'.[32] Cromwell also maintained twelve children as musicians,[33] something that almost anyone 'with pretensions to rank or position' chose to do.[34] The abbot of St Albans was certainly impressed by those in Cromwell's service. He commended the 'Grett chere' which he received while 'at Sopper' in Cromwell's house 'with all mesyke plesant' in 1533.[35]

It has already been noted that Cromwell employed many of his most trusted servants on the king's business as well as his own. Of his principal household officers, however, only his cofferer, William Body, was involved in matters of state during the early 1530s. When Body joined Cromwell's household is uncertain. He is mentioned in Cromwell's will, first drawn up in 1529, but his name has been added in Cromwell's hand, presumably as part of Cromwell's later amendments to the will sometime after 1532.[36] By November of that year Body was being sent by Cromwell to collect the £200 owing from the archbishop of York for his temporalities. He also had the custody of a great deal of the king's money, which Cromwell received as master of the jewels.[37] William Brabazon, John Whalley, John Smith, Stephen Vaughan and William Candisshe were other men who have already been shown working for Cromwell during the 1520s, and would later continue to assist him in the king's business. Richard Swift was another who served Cromwell in a private capacity before also being employed on royal work.[38] In 1529, for example, Swift was attending to such domestic duties as harvesting Cromwell's corn, while in 1533 he can be shown handling the king's money for the building of ditches at Lesnes, Kent.[39] Another notable servant was Ralph Sadler, Cromwell's most senior clerk. He lived with his master,[40] and not only drafted some of Cromwell's letters to the king,[41] but was even entrusted with the custody of the signet in 1532, when Cromwell held it temporarily for the absent Gardiner.[42] Each of these men deserves recognition for playing an important role (often overlooked) in assisting Cromwell's rise. The increasing amount of government work which Cromwell undertook from late 1531 onwards would fast ensure his indispensability to Henry VIII, and his emergence as chief minister. But Cromwell's successful management of this workload depended, in part, on his ability and willingness to delegate some of its implementation to men in his own service. These were men who had similar skills to those Cromwell possessed, and they had acquired these skills through earlier work for him. Brabazon, Sadler, Vaughan, Whalley and Candisshe, for example, had all cut their teeth under Cromwell by undertaking various legal and administrative tasks connected with Wolsey's colleges, just as Cromwell himself had.

It was not merely Cromwell, however, who benefited from the employment of these men; a position in the minister's establishment carried its own rewards. First of all, service in Cromwell's household might provide a form of education, enabling many to obtain skills and experience through the work they were required to do. Some might even receive formal instruction. Thomas Avery, for example, was a servant sent by Cromwell to Stephen Vaughan in Antwerp in 1530 'to be taught and brought vp in the knowledge and exercise of thinges 'meate for his age and capacitie'.[43] In 1532 he was sent back to Cromwell, and during the later 1530s Avery would serve as Cromwell's household cofferer.[44] Servants were also rewarded financially for their work. In 1533 Ralph Sadler and William Body received £5 and £20 respectively from the king,[45] while Cromwell himself secured fees, annuities and positions for many men in his service.[46] Working in the household of a rising figure might also present opportunities for social advancement. After all, service under Wolsey had been significant in the development of Cromwell's career, and many of those who now served in his household would later advance greatly from their own humble origins. Three examples are sufficient here. William Brabazon was made under-treasurer and receiver-general of Ireland in 1534 and one of Cromwell's deputy viceregents there in 1539; in 1543 he would become lord justice of Ireland.[47] Ralph Sadler and Thomas Wriothesley, who had both been in Cromwell's service since the 1520s, would jointly replace him as secretary in the months before his fall.[48]

Because of the opportunities, rewards and advancement it might bring, membership of Cromwell's household became an increasingly sought-after position as he became a figure of growing importance. One man remarked to Cromwell that his kinsman desired to be Cromwell's servant 'not to put you to charge of wagis but only to deserve and have your Favour'.[49] Another was prepared to promise Cromwell that his suitor would 'neuer take wages of youer maystershipp', if he was allowed to serve him.[50] Richard Jones valued a place in Cromwell's establishment so highly that he beseeched him to 'admytte me to your seruyce not as a seruant but as one of your dogges'.[51] Some were even prepared to cover their own costs and expenses for a place in Cromwell's service. Richard Phillips promised Cromwell £20 if he allowed his son to work for him, and claimed that he would give the boy £40 a year to live on.[52] Cromwell's rising status also ensured that his household became a recognised centre of influence for aspiring members of the gentry and figures at court. Leading families had long sought to place their children in the homes of their kinsfolk, friends and patrons in order to strengthen their own positions and networks of influence.[53] Sir John Gage was one such figure who wanted his son to be placed in Cromwell's service; so too did Sir Thomas Worsley.[54] That the social elite now saw Cromwell's household as a centre of power and influence illustrates that he had come to be seen as a dispenser of patronage in his own right.

A final point worth noting here relates to some of the skills that hopeful applicants thought Cromwell might require from his servants. David Cecil told the minister that his suitor 'wrytethe a gude secretary hand, and Romans, vnderstondeth well and speketh lattyn', while John Amadas similarly told Cromwell that his son knew French and Latin, wrote a good secretary hand and had studied the common law.[55] One person hoping to join Cromwell's growing household was even asked to send three examples of his handwriting: one in English, one in French and one in Latin.[56]

Members of Cromwell's household would have attended on their master wherever he was resident. From 1523 until his fall in 1540, the minister's principal residence was his capital house in Throgmorton Street, next to the Austin Friars.[57] An inventory of this property from the 1520s suggests that this was a relatively modest house, originally containing over fourteen rooms. These included several chambers and parlours, a kitchen and a hall.[58] Following his entry into the king's service, Cromwell then began to enlarge the building into a house more befitting of a royal minister. On 4 June 1532 he took out a ninety-nine year lease on 'two mesuages ... late of newe buyelded ... seuerall gardens belonginge to thesaide two tene-ments ... A greate warehouse lienge and belonginge to oon of the sayde mesuages' and a tenement called 'the Swane', all of which lay against the west end of the Augustinian friary churchyard wall.[59] During Cromwell's attendance upon the king at Calais in late 1532, his servants set about enlarging and transforming his existing property to incorporate these new acquisitions.[60] John Aleyn informed Cromwell on 25 October 1532 how his household and friends were preparing 'anew Altered howse', which 'haryng saye ... shall content your mynde'.[61] Two days earlier, John Whalley had similarly reported to him that a thousand loads of rubbish had been 'taken owte of the sellours & prevy kechyn and other lodgynges ... your hous yt goyth well forwards / ye shall see a greate thinge done there in so litle awhile'.[62] Unfortunately, there is no indication as to what Cromwell's capital house looked like at this point, although John Stow, writing later, recollected that Cromwell built a 'very large and spacious' house 'in the place of olde and small Tenementes'.[63] A description of the residence as it stood in 1543, following its purchase from the Crown by the Drapers' Company, has also survived; so too has a seventeenth-century survey of the property and surrounding area.[64] These show a three-storey house, based around a large central courtyard, with over fifty rooms, which included numerous chambers and halls, cellars 'for wyne Ale & bere', 'A fayre grete chamber or hall fyled & matted with iiii bay glas windows & a chy[m]ney over the greate gate' and a 'greate Garden'.[65] But the building programme embarked on in 1532 was the first in a continuing series of alterations made to the property throughout the decade. The most significant of these seems to have been completed between 1535 and 1536, after Cromwell had purchased the earlier leases in full from the friary in May 1534, as well as adding several further tenements.[66] It is difficult, therefore, to establish exactly what was added when. Nevertheless, it is clear that on his fall in 1540 Cromwell possessed one of the grandest houses in London.

The first enlargement of the Austin Friars house was an obvious indica-tion of Cromwell's rising status in 1532. He now had the wealth to build on a significant scale and, like other rising courtiers, he was keen to announce his newly established position by developing his home into a more impres-sive building. But the suggestion that Cromwell's house was intended as an expression of his power should be pushed only so far. Grand as it undoubtedly became, an urban residence did not have the same potential as a country house, from which a landed power base might be constructed. During the 1520s and early 1530s, Cromwell's house had a practical function as a home and working office. That he played bowls in the garden, and later built a bowling alley and tennis courts there, confirms that it was also a place for rest and relaxation.[67] Of greater significance here is that Cromwell himself often worked from his home during these years. In the 1543 description of the property, one of its rooms is described as 'An office to wryte in',[68] while an account of Cromwell's expenses incurred on Wolsey's college projects records money paid out 'for the carriage of Theuydences of Saynt Frediswide from yorke place to my house in London', which hints that the preparation of legal documents was undertaken there.[69] In 1529 Stephen Vaughan also told Cromwell that he had 'Diligently sought in your countynghouse and other places for suche wrytynges' concerning several monasteries.[70] Cromwell's papers, both private and those relating to the governance of the realm, were often kept at his Austin Friars house. According to a 'catholog' of the papers in Cromwell's 'closet', many of the 'billes and other thinges' which were in his possession from February 1533 were kept 'in his chamber', while others were housed in his 'new cawberd'.[71] It is even possible to offer a tentative reconstruction of how some of Cromwell's papers might have been stored. A book, listing 'certayn Euydences and specyalties' in Cromwell's possession, reveals that many papers were kept in 'great rounde boxes standing vnder the drawing boxes on the right hande [of] the dore' or 'In a longe box with a particion'.[72] Interestingly, some of Cromwell's correspondence also contains annotations on the back in his hand, or in that of one of his clerks, recording the surname of the writer.[73] This suggests that Cromwell's papers were originally stored by him in alphabetical bundles, some of which were also arranged in chronological sequence.[74] Although Cromwell would later acquire other residences, including houses at Stepney and Hackney, it is likely that much of his correspondence was kept at the Austin Friars. Rather than being a 'power house', therefore, Cromwell's London residence is more accurately seen as a working home, and a base for Cromwell's early ministry. It would continue to remain so throughout the 1530s. During his later political career, Cromwell would entertain many important guests there, including the king and the French and Imperial ambassadors. Members of the council would also convene at his capital house from time to time.[75]

Wealth and Landed Interests, 1531–1534

Service under the king offered considerable opportunity for enrichment, and Cromwell's personal wealth grew significantly during his first four years as a royal minister. The limited evidence available suggests that Cromwell's wealth almost doubled between 1529 and the end of 1532. It will be recalled that Cromwell's will bequeathed cash bestowals of over £900 when it was first drawn up in 1529. When the will was amended sometime after, but probably close to, September 1532, many of the bequests were doubled in value, and collectively it then bequeathed well over £1,830 in cash alone.[76] Cromwell had clearly made considerable financial gains in the space of less than three years. There is even some suggestion that by 1533 he was wealthier than some of the Crown's more longstanding servants and officials. It was in that year that Christopher Hales, the attorney general, rejected Cromwell's accusation of covetousness for withholding certain lands belonging to Cromwell's servant. Hales responded by telling him that 'if ye know aswell the value of my treasor as ye do of your owne' he would not have grounds to think that.[77]

How had Cromwell amassed such a considerable fortune in less than four years? One of the most persistent accusations surrounding Cromwell is that he was a corrupt and unscrupulous minister, keen to enrich himself through the acceptance of bribes. In 1538 allegations were made that Cromwell was a 'great ... taker of money / For he woll speke solicite or doo for noo man but all for money'.[78] On his fall in 1540 the act of attainder which condemned Cromwell also alleged that he had 'acquired and obteyned into his possession by oppression bribery extort power and false promises ... Innumerable somes of money and Treasure'.[79] These are charges which have continued to find support among several modern historians. R. B. Merriman believed Cromwell to have been notoriously susceptible to bribes, particularly concerning monastic suppressions.[80] Neville Williams broadly concurred with this.[81] So too did M. St Clare Byrne: she accused Cromwell of 'taking money for every favour granted', and claimed that he 'pocketed annuities, bribes and fees from gentle and simple, rich and poor ... The so-called fees sent to him by most abbots and abbesses ... were nothing but bribes.'[82] In his final paper on Cromwell in 1993, however, the late Sir Geoffrey Elton sought to defend the minister against these charges of corruption and venality. Although anxious not to 'make Cromwell out to be lily-white', and conceding that 'He probably did on occasion take what to modern eyes would look like straightforward bribes', Elton emphasised the complex system of payments in operation in the sixteenth-century world, which included the giving of fees for services rendered that were 'totally above board'.[83] He also criticised Merriman and St Clare Byrne for failing to provide adequate examples of Cromwell's venality.[84] Other historians have concurred with Elton's interpretation of the payment system, also highlighting the difficulty in distinguishing between unscrupulous payments made to royal officials and those which were deemed acceptable.[85] And yet, although the charges brought against Cromwell in 1540 in no way prove that he took bribes, they do confirm that venality among royal servants was a genuine concern in the sixteenth century. Accusations of corruption are not, therefore, an anachronistic imposition. If the claims of corruption against Cromwell are to be satisfactorily assessed, then it becomes necessary to identify the types of income he was receiving, and to try to draw some distinction between those which were deemed acceptable in Henry VIII's England and those which were not.

Perhaps the most straightforward sums of money that Cromwell received during his early political career were the salaries for the various offices and positions he held. In January 1532 the king reappointed Cromwell as receiver-general of Wolsey's former college lands.[86] Although no fee is mentioned in the patent for this office, Cromwell presumably continued to receive the £20 granted to him in 1528 by Cardinal College, Oxford, for this position.[87] In April 1532 he was then made master of the king's jewels, while in July he was made clerk of the hanaper.[88] These offices came with salaries of £50 and approximately £65 a year respectively.[89] In April 1533, Cromwell was also made chancellor of the Exchequer, for which he received an annual fee of £26 13s 4d.[90]

Sixteenth-century office holders did not generally receive significant salaries for the positions which they held. The salaries for most offices had usually been fixed long ago when they were first established, and they were rarely altered in line with inflation. Instead, royal officials and office holders were sincerely expected to supplement these relatively modest salaries through a variety of payments and rewards made by people for whom they undertook additional favours and requests. The numerous gifts and tokens that Cromwell received during his early years in the king's service would be one example of such remuneration. First and foremost, of course, such gifts were given as a sign of friendship. Cromwell sent his friend John Benolt a 'litle hoby' in 1531 and received 'a casse of knyffes' in return.[91] Christopher Hales sent a lean doe and a dish of wild fowl to Cromwell around the same time,[92] and Sir William Fitzwilliam and his wife also sent him fowl and 'a piece of a Reddere' in 1533.[93] Nevertheless, gifts might also be given in order to encourage or reward ministers when undertaking minor favours. In 1532 Cromwell was sent a gift of twenty-four partridges and six plovers, along with a request 'to obteyne the signature of the kings highness' for a bill.[94] In the same year, Cromwell was informed that the townsfolk of Cambridge

> for the harty goode mynde and service that they owe vnto your saide maistershyppe have sent ... A small present of suche commodetyes as be in this partyes viz 20 pykes and 10 Tenches ... besechyng you to be goode maister to the poore Towne of Cambrigge and to bear your lawfull and indifferent favour to the same.[95]

Food such as this was commonly given or exchanged as gifts,[96] but other items could also be offered in return for a favour. Among the more unusual gifts that Cromwell received during these years was a piece of turquoise,[97] a 'Rowll off lechis',[98] four pieces of tin from which to make pewter vessels for his household,[99] several knives,[100] a pair of perfumed gloves,[101] and a precious stone.[102] Another regular gift or recompense given to Cromwell was horses,[103] and he himself gave them as gifts on several occasions, even offering Eustace Chapuys one in July 1533.[104] Many gifts given, however, were of small value and were often sent as 'sweeteners' when the person requesting something was unable immediately to provide a greater incentive. In 1532, for example, Cromwell was sent a 'Tothepicke with a wystell of golde' as a 'Remembraunce' from a widow who wanted her warrant signed. She promised to recompense Cromwell for his efforts more fully at a later date.[105]

Equally frequent, and perhaps more of an incentive, was the payment of money to royal ministers in return for services rendered. In 'modern' eyes many of these exchanges have the uncomfortable appearance of being bribes. But here too it is important to distinguish between the different types of payments offered, most of which were entirely conventional in the eyes of sixteenth-century men and women. For example, many office-holders were entitled to levy small charges on the suitors to their office, in addition to their fixed salaries. The clerks of the signet, for instance, charged fixed fees for applying the seal to an individual's warrant.[106] As clerk of the hanaper, Cromwell was involved in the sealing process in Chancery, and would have drawn additional fees of 2s 6d from every suitor requiring a document to be sealed there.[107] When he became secretary in April 1534 Cromwell would also have been entitled to his share of the signet fees, which brought him approximately £60 per annum.[108]

Cromwell was also given a considerable number of annuities between 1531 and 1534. These were annual payments, often referred to as 'fees', which were paid by private individuals, religious houses and professional corporations in order to retain Cromwell's services or to encourage him to speak, lobby or act on the grantors behalf as and when required. The abbot of Pipewell gave Cromwell an annuity of 26s 8d on 4 June 1531. According to the grant for this it was given for Cromwell's 'good and gratuitous counsel and aid, and for his good will already shown to us and to be shown'.[109] In 1533 the earl of Westmorland told Cromwell, 'im verye desirous to haue your favour ... wherefore I Requyre you to be contented to accept oon yerely annuytie of £10'.[110] Other fees were offered in the hope of eliciting Cromwell's assistance or favour concerning land disputes.[111] Sir Henry Everingham, for instance, made Cromwell 'stuard off hys holl landes' in August 1533, with a fee of 53s 4d. This was to encourage him to assist Everingham with 'a Forward fellow ... whyche wold occupy hys land agaynst hys wyll'.[112] It was probably no coincidence that John, Lord Scrope of Bolton also gave Cromwell an annuity of £6 13s 4d in March 1534. This coincided with Cromwell's efforts to conclude the arrangements of a land exchange between Scrope and the king.[113]

Perhaps more important in terms of Cromwell's overall income, were the wider sums of money that were offered or given to royal servants in return for specific favours and patronage. These were not annual payments, but rather ad hoc ones given for particular requests. Thomas Pope promised to 'recompense' Cromwell's pains if he obtained the king's signature for a bill, while the abbot of York sent him £5 as 'a poore rewarde for your goodness to me shewyd concernyng my discherge for my apperaunce at london' during Anne Boleyn's coronation.[114] Thomas Leson sent the minister 20 nobles for his favour and counsel toward his brother concerning a lease on a parsonage.[115] The same amount was also sent to Cromwell by Sir William Stourton's father at the beginning of 1532, in order to be absent from parliament.[116] Again, such sums of money might have the appearance of being bribes, but it would be better to see these as gratuity payments – small sums of money offered in return for services rendered. These sorts of payment were widespread throughout sixteenth-century government. The king's secretary could expect to receive around £5 or £6 for forwarding suits to the king.[117] Richard Hart, a canon at Bruton, also told Lady Lisle how 'master Weston got my byll synd of the kyng & had of me £20 for hys labor master Crumwell dyd red the byll to the kyng & gaue hytt hys good worde & he had £5'.[118] How much Cromwell and other ministers accumulated from these sorts of payments is impossible to calculate. Nevertheless, there was clearly potential for any industrious man to exploit his position for considerable financial gain.

Each of the incomes just discussed was a customary way for Crown servants to supplement their relatively modest salaries. In an age when the cost of government fell on royal expenses, the Crown relied on this system to pay and enrich its servants, being unable – or perhaps unwilling – to raise taxes so that it could do so itself. Moreover, the Crown participated in this system and therefore actively encouraged it.[119] Gifts were given from the king at New Year and at other times, while the Crown also used sinecures as a further method of reward. Cromwell himself received two 'gilte saltes with a couer', 'a gilte boolle', 'a gilte truse glasse fasshion', 'a Ring with a Ruby & abox with the Imagis of the frenche kinges children' and two bucks from the king during these early years.[120] In February 1534 Henry also granted him the constableship of Hertford Castle, with an annual fee of £12 14s.[121] Another resource with which the king might recompense courtiers was land. In May 1532 Cromwell was given the manor of Rompney, or Rumney, in Monmouthshire, South Wales, by Henry.[122] According to an abstract of Cromwell's lands from mid-1535, Rompney was worth 100 marks a year,[123] while William Walwyn, auditor of the duchy of Lancaster, told Cromwell that its lands were 'verry goode for all kyndes of corne'.[124] In 1533 Cromwell and several other men also received a fifty-year lease from the king on some lead mines in Dartmoor Forest.[125]

Yet despite Elton's vigorous defence of Cromwell, and even bearing in mind the numerous legitimate incomes which the minister received, he clearly did enrich himself through the acceptance of bribes. Two instances where he almost certainly took bribes while in the royal service have already been discussed in previous chapters.[126] They have been detectable because those offering Cromwell the bribe hinted in their letters that they were aware that what they were doing was unscrupulous. Attempts to identify further bribes in a system which relied on customary exchanges of gifts and money is somewhat problematic. Joseph Block has suggested that a bribe in this period should be defined as 'a conditional offer for a material reward in pursuit of a desired objective'.[127] Yet this is not a satisfactory definition given that many of the fees paid to Cromwell outlined above would fit this criterion, and were entirely acceptable. Ultimately, with no clear indication from contemporaries as to what they saw as constituting bribery, one needs to try to distinguish between the routine and the exceptional, not least in size and amount. What can be said is that the customary gifts and gratuities discussed above tended to be of relatively small denominations – generally between 40s and £10, depending on the nature of the request. Significantly larger offers to Cromwell are much more likely to constitute bribery. For instance, in 1534 he was offered £100 and the stewardship of Wilton, which came with a yearly fee of £10, if he advanced a candidate to succeed as abbess there.[128] In 1532, when William Owen wanted to be made 'the Kynges justice' in North Wales, he offered Cromwell 'a £100 for your so doing / or asmoche as any otherman will offyr'.[129] Martin Bowes and his associate deputy worker at the Tower Mint also asked Cromwell to be 'our solysitour to the kyng' so that they might have the office of master worker. In return they promised him a chain of gold worth £30.[130] Each of these proposed payments appears conspicuously large for what were relatively routine requests. If these were not outright bribes, then Cromwell was certainly being presented with a strong financial incentive. Also of note is Sir Richard Bulkeley's offer to give Cromwell £20 'for your paynys' if he moved the king to appoint his brother to a benefice. His brother, Bulkeley added, would continue to give Cromwell a third of that benefice's value each year.[131]

Does this make Cromwell an unscrupulous and corrupt minister? Ultimately, yes: he certainly took bribes, and probably made considerable sums when doing so. Moreover, given that contemporaries did not approve of venality among Crown officials, this is not an anachronistic judgement from a 'modern' point of view. What needs stressing is that Cromwell was by no means unique in capitalising on his position. Other Crown servants and courtiers also enriched themselves in similar ways.[132] John Williams, Cromwell's successor as master of the jewels, and treasurer of the Court of Augmentations, for example, managed to embezzle £31,000 from the Augmentations.[133] During Elizabeth I's reign, Robert Cecil amassed an enormous fortune from a collection of similar fees, gifts and bribes.[134] It should also be emphasised that the allegation made by Merriman and St Clare Byrne – that Cromwell was especially rapacious in his pursuit of bribes – probably reflects the survival of Cromwell's considerable correspondence, and the lack of an equivalent archive for other men in comparable positions. None of this is to excuse Cromwell's actions, but political corruption of this sort has been a recurring feature of governments throughout the early modern period and beyond, right up to the present day. Cromwell was not exceptional in what he did, but his rising favour with the king meant that the scale of his operations was much larger and the sums he collected by way of fees and gifts much greater than those of lesser officials.

Although it is clear, then, that Cromwell's position close to the centre of power enabled him to enrich himself considerably, exactly how much wealth he accumulated through this is difficult to assess. Indeed, frustratingly little detail is known generally about the incomes of royal servants in the sixteenth century.[135] Although private correspondence does yield occasional reference, as we have seen, to the unofficial (although by no means illegal) payments that were given in return for favour or patronage, such examples have not survived in anything like the quantity necessary to estimate annual incomes. It is of considerable interest, therefore, that an uncalendared document among Cromwell's papers offers a fairly comprehensive picture of the revenues he was receiving from one of these sources. This is an account written in the hand of Cromwell's cofferer, William Body, which lists almost all of the annual fees and annuities granted to Cromwell between March 1525 and June 1534.[136] It will be recalled that such fees were usually given to ensure a minister's continuing favour and, significantly, the ninety-four annuities recorded as being granted to Cromwell for this purpose are dated and arranged chronologically on this account. It therefore provides a unique glimpse of just how lucrative Cromwell's work for both Wolsey and the king could be during the very years which concern us here.

It is no coincidence that the first of the annual fees recorded on this list – the 26s 8d given by the priory of Shulbred, Sussex – was granted to Cromwell on 10 March 1525.[137] As we saw in Chapter One, that was less than a year after Cromwell had begun working for Cardinal Wolsey, a man who, next to the king, was the most powerful figure in England during the 1520s. Evidently individuals were prepared to pay annual fees to those in close proximity to Wolsey in the hope of benefiting from this. Between March 1525 and September 1529, a total of thirteen such annuities is recorded as being granted to Cromwell for this purpose. These range in value from 20s to £13 6s 8d, and reflect the fact that during the late 1520s Cromwell had become one of the cardinal's most trusted and influential servants. Admittedly, one or two of the annuities granted may have

been given to retain his legal services, as he also continued to operate independently as a lawyer throughout the 1520s. Yet it is of note that on Wolsey's
fall in October 1529, and throughout the cardinal's disgrace in 1530, no
new annuities are recorded. This further suggests that Cromwell was chiefly
valued for his position and influence with Wolsey. By mid-1530, however,
Cromwell had begun to work for the king, and in December he was sworn
a member of the King's Council. New annuities quickly followed. The
'Gylde of Boston' is recorded as giving him an annual fee of £4 on 4
February 1531, and nine similar grants were made in that year.[138] These
ranged from the 13s 4d given by the prior and chapter of Rochester to the
£10 paid by the convent of St John of Jerusalem, London. Throughout
1532 Cromwell's influence was extended further still. This was reflected by
the twenty-one new annuities made to him in that year, ranging from 40s
to £20. A further thirty-three annuities were granted in 1533, by which
point Cromwell had indisputably emerged as the king's leading minister.
During the first half of 1534 another eleven were also given to him.
Significantly, many of the amounts granted in these later years were considerably higher than before. Although amounts given still ranged from 40s
to £13, in 1533 Cromwell received – among others – five annuities of £10,
four of £5, three worth £4 and seven worth 5 marks (or £3 6s 8d).
Between January and June 1534, however, no new fee was granted to him
worth less than 5 marks. The most frequent value granted to him in that
year was 10 marks (or £6 13s 4d), followed by two annuities of £4 and
5 marks respectively.

Needless to say, the cumulative receipt of all these annuities was considerable. According to the figures recorded, by 1529 Cromwell was receiving
annual fees worth over £54. By 1531, with over £40 of new grants made
then, the figure was more than £94. In 1532 the total of new annuities
came to over £129. By then Cromwell was receiving over £223 in annuities.
In 1533 over £214 of new fees were made to him, taking his overall annual
income from these to over £437. During the first six months of 1534
he then received a further £67 7s 4d. Assuming that these obligations
all continued to be met, by June 1534 Cromwell was receiving annuities
that comfortably amounted to over £500.

How does this income compare with that of other royal servants? Such
a comparison is difficult to make given the lack of detail about the incomes
of equivalent figures. Cardinal Wolsey's total income in 1519 was estimated
by the Venetian ambassador to be approximately £9,500, while in 1531 his

successor thought it was around £35,000.[139] Much of this, however, came from Wolsey's numerous spiritual positions and landed estates; it is unclear how much he received in the form of annual fees. Sir William Compton, a courtier and groom of the stool under Henry VIII, amassed a considerable fortune in the royal service. The income from his lands alone amounted to over £1,689 for 1524–1525.[140] Again, what is lacking is any breakdown of how much Compton might have received in the form of fees and annuities.[141] The most detailed account of a royal servant's income from the perquisites of office holding is probably that offered by A. J. Slavin. He estimated that Sir Ralph Sadler, Cromwell's clerk, who would later go on to become a significant political figure in his own right, received around £488 per annum during the 1540s, from a comparable income of annuities, salaried positions and fees for various stewardships.[142] It should be stressed, however, that in the 1540s Sadler was at the height of his powers. During the years covered by Cromwell's account, he himself had not yet scaled the full height of his political career. A later set of Cromwell's accounts, kept by Thomas Avery, his household receiver, is instructive here. This set covers the years from 1537 to 1539, and records Cromwell's income and expenditure, including his fees and annuities, month by month.[143] Although it is too large to be considered in detail here, Elton analysed two months' worth of entries, which can offer another brief comparison with Cromwell's position in 1534.[144] Of the £996 2s 8d Avery received on Cromwell's behalf in January 1537, for example, Elton estimated that a minimum of £215 2s 6d came from annual fees. In October 1537, with many fees and obligations often due at Michaelmas, Cromwell's income was much higher. The total income received then was a staggering £1,255 11s 4d, of which £510 8s 8d came from annuities. In 1537, therefore, Cromwell received more in fees in one month alone than he would have done throughout the entire year of 1533 – an indication of just how wealthy he eventually became.

Cromwell had several sources of income in addition to the wealth directly generated by his work for the Crown. It will be recalled that during 1531 and early 1532 he continued to dabble in trade, while moneylending also continued. A further source of income was provided by the wardships Cromwell obtained in relation to Lawrence Courtenay, Anthony Stydoffe and Thomas Rotherham. Wardship was a right whereby a landlord took control of a tenant's estate during the minority of the tenant's heir. Until they reached the age of twenty-one, all the profits of the land went to the landlord, who also possessed the right to arrange the ward's marriage and

raise him or her as he saw fit. Wardships could be highly lucrative, therefore, and were often sold to the highest bidder.[145] Unfortunately, very little
information can be discerned about Cromwell's wards. Lawrence Courtenay
may have worked for him as a servant during his minority,[146] while the sum
of £4 12s 11d is recorded as coming from the wardship of Anthony
Stydoffe on one of Cromwell's accounts between January and July 1533.[147]
Evidently this wardship was valuable enough to justify Cromwell's letter to
a judge of the Common Bench defending his title to it when questions
were raised.[148] Finally, Thomas Rotherham, who would inherit land in
Bedfordshire worth 100 marks when he came of age, became Cromwell's
ward in 1533. According to the draft indenture arranging this, Cromwell
intended to have him marry his niece, Alice Wellyfed, when Rotherham
reached the age of his majority at twenty-one.[149]

Cromwell also continued to invest personally in land during his
early political career, although his acquisitions – even including the land
which the king rewarded him with – continued to be small and piecemeal,
with no discernible intent beyond profit and investment.[150] In fact, the only
significant property that Cromwell acquired between 1531 and 1534
(besides Rompney) was the sixty-year lease he took out on the manors of
Canonbury and Cutlers, in Islington parish, Middlesex, in September
1532.[151] Canonbury, in particular, was described as 'a greate tenement',
which included 'A greeite gardeyn therto lienge and two stables and A
Berne', along with other 'houses edifices buyeldynges yards gardeyn courtes
... waters pondes fysshe poles' and numerous fields.[152] In the *Valor
Ecclesiasticus* of 1535, its lands were valued at over £26.[153] Canonbury would
serve as another residence for Cromwell. He lived there on occasion,[154] and
spent over £58 'for the settynge vpp of the Pale att Canbury and for the
prouysyon of the Tymber and stuffe for the same' between January and
March 1533.[155] There were also other, smaller land acquisitions. Cromwell
purchased the manor of Bourne from Sir Robert Waterton, a Yorkshire
knight, paying out over £162 to secure this in 1533.[156] In September of that
year he also attempted to lease the farm of Nasingbury from William Parry,
and finally obtained the property in 1534.[157] It would also appear that in
1533 Cromwell purchased a house in Stepney.[158]

It is interesting, however, that between 1531 and 1534 Cromwell did
not seek to transform Henry VIII's favour into something more permanent
by establishing himself and his family with landed power. Cromwell was
not yet sufficiently wealthy to embark on that. And in these years he was

still rising, establishing and consolidating his position, and undoubtedly very busy. As Mary Robertson has noted, during Cromwell's early career his land purchases were small, with no geographic pattern or attempt to concentrate them in one area, beyond an obvious proximity to London.[159] In fact, the properties which Cromwell leased or purchased during the early 1530s were even fewer than Robertson realised. With regard to two of the properties he ostensibly acquired in this period, Cromwell was actually acting on behalf of someone else. Coggeshall and Fyllolshall, Essex, were acquired by Cromwell in 1532 on the king's behalf, and the lands were used to endower Anne Boleyn.[160] Similarly, his attempt to acquire the lease to the farm of Alton, Wiltshire, from New College, Oxford, was made on behalf of one of Cromwell's friends.[161] Between 1531 and 1534, therefore, Cromwell's own land and property purchases were merely intended as another form of investment. A summary of his lands as they stood in mid-1535 (by which point one or two further properties had also been bought) suggests that land provided Cromwell with an income of about £500 per annum, a sizeable but by no means enormous amount.[162] Helen Miller has shown that the average annual income for a member of the nobility in 1534 was £921.[163] Robertson herself noted that subsidy rolls for Sussex in 1524–1525 show that at least twenty-four men and three women of gentry status or lower had landed incomes greater than Cromwell [did] in mid-1535.[164] Before 1536, then, Cromwell made no serious attempt to build a landed power base for his political career, nor was the wealth generated from the properties he owned conspicuously large.

It was not until the dissolution of the smaller monasteries in 1536 that Cromwell began to invest notably in land.[165] Following several smaller acquisitions in 1535 and 1536, he would acquire the dissolved priory of Michelham, Sussex, in 1537. This property included fifteen manors, which brought in over £170 per annum.[166] In early 1538 Cromwell was then granted the wealthy priory of St Pancras at Lewes.[167] Thereafter Cromwell began a policy of building up and consolidating his landholding in the south-east of England.[168] This culminated in April 1540 when he was created earl of Essex, an honour which came with twenty-three manors in that county.[169] Cromwell's later land acquisitions have been seen by Robertson as a 'continuation of politics by other means', that is, as an extension of the alleged factional battles at court, particularly with the duke of Norfolk.[170] Although it falls outside the years with which this study is primarily concerned, it is worth noting that this suggestion is largely unconvincing. A good deal of the land which Cromwell would obtain in 1538 was acquired from the duke with his consent: rather than factional hostility, there seems to have been a good deal of amicable co-operation between Norfolk and Cromwell. The two men carved up the spoils of Lewes Priory together in 1538,[171] while the duke had previously entrusted Cromwell with his will during his absence serving in the north throughout the Pilgrimage of Grace.[172] Cromwell's later consolidation of his land holdings in the south-east was because of their convenience and proximity to London. What drove his behaviour was a desire to ensure that he possessed enough land to reflect his rising status (he was created a baron in 1536, before his later elevation to the earldom), and to try to turn the king's favour, which might be fleeting, into something more lasting. It is revealing that his son Gregory and his wife were sent to live at Lewes almost immediately.[173] In his later career, then, Cromwell made efforts to establish his family with a landed power base.

Personality and Politics

Can Cromwell's personal life or character reveal anything of significance about his political career and its development? Several references in letters to Cromwell make it plain that he enjoyed gardening as a pastime. Seeds were sent for him to plant in his garden, for instance, while Thomas Audeley's wife asked to be sent news of what Cromwell was growing.[174] The chronicler John Stow also remembered how Cromwell arbitrarily expanded his own garden at his Austin Friars residence by causing 'the pales of the Gardens adioyning to the northe parte' of this 'to bee taken downe' suddenly. Twenty-two foot was then 'measured into the north of euery mans ground', a line drawn, 'a trench . . . cast, a foundation laid, and a high bricke Wall . . . builded'. Stow's father 'had a Garden there, and an house' standing close by. This house the workmen 'lowsed from the ground, & bare vpon Rowlers into my Fathers Garden 22. Foot'. No warning was given, and no answer provided, when Stow's father 'spake to the surueyers of that worke'. All that they would say was that Cromwell had 'commanded them so to doe', '[and] no man durst go to argue the matter'.[175] In another possible hint at Cromwell's horticultural interests, Edward Hasted claimed in his survey of Kent that 'the perdrigon plum, with two kinds more, were first made natives of this soil by Thomas, Lord Cromwell' when he returned from his youthful travels.[176]

In addition to an interest in gardening, Cromwell enjoyed hunting,[177] and kept hawks and greyhounds for this purpose.[178] He was also personally well travelled, and presumably had an interest in geography and history. The MP Edward Hall sent Cromwell a map of Hungary in 1533, while two world maps were among Cromwell's possessions during the 1520s.[179] Stephen Vaughan obtained a globe for Cromwell from Antwerp, and tried to locate for him a copy of the *Cronica Cronicarum cum figuris*, an illustrated history of the world published in 1493.[180] In 1531 Vaughan also recommended that Cromwell read *De vanitate scientiarum* by Cornelius Agrippa. Vaughan described Agrippa as 'a man of great litterature and knowlag', and urged Cromwell to 'Rede it for your pastyme'.[181]

Revelations about Cromwell's interests and leisure activities are of course useful when seeking to present a well-rounded picture of a man, but they tell us very little about the politics of the period, or what Cromwell himself was really like. Perhaps the most salient point worth making about Cromwell's private life is that he never remarried. In the early 1510s Cromwell had married a widow, Elizabeth Wykys, a union that may well have been motivated by Elizabeth's inheritance or perhaps the opportunity of assisting her father in business. The only known letter from Cromwell to 'my wel beloved wyf Elyzabeth' is short and perfunctory in tone, but it would be wrong to read too much into their relationship on the basis of this single letter.[182] In any event, Elizabeth was dead by the time Cromwell joined Henry VIII's service. Yet remarkably, Cromwell never then sought to advance his own political career through a favourable second marriage. It is true that Chapuys later reported a rumour that Cromwell intended to wed Princess Mary, but the ambassador rightly dismissed this as gossip.[183] Cromwell certainly arranged a favourable marriage for his son Gregory, who married Elizabeth Oughtred, widow of Sir Anthony Oughtred and sister to Jane Seymour, in the mid-1530s. This made Gregory brother-in-law to Henry VIII and uncle to the future King Edward VI. Nevertheless, Cromwell himself never remarried. It is somewhat surprising given that this was a period when courtiers and leading figures actively sought to strengthen their positions and networks of influence through marriage, and Cromwell's reasons for not doing so are unclear. Perhaps a suitable second wife never materialised; perhaps Cromwell was still attached to his first wife or perhaps he was simply too busy to find the time.

Given that Cromwell did not remarry, is there any evidence that he had a mistress? G. W. Bernard has referred to T. B. Pugh's suggestion that the countess of Worcester may have been Cromwell's mistress by the mid-1530s.[184] Yet most of the evidence for this rests on a letter from the countess to Cromwell thanking him for his kindness concerning £100 she had borrowed discreetly from Anne Boleyn.[185] Although letters from married noblewomen to ministers are unusual, it would be some stretch to suggest on this basis that the countess and Cromwell were lovers. There is, however, at least a passing reference to Cromwell and matters of the flesh from 1537. When enquiring whether Cromwell would lodge with one Tristram Teshe in York, the duke of Norfolk remarked to him that 'if ye Lust not to daly with his wif, he [Teshe] hath a yowng woman with praty proper tetins'.[186] Perhaps more intriguingly, there is a later reference to a possible illegitimate daughter of Cromwell. Arthur Collins, in his *The History of the Lives and Actions of Thomas Cromwel Earl of Essex and his Descendants* of c.1761, made reference to Cromwell's son Gregory 'and a daughter Jane', who he claimed had married one William Hough, Esquire.[187] Cromwell's only known daughters, Anne and Grace, had both died young. But there is another curious allusion to a daughter in a letter to Cromwell from Richard Southwell in 1537. Southwell remarked to Cromwell that 'I sawe a child of my ladye your daughters at a nonrye in yorkshire'.[188]

What did Cromwell himself look like? There is a handful of contemporary or near contemporary portraits that offer an indication of his appearance. The National Portrait Gallery, London, possesses a couple of miniatures of Cromwell, one dating to c.1532–1533, the other to c.1537, after his election to the Order of the Garter.[189] A medal commemorating this event also contains an image of Cromwell, and dates to 1538.[190] Without doubt, however, the best-known image of the minister is Hans Holbein's magnificient portrait, which can found in the Frick Collection, New York.[191] The Holbein portrait captures Cromwell during the very years which are of interest here. It shows Cromwell seated at a desk, with letters and dispatches before him. One of these letters is addressed to him as master of the king's jewels; this dates the portrait to 1532–1533. It shows that Cromwell was a solidly built man, clean-shaven, with dark hair. It is interesting to note that a contemporary writing to Cromwell in 1532 also remarked that Cromwell was 'sumwhat disposed to be Fatt', which further suggests that by the time he reached his early forties Cromwell was a man of ample size.[192] What is perhaps most remarkable about the Holbein portrait is how the painter captured his subject. Cromwell, amid letters and documents, is wearing the black cap and gown of a lawyer or royal official, trimmed with a fur collar.

Thus, Holbein portrayed Cromwell very much as this study has found him: as a lawyer turned royal minister, at work, engaged with administration and government.

Cromwell's correspondence, which is almost exclusively focused on his work and matters of state, reveals frustratingly little of his personality or motives during the 1530s. It is beyond dispute that he must have been hard working and extremely driven. But what motivated him is less clear. Pure ambition and a desire for advancement are more likely characteristics than the religious zeal, political ideals or commonwealth concerns usually given. Judgements on Cromwell by his contemporaries and near contemporaries are equally sparse. The Imperial ambassador Eustace Chapuys described Cromwell as 'a man of wit, well versed in Government affairs, and reasonable enough to judge correctly of them' in 1533.[193] He also noted in 1535 that Cromwell was 'eloquent in his own language' and could speak 'Latin, French, and Italian tolerably', as well as being 'liberal both of money and fair words'.[194] Both John Foxe and the Italian novelist Bandello were impressed that Cromwell was a man who did not forget his old friends and acquaintances, even after his meteoric rise.[195] The opinion of Cromwell given by Cardinal Reginald Pole in 1539, however, was far less positive. According to Pole, Cromwell was a 'messenger' and 'ambassador' of Satan,[196] and in the first preface to his treatise *In Defence of the Unity of the Church*, he recalled a conversation with Cromwell from 1528 in which the two men had discussed what makes a prudent counsellor.[197] Cromwell told Pole that an effective counsellor 'worked in secret and always tried to discern what the prince wanted. His job was to make the prince appear virtuous, while yet having his way.' Shortly following this, Cromwell offered the cardinal an unnamed book on statecraft, which Pole later assumed must have been Machiavelli's *The Prince*.[198]

Pole's remarks have led several historians to conclude that Cromwell was a disciple of Machiavelli, and this has sometimes been seen as key to an understanding of his character and philosophy. R. B. Merriman accepted Pole's story wholeheartedly, and argued that Cromwell 'read and studied his Machiavelli', which served as 'a guide to his future political career'.[199] A. D. Innes similarly believed that 'The "Prince" became Cromwell's political textbook, whose principles and maxims he was prepared to apply with appalling thoroughness if ever the opportunity offered'.[200] Yet there are difficulties in accepting Pole's testimony on Cromwell. Although Pole may have sincerely believed that Cromwell had poisoned the mind of Henry VIII and caused the destruction of the Church in England, it is by no means clear that the book which Cromwell offered Pole was Machiavelli. As the cardinal's account makes plain, Cromwell did not name the work, and the notion that Cromwell could have read Machiavelli in 1528 has been dismissed. P. Van Dyke has noted that the book itself, although written in 1513, was not printed until 1532.[201] Instead, he suggested Castiglione's *The Courtier* as the book which Cromwell had recommended to Pole.[202] A letter from Edmund Bonner reveals that Cromwell certainly possessed Castiglione's work, while one from Lord Morley in 1539 implies that Cromwell had not read *The Prince*.[203] Although it is not inconceivable that Cromwell read a manuscript copy of Machiavelli on his youthful travels in Italy, there is certainly no evidence – besides Pole's questionable testimony – to suggest that Cromwell had any interest in his writings.

No attempt has been made in this book to offer judgement on whether Cromwell was a particularly 'good' or 'bad' man. As one historian has put it, most human beings 'are mixtures of good and not so good qualities', and Cromwell was no different.[204] In many respects, the question of whether Cromwell should be seen as a hero or villain is something of a distraction, obscuring the truly significant historical questions about how his actions and policies shaped the development of the English state. In popular imagination, however, the ruthless Machiavellian outlined by Merriman has held sway. Robert Bolt's play *A Man for All Seasons*, focusing on the life of Thomas More, has also done much to compound the image of Cromwell as a sinister villain, cloaked in black. More recently, Hilary Mantel's novels *Wolf Hall* and *Bring Up the Bodies* have rescued Cromwell from the scorns of popular imagination. They have rightly been lauded as superb novels, and it is refreshing to see an attempt made to present Cromwell as a man of flesh and blood, with hopes and aspirations. Yet it is worth remembering that Mantel's tales are not history; nor has she claimed them to be. Although both books are clearly well researched, Mantel's work focuses heavily on Cromwell's private life, something about which the historical record offers precious little. As a novelist, Mantel has licence to speculate on Cromwell's thoughts and motives – an approach that is usually inappropriate for the historian. The picture she offers of Cromwell's rise to power is one tied closely to his ability to secure the king his divorce, and she makes much of Cromwell's alleged personal rivalries with Stephen Gardiner and Thomas More. This contrasts with the more prosaic picture of Cromwell's ascent offered here. This book has placed greater emphasis on the day-to-day government work that Cromwell undertook rather than power vacuums and factional clashes. These might make for entertaining reading but they are difficult to substantiate from the surviving sources. Although Mantel at times offers seemingly plausible explanations for events or actions, it cannot be stressed enough that what she offers is historical fiction.

An impression of Cromwell's character is particularly difficult to glean from the State Papers. His personal correspondence is tightly focused on business, so much so that it seems likely that he did not keep many letters that were personal or unrelated to his work. Even the single surviving letter to his wife, in which Cromwell asked who had called for him in his absence and instructed his wife to send his servant, Richard Swift, to him at 'Begham or Tonbridge', relates to his work on Wolsey's colleges.[205] In the absence of any statement of motives or beliefs, some scholars have looked to Cromwell's actions when trying to identify his personality and political outlook. T. M. Parker has suggested that, regardless of whether or not Cromwell read *The Prince*, he was still 'essentially Machiavellian' in his character and principles.[206] The majority, however, have followed Elton, who argued that Cromwell's political beliefs were centred on a determination to remake the body politic by subjecting the Church to the State, and establishing the supremacy of king-in-parliament.[207] The writings of Marsilius of Padua have therefore been seen by many scholars as a stronger influence on Cromwell than Machiavelli.[208] Yet although the *Defensor pacis* was certainly used by Cromwell to defend government policy, this was primarily for anti-papal purposes, and there is little indication that he was personally taken with its arguments.[209]

Nevertheless, if Cromwell was not a disciple of Machiavelli and had little interest in the teachings of Marsilius of Padua, this does not mean that he did not hold any principles worth discussing. To search in Cromwell's actions for an ideology or set of all-encompassing principles is probably unrealistic. Cromwell was a political animal by nature, and many of his actions and policies during the 1530s were surely made in response to events or circumstances, rather than being the implementation of some master plan based on a set of governing principles. Yet it is odd that one of the most formative areas of Cromwell's life – his background in law – has been so neglected by historians. For the vast majority of his life, Cromwell was a lawyer; and his work for Wolsey shows that he believed in the legitimacy that the law provided. During his political career in the 1530s, however, there is little to suggest that Cromwell was a notable defender of the common law; instead, he seems to have been more of a believer in the royal prerogative. We have seen, for instance, how during his first few years under Henry, Cromwell consistently acted to protect the king's rights towards the monasteries and claims to land. His memoranda during the 1530s also show that he very much took his lead from the king on important issues. For example, he frequently reminded himself 'to knowe whether the king will haue all the rest of the monkes and Freers [friars] sent for', 'to know what the kyng will haue done with [the] none [of kent] and her complycys' and 'to knowe whom the king will appoint to go with Doctor Lee to Lubeck'.[210] When analysing the language used in such memoranda, one historian has claimed that they show Cromwell emerging as little more than 'the executor of the king's wishes'.[211] Perhaps this is true; but even if Cromwell was only following orders when attending to much of the business of government, this reveals a frame of mind that was notably different from other men's, such as Thomas More who refused to accept the Royal Supremacy, or even a 'critical friend' of the king such as Sir Thomas Elyot.[212] 'Only following orders' is not really a sufficient explanation for someone's actions. What should interest us is the self-rationalisation behind this choice: how Cromwell justified his actions to himself or would have explained them to others. In his description of political thought in the later fifteenth century, John Watts has shown that many beliefs which might seem trite or commonplace really did matter, because they helped determine how people thought about their actions.[213] Personal bonds of obligation and doctrines of obedience have received little serious analysis as an explanation for people's attitudes during the Reformation, yet such notions were strong in the sixteenth-century world. When one considers a third element – the magic of kingship – it becomes that bit easier to understand people such as Cromwell, who, whatever private reservations they might have harboured, were ultimately prepared to follow or cleave to the king, and to understand why they acted as they did.

At least one historian has characterised Cromwell as a 'modern' man, who manifestly belonged to the 'modern age'.[214] He has elsewhere been described rather vaguely as a 'practical man' and a 'ways and means man', apparently implying that Cromwell was someone who might be equally at home running a modern multinational company as Henry VIII's England.[215] In reality, Cromwell was very much a product of his age, and the person to whom he appears most comparable was his former master, Thomas Wolsey. Although the cardinal and the minister are sometimes held to have been opposites, they actually shared many of the same characteristics which made them so successful under Henry VIII.[216] Both men emerged from humble origins: Wolsey was the son of an Ipswich butcher; Cromwell, the son of a Putney blacksmith and brewer. Both were clearly men who enjoyed handling the routine matters of State, and were prepared to rid the king of the daily requirements of government. They also probably got on personally, as Cromwell's loyalty to Wolsey on his fall in 1529 hints at. Strikingly, there are even intriguing similarities in the way that both men's position as Henry's leading counsellor was finally consolidated. Wolsey had risen to power gradually, but thanks in no small part to the patronage and support of Richard Fox, bishop of Winchester.[217] Nevertheless, George Cavendish, Wolsey's gentleman-usher and earliest biographer, also recollected how Wolsey played an important role in preparing the English army for the king's French campaign in 1513:

> Yt chaunced that the warres bytwen the Realmes of Englond & ffraunce to be opyn ... Wherfore it was thought very necessary that this Royall enterprise shold be spedely provyded and plentifully ffurnysshed in euery degree of thynges apte and convenyent for the same / Thexpedycion wherof the kynges highnes thought no oon mans wytt so mete for pollecy and paynfull travayll as his welbeloved Almosyner [Wolsey] was / To whome therfore he committed his hole affiaunce and trust ther in / And he [Wolsey] ... brought all thynges to a good passe & purpose in a right decent order as of all manner of victualles, provisions, and other necessaryes convenyent for so nobyll a voyage & pieusaunt Armye.[218]

Although the competent handling of the French campaign was not the cause of Wolsey's rise, it undoubtedly helped to cement his position as Henry's first chief minister. As J. J. Scarisbrick has noted, 'If Wolsey mattered, as he did, by 1512, he mattered still more by the end of 1513. It was his firm hands which had largely shaped the campaign in France of that year, providing Henry with a well-fed, remarkably healthy, disciplined and well-equipped army.'[219]

What has not been acknowledged is that Cromwell's own advance followed a surprisingly similar pattern, and required him to draw on the same personal attributes as Wolsey. As we have seen, Cromwell had risen gradually in the king's esteem through his ability to handle all manner of tasks, from responsibilities connected to various Crown lands and building projects to church administration and finance. Like Wolsey before him, Cromwell then further demonstrated his potential by competently handling Henry VIII's military activities. In late 1532 a small war broke out between England and Scotland, during which Cromwell supplied most of the money being sent north for the wages of the Berwick garrison.[220] When doing so he worked closely with Sir George Lawson, treasurer of Berwick, who was receiving the money which Cromwell was sending north. A brief examination of their correspondence shows that Cromwell was highly efficient at ensuring that the troops were paid on time. Before one set of wages was due to the first garrison on 8 January, for instance, Cromwell sent north a new supply of £2,034 13s 4d, which Lawson received on 6 January.[221] Cromwell's warrant authorising this money to be sent is dated 28 December.[222] When it is considered that Lawson wrote on 23 December requesting that money be sent to meet these wages, and that the time taken to travel between London and the borders during the war appears to have been five days (at a minimal estimate), this means that Cromwell probably obtained his warrant and began arranging the supply on the day he received Lawson's request.[223] Such characteristic efficiency continued throughout this military campaign. On 1 February Lawson wrote that he had received a further £3,000 from Cromwell, and that the first thousand men were now paid until 5 March.[224] Cromwell's warrant for this amount is dated 6 February, meaning that he sent the money before having obtained his warrant.[225] In the same letter Lawson remarked how the second garrison of one thousand, five hundred men clamoured to be 'equall with ther moneth wages' as the first thousand men were, and informed Cromwell that this would require an extra £1,500.[226] A subsequent letter reveals that Lawson received the requested sum by 21 February, at the latest.[227]

Like Wolsey before him, then, Cromwell relied on his organisational and administrative skills when handling Henry's military affairs, and underlined his usefulness to the king. Cromwell's punctual arrangement for the delivery of money ensured that the wages for soldiers on the borders were consistently met, with Cromwell often sending money north before he had received a request to do so. A medieval government's ability to ensure that its armies were sufficiently well supplied in the field has been held as an example of one of the most strenuous tests that it faced during this period.[228] Cromwell successfully passed this test, and when doing so he relied on his most important characteristic: efficiency when dealing with the routine requirements of government. Under these circumstances, it is not difficult to see why Henry's confidence in Cromwell first became manifest during the final months of the war with Scotland. Indeed, it was in April 1533, at the height of military activity in the north, that the Imperial ambassador noted that Cromwell was 'the man who has most influence with the King just now'.[229]

Conclusion

Cromwell's rise to power was aided in no small part by the men who worked for him in a private capacity. In an age without a civil service, Cromwell relied on these servants to help him deal with matters of state, and he was evidently someone who was comfortable delegating work to others. This important characteristic no doubt explains how he was able to accomplish so much during these years. Cromwell has also emerged once again as a man of considerable competence and efficiency, much like his former master, Cardinal Wolsey. Indeed, the similarity between Wolsey's rise and Cromwell's own is striking. Yet with regard to wider biographical evidence, particularly evidence of Cromwell's personal affairs, relationships with family members, motives and beliefs, the historical record is frustratingly silent. While this means that it is difficult to penetrate Cromwell's private life and inner character, it is nonetheless clear that he was a man of flesh and blood, and that the things motivating him were the same things which motivate most men. Cromwell sought wealth, and exploited his political position to get it. He bought land and was keen to display his personal and social advancement through his entourage and building works. At times, Cromwell was even willing to enrich himself through the acceptance of bribes. Such a conclusion – that Cromwell exploited his emergence into a position of tremendous political influence – might seem unremarkable. But not all biographical evidence needs to be earth-shattering. Given that some historians have sought to portray Cromwell as driven by high political or evangelical goals, this chapter serves as a reminder that he could equally have been motivated by personal advancement and private gain.

CHAPTER SEVEN

THE BREAK WITH ROME

EXISTING ACCOUNTS OF Thomas Cromwell's rise have usually placed considerable emphasis on his role in Henry VIII's break with Rome. Two of the earliest commentators on this subject, Cardinal Reginald Pole and John Foxe, both recounted a momentous first meeting between king and minister during which Cromwell suggested that Henry should end his allegiance to Rome and settle the validity of his marriage to Catherine of Aragon in England.[1] Later historians also argued that Cromwell was the architect behind the Anglo-papal schism. R. B. Merriman accepted Pole's and Foxe's accounts, and saw the 'important services' with which Cromwell provided the king during the divorce as crucial to his becoming chief minister.[2] It was Elton, however, who was most vociferous in arguing that the break with Rome was Cromwell's innovative solution to the king's marital problem. For Elton, the years 1529–1532 were 'years without a policy', with neither the king nor his counsellors capable of solving the conundrum of how to proceed.[3] Elton attributed what he saw as a radical shift in royal policy in 1532 to Cromwell's growing importance as a member of Henry's council.[4] Although he had rightly emphasised the importance of Cromwell's administrative hack-work when discussing his rise to prominence on the council,[5] for Elton it was Cromwell's responsibility for the idea of schism which was crucial in securing the king's confidence. This was argued to have been vital in his emergence as chief minister, and something that Elton believed Cromwell 'first secured in the year 1532' through his plan to resolve the king's 'great matter'.[6]

Admittedly, few historians now would subscribe to the view that Cromwell was responsible for the concept of a break with Rome. Graham Nicholson and John Guy have both shown that the intellectual origins behind this were being formulated well before Cromwell's ascendancy, while G. W. Bernard has demonstrated that there was a good deal more consistency to Henry VIII's earliest efforts to secure a divorce than is generally thought.[7] Nevertheless, if Cromwell is no longer seen as the originator of these ideas, the important part he played in the break with Rome, particularly in drafting the various Reformation statutes, remains undisputed and is still seen as decisive in his rise to power.[8] This is in spite of the fact that there is still no convincing account of Cromwell's precise role in all of this. Two of the most notable historians to have discussed Cromwell in relation to these events have both performed reversals on their earlier positions.[9] This chapter is therefore intended to establish a truly comprehensive account of Cromwell's role in the break with Rome, while also assessing the significance of these events in the context of his own unfolding political career. Its focus is primarily on the aspects of royal policy with which Cromwell was involved. This included drafting much of the legislation connected with the schism, the production and dissemination of propaganda justifying the king's actions and the enforcement of the government's policy in the localities. But before we look at Cromwell, and the events he was involved with in the early 1530s, it is necessary to begin by considering Henry VIII's own role in the Anglo-papal schism.

Henry VIII and Imperial Kingship

Henry VIII did not want to break with Rome in the early 1530s. What the king wanted was recognition – papal recognition – that his marriage to Catherine of Aragon was invalid in the eyes of God, so that he was free to marry someone else. Since the late 1520s the king had been convinced of the righteousness of this conviction, and sought to persuade both the pope and wider European opinion that his first marriage should be annulled. We have already seen how Henry sought dispensations to this end from Rome in 1527 and 1528, and that Cardinal Wolsey tried in vain to obtain papal permission to pronounce domestically on the king's 'great matter'. Wolsey's failure led to his fall from power, and the king carried on regardless. Yet it would prove a long, difficult struggle. There was a gap of almost six years between Henry's first attempts to obtain an annulment and the passage of the act in restraint of appeals in 1533, which enabled him to marry Anne Boleyn. A surprising number of historians have taken this length of time as evidence that the king did not know how best to proceed to secure a divorce. Henry supposedly boasted, blustered and continually changed tack because he was 'bankrupt in ideas'.[10] Royal policy towards the divorce had 'no clear strategy', argued Christopher Haigh, while it remained in a 'state of flux' if we follow John Guy.[11] According to this consensus, it was only when it was suggested to Henry that he – and not the pope – was head of the English Church, and already possessed the necessary jurisdiction, that the king realised he might settle the question of his marriage to Catherine domestically. For Elton, these concepts, and the policy of using parliament to realise them, emerged in 1532 with the ascent of Cromwell.[12] For others, a 'think tank' of scholars, including Thomas Cranmer and Edward Foxe, proposed them in late 1530.[13] Only a few historians have been willing to recognise that the king himself was already aware of the possibility of a break with Rome to achieve his divorce. Given the implications such a suggestion carries for Cromwell's own role in these events, this is a claim which deserves much greater attention here.

Henry VIII had always held a high concept of his own authority. Like his father before him, Henry continued to use iconography and imagery to lay claim to an imperial kingship, a medieval notion that the ruler held supreme temporal authority within a territory or kingdom.[14] A new variety of coin minted in 1489 had depicted Henry VII wearing a closed or arched crown (as opposed to the traditional open one), which was a recognised symbol of imperial authority.[15] In 1513 Henry VIII had given two of his newest warships imperial titles, naming one the *Henry Imperial* and another the *Mary Imperial*.[16] Several years later, when Wolsey was ordered to have a new great seal engraved, it was instructed that the king should be depicted on it 'sittyng in magestie in a cheire crowned with a crowne imperyall'.[17] Cuthbert Tunstall's remarks to the king in 1517, that 'the crown off englond is an empire off hit self . . . for which cause your grace werith a close crown', also makes it clear that the term 'empire', and the image of the closed crown, had come to symbolise sovereignty and imperial kingship by this point.[18] Of course, all of this was entirely in keeping with earlier rulers' understanding of their power and authority. Previous kings had made claims to *imperium* and empire (sovereignty), and a distinction was drawn between the temporal sovereignty of secular rulers and the spiritual sovereignty of Church and pope.[19] Although it would not be overbold to suggest that under both Henry VII and Henry VIII there had been an increase in claims to imperial kingship, Henry VIII continued to uphold this medieval distinction throughout the early years of his reign. In his anti-Lutheran tract, the *Assertio septem sacramentorum*, for example, Henry had professed the pope to be the 'Supreme Judge upon earth' to whom all kingdoms owed subjection.[20] If an account of Sir Thomas More's recollection in 1534 is to be trusted, Henry had even told him in 1521 that 'We are so muche bounden vnto the Sea of Room that we cannot doe to muche honor vnto it ... For we receaued from that Sea our crowne Imperiall'.[21] If the king had made this comment in 1521, and meant it sincerely, then he was asserting a surprisingly hierocratic understanding of kingship. Indeed, this was a view similar to that deployed by canon lawyers in the twelfth and thirteenth centuries, when they claimed that secular rulers received their power through the Church and pope.[22]

What Henry would claim in 1533 was something radically different. The act in restraint of appeals of that year pronounced a novel 'theory of the imperial crown of England sovereign within its own realm over both laity and church'.[23] The act's preamble referred to an 'imperiall crowne', under which a 'body politike' was bound, composed of the spirituality and temporality, with no superior other than God. And the act went on to refer to 'progatyves libities and pemynences of the said imperiall crowne of this realme, and of the *jurisdictions spirituall and temporall* of the same'.[24] In some of the earliest drafts of the appeals act, Henry VIII himself had even inserted remarks that both temporal and spiritual jurisdiction proceeded 'of & from the seid imperiall Crowne and none other wyse' (significantly, these remarks were later removed by Cromwell).[25] The act of supremacy, passed the following year, even went on to define exactly what the king's spiritual powers were. That act declared that Henry had full power and authority to 'visite represse redresse reforme ordre correct restrayne and amende all such errours heresies abuses offences contemptes and enormytes what so ever they be'.[26] By 1533, then, Henry VIII was claiming both temporal and spiritual powers: specifically, the right to reform the Church, eradicate heresy and to pronounce on theological doctrine. This was a revolutionary break from medieval political thought, and one which is usually attributed either to Cromwell or to a group of scholars who produced a collection of 'historical' precedents and biblical examples in 1530 to support the king's sudden claim to these powers.

Yet, significantly, Henry himself may have been closer to making this leap on his own than is sometimes realised. It is worth pointing out that

there was something of an uneasy tension generally in the relation of medieval monarchs to the Church. Kings had long been associated with spiritual
powers, despite the claim that spiritual jurisdiction – that is, matters relating
directly to salvation, the soul or man's relationship with God – was recognised as belonging to Church and pope. The coronation of an English
monarch offers one example of how the concept of kingship was entwined
with spiritual and religious significance. Central to the coronation ceremony
was the anointing of the monarch with holy oil, an act widely seen as
endowing him or her with a spiritual authority. Peter of Blois had remarked
in the twelfth century that the 'king himself is holy; he is the Anointed of
the Lord'; and spiritual, Christ-like powers continued to be attributed to
monarchs.[27] Medieval kings maintained the practice of touching to cure the
'king's evil' (or scrofula), while both Henry VII and Henry VIII also
continued the practice of giving out cramp rings. Although the coronation
oath, in which the monarch swore to 'kepe and mayntene the right and
libertees of holie churche of old tyme graunted by the rightuous Cristen
kinges of Englond', may have attempted to qualify the boundaries between
Church and state,[28] the notion that a king could regulate and reform the
Church itself was not unfounded. John Wyclif and the Lollards had claimed
throughout the fourteenth century that it was the secular prince, and not the
'bisshop of Rome', who held the authority to put the Church in order.[29]
Evidently, similar notions were still common at the accession of Henry VIII.
Edmund Dudley's political treatise *The Tree of Commonwealth* asserted in
1510 that it was the king's purpose to 'assitith his maker and redeemer of
whome he hath all his power and auctoritie', and that the 'root of the love
of God ... within this realm must chiefly grow by our sovereign lord the
king'.[30] As Gywn has noted, such a claim almost suggests that Dudley
'envisaged a spiritual function for the prince'.[31] At the very least, when
arguing that 'any manour of grudge' between the king's 'subiectes of the
spiritualtie and his subiectes of the temporaltie' could only be 'stablisshed
and reformyd' by the king, Dudley's treatise indicates more generally that
at the beginning of Henry's reign there remained those who maintained
that a monarch was entitled to regulate the Church.[32]

   Did Henry VIII himself hold such views? While we have seen that
throughout his early reign Henry clung to the entirely conventional belief
that spiritual sovereignty fell to Church and pope, at times the king also
exhibited a belief that he was entitled to interfere in certain church affairs.
The use of praemunire writs, which declared it illegal to cite a case before

ecclesiastical courts if it was perceived to fall under the king's jurisdiction, increased notably during the early years of Henry's reign. These were based on the fourteenth-century statutes of praemunire and provisors, which had been enforced sporadically during earlier periods. Yet implicit in any charge of praemunire was an assertion of royal authority at the expense of papal power, and between 1500 and 1532 over fifty cases involving praemunire would appear before King's Bench.[33] True, the majority of these were private suits made by lawyers no doubt keen to increase their business. But the Crown implicitly endorsed the use of these writs when failing to respond to calls from leading clerics to stop encroachment on the Church's ecclesiastical rights.[34] In 1512 Henry's parliament also passed an act which severely limited the clerical privilege known as benefit of clergy, which prevented clerics from being sentenced for a crime by a secular court.[35] Three years later, in a cause célèbre over this ecclesiastical liberty, Henry VIII even declared to a conference of his clergy that

> By the ordinance and sufferance of God we are king of England, and the kings of England in times past have never had any superior but God alone. Therefore take good heed that we wish to maintain the right of our crown and of our temporal jurisdiction, both in this point and in all other points, in as ample a manner as any of our forbears have done before our time.[36]

Some historians have seen these remarks as an indication that Henry already held views which would develop more fully in the early 1530s.[37] Yet Henry's use of the term 'temporal' jurisdiction here does suggest that he continued to acknowledge 'the reality of papal spiritual jurisdiction' at this point.[38] Nevertheless, this was still a confident declaration of power and authority, and Henry's refusal to adjourn the dispute over these liberties to Rome hints that his understanding of kingship was more nuanced than a straightforward distinction between spiritual and temporal powers allows for.[39]

Interestingly, a similar conference presided over by the king a few years later offers greater clarity on Henry's view of his authority. This time the ecclesiastical liberty under scrutiny was sanctuary, a right which enabled every church and ecclesiastical institution to offer any claimant protection and immunity from prosecution under common law for a period of forty days.[40] By the late medieval period this practice was widely seen as corrupt and in need of reform. When a particularly acrimonious case of sanctuary finally came before the king and his council in 1519, after hearing both clerical and secular arguments surrounding the privilege, Henry VIII offered his own verdict:

> I do not suppose that St Edward, King Elgar, and the other Kings and holy fathers who made the sanctuary ever intended to serve for the voluntary murder and larceny done outside the sanctuary in hope of returning . . . I believe the sanctuary was not so used in the beginning. And so I will have that reformed which is encroached by abuse, and have the matter reduced to the true intent of the making thereof in the beginning.[41]

Henry's language here is striking: 'I will have that reformed'. It suggests that the king already perceived this to be an area of the Church which fell under royal control. Significantly, nothing in Henry's actions or comments suggests that he believed papal or clerical permission necessary to undertake this. Yet sanctuary, like benefit of clergy, struck at the heart of the Church's privileges and jurisdiction. What Henry was laying claim to here was not a spiritual jurisdiction over the Church, therefore, but an ecclesiastical one. The king seems to have believed that the Church's external matters, such as jurisdiction, organisation and discipline – areas not directly related to salvation – fell under his royal authority. Many leading churchmen clearly felt uneasy about this, as their repeated refusal to cooperate with attempts to reform such privileges shows.[42]

It is true, however, that Henry VIII's relationship with the papacy was 'warm' before 1527.[43] In 1513, for example, Henry had written to the new pope, Leo X, to 'express his joy' and congratulations at his election, and promised to send ambassadors to declare his obedience.[44] Most notably, in his *Assertio septem sacramentorum* of 1521, the king had even declared that he had 'no intention of insulting the pope by discussing his prerogative as though it were a matter of doubt . . . all the churches accept and revere the holy Roman see as mother and ruler of the faithful'.[45] Yet Henry's regard for the papacy was often peculiarly self-serving. In August 1515 Wolsey had told the English ambassador in Rome that the pope would never have a better friend than the king of England, '*if he comply with his desires*'.[46] In 1515 the king himself had also told the Venetian ambassador that he was the pope's 'good son', but that he also had 'sufficient power with the pope to warrant hopes of my making him adhere to whichever side I choose'.[47]

The absentee bishop of Worcester, Silvestro de Gigli, also complained in 1520 that the pope had received no correspondence from England for over eight months. When a letter finally arrived, the pope remarked that the English 'never wrote except to beg something'.[48] Henry's minor confrontation with the papacy over Tournai in 1517 has even been presented by one historian as being 'on the road to 1534'.[49] The king clashed with the papacy over this recently conquered territory after the pope promulgated bulls in support of the deposed bishop-elect there. Henry was furious, telling his ambassador in Rome that he had 'supreme powere as lord and kynge in the regalie of Torney without recognisione of any superior'.[50] Yet Henry's claims, although seemingly grandiose, related only to traditional temporal matters, and stopped 'a long way short' of repudiating papal power.[51] Perhaps more interesting are the tactics that Henry used in order to get his own way. In his instructions to his ambassador in Rome regarding Tournai, Henry emphasised 'all the benefittes we have doon to hym [the pope] and the churche of Rome', with the clear implication that because the king had 'don so moche for the churche' the pope should comply with Henry's request.[52] When asking the pope to annul the king's first marriage in 1527 and 1528, Wolsey would adopt very similar tactics, reminding Henry's agents in Rome to stress 'what a benefactor' Henry had been to the Church.[53] What is more, the language used by Henry against the pope in 1517 really '*is* striking'.[54] He declared that if the pope 'rigerously without ground of justice proceed against vs wee would not suffer it', and warned the pontiff that he should 'be well warie how he graunte . . . bulles againste the soveraignety of princes herafter remembringe the daunger that may ensue vnto hym by the same'.[55] Even Henry's ambassador was struck by the 'most bitter letter' which the king had sent and never expected such proof of Henry's 'displeasur'.[56] Of course, Henry had no intention of splitting with Rome in 1517 over such a minor diplomatic incident. But as one historian has put it, Henry's letter regarding Tournai 'does reveal a frame of mind, a perfectly conventional frame of mind, but nonetheless one that could, in some quarrel between king and pope that could not readily be resolved, ultimately lead to a chain of events culminating in a renunciation of papal authority'.[57]

All this is highly significant as it undermines Elton's belief that a break with Rome was unthinkable without Cromwell.[58] Yet almost from the very beginning of his divorce campaign, as soon as it became clear that the pope would not or could not grant an annulment, Henry began to threaten and hint that he might ultimately be prepared to act independently.[59] As early as December 1527 Wolsey was instructing Henry's man in Rome, Gregory Casale, to inform the pope that the king was determined to 'satisfy his conscience', and that his disregard for the papacy grew daily. Casale was urged to stress that Henry's enmity was 'fraught with the most terrible consequences', and that Wolsey had 'knowledge' of what the result would be.[60] In April 1528 Stephen Gardiner had told the pope while on a diplomatic sojourn in Rome that if he would not comply with Henry's wishes, 'the kinges highness wold doo it without him'.[61] Less than a year later, in January 1529, the French ambassador reported that Gardiner had been instructed to tell the pope that if the divorce was not hurried, the king would throw off his allegiance to Rome.[62] A surprising number of historians have failed to give these early threats their due weight. Too often they are dismissed as a mere 'tactic to secure a favourable decision'.[63] But Wolsey's warning that the pope would 'lose the king and the devocion of this Realme from hym and the see apostolique' could scarcely have been clearer.[64] Well before the advent of Cromwell or the work of a 'think tank' of scholars active in late 1530, Henry was alert to the possibility of independent action. Indeed, the king's attitude was neatly observed by Cardinal Campeggio in 1528, shortly after he had arrived in England. 'The king,' Campeggio informed the pontiff, 'does not want to determine anything on his own judgement, but leaves all to the Holy See.' If, however, the pope did not provide Henry with the necessary remedy then 'it will be all over with this King and kingdom ... the Apostolic dignity will be destroyed'.[65]

So Henry was already alert to the possibility of independent action before Cromwell's emergence; what is more, he had some idea of how it might be achieved. Right from the beginning, the king had challenged papal power by questioning whether the pope was able to grant the original dispensation which had allowed him to marry Catherine.[66] From 1529 onwards, Henry then consistently threatened and restricted papal power in England, pressuring the pope to allow the case to be heard there, while simultaneously maintaining that he had the right to act independently.[67] The pluralities act of 1529 prevented anyone in England from procuring or obtaining from Rome any 'licences, union, tolleracyon [or] dyspensacyon to receive and take any more benefices with cure' than the act allowed.[68] A royal proclamation the following September forbade anyone from seeking or publishing anything from Rome which was deemed prejudicial to the authority of the realm.[69] Perhaps of greater significance, given the claims that have been made of Cromwell, is that Henry was also aware that parliament might be of use in his quest for a divorce. As early as September 1529 Chapuys reported that Queen Catherine was 'concerned and frightened' at the calling of the new parliament, and the ambassador added that the king might be tempted to obtain through this means that which 'he has not yet been able to get'.[70] Rumours surrounding parliament's purpose then continued into 1530. In April a French agent reported that if the pope continued to oppose Henry, he intended to 'settle' his 'great matter' 'within his realm by the advice of Council and Parliament'.[71] Perhaps most strikingly, in October 1530 the king assembled his clergy and lawyers together and asked them whether parliament could enact the divorce as decided by the archbishop of Canterbury. To this, the clergy and lawyers had answered no, and being 'very angry', Henry prorogued parliament until the following February in an attempt to bring them over to his means.[72]

It has been argued that all these early threats and manoeuvres meant precious little because Henry did nothing until 1532.[73] Yet one should not equate the king's reluctance to act with an ignorance of how to go about it. During his earliest attempts in the late 1520s, Henry quite reasonably expected the pope to grant him what he wanted. Papal dispensations were not particularly hard for a monarch to obtain.[74] And if the pope had agreed, the break with Rome would never have happened, and English history would have played out very differently. As months turned to years, however, and with Henry still no closer to securing what he wanted, he began to consider the threat of independent action much more viable. Yet a break with Rome was an incredibly dangerous move, and the king was justifiably fearful of opposition. In April 1530 the duke of Norfolk questioned the Spanish ambassador over whether Charles V would make war on England if the king were to settle his 'great matter' independently.[75] Similarly, in February 1533, shortly before much of the legislation that would enable the break with Rome had been passed, Anne Boleyn noted that Henry had resisted acting independently for so long 'from fear of his subjects'.[76] Unlike historians, Henry was not gifted with hindsight; he did not know what would happen. He also needed an approach which was flexible and adaptable in case the situation changed. Perhaps the pope might be willing to grant an annulment if the alignment of European politics altered. Perhaps Clement VII might die and the next pope be more willing to give Henry what he wanted. Perhaps Catherine of Aragon would die, thereby removing the most immovable of impediments.[77] A split with Rome was a last resort for the king, therefore, and Henry's cautious approach towards implementing the split should not be taken to show that he 'did not know how to proceed'.[78]

Where, then, does this leave Cromwell? If the preceding interpretation is correct, then before we even turn to look at his precise role, he has already emerged as a less important figure in the break with Rome than has sometimes been claimed. Rather than being the man behind it all, many of the concepts of sovereignty and claims to an imperial kingship that would be declared so stridently in the Reformation statutes of the early 1530s were actually present well before he had joined Henry's council in late 1530. But if Cromwell was not the originator of these ideas, then was he, as it is sometimes more reasonably claimed, Henry's 'fixer': the man who turned these seemingly abstract political concepts into legally enforceable statutes? If so, just how significant was this in his emergence as Henry's chief minister? To answer these questions we must now turn to the principal events that enabled the break with Rome, and try to identify Cromwell's role in these.

Legislating Schism

In mid-1530 threats and accusations were made by the Crown against members of the English Church, marking the opening stages of a struggle of authority that would continue throughout the next few years. The Crown began these manoeuvres by targeting individual members of the clergy in an attempt to intimidate churchmen, assert the king's supremacy over them and prepare the way for possible independent action over the royal divorce. Cromwell has sometimes been accorded an important role in these proceedings, which eventually resulted in the entire English clergy acknowledging the king as 'supreme head of the English Church' in 1531.[79] It all began in July 1530 when charges of praemunire were brought against fifteen members of the English Church. Although it has been argued that all the Crown wanted from the clergy at this early stage was money, the specific use of praemunire (which carried an implicit attack on papal power and an assertion of the king's supremacy) suggests that the Crown was already looking for ways to emphasise its authority over the Church, in case it did ultimately have to act unilaterally over the divorce.[80] But how far was Cromwell behind these events?

The attacks commenced on 11 July 1530, before Cromwell had even joined Henry VIII's service. Eight bishops and three abbots were among the fifteen members of the clergy originally cited to appear in King's Bench at Michaelmas on grounds of praemunire. In a possible act of defiance, however, nine of them failed to appear, and the case was postponed. When these matters were resumed in early 1531 (by which time Cromwell was a councillor) the entire English clergy suddenly felt sufficiently threatened to agree to pay the king a £100,000 'subsidy' in return for a pardon.[81] Although it is unclear whether a general charge of praemunire was ever levied against the clergy as a whole (this was technically impossible, as it did not constitute a corporate entity), there can be no doubt that there was a 'shift in emphasis' during these events.[82] The fifteen clerics in 1530 had originally been charged with abetting and complying with Wolsey's legatine authority. The pardon eventually granted in March 1531 absolved the entire English clergy of the illegal exercising of their spiritual jurisdiction.[83] Cromwell has been singled out and put forward as the mastermind behind this transformation in royal policy. According to Elton, Cromwell saw a much more ambitious opportunity in the early charges brought against the fifteen, and implemented a decisive change in strategy by threatening the whole clergy with praemunire. His intent was supposedly to emphasise the king's authority over the Church.[84] In support of this argument, Elton noted Cromwell's cryptic comments to Cardinal Wolsey in a letter of 21 October 1530: 'the Parlyment ys prorogyd [until the] vi daye of January. The prelattes shalnot appere [in the] premunire Ther ys Another way deuysyd in [place thereof] as your grace shall Ferther know.'[85] These remarks do indeed intimate that Cromwell was aware of a change in how the government intended to proceed. But whether this change referred to *the* change that actually occurred is less clear, and must be called into doubt given that Guy has put forward a convincing case that there was no dramatic shift in emphasis until early 1531.[86]

For our purposes, what is significant is that whoever or whatever lay behind the decision to alter the framing of the praemunire manoeuvres, there is nothing to link Cromwell with this decision, or with these attacks more generally. Although Scarisbrick and Guy disagreed with one another over when the shift in royal policy occurred, both were in agreement that Cromwell played no part in formulating this.[87] Guy highlighted the lack of evidence to suggest that Cromwell 'was anything more than Henry VIII's executive agent in 1530 and 1531',[88] while Scarisbrick questioned whether Cromwell would have had sufficient influence to impact on these events so early in his royal career.[89] This book has in fact gone further, by demonstrating that Cromwell was preoccupied with the Crown's landed interests during these early months, and was not entrusted with the implementation of government policy until the second half of 1531. What Cromwell's remark to Wolsey the previous October does suggest, however, is that he was by then close enough to the centre of power to be sufficiently aware of the threats and rumours against the Church. But it is entirely possible that his comment was nothing more than a matter-of-fact remark about parliament's prorogation meaning that affairs were being adjusted.[90]

Cromwell did, however, play a minor role in the subsequent manoeuvres which followed in convocation in early 1531.[91] The southern clergy had convened at St Paul's on 12 January to address the threats of praemunire against its members. Convocation was transferred to the chapterhouse of Westminster Abbey on 19 January, where it responded to recent events and begrudgingly offered the king £100,000 in return for a pardon, the confirmation of clerical rights and a clear definition of praemunire. It was in a rejoinder to this that the king demanded to be recognised as 'supreme head of the English church and clergy', and several of the king's councillors attended convocation during a critical week in early February when the king's new conditions were being debated.[92] Cromwell was one of the council members in attendance on 10 February, and he held a private conversation with Archbishop Warham on the king's behalf.[93] For Elton, Cromwell's 'decisive appearance' was enough to prove 'who stood behind the policy of subduing the clergy by forcing them to buy a pardon and make sweeping concessions'.[94] But the accounts of convocation make it plain that many of the king's councillors attended during this critical week, and took part in the negotiations and arm-twisting.[95] Francis Atterbury, working from convocation records now lost, stated that over the period 7–12 February 'at least seven or eight Menacing Messuages were sent from the King by the Great Men of the Law, or by some of his Privy Councellors and Nobles'.[96] Cromwell was therefore one of many sent to cajole the clergy, and it is far from clear whether he played any notable role. Although it has been claimed that it was probably Cromwell or Thomas Audeley who was responsible for the clause 'as far as the word of God allows', which was added to the king's newly claimed title to make it more palatable to convocation, 'we do not know who suggested this saving clause'.[97] And given that Cromwell had joined the council less than two months before, it was surely Henry's leading councillors – Norfolk, Gardiner and the earl of Wiltshire – who were co-ordinating these events.

A letter showing Cromwell's handling of the northern convocation in May 1531 was also cited by Scarisbrick and Michael Kelly in general support of the notion that Cromwell might have had a hand in the pardon of the clergy.[98] Elton also alluded to this in order to strengthen his overarching argument that Cromwell masterminded a dramatic change in royal policy.[99] But the letter in question, although dated to 1531 in *Letters and Papers*, was actually sent to Cromwell in May 1533.[100] Another letter, however, which has not been cited by any of these historians, could tentatively suggest Cromwell's involvement with the pardon through his handling of the northern synod. This was sent from Brian Higdon, dean of York, and William Strangways, the vicar-general there, on 14 May 1531. They told Cromwell that they had

recevyd your lettres In the favour of the lord of sanct Johns that the church belonging to [the] said lord of sanct Johns might bee [*sic*] the conuocacion here bee discharged of making to the kynges subside … wee dyd owr best to move … the clergie assembled In this conuocacion to aylowe the pryuyleges and chartres wuch wher exhybytyt In the conuocacion as suffycynnt for discharge … but aysuredlie the clergie wold In noo wyse consent.[101]

In an earlier letter, then, Cromwell had requested that the Crown's ecclesiastical agents in the north make arrangements in convocation for an exemption to the praemunire fine for the priory of St John of Jerusalem, London, which might just be used to support the notion that Cromwell was overseeing the whole matter. It will be remembered, however, that Cromwell had been one of four councillors who had concluded terms with the priory for a land exchange on the king's behalf on 30 May 1531.[102] It would be more realistic, therefore, to see Cromwell's request to Higdon and Strangways as a private agreement extracted by the prior of St John when negotiating the terms of this exchange. Cromwell was neither formulating nor executing the arrangements of either clergyman's pardon during these months; he was a middle-ranking councillor who could secure concessions from those who were. Cuthbert Marshall's letter to Cromwell, thanking him for 'laboring to the Kinges highnes' that he should not be exempt from the pardon granted to the York convocation in April 1531, similarly supports these conclusions.[103] Cromwell's first notable involvement with these matters did not in fact occur until August 1531, when several of the instructions that the king ordered him to deliver to the council concerned the conclusion of individual clerical fines for praemunire offences.[104] From December 1531 onwards Cromwell then began to receive some of these personal fines on the king's behalf.[105]

The important role Cromwell has been accorded in the break with Rome has more reasonably been attributed to the fact that he drafted, corrected or amended a great deal of the parliamentary legislation that would help implement it. Cromwell's first involvement with this did not occur until 1532. As Edward Hall recollected, it was early in that year that an act had been made in parliament 'that Bysshops shoulde pay no more Annates or money for their Bulles to the Pope'.[106] These annates (or first fruits) were payments made to Rome when bishops were appointed to their sees. Although they usually amounted to little more than £4,500 per annum,[107] the threat to cut this revenue off was a clear attempt to provide the king with a financial bargaining chip in his struggle with the papacy. A parliamentary petition, lamenting the 'uniuste exactions' of annates, had ostensibly initiated the call for this legislation. The petition even urged the king to withdraw himself and his people from obedience to Rome entirely should the pope launch any process in retaliation.[108] Given the eventual opposition to the annates bill in both the Lords and the Commons, this petition was almost certainly a government initiative, promoted in parliament by the king's men, of whom Cromwell was probably one.

Nevertheless, the idea of using annates as a means of enacting financial sanctions had not emerged with Cromwell. As early as December 1529, well before he had started to work for the king, Henry had remarked to Chapuys that 'He was ... about to undertake the annats'.[109] This hints that the idea of threatening papal revenue from England was already being mooted. Cromwell's involvement in 1532 was patently that of a legal draftsman. Corrections in his hand can be found alongside those of others on an early draft of the act,[110] while Elton also drew attention to a draft clause, wholly in Cromwell's hand, which he thought was probably the 'origin' of the act itself.[111] Given that this draft clause delayed the decision on the cessation of paying annates to Rome until Easter 1533, it might be more logical to see it as a subsequent amendment to the bill, conceded in order to ease its passage through parliament in the face of opposition. Cromwell himself was evidently unsure of the bill's chances, remarking to Gardiner in January how 'thys day was Redd in the higher house a bill touching the Annates of busshopriches to what ende or effecte it will succede suerlie I know not'.[112] Chapuys similarly reported opposition to it in both Houses,[113] and Henry VIII had personally to attend parliament on three occasions, before finally ordering a division in his presence as to who would or would not support the act. Several of those who opposed it 'for fear of the King's indignation went over to the King's side', and in that manner a majority was obtained.[114] No doubt Cromwell, sitting there as MP for Taunton, was vocal on the king's behalf. But nothing suggests his involvement with the annates act was anything more than his role as executor of the royal will would require: drafting and amending the legislation, and helping to secure its passage through parliament.

Far greater importance, both in terms of the practical resolution of the royal divorce, and in Cromwell's own rise under the king, is often placed on his role in the Commons' Supplication against the Ordinaries. This began in the same parliamentary session as the annates, and, according to Hall, emerged from spontaneous grievances in the Lower House against ecclesiastical officials who exercised jurisdiction in church courts (Ordinaries). Hall recounted how,

> After Christemas the. xv. Daye of January the Parliament began to sytte, & amongst dyuers griefes which the Commons were greued with, they sore complained of the crueltie of the Ordinaries . . . this matter and other Exactions done by the Clergy in their Courtes were long debated in the Common House.[115]

The duke of Norfolk's remark about 'the Infenyte clamors of the temporaltye here in parl[a]ment agaynst the mysusyng of the sprytuell jurysdiccion' at the end of February 1532 also adds some support to Hall's account.[116] Yet the chronicler's recollections were dismissed by Elton, who argued that Chapuys's remark that 'nothing had been done in parliament' at the end of February suggests that these grievances did not emanate from the Commons.[117] Instead, Elton put forward a detailed argument that Cromwell, having witnessed first hand the anticlerical sentiment in parliament during 1529, kept the petitions produced against the clergy in the first session, and resurrected them in the third session in 1532.[118] On Elton's reading, the Supplication was a government initiative masterminded by Cromwell, and its overriding purpose was to elicit a response from the clergy that would culminate in the loss of their independent law-making jurisdiction.

Chapuys's silence, however, is insufficient proof of the goings-on in parliament. After all, Chapuys was still unaware of the Supplication on

20 March, again writing that no other important measure had been discussed besides the annates act.[119] Yet this was two days after the Supplication had in fact been presented to the king. Moreover, Elton's proof for Cromwell's role largely rested on the basis that his hand was again to be found on drafts of the Commons' complaints, several of which he also argued should be redated. Five drafts survive, which Elton designated A, B, C_1, C_2, D and E.[120] Drafts A, B, C_1 and C_2, which all contain corrections by Cromwell, were claimed by Elton to belong to the 1529 session.[121] D and E, by contrast, were thought to have been produced by the government in 1532. Draft D, in particular, again contained corrections by Cromwell, and Elton believed this preceded the first appearance of the Supplication in parliament, having been produced by Cromwell's office from the earlier petitions.[122] According to Elton, 'Cromwell himself took up the idea of attacking the church through its courts' and, having seen 'where Henry's actions were leading him', Cromwell 'prepared a plan which he put into practice as soon as he convinced the king of its efficacy'.[123]

The problem with Elton's argument is that there is no convincing reason to date drafts A and C_1 to the first session of the Reformation parliament, or to think that D was produced before these matters emerged in the Commons in 1532.[124] Drafts B and C_2 are more difficult to date with certainty. Corrected by Cromwell, B was concerned with the excessive fees charged by the officials of ecclesiastical courts for probate of testaments, and would fit with the anticlerical grievances aired in the first session of the Reformation parliament.[125] So, too, would C_2, a copy of B incorporating Cromwell's corrections and containing further amendments by him.[126] The complaints in these regarding the excessive charges for probate of wills might suggest that both were written before the 1529 act, which tried to regulate this.[127] Nevertheless, a date of 1532 cannot be ruled out, particularly if the act of 1529 was ineffective. Indeed, this would be a prerequisite for accepting Elton's wider argument, as it is difficult to see how Cromwell could have resurrected grievances about probate from 1529 if these were not still perceived to be a genuine problem in 1532. Ultimately, the drafts of the Supplication are frustratingly inconclusive. With no convincing reason to discount Hall's testimony about the spontaneity of these complaints, acceptance of Elton's assertions would require a tremendous leap of faith.

Despite this they have enjoyed notable support. Haigh, Ives and Redworth have all broadly endorsed Elton's conclusions.[128] Guy went even further, arguing that the king himself was unaware of Cromwell's plan. He suggested that the minister tricked parliament into believing that Henry supported the grievances, not only to deprive the Church of its independence, but also to enable Cromwell to personally triumph over his conservative opponents, notably Thomas More, on the council.[129]

But Cromwell's role is easier to understand if he is seen not as some scheming politician but as one of the royal servants, who were required to deal with what were spontaneous grievances in 1532, before they were submitted to the king. Hall recollected that, after the Commons had raised these matters, 'it was concluded & agreed, that all the griefes . . . shoulde be putte in writyng and delyuered to the Kyng, whiche *by great aduyce was done*'.[130] As one of the king's councillors who also sat in parliament, Cromwell was ideally placed to act as a channel of communication between the Crown and the Lower Chamber. It is also significant that Cromwell's close associate Thomas Audeley, the speaker of the Commons, acted in a similar capacity. Audeley corrected draft D, and personally delivered the final petition to the king before Easter.[131] That both Cromwell and Audeley made corrections to the drafts very much suggests that they were responding to the issue as it arose, rather than producing the Supplication on their own initiative. Why, for instance, did Cromwell not just prepare a complete text in his own hand?[132] What they were doing was amending genuine grievances on the Commons' behalf to try to ensure that they were acceptable to the king. In draft B, for instance, when Cromwell altered part of the petition complaining of the excessive fees charged by officials of ecclesiastical courts for probate of testaments, he softened some of the language to read as follows:

> So many judges scribes apparitours somoners . . . and other mynistres for the approbation of testaments ~~which like a sorte of Rauenous Wooluys nothing elles attending but~~ *which coueting somoche* there ~~onelie~~ pryuate Lucres and *the* satisfaction ~~of the couetous and Insatiable~~ *of the* appetites of the said prelates and ordynaries . . . *exsessyuelye* take of theme . . . ~~suche~~ *so large* ~~excessiue~~ fees ~~bribes~~ and rewardes for the same . . . ayenst all Justice law equytie and good consciens.[133]

These changes were presumably to make the petition more palatable to the king; and the claim of bribery was subsequently dropped entirely by Cromwell in C_2.

The changes Cromwell made to draft A are perhaps more significant. In this, Cromwell rewrote the first complaint raised, removing the opening remarks about the clergy having a 'libertie and a voyce of assent' over statute law, and went straight to the issue of the clergy's own laws being made without the king's 'Royal assent or knowlage or the assent or consent of Any of your laye subiectes'.[134] This has the effect of sharpening the complaint somewhat, but it would seem fanciful to suggest, as Elton does, that Cromwell had seized on the 'larger issues' of clerical independence here. The complaint itself was fundamentally unaltered by Cromwell, and remained rooted as a grievance of the laity. His changes continued to focus on how the king's lay subjects were bound 'in thayr Bodyes possessyons and goodes' by the clergy's laws, none of which, it is complained, were written in English or published.[135] Moreover, the remarks about the king's royal assent had been present right from the start, and might more plausibly be seen as an attempt by the Commons to win the king's sympathy for their grievances. Above all, despite Cromwell's modifications, the Supplication in its final form remains a 'remarkable miscellany of grievances'.[136] This again raises the likelihood that they were – as Hall suggested – spontaneous concerns raised in parliament. If its principal aim was to deprive the clergy of their independent law-making jurisdiction, it was a poor attempt at framing this.

The king's reaction to the Supplication adds further weight to the argument that it was not a government initiative. What has not been sufficiently recognised is that, on receiving the petition from Audeley, Henry did not seize on it and proceed against the Church. Instead, Henry agreed to act as an arbitrator between the Commons and clergy, but only if the Commons would look favourably on the contentious bill of uses.[137] This bill was an attempt to deal with the issue of land being held by trustees for the 'use' or profit of another, which denied the Crown certain feudal dues.[138] Bernard has suggested that Henry's unenthusiastic stance on receiving the Supplication was 'play-acting', and that the king quickly realised how the Commons' grievances might be turned to his advantage in his struggle against the Church.[139] But what is striking is just how much emphasis Hall placed on Henry's concern for the passage of the bill of uses, perhaps suggesting that this was of greater importance to Henry at this point.[140] It might be misleading to view every royal action during these years as being one-dimensionally focused on the divorce. The salient point is that it was only after receiving convocation's reply to the Supplication that the king became concerned with the matter, remarking to Speaker Audeley that 'we thynke their answere will smally please you, for it semeth to vs very slender'.[141] Perhaps until then Henry had been quite content with the recognition he extracted from his clergy in 1531, when they declared him 'supreme head' of the Church, and already believed them to be sufficiently compliant. Did the clergy's response to the Supplication take Henry and his closest councillors, including Cromwell, by surprise? After all, the clergy did not merely deny the charges brought against them, but also went further, defending church liberties and the right of clerical independence.[142] Such a resolute defence would have alarmed an unsuspecting king, undermined the acknowledgement Henry had extracted in 1531 and alerted him to the likelihood that his clergy were not yet sufficiently submissive.

On such a reading, Cromwell's role in the Supplication itself appears limited. What cannot be doubted, however, was his close involvement in the government's response to convocation following this. In early May, having been enraged by the clergy's reply, Henry sent demands to convocation that they were not to enact laws without the royal assent.[143] At the same time, pressure was increased on the Church in parliament, with the king telling eight members of the House of Lords, a dozen members of the Commons and Speaker Audeley how

> we thought that the clergie of our realme, had been our subiectes, yea, and scace our subiectes: for all the Prelates at their consecracion, make an othe to the Pope, clene contrary to the othe that they make to vs, so that they seme to be his subiectes, and not ours.[144]

Again, it is likely that this was in response to remarks from the bishops, who had claimed that they could not assent to the king's divorce without the pope's consent, because, when created, they had sworn not to oppose the pope's wishes.[145] But what seems interesting is that John Foxe associated this useful argument with Cromwell, who he thought had made it

> manifest vnto his highness, how his princely authoritie was abused within his owne realme, by the Pope and hys Clergie, who beyng sworne vnto hym, were afterward dispensed from the same, and sworne a new vnto the Pope, so that he was but halfe a king, & they but halfe his subiectes.[146]

Given the scepticism already raised over the reliability of Foxe, these assertions alone would carry little weight. They do, however, find some support from Cromwell's own papers, among which there were at least two copies of 'the othes of the prelates made to the pope'.[147] Evidently, if Cromwell did not personally come up with this argument, he was certainly one of those involved in deploying it in parliament, with an intent of persuading its members to 'inuent some ordre' so that the king 'bee not thus deluded' of his spiritual subjects.[148]

The 'ordre' envisaged was probably a bill – two drafts of which survive, both corrected by Cromwell – which the government presumably introduced following the clergy's oath having been read there. It was similar in tone and intent to the articles of submission sent to convocation simultaneously in May.[149] In particular, it specified that no ordinance made in convocation would hold effect unless ratified by parliament, and also contained remarks about convocation being 'called by the kynges wrytte . . . as hathe be acustomed'.[150] This bill hints, as Kelly has suggested, that the government intended to proceed simultaneously against the clergy in both convocation and parliament, before eventually abandoning the latter following the clergy's submission on 16 May.[151] Cromwell, who was present as one of five councillors who witnessed the clergy's surrender to the king, was evidently closely involved with these events.[152] Yet frustratingly, his precise role, beyond that of parliamentary draftsman, remains tantalisingly unclear.

For both Elton and Guy, the Supplication against the Ordinaries and the surrender of the clergy were crucial to Cromwell becoming Henry VIII's chief minister. It was through these events, Elton argued, that 'Cromwell had gained the king's ear, and for the next eight years he was to be, next to Henry, the most powerful man in England'.[153] Similarly, for Guy, Cromwell had not only won 'the factional battle for control of . . . Henry VIII's policy', but he had also eliminated a political rival in Sir Thomas More, who resigned as lord chancellor within hours of the clergy surrendering their independence to the king.[154] More was hostile to any radical measures against the Church, and, knowing this, Cromwell supposedly put forward the Supplication, not only to manipulate Church and Commons but also to remove More.[155] But the suggestion that by the end of May 1532 Cromwell was established as Henry's leading minister is premature, as the concluding chapter of this book will show. It may also be revealing that it was Thomas Audeley (who also had a hand in the Supplication, and who delivered it to the king personally) who was subsequently knighted and made keeper of the great seal following More's resignation. Did he perhaps play a more significant role than Cromwell? Above all, the notion that Cromwell had deliberately planned the removal of his alleged rivals not only exaggerates the factional divisions and scheming among Henry's councillors, but it also suggests a level of prescience on Cromwell's part which is patently unlikely, and certainly unsupportable from the evidence.

Nevertheless, the Supplication, or perhaps more specifically the clergy's response to it, was significant in the development of Cromwell's own career in one notable respect: it severely diminished the king's trust in Stephen Gardiner, bishop of Winchester, who had been acting as the king's secretary since 1529. It was Gardiner who had drafted convocation's initial response to the Supplication, and either as the result of a severe misunderstanding of Henry's attitude towards his clergy, or perhaps through genuine belief in the need to stand up for the Church's independence, Gardiner produced a resolute answer, which met with strong royal disapproval.[156] As a result, the bishop went into exile from court and took some time to regain Henry's trust.[157] It is not an endorsement of factional scheming to say that Cromwell undoubtedly benefited from Gardiner's temporary loss of royal favour. In early 1532 Cromwell was a leading member of the King's Council and one of the royal servants charged with managing parliament. Gardiner, by contrast, was a far more significant figure about the king, and was even allowed to amend royal dispatches as he saw fit.[158] In January 1532, while Gardiner was in France on a diplomatic mission, Cromwell even wrote to the bishop, telling him how the king deeply regretted Gardiner's absence, which he lamented as 'the lacke of my right hand for I am now so moche pestred with busynes and haue no bodie to rydde ne depeche the same'.[159] Not only do these remarks reveal that Gardiner had been handling many of the king's closest matters, but they also show that Cromwell was not yet Henry's man of business. But by spectacularly losing Henry's trust during the Supplication, Gardiner would offer the ambitious and hardworking Cromwell the opportunity to replace him as one of the king's most trusted servants.

Certainly, by 1533 Cromwell had succeeded in doing so. From the beginning of that year the minister was overseeing the final stages of Henry's quest for a divorce. On 5 February, for instance, the Imperial ambassador reported that 'one of the principal members of the Privy Council' had assembled a number of doctors, churchmen and lawyers, and had shown them a document asserting that Queen Catherine had been 'cognue' by Arthur, and so her second marriage to the king was null and void.[160] Chapuys did not mention Cromwell by name in this dispatch, and in fact never did so until 15 February 1533. Nevertheless, it was almost certainly Cromwell he was referring to here. Had it been another leading figure on the council, such as Norfolk or Wiltshire, both of whom the ambassador frequently mentioned by name, Chapuys would undoubtedly have said so. The meeting which Chapuys was referring to had been convened by Cromwell to prepare the way for the new archbishop of Canterbury, Thomas Cranmer, to pronounce on the king's marriage to Catherine. Its outcome was that those assembled had agreed 'that the King, by the authority of the archbishop of Canterbury, legate of England, ought to carry out his undertaking at once'.[161]

Debates were also held in the southern convocation towards the end of March to prepare for Cranmer's pronouncement. Conclusions in favour of the king were passed there in relation to several thorny questions on which the divorce had long hinged.[162] Cromwell was presumably closely involved with these debates; he certainly oversaw the passage of parallel conclusions on the same matters in the northern synod in April and May. Thomas Magnus, archdeacon of the East Riding, told him on 21 April how Rowland Lee had 'shewed vnto me the kinges mooste gracious pleasure and your aduertisementes for my going northwards to the convocacion at yorke'.[163] Magnus was to assist Lee in getting the northern clergy to agree to the same conclusions as its southern counterpart, and he continued to keep Cromwell informed on his progress.[164] Brian Higdon, dean of York, and Cuthbert Marshall, archdeacon of Nottingham, were two other prelates whom Cromwell instructed to ensure convocation's compliance.[165] Marshall, in particular, told Cromwell how 'acordingly to your desir I haue not onli condiscendid . . . to ye passing of certain conclusions in the conuo-cacion . . . but also did solicitt other takyng and remouing scrupilles out off ther consciens'.[166] In this, Cromwell's involvement as the Crown's executive agent is once again clear. What is perhaps more interesting are the methods he employed to achieve this. Several royal agents based permanently in the north worked under his direction cajoling other clergy, while books and carefully prepared writings were also sent north in an attempt to persuade reluctant members of the validity of Henry's case.[167] Cromwell also dispatched one of his most trusted associates, Rowland Lee, to oversee these affairs personally,[168] and even used a promotion as a reward for a man who assisted Lee in these matters.[169]

During the early months of 1533 Cromwell was also busy preparing the famous act in restraint of appeals. Introduced in parliament on 14 March, and finally passed in April,[170] this act has long been seen as another important stage in the break with Rome, and one in which Cromwell played a formative part. 'The act against appeals was his act,' argued Elton; 'it embodied his [Cromwell's] political thought', namely, a belief in the 'theory of the imperial crown of England sovereign within its own realm over both laity and church'.[171] It is of course true that Cromwell was instrumental in drafting and correcting much of the appeals act. His handwriting can be found on several early versions of it,[172] and he also presumably played some part in navigating the bill through parliament. But it does not necessarily follow that the draftsman of an act is the originator of the concepts and ideas embodied within it.[173] As we have already seen, convincing evidence suggests that the concepts which Elton claimed came uniquely from Cromwell were already part of the wider intellectual discourse of the time.[174] Moreover, it was Henry VIII himself – and not Cromwell – who on one early version of the appeals act, re-inserted remarks previously removed, which stated that both temporal and spiritual jurisdiction proceeded 'off and frome the sayd imperiall crowne'.[175] The king's remarks were again removed in a subsequent draft.[176]

Another intriguing point which Elton was quick to play down was that the earliest version of the act of appeals was not drafted by Cromwell at all, but by his close associate Thomas Audeley.[177] This 'abortive predecessor of the Act against Appeals' was written wholly in Audeley's hand, which is in contrast to the later drafts of the appeals act that are merely corrected by Cromwell, and it has some striking similarities to the eventual form the act of appeals would take.[178] Audeley's draft bill would have enabled the two English archbishops (Cranmer and Edward Lee) – or 'oon of theym' – to pronounce on Henry's first marriage domestically, and it specified that if the pope issued any censures in response, these were 'not [to] be obeyed allowed Accepted admytted nor executed within this realme'. Moreover, any person who appealed to Rome against the archbishops' decision was liable under the statute of provisors.[179] Audeley's bill even referred to 'the Imperiall crown of this realme'.[180] Many of these points would of course have echoes, not only in the act of appeals itself, but also in how the king's 'great matter' was finally resolved. If responsibility can be apportioned solely on the basis of drafting legislation alone – an implication inherent in Elton's reasoning – then perhaps Audeley deserves similar credit to that accorded to Cromwell by Elton. After all, he was not only involved in the appeals act, but Audeley also amended or drafted several other bills connected with the Anglo-papal schism, including a draft of the Commons Supplication in 1532.[181]

Where Cromwell did play a formative part in the appeals act, however, was in the detail of the act itself. Although Elton was greatly concerned with the novel theory of empire he believed it proclaimed, it is all too easily overlooked that the appeals act was intended for a fundamentally practical purpose. It prevented all 'Causes of Matrimony and Divorces, rightes of Tithes Oblacions, and Obvencions' from going to Rome, in order to inhibit Catherine of Aragon from appealing there and ensuring that the validity of her marriage to the king would be settled in England.[182] As a result, a new appeals procedure was needed to replace the one the act revoked; unsurprisingly, much of the act outlined the process intended to replace the traditional appeals procedure to the papal curia. Judging by the extent of Cromwell's corrections and amendments, it was with these details that he was mainly concerned. The drafts containing the famous preamble and the justification for the act only possess a few additions in Cromwell's hand, and these mainly served to tighten or reword some of the phrasing.[183] By contrast, several detailed alterations were made by him to the new appeals process erected by the act.[184] In one draft, for instance, an entire clause was devised and added by Cromwell specifying that matters affecting the king or his realm were now to go to the convocation of the province concerned.[185] As Elton noted, it was only when Cromwell got to work on the procedural part of the act 'that real changes were made'.[186] Yet, despite forensically outlining Cromwell's changes, Elton did not grasp their significance.[187] It was the administrative detail of the new appeals system that patently occupied most of Cromwell's time; and this is entirely understandable given the immediate need to provide a system to replace the existing papal one. If responsibility for any aspect of the act in restraint of appeals can be apportioned solely to Cromwell, then it should be the administrative and technical details, rather than an intangible theory of national sovereignty.

Once the appeals act was in place, Archbishop Cranmer could finally pronounce on the validity of Henry VIII's marriage. A court was held by Cranmer at Dunstable for this purpose, and Cromwell was kept regularly informed of its proceedings.[188] Once a verdict declaring the king's marriage invalid had been reached, Cromwell then began preparations for the coronation of Henry's new queen, Anne Boleyn. Spread over four days, and including a water pageant, processions through the City of London and a great banquet in Westminster Hall, the queen's coronation must have been an operational and logistical nightmare.[189] Hall records that 'great preparacion was made for all thynges necessary for suche a noble triumph'.[190] Cromwell himself was engaged with much of this. One of his memoranda from 1533 reminded him 'to devyse for the coronacyon and to see presendmenttes for the same',[191] while several letters suggest that he was arranging for people's attendance, and ordering the preparation of presents.[192] The reconstruction of new royal apartments at the Tower of London, where the king and queen would lodge during these festivities, had also been overseen by him.[193] He even recorded 'the coronacyon of queen Anne' on his list of things done since entering the king's service.[194] Of course, Cromwell was not single-handedly responsible for all these preparations. Hundreds of people were involved with the coronation, including many of the City of London's guilds and corporations.[195] Nevertheless, Sir Anthony Browne, writing to Cromwell only days after these events, noted that

> the honorablle crowen[ing] of the Qwens grace, wych was so honorably doon, that lycke has not byn sene be fore … was not a lyttyl to your prayes [praise] in my myend / for I am sewer ther was none that had the payen and trabell that yow … have.[196]

Judging by Browne's remarks, Cromwell was thought responsible for much of the coronation's success. The event is further proof, therefore, that Cromwell was by this stage Henry's factotum, as well as being yet another testimony to his organisational abilities.

Although by 1533 Cromwell was overseeing almost every aspect of the king's 'great matter', it is important to note that other royal councillors were also highly active in these affairs, and, more often than not, were working closely with one another. From the very beginning, Henry VIII's quest for a divorce had been something of a 'team' effort. Virginia Murphy has shown that a group of scholars was working on arguments in support of the king's position as early as 1527, while Guy has argued that a similar group was behind the production of the *Collectanea satis copiosa*, a piece of research used to substantiate many of Henry VIII's bold claims towards the English Church.[197] That collaboration continued, and was pervasive among many of the king's closest servants and councillors, is neatly illustrated by a letter sent to Cromwell in 1533. In this, Thomas Audeley informed him how my lord of norffolk required me to wryte to you / For the Instrument concernyng the opynyons of doctors And many lerned men in the Kynges great case he hath wrytten to my lord of Canterbury but it seyeth by report of my lord of Wilteshire that he hath them no[t] And if they be not with you / then they be supposed to be at yorke place or ells with doctor lee . . . the kynges pleasure ys that they shod with spede be sent to my lorde of Wynchester And if ye can Fynde them . . . send them to the court with spede.[198]

What is noteworthy here is the high level of involvement of several notable figures – Norfolk, Audeley, Cromwell, Cranmer, Wiltshire, Lee and Gardiner – all of whom were so closely embroiled in Henry's 'great matter' that no one was quite sure who possessed the sought-after material. Another letter to Cromwell from Thomas Bedyll, suggesting that the *Determination of the Universities* be looked over by Gardiner and Edward Foxe before being sent overseas for diplomatic purposes, also reinforces the impression of royal servants working together.[199] So too does a brief correspondence between Norfolk and Cranmer that shows both the duke and Cromwell seeking the writings of learned men,[200] and a letter of 1533 from Cromwell to Audeley in which he instructed the lord chancellor to make 'the ratificacions' to the act of annates.[201] The dispatches of the Imperial ambassador Eustace Chapuys also revealed that between 1531 and 1534 the likes of Norfolk, Gardiner and Wiltshire – among many others – were constantly working to promote Henry VIII's divorce. This is significant because it helps to place Cromwell's role within its proper context. Since 1532 Cromwell had been an important member of the council, contributing heavily to the efforts of resolving the king's 'great matter'. By early 1533 he had the oversight of the whole affair. But throughout, others were also closely involved. The divorce campaign was not simply a matter of king and minister working together; it had been very much a collective effort.

Justifying Schism

Alongside his work drafting the statutes which would legislate the break with Rome, Cromwell was also closely involved in the propaganda campaign that attempted to justify it. Since the beginning of his efforts to secure a divorce, the king had employed scholars and polemicists to produce written arguments in favour of his position. These were intended to persuade prominent elements of society, including leading churchmen and lawyers, of the righteousness of Henry's case.[202] Once the king's threats against the papacy and the independence of the Church intensified, the battle for hearts and minds also needed to extend to the broader population in order to eradicate support for papal authority and minimise or prevent domestic unrest. Much of the literature justifying Henry's actions was therefore dispersed more widely. Henry Falsted referred to 'certeyn bokes of the kynges print . . . putt forth among the kinges louyng subiectes' in March 1533,[203] while proclamations outlining the act of appeals were to be made throughout the realm, and the act itself was printed and pinned on every church door.[204] Cromwell's own memoranda also hint at a preaching campaign he was orchestrating, with 'Deuyces' planned 'for the Bisshoppes to set fourth and preache the kings grete cause and also ayenst the censures' from Rome.[205]

A second audience in need of persuasion was the international one. In breaking with Rome, England could have become dangerously isolated, and vulnerable to possible retaliation by Catherine of Aragon's nephew, Charles V. Francis I of France was therefore courted for support in an attempt to counteract this threat. The *Determinations of the Universities* favourable to the king's cause were sent abroad for these purposes in 1533.[206] In the same year Thomas Bedyll told Cromwell that there were 'ii or iii thinges' which would need amending in a paper they intended to send abroad to 'animat the frenche king'.[207] In December 1533 the council also devised a set of articles asserting the invalidity of Henry's first marriage and the right for the matter to be settled in England.[208] These were distributed with 'profusion' at the English court, and shown to the Scottish ambassador before being translated into French and sent abroad for wider circulation.[209] These domestic and foreign propagandistic efforts have already received some attention from historians.[210] Of interest here is not the propaganda itself, but Cromwell's role in the production and promulgation of this material.

In the early 1530s it was necessary for the government to take an antipapal stance in order to defend what Henry VIII was doing. Unsurprisingly, the Crown was therefore often required to turn to men who held radical religious beliefs in order to produce literature in support. In some circles, Cromwell's backing and protection of such men have been taken as proof that he shared their religious beliefs. In fact, this support had less to do with Cromwell's own religious outlook than with the immediate need to justify the Anglo-papal schism. It will be recalled, for instance, that in late 1530 and early 1531 Cromwell's agent Stephen Vaughan was operating in Flanders, under the king's approval, attempting to persuade William Tyndale to return to England.[211] What is interesting is that Vaughan appears to have had a wider mandate, having been instructed to keep both Cromwell and the king informed of other written works circulating in Flanders, and of any religious radicals who might be of use when seeking to justify Henry's 'great matter'. In January 1531, alongside an update on his progress with Tyndale, Vaughan sent Cromwell 'The dyaloge of Okham', something which would shortly be used in the government's propaganda efforts in England.[212] Similarly, in May Vaughan wrote to inform the king of a work by Luther 'lately put forthe . . . agenst themperor in the German tongue, whiche I wold cause to be translated into laten'. Vaughan added that 'in it wer many thinges to be seen', and he promised to 'send it to your magestie, if I knew your gracious pleasure'.[213] That Vaughan sought Henry's permission underlines that what he and Cromwell were doing had royal sanction. That Vaughan received the king's affirmative response via Cromwell also illustrates that king and minister were working together.

By the time Vaughan received the king's answer via Cromwell, however, he could no longer obtain Luther's book. Instead, he offered Cromwell another one 'by melanchton in the laten tonge', adding 'I wold gladly sende suche thinges to his highnes, but I am enformed he loketh not vpon them hym self but commyttethe them to other'.[214] It is important to acknowledge that Vaughan was fearful that the king might be swayed by those about him who would be unenthusiastic about receiving a Lutheran work. Nevertheless, he continued to seek out other potentially useful works on Cromwell's behalf, telling him in June that he would write 'more largely concernyng all these that write and theyr books by my next lettres'.[215] In November he supplied Cromwell with Tyndale's *The Exposition of the First Epistle of St John* and a work by the Lutheran Robert Barnes, both of which were 'to be by yow puted to the kynges magesty'.[216] It is likely that Vaughan was hopeful that Cromwell would lend these his good word; Vaughan was undoubtedly evangelical, and in one letter he even requested that Cromwell 'healpe that doctor barnes might declare thopinions of his booke bifore the kynges magestye'.[217] Yet there seems little reason to doubt that Cromwell was operating with the king's broad approval. It is of note that when Barnes's book did not reach Cromwell, Vaughan was suspicious that its bearer either dared not deliver it, 'or ells to pike a thanke delyuered [it] to the dukes grace of Norfolk / hauyng other lettres written to his grace from hens'.[218] This might be read as an indication that Vaughan thought Norfolk unsympathetic to such views, and keen to prevent them circulating. But this might better be taken as an indication that Cromwell was not alone among Henry's councillors in seeking out works of potential use. Vaughan's sending Cromwell another copy, along with instructions that if the first turned up he should give it to Lord Chancellor More, would seem surprising if he and Cromwell were trying to operate in a clandestine fashion.

Cromwell's efforts in 1531 to recruit the religious radical John Frith offer a clearer picture of the minister's intentions when dealing with reformers. Frith was undoubtedly a staunch evangelical, and would be burned at the stake in 1533 for denying the corporeal presence of Christ during Mass.[219] In 1529, however, he had written *The Revelation of the Antichrist*, which offered 'a comparison between "Christ's acts and our holy father the Pope's", inevitably greatly to the latter's disadvantage'.[220] It is not difficult to see how the author of such an anti-papal tract might be attractive to a government seeking to discredit the papacy. Frith was therefore another of those whom Vaughan contacted while in Antwerp in early 1531, and he sent letters to the king 'towching a yong man being in these parties named Frithe' in May.[221] Cromwell was again working closely with the king as his executive agent on this matter. He informed Vaughan that

> As touching Frith mencyoned in your said lettres the kings highnes heryng tell of his towardnes in good lettres and lernyng ~~dothe Regrete and~~ *moche* lament that he should in such wise as he doth set fourth shew and applye his lerning and doctrine in the semynacyon ~~and sowing~~ *and sewing* such euill seedes of dampnable and detestable heresies / mayntening bolstring and aduancyng the venomous and pestyferous works erronyous and sedycyous opynyons of the saide Tyndale.[222]

Yet Cromwell added that the king thought that Frith was not totally lost to heresy, and '*moche desyryng the reconsylyacyon of the sayd fryth*', had instructed him '*to wryt vnto yow that ye ... will* with your frendelie persuasions ... counseull and aduyse the saide Fryth ... to retorne ... *unto his natif cuntrey wher he assurydyly shall Fynde the kynges highness most mercyfful*'.[223]

Although Vaughan was successful in his attempts to persaude Frith to return to England,[224] the intention of having him write in support of the king's 'great matter' did not go according to plan. In late 1531 Frith published *A Disputation of Purgatory*, which was quickly blacklisted as

heresy,[225] and by October 1532 he was a prisoner in the Tower.[226] Edmund
Walsingham, the lieutenant there, wrote to Cromwell on 21 October
informing him of the condition of several prisoners, and his comments on
Frith point to Cromwell's own attitude. Walsingham felt that Frith 'lackyth
nott wytt nor plesunte tonge [but] hys lernynge passyth my jugement Sir
as ye sayd hytt were greate pytte to lose hym yf he may be reconsylyd'.[227] Both
Walsingham and Cromwell were apparently impressed by Frith's erudition,
yet what is striking is that Cromwell felt he was only of use if he could be
'reconsylyd', that is, persuaded to recant his wider beliefs. The significant
point here, then, is that, whatever private sympathies Cromwell may have
harboured, he was prepared to follow the king's lead on the terms under
which reformers would be tolerated and utilised by the Crown.

During the early 1530s Cromwell also supported a number of scholars
who would produce propaganda in support of the king. In December 1531,
for instance, John Hastings remarked how 'yit hathe pleside you to be so
gude to me that ye haue gote me a rowme yn the kings college in oxford off
the kings grace'.[228] The following year he reminded Cromwell that 'y
promyste to wrytte sumwhatt in the kynges matter . . . ye shall haue yit . . .
sumtyme thys weyke or the nexte att the ferthyste'.[229] Cromwell paid
William Marshall for the production of the anti-papal tracts the 'Donation
of Constantine' and the *Defensor pacis.*[230] S. W. Haas has also claimed that
Cromwell was 'almost certainly involved' with the treatise *A Document of the
Year 1531 on the Subject of the Pope's Supremacy,*[231] and with several tracts
delivered to convocation in February 1531.[232] Although there is no evidence
connecting Cromwell to these works, the link is at least plausible given that
his earliest involvement in the attacks on the Church saw him working
with Stephen Vaughan to obtain useful writings which might support
Henry's position. It was George Boleyn, viscount Rochford, however, who
introduced these works in convocation, underlining once again that
Cromwell was still at that point a middle-ranking councillor.[233]

Haas more credibly links Cromwell with the printing of the *Disputatio
inter clericum et militem* in mid-1531.[234] The *Disputatio* had emerged in
France during the thirteenth century, as a result of Philip the Fair's clash
with Pope Boniface VIII. By the sixteenth century, the *Disputatio* was
mistakenly attributed to William of Ockham.[235] Stephen Vaughan had
sent Cromwell 'The dyaloge of Okham' at the end of January 1531 as part
of his efforts to secure useful books.[236] By June of that year Chapuys was
reporting to Charles V that 'After all the . . . defying of Papal authority . . .

these people have only caused a small book to be printed in the form of a dialogue'.[237] There is clearly a strong likelihood that this was the same work. Admittedly, the *Disputatio* was primarily an anti-clerical tract, which called for the clergy to contribute to the defence of the realm, and advocated that if they did not, the privileges of the Church should be revoked by the secular ruler. But the 1531 and 1533 versions of this tract were deliberately edited to 'bolster the royal *imperium*'.[238] Whether Cromwell had much role in its printing and promulgation, beyond acting as a middle-man between Vaughan in Antwerp and the royal court in England, is unclear.

Cromwell's involvement with Henry VIII's *A Glasse of Truthe* the following year, however, cannot be doubted.[239] Unlike the *Disputatio*, which was initially published in Latin before being reprinted in English, *A Glasse* was published in the vernacular from the outset, and was clearly intended for a much wider domestic audience. Along with the *Determination of the Universities*, published in November 1531,[240] *A Glasse of Truthe* was the most significant piece of propaganda produced by the government during the early 1530s. It outlined to its readers how the pope did not have the authority to dispense from divine Scripture, or the right to settle a matter in Rome which should be heard in England. Instead, *A Glasse* advocated that parliament and the English archbishops should resolve the royal divorce.[241] This work was most likely in production by mid-1532;[242] on 17 September Cromwell was written to by Richard Croke, the sub-dean at Oxford:

> after my departing vnto to yow Bartelot the printer shewed me that master Goodrycke shulde aduertyse hym to aduertyse the kinge off certayne errors in the glasse of treuthe how beyt Bertelat tolde me that he wolde not ... forasmoche as that he had mouyd the kinge in sutche mater aforetyme and perceuyd that his grace was not contente therewith.[243]

Cromwell was evidently closely involved with its production because Croke added, 'I thynke yt better to get ouht [*sic*] by policye the thynges that master goodryke noteth whiche I douht [doubt] not but yowr wysdome can right wel do'.[244] Most likely Cromwell had played some role in organising its printing. Print was a medium with which he was already familiar, having arranged for the production of four thousand briefs from the king's printer on behalf of a man from Boston in 1523.[245] A second letter from Croke also suggests that Cromwell was giving direction on *A Glasse of Truthe*'s distribution, having told the sub-dean to disperse copies at Oxford in order to persuade members of the university of the merits of the king's case.[246]

Once again, it is important to acknowledge that Cromwell was not alone in producing material which could be used to justify the royal divorce and the break with Rome. The *Collectanea satis copiosa* and the *Determination of the Universities* are two of the most obvious examples of literature compiled by other royal servants. It is also interesting to note that English diplomats abroad were instructed, like Stephen Vaughan, to source foreign works of potential use. Nicholas Hawkins, Henry's ambassador to the Low Countries, recollected to the king that 'it was youre hines commandement, that we shuld seke owte suche bookis, as be found here de potestate papae'.[247] In December 1532 he sent the king 'for youer Inglishe Dialogue [*A Glass of Truthe*], a Dialogue for in smale eloquence latinised', while in 1533 he reported a book he had seen in Barcelona with an exposition on the crucial passage of Leviticus, which was central to Henry's divorce.[248]

Nevertheless, by mid-1532 Cromwell was notably involved in the government's propaganda efforts. In May of that year Dr John London, warden of New College, Oxford, had informed him that he had made 'serche in all the libraries in our contrie' for further learned opinions on the validity of the king's marriage. His subsequent comment that Cromwell had 'herde many great lernyd men spek in thys cause and ... redd manye of theyr doings wherby your gudde masterschipp ys riperlye instructe in thys mater' underlines that Cromwell was now close to the centre of attempts to justify the king's position.[249] By the beginning of 1533, Cromwell was managing this battle for heart and minds. Thomas Berthelet, the king's printer, felt that Cromwell was a figure who might be in need of his particular skills, asking him in January of that year to 'accept me ... to your mastershipes seruice'.[250] Among the papers in Cromwell's possession was 'a boke resityng the powers of the pope made and noted with figures and handes' and 'iii rolles knyt with a red silke point concernyng the kynges matter', as well as many others which were produced to justify the king's position.[251] The actions of Cromwell's friend Sir George Lawson, treasurer of Berwick, are also interesting. In May 1534 he had come across 'a table hangyng apon the walle' in York Cathedral on which were inscribed 'the reigne[s] of diuers kinges of this realme'. Among these Lawson had 'found one lyne of a king that took this kingdom of the pope by tribute to hold of the churche of roome'. That Lawson sent Cromwell 'the title therof as it was in the said table' underlines that contemporaries saw him as a figure responsible for collecting useful material.[252] It is also significant that when Nicholas Hawkins sent the king foreign books on the pope's power in November 1532, he added that 'Crumwol' would need 'to finde an interpreter' for this work.[253] Evidently, although many were involved in the efforts to collect literature, Cromwell was perceived to be at the centre of these operations. Significantly, this would explain why Christopher Mont was at work in Cromwell's house translating foreign texts.[254] That he was paid by Cromwell using the king's money confirms that these translations had official sanction.[255]

How effective was the propaganda campaign that Cromwell was helping to co-ordinate? To such a question, no straightforward answer can be given. It is true that Richard Croke told Cromwell that when he had dispersed *A Glasse of Truthe* at Oxford, 'many by the reding off thys boke hathe here alteryd theyr stouburne and affectionate mynde towarde the contrarye'.[256] But Chapuys reported that the Scottish ambassador was unimpressed with the anti-papal tract which Cromwell had shown him in January 1534, and claimed that rather than justifying himself in the eyes of his people, Henry had only succeeded in stirring up 'those among his subjects who were a little contaminated by Lutheranism'.[257] Cromwell's preaching campaign, with 'Deuyces' intended 'for the Bisshoppes to set fourth and preache the kings grete cause', was probably the most effective method of getting the government's message across – at least if success is measured by the number of people it reached.[258] Yet it is all too easy to assume that the Crown's propaganda was passively accepted. When Cromwell sent books north to persuade the northern clergy to pass conclusions in their convocation, Cuthbert Marshall told him, 'i was not mouyd be [the] argumentes or reasoning' contained in them.[259] As one historian has rightly noted, there has often been a tendency to see the sixteenth-century audience 'in a patronising way as mere objects to be manipulated, rather than as human beings to be coaxed and persuaded'.[260] In many cases, the king's subjects actually opposed what he was doing, and, by implication, the arguments the Crown put forward to justify it. Other, more coercive methods were therefore needed to ensure that the break with Rome was successful.

Enforcing Schism

Although it might appear with hindsight that the revolutionary changes of the early 1530s were implemented with surprisingly little widespread opposition, at the time the Crown understandably feared resistance. Another of Cromwell's multifarious responsibilities during these years was therefore to enforce the changes that he had helped bring about, and to eliminate opposition. His efforts when doing so have sometimes been seen as the opening stages of a reign of terror spanning the entire decade. R. B. Merriman claimed that 'Early in 1532 Cromwell began to create a system of espionage, the most effective that England had ever seen ... It was impossible to tell who the government spies were: impossible to know when or against whom the next accusation would be made.'[261] This was a view shared by A. D. Innes and Peter Wilding,[262] but one which would be contested by Elton, who, in his general rehabilitation of Cromwell, denounced the disdain of earlier historians and presented the minister in a much more favourable light:

> Cromwell wanted, not to kill men, but to bring them to a better condi-
> tion, and his undoubted ruthlessness against genuine opposition owed
> more to the pressure of his positive convictions than to lust for power ...
> It was because he had a vision of an England reformed in body and soul
> that he proceeded as he did.[263]

Enforcement during the Cromwellian decade is therefore an area which has received a good deal of attention from historians. Yet by delving deeper into the minister's early career, fresh light can be shed on the coercive methods he employed for such enforcement, as well as offering further glimpses into Cromwell's own character. When considering this, the well-studied resistance of individuals such as Thomas More, John Fisher and the Nun of Kent need not be repeated. Instead, the focus here is once again on the more quotidian aspects of government enforcement, and the difficulties which Cromwell and the Crown faced in relation to the Anglo-papal schism.

Cromwell's role in enforcing the break with Rome is amply demonstrated by the contents of his correspondence. Reports of seditious speech and copies of books attacking the king were sent to him.[264] He was also kept informed on prisoners held in the Tower, and maintained a close eye on the licensing of preachers.[265] Nevertheless, Merriman's accusation that Cromwell erected a system of espionage to eradicate dissent is largely unfounded. Although it is true that in July 1533 Cromwell told the king that 'the Freres obseruantes that were with the prynces dowaiger ... were first espied at ware by such espialles as I leyed for the purpose', this, along with Norfolk's and Cromwell's responsibility for sending spies to Scotland when relations with the Scots began to sour, are the only documented instances where Cromwell used spies.[266] During the early 1530s Cromwell was written to by a variety of people who acted as informants, and no system, or even any obvious affiliation, emerges from this correspondence. Instead, the picture that forms is one of a government relying, as it always had, on the co-operation of magnates and gentry to maintain order in the regions and report opposition. Such co-operation was of course mutually beneficial for the maintenance of law and order. For instance, Simon Mountfort suggested that the council call up one Richard Howe, who was suspected of 'robyng . . . sertayne churchys', believing that in this way the council would help 'breke suche anest [of thieves] as has not byn sen in a contrey'.[267] Yet what motivated many in the localities to report 'cedycyus & heynous wurdes' spoken 'Ayenst the kynges highness as Ayenst the quenes grace' in the years surrounding the break with Rome was often a sense of allegiance and obligation towards the Crown.[268] When Sir Edward Guildford, lord warden of the Cinque Ports, wrote to Cromwell about a 'lewed prist' who had been examined before the mayor and jurats of Rye, he referred to the words used by the priest 'contrarie to his duetie of his allegiaunce to the kings highenes'.[269] Similarly, when Sir Giles Strangway told Cromwell of people accused of speaking ill of the king and his new queen, he had felt it his 'dewtye . . . to enforme yow as one of the kings moste honorable cowncell'.[270]

Murmurs of dissent in the regions and localities, however, were difficult to eradicate. Cromwell ordered Sir Piers Edgecombe to punish 'by pyllory and stockes in markett places' any person who spoke seditiously or opprobriously about Henry's new queen, and this would have served as a warning as much as a punishment.[271] Yet grumblings in the regions had to be reluctantly tolerated by a government that lacked the means to enforce its position there more thoroughly. In the debate over Cromwell's wider ability to control and direct the efforts of the gentry in the localities, Helen Speight's argument is convincing. She proposes central government had limited control, and that Cromwell often had little choice but to defer enforcement to local governors, who operated with considerable independence.[272] Dissent in the localities was only a significant cause for alarm for those in central government if it became concentrated under local leadership. Regional magnates might provide this, although the nobility presented no such threat during the early 1530s.[273] Priests and friars preaching in villages and towns, and the religious orders more generally, comprised another group capable of inciting a more concentrated level of opposition. This explains why a high number of reports sent to Cromwell during these years were concerned with seditious words spoken by preachers, and with the goings-on at suspect monastic houses.[274] It was also overwhelmingly recalcitrant priests and monks whom Cromwell instructed the Crown's agents to 'put in safe kepyng' or have 'commyttyd . . . to warde'.[275] In April 1534 he instructed one Henry Huttoft and the mayor of Southampton to arrest a friar Observant preaching there, and to send him up to Cromwell in London.[276] Many more priests and monks were sent to him for examination and interrogation.[277] The suspicion must remain, therefore, that dissenting members of the clergy were a significant cause for concern, given both their standing in society and their ability to convey their opinions quickly to a wide audience. The efforts to silence and discredit Elizabeth Barton, the Nun of Kent, are perhaps the most striking illustration of this.[278]

The threat of recalcitrant preaching against the king's 'great matter' explains why the licensing of preachers was something that the government attempted to control as best it could. It is revealing, for instance, that Archbishop Cranmer, having received a request for a licence to preach from the friar Dr John Hisley, wrote to Cromwell asking whether he and the council thought this should be granted.[279] In April 1533 Thomas Bagarde, chancellor of Worcester, also informed Cromwell that William Hubberdyne had 'come to me desyryne me to haue a licence to preach . . . I warraunt you he [will] get no licence off me as long as hyt schall please godde the kynges grace and your maisterschype'.[280] Bagarde had also thought, perhaps mistakenly, that he had Cromwell's 'expresse consent' to inhibit Hugh Latimer from preaching.[281] All this concerned a 'battle of the pulpits' which was underway in Bristol between Hubberdyne and Latimer in April and May 1533, which Cromwell was attempting to control. Latimer, a well-known evangelical, had been appointed to preach there by the mayor of Bristol during Lent and Easter.[282] Yet many had abhorred his preaching against pilgrimages and attacks on the Virgin Mary,[283] and several clerics, notably Dr Edward Powell and Hubberdyne himself, began preaching against him in response. Complaints against both sets of preachers were then sent to Cromwell and the King's Council. Latimer was accused of preaching 'sysmatyke & yrronyous opinions', while Hubberdyne had supposedly attacked the king in his preaching, and defended the pope.[284] Cromwell investigated both parties, and instructed commissioners to research 'the behauynge as well of Latomer as of huberdyn & ther prechyns *& spesyally what wordes hyberdyn schold haue consernyge the kynges hyhe magesty*'.[285] What is striking here is the emphasis that Cromwell placed on what might have been spoken against the king. It gives an indication of the government's principal concerns, and also perhaps hints at an element of insecurity on the Crown's part. Undoubtedly, it was Hubberdyne's support for the papacy and criticism of the king which resulted in him being sent to the Tower in July.[286] Latimer, by contrast, escaped punishment. This was most likely thanks to the support of the Bristol authorities,[287] but also perhaps because the Crown felt he might be of use to them as a supporter of the royal divorce.[288] Meanwhile Cromwell continued to clamp down on those who had preached against Henry, and in August he ordered that Dr Powell be sent to him in London for examination.[289]

There can be no doubt that Cromwell was an extremely effective interrogator. Richard Gwent, a chaplain to the king, remarked in August 1533 that if it were not for Cromwell's 'interogatores' then the Nun of Kent 'wold [haue] confessyd no thyng'.[290] Christopher Hales similarly told Cromwell that he could find nothing to implicate the parson of Aldington with the Nun, and that he found him 'a man of gode Fame'; 'Neuerthelesse', Hales added, 'your industry herin to make the matter opine in gode or evyll, as truthe it is, shalbe moche laudable.'[291] Writing to the king, Cromwell even advocated using torture during an interrogation, remarking that several monks 'wolde confesse sum grete matier if they might be examined as they ought to be that is to sey by paynes'.[292] Such comments might make uneasy reading for modern eyes, but neither Gwent nor Hales reveals any hint of disapproval at Cromwell's interrogatory abilities or methods. This prompts questions about how such activities were understood. Those whom Cromwell wished to examine under 'paynes' were suspected by him of being 'moche gyuen to sedycyon'. Perhaps it was acceptable to use physical force in certain situations, if it ensured obedience, good public order and the harmony of the realm.

One or two of Cromwell's wider practices for combating dissent are also worthy of brief comment. In 1533 he informed the king that two friars had entered the realm with 'pryuy letteres' and intended to meet with Catherine of Aragon. Cromwell's advice was that

in my poore oppynyon it shalbe right well done that thaye might be sent
For by sum trustye persone howbeit yt were best that theye Fyrst sholde

be sufferyd to speke with her [Catherine of Aragon] and suche other of hers as woolde peraduenture delyuer to them anything wherbye theyr Farther practysys might be persayuyd and so thayr cankyrd Intenttes might be therbye dysyfferyd.[293]

Although there is no evidence that Cromwell was a disciple of Machiavelli, as some historians have alleged, there was clearly a degree of hard-nosed calculation in his counsel that the friars should be allowed to make contact, reveal additional information and perhaps implicate themselves further. In the same letter he also reported a London merchant who was assisting the friars, adding, 'yf it be trew he ys worthye to suffer to make other beware'.[294] Clearly Cromwell saw the benefit of using forceful punishment to coerce people more widely.

Did Cromwell deal lawfully with those whom he suspected of sedition or treason? Although historians disagree on the tyrannical nature of the regime during the Cromwellian decade, most are in agreement that the numbers executed for treason between 1532 and 1540 were not 'unduly high'.[295] (We might ask, however, exactly what constitutes an acceptable number of people tortured or killed?) Cromwell himself certainly spoke 'amyable wordys' before the council on behalf of Richard Masters, parson of Aldington, over his involvement with the Nun of Kent, and obtained a pardon for him.[296] The implication here must be that, having examined the parson, Cromwell did not think there was sufficient evidence to condemn him. Nevertheless, to conclude that Cromwell dealt judiciously with those suspected of crimes would leave an overly favourable impression of him. Cromwell's letter to Bishop Fisher, who had failed to report the revelations of the Nun of Kent in 1534 and was suspected of sympathising with her, was threatening and menacing in tone, and makes uncomfortable reading.[297] A far more damning reflection of Cromwell's willingness to act unscrupulously in order to secure obedience was his close involvement with the Crown's attempts to enhance the treason legislation, which culminated in the new treason act of 1534, and extended its scope to include words spoken maliciously against the king.[298] Indeed, it is hard to avoid the conclusion that in doing this the government was altering the law to suit its own immediate needs. True, in a handful of fifteenth-century cases words had already been construed as constituting treason.[299] But the act of 1534 made this explicit; whether words spoken proved the intent to compass or imagine the king's death had previously been a matter for judges to interpret.[300] The act of 1534 removed any ambiguity in the law greatly to the Crown's advantage, and potentially made a mere passing comment punishable by death. Contemporaries in parliament were concerned enough by this to insist that the words must be spoken 'maliciously' against the king to constitute treason.[301] On Cromwell's fall the act was also held against him by some, and it is pertinent to acknowledge that in 1547 much of the treason act was repealed by Protector Somerset.[302] Cromwell's role in this somewhat repressive extension of the Crown's powers therefore requires some comment.

It was once thought that the earliest version of the government's treason legislation, prepared towards the end of 1530 for the parliamentary session in early 1531, was corrected by Cromwell.[303] Examination of the drafts, however, reveals that Elton was correct to argue that these alterations are in the hand of Thomas Audeley, not Cromwell, and were probably made in the Michaelmas term of 1531, when both he and Cromwell began to work on the earlier legislation following instructions from the king.[304] The changes made at this stage were hardly innovative, and for some unknown reason the legislation was not brought before parliament.[305] The first hints at an intent to extend treason explicitly to cover words did not emerge until the drafting stage of the bill of succession in early 1534. One of Cromwell's memoranda concerns discussions he had held with the king's legal counsel over this act. It reveals that, with regards to the 'woord wrytyng or dede', these legal experts 'be contentyd that woord dede & writing shalbe treson And woorde to be mysprisyon'.[306] This is significant because it suggests that words constituting treason was something that Henry's senior legal advisers had initially rejected; and the succession act of March 1534 indeed laid out that verbal attacks on the king were only 'mesprision of treason' and punishable by imprisonment and the loss of possessions.[307]

The treason act of 1534 was passed only months after this, but now declared that anyone who 'malicyously' spoke ill of the king and queen, their heirs, or called Henry a 'heretyke scismatike Tiraunt ynfidell or Usurper of the Crowne' was guilty of high treason, punishable by death.[308] Cromwell was put forward by Elton as the person who had proposed extending the definition of treason to include the spoken word,[309] but the evidence for this is far from convincing, and largely rests on a slip of Cromwell's pen.[310] It is far from clear whether one individual was responsible for this particular element of the act, and it would be more reasonable to attribute these changes to a continuing dialogue between the king and his legal advisers. Cromwell was certainly closely involved, and corrected parts of the various treason bills drafted between 1531 and 1534.[311] But even a cursory glance at the surviving drafts makes it plain that the hand of Thomas Audeley is far more evident on those prepared in late 1533, when words were declared treason.[312] It was Audeley, for instance, who removed a phrase which would have made it treason to have spoken words that caused 'derogacion of the kinges honor' or that might have brought the royal personages 'in hatered or euyll opynyon', when the legislation was returned to in late 1533.[313] Audeley replaced this with a clause making words deemed dangerous to the unity of the realm, misprision of treason, if they were not already classed by the act as treason.[314] This clause was later dropped, but such detailed legal amendments highlight that Cromwell made only a single and extremely minor alteration, moving the date on which the 1533 legislation would become active to 'January next ensuying'.[315] Cromwell's most notable alterations were to the earlier drafts prepared in late 1531 and early 1532.[316] His most significant contribution seems to have been the removal of a passage from the aborted 1532 bill which offered a reward to informers.[317] This had been suggested by the king, but was clearly impractical in that it almost invited false accusations.[318] Despite Elton's assertions, therefore, the strong likelihood is that Cromwell actually played very little part in formulating the treason legislation in 1533, when the crucial changes were made. Instead, it was Thomas Audeley, a man who had received formal legal training, who seems to have played a far more significant role in drafting the legislation. Perhaps a likely explanation of events is that during 1531 and 1532 Cromwell and Audeley were working on this legislation together, which explains why Cromwell's hand is to be found more copiously on the earlier drafts. The legislation was then returned to in mid- to late 1533, by which time Cromwell was undeniably established as Henry's chief minister. In this role he probably had less time to attend to the technicalities of drafting an act, and left it to the more legally minded Audeley. These considerations show that apportioning sole responsibility for the act is unrealistic: both men must have shared it – along, perhaps, with the king.

Conclusion

In this chapter, the first comprehensive account of Cromwell's role in the break with Rome has been established. Despite the considerable consensus of historians who have thought otherwise, Cromwell was not notably involved in the attacks against the Church in late 1530, and only became fully involved with the king's 'great matter' in 1532. Through sheer hard work, efficiency and thoroughness, it was Cromwell who helped devise and put in place the necessary legislation which would help Henry VIII to end his marriage to Catherine. Cromwell has therefore emerged from this chapter less as the formulator of the Crown's policy, and more as its principal executor. Interestingly, this was how Cromwell himself recollected these events in 1536, when he told the Imperial ambassador that he had 'paved the way' for the king to marry Anne.[319] When performing his duties Cromwell was often responding to events – such as the Supplication against the Ordinaries – rather than implementing some preconceived plan. And instead of being the mastermind or architect behind the submission of the clergy, Cromwell appears instead to have been the beneficiary of its fall-out. Significantly, Cromwell has also been shown here working alongside others when drafting many of the acts which enabled the Anglo-papal schism. Indeed, one of the most important conclusions to emerge from this chapter is that Thomas Audeley played a much bigger part in this than has previously been acknowledged. Audeley's role was actually very similar to the one Elton claimed for Cromwell.

It has been a central argument of this book, however, that no single responsibility undertaken by Cromwell was key to his securing the king's confidence, but rather that Cromwell's ever-increasing workload saw him gradually emerge as Henry's factotum. The analysis of Cromwell's role in the break with Rome offered here has neither modified nor altered this conclusion. Instead, it has reinforced it, by demonstrating further responsibilities that he oversaw on the king's behalf which contributed to Cromwell becoming the king's leading councillor. All that remains to be seen is exactly when Cromwell succeeded in achieving that position. It is to this question that the conclusion of the book will now turn.

CONCLUSION

IN THIS BOOK, THE full extent of Thomas Cromwell's life, responsibilities and interests between 1485 and 1534 has been examined for the first time. The Cromwell who emerges from the study of these years was not the fervent evangelical, Machiavellian schemer or revolutionary administrator, whom Foxe, Merriman and Elton respectively emphasised. Instead, Cromwell appears as a middle-ranking lawyer and merchant, who moved, like many figures of the legal profession during this period, into the royal service. He then went on to prove himself to be a highly competent and efficient servant of the Crown. In short, placing Cromwell's early life and career under the microscope reveals him to have been a much less unique figure than previously thought.

It has also become clear that Cromwell emerged as Henry VIII's chief minister because of his ability to cope with the ever-increasing workload that he had gradually been entrusted with. Far from being a visionary, Cromwell was the conventional Tudor man-of-business, distinguished from his peers perhaps only by his aptitude and skills; and who was less central to the momentous events surrounding the break with Rome than has previously been claimed. Such an interpretation runs counter to the longstanding and widely accepted view that those events were crucial to Cromwell becoming chief minister. Instead, it has been shown here that if any one aspect of Cromwell's work for the king was responsible for his meteoric rise, then it was probably his duties concerning Crown lands. It was this that had enabled his transition into the king's service in the first place, and it was this that continued to consume the majority of Cromwell's attention during his initial year as a royal councillor. Managing these lands allowed Cromwell to demonstrate his skills to the king.

The most obvious of these skills was Cromwell's organisational efficiency. Again and again, Cromwell has emerged from this book as a highly competent and efficient royal servant: somebody who got things done and resolved problems quickly. Alongside this, and closely linked to it, were Cromwell's administrative and financial talents. These were acquired and sharpened during his careers as a lawyer and merchant, and as Cardinal Wolsey's man of business in the 1520s. The same skills were then exhibited during his work on the Crown's lands.

Of course, other factors also contributed to Cromwell's entry and rise in the king's service. Throughout the period of Wolsey's disgrace, Cromwell relied enormously on the goodwill of those close to the king for his survival. Luck naturally played its part, with Henry VIII needing someone who was familiar with Wolsey's college lands to manage their legal transfer into his possession. Once in the royal service, Cromwell then worked co-operatively and effectively with other royal ministers, a point that has often been obscured in studies that adopt a narrow focus purely on the minister. All of these factors and qualities contributed to Cromwell's rise, but perhaps none were more significant than his competence and efficiency. It was these skills that resulted in more and more work being entrusted to him, including the management of the English Church and the routine tasks of government. Gradually, through the accumulation of this enormous workload, Cromwell emerged as Henry VIII's chief minister.

But when exactly did Cromwell attain this position? Previous studies have tended to circumvent attempts at pinpointing when Cromwell became Henry's factotum. Most allude to his rise as part of a general narrative of the break with Rome.[1] The month of May 1532, following the surrender of the clergy and Cromwell's supposed triumph over More and Gardiner, is a frequently implied date of significance.[2] Merriman opted for the beginning of 1533, as did Robertson, although both felt his position was secured much earlier.[3] Guy has even suggested a notably later date, claiming that Cromwell only 'reached the summit of his career . . . after Anne Boleyn's fall' in May 1536, with the 'putsch' of that year supposedly giving Cromwell 'the pre-eminent ascendancy he had hitherto lacked'.[4] Elton has probably offered the most definite dating, but he very much hedged his bets, and subsequently changed his mind. In 1949, for instance, Elton was arguing that Cromwell emerged as Henry's chief minister around April 1533, following his success with the act of appeals.[5] In 1953 he repeated this claim but immediately qualified it by adding that Cromwell 'had been very nearly that for about a year', being 'supreme' in the king's 'circle of advisers on policy' from early 1532.[6] In an article the following year, Elton then suggested that the duke of Norfolk's use of the term 'empire' in January 1531 'Possibly . . . reflects the beginning of Cromwell's real influence'.[7] By the late 1970s, however, Elton was claiming that Cromwell was influencing policy as early as the middle of 1530.[8] Then, in one of his final pieces on Cromwell in 1991, Elton implied that Cromwell became the king's chief minister in May 1532, having won 'the battle for ascendancy in the king's Council'.[9]

Here, a slightly different date is offered to those given above. A letter from Philip Champernon suggests that as late as the end of July 1532 Cromwell's standing with Henry had not notably changed. Champernon was writing to Sir George Carew about treasonous activities that he wanted declared to the king and his councillors. Of interest here are his instructions that if Carew 'cannott speke with my lord marques / thens I wyll desyr yow / to schew thys letter . . . to my lord of norffolke / or master Cromwell / or master controllerr'.[10] What seems revealing is that Champernon did not specify that Cromwell alone should be informed; he listed a number of prominent figures, which might suggest that Cromwell was not yet seen as Henry's factotum. This deduction is also supported by Cromwell's own correspondence with the king. Six letters sent from Cromwell to Henry VIII survive for the period 1531 to April 1534. Two of these were sent in May and June 1532, the commonly asserted point of Cromwell's ascendancy. Both are notably short, and the matters on which Cromwell wrote can hardly be described as high policy.[11] At this point, Cromwell was merely receiving general news from abroad and summarising this briefly for the king. By contrast, a letter Cromwell sent to Henry in September was somewhat longer, and begins to hint that they were now working in closer proximity.[12] True, the subject matter still appears to be relatively minor, but Cromwell can at least be seen implementing the king's instructions. The remaining letters, all sent from July 1533 onwards, confirm that Cromwell was by then executing high policy. He was interrogating monks, dealing with the threat posed by the Nun of Kent and reporting affairs in parliament.[13] All this suggests that Cromwell's position did not alter until some point between September 1532 and July 1533.

A perceptible change in Cromwell's position is indeed detectable at the beginning of October. It was during that month that he accompanied the

king to Calais and Boulogne for his meeting with Francis I.[14] That
Cromwell was part of the king's entourage suggests in itself that he was by
then indispensable to Henry VIII. This point is confirmed not only by
evidence that Cromwell could now be found amending the royal warrant
ordering provisions for the trip, but also by the observations of Cromwell's
close associates.[15] When making arrangements for accommodation in
Calais, Christopher Hales revealingly remarked to Cromwell that 'consid-
eryng that *ye must nedes haue dayly accesse vnto the kynges persone* ye shall ...
lye in a Frendes house of myne where no persone shall inquyet you'.[16] On
11 October Thomas Audeley wrote informing Cromwell that the king
would receive letters detailing the council's work in England, before adding,
'I do not dowt but that ye shal haue knowlegg by the sight of the same
lettres'.[17] What is striking here is that both men now recognised that
Cromwell was working closely with Henry. According to Hales, Cromwell
had 'dayle accesse', while Audeley thought that the two were now so close
that Cromwell was shown the king's correspondence.

Other men were also aware of Cromwell's elevated position and
increasing favour. Thomas Winter, Wolsey's illegitimate son, requested
Cromwell's help on 20 October, believing that Cromwell was 'now placed
in that position which I and all your friends have long wished for'.[18]
Thomas Alvard remarked to Cromwell on 2 November that he had heard
'howe the kynges grace hath you in so great Favour / And the Frenche
kyng also'.[19] Sir Thomas Elyot similarly referred to 'the kings goode opinion
& favor towardes you' in a letter to Cromwell on 18 November.[20] This
recognition then continued during the final month of 1532. In December
Cromwell was complimented on his progress in the king's favour,[21] while
another man noted that Cromwell was increasingly busy.[22] All this is in
stark contrast to his position just a few months earlier, and it suggests that
from October 1532 Thomas Cromwell was Henry VIII's chief minister.

Redating Cromwell's emergence as Henry's leading minister to October
rather than May 1532 or April 1533 may seem to be splitting hairs, particularly as the period in question is only a matter of months. Yet a more
precise outline of the chronology of Cromwell's rise is important if the
correct conclusions are to be drawn about his role and influence during this
period. Not only is there little evidence in support of claims that a factional
battle was taking place around May 1532, but, significantly, Cromwell's
own position did not change at that point. This supports the inference
drawn in the previous chapter: namely, that Cromwell was a less important

figure during the struggles against the Church in Easter 1532 then is generally assumed. A conclusion more attentive to the evidence would be that the removal of More and Gardiner provided Cromwell with the opportunity to proceed further in Henry's favour by taking on more work which might previously have gone elsewhere. This took a number of months, but was recognised to have occurred by October.

Cromwell's position as Henry's chief minister was even more widely perceived early the following year. In January 1533 there was the first of many mistaken assumptions that the king had made Cromwell a knight.[23] On 15 February the Imperial ambassador mentioned Cromwell by name for the first time in his dispatches.[24] In April he then confirmed that Cromwell was 'the man who has most influence with the King just now'.[25] John, Lord Scrope remarked in May that Cromwell was 'soo busye with gret matters of the kinge' that he had 'no laysour' to finish a matter of his.[26] This sentiment was reiterated in November by Chapuys, who mentioned that he could not meet with Cromwell because the minister was 'very much engaged' with business.[27] Evidently Cromwell was now heavily preoccupied with the king's affairs, and this explains why towards the end of 1533 he took temporary possession of the signet from the absent secretary, Stephen Gardiner.[28] The signet was the king's personal seal, used to authenticate Henry's instructions and official correspondence. That it was given to Cromwell confirms that king and minister were now working closely together. By April 1534 Cromwell held the signet permanently, having formally replaced Gardiner as royal secretary.[29] As Elton noted,

> Cromwell was never more powerful, more ubiquitous in the administration, more completely in control of the day-to-day government of the country, than he was through the office of principal secretary.[30]

This appointment was a reflection of his emergence into a position of extraordinary political influence, and marked the culmination of Cromwell's early career under the king.

The relationship between Cromwell and Henry VIII has featured heavily in many chapters of this book. Can any final conclusions be drawn about the nature of this relationship? Over the past sixty years, a broad division has emerged between those who interpret Henry VIII as the puppet of his ministers and those who interpret him as the puppeteer. One of the benefits of the sharper focus adopted in this book is that it has allowed a more detailed scrutiny of the work which Cromwell was doing for the king, which, in turn, has produced a more rounded conclusion of his role and influence. Certainly Henry VIII was a king willing to allow his ministers to rid him of the daily toils of government, and as several chapters have illustrated here, there were areas over which Cromwell had very real influence – even a measure of independence. With regard to the Crown lands, for example, on at least one occasion Henry refused to make a decision without first taking Cromwell's advice. He has also been shown promoting legislation in parliament of which the king had very little knowledge. But more often than not, Cromwell's independence was over the execution of policy, not its formulation. The significant point to emerge from many chapters here is that during the years 1531–1534, Cromwell was working for, and taking his lead from, his royal master. Repeatedly, his memoranda reminded him 'to speke with the kinges highness' or 'to knowe the kinges pleasure' touching all manner of matters on which he was engaged.[31] As these are private memoranda, it is hard not to conclude that they are a revealing reflection of Cromwell's actions and intent.

Yet even here it is probable that Cromwell had a good deal more influence than seems to be the case at first sight. As this book has argued that Cromwell was a highly efficient servant of the Crown, it should be stressed that efficiency in government itself is something of an ideological choice.[32] In his memoranda, Cromwell was not simply marshalling decisions for the king to take but must also have been selecting from a whole series of issues and prioritising those he thought important. It is even possible that Cromwell left some things out entirely, having decided not to bother Henry with them. Although often dealing with the seemingly mundane, Cromwell's memoranda reveal his frame of mind, and the choices he thought needed to be made in order for government to run smoothly. On a more general note, it is worth pointing out that many contemporaries believed that royal servants used their positions to nudge the king in certain directions. Cromwell, for example, was asked frequently to 'move the king' on particular issues or requests; and in many respects, whether he succeeded does not matter. What is significant is that royal councillors were not expected to be impartial civil servants: Henry wanted and valued their opinions.

Yet decisions and policies were not formulated between Cromwell and the king alone. Practical realities and particular circumstances heavily influenced any decision. Other councillors were also comprehensively involved in the decision-making process – an obvious point perhaps, but one frequently obscured by the survival of Cromwell's papers. The 'king or minister' debate is therefore somewhat misleading, because it conceals the multi-dimensional reality of policy making. A neat illustration of this point can be seen during the greatly neglected Anglo-Scottish war of December 1532 to May 1533. Other than letters to Henry and Cromwell, no correspondence survives regarding the war for any other 'central' government figure. This very much reinforces the impression that Henry and Cromwell were at the centre of everything. Yet Cromwell's correspondence, closely scrutinised, hints at the role and involvement of others. There is a brief allusion to Stephen Gardiner's participation.[33] Sir John Gage, Henry's vice-chamberlain, was sent to the borders in late 1532, and on his return it was felt that he was capable of discussing matters with the king and Cromwell.[34] Perhaps most significant of all, the duke of Norfolk was kept closely informed on affairs in the north, and much of his contribution was in a capacity very similar to that of Cromwell. It was Norfolk who had told Henry in Easter 1532 of the need for better border defences.[35] In early December Sir George Lawson, the treasurer at Berwick with whom Cromwell was in constant communication, had also written 'a letter to my lord of Norffolkes grace' concerning the damage done to the walls and towers of the castle of Berwick.[36] Norfolk even emerges as a man who, like Cromwell, was concerned with the war's finances. Cromwell was sent accounts of all the receipts and expenditures on the borders,[37] but at some point before 14 December Norfolk had asked that Lawson keep the king separately informed of the need for money, while the duke himself was similarly kept up to date.[38] On at least two occasions when detailing the payment of the garrison to Cromwell, Lawson requested that his letters be shown to both Henry and Norfolk.[39] He also sent a servant to the duke to inform him of affairs on the borders, and when sending Cromwell the war's financial accounts he requested that 'the kinges highness and my lord of Norffolkes grace maye see the same'.[40] It is important to recognise, therefore, that the conduct of the war was not decided on the basis of a one-dimensional dialogue between Henry and Cromwell. Other figures were kept up to date, and were expected to discuss matters with the king, who was himself well informed. This makes it difficult to see how Cromwell could have manipulated or led Henry in the way some historians suggest. But it also makes apportioning exclusive responsibility for actions or policy even more unrealistic.

Perhaps rather than interpreting events during the 1530s as being the work of either the king or minister, it would be more reasonable to see the two men working together to deal with matters as they unfolded. This is the impression that should be drawn from several chapters of this book. It is also something particularly noticeable in the two men's conduct of foreign policy during these years. Memoranda frequently reminded Cromwell to 'remember to shew the king the lettres' that came from ambassadors abroad,[41] and 'to speke with the kyng For Answer' to these.[42] During the war with Scotland both Henry and Cromwell were kept informed on events on the borders, and were often sent simultaneous accounts.[43] None of this was because Cromwell was seen as an *alter rex*; on the contrary, those conducting the war in the north continually looked to Henry when decisions were needed.[44] Cromwell was kept updated to ensure that he was capable of discussing, making recommendations and, at times, briefing the king, who could not possibly hope to remain on top of all the information he was sent – whatever his attitude towards government work may have been. It is revealing that when the English commissioners were meeting with their Scottish counterparts to negotiate an end to the conflict, many of the letters they sent to Cromwell were notably brief. The reason for this was stated openly to him:

> Vpon Tuesdaie next I truste we shall haue woorde frome the king of Scottes and suppoos the same shalbe good / As it shall chaunce ye shalbe aduertised / yet neuertheles I doubte not but ye ar and shalbe prevea to such oure letteres as doe and shall come to the kinges highness / soe that therfore I shall not nede to write further in this behalue vnto you.[45]

Those in the north evidently expected Cromwell and Henry to read and work from the same letters. And this was certainly no isolated case: in an earlier correspondence Cromwell was told that the commissioners had 'written all at large vnto the kinges highness. Whernto I doubte not but your mastership shalbe made privea'.[46] On 27 July, when letters were sent to the king concerning the Scots' response to his terms for peace, the commissioners similarly added to Cromwell that they 'doubte not but your mastership shalbe privea to the same'.[47] Cromwell even occasionally received letters for the king, before forwarding them on.[48] Again, this very much reinforces the argument that the two men were working together.

Nevertheless, if it is possible to speak of a partnership between the two men, then it was one in which Henry was not merely the senior partner, but also a highly active one. That Cromwell forwarded letters on to Henry suggests that he expected the king to read them. Similarly, one of Cromwell's memoranda relating to the year-long truce finally agreed with the Scots reminded Cromwell to discover 'what order the kings highness will take if the Scottes do not sew for peace after the treues and what provision shalbe made because the treues lastith but for a yere'.[49] This neatly underlines that the two men discussed policy, but that decisions were ultimately taken by the king. During the years 1531–1534, therefore, Thomas Cromwell was very much the king's hardworking and efficient servant.

Cromwell's appointment as the king's secretary was by no means the apogee of his political career under Henry VIII. Over the next six years Cromwell would continue to progress further in the royal service, attracting and accumulating offices, honours and rewards. In October 1534 he would become master of the rolls, a position in Chancery chiefly responsible for its records.[50] This was followed by his appointment as the king's vicegerent in spirituals in 1535, which effectively made Cromwell Henry VIII's deputy as head of the English Church. The year 1536 saw a notable increase in Cromwell's social status. In that year he succeeded the earl of Wiltshire as lord privy seal, one of the great offices of state, and became Baron Cromwell of Oakham. The following August he was then made a knight of the garter. Finally, in April 1540, Cromwell was given the earldom of Essex, one of the oldest peerages in the realm, and was appointed to the position of great chamberlain, a prestigious office in the royal household.[51] Barely two months later, Cromwell would be arrested for treason while attending a meeting of the Privy Council.[52] Although not one of the charges which condemned Cromwell under the act of attainder stands up to any sort of scrutiny, he was beheaded on Tower Hill in July 1540.[53]

The focus in this book on Cromwell's early life and political career up to 1534 should not be taken to suggest that his later ministerial career was unimportant or of less significance than his rise to power under Henry. Nevertheless, there can be no attempt here to reconstruct even a cursory account of Cromwell's later ministry, as this would not do it sufficient justice. A good deal of further work still needs to be done if we are fully to understand and isolate Cromwell's precise role in the momentous events of the 1530s. Cromwell's role as vicegerent, in particular, remains a much neglected area of study, and it would be interesting to know, since we have seen that by 1534 Cromwell had established a mastery over the English Church, how far he continued to involve himself in the more routine aspects of the Church, in terms of its administration, finance and organisation. A study of Cromwell's later political career to the depth and with the perspectives of that undertaken here is likely to throw up some new surprises.

It is nonetheless revealing that the final verdict on Cromwell, given by Henry VIII himself, echoes the conclusions drawn in this study of the minister's rise. Lamenting Cromwell's execution less than a year after its occurrence, the king would acknowledge that he had 'put to death the most faithful servant he ever had'.[54]

ABBREVIATIONS

Each reference has been given in full on its first appearance in the text. Thereafter the following abbreviations are used.

BL   British Library, London
CSP, Spanish   *Calendar of Letters, Despatches, and State Papers,*
                   Spanish, Henry VIII, ed. G. A. Bergenroth, P. de
                   Gayangos and M. A. S. Hume (15 vols in 20 parts,
                   London, 1862–1954)
DCR   Drapers' Company Records
LP   *Letters and Papers, Foreign and Domestic, of the Reign of*
                   Henry VIII, 1509–1547, ed. J. S. Brewer, J. Gardiner
                   and R. H. Brodie (21 vols and addenda, London,
                   1862–1932)
ODNB   *Oxford Dictionary of National Biography,* ed. B.
                   Harrison and H. C. G. Matthew (Oxford, 2004)
State Papers   *State Papers Published Under the Authority of His*
                   Majesty's Commission, King Henry VIII, Public Record
                   Office (London, 1830–1852).
STC   *The Short Title Catalogue of Books Printed in England,*
                   Scotland, and Ireland, 1475–1640, second edn, revised
                   and enlarged by W. A. Jackson and F. S. Ferguson and
                   completed by K. F. Pantzer (3 vols, London,
                   1976–1986)

TNA, PRO   The National Archives, Public Record Office, Kew
VCH   *Victoria History of the Counties of England*
WAM   Westminster Abbey Muniments, London

NOTES

Preface

1. G. R. Elton, *The Practice of History* (second edn, Oxford, 2002), pp. 123–124.
2. G. R. Elton, 'Thomas More and Thomas Cromwell', in G. J. Schochet, ed., *Reformation, Humanism, and 'Revolution'* (Washington, D.C., 1990), pp. 97–98. Elton claimed a biography of Cromwell would be an 'absurdity'.
3. For the debate on the academic merits of biography, see P. O'Brien, 'Is Political Biography a Good Thing?', *Contemporary British History*, 10 (1996), pp. 60–67; P. Croft, 'Political Biography: A Defence', *Contemporary British History*, 10 (1996), pp. 67–75; J. Derry, 'Political Biography: A Defence (2)', *Contemporary British History*, 10 (1996), pp. 75–81; N. Hamilton, 'In Defence of the Practice of Biography', *Contemporary British History*, 10 (1996), pp. 81–97. Also see the *American Historical Review*'s Roundtable discussion on historians and biography, *American Historical Review*, 114 (2009), pp. 573–661, and the articles on biography and history in the *Journal of Interdisciplinary History*, 40 (2010).
4. M. Prestwich, 'Medieval Biography', *Journal of Interdisciplinary History*, 40 (2010), p. 326.
5. Derry, 'Political Biography: A Defence (2)', p. 77.
6. This is a problem familiar to historians of the medieval period. See Prestwich, 'Medieval Biography', p. 345.
7. Elton, 'Thomas More and Thomas Cromwell', p. 97.

Introduction

1. T[he] N[ational] A[rchives], P[ublic] R[ecord] O[ffice], C82/654 and C66/659 m. 36 (*L[etters and] P[apers], Foreign and Domestic, of the Reign of Henry VIII*, ed. J. S. Brewer, J. Gardiner and R. H. Brodie (21 vols and addenda, London, 1862–1932), [Volume] V, 978 [13]); TNA, PRO C82/658 and C66/660 m. 33 (*LP* V, 1207 [36]); C82/658 and C66/660 m. 33 (*LP* V, 1207 [36]); C82/667 and C66/661 m. 27 (*LP* VI, 417 [22]). The office of principal secretary was not one confirmed by patent, but the first warrant Cromwell signed as secretary is dated 19 April 1534. See TNA, PRO, C82/681 (*LP* VII, 587 [26]).
2. TNA, PRO, C82/689 and C66/665 m. 1 (*LP* VII, 1352 [3]).
3. No patent exists for the position of vicegerent, an office which, to date, only Cromwell has held. He was appointed to this in January 1535, although there has been some debate as to whether this was initially intended as a permanent position. See S. E.

Lehmberg, 'Supremacy and Vicegerency: A Re-examination', *English Historical Review*, lxxxi (1966), pp. 225–236; F. D. Logan, 'Thomas Cromwell and the Vicegerency in Spirituals: A Revisitation', *English Historical Review*, ciii (1988), pp. 658–668.

4. TNA, PRO, C82/714 and C66/669 m. 3 (*LP* XI, 202 [3]).

5. TNA, PRO, C82/765 (*LP* XV, 611 [37 and 38]).

6. J. J. Scarisbrick, *Henry VIII* (second edn, London, 1997), p. 383.

7. There were four editions of *Acts and Monuments* (commonly known as the 'Book of Martyrs') published during Foxe's lifetime: 1563, 1570, 1576 and 1583. Foxe added to, amended and altered the text of his work in each version as new material and new accounts of the lives of his 'martyrs' became known to him. Although his account of Cromwell's life contains such amendments and alterations, nothing new of significance was added to the 1576 and 1583 editions. References to Foxe are taken from the online editions published on the website of the Humanities Research Institute, University of Sheffield. The above quotation is from the 1563 edition: John Foxe, *The Unabridged Acts and Monuments Online* (1563 edn) (Sheffield, 2011), p. 654. Available from www.johnfoxe.org. Hereafter the online *Acts and Monuments* is cited as: Foxe, *Acts and Monuments*.

8. Foxe, *Acts and Monuments* (1570 edn), p. 1392.

9. R. Holinshed, *Chronicles of England, Scotland and Ireland* (6 vols, London, 1807–1808), iii. 818.

10. G. Burnet, *The History of the Reformation of the Church of England* (4 vols, London, 1837), i. 281, 457.

11. J. Collier, *An Ecclesiastical History of Great Britain* (9 vols, London, 1840–1841), v. 73.

12. J. A. Froude, *History of England from the Fall of Wolsey to the Death of Elizabeth* (12 vols, London, 1856–1870), iii. 521, 525.

13. Ibid., 525.

14. A. Galton, *The Character and Times of Thomas Cromwell: A Sixteenth-Century Criticism* (Birmingham, 1887), pp. 208, 209. Galton also felt that although 'no impartial historian can believe in the motives of Henry VIII, or admire the methods of Cromwell, it is possible to see that their work was, on the whole, indispensable' (p. 176).

15. J. J. Ellis, *Thomas Cromwell* (London, 1891), p. 2.

16. Ibid., pp. 103, 105.

17. R. B. Merriman, *Life and Letters of Thomas Cromwell* (2 vols, Oxford, 1902), i. 87.

18. Ibid., i. 87.

19. Ibid., 88.

20. A. Innes, *Ten Tudor Statesmen* (London, 1906), pp. 115, 149.

21. P. Wilding, *Thomas Cromwell* (London, 1935), p. 66.

22. A. F. Pollard, *Henry VIII* (London, 1913), p. 323.

23. P. Van Dyke wrote a more balanced account of Cromwell's life in his book *Renascence Portraits* (New York, 1905). This included an appendix refuting the charges that Cromwell was a disciple of Machiavelli, an accusation that was first levelled at him by Cardinal Reginald Pole in 1538 or 1539. See *Renascence Portraits*, pp. 138–259 for the life of Cromwell, and pp. 377–426 for the appendix. The appendix had also been published separately a year earlier as P. Van Dyke, 'Reginald Pole and Thomas Cromwell: An Examination of the Apolgoia Ad Carolum Quintum', *American Historical Review*, 9 (1904), pp. 696–724.

24. G. R. Elton, 'Thomas Cromwell: Aspects of his Administrative Work' (University of London PhD thesis, 1948); G. R. Elton, *The Tudor Revolution in Government: Administrative Changes in the Reign of Henry VIII* (Cambridge, 1953).

25. G. L. Harriss and P. Williams, 'A Revolution in Tudor History?', *Past and Present*, 25 (1963), pp. 3–59; J. P. Cooper, 'A Revolution in Tudor History?', *Past and Present*, 26 (1963), pp. 110–113; G. R. Elton, 'The Tudor Revolution: A Reply', *Past and Present*, 29 (1964), pp. 26–50; G. L. Harriss and P. Williams, 'A Revolution in Tudor History?', *Past and Present*, 31 (1965), pp. 87–97; G. R. Elton, 'A Revolution in Tudor History?', *Past and Present*, 32 (1965), pp. 103–110.

26. C. Coleman and D. Starkey, eds, *Revolution Reassessed: Revisions in the History of Tudor Government and Administration* (Oxford, 1986). Other notable criticisms of Elton's interpretation of Cromwell and his work in government include: R. B. Wernham,

'Review: The Tudor Revolution in Government', *English Historical Review*, lxxi (1956), pp. 92–95; G. W. Bernard, 'Politics and Government in Tudor England', *Historical Journal*, 31 (1988), pp. 159–182; C. S. L. Davies, 'The Cromwellian Decade: Authority and Consent', *Transactions of the Royal Historical Society*, Sixth Series, vii (1996), pp. 177–195; C. Russell, 'Thomas Cromwell's Doctrine of Parliamentary Sovereignty', *Transactions of the Royal Historical Society*, Sixth Series, vii (1996), pp. 235–247; K. B. McFarlane, *Letters to Friends, 1940–1966*, ed. G. L. Harriss (Oxford, 1997), pp. 97-98; G. W. Bernard, 'Elton's Cromwell', *History*, 83 (1998), pp. 587–607, reprinted in G. W. Bernard, *Power and Politics in Tudor England* (Aldershot, 2000), pp. 108–129. The most recent contribution to the debate has been an article by Ian Harris, which examines the origins of Elton's concept of a revolution in government. See I. Harris, 'Some Origins of a Tudor Revolution', *English Historical Review*, cxxvi (2011), pp. 1355–1385.

27. Elton's works with the most direct relevance to Cromwell, beyond those already cited, are: *England under the Tudors* (third edn, London, 1991); *Policy and Police: The Enforcement of the Reformation in the Age of Thomas Cromwell* (Cambridge, 1972); *Reform and Renewal: Thomas Cromwell and the Common Weal* (Cambridge, 1973); 'Taxation for War and Peace in Early-Tudor England', in J. M. Winter, ed., *War and Economic Development: Essays in Memory of David Joslin* (Cambridge, 1975), pp. 33–49; *Reform and Reformation: England, 1509–1558* (London, 1977). Elton also wrote several important articles on Cromwell, which have since been published in his collective works. See G. R. Elton, *Studies in Tudor and Stuart Politics and Government* (4 vols, Cambridge, 1974–1992). For a more thorough list of Elton's works on Cromwell, see the bibliography at the end of this book.

28. Elton, *Reform and Reformation*, p. 172.

29. G. R. Elton, 'The Political Creed of Thomas Cromwell', in G. R. Elton, *Studies in Tudor and Stuart Politics and Government* (4 vols, Cambridge, 1974–1992), ii. 225, 234.

30. Elton, *England under the Tudors*, pp. 165–175.

31. Elton, *Tudor Revolution in Government*, p. 175.

32. G. R. Elton, 'King or Minister? The Man behind the Henrician Reformation', *History*, 39 (1954), p. 218. Reprinted in G. R. Elton, *Studies in Tudor and Stuart Politics and Government* (4 vols, Cambridge, 1974–1992), i. 173–189.

33. G. R. Elton, 'Thomas Cromwell Redivivus', in G. R. Elton, *Studies in Tudor and Stuart Politics and Government* (4 vols, Cambridge, 1974–1992), iii. 373.

34. M. L. Robertson, 'Thomas Cromwell's Servants: The Ministerial Household in Early Tudor Government and Society' (University of California PhD thesis, 1975); M. L. Robertson, '"The Art of the Possible": Thomas Cromwell's Management of West Country Government', *Historical Journal*, 32 (1989), pp. 793–816; M. L. Robertson, 'Profit and Purpose in the Development of Thomas Cromwell's Landed Estates', *Journal of British Studies*, 29 (1990), pp. 317–346. See also H. M. Speight, '"The Politics of Good Governance": Thomas Cromwell and the Government of Southwest England', *Historical Journal*, 37 (1994), pp. 623–638; M. L. Robertson, 'A Reply to Helen Speight', *Historical Journal*, 37 (1994), pp. 639–641.

35. P. J. Ward, 'The Origins of Thomas Cromwell's Public Career: Service under Cardinal Wolsey and Henry VIII, 1524–1530' (University of London PhD thesis, 1999).

36. N. Williams, *The Cardinal and the Secretary* (London, 1975); B. W. Beckingsale, *Thomas Cromwell: Tudor Minister* (London, 1978).

37. H. Mantel, *Wolf Hall* (London, 2009); H. Mantel, *Bring Up the Bodies* (London, 2012).

38. R. Hutchinson, *Thomas Cromwell: The Rise and Fall of Henry VIII's Most Notorious Minister* (London, 2007); J. Schofield, *The Rise and Fall of Thomas Cromwell: Henry VIII's Most Faithful Servant* (London, 2008); J. P. Coby, *Thomas Cromwell: Henry VIII's Henchman* (London, 2012); D. Loades, *Thomas Cromwell: Servant to Henry VIII* (Stroud, 2013); T. Borman, *Thomas Cromwell: The Untold Story of Henry VIII's Most Faithful Servant* (London, 2014).

39. A. G. Dickens, *Thomas Cromwell and the English Reformation* (London, 1959).

40. Williams, *Cardinal and the Secretary*, pp. 261–263; C. S. L. Davies, *Peace, Print and Protestantism* (London, 1976), p. 190; J. Block, 'Thomas Cromwell's Patronage of Preaching', *Sixteenth Century Journal*, 8 (1977), pp. 37–50; A. J. Slavin, 'Cromwell, Cranmer

and Lord Lisle: A Study in the Politics of Reform', *Albion*, 9 (1977), pp. 316–336; Beckingsale, *Thomas Cromwell*, pp. 75–77; S. Brigden, 'Thomas Cromwell and the "Brethren"', in C. C. Cross, D. Loades and J. J. Scarisbrick, eds, *Law and Government under the Tudors: Essays Presented to Sir Geoffrey Elton* (Cambridge, 1988), pp. 31–50; J. Guy, *Tudor England* (Oxford, 1990), pp. 180–181; D. MacCulloch, *Reformation: Europe's House Divided, 1490–1700* (London, 2003), p. 199. This list could be considerably lengthened.

41. Elton, *England under the Tudors*, p. 151; G. R. Elton, 'Thomas Cromwell', *History Today*, 6 (August, 1956), p. 531.

42. Elton, *Policy and Police*, p. 424; Elton, *Reform and Reformation*, p. 172; Elton, *Reform and Renewal*, pp. 34, 36. See also G. R. Elton, *Thomas Cromwell* (Bangor, 1991), pp. 35–36. Although, in a neat illustration of the argument made here, Elton continued to understand everything as working towards, or contributing to, Cromwell's desire to reform the body politic, even his religion: 'He [Cromwell] had in effect become convinced that only a form of Protestantism could serve the polity he was building' (Elton, *Reform and Reformation*, p. 172).

43. D. Starkey, *The Reign of Henry VIII: Personalities and Politics* (London, 1985), p. 105. For a similar view, see J. Block, *Factional Politics and the English Reformation, 1520–1540* (Woodbridge, 1993), pp. 52, 59.

44. Guy, *Tudor England*, p. 124.

45. Brigden, 'Cromwell and the "Brethren"', p. 32.

46. Guy, *Tudor England*, pp. 181, 183.

47. Davies, *Peace, Print and Protestantism*, pp. 190, 212; Block, 'Cromwell's Patronage of Preaching', pp. 37–50; Slavin, 'Cromwell, Cranmer and Lord Lisle', pp. 316–336; J. A. Guy, 'Reassessing Thomas Cromwell', *History Sixth*, 6 (1990), pp. 4–5; W. Underwood, 'Thomas Cromwell and William Marshall's Protestant Books', *Historical Journal*, 47 (2004), pp. 517–539.

48. H. Leithead, 'Cromwell, Thomas (*c.*1485–1540)', *Oxford Dictionary of National Biography (ODNB)*.

49. Foxe, *Acts and Monuments* (1570 edn), p. 1387; Merriman, *Life and Letters of Thomas Cromwell*, i. 89–92; Hutchinson, *Thomas Cromwell*, pp. 47–70; Schofield, *Rise and Fall*, pp. 45–57; Loades, *Thomas Cromwell*, pp. 57–84; Borman, *Thomas Cromwell*, pp. 117–120, 126–127, 129–134, 148–153

50. Elton, *Tudor Revolution in Government*, pp. 89–90, 97.

51. Elton, 'King or Minister?', in Elton, *Studies*, i. 173–189.

52. Elton, *England under the Tudors*, pp. 128, 129; Elton, *Reform and Reformation*, pp. 152–156; Elton, *Thomas Cromwell*, p. 11.

53. See, for example, J. A. Guy, *The Public Career of Sir Thomas More* (Brighton, 1980), pp. 130–138, 161, 175–201; although Guy later modified this somewhat in 'Henry VIII and the *Praemunire* Manoeuvres of 1530–1531', *English Historical Review*, xcvii (1982), pp. 481–503; C. Haigh, *English Reformations: Religion, Politics, and Society under the Tudors* (Oxford, 1993), pp. 105–120; S. Brigden, *New Worlds, Lost Worlds* (London, 2000), pp. 117–119; H. Leithead, 'Cromwell, Thomas (*c.*1485–1540)', *ODNB*; Hutchinson, *Thomas Cromwell*, pp. 47–70; Schofield, *Rise and Fall*, pp. 45–57; Loades, *Thomas Cromwell*, pp. 57–84; Borman, *Thomas Cromwell*, pp. 123–171.

54. Mantel, *Wolf Hall*.

55. Elton, *Tudor Revolution in Government*, pp. 98, 109–110, 119.

56. Starkey, *Reign of Henry VIII*, p. 84.

57. Ibid., pp. 83–84; D. R. Starkey, 'Intimacy and Innovation: The Rise of the Privy Chamber, 1485–1547', in D. R. Starkey, ed., *The English Court from the Wars of the Roses to the Civil War* (London, 1987), pp. 108–109.

58. D. R. Starkey, 'The King's Privy Chamber, 1485–1547' (University of Cambridge PhD thesis, 1973); D. Starkey, 'Court and Government', in D. Starkey and C. Coleman, eds, *Revolution Reassessed: Revisions in the History of Tudor Government and Administration* (Oxford, 1987), pp. 29–58; Starkey, 'Intimacy and Innovation', pp. 71–118; D. Starkey, 'Representation Through Intimacy: A Study of the Symbolism of Monarchy and Court Office in Early Modern England', in I. Lewis, ed., *Symbols and Sentiments: Cross-Cultural Studies in Symbolism* (London, 1977), pp. 187–224.

59. G. W. Bernard, *The Power of the Early Tudor Nobility: A Study of the Fourth and Fifth Earls of Shrewsbury* (Brighton, 1985).

60. J. A. Guy, 'Tudor Monarchy and Political Culture', in J. Morrill, ed., *The Oxford Illustrated History of Tudor and Stuart Britain* (Oxford, 1996), pp. 219–238; J. Guy, 'General Introduction', in J. Guy, *The Tudor Monarchy* (London, 1997), pp. 7–8; W. T. MacCaffrey, 'Place and Patronage in Elizabethan Politics', in S. T. Bindoff, J. Hurstfield and C. H. Williams, eds, *Elizabethan Government and Society: Essays Presented to Sir John Neale* (London, 1961), pp. 95–126; Davies, *Peace, Print and Protestantism*; P. Williams, *The Tudor Regime* (Oxford, 1979); P. Collinson, 'The Monarchical Republic of Queen Elizabeth I', *Bulletin of the John Rylands University Library of Manchester*, 69 (1987), pp. 394–424; B. J. Harris, 'Women and Politics in Early Tudor England', *Historical Journal*, 33 (1990), pp. 259–281; S. J. Gunn, *Early Tudor Government, 1485–1558* (Basingstoke, 1995).

61. N. Mears, 'Courts, Courtiers and Culture in Tudor England', *Historical Journal*, 46 (2003), p. 704. See also S. Alford, 'Politics and Political History in the Tudor Century', *Historical Journal*, 42 (1999), pp. 535–548.

62. I owe this point to Dr Paul Cavill, who discussed these ideas with me.

63. Where the reason for redating a document is not obvious, an explanatory footnote is given.

64. *LP* V, p. vi.

Chapter One London Lawyer and Merchant

1. One exception to this rule is Philip Ward's excellent PhD thesis, 'The Origins of Thomas Cromwell's Public Career'. Ward's thesis, however, is only concerned with Cromwell's work for Cardinal Wolsey, and does not examine Cromwell's private work as a lawyer or his mercantile interests.

2. E. W. Ives, 'The Common Lawyers in Pre-Reformation England', *Transactions of the Royal Historical Society*, Fifth Series, xviii (1968), p. 153; R. L. Storey, 'Gentleman-bureaucrats', in C. H. Clough, ed., *Profession, Vocation and Culture in Later Medieval England* (Liverpool, 1982), p. 104; E. W. Ives, *The Common Lawyers of Pre-Reformation England: Thomas Kebell, A Case Study* (Cambridge, 1983), pp. 222–247; J. A. Guy, 'Law, Faction, and Parliament in the Sixteenth Century', *Historical Journal*, 28 (1985), p. 441; Gunn, *Early Tudor Government*, p. 15.

3. Ives, *Common Lawyers*, pp. 247–263.

4. D. Lyson, ed., *The Environs of London* (4 vols, London, 1792), i. 404–435; H. E. Malden, ed., *A History of the County of Surrey* (4 vols, London, 1912), iv. 78–83.

5. J. Phillips, 'The Cromwells of Putney', *Antiquarian Magazine*, ii (1882), 56–62 and 178–186, at p. 184.

6. *Statutes of the Realm*, ed. A. E. Luders *et al.* (11 vols, London, 1810–1828), 28 Henry VIII, c. 50; *LP* X, 1087.

7. C. S. S. Higham, *Wimbledon Manor House under the Cecils* (London, 1962), pp. 3–17.

8. For the ancestry of the Cromwell family, see Phillips, 'Cromwells of Putney', pp. 56–62, 178–186; Merriman, *Life and Letters of Thomas Cromwell*, i. 1–8; *Calendar of Close Rolls, Henry VII*, ed. K. H. Ledward and R. A. Latham (2 vols, London, 1955–63), ii. 57 (p. 18); TNA, PRO, C1/296/4.

9. Merriman, *Life and Letters of Thomas Cromwell*, i. 3; Phillips, 'Cromwells of Putney', p. 57.

10. Merriman, *Life and Letters of Thomas Cromwell*, i. 3; *Extracts from the Court Rolls of the Manor of Wimbledon, extending from I Edward IV to AD 1864*, ed. P. H. Lawrence (London, 1866), pp. 73–75.

11. Phillips, 'Cromwells of Putney', p. 179.

12. Ibid., p. 179.

13. TNA, PRO, SP1/77 fo. 77 (*LP* VI, 696); Phillips, 'Cromwells of Putney', p. 179.

14. TNA, PRO, SP1/54 fo. 244 (Merriman, *Life and Letters of Thomas Cromwell*, i. 56–63; *LP* IV, iii. 5772).

15. *Calendar of Letters, Despatches, and State Papers, Spanish, Henry VIII (CSP, Spanish)*, ed. G. A. Bergenroth and P. de Gayangos (14 vols, London, 1862–1886), V, i, 165.

16. *LP* I, i 1602 [22]; TNA, PRO, SP1/12 fo. 51 (*LP* II, i, 1369). For Robert Cromwell, see also S. Thurley, 'The Domestic Building Works of Cardinal Wolsey', in S. J. Gunn and P. G. Lindley, eds, *Cardinal Wolsey: Church, State and Art* (Cambridge, 1991), p. 80.

17. A transcription of Chapuys's remarks on Cromwell, upon which I have relied here, can be found in W. Thomas, *The Pilgrim*, ed. J. A. Froude (London, 1861), pp. 106–108. See also *CSP, Spanish*, V, i, 228.

18. Foxe, *Acts and Monuments* (1570 edn), p. 1386.

19. *The Novels of Matteo Bandello*, trans. J. Payne (6 vols, London, 1890), iv. 107.

20. Thomas, *The Pilgrim*, p. 107; *CSP, Spanish*, V, i, 228.

21. *Novels of Matteo Bandello*, iv. 107. According to Foxe, Cromwell was 'in the warres of Duke Bourbon at the siege of Rome'. See Foxe, *Acts and Monuments* (1570 edn), p. 1386.

22. *Novels of Matteo Bandello*, p. 107.

23. Archivio Vaticano, Archivio della Rota, Manualia Actorum et Citationum 92, fo. 350, cited in A. J. Slavin, 'The Gutenberg Galaxy and the Tudor Revolution', in G. P. Tyson and S. S. Wagonheim, eds, *Print and Culture in the Renaissance: Essays on the Advent of Printing in Europe* (Newark, NJ, 1986), p. 95.

24. Slavin, 'Gutenberg Galaxy', pp. 95–96.

25. G. Parks, *The English Traveller to Italy* (Rome, 1954), pp. 376, 417; D. S. Chambers, *Cardinal Bainbridge in the Court of Rome* (Oxford, 1965), pp. 77–78.

26. Chambers, *Cardinal Bainbridge*, pp. 113–115.

27. Foxe, *Acts and Monuments* (1570 edn), pp. 1385–1386.

28. For the history of the Boston indulgences, see R. N. Swanson, *Indulgences in Late Medieval England: Passports to Paradise?* (Cambridge, 2009), p. 449; W. E. Lunt, *Financial Relations of the Papacy with England, 1327–1534* (Cambridge, MA, 1962), pp. 495–510.

29. Foxe, *Acts and Monuments* (1576 edn), p. 1173.

30. BL, Egerton MS 2886 fo. 181v.

31. Foxe, *Acts and Monuments* (1570 edn), p. 1385; TNA, PRO, C1/482/33.

32. TNA, PRO, SP1/104 fo. 211 (*LP* X, 1218).

33. *CSP, Spanish*, V, i, 228.

34. Merriman, *Life and Letters of Thomas Cromwell*, i. 11–12; Williams, *Cardinal and the Secretary*, p. 144; Robertson, 'Thomas Cromwell's Servants', p. 43.

35. TNA, PRO, SP1/52 fos 36–51v (*LP* IV, iii, 5330).

36. TNA, PRO, SP1/3 fo. 73v (*LP* I, i, 1473).

37. Elton, 'Thomas Cromwell Redivivus', in Elton, *Studies*, iii. 375. Elton also gave an undated petition (TNA, PRO, STAC 2/2/274) addressed to Cromwell as 'oone of the lorde Cardynalles honerable Councell', which concerned a theft on St Bartholomew's Eve, 1519, as evidence that Cromwell was in Wolsey's service by that year. As the petitioner was asking Cromwell to 'avyse me' on the matter, this might also attest to Cromwell's legal activities then. For its re-dating, see p. 29.

38. TNA, PRO, REQ2/4/45 fos 1–5; TNA, PRO, STAC 2/13 fos 139–141. A copy of the petition, incorporating Cromwell's corrections, follows, on fos 142–143.

39. TNA, PRO, SP1/31 fos 31–32 (*LP* IV, i, 368); SP1/21 fos 119–120 (*LP* III, i, 1026).

40. TNA, PRO, C244/162/92. I am very grateful to Dr Paul Cavill, who drew my attention to this writ, and to Dr Simon Payling, who assisted with the translation.

41. D. A. L. Morgan, 'The Individual Style of the English Gentleman', in M. Jones, ed., *Gentry and the Lesser Nobility in Later Medieval England* (Gloucester, 1986), p. 25.

42. Ives, *Common Lawyers*, p. 10.

43. For the legal training provided by the Inns, see Ives, ibid., pp. 36–60; J. H. Baker, *The Reports of Sir John Spelman* (2 vols, London, 1978), ii. 125–135.

44. Ives, 'Common Lawyers', p. 146.

45. N. Ramsay, 'What was the Legal Profession?', in M. Hicks, ed., *Profit, Piety and the Professions in Later Medieval England* (Gloucester, 1990), p. 68; Ives, *Common Lawyers*, p. 20.

46. D. Youngs, *Humphrey Newton (1466–1536): An Early Tudor Gentleman* (Woodbridge, 2008), pp. 41–69.

47. *LP* I, 438 [2]; *LP* I, 438 [1]; Ives, 'Common Lawyers', p. 148.

48. Ramsay, 'What was the Legal Profession?', p. 68.

49. J. H. Baker, 'The English Legal Profession, 1450–1550', in J. H. Baker, *The Legal Profession and the Common Law: Historical Essays* (London, 1986) p. 76.

50. Youngs, *Humphrey Newton*, p. 42; P. Brand, *The Origins of the English Legal Profession* (Oxford, 1992), p. vii.

51. Ives, 'Common Lawyers', p. 148.

52. S. Gunn, 'Sir Thomas Lovell (*c*.1449–1524): A New Man in a New Monarchy?' in J. L. Watts, ed., *The End of the Middle Ages? England in the Fifteenth and Sixteenth Centuries* (Stroud, 1998), p. 122.

53. S. T. Bindoff, *History of Parliament: The House of Commons, 1509–1558* (3 vols, London, 1982), i. 350.

54. Ibid., ii. 274–275.

55. Ibid., 620.

56. There is one exception. In a letter dated 30 August, and placed in 1531 in *Letters and Papers*, Lawrence Stubbs wrote to Cromwell concerning a suit which Robert Barfote, mercer, had against him in 'the common place at Westminster' over a debt. Stubbs remarked to Cromwell that 'ye showed me at our last beynge to geddere ye cowd discharge me of this suyte'. See TNA, PRO, SP1/67 fo. 8 (*LP* V, 386). Without further evidence, however, this letter is insufficient proof that Cromwell pleaded in the Court of Common Pleas. All that can be said of Stubbs's request is that he asked Cromwell, by his 'wisdom pollicy & lernyngs', to find some way of discharging him. If he could not, Cromwell was asked to prepare a bill to remove the suit to Chancery.

57. J. Foster, *The Register of Admissions to Gray's Inn, 1521–1889* (London, 1889), p. 4. He was appointed an ancient there in 1534. See W. R. Douthwaite, *Gray's Inn, Its History and Associations* (London, 1886), pp. 198, 221.

58. Baker, 'English Legal Profession', pp. 76–77.

59. J. H. Baker, 'Oral Instruction in Land Law and Conveyancing, 1250–1500', in J. A. Bush and A. Wijffels, eds, *Learning the Law: Teaching and the Transmission of English Law, 1150–1900* (London, 1999), pp. 157–175; J. H. Baker, *Legal Education in London, 1250–1850* (London, 2007).

60. Ives, *Common Lawyers*, p. 20; Ramsay, 'What was the Legal Profession?', p. 68.

61. C. W. Brooks, *Pettyfoggers and Vipers of the Commonwealth: The Lower Branches of the Legal Profession in Early Modern England* (Cambridge, 1986).

62. Ives, *Common Lawyers*, p. 12.

63. Estimates place the combined total of serjeants and apprentices somewhere between 120 and 180 during this period. Attorneys numbered slightly higher, with around two hundred working and operating in Westminster alone. See Baker, 'English Legal Profession', pp. 85, 87, 88–89; Ives, *Common Lawyers*, p. 18.

64. F. Metzger, 'The Last Phase of the Medieval Chancery', in A. Harding, ed., *Law-Making and Law-Makers in British History* (London, 1980), pp. 79–90; J. A. Guy, *The Cardinal's Court: The Impact of Thomas Wolsey in Star Chamber* (Hassocks, 1977), p. 112.

65. Brooks, *Pettyfoggers and Vipers*, p. 25; J. A. Guy, *The Court of Star Chamber and Its Records to the Reign of Elizabeth I* (London, 1985), pp. 15–16.

66. TNA, PRO, SP1/53 fo. 168 (*LP* IV, iii, 5437).

67. TNA, PRO, SP1/235 fo. 219 (*LP* Add[enda] I, i, 542). For further examples of requests for Cromwell's counsel and advice on legal matters, see TNA, PRO, SP1/25 fo. 140 (*LP* III, ii, 2461); SP1/58 fo. 198 (*LP* IV, iii, 6783); SP1/236 fo. 1 (*LP* Add. I, i, 606).

68. TNA, PRO, SP1/46 fos 33–34 (Merriman, *Life and Letters of Thomas Cromwell*, i. 316; *LP* IV, ii, 3741). What appears to be an earlier draft of this letter can be found in TNA, PRO, SP1/235 fos 252–253 (*LP* Add. I, i, 561).

69. TNA, PRO, SP1/46 fo. 34 (Merriman, *Life and Letters of Thomas Cromwell*, i, 316; *LP* IV, ii, 3741).

70. For the litigation connected to this suit, see TNA, PRO, C131/108/30–31; C131/269/2; C131/269/4; C1/488/45; C1/490/33.

71. J. H. Baker, *The Oxford History of the Laws of England*, Volume VI, *1483–1558* (Oxford, 2003), pp. 171–190, 195–200; N. Pronay, 'The Chancellor, the Chancery, and the Council at the End of the Fifteenth Century', in H. Hearder and H. R. Loyn, eds, *British Government and Administration: Studies Presented to S. B. Chrimes* (Cardiff, 1974), pp. 87–103.

72. For Star Chamber's development, see Guy, *Cardinal's Court, passim.*

73. Baker, *Laws of England*, p. 197.

74. Metzger, 'Medieval Chancery', p. 84; Ives, *Common Lawyers*, pp. 194–195; Guy, *Cardinal's Court*, pp. 51–79; Baker, *Laws of England*, p. 197.

75. TNA, PRO, C1/558/27. A draft of this petition, written in Cromwell's hand, can be found in TNA, PRO, SP1/29 fos 136–137v (*LP* III, ii, 3681).

76. TNA, PRO, C1/569/41; C1/484/11; C1/507/43; C1/494/35.

77. TNA, PRO, SP1/236 fo. 1 (*LP* Add. I, i, 606).

78. TNA, PRO, SP1/31 fo. 54 (*LP* IV, i, 385). Another (probably earlier) draft of this petition, again in Cromwell's hand, is SP1/81 fos 80–80v (*LP* VI, 1625 [iv]). The formal petition for this in Chancery is not signed by Cromwell, nor is his name or handwriting to be found on it. See TNA, PRO, C1/498/32.

79. TNA, PRO, SP1/55 fo. 100 (*LP* IV, iii, 5930).

80. TNA, PRO, STAC 2/13 fos 139–141.

81. TNA, PRO, STAC 2/26/36; STAC 2/24/410; STAC 2/26/19; TNA, PRO, SP1/235 fo. 122 (*LP* Add. I, i, 511).

82. TNA, PRO, SP1/33 fo. 117 (*LP* IV, i, 1048).

83. TNA, PRO, SP1/23 fo. 271 (*LP* III, ii, 1963).

84. TNA, PRO, SP1/235 fo. 30 (*LP* Add. I, i, 469).

85. TNA, PRO, SP1/36 fo. 100 (*LP* IV, i, 1732). For Cromwell's other legal work for Lawrence Giles, see SP1/36 fos 10–10v (*LP* IV, i, 1620); SP1/40 fo. 66 (*LP* IV, ii, 2701).

86. TNA, PRO, SP1/235 fos 20–24 (*LP* Add. I, i, 469); SP1/235 fos 26–28 (*LP* Add. I, i, 469); SP1/235 fo. 30 (*LP* Add. I, i, 469). Once again, the formal Chancery petition does not reveal that Cromwell was involved with the suit, see TNA, PRO, C1/512/69–71b.

87. TNA, PRO, SP1/40 fo. 66 (*LP* IV, ii, 2701).

88. TNA, PRO, SP1/236 fo. 70 (*LP* Add. I, i, 633). The editors of *Letters and Papers* believed this letter to have been sent in January 1526, but this seems unlikely. If it was sent then, then Cromwell had handled the dispute unbelievably quickly. Yet litigation in matters such as this usually took several months, and Giles's remark, 'that I maye knowe the conclusion . . . which I haue a long season desired', suggests that this matter had indeed taken some time. Another letter, dated 19 July 1526, in which Giles asked Cromwell for good news on his 'mater', also suggests the dispute was not resolved by early 1526. See TNA, PRO, SP1/38 fo. 243 (*LP* IV, i, 2329).

89. TNA, PRO, SP1/26 fo. 119 (*LP* III, ii, 2628); SP1/25 fo. 76 (*LP* III, ii, 2441 [i]).

90. TNA, PRO, SP1/26 fo. 35 (*LP* III, ii, 2557).

91. Ibid.

92. TNA, PRO, SP1/26 fo. 119 (*LP* III, ii, 2628 [ii]). See also SP1/233 fos 148–155v (*LP* Add. I, i, 345), which are badly mutilated bonds and other documents connected with this dispute.

93. TNA, PRO, SP1/26 fo. 119 (*LP* III, ii, 2628 [ii]).

94. Although no trace of this dispute survives in the Chancery records, drafts of undated Chancery proceedings relating to it, which also refer to the attempts at arbitration in Calais, can be found among the State Papers. See TNA, PRO, SP1/25 fos 77–112 (*LP* III, ii, 2441 [ii]).

95. The case is also briefly discussed in Guy, *Cardinal's Court*, p. 100, although it is not noted there that Cromwell was involved.

96. TNA, PRO, SP1/39 fos 199–201v (*LP* IV, ii, 2553). This is a draft petition for Star Chamber, amended and corrected by Cromwell. The formal bill is TNA, PRO, STAC 2/21/182 fo. 4. Another draft of this is STAC 2/21/167.

97. TNA, PRO, SP1/235 fo. 88 (*LP* Add. I, i, 501); SP1/42 fo. 59 (*LP* IV, ii, 3154); SP1/54 fo. 44 (*LP* IV, iii, 5622); SP1/53 fo. 176 (*LP* IV, iii, 5459); SP1/54 fo. 55 (*LP* IV, iii, 5623). As with several of the cases mentioned above, the records of Star Chamber offer no

indication of Cromwell's involvement. The draft petition on behalf of Clay, which survives among the State Papers, however, is heavily corrected and altered by Cromwell, while the formal petition located in the Star Chamber proceedings is a word-for-word copy of this draft, incorporating Cromwell's corrections. See TNA, PRO, SP1/39 fos 199–200 (*LP* IV, ii, 2553); TNA, PRO, STAC 2/21/167; TNA, PRO, STAC 2/21/182 fo. 4.

98. TNA, PRO, STAC 2/21/182 fos 2, 3.
99. TNA, PRO, SP1/235 fos 87–88 (*LP* Add. I, i, 501). Ap Powell apparently owed Thomas Hinde £77.
100. TNA, PRO, SP1/235 fos 87–89 (*LP* Add. I, i, 501).
101. TNA, PRO, SP1/42 fo. 59 (*LP* IV, ii, 3154). Bundles relating to the questions the commissioners should seek answers to can be found in TNA, PRO, STAC 2/19/332.
102. TNA, PRO, STAC 2/19/9; BL, Cotton MS, Appendix L fo. 38 (*LP* IV, iii, 5402); BL, Cotton MS, Galba B IX fo. 187 (*LP* IV, iii, 5436); BL, Cotton MS, Galba B IX fos 165–170 (*LP* IV, iii, 5461); BL, Cotton MS, Galba B IX fos 173–174.
103. TNA, PRO, STAC 2/19/304; STAC 2/19/9.
104. Guy, *Cardinal's Court*, pp. 97–105.
105. *The Complete Works of St Thomas More*, ed. E. Surtz and J. H. Hexter (15 vols, London, 1965), iv. 39.
106. TNA, PRO, SP1/32 fo. 239 (*LP* IV, i, 955 [iv]); SP1/44 fos 194–194v (*LP* IV, ii, 3534 [i]); SP2/C fos 10–15 (*LP* IV, ii, 2972 [4]); SP1/41 fos 99–102 (*LP* IV, ii, 2991); SP1/234 fos 197–202v (*LP* Add. I, i, 447); SP1/56 fo. 119–120 (*LP* IV, iii, 6102); SP1/56 fos 170–171 (*LP* IV, iii, 6126).
107. TNA, PRO, SP1/41 fos 141–144 (*LP* IV, ii, 3032).
108. For the details of the dispute, see TNA, PRO, SP1/41 fos 187–190 (*LP* IV, ii, 3086 [i]); SP1/41 fo. 191 (*LP* IV, ii, 3086 [ii]). The final petition can be found in the formal records of Chancery; see TNA, PRO, C1/490/11.
109. TNA, PRO, SP1/52 fos 72–78 (*LP* IV, ii, 5126). Some of the amendments in this award are in Cromwell's hand.
110. Guy, *Cardinal's Court*, p. 98.
111. TNA, PRO, SP1/52 fo. 76 (*LP* IV, ii, 5126).
112. TNA, PRO, SP1/52 fos 76–78 (*LP* IV, ii, 5126).
113. TNA, PRO, SP1/31 fo. 128 (*LP* IV, i, 437); SP1/31 fo. 142 (*LP* IV, i, 461); SP1/40 fos 243–246 (*LP* IV, ii, 2844); TNA, PRO, SP2/C fos 1–3 (*LP* IV, ii, 1375 [1]); SP2/C fos 4–7a (*LP* IV, ii, 2375 [2]); SP2/C fos 16–34 (*LP* IV, ii, 2375 [5]); SP2/C fos 35–47 (*LP* IV, ii, 2375 [6]); SP2/C fos 48–61v (*LP* IV, ii, 2375 [7]); SP2/C fos 62–73 (*LP* IV, ii, 2375 [8]).
114. Youngs, *Humphrey Newton*, p. 46.
115. TNA, PRO, SP1/34 fo. 34 (*LP* IV, i, 1150); SP1/235 fo. 53 (*LP* Add. I, i, 485). This second letter was placed in 1526 by the editors of *Letters and Papers*. It would be more reasonable to date it to 1525, on the grounds that the office had become vacant following the death of the previous incumbent in March of that year.
116. It certainly did not entitle Cromwell to select the local mayor. *Letters and Papers* erroneously describes Thomas Chaffyn, who wrote to Cromwell regarding the clerkship, as proposing 'that the mayor be appointed by Cromwell himself'. This is a misreading of the line 'hitt maye be your pleasure that he [John Acton, the man who would act as Cromwell's deputy there] maye be surly Appoyntyd by your owne selffe'. See TNA, PRO, SP1/56 fo. 190 (*LP* IV, iii, 6136).
117. T. E. Headrick, *The Town Clerk in English Local Government* (London, 1982), p. 15.
118. TNA, PRO, SP1/34 fo. 34 (*LP* IV, i, 1150); SP1/236 fo. 292 (*LP* Add. I, i, 683); SP1/56 fo. 190 (*LP* IV, iii, 6136); SP1/235 fo. 53 (*LP* Add. I, i, 485).
119. TNA, PRO, SP1/236 fo. 17 (*LP* Add. I, i, 614).
120. Brooks, *Pettyfoggers and Vipers*, p. 39.
121. P. D. A. Harvey, *Manorial Records* (London, 1977), p. 51.
122. *Court Rolls of the Manor of Tottenham, 2 Henry VIII to 22 Henry VIII*, ed. F. H. Fenton (London, 1960), pp. 225–242.
123. TNA, PRO, SP1/26 fo. 57v (*LP* III, ii, 2577); J. Stow, *A Survey of London*, ed. C. L. Kingsford (2 vols, Oxford, 1908), i. 138–139, 146–147.

124. TNA, PRO, SP1/29 fo. 117 (*LP* III, ii, 3657); SP1/30 fo. 240v (*LP* IV, i, 166).
125. For further examples of Cromwell's work for merchants, see TNA, PRO, SP1/31 fo. 57 (*LP* IV, i, 387); SP1/36 fos 152–157 (*LP* IV, i, 1794 [i]); SP1/36 fos 158–159 (*LP* IV, i, 1794 [ii]); TNA, PRO, SP2/C fos 1–3 (*LP* IV, ii, 2375 [1]); SP2/C fos 4–7a (*LP* IV, ii, 2375 [2]); SP2/C fos 16–34 (*LP* IV, ii, 2375 [5]); SP2/C fos 35–47 (*LP* IV, ii, 2375 [6]); SP2/C fos 48–61v (*LP* IV, ii, 2375 [7]); SP2/C fos 62–73 (*LP* IV, ii, 2375 [8]).
126. TNA, PRO, SP1/26 fos 248–249 (*LP* III, ii, 2753).
127. TNA, PRO, SP1/235 fos 108–109 (*LP* Add. I, i, 507).
128. TNA, PRO, SP1/59 fos 123–125v (*LP* IV, iii, App. 229).
129. TNA, PRO, SP1/31 fo. 11 (*LP* IV, i, 304 [i]), annotated by Cromwell; TNA, PRO, SP1/31 fo. 12 (*LP* IV, i, 304 [ii]), wholly in Cromwell's hand; TNA, PRO, SP1/31 fos 15–16 (*LP* IV, i, 311).
130. TNA, PRO, SP1/53 fo. 168 (*LP* IV, iii, 5437).
131. BL, Egerton MS 2886 fo. 181v.
132. TNA, PRO, SP1/26 fo. 119 (*LP* III, ii, 2628); SP1/25 fo. 76 (*LP* III, ii, 2441); SP1/26 fo. 119 (*LP* III, ii, 2628); SP1/36 fo. 10 (*LP* IV, i, 1620); SP1/36 fo. 100 (*LP* IV, i, 1732).
133. TNA, PRO, SP1/34 fos 193–206 (*LP* IV, i, 1348).
134. TNA, PRO, SP1/235 fo. 360 (*LP* Add. I, i, 602); SP1/236 fo. 1 (*LP* Add. I, i, 606).
135. TNA, PRO, SP1/23 fo. 271 (*LP* III, ii, 1963); SP1/25 fo. 140 (*LP* III, ii, 2461); SP1/26 fo. 57 (*LP* III, ii, 2577); SP1/236 fos 344–354 (*LP* Add. I, i, 705).
136. Guernsey: TNA, PRO, SP1/55 fo. 100 (*LP* IV, iii, 5930). Hertfordshire: TNA, PRO, C1/569/41. Suffolk: TNA, PRO, C1/667/9; C1/484/11; TNA, PRO, STAC 2/17/252; TNA, PRO, SP1/40 fos 243–246 (*LP* IV, ii, 2844).
137. Brooks, *Pettyfoggers and Vipers*, p. 31.
138. TNA, PRO, SP1/54 fo. 235 (*LP* IV, iii, 5772). Cromwell's will is also printed in full in Merriman, *Life and Letters of Thomas Cromwell*, i. 56–63.
139. TNA, PRO, SP1/52 fo. 97 (*LP* IV, iii, 5143).
140. TNA, PRO, SP1/53 fos 36–51v (*LP* IV, iii, 5330).
141. Listed, among others, were: the dean of Cardinal's College, for £100 (TNA, PRO, SP1/53 fo. 41); the abbot of Welbeck, for £4 10s (fo. 41); the abbot of St James, for 26s 4d (fo. 41); the prior of Christchurch, for 10s (fo. 41); the prior of Lewes Abbey for 20s (fo. 41); the prior of Wenlock, for £13 6s 8d (fo. 41v); the prior of Butley, for £6 8s 4d (fo. 42); the prior of Lynton, for £5 (fo. 42).
142. TNA, PRO, SP1/29 fos 136–137v (*LP* III, ii, 3681 [i]); SP1/29 fo. 138 (*LP* III, ii, 3681 [i]); TNA, PRO, C1/558/27.
143. TNA, PRO, SP1/30 fos 33–34v (*LP* IV, i, 39). See also TNA, PRO, SP1/29 fos 134v–135v (*LP* III, ii, 3680 [ii]); much of this indenture is in Cromwell's hand.
144. TNA, PRO, SP1/55 fo. 16v (*LP* IV, iii, 5809).
145. TNA, PRO, SP1/31 fos 31–32 (*LP* IV, i, 360).
146. TNA, PRO, SP1/31 fos 31–32 (*LP* IV, i, 368); SP1/234 fo. 95, fos 97–98 (*LP* Add. I, i, 427).
147. Ives, *Common Lawyers*, p. 135.
148. Ibid., p. 133.
149. Elton, 'Thomas Cromwell Redivivus', in Elton, *Studies*, iii. 374; Elton, *Thomas Cromwell*, p. 3. Elton's chronology has been adopted by several other historians. See J. A. Guy, 'Thomas Wolsey, Thomas Cromwell and the Reform of Henrician Government', in D. MacCulloch, ed., *The Reign of Henry VIII: Politics, Policy and Piety* (Basingstoke, 1995), p. 41; Schofield, *Rise and Fall*, p. 14; Loades, *Thomas Cromwell*, p. 18.
150. BL, Egerton MS 2886.
151. TNA, PRO, STAC2/2/274; Ward, 'Origins of Thomas Cromwell's Public Career', pp. 32–33.
152. TNA, PRO, SP1/25 fo. 126 (*LP* III, ii, 2447); SP1/26 fo. 250 (*LP* III, ii, 2754). Deovanture was active in England around this time; Cromwell himself had drafted a licence for him in 1523. See TNA, PRO, SP1/26 fos 248–249 (*LP* III, ii, 2753).

153. TNA, PRO, SP1/21 fos 119–120v (*LP* III, i, 1026). See also TNA, PRO, SP1/22 fos 108–143v (*LP* III, ii, 1289 [1–3]); SP1/29 fos 136–137v, 138 (*LP* III, ii, 3681 [i, ii]); SP1/233 fos 71–77 (*LP* Add. I, i, 322 [2]).

154. Beckingsale and Williams also accepted 1524. See Beckingsale, *Thomas Cromwell*, p. 15; Williams, *Cardinal and the Secretary*, p. 148.

155. Merriman, *Life and Letters of Thomas Cromwell*, i. 13.

156. BL, Cotton MS, Vespasian F XIII fo. 173v (*LP* III, ii, 2437); TNA, PRO, SP1/41 fo. 160v (Merriman, *Life and Letters of Thomas Cromwell*, i. 316; *LP* IV, ii, 3053). *Cf.* Elton's comments on the Dorset link in *Thomas Cromwell*, p. 3.

157. TNA, PRO, SP1/31 fo. 3 (Merriman, *Life and Letters of Thomas Cromwell*, i. 316; *LP* IV, i, 294).

158. A document headed 'the expences and costes of John Alyen' relating to the sale of the Kexby lands, included items listed 'for the costes of master Cromwell'. See TNA, PRO, SP1/44 fo. 312 (*LP* IV, ii, 3536 [3]). *Cf.* Ward, 'Origins of Thomas Cromwell's Public Career', pp. 25–26.

159. Dickens, *Thomas Cromwell*, pp. 19–20. For the speech, see TNA, PRO, SP1/27 fos 193–207v (Merriman, *Life and Letters of Thomas Cromwell*, i. 30–43; *LP* III, ii, 2958).

160. Robertson, 'Thomas Cromwell's Servants', pp. 43–46.

161. TNA, PRO, SP1/30 fo. 120v (*LP* IV, i, 99).

162. For Ward's convincing discussion of Cromwell's entry into Wolsey's services, see 'Origins of Thomas Cromwell's Public Career', pp. 21–45.

163. Ibid., pp. 39–44. The indentures connected with Cromwell, made in June 1524, on behalf of Hennage, can be found in TNA, PRO, SP1/31 fo. 142 and fos 143–147 (*LP* IV, i, 461). The first indenture is wholly in Cromwell's hand; the second, a further draft of the same, is corrected by him.

164. TNA, PRO, E40/683.

165. Papal approval was given for the suppression of St Frideswide's monastery, Oxford, on 3 April 1524. The royal assent was given on 19 April; see TNA, PRO, SP1/30 fos 317–320 (*LP* IV, i, 264). For a thorough discussion of the collegiate foundations, see the accounts given in D. Knowles, *The Religious Orders in England* (3 vols, Cambridge, 1959), iii. 161–164; J. Newman, 'Cardinal Wolsey's Collegiate Foundations', in S. J. Gunn and P. G. Lindley, eds, *Cardinal Wolsey: Church, State and Art* (Cambridge, 1991), pp. 103–116; R. B. Pugh, ed., *Victoria History of the Counties of England: A History of the County of Oxfordshire* (10 vols, London, 1907–1979), iii. 228–238; W. Page, ed., *Victoria History of the Counties of England: A History of the County of Suffolk* (2 vols, London, 1907–1911), ii. 142–144.

166. *LP* IV, i, 1137.

167. TNA, PRO, C82/550/101 (*LP* IV, i, 697). The monasteries listed for suppression were: Canwell, Staffordshire; Sandwell, Staffordshire; Littlemore, Oxfordshire; Tickford, Buckinghamshire; Wallingford, Berkshire; Ravenstone, Buckinghamshire; Daventry, Northamptonshire; Bradwell, Buckinghamshire; Tonbridge, Kent; Lesnes, Kent; Bayham, Sussex; Calceto, Sussex; Wix, Essex; Tiptree, Essex; Blackmore, Essex; Stanesgate, Essex; Horkesley, Essex; Thoby, Essex; Poughley, Berkshire; Dodnash, Suffolk; and Snape, Suffolk. To these should be added the nunnery of Pré, Hertfordshire, which was suppressed at a later date.

168. The papal bulls authorising the suppression of St Peter's and the other houses intended for dissolution were given on 14 May 1528. See TNA, PRO, SC 7/63/8 (*LP* IV, ii, 4259 [1]); SC 7/63/9 (*LP* IV, ii, 4259 [2]). Royal assent followed on 26 May; see TNA, PRO, C66/652 m. 35 (*LP* IV, ii, 4297 [1]) and E24/1/2 (*LP* IV, ii, 4297 [2]). The other houses suppressed for Cardinal College, Ipswich, were Rumburgh, Suffolk; Felixstowe, Suffolk; Bromehill, Norfolk; and Mountjoy, Norfolk. The priory of Blythburgh, Suffolk, was also included in the bull, but was not suppressed by Wolsey; see *VCH, Suffolk*, ii. 93.

169. E. Hall, *The Union of the Two Noble and Illustre Famelies of Lancastre and York*, ed., H. Ellis (London, 1809), p. 769. Henceforth referred to as Hall, *Chronicle*.

170. Foxe, *Acts and Monuments* (1570 edn), p. 1386. Eustace Chapuys similarly alluded to Cromwell's role in Wolsey's suppressions when describing Cromwell in 1535. See Thomas, *The Pilgrim*, pp. 106–108; *CSP, Spanish*, V, i, 228.

171. Ward, 'Origins of Thomas Cromwell's Public Career', *passim*. Several of the following paragraphs draw on this thesis.
172. TNA, PRO, E24/22/2; E24/23/1 (*LP* IV, i, 989). Medmenham and Finchbrooke escaped suppression.
173. TNA, PRO, SP1/53 fo. 174 (*LP* IV, iii, 5458).
174. Ibid.
175. TNA, PRO, SP2/E fo. 123v.
176. J. Youings, *The Dissolution of the Monasteries* (London, 1971), p. 27.
177. *Cf.* Ward, 'Origins of Thomas Cromwell's Public Career', p. 51.
178. *LP* IV, i, 1137 [1–20]; J. E. Oxley, *The Reformation in Essex to the Death of Mary* (Manchester, 1965), p. 71.
179. Youings, *Dissolution of the Monasteries*, p. 28; Knowles, *Religious Orders in England*, iii. 163; *Statutes of the Realm*: ii, 8 Henry VI, c. 16; ii, 18 Henry VI, c. 6, 7; iii, 1 Henry VIII, c. 8.
180. This practice attracted some controversy at the time. The chronicler Hall recollected how Wolsey 'caused thexcheter' to 'founde the kynge founder, where other men wer founders' during these suppressions. See Hall, *Chronicle*, p. 794.
181. TNA, PRO, SP1/47 fo. 153 (Merriman, *Life and Letters of Thomas Cromwell*, i. 318; *LP* IV, ii, 4135).
182. TNA, PRO, E101/518/14 fos 4–5 (*LP* IV, ii, 5117 [1]).
183. See, for example, TNA, PRO, C142/76/3; C142/76/3, 4, 5, 6, 9, 12, 13, 15, 16, 17, 18, 19, 21, 22, 23, 30, 31, 37, 38, 39, 41, 42, 45, 46, 48, 49, 50, 51.
184. The licence to found the college on the site of St Frideswide can be found in TNA, PRO, C82/ 562 (*LP* IV, i, 1499 [1]); for a corrected draft, bearing Cromwell's hand, see TNA, PRO, SP1/35 fos 58–65v and TNA, PRO, C66/647 m. 1 (*LP* IV, i, 1499 [3]). The grant of the sites of the suppressed monasteries to be used for this can be found in TNA, PRO, C82/ 567 and TNA, PRO, C66/646 m. 20 (*LP* IV, i, 1833 [1]); for a draft of the same, in Thomas Wriothesley's hand, with amendments by Cromwell, see SP1/35 fos 171–180 (*LP* IV, i, 1833 [3]).
185. TNA, PRO, SP1/47 fo. 153 (Merriman, *Life and Letters of Thomas Cromwell*, i. 318; *LP* IV, ii, 4135).
186. TNA, PRO, SP1/50 fo. 70 (Merriman, *Life and Letters of Thomas Cromwell*, i. 322; *LP* IV, iii, 4697).
187. TNA, PRO, SP1/53 fo. 23 (*LP* IV, iii, 5304).
188. TNA, PRO, SP1/44 fo. 207 (*LP* IV, ii, 3536 [i]).
189. TNA, PRO, SC12/18/60 fos 77v–86 (*LP* IV, i, 1845 [iv]); not SC11/18/60, as given in the TNA, PRO 'List and Index' guide to *Letters and Papers*.
190. TNA, PRO, SP1/51 fo. 112v (*LP* IV, ii, 5052).
191. When Cromwell became receiver-general is unclear, but for his accounts in this position, covering the period between Michaelmas 1524 and Michaelmas 1527, see TNA, PRO, SC6/HENVIII/2913 (*LP* IV, ii, 3461 [1]).
192. TNA, PRO, E101/479/11 (*LP* IV, ii, 3676). See also TNA, PRO, SP1/54 fo. 351 (*LP* IV, iii, 5792); SP1/43 fo. 6v (*LP* IV, iii, 3334).
193. TNA, PRO, SP1/52 fos 146–146v (Merriman, *Life and Letters of Thomas Cromwell*, i. 323–325; *LP* IV, iii, 5186).
194. BL, Cotton MS, Titus B I fo. 281 (*LP* IV, ii, 4778).
195. TNA, PRO, SP1/49 fo. 1 (Merriman, *Life and Letters of Thomas Cromwell*, i. 320; *LP* IV, ii, 4441).
196. TNA, PRO, SP1/44 fos 365–367 (*LP* IV, ii, 3539); TNA, PRO, E40/14609.
197. TNA, PRO, SP1/50 fo. 71 (Merriman, *Life and Letters of Thomas Cromwell*, i. 322–323; *LP* IV, ii, 4697 [ii]).
198. Oxley, *Reformation in Essex*, p. 72.
199. For other references to payments made 'to yong children at the possession taking' of several monasteries, see TNA, PRO, SP1/44 fo. 218v (*LP* IV, iii, 3536 [3]); TNA, PRO, E101/518/14 fo. 3r (*LP* IV, iii, 5117 [1]).
200. Hutchinson, *Thomas Cromwell*, p. 119.
201. TNA, PRO, SP1/44 fo. 299v (*LP* IV, ii, 3556 [iii]).

202. TNA, PRO, SP1/44 fo. 218 (*LP* IV, ii, 3536 [iii]).
203. TNA, PRO, SP1/44 fo. 233r–233v, 275r.
204. Ward, 'Origins of Thomas Cromwell's Public Career', p. 65.
205. Ibid., pp. 64–65.
206. TNA, PRO, SP1/39 fo. 3v (*LP* IV, i, 2347); SP1/39 fo. 4v (*LP* IV, i, 2348); SP1/41 fo. 180v (*LP* IV, ii, 3079); SP1/49 fo. 158v (*LP* IV, ii, 4573); SP1/49 fo. 159v (*LP* IV, ii, 4581); SP1/49 fo. 203v (*LP* IV, ii, 4614); SP1/50 fo. 64v (*LP* IV, ii, 4690); SP1/52 fo. 95 (*LP* IV, ii, 5131); SP1/53 fo. 165v (*LP* IV, iii, 5431).
207. TNA, PRO, SP1/51 fos 260–264 (*LP* IV, ii, 5107). The draft indenture is in Thomas Wriothesley's hand, then in Cromwell's service, and is corrected by Cromwell.
208. TNA, PRO, SP1/52 fos 50–57 (*LP* IV, ii, 5117 [5]), this draft indenture is corrected by Cromwell; TNA, PRO, SP1/52 fos 58–63 (*LP* IV, ii, 5117 [6]). For the final indenture of this, see TNA, PRO, E40/716.
209. TNA, PRO, E101/518/14 fos 12–13 (*LP* IV, ii, 5117 [iii]); TNA, PRO, SP1/236 fo. 73 (*LP* Add. I, i, 636).
210. TNA, PRO, SP1/59 fos 106–107 (*LP* IV, iii, App. 109). Wolsey had been involved with the wardship from the very beginning, negotiating its terms on behalf of the king in January 1524. See TNA, PRO, SP1/30 fo. 39 (*LP* IV, i, 48). The young Monteagle had also been placed in Wolsey's household during his minority; see S. J. Gunn, *Charles Brandon, Duke of Suffolk, c.1484–1545* (Oxford, 1988), p. 93.
211. TNA, PRO, SP1/53 fo. 250 (*LP* IV, iii, 5526); SP1/54 fo. 4 (*LP* IV, iii, 5550); SP1/55 fo. 101 (*LP* IV, iii, 5933). TNA, PRO, SP1/82 fo. 267 (*LP* VII, 341) is also connected with this, but has been erroneously placed in 1534 by the editors of *Letters and Papers*. For another example of Cromwell's private work for Capon, see TNA, PRO, SP1/57 fo. 24 (*LP* IV, iii, 6230).
212. TNA, PRO, SP1/46 fo. 35 (*LP* IV, ii, 3442).
213. TNA, PRO, SP1/48 fo. 125 (*LP* IV, ii, 4342).
214. TNA, PRO, SP1/33 fos 163–170 (*LP* IV, i, 1091 [1]); SP1/33 fos 171–177 (*LP* IV, i, 1091 [2]);SP1/33 fo. 178 (*LP* IV, i, 1091 [3]).
215. TNA, PRO, SP1/70 fo. 203 (*LP* V, 1239).
216. TNA, PRO, SP1/71 fo. 17 (Merriman, *Life and Letters of Thomas Cromwell*, i. 348; *LP* V, 1298); SP1/71 fo. 38 (*LP* V, 1323 [1]); SP1/71 fo. 38v (*LP* V, 1323 [2]); SP1/76 fo. 1 (*LP* VI, 420).
217. TNA, PRO, SP1/74 fo. 169 (*LP* VI, 171); SP1/74 fo. 183 (*LP* VI, 189).
218. TNA, PRO, SP1/26 fo. 108 (*LP* III, ii, 2624).
219. TNA, PRO, SP1/27 fo. 286 (*LP* III, ii, 3015). For further mercantile activities, see BL, Cotton MS, Vespasian F XIII fo. 173 (*LP* III, ii, 2437).
220. TNA, PRO, SP1/42 fo. 59v (*LP* IV, ii, 3154).
221. TNA, PRO, SP1/34 fos 233 (*LP* IV, i, 1385).
222. TNA, PRO, SP1/27 fo. 286 (*LP* III, ii, 3015). For Cromwell's involvement with printing more generally, see Slavin, 'Gutenberg Galaxy', pp. 90–109; A. J. Slavin, 'Thomas Cromwell and the Printers: The Boston Pardons', in G. J. Schochet, ed., *Reformation, Humanism, and 'Revolution'* (Washington, DC, 1990), pp. 235–249.
223. TNA, PRO, SP1/48 fo. 175 (*LP* IV, ii, 4388).
224. TNA, PRO, SP1/25 fo. 55 (*LP* III, ii, 2394); SP1/26 fo. 108 (*LP* III, ii, 2624).
225. BL, Cotton MS, Galba B IX fo. 13 (*LP* IV, ii, 4018).
226. TNA, PRO, SP1/49 fo. 149 (*LP* IV, ii, 4555).
227. TNA, PRO, SP1/235 fo. 354 (*LP* Add. I, i, 598); SP1/81 fo. 111 (*LP* VI, 1657), misdated to 1533 in *Letters and Papers*.
228. TNA, PRO, SP1/50 fo. 23–23v (*LP* IV, ii, 4662 [i]); SP1/50 fo. 44–44v (*LP* IV, ii, 4662 [xi]); SP1/50 fo. 23 (*LP* IV, ii, 4662 [i]).
229. TNA, PRO, SP1/49 fo. 201v (*LP* IV, ii, 4613); SP1/59 fo. 88 (*LP* IV, iii, App. 78); SP1/55 fo. 138 (*LP* IV, iii, 5971); SP1/73 fo. 132 (*LP* V 1756 [2]).
230. TNA, PRO, SP1/57 fo. 23 (*LP* IV, iii, 6223).
231. TNA, PRO, SP1/53 fo. 39 (*LP* IV, iii, 5330).
232. TNA, PRO, SP1/51 fo. 131 (*LP* IV, ii, 5077).
233. TNA, PRO, SP1/235 fo. 219 (*LP* Add. I, i, 542).

234. TNA, PRO, SP1/58 fo. 173 (*LP* IV, iii, 6754).
235. TNA, PRO, SP1/49 fos 201v (*LP* IV, ii, 4613).
236. *Cf.* Robertston, 'Profit and Purpose', pp. 320–322 on Cromwell's earliest acquisition of land.
237. TNA, PRO, SP1/29 fo. 26 (*LP* III, ii, 3502); TNA, PRO, C1/492/17–21. See also TNA, PRO, C1/494/55, which is connected to this; TNA, PRO, SP1/32 fo. 236–236v (Merriman, *Life and Letters of Thomas Cromwell*, i. 314–316; *LP* IV, i, 955 [3]).
238. TNA, PRO, SP1/65 fo. 119 (*LP* V, 84). The letter is dated to 1531 in *Letters and Papers*, but the references in it to William Brabazon and Richard Swift's work surveying Daventry, Northamptonshire, suggest it should be dated to 1527.
239. TNA, PRO, SP1/44 fos 198–206 (*LP* IV, ii, 3535).
240. TNA, PRO, SP2/J fos 159–170 (*LP* IV, iii, 6336 [i]); SP2/J fos 170–172 (*LP* IV, iii, 6336 [ii]); SP2/K 1–5 (*LP* IV, iii, 6336 [iii]); TNA, PRO, SP1/57 fo. 23 (*LP* IV, iii, 6223); SP1/57 fo. 16 (*LP* IV, iii, 6221).
241. TNA, PRO, SP2/K fos 1–5 (*LP* IV, iii, 6336 [iii]).
242. TNA, PRO, C82/638 and C66/657 m. 30 (*LP* V, 119). The lease for this was originally for thirty years, but Cromwell gave up his interest to Bowland in May 1529.
243. TNA, PRO, SP1/58 fos 199–205. Cromwell also purchased a lease on the manor of Filston, 'lying within the paroche of Shorham … within the countye of Kent', from William Petley on 24 May 1528. See TNA, PRO, SP1/48 fos 37–40 (*LP* IV, ii, 4295). In this instance, however, Cromwell was himself acting as a middleman for Robert Studley, who had been trying to acquire the lease on the farm for some time. See TNA, PRO, SP1/52 fo. 102 (*LP* IV, iii, 5146); SP1/52 fo. 101 (*LP* IV, iii, 5145), placed in 1529 in *Letters and Papers*, but it is from 1528.
244. Ives, *Common Lawyers*, pp. 330–354.
245. W. Roper, *The Lyfe of Sir Thomas Moore, Knighte*, ed. E. V. Hitchcock (London, 1935), p. 9; Ives, *Common Lawyers*, pp. 328, 447.
246. Ives, *Common Lawyers*, pp. 299, 304.
247. TNA, PRO, SP1/32 fo. 235 (*LP* IV, i, 955).
248. TNA, PRO, SP1/44 fo. 222v (*LP* IV, ii, 3536 [3]).
249. Ibid., fo. 221v.
250. TNA, PRO, SP 1/44 fos 218r, 221r (*LP* IV, ii, 3536 [3]).
251. TNA, PRO, E179/69/8 (*LP* IV, ii, 2972 [9]).
252. TNA, PRO, E179/69/1 (*LP* IV, ii, 2972 [1]). In another valuation of Wolsey's entourage from the same period, Thomas Audeley was valued in lands worth a mere £7. See TNA, PRO, E179/69/10 (*LP* IV, ii, 2972 [8]).
253. TNA, PRO, SP1/54 fos 235–248 (*LP* IV, iii, 5772). The will is printed in full in Merriman, *Life and Letters of Thomas Cromwell*, i. 56–63.
254. TNA, PRO, SP1/54 fos 235–248 (Merriman, *Life and Letters of Thomas Cromwell*, i. 56–64; *LP* IV, iii, 5772). Many of these cash bestowals in Cromwell's will were amended and increased when he revised it after September 1532.
255. Their entries in the will were crossed out by Cromwell in a subsequent revision.
256. Merriman, *Life and Letters of Thomas Cromwell*, i. 50.
257. TNA, PRO, C244/169/19. See also Guy, *Cardinal's Court*, p. 90.
258. TNA, PRO, STAC 2/7 fos 107–108.
259. TNA, PRO, SP1/59 fo. 104 (*LP* IV, iii, App. 103). See also TNA, PRO, SP1/52 fo. 219–219v (*LP* IV, iii, 5285), which was placed in 1529 in *Letters and Papers* but which dates to the suppression of Poughley, Berkshire, in 1525.
260. TNA, PRO, E36/140 fo. 29r.
261. TNA, PRO, SP1/65 fo. 136 (*LP* V, 106). This was placed in 1531 in *Letters and Papers*, but it clearly refers to the fee recorded on Cromwell's list of fees and annuities granted in 1525; see TNA, PRO, E36/140 fo. 29r. An undated draft of this grant was also mistakenly placed in 1533; see TNA, PRO, SP2/O fo. 133 (*LP* VI, 1625 [7]).
262. TNA, PRO, C82/550/101 (*LP* IV, i, 697).
263. TNA, PRO, SP1/65 fo. 136 (*LP* V, 106); SP1/65 fo. 137 (*LP* V, 107). Both letters are of the year 1525.

264. BL, Add. MS, 48028 fo. 164. Cromwell's attainder is not printed in *Statutes of the Realm*. A printed copy can be found in Burnet, *History of the Reformation*, iv. 105–109.

265. TNA, PRO, SP1/52 fo. 130 (*LP* IV, iii, 5169).

266. TNA, PRO, SP1/37 fo. 6 (*LP* IV, i, 1881). This is dated January, and placed in 1526 in *Letters and Papers*; given that Tickford and Ravenstone were suppressed in February 1525, it may well date to that year.

267. TNA, PRO, SP1/47 fo. 222 (*LP* IV, ii, 4201). Cromwell was asked to 'helpe he may haue graunte and auctoritie of my lordes grace to contenew & be in the said mynt'.

268. C. E. Challis, *The Tudor Coinage* (Manchester, 1978), p. 76. For other examples of Cromwell's perceived influence with Wolsey, see TNA, PRO, SP1/51 fo. 122 (*LP* IV, ii, 5069); SP1/50 fo. 207 (*LP* IV, ii, 4877); SP1/59 fo. 273 (*LP* IV, iii, App. 272).

269. TNA, PRO, SP1/53 fos 36–51v (*LP* IV, iii, 5330).

270. Ibid., fos 38, 43v, 49.

271. Ibid., fos 39, 41, 49v.

272. The earliest is from June 1521, and so cannot be linked to Cromwell's association with Wolsey. Ibid., fos 40, 46, 49v, 50v.

273. TNA, PRO, SP1/59 fos 106–107v (*LP* IV, iii, App. 109).

274. TNA, PRO, SP1/235 fo. 363 (*LP* Add. I, i, 604); SP1/236 fo. 68 (*LP* Add. I, i, 631).

275. TNA, PRO, SP1/235 fo. 56 (*LP* Add. I, i, 488).

276. On this friendship, see pp. 58–59.

277. Elton, 'Thomas Cromwell Redivivus', in Elton, *Studies*, iii. 376; Elton, *Reform and Reformation*, p. 170.

278. TNA, PRO, SP1/29 fos 117–122 (*LP* III, ii, 3657).

279. A. E. McCampbell, 'The London Parish and the London Precinct, 1640–1660', *Guildhall Studies in London History*, 2 (1976), pp. 117–119.

280. *LP* IV, i, 969 [4].

281. R. Schofield, *Taxation under the Early Tudors, 1485–1547* (Oxford, 2004), p. 96.

282. Ibid, pp. 116–118.

283. TNA, PRO, SP1/27 fos 193–207v (*LP* III, ii, 2958). The speech is printed in Merriman, *Life and Letters of Thomas Cromwell*, i. 30–43.

284. *LP* IV, iii, 6043 [2].

285. Elton, 'Political Creed of Thomas Cromwell', in Elton, *Studies*, ii. 225; Elton, *Reform and Reformation*, p. 121.

286. Elton, *Tudor Revolution in Government*, p.80.

287. Elton, 'Political Creed of Thomas Cromwell', in Elton, *Studies*, ii. 225; Elton, *England under the Tudors*, pp. 128–129, 160–192.

288. G. Cavendish, *The Life and Death of Cardinal Wolsey*, ed. R. S. Sylvester (London, 1959), pp. 105, 112.

289. Elton, *Tudor Revolution in Government*, p. 80.

290. S. J. Payling, 'The Rise of Lawyers in the Lower House, 1395–1536', *Parliamentary History*, 23 (2004), pp. 103–120.

291. TNA, PRO, SP1/28 fo. 154 (Merriman, *Life and Letters of Thomas Cromwell*, i. 313; *LP* III, ii, 3249).

292. Merriman, *Life and Letters of Thomas Cromwell*, i. 27; Innes, *Ten Tudor Statesmen*, p. 119; H. A. L. Fisher, *The Political History of England*, Volume V: *From the Accession of Henry VII to the Death of Henry VIII, 1485–1547* (London, 1906), p. 247.

293. Dickens, *Thomas Cromwell*, p. 20; Williams, *Cardinal and the Secretary*, p. 147; Beckingsale, *Thomas Cromwell*, p. 15; Schofield, *Rise and Fall*, p. 17; Loades, *Thomas Cromwell*, p. 31; Borman, *Thomas Cromwell*, p. 39.

294. Elton, 'Political Creed of Thomas Cromwell', in Elton, *Studies*, ii. 224. Elton claimed that 'this is no weighty and pompous judgement, but a man of affairs laughing at himself and his fellows'.

295. H. Miller, 'London and Parliament in the Reign of Henry VIII', *Bulletin of the Institute of Historical Research*, 35 (1962), pp. 128–149; I. Archer, 'The London Lobbies in the Later Sixteenth Century', *Historical Journal*, 31 (1988), pp. 17–44.

296. Miller, 'London and Parliament', pp. 136, 137, 139.

297. TNA, PRO, SP1/233 fo. 291 (*LP* Add. I, i, 384).

298. TNA, PRO, SP1/41 fo. 157 (*LP* IV, ii, 3053 [4]); SP1/235 fo. 203 (*LP* Add. I, 532 [1]). TNA, PRO, SP1/235 fo. 205 (*LP* Add. I, i, 532 [2]) is a copy of this.
299. TNA, PRO, SP1/235 fos 203 (*LP* Add. I, i, 532).
300. TNA, PRO, SP1/236 fo. 169 (*LP* Add. I, i, 663). Cromwell's endorsement, along with those of Paul Withypoll, Edward Hall, John Branings and Henry Seye, is on fo. 168, but no longer visible. The names that can still be made out, however, indicate that the *Letters and Papers* summary is correct.
301. G. L. Harriss, 'Medieval Government and Statecraft', *Past and Present*, 25 (1963), p. 21.
302. M. A. R. Graves, 'The Management of the Elizabethan House of Commons: The Council's "Men of Business"', *Parliamentary History*, 2 (1983), p. 16.
303. Ives, 'Common Lawyers', p. 153.
304. Gunn, *Early Tudor Government*, p. 15.
305. Guy, *Tudor England*, pp. 122–123; S. Gunn, 'Edmund Dudley and the Church', *Journal of Ecclesiastical History*, 51 (2000), pp. 509–526.

Chapter Two Entry into the King's Service, 1529–1530

1. The best account of Cromwell's entry into the king's service is Ward, 'Origins of Thomas Cromwell's Public Career', pp. 194–240; the most accessible remains Elton, *Tudor Revolution in Government*, pp. 71–88. See also Hutchinson, *Thomas Cromwell*, pp. 27–46; Schofield, *Rise and Fall*, pp. 26–32; Loades, *Thomas Cromwell*, pp. 46–58; Borman, *Thomas Cromwell*, pp. 80–100.
2. Elton, *Tudor Revolution in Government*, pp. 84, 82.
3. Ibid., p. 84.
4. There was, however, a contrary set of instructions in Deuteronomy 25:6. For the best discussions of Henry's case in canon law, see G. W. Bernard, *The King's Reformation: Henry VIII and the Remaking of the English Church* (New Haven, CT and London, 2005), pp. 17–24; Scarisbrick, *Henry VIII*, pp. 163–197.
5. *LP* IV, ii, 3140.
6. *LP* IV, ii, 3400.
7. J. Sharkey, 'Between king and pope: Thomas Wolsey and the Knight Mission', *Historical Research*, 84 (2011), pp. 236–248.
8. Scarisbrick, *Henry VIII*, p. 204.
9. *LP* IV, ii, 3693.
10. *LP* IV, ii, 4345; *LP* IV, ii, 4380; *LP* IV, ii, 4897.
11. For the complex international dimension, see P. Gwyn, *The King's Cardinal: The Rise and Fall of Thomas Wolsey* (London, 1990), pp. 530–548.
12. Hall, *Chronicle*, p. 756.
13. Cavendish, *Life and Death of Cardinal Wolsey*, p. 85.
14. G. W. Bernard, 'The Fall of Wolsey Reconsidered', *Journal of British Studies*, 35 (1996), pp. 299, 300; *CSP, Spanish*, IV, i, 83.
15. Gwyn, *King's Cardinal*, p. 591; Bernard, 'Fall of Wolsey', pp. 300–304.
16. *CSP, Spanish*, IV, i, 152.
17. Cavendish, *Life and Death of Cardinal Wolsey*, pp. 92–6; BL, Cotton MS, Vitellius B XII fo. 168 (*LP* IV, iii, 5953).
18. *CSP, Spanish*, IV, i, 132.
19. *LP* IV, iii, 5945; *LP* IV, iii, 5946.
20. BL, Cotton MS, Vitellius B XII fo. 168 (*LP* IV, iii, 5953).
21. Starkey, *Reign of Henry VIII*, p. 101; Guy, *Public Career*, pp. 97, 106–107; Haigh, *English Reformations*, pp. 93–94, 111; E. W. Ives, 'The Fall of Wolsey', in S. J. Gunn and P. G. Lindley, eds, *Cardinal Wolsey: Church, State and Art* (Cambridge, 1991), pp. 286–316.
22. Gwyn, *King's Cardinal*, pp. 504–598; Bernard, 'Fall of Wolsey Reconsidered', pp. 277–310.
23. *LP* IV, iii, 6035.
24. *LP* IV, iii, 6025.
25. TNA, PRO, E30/1458 (*LP* IV, iii, 6017).
26. TNA, PRO, SP1/55 fo. 198 (*LP* IV, iii, 6036).

27. *LP* XIV, i, 200 (p. 82).
28. Cavendish, *Life and Death of Cardinal Wolsey*, p. 105.
29. TNA, PRO, SP1/56 fo. 124 (*LP* IV, iii, 6110).
30. TNA, PRO, SP1/56 fo. 1 (*LP* IV, iii, 6039); SP1/56 fo. 86 (*LP* IV, iii, 6055); SP1/56 fo. 88 (*LP* IV, iii, 6061).
31. TNA, PRO, SP1/56 fos. 119–120 (*LP* IV, iii, 6102); SP1/38 fos 28–29, 35–39v (*LP* IV, i, 2109 [1 and 4]); SP1/54 fo. 80 (*LP* IV, iii, 5673);SP1/55 fo. 85 (*LP* IV, iii, 5901); SP1/55 fos 107–117 (*LP* IV, iii, 5948); SP1/55 fo. 154 (*LP* IV, iii, 6005);SP1/56 fos 191–192v (*LP* IV, iii, 6137); TNA, PRO, SP2/J fos 72v–72va (*LP* IV, iii, 6336 [2]).
32. BL, Cotton MS, Cleopatra E IV fo. 211 (Merriman, *Life and Letters of Thomas Cromwell*, i. 67–68; *LP* IV, iii, App. 238).
33. BL, Cotton MS, Appendix L fo. 30 (*State Papers Published Under the Authority of His Majesty's Commission, King Henry VIII, Public Record Office [11 vols, London, 1830–1852]*), i. 352; *LP* IV, iii, 6098). In *Letters and Papers*, much of Wolsey's correspondence to Cromwell during his fall is erroneously labelled as being in Cotton Appendix XLVIII. Those listed as such are in fact in Appendix L, as correctly cited here.
34. BL, Cotton MS, Appendix L fo. 29 (*State Papers*, i. 355; *LP* IV, iii, 6181).
35. BL, Cotton MS, Appendix L fo. 24 (*State Papers*, i. 360; *LP* IV, iii, 6262).
36. BL, Cotton MS, Appendix L fo. 27 (*State Papers*, i. 356; *LP* IV, iii, 6226).
37. Cavendish, *Life and Death of Cardinal Wolsey*, pp. 112–113.
38. TNA, PRO, SP1/57 fos 168–172v (*LP* IV, iii, 6467 [1]).
39. BL, Cotton MS, Appendix L fo. 7 (Merriman, *Life and Letters of Thomas Cromwell*, i. 329–330; *LP* IV, iii, 6482).
40. TNA, PRO, SP1/55 fo. 20 (*LP* IV, iii, 5812); this was placed in July 1529 in *Letters and Papers*, but was redated by Pollard to October. See A. F. Pollard, *Wolsey* (London, 1929), p. 240, n. 2.
41. From a letter now lost. See Merriman, *Life and Letters of Thomas Cromwell*, i. 327.
42. *Cf.* Ward, 'Origins of Thomas Cromwell's Public Career', p. 201. In a similar vein, during the 1530s, when Cromwell was firmly established in a position of immense power, he would continue to help and support Wolsey's illegitimate son, Thomas Winter. See TNA, PRO, SP1/73 fo. 166 (*LP* V, App. 24); TNA, PRO, C82/651 (*LP* V, 766 [12]); TNA, PRO, SP1/73 fo. 167 (*LP* V, App. 27); BL, Cotton MS, Nero B VI fos 126–126v (*LP* VI, 314), this is 1532, not 1533 as in *Letters and Papers*; TNA, PRO, SP1/70 fos 182–183 (*LP* V, 1210); SP1/71 fos 124–124v (*LP* V, 1452); SP1/80 fo. 99 (*LP* VI, 1428), this is 1532, not 1533 as in *Letters and Papers*; TNA, PRO, SP1/68 fo. 80 (*LP* V, 572), this is 1532, not 1531 as in *Letters and Papers*; TNA, PRO, SP1/73 fo. 13 (*LP* V, 1688); SP1/72 fo. 165v (*LP* V, 1670 [1]); SP1/74 fo. 16v (*LP* VI, 25); SP1/74 fos 170–170v (*LP* VI, 172); SP2/O fo. 34 (*LP* VI, 841).
43. TNA, PRO, E30/1458 (*LP* IV, iii, 6017).
44. *LP* IV, iii, 6030.
45. *CSP, Spanish*, IV, i, 257.
46. Cavendish, *Life and Death of Cardinal Wolsey*, pp. 123–124.
47. TNA, PRO, C82/624 (*LP* IV, iii, 6213 [1]); TNA, PRO, E24/23/32 (*LP* IV, iii, 6213 [2]).
48. *CSP, Spanish*, IV, i, 194; Cavendish, *Life and Death of Cardinal Wolsey*, pp. 102, 111, 120–121.
49. *LP* IV, iii, 6151; Cavendish, *Life and Death of Cardinal Wolsey*, p. 120.
50. Gwyn, *King's Cardinal*, pp. 593–596, 616–635.
51. *CSP, Spanish*, V, i, 228.
52. The *Apologia Reginaldi Poli ad Carolum V. Caesarem super quatuor Libris a se scriptis de Unitate Ecclesiae*, to give it its full title, was the first of three prefaces, all written for Pole's treatise *In Defence of the Unity of the Church* (*Pro Ecclesiasticae Unitatis Defensione*). No English translation of the *Apologia* exists. Merriman has printed extracts of it (*Life and Letters of Thomas Cromwell*, i. 18–19), but here P. Van Dyke's detailed treatment of it has been relied upon, along with the summarised version in *Letters and Papers*. See P. Van Dyke, 'Reginald Pole and Thomas Cromwell: An Examination of the *Apologia*

Ad Carolum Quintum', *American Historical Review*, 9 (1904), pp. 696–724; *LP* XIV, i, 200 (esp. p. 82).

53. Van Dyke, 'Reginald Pole and Thomas Cromwell', p. 704.
54. *LP* XIV, i, 200 (p. 82); Van Dyke, 'Reginald Pole and Thomas Cromwell', p. 706.
55. Foxe, *Acts and Monuments* (1570 edn), p. 1387. It is interesting to note that the first edition of *Acts and Monuments*, published in 1563, did not report this story. Instead, in his earliest version Foxe alleges that it was Wolsey who facilitated Cromwell's entry into the king's service: 'he was commended by the Cardinall vnto the kyng, and after that, he was translated into his court, by and by he was set to beare office'. See and compare with Foxe, *Acts and Monuments* (1563 edn), p. 648.
56. J. A. Guy, 'Thomas Cromwell and the Intellectual Origins of the Henrician Reformation', in A. Fox and J. A. Guy, eds, *Reassessing the Henrician Age: Humanism, Politics and Reform, 1500–1550* (Oxford, 1986), pp. 151–178.
57. *LP* XIV, i, 200 (p. 82); Van Dyke, 'Reginald Pole and Thomas Cromwell', p. 708.
58. Elton, *Tudor Revolution in Government*, pp. 72–75. Elton would later claim that he could identify Cromwell's influence on policy as early as 1530. He therefore felt that, although the accounts of Pole, Chapuys and Foxe were 'a bit garbled', they should not be disregarded. See Elton, *Reform and Reformation*, p. 136 and n. 12.
59. Elton, *Tudor Revolution in Government*, pp. 75–76.
60. Hall, *Chronicle*, p. 769.
61. Elton, *Tudor Revolution in Government*, p. 83. Most modern historians have accepted this. See Dickens, *Thomas Cromwell*, pp. 34–35; Robertson, 'Thomas Cromwell's Servants', pp. 65–66; Williams, *Cardinal and the Secretary*, p. 155; Guy, 'Thomas Wolsey, Thomas Cromwell and the Reform of Henrician Government', p. 41; Schofield, *Rise and Fall*, p. 29.
62. TNA, PRO, SP1/65 fo. 122 (*LP* V, 86).
63. Elton, *Tudor Revolution in Government*, p. 83; *LP* IV, iii, 6196.
64. Elton, *Tudor Revolution in Government*, p. 87.
65. TNA, PRO, SP1/236 fo. 305 (*LP* Add. I, i, 687).
66. Elton, *Tudor Revolution in Government*, p. 87.
67. Cavendish, *Life and Death of Cardinal Wolsey*, pp. 122–123.
68. From a letter now lost. See Merriman, *Life and Letters of Thomas Cromwell*, i. 327.
69. TNA, PRO, SP1/236 fo. 171 (*LP* Add. I, i, 665). In another letter to Cromwell from one James Beck, placed with this letter to Wolsey, Beck refers to having spoken with Cromwell 'in the kings chamber'. See TNA, PRO, SP1/236 fo. 173 (*LP* Add. I, i, 666). The subject of the letter very much suggests it was written in 1531 or 1532, when Cromwell was engaged on matters of state.
70. From a letter now lost. See Merriman, *Life and Letters of Thomas Cromwell*, i. 327.
71. Cavendish, *Life and Death of Cardinal Wolsey*, pp. 123–126.
72. TNA, PRO, SP1/57 fo. 139 (*LP* IV, iii, 6420).
73. BL, Cotton MS, Appendix L fo. 30 (*State Papers*, i. 352; *LP* IV, iii, 6098).
74. BL, Cotton MS, Appendix L fo. 18 (*State Papers*, i. 350; *LP* IV, iii, 6263); BL, Cotton MS, Appendix L fo. 25 (*State Papers*, i. 354; *LP* IV, iii, 6204).
75. For Gage's career, see D. Potter, 'Sir John Gage, Tudor Courtier and Soldier (1479–1556)', *English Historical Review*, cxvii (2002), pp. 1109–1147.
76. BL, Cotton MS, Titus B I fo. 375 (*LP* IV, iii, 6112). The letter is undated, but must have been sent before February 1530 as it was addressed to Cromwell at the cardinal's house at 'Asshire'.
77. TNA, PRO, SP1/53 fo. 39 (*LP* IV, iii, 5330).
78. TNA, PRO, SP2/J fos 159–169 (*LP* IV, iii, 6336 [i]); TNA, PRO, SP1/65 fo. 51 (*LP* V, 36). This letter was placed in January 1531 by *Letters and Papers*, but probably dates to the mid to late 1520s, when Cromwell was more active on mercantile matters. See also TNA, PRO, SP1/53 fo. 39 (*LP* IV, iii, 5330).
79. TNA, PRO, SP1/78 fo. 104 (*LP* VI, 965). My italics for emphasis.
80. TNA, PRO, SP1/57 fo. 67 (*LP* IV, iii, 6335).
81. BL, Cotton MS, Cleopatra E IV fos 211–211v (Merriman, *Life and Letters of Thomas Cromwell*, i. 67–68; *LP* IV, iii, App. 238).

82. Merriman and *Letters and Papers* both mistakenly transcribed this burgess as Oxford. Examination of the original manuscript confirms Elton was correct to note it as Orford in Suffolk.
83. *LP* IV, iii, 6043 [2].
84. BL, Cotton MS, Cleopatra E IV fo. 211 (Merriman, *Life and Letters of Thomas Cromwell*, i. 67–68; *LP* IV, iii, App. 238).
85. Elton, *Tudor Revolution in Government*, pp. 78, 79. A. J. Slavin, in his biography of Ralph Sadler, followed Elton on the details of this episode. See A. J. Slavin, *Politics and Profit: A Study of Sir Ralph Sadler* (Cambridge, 1966), pp. 18–21.
86. BL, Cotton MS, Cleopatra E IV fo. 211 (Merriman, *Life and Letters of Thomas Cromwell*, i. 67–68; *LP* IV, iii, App. 238). My italics for emphasis.
87. A letter from Thomas Shell to Cromwell, dated 27 November, in which Shell remarks that 'you be in fauour hilie with the kynges grace lords and the commumy-altie aswell spirituall as temporall', was placed in 1531 in *Letters and Papers*, with a note from the editors that it might be of 1530. Elton concurred that it was probably of 1530 (*Tudor Revolution in Government*, p. 88). Yet the reference to parliament, which did not meet at all in 1530, and Shell's comment that 'you wer in grete troble for my lorde cardynalles causez and matters' make little sense in either 1531 or 1530. It is highly probable, then, that this letter was sent in November 1529, shortly after Cromwell had secured his seat. See TNA, PRO, SP1/68 fo. 58 (*LP* V, 551). *Cf.* Ward, 'Origins of Thomas Cromwell's Public Career', p. 206 n.71.
88. *LP* IV, iii, 6019.
89. BL, Cotton MS, Appendix L fo. 30 (*State Papers*, i. 352; *LP* IV, iii, 6098).
90. BL, Cotton MS, Vespasian F XIII fo. 147 (*State Papers*, i. 349; *LP* IV, iii, 6080).
91. TNA, PRO, SP1/56 fo. 86 (*LP* IV, iii, 6055).
92. Cavendish, *Life and Death of Cardinal Wolsey*, p. 124.
93. Ibid., p. 115.
94. BL, Cotton MS, Appendix L fo. 29 (*State Papers*, i. 355; *LP* IV, iii, 6226).
95. TNA, PRO, E30/1458 (*LP* IV, iii, 6017).
96. *LP* IV, iii, 6220. Although Wolsey remained bishop of Winchester and head of St Albans.
97. Cavendish, *Life and Death of Cardinal Wolsey*, p. 125.
98. Ibid.
99. TNA, PRO, SP1/236 fo. 319 (*LP* Add. I, i, 693).
100. TNA, PRO, SP1/236 fo. 320 (*LP* Add. I, i, 694).
101. TNA, PRO, SP1/57 fo. 139 (*LP* IV, iii, 6420). My italics for emphasis.
102. Elton, *Tudor Revolution in Government*, p. 85.
103. *Cf.* Ward, 'Origins of Thomas Cromwell's Public Career', pp. 221–222.
104. Two drafts of this grant from Wolsey to Sandys have survived, one of which is complete (TNA, PRO, SP1/57 fo. 162; *LP* IV, iii, 6420 [2]); the second is only the latter part of the grant (TNA, PRO, SP1/57 fo. 164; *LP* IV, iii, 6460 [3]). The editors of *Letters and Papers* believed the second to be corrected in Cromwell's hand; but it is not evidently Cromwell's.
105. TNA, PRO, SP1/57 fo. 148 (*LP* IV, iii, 6432).
106. TNA, PRO, SP1/57 fo. 150 (*LP* IV, iii, 6435). See also SP1/57 fo. 160 (*LP* IV, iii, 6460 [1]).
107. Paulet also wrote on the matter as late as September, having finally sent Henry Norris's sealed patent to Cromwell, along with another for a Master Chomely. See TNA, PRO, SP1/236 fo. 326 (*LP* Add. I, i, 697).
108. Cavendish, *Life and Death of Cardinal Wolsey*, pp. 125, 126.
109. *Cf.* Ward, 'Origins of Thomas Cromwell's Public Career', pp. 224–233.
110. *LP* IV, iii, 6555, 6575, 6576, 6577.
111. TNA, PRO, SP1/56 fo. 86 (*LP* IV, iii, 6055).
112. TNA, PRO, SP1/56 fo. 88 (*LP* IV, iii, 6061).
113. TNA, PRO, SP1/56 fo. 124 (*LP* IV, iii, 6110).
114. TNA, PRO, SP1/57 fo. 90 (*LP* IV, iii, 6377).
115. TNA, PRO, SP1/57 fos 227–227v (*LP* IV, iii, 6510).

116. TNA, PRO, SP1/57 fo. 227 (*LP* IV, iii, 6510).
117. TNA, PRO, SP1/57 fos 276–277 (*LP* IV, iii, 6579).
118. In a letter now lost. See Merriman, *Life and Letters of Thomas Cromwell*, i. 327.
119. Ibid.
120. TNA, PRO, SP1/57 fo. 227 (*LP* IV, iii, 6510).
121. TNA, PRO, SP1/66 fo. 158 (*LP* V, 335). My italics for emphasis. Incorrectly dated to 1531 in *Letters and Papers*; it clearly belongs to 1530.
122. TNA, PRO, SP1/57 fo. 265 (*LP* IV, iii, 6556).
123. TNA, PRO, SP1/58 fo. 124 (*LP* IV, iii, 6698).
124. TNA, PRO, SP1/58 fos 19–20 (*LP* IV, iii, 6598 [1 and 2]).
125. Ward, 'Origins of Thomas Cromwell's Public Career', p. 230; TNA, PRO, C66/656 mm 8d, 9d (*LP* IV, iii, 6516 [1]).
126. Cavendish, *Life and Death of Cardinal Wolsey*, pp. 125, 126. My italics for emphasis.
127. Ibid., p. 126.
128. TNA, PRO, SP1/57 fos 270–273 (Merriman, *Life and Letters of Thomas Cromwell*, i. 331–334; *State Papers*, i. 365; *LP* IV, iii, 6571); BL, Cotton MS, Appendix L fo. 81 (Merriman, *Life and Letters of Thomas Cromwell*, i. 334–335; *LP* IV, iii, 6699); *LP* IV, iii, 6582, 6583, 6584, 6585, 6586, 6587, 6588.
129. TNA, PRO, SP1/58 fo. 147 (*State Papers*, vii. 268; *LP* IV, iii, 6744); SP1/58 fo. 173 (*LP* IV, iii, 6754). This episode is discussed in the next chapter.
130. N. H. Nicolas, *The Privy Purse Expenses of Henry the Eighth, 1529–1532* (London, 1827), p. 101; TNA, PRO, SP1/65 fo. 47 (*LP* V, 32); *LP* V, p. 753.
131. TNA, PRO, SP1/65 fo. 58v (*LP* V, 38).
132. TNA, PRO, SP1/68 fo. 181v (*LP* V, 168); SP1/65 fo. 187v (*LP* V, 181); SP1/65 fo. 201v (*LP* V, 196).

Chapter Three The Crown Lands and King's Works

1. TNA, PRO, SP1/66 fo. 171 (*LP* V, 360); SP1/68 fo. 37 (*LP* V, 507); SP1/68 fo. 56 (*LP* V, 543); SP1/68 fo. 135 (*LP* V, 650); SP1/68 fo. 140 (*LP* V, 655).
2. TNA, PRO, SP1/65 fos 82–86 (*LP* V, 52 [1]). The draft contains clauses for enactment in March 1531. I. D. Thornley, 'The Treason Legislation of Henry VIII (1531–1534)', *Transactions of the Royal Historical Society*, Third Series, xi (1917), pp. 87–123. The act finally passed in 1534 is *Statutes of the Realm*, iii. 26 Henry VIII, c. 13.
3. For examples of Audeley's handwriting for comparison, see TNA, PRO, SP1/71 fo. 91 (*LP* V, 1408); SP1/71 fo. 150 (*LP* V, 1476). *Cf.* Elton, *Tudor Revolution in Government*, p. 95, Elton, *Policy and Police*, p. 265 n. 2.
4. TNA, PRO, SP1/65 fo. 189 (*LP* V, 182).
5. Elton, *Tudor Revolution in Government*, p. 89.
6. A letter from William Stockill to Cromwell, dated 29 March and placed in 1531 by the editors of *Letters and Papers*, also has the appearance of 'official' work. Stockill wrote informing Cromwell that he had 'sene the ship' which 'ys fare owt of redynes', lacking a sail, mast and part of its tackle. See TNA, PRO, SP1/65 fo. 175 (*LP* V, 160). Although this letter shows that Cromwell was clearly in a position of some authority, it can securely be dated to 1528, and relates to his work for Wolsey. See TNA, PRO, SP1/47 fo. 222 (*LP* IV, ii, 4201); SP1/52 fos 18–19 (*LP* IV, ii, 5111 [3]).
7. TNA, PRO, SP1/68 fo. 109 (*LP* V, 628).
8. Elton, *Tudor Revolution in Government*, pp. 90–91.
9. S. E. Lehmberg, *The Reformation Parliament, 1529–1536* (Cambridge, 1970), pp. 130–131.
10. TNA, PRO, SP1/65 fos 87–90 (*LP* V, 52 [2]).
11. BL, Cotton MS, Cleopatra E IV fo. 211 (Merriman, *Life and Letters of Thomas Cromwell*, i. 67–68; *LP* IV, iii, App. 238).
12. TNA, PRO, SP1/68 fo. 53 (*LP* V, 538); SP1/68 fo. 123 (*LP* V, 639).
13. TNA, PRO, SP1/66 fos 33–33v (Merriman, *Life and Letters of Thomas Cromwell*, i. 339–340; *LP* V, 277); SP1/66 fo. 155 (*LP* V, 332).

14. TNA, PRO, SP1/68 fos 142–143 (*LP* V, 657) is a list of fines owed to the king. It was placed at the end of 1531 in *Letters and Papers*, but actually dates to sometime after February 1532. One of the fines is for £700 owing from the bishop of Bath and Wells, of which £300 is recorded as being 'payed alredie' into the king's coffers. A warrant dated 25 February 1532 records Cromwell's receipt of this sum. See TNA, PRO, E101/421/5 (*LP* V, 825). It would also seem reasonable to redate a 'memoriall' declaring the king's revenues, partially in Cromwell's hand, to at least 1532, when Cromwell was taking a far greater financial role on the king's behalf. See TNA, PRO, SP1/67 fos 28–33 (*LP* V, 397).

15. BL, Cotton MS, Titus B I fos 483–484 (*State Papers*, i. 380; *LP* V, 394).

16. TNA, PRO, SP1/67 fo. 83 (*LP* V, 429).

17. TNA, PRO, SP1/68 fo. 79 (*LP* V, 571); SP1/68 fo. 83 (*LP* V, 578); SP1/68 fos 102–103 (*LP* V, 612); BL, Cotton MS, Titus B I fo. 371 (*LP* V, 625); TNA, PRO, SP1/68 fo. 128 (*LP* V, 644); SP1/72 fo. 164 (*LP* V, 1669).

18. *Calendar of State Papers, Venetian*, Volume IV, *1527–1533*, ed. R. Brown (London, 1871), 694 (p. 297).

19. Ibid., pp. 294–295.

20. TNA, PRO, SP1/69 fo. 12 (*LP* V, 712).

21. TNA, PRO, SP1/68 fo. 107 (*LP* V, 623); SP1/68 fo. 108 (*LP* V, 624).

22. TNA, PRO, SP1/69 fo. 13v (*LP* V, 712).

23. Ibid., fo. 12.

24. TNA, PRO, SP1/69 fo. 15 (*LP* V, 717). My italics for emphasis.

25. TNA, PRO, SP1/69 fo. 12v (*LP* V, 712).

26. For examples of letters that probably belong to the 1520s, see TNA, PRO, SP1/65 fo. 162 (*LP* V, 141); SP1/66 fo. 34 (*LP* V, 279); SP1/66 fo. 122 (*LP* V, 312); SP1/67 fo. 8 (*LP* V, 386); SP1/67 fo. 77 (*LP* V, 417); SP1/67 fo. 86 (*LP* V, 440); SP1/67 fo. 87 (*LP* V, 441); SP1/68 fo. 9 (*LP* V, 466); SP1/68 fo. 23 (*LP* V, 481); SP1/68 fo. 53 (*LP* V, 538).

27. TNA, PRO, SP1/65 fo. 58v (*LP* V, 38).

28. TNA, PRO, SP1/65 fo. 163 (*LP* V, 142); SP1/53 fos 8–10 (*LP* IV, iii, 5293).

29. BL, Cotton MS, Vespasian F XIII fo. 256 (*LP* V, 499); SP1/73 fo. 144 (*LP* V, 1767); SP1/73 fo. 145 (*LP* V, 1768); SP1/73 fo. 130 (*LP* V, 1755). These last three letters are all undated, but were placed in 1532 in *Letters and Papers*. It would be more reasonable to date all of them to 1531, when Cromwell was far less preoccupied with government work.

30. TNA, PRO, SP1/72 fo. 100 (*LP* V, 1610); SP1/72 fo. 135v (*LP* V, 1639); SP1/73 fo. 133 (*LP* V, 1757); SP60/2 fo. 49 (Merriman, *Life and Letters of Thomas Cromwell*, i. 357–358; *LP* VI, 791); SP 60/2 fo. 3 (*LP* VI, 857).

31. TNA, PRO, SP1/58 fo. 147 (*LP* IV, iii, 6744); BL, Cotton MS, Galba B X fo. 47 (*LP* V, 65); TNA, PRO, SP1/66 fo. 121 (*LP* V, 311); SP1/68 fo. 55 (*LP* V, 542); BL, Cotton MS, Galba B X fo. 3 (*LP* V, 804); BL, Cotton MS, Galba B X fo. 5 (*LP* V, 808); BL, Cotton MS, Galba B X fo. 3 (*LP* V, 813).

32. Hall, *Chronicle*, p. 775.

33. TNA, PRO, SP1/65 fo. 181 (*LP* V, 168); SP1/65 fo. 187 (*LP* V, 181); see also TNA, PRO, SP1/73 fo. 123 (*LP* V, 1748), which is undated but possibly connected with this; TNA, PRO, SP1/65 fo. 222 (*LP* V, 205); SP1/66 fo. 49 (*LP* V, 305); SP1/66 fo. 172 (*LP* V, 365); SP1/68 fo. 53 (*LP* V, 538); SP1/68 fo. 94 (*LP* V, 597); SP1/68 fo. 118 (*LP* V, 624); SP1/68 fo. 123 (*LP* V, 639).

34. The documents placed in 1531 that should be redated are: TNA, PRO, SP1/65 fo. 239 (*LP* V, 224); SP1/66 fo. 45 (*LP* V, 294); SP1/66 fo. 46 (*LP* V, 300); SP1/68 fo. 34 (*LP* V, 501); SP1/77 fo. 44 (*LP* V, 295); SP1/66 fo. 174 (*LP* V, 367); SP1/65 fo. 129 (*LP* V, 95); SP1/65 fo. 130 (*LP* V, 96). The redating is discussed in the next chapter.

35. TNA, PRO, SP1/68 fo. 26 (*LP* V, 486); SP1/67 fo. 80 (*LP* V, 426); SP1/66 fo. 160 (*LP* V, 339); SP1/68 fo. 33 (*LP* V, 500); SP1/68 fo. 78 (*LP* V, 570); SP1/68 fo. 108 (*LP* V, 624).

36. TNA, PRO, SP1/237 fo. 25 (*LP* Add. I, i, 732).

37. TNA, PRO, SP1/66 fo. 156 (*LP* V, 333).

38. TNA, PRO, SP1/66 fo. 172 (*LP* V, 365).

39. TNA, PRO, SP1/68 fo. 94 (*LP* V, 597).

40. TNA, PRO, SP1/67 fo. 159 (Merriman, *Life and Letters of Thomas Cromwell*, i. 341; *LP* V, 458 [1]).

41. G. Redworth, *In Defence of the Church Catholic: The Life of Stephen Gardiner* (Oxford, 1990), p. 22.

42. BL, Cotton MS, Vespasian F XIII fo. 257 (Merriman, *Life and Letters of Thomas Cromwell*, i. 340–341; *LP* V, 302).

43. *The Letters of Stephen Gardiner*, ed. J. A. Muller (Cambridge, 1933), pp. 44–49; *LP* V, 1025.

44. TNA, PRO, SP1/66 fo. 162 (*LP* V, 346).

45. For further details, see Elton, *Tudor Revolution in Government*, pp. 91–93; W. C. Richardson, *Stephen Vaughan: Financial Agent of Henry VIII* (Baton Rouge, LA, 1953), pp. 25–35.

46. TNA, PRO, SP1/58 fo. 147 (*LP* IV, iii, 6744); SP1/58 fo. 173 (*LP* IV, iii, 6754); BL, Cotton MS, Galba B X fo. 46v (*LP* V, 65). In the summary given in *Letters and Papers* for the first two letters cited here, 'Master Treasurer' is thought to refer to Sir Brian Tuke, treasurer of the Chamber. Given that Vaughan refers to Fitzwilliam, treasurer of the household, in his letter to the king, this was probably the treasurer he referred to in all these letters.

47. Nor, incidentally, was Vaughan the only agent Cromwell was using to contact Tyndale. Thomas Jermyn wrote to Cromwell in June 1531 to inform him that 'accordynge to your mynde I haue sent to master tyndall ... the kynges lettre to hym'. See TNA, PRO, SP1/66 fo. 48 (*LP* V, 304).

48. BL, Cotton MS, Galba B X fo. 46 (*LP* V, 65).

49. BL, Cotton MS, Galba B X fo. 46v (*LP* V, 65).

50. BL, Cotton MS, Galba B X fos 354–355 (*LP* V, 248; Merriman, *Life and Letters of Thomas Cromwell*, i. 336–337). Cromwell's letter to Vaughan is written in the hand of one of Cromwell's clerks, but heavily altered by Cromwell himself, with crossings-out and additional remarks in his own hand. The italicised parts of the extracts here are those written in Cromwell's own hand.

51. He continued to obtain and send works circulating in Antwerp to both Cromwell and the king, at the request of the latter. See, for example, TNA, PRO, SP1/66 fo. 47 (*LP* V, 303); SP1/68 fos 51–52 (*LP* V, 533). The attempts to obtain these works are discussed in Chapter Seven.

52. *VCH, Suffolk*, ii. 331; TNA, PRO, SP1/57 fos 242–243 (*LP* IV, iii, 6523); SP1/58 fos 94–95 (*LP* IV, iii, 6663); SP1/58 fo. 107 (*LP* IV, iii, 6666); SP1/58 fos 122–123 (*LP* IV, iii, 6688).

53. TNA, PRO, SP2/M fos 21–28 (*LP* V, 1180); SP2/M fo. 29 (*LP* V, 1181 [1]); SP2/M fo. 30 (*LP* V, 1181 [2]); J. McConica, ed., *The History of the University of Oxford, Volume III: The Collegiate University* (Oxford, 1986), p. 32.

54. TNA, PRO, SP1/69 fo. 9 (*LP* V, 701).

55. TNA, PRO, E36/102 fos 59–68 (*LP* IV, iii, 6651). Cromwell's annotations are on fos 64 and 66.

56. TNA, PRO, SP1/65 fo. 117 (*LP* V, 83).

57. TNA, PRO, SP1/65 fo. 186 (*LP* V, 175).

58. TNA, PRO, SP1/69 fo. 80 (*LP* V, 769); this was incorrectly placed in 1532 in *Letters and Papers*. TNA, PRO, SP1/65 fo. 185 (*LP* V, 174), SP1/66 fo. 21 (*LP* V, 273). A letter to Cromwell from Thomas Whalley, dated February and placed in 1531 in *Letters and Papers*, actually relates to the surveying of Daventry, Northamptonshire, for Cardinal College, Oxford, in 1527; see TNA, PRO, SP1/65 fo. 119 (*LP* V, 84). Two further letters from Whalley to Cromwell concerning other college matters were also erroneously placed in 1532; see TNA, PRO, SP1/70 fo. 190 (*LP* V, 1221); SP1/70 fo. 218 (*LP* V, 1252). These also belong to 1527.

59. TNA, PRO, SP1/65 fo. 185 (*LP* V, 174).

60. Knight was receiver at Raunston, but was dead by November 1532. See TNA, PRO, SP2/N fo. 107 (*LP* VI, 228 [i]); *LP* V, 1598 [24].

61. TNA, PRO, SP1/51 fo. 101 (*LP* IV, ii, 5024 [i]).

62. TNA, PRO, SP1/75 fo. 30 (*LP* VI, 249). See also TNA PRO, SP1/74 fo. 197 (*LP* VI, 203).

63. TNA, PRO, SP1/75 fo. 132 (*LP* VI, 342).
64. TNA, PRO, C82/638 and C66/656 m. 6 (*LP* V, 119 [48]).
65. TNA, PRO, E36/143 fo. 7 (*LP* VI, 299 [ii]).
66. TNA, PRO, C82/639 and C66/656 m. 19 (*LP* V, 166 [37/i]). The manor had belonged to the abbey of Lesnes, Kent, which was suppressed by Wolsey in February 1525. See *VCH, Kent*, ii. 166.
67. TNA, PRO, SP1/65 fos 179–180 (*LP* V, 166 [37/ii]); Cromwell's endorsement is on fo. 179v.
68. TNA, PRO, C66/656 m. 17 (*LP* V, 220 [11]).
69. TNA, PRO, SP1/71 fos 65–68 (*LP* V, 220 [11/ii]).
70. TNA, PRO, C66/656 m. 17 (*LP* V, 220 [3 and 4]), C82/640 and C66/656 m. 21 (*LP* V, 220 [10]).
71. TNA, PRO, SP1/73 fo. 149 (*LP* V, 1778). Among Cromwell's jottings was a list of manors, including 'romborow ... For master Downes'.
72. TNA, PRO, SP1/65 fo. 186 (*LP* V, 175).
73. TNA, PRO, C82/646 and C66/659 m. 4 (*LP* V, 392 [9]). Cromwell's draft is TNA, PRO, SP1/237 fo. 32 (*LP* Add. I, i, 737).
74. TNA, PRO, SP1/65 fo. 45 (*LP* V, 23). 'Bromefelde' was a farm belonging to the late priory of Bromehill, Norfolk, suppressed by Wolsey in September 1528 and used to endower his Ipswich college.
75. TNA, PRO, SP1/65 fo. 186 (*LP* V, 175).
76. TNA, PRO, SP1/75 fo. 30 (*LP* VI, 249). For its redating, see p. 74.
77. TNA, PRO, SP1/69 fo. 80 (*LP* V, 769); incorrectly dated in *Letters and Papers*.
78. TNA, PRO, SP1/66 fo. 21 (*LP* V, 273).
79. S. Thurley, *The Royal Palaces of Tudor England: Architecture and Court Life, 1460–1547* (London, 1993), p. 49.
80. W[estminster] A[bbey] M[uniments] 3231.
81. TNA, PRO, SP1/66 fos 13–17 (*LP* V, 264). Quotation on fo. 13.
82. *VCH, Middlesex*, ii. 325–326.
83. In the draft articles the councillors are merely described as A, B, C and D; see TNA, PRO, SP1/66 fo. 13.
84. A draft of the grant, corrected by Cromwell, lacks the day and month it was made, but is dated 1531; see TNA, PRO, SP1/66 fos 36–37 (*LP* V, 285 [1]). See also TNA, PRO, SP1/66 fos 38–41 (*LP* V, 285 [2]), which is another corrected draft. The grant was confirmed in the third session of the Reformation parliament, and the act provides the date of 5 June. See *Statutes of the Realm*, iii. 23 Henry VIII, c. 26.
85. For the offices of Attorney and Solicitor-General, see Baker, *Laws of England*, vi. 425–426.
86. *LP* V, 80 [11 and 28].
87. Among his papers, for instance, were those that contained the values of the suppressed lands of Wolsey's colleges. See TNA, PRO, SP1/65 fo. 63 (*LP* V, 47 [2]); SP1/65 fo. 64 (*LP* V, 47 [3]).
88. TNA, PRO, SP1/66 fos 13–17 (*LP* V, 264); SP1/66 fos 36–37 (*LP* V, 285 [1]).
89. TNA, PRO, SP1/66 fos 36–37 (*LP* V, 285 [1]); *Statutes of the Realm*, iii. 23 Henry VIII c. 26.
90. TNA, PRO, SP1/67 fos 39–53 (*LP* V, 403 [2]).
91. TNA, PRO, SP1/67 fo. 39 (*LP* V, 403 [2]). The italics indicate parts in Cromwell's hand.
92. TNA, PRO, SP1/67 fos 40–41 (*LP* V, 403 [2]). The final indenture for this agreement is TNA, PRO, E41/149 (*LP* V, 403 [1]).
93. TNA, PRO, SP1/67 fo. 42 (*LP* V, 403 [2]).
94. TNA, PRO, SP1/67 fo. 7 (*LP* V, 385).
95. TNA, PRO, E41/214 (*LP* V, 405 [1]). See also E41/215 (*LP* V, 508), which is a deed giving part effect to E41/214.
96. TNA, PRO, E41/216 (*LP* V, 406 [1]); TNA, PRO; SP1/67 fos 58–60 (*LP* V, 406 [2]); SP1/67 fos 61–62 (*LP* V, 406 [3]).

97. TNA, PRO, E41/213 (*LP* V, 404 [1]); TNA PRO; SP1/67 fos 54–57 (*LP* V, 404 [2]). The convent's indenture for this grant can be found in WAM, 32345.
98. Sheen's warrant for the Great Seal is TNA, PRO, C82/650 (*LP* V, 627 [22]); St Peter's is C82/650 and its enrolment on the Patent Rolls is C66/659 m. 22 (*LP* V, 627 [23]); TNA, PRO, SP1/237 fos 84–90 (*LP* Add. I, i, 748) is a similar draft of this; St Albans is C82/650 and C66/659 m. 24 (*LP* V, 627 [24]); Eton College's is C82/650 and C66/659 m. 27 (*LP* V, 627 [28]). The acts of parliament, respectively, are *Statutes of the Realm*: iii. 23 Henry VIII c. 27; 23 Henry VIII c. 21; 23 Henry VIII c. 25; 23 Henry VIII c. 24.
99. TNA, PRO, C82/651 and C66/659 mm. 26–27 (*LP* V, 766 [2]); C66/659 m. 23–24 (*LP* V, 766 [4]) and TNA, PRO, SP2/L fos 116–128 (*LP* V, 766 [4/ii]), which is a draft of this. The acts of parliament confirming the exchange are *Statutes of the Realm*: 23 Henry VIII c. 23 (Waltham); 23 Henry VIII c. 22 (Cambridge).
100. TNA, PRO, C54/400 m. 13d (*LP* V, 600). Candisshe is described as Cromwell's 'clerk' in TNA, PRO, SP1/73 fo. 96 (*LP* V, 1722).
101. TNA, PRO, SP1/67 fo. 59 (*LP* V, 406 [2]).
102. TNA, PRO, C54/400 m. 13d (*LP* V, 619 and 622).
103. J. D. Alsop, 'Cromwell and the Church in 1531: The Case of Waltham Abbey', *Journal of Ecclesiastical History*, 31 (1980), pp. 327–330.
104. TNA, PRO, E407/8/180/4. Alsop believed the entire draft was in Cromwell's hand, and amended by him (Alsop, 'Cromwell and the Church', p. 328). While the amendments are his, the original writing is not obviously in Cromwell's distinctive hand.
105. Alsop, 'Cromwell and the Church', p. 328.
106. TNA, PRO, SP2/L fos 66–71 (*LP* V, 673). See also WAM, 32335, which grants power of attorney from the abbot, prior and convent of Westminster to William Middletone and Willam Russell to deliver seisin on this messuage to Norwich, Lister, Paulet, Audeley, Hales, Mallet and Cromwell. It is dated 1 November in the chapterhouse at Westminster.
107. TNA, PRO, C82/650 and C66/659 m. 22 (*LP* V, 627 [23]); WAM, 32345.
108. TNA, PRO, SP1/102 fo. 220v (*LP* X, 1231).
109. For Anne Boleyn's lands, see p. 83. Many of the Cambridge lands were joined to the manor of Hunsdone. See *Statutes of the Realm*, iii. 23 Henry VIII c. 30. Henry Norris was made steward of the manors of Lewisham and East Greenwich, Kent, acquired from the charterhouse of Sheen. See TNA, PRO, C82/654 (*LP* V, 1065 [22]); *LP* V, 1075.
110. W. C. Richardson, *Tudor Chamber Administration, 1485–1547* (Baton Rouge, LA, 1952), pp. 10–14.
111. BL, Cotton MS, Titus B IV fos 119–119v (*LP* V, 1713).
112. TNA, PRO, SP1/70 fo. 57 (*LP* V, 1051); SP1/74 fo. 132 (*LP* VI, 128). Sir William Spencer held considerable lands in Northamptonshire and Warwickshire, and Cromwell was told that the king was in danger of losing 500 marks. See TNA, PRO, C142/55; C142/60; C142/290 for the lands. Exactly how the king was being defrauded is not clear. In September Cromwell told the king that a dispute between Lady Spencer and the executors of her husband's will was heard 'before my lorde the keper of your greate seale [Thomas Audeley] Sir Willyam Poulet and me'. Cromwell informed Henry that one of the executors, Edmund Knightley, had 'trauayled asmoche as in him ... to sett pyke between the sayd ladye and the executors and to defeate your grace of your title to the heire of the saide spencer'. See TNA, PRO, SP1/71 fo. 17 (Merriman, *Life and Letters of Thomas Cromwell*, i. 348–349; *LP* V, 1298). In a series of letters to Cromwell, Thomas Audeley reveals that the two men were working in conjunction to protect the king's rights. How the matter was resolved is uncertain, but the king did successfully obtain his rights to these lands. See BL, Cotton MS, Titus B I fos 89v–90 (*LP* V, 1518); BL, Cotton MS, Titus B I fo. 351 (*LP* V, 1542); TNA, PRO, SP1/74 fo. 132 (*LP* VI, 128); TNA, PRO, C82/685 and C66/665 m.15 (*LP* VII, 922 [20]).
113. For the construction of Whitehall, see S. Thurley, *Royal Palaces*, pp. 50–56; S. Thurley, *Whitehall Palace: An Architectural History of the Royal Apartments, 1240–1690* (London, 1999), pp. 37–39; M. H. Cox and P. Norman, *Survey of London, Volume*

XIII: The Parish of St Margaret, Westminster, Part II (London, 1930), pp. 8–22; H. M. Colvin, ed., *The History of the King's Works* (6 vols, London, 1963–1982), iv. 305–315.

114. G. Rosser and S. Thurley, 'Whitehall Palace and King's Street, Westminster: The Urban Cost of Princely Magnificence', *London Topographical Record*, xxvi (1990), pp. 57–78.

115. *CSP, Venetian*, IV, 664.

116. *CSP, Spanish*, IV, ii, 720.

117. WAM, 18048; 18049a; 18049b; 18049c; TNA, PRO, SC/12/3/13. Was Cromwell one of the surveyors?

118. TNA, PRO, SP1/67 fos 66–69 (*LP* V, 408).

119. TNA, PRO, E40/1526; E40/1536; E40/1559; E40/1560; E40/1563; E40/1565; E40/13086; E40/1566; TNA, PRO, SP1/67 fos 70–73 (*LP* V, 409); TNA, PRO, E40/13406; E40/13077; E40/13446; E40/12837; E40/6071; E40/13447; E40/12383; E40/1560; E40/13448. A further eight leases are recorded on TNA, PRO, SP1/67 fos 67–69 (*LP* V, 408), for which no separate indentures have survived.

120. Cromwell was still in correspondence with John Bourchier, Lord Berners in August 1532 concerning his lease of 'pete caleys' in King's Street. See TNA, PRO, SP1/69 fos 154–154v (*LP* V, 857); SP1/70 fo. 188 (*LP* V, 1219).

121. WAM, 3231; TNA, PRO, C54/400 m. 13d (*LP* V, 622), C82/651 and C66/659 mm. 26–27 (*LP* V, 766 [2]); *Statutes of the Realm*, iii. 23 Henry VIII c. 23.

122. TNA, PRO, E101/518/15 (*LP* V, 173), not E101/578/15, as listed in the TNA, PRO *List and Index* guide to *Letters and Papers*.

123. TNA, PRO, SP2/K fo. 102.

124. TNA, PRO, SP1/66 fo. 151 (*LP* V, 329).

125. TNA, PRO, SP1/71 fo. 99 (*LP* V, 1423); my italics for emphasis.

126. TNA, PRO, SP1/77 fo. 54 (*LP* VI, 673).

127. TNA, PRO, SP1/66 fo. 157 (*LP* V, 334); my italics for emphasis. This was placed in 1531 in *Letters and Papers*, but probably dates to 1533. The letter was written 'from King henry the viii^th college', suggesting it was sent after the formal refounding in July 1532.

128. TNA, PRO, SP1/82 fo. 146 (*LP* VII, 174).

129. TNA, PRO, SP1/68 fo. 91 (*LP* V, 590); SP1/69 fo. 190 (*LP* V, 899), misdated in *Letters and Papers*, it is of the year 1533; SP1/70 fo. 168 (Merriman, *Life and Letters of Thomas Cromwell*, i. 346; *LP* V, 1185 [i]); SP1/75 fo. 30 (*LP* VI, 249); SP1/76 fos 26–28 (*LP* VI, 453) and SP1/76 fo. 78r (*LP* VI, 1519); SP1/77 fo. 76 (*LP* VI, 695); SP1/82 fo. 103 (*LP* VII, 98); SP1/82 fo. 228 (*LP* VII, 294); SP1/82 fos 229–229v (*LP* VII, 295); SP1/83 fo. 63 (*LP* VII, 439); SP1/86 fos 84–86 (*LP* VII, 1301); SP2/N fo. 107 (*LP* VI, 228).

130. *CSP, Spanish*, IV, ii, 796, 853.

131. For the family, see R. A. Griffiths, *Sir Rhys ap Thomas and his Family: A Study in the Wars of the Roses and Early Tudor Politics* (Cardiff, 1993), especially pp. 88–112.

132. TNA, PRO, SP1/237 fo. 78 (*LP* Add. I, i, 743).

133. Baker, *Reports of John Spelman*, i. 47.

134. TNA, PRO, SP1/68 fos 216–220 (*LP* V, 683). Quotation on fo. 216; italics indicate parts in Cromwell's hand.

135. TNA, PRO, SP1/67 fo. 218 (*LP* V, 683).

136. TNA, PRO, SP1/69 fos 43–45 (*LP* V, 724 [9]). In this later version, three further instructions have been added that are not present on the earlier draft, but these appear at the end.

137. TNA, PRO, SP1/69 fo. 43 (*LP* V, 724 [9]).

138. In April 1532 Jones was rewarded for his work as a commissioner by being given the offices of steward, surveyor and receiver of several of ap Gruffyd's former lands; see TNA, PRO, C82/654 (*LP* V, 978 [3]). A draft bond for these offices, by which Jones agreed to furnish true accounts of the lands, was drawn up by Cromwell; see TNA, PRO, SP1/237 fo. 166 (*LP* Add. I, i, 166).

139. Griffiths, *Sir Rhys ap Thomas*, p. 114.

140. TNA, PRO, SP1/69 fo. 43 (*LP* V, 724 [9]).

141. TNA, PRO, SP1/44 fos 213 and 219 (*LP* IV, ii, 3536 [1]); SP1/47 fo. 287 (*LP* IV, ii, 4229 [9]).

142. While in Calais, Cromwell sent and received patents for these endowments to and from Thomas Audeley. See BL, Cotton MS, Vespasian C XIV fos 166–167 (*LP* V, 1430); TNA, PRO, SP1/71 fo. 113 (*LP* V, 1437); SP1/71 fo. 121v (*State Papers*, i. 385; *LP* V, 1450). Draft copies of several of these grants have also survived (among Cromwell's papers?), one of which is written in Wriothesley's hand, who was working with Cromwell during these years. The grants are: TNA, PRO, C82/660 and C66/660 m. 25 (*LP* V, 1370 [3/i]), a corrected draft of this is SP2/M fos 96–97 (*LP*, 1370 [3/ii]); C66/662 mm. 44–47 (*LP* V, 1499 [23/i]), a draft of this in Wriothesley's hand is SP2/M fos 98–120 (*LP* V, 1499 [23/2]). Valuations of the lands granted to Anne, presumably those which have survived in TNA, PRO, SP1/71 fo. 6 (*LP* V, 1274 [6]), were also returned to Cromwell; see TNA, PRO, E36/143 fo. 14 (*LP* VI, 299 [iii]).

143. For examples of Brabazon's work for Cromwell on Wolsey's suppression, including the surveying of lands, see: TNA, PRO, SP1/48 fo. 23 (*LP* IV, ii, 4275); SP1/54 fo. 351 (*LP* IV, iii, 5792); SP1/55 fo. 196 (*LP* IV, iii, 6033); SP1/57 fo. 2 (*LP* IV, iii, 6217), probably earlier than 1530 (as in *Letters and Papers*); SP1/57 fo. 16 (*LP* IV, iii, 6221). John Smith appears to have been an auditor in Wolsey's entourage during the 1520s (*LP* IV, i, 1834 [i]), and worked alongside Cromwell in Wolsey's suppressions. Smith and Cromwell acted together as attorneys taking possession of several sites intended for the collegiate foundations, as well as settling rents, and surveying monastic lands together. See TNA, PRO, SP1/33 fo. 73 (*LP* IV, i, 990 [i]); TNA, PRO, E24/9/1 (*LP* IV, i, 1964); TNA, PRO, SC12/18/60 fos 78–86 (*LP* IV, i, 1845 [iv]); SP1/44 fo. 62 (*LP* IV, ii, 3406); SP1/44 fo. 114a (*LP* IV, ii, 3448); SP1/44 fo. 146 (*LP* IV, ii, 3489); SP1/44 fo. 218 (*LP* IV, ii, 3536 [i]); SP1/53 fo. 174 (*LP* IV, iii, 5458). Whether Smith ever formally entered Cromwell's household after Wolsey's fall seems doubtful, although Edward Fetyplace did refer to one 'master Smythe your Auditor' in a letter to Cromwell, probably from 1527; see TNA, PRO, SP1/59 fo. 104 (*LP* IV, iii, App. 103). For Smith's and Brabazon's later careers, see Robertson, 'Thomas Cromwell's Servants', pp. 451–452 and 560–561.

144. TNA, PRO, C82/664 (*LP* VI, 74). See also *LP* V, 1274 [5], which has been misdated to September 1532. TNA, PRO, SP1/74 fo. 196 (*LP* VI, 200).

145. TNA, PRO, SP1/69 fo. 42 (*LP* V, 724 [7]).

146. Among the papers in Cromwell's possession were the 'accompte of Willi[a]m Brabson ... of all the londes and tenantes late Res ap Gryffith' and 'the accompt of Res ap Gryffith gooddes [*sic*] londes tenantes and possessions at the tyme of his atteyndure'. See TNA, PRO, E36/143 fos 26 and 39 (*LP* VI, 299 [ix] and [xi]). At least some of these papers were surely: TNA, PRO, E36/151 fos 1–12 (*LP* V, 724 [1]); fos 13–18 (*LP* V, 724 [2]); fos 19–20 (*LP* V, 724 [3]); fos 21–24 (*LP* V, 724 [4]); fos 25–27 (*LP* V, 724 [5]); fos 28–33 (*LP*, 724 [6]); TNA, PRO, SC6/HenVIII/4882–4888.

147. TNA, PRO, SP1/67 fo. 104 (*LP* V, 448).

148. TNA, PRO, SP2/N fo. 109 (*LP* VI, 228 [i]).

149. Elton, *Tudor Revolution in Government*, p. 110.

150. Cromwell became master of the king's jewels on 14 April 1532, TNA, PRO, C82/654 and C66/659 m. 36 (*LP* V, 978 [13]); clerk of the hanaper on 16 July 1532, C82/658 and C66/660 m. 33 (*LP* V, 1207 [36]); and chancellor of the exchequer on 12 April 1533, C82/667 and C66/661 m. 27 (*LP* VI, 417 [22]). The holder of each of these offices was appointed by patent for life, and Cromwell was appointed to each following the death of the previous incumbent.

151. Elton, *Tudor Revolution in Government*, p. 119.

152. Ibid., p. 120.

153. Ibid., pp. 109–110.

154. Ibid., p. 98.

155. *Cf.* Gywn, *King's Cardinal*, p. 104, on the office of lord chancellor.

156. TNA, PRO, E101/421/1 (*LP* V, 341).

157. TNA, PRO, SP1/68 fo. 82 (*LP* V, 577). The remaining 400 marks formed part of a fine owed to the king by the bishop of Bangor.

158. TNA, PRO, E36/141 fo. 39 (*LP* V, 1285 [ix]). This is recorded on a list of Cromwell's warrants signed by the king. The warrant itself does not appear to have survived.

159. TNA, PRO, SP1/69 fo. 9 (*LP* V, 701).

160. TNA, PRO, SP1/69 fo. 83 (*LP* V, 774).

161. TNA, PRO, E36/141 fo. 40 (*LP* V, 1285 [ix]). This warrant does not appear to have survived, but is recorded in Cromwell's book listing the warrants directed to him from the king.

162. TNA, PRO, SP1/69 fo. 139 (*LP* V, 842). The amount owed was actually £40, but £13 6s 8d was paid to one Robert Holdyche, treasurer of the duke's household, for 'twoo yeres ffee'.

163. TNA, PRO, SP1/70 fo. 49 (*LP* V, 1040).

164. TNA, PRO, E101/421/5 (*LP* V, 825).

165. Nicolas, *Privy Purse Expenses*, p. 101; *LP* V, p. 753; TNA, PRO, SP1/65 fo. 47 (*LP* V, 32). He also made later payments for this, see SP1/70 fo. 204 (*LP* V, 1244).

166. TNA, PRO, SP1/104 fos 220–222 (*LP* X, 1231); quotation on fo. 220.

167. TNA, PRO, SP1/69 fo. 140 (*LP* V, 403); SP1/70 fo. 137 (*LP* V, 1136); SP1/69 fo. 140 (*LP* V, 403); SP1/69 fo. 108 (*LP* V, 798); SP1/70 fo. 137 (*LP* V, 1136); SP1/71 fos 26–27 (*LP* V, 1309); SP1/73 fo. 120 (*LP* V, 1745); SP1/78 fo. 10 (*LP* VI, 848); SP1/82 fo. 13 (*LP* VII, 16); SP1/92 fo. 41 (*LP* VIII, 571); BL, Cotton MS, Faustina CIII fo. 483 (*LP* VIII, 577).

168. TNA, PRO, E40/13578 (*LP* V, 1537); E40/13579 (*LP* V, 1571); E40/13500 (*LP* V, 1580); E40/13580 (*LP* V, 1581); E40/13581 (*LP* V, 1606); E40/13582 (*LP* V, 1607); E40/13583 (*LP* V, 1611) – not E40/13582 (as listed in TNA, PRO, *List and Index* guide to *Letters and Papers*); E40/13584 (*LP* V, 1615).

169. TNA, PRO, SP2/L fos 150–151 (*LP* V, 814). A draft of this grant, corrected by Cromwell, is SP2/L fos 56–61 (*LP* V, 658).

170. TNA, PRO, SP1/68 fo. 105 (*LP* V, 620); TNA, PRO, E36/143 fo. 35 (*LP* VI, 299 [ix]).

171. TNA, PRO, SP1/70 fo. 138 (*LP* V, 1139 [24]).

172. TNA, PRO, E36/182 fos 37–41 (*LP* VII, 63 [2]). These are articles of agreement made between Cromwell and the abbot and convent, written in Cromwell's hand. They are undated, but were placed in 1534 in *Letters and Papers* on the grounds that the exchanges were finally ratified in parliament in that year. According to these articles, in return for the manor and park of Coppydhall the abbey was to receive lands 'which the kinges highness shall purchase of humffrey Browne sergeant of the law' (fo. 37). The significant point here is that Browne was one of the king's serjeants between 1530 and 1532, and then from 1535, but not in 1533 or 1534. See J. Sainty, *A List of English Law Officers, King's Counsel and Holders of Patents of Precedence* (London, 1987), p. 14; J. H. Baker, *The Order of Serjeants at Law* (London, 1984), p. 502. In 1533 Browne himself wrote to Cromwell, notifying him that he would be happy to exchange his Waltham lands for 'A lettell house callyd Alderbroke the wyche was heronz' while also asking Cromwell to have him in remembrance for '*woon of the kynges sergeantes to be made*'. See TNA, PRO, SP1/81 fo. 90 (*LP* VI, 1635); my italics for emphasis. It seems highly probable, therefore, that these articles were first drawn up in 1532, not 1534.

173. TNA, PRO, SP1/73 fo. 7 (*LP* V, 1684).

174. The acts of parliament ratifying the exchange were passed in early 1534. See *Statutes of the Realm*, iii. 25 Henry VIII c. 26; *Statutes of the Realm*, iii. 26 Henry VIII c. 24. The trustees of the lands on behalf of the king again included Cromwell, along with Audeley, Tuke and Richard Riche, the solicitor-general.

175. An item among Cromwell's remembrances was 'To remember my lord of Waltham's recompense for Copped Hall park'. See *LP* VII, 143 [ii]. Another memorandum in his own hand, written on the back of a letter from the bishop of Ely, is headed, 'landes to be appointed for the Abbot of Waltham in the leu of coppydhall park and the manor of Epping'. It goes on to list a number of lands, each of which is valued. See TNA, PRO, SP1/75 fo. 73 (*LP* VI 312).

176. TNA, PRO, E36/182 fo. 37 (*LP* VII, 64 [2]).

177. TNA, PRO, SP1/71 fo. 118 (*LP* V, 1445).

178. See pp. 76, 78. In February 1532 Hales and Cromwell, along with Baldwin Mallet, had also bought Giles Heron's house, which was called Alderbroke, in Wanstead, Essex, on behalf of the king, following negotiations in late 1531. See TNA, PRO, SP1/68 fo. 105 (*LP* V, 620); SP2/L fos 150–151 (*LP* V, 814). A draft of this grant, corrected by Cromwell, is SP2/L fos 56–61 (*LP* V, 658).

179. Foxe, *Acts and Monuments* (1570 edn), pp. 1386–1387. Foxe claimed that Hales was one of the figures who recommended Cromwell to the king in 1530, following Wolsey's fall: 'There was at the same tyme one Syr Christofer Hales Knight, Maister of the Rolles, who notwithstādyng was then a mighty Papiste, yet bare he such fauour and good lykyng to Cromwell, that hee commended hym to the kyng, as a man most fitte for hys purpose, hauyng then to do agaynst the Pope'.

180. TNA, PRO, SP1/71 fo. 118 (*LP* V, 1445).

181. TNA, PRO, SP1/71 fo. 141 (*LP* V, 1466); *Feet of Fines for Essex, Volume IV: 1423–1457*, ed. P. H. Reaney and M. Fitch (Colchester, 1964), p. 196 n. 21.

182. TNA, PRO, SP1/71 fo. 145 (*LP* V, 1470). Robert's lands were also in Waltham and are itemised on Cromwell's list of 'Thynges done by the kinges highness sythyn I came to his seruyse'. The account of payments Cromwell made on behalf of the king between 22 November 1532 and 11 March 1533 records that he delivered the £220 to Richard Riche to purchase these lands. See TNA, PRO, SP2/N fo. 110 (*LP* VI, 228).

183. TNA, PRO, SP1/70 fo. 57 (*LP* V, 1051); SP1/74 fo. 132 (*LP* VI, 128); SP1/71 fo. 17 (Merriman, *Life and Letters of Thomas Cromwell*, i. 348–349; *LP* V, 1298); SP1/71 fo. 130 (*LP* V, 1455); BL, Cotton MS, Titus B I fos 89v–90 (*LP* V, 1518); BL, Cotton MS, Titus B I fo. 351 (*LP* V, 1542); TNA, PRO, SP1/71 fo. 130 (*LP* V, 1455).

184. TNA, PRO, SP1/71 fo. 34 (*LP* V, 1317); SP1/71 fo. 41v (*LP* V, 1327); SP1/71 fo. 120 (*LP* V, 1447); SP1/76 fo. 115v (*LP* VI, 551).

185. Elton, *Tudor Revolution in Government*, pp. 428–430.

186. TNA, PRO, SP1/73 fo. 128 (*LP* V, 1753); SP1/77 fos 203–204 (*State Papers*, vii. 481; *LP* VI, 830); SP1/83 fo. 139 (*LP* VII, 527); SP1/83 fo. 140 (*LP* VII, 528); SP1/88 fo. 85 (*LP* VII, 1653).

187. TNA, PRO, SP1/88 fo. 85 (*LP* VII, 1653).

188. When Cromwell was appointed master of the king's woods is unclear, because no patent has survived. The earliest evidence of his acting in this capacity is a letter from March 1533, addressed to Cromwell as 'one of the masters of the kynges woddes'. See TNA, PRO, SP1/74 fo. 205 (*LP* VI, 209). An undated draft patent appointing Cromwell and Paulet masters of the king's woods in the duchy of Lancashire was also placed in 1533 in *Letters and Papers*. See TNA, PRO, SP2/O fos 116–117 (*LP* VI, 1623). For Cromwell's forest policy, see Richardson, *Tudor Chamber Administration*, pp. 271–273.

189. TNA, PRO, SP1/74 fo. 206 (*LP* VI, 210); SP1/75 fo. 23 (*LP* VI, 231); SP1/75 fos 187–193 (*LP* VI, 406); SP1/81 fo. 31 (*LP* VI, 1575); SP1/81 fo. 32 (*LP* VI, 1576). Several documents also show Paulet active by himself. See TNA, PRO, SP1/238 fos 137–145v (*LP* Add. I, i, 876 [1 and 2]); SP1/82 fos 139–140 (*LP* VII, 154).

190. TNA, PRO, SP1/73 fo. 128 (*LP* V, 1753); undated and placed in 1531 in *Letters and Papers*. It would be more reasonable to date this to 1532 or 1533. My italics for emphasis.

191. TNA, PRO, SP1/69 fo. 208 (*LP* V, 916). See also TNA, PRO, SP1/69 fo. 207 (*LP* V, 915).

192. A surviving fragment of an indenture between Lord Scrope on the one part, and Cromwell, Audeley, Brian Tuke, Hales and Mallet on the other, was placed in 1527 in *Letters and Papers*. See TNA, PRO, SP1/46 fos 31–32 (*LP* IV, ii, 3740). It is connected with this exchange, and should be dated to the early 1530s.

193. TNA, PRO, SP1/71 fo. 118 (*LP* V, 1445); SP1/71 fo. 141 (*LP* V, 1466).

194. TNA, PRO, SP1/70 fo. 28 (*LP* V, 1015). This letter was placed in 1532, but was surely sent in response to Cromwell's letter dated 24 April, which was placed in 1533 in *Letters and Papers*. See TNA, PRO, SP1/75 fo. 168 (Merriman, *Life and Letters of Thomas Cromwell*, i. 352–353; *LP* VI, 383). Both probably belong to 1532.

195. TNA, PRO, SP1/74 fo. 37 (*LP* VI, 43).

196. TNA, PRO, SP1/75 fo. 139 (*LP*, 348 [ii]). John, Lord Scrope was son and heir to Henry, who had died in 1533, before negotiations were complete. See TNA, PRO, C82/677 and C66/663 m. 19 (*LP* VI, 1595 [27]).

197. TNA, PRO, SP1/75 fo. 139. My italics for emphasis.

198. TNA, PRO, SP1/74 fo. 37 (*LP* VI, 43); BL, Cotton MS, Vespasian F XIII fo. 208 (*LP* VI, 348 [i]).

199. BL, Cotton MS, Vespasian F XIII fo. 208 (*LP* V, 348 [i]); TNA, PRO, SP1/74 fo. 37 (*LP* VI, 43).

200. TNA, PRO, SP1/75 fo. 168 (Merriman, *Life and Letters of Thomas Cromwell*, i. 353–353; *LP* VI, 383).

201. *Statutes of the Realm*, iii. 25 Henry VIII c. 31; TNA, PRO, SP1/76 fos 26–27 (*LP* VI, 453); SP1/79 fo. 79 (*LP* VI, 520); TNA, PRO, E36/143 fo. 43 (*LP* VII, 50); TNA, PRO, SP1/86 fo. 150 (*LP* VII, 1364). For details of the final settlement, see H. Miller, *Henry VIII and the English Nobility* (Oxford, 1986), pp. 219–220.

202. TNA, PRO, SP1/74 fo. 134 (*LP* VI, 133). Poyntz's grant for this office is TNA, PRO, C82/665 and C66/660 m. 9 (*LP* VI, 196).

203. TNA, PRO, SP1/75 fo. 138 (*LP* VI, 347); SP1/76 fo. 7 (*LP* VI, 426), which are incorrectly placed in 1533 in *Letters and Papers*. They belong to 1532.

204. *VCH, Hertfordshire*, ii. 376. For a succint history of the More, see M. Biddle, L. Barfield and A. Millard, 'The Excavation of the Manor of the More, Rickmansworth, Hertfordshire', *Archaeological Journal*, 116 (1959), pp. 138–142.

205. TNA, PRO, SP1/75 fo. 138 (*LP* VI, 347). The king believed that Russell received enough of the revenues to do it himself.

206. TNA, PRO, SP1/75 fo. 182 (*LP* VI, 401); SP1/76 fo. 7 (*LP* VI, 426). Both incorrectly placed in 1533 in *Letters and Papers*. They belong to 1532.

207. TNA, PRO, SP1/69 fo. 266 (*LP* V, 976). My italics for emphasis.

208. Ibid.

209. TNA, PRO, SP1/75 fo. 138 (*LP* VI, 347); SP1/75 fo. 182 (*LP* VI, 401).

210. TNA, PRO, SP1/75 fo. 138 (*LP* VI, 347).

211. TNA, PRO, SP1/76 fo. 45 (*LP* VI, 483). This is also from 1532, not 1533 as in *Letters and Papers*. A record of Cromwell's warrants lists one 'bering date the 22 day of May in the 24 yere of king henry the viii[th] [i.e. 22 May 1532] of and for the payment of £40 to Sir John Russell knight to be imployed about the paling of the parke at more'. See TNA, PRO, E36/141 fo. 41 (*LP* V, 1285 [ix]).

212. TNA, PRO, SP1/82 fo. 228 (*LP* VII, 294); SP1/82 fo. 229 (*LP* VII, 295); SP1/69 fo. 231 (*LP* V, 950).

213. TNA, PRO, SP 1/68 fo. 91 (*LP* V, 590). Cromwell had obtained the lease and position of receiver for Cave during the 1520s. See TNA, PRO, SP 1/48 fo. 175 (*LP* IV, ii, 4388); SP 1/49 fo. 88 (*LP* IV, ii, 4481).

214. TNA, PRO, SP 1/82 fo. 146 (*LP* VII, 174).

215. TNA, PRO, SP1/70 fo. 184 (*LP* V, 1212); SP1/71 fo. 95 (*LP* V, 1415); SP1/73 fo. 125 (*LP* V, 1750); SP1/76 fo. 17 (*LP* VI, 443); SP1/76 fo. 36v (*LP* VI, 473); SP1/81 fo. 91 (*LP* VI, 839); SP1/79 fo. 168 (*LP* VI, 1279); SP1/79 fo. 189 (*LP* VI, 1307); SP1/81 fo. 93 (*LP* VI, 1640); SP1/82 fo. 172 (*LP* VII, 218); SP1/83 fo. 84 (*LP* VII, 482).

216. TNA, PRO, SP1/76 fo. 9 (*LP* VI, 430).

217. TNA, PRO, SP1/70 fo. 200 (*LP* V, 1233).

218. TNA, PRO, SP 60/2 fo. 3 (*LP* VI, 857).

219. TNA, PRO, SP1/71 fo. 83 (*LP* V, 1395).

220. TNA, PRO, SP1/73 fos 101–102 (*LP* V, 1727). Quotation on fo. 101. Cromwell also assisted Henry Percy, sixth earl of Northumberland, with a complicated sale of lands to the king in order to alleviate the earl's debts. Exactly when Cromwell began acting in this is unclear. Several documents connected with the king's purchase of various Percy lands were placed in 1531 by the editors of *Letters and Papers*. See SP1/67 fos 25–27 (*LP* V, 395); SP1/67 fo. 85 (*LP* V, 435). Yet it appears these date to 1534, shortly before a renegotiated settlement for Northumberland's lands was made in February 1535. See R. W. Hoyle, 'Henry Percy, Sixth Earl of Northumberland, and

the Fall of the House of Percy', in G. W. Bernard, ed., *The Tudor Nobility* (Manchester, 1992), p. 193 (and nn. 64 and 65).

221. BL, Cotton MS, Vespasian C XIV fo. 166v (*LP* V, 1430).
222. TNA, PRO, SP1/75 fo. 32 (*LP* VI, 251), incorrectly placed in 1533 in *Letters and Papers*; SP1/237 fo. 161 (*LP* V, 773).
223. TNA, PRO, SP1/75 fo. 32 (*LP* VI, 251); SP1/71 fo. 171 (*LP* V, 1496).
224. TNA, PRO, SP1/237 fo. 216 (*LP* Add. I, i, 788).
225. TNA, PRO, SP1/71 fo. 96 (*LP* V, 1416). He told Cromwell, 'if I had made no form[er] graunte I wolde haue been glad to haue Accomplyshed your mynde.'
226. TNA, PRO, SP1/76 fo. 102 (*LP* VI, 536).
227. TNA, PRO, SP1/77 fo. 63 (*LP* VI, 681).
228. TNA, PRO, SP1/74 fo. 89 (*LP* VI, 95); SP1/74 fo. 83 (*LP* VI, 82).
229. TNA, PRO, SP1/65 fos 255–257 (*LP* V, 253).
230. TNA, PRO, SP1/65 fos 262–267 (*LP* V, 260).
231. TNA, PRO, E36/251; E36/252 (*LP* V, 952).
232. TNA, PRO, SP1/73 fo. 91 (Merriman, *Life and Letters of Thomas Cromwell*, i. 351–352; *LP* V, 1719).
233. Colvin, *History of the King's Works*, iii. 264. What appears to be a survey of the work required at the Tower can be found in TNA, PRO, E101/474/18.
234. TNA, PRO, E101/474/12 (*LP* V, 1307); E101/474/13 (*LP* VI, 5).
235. Thurley, *Royal Palaces*, p. 55; *Whitehall Palace*, pp. 37–39.
236. TNA, PRO, SP1/103 fo. 220v (*LP* X, 1231); Thurley, *Royal Palaces*, p. 54.
237. TNA, PRO, SP1/103 fo. 220v (*LP* X, 1231).
238. TNA, PRO, SP1/70 fos 101–103 (*LP* V, 1086 [1]); quotation on fo. 103.
239. TNA, PRO, SP1/70 fos 104–104v (*LP* V, 1086 [2]); TNA, PRO, E40/5944.
240. TNA, PRO, SP1/65 fo. 268 (*LP* V, 261). This latter reference is an undated receipt in Cromwell's hand, which records that 'Nycholas Tyrrye hath solde to Thomas Crumwell to thuse of our soueraigne lorde the king' 200 tons of luke stone, and 300 tons of cane stone, for delivery at the Tower next Michaelmas. It was placed in 1531 in *Letters and Papers*, but probably dates to 1532. See TNA, PRO, SP1/71 fo. 156 (*LP* V, 1487).
241. TNA, PRO, SP1/73 fo. 91 (Merriman, *Life and Letters of Thomas Cromwell*, i. 351–352; *LP* V, 1719).
242. For Heritage in Wolsey's service, see: TNA, PRO, SP1/48 fo. 230v (*LP* IV, ii, 4438); SP1/49 fo. 93v (*LP* IV, ii, 4486); SP1/49 fo. 102 (*LP* IV, ii, 4497); SP1/53 fo. 174 (*LP* IV, iii, 5458). For Alvard, see: BL, Cotton MS, Titus B I fo. 282 (*LP* IV, ii, 4778); TNA, PRO, E24/5/4 (*LP* IV, ii, 4461); TNA, PRO, SP1/44 fos 315–317 (*LP* IV, ii, 3539); SP1/51 fo. 101 (*LP* IV, ii, 5024); SP1/38 fos 233–236v (*LP* IV, i, 2321).
243. Alvard addressed Cromwell as 'hys Rythe hartely lovyd Frende' in a letter of the late 1520s, and his will, drawn up on 26 January 1535, named Cromwell as one of the executors, and bequeathed him Alvard's 'best chaine of golde'. Cromwell also left Alvard money in his will. See TNA, PRO, SP1/50 fo. 116v (*LP* IV, ii, 4793); TNA, PRO, PROB 11/27 (Dyngeley). Alvard died in 1538.
244. TNA, PRO, SP1/71 fo. 146 (*LP* V, 1472); SP1/71 fo. 148 (*LP* V, 1473).
245. BL, Cotton MS, Titus B I fo. 328 (*LP* IV, iii, 6390). In April 1531 he had been made master carpenter of the king's works, followed by clerk of the works in 1533. See *LP* V, 220 [20]; TNA, PRO, SP1/73 fo. 135 (*LP* V, 1759); *LP* VI, 418 [9].
246. For Whalley's career under Cromwell, see Robertson, 'Thomas Cromwell's Servants', p. 586.
247. TNA, PRO, SP1/71 fo. 106 (*LP* V, 1432); SP1/71 fo. 128 (*LP* V, 1454); SP1/71 fo. 143 (*LP* V, 1467); SP1/71 fo. 156 (*LP* V, 1487); SP1/73 fo. 143 (*LP* V, 1766).
248. TNA, PRO, SP1/71 fos 114–115 (*LP* V, 1442); SP1/71 fo. 106 (*LP* V, 1432); SP1/71 fo, 136 (*LP* V, 1461); SP1/71 fo. 137 (*LP* V, 1462); SP1/71 fo. 139 (*LP* V, 1464); SP1/71 fo. 143 (*LP* V, 1467); SP1/71 fo. 156 (*LP* V, 1487).
249. TNA, PRO, SP1/70 fo. 128 (*LP* V, 1119).
250. TNA, PRO, E101/421/5 (*LP* VI, 220).
251. TNA, PRO, SP2/O fo. 29 (*LP* VI, 717).

252. TNA, PRO, SP1/69 fo. 235 (*LP* V, 953). This was money that had previously belonged to Cardinal Wolsey.

253. It is recorded as being paid by Alvard from the king's money he had been receiving since October 1529; see TNA, PRO, SP1/69 fo. 235 (*LP* V, 953).

254. Nicolas, *Privy Purse Expenses*, p. 228.

255. TNA, PRO SP2/N fo. 109 (*LP* VI, 228 [ii]); SP1/75 fo. 57v (*LP* VI, 284).

256. TNA, PRO, SP1/238 fo. 36 (*LP* Add. I, i, 825).

257. The memorandum also lists a warrant required for £1,266 13s 4d 'delyuerid to master Gunston for ryggyng of the kings shippys'. Cromwell made payments to Gonson for this, but apparently from October 1533 to December 1534. See *LP* VII, 1564.

258. TNA, PRO, E101/474/18.

259. TNA, PRO, E351/3322.

260. Colvin, *History of the King's Works*, iii. 265. They are TNA, PRO, E101/474/12 (*LP* V, 1307); E101/474/13 (*LP* VI, 5).

261. TNA, PRO, E36/139 fo. 99 (*LP* VII, 923).

262. BL, Cotton MS, Titus B I fo. 455 (*LP* VII, 143).

263. Thurley, *Royal Palaces*, p. 52.

264. TNA, PRO, SP1/102 fo. 220v (*LP* X, 1231).

265. Ibid., fos 200 and 200v.

266. Hall, *Chronicle*, p. 786.

267. TNA, PRO, E41/216 (*LP* V, 406 [1]).

268. TNA, PRO, E41/156 (*LP* VI, 1526); TNA, PRO, SP1/80 fo. 107 (*LP* VI, 1450).

269. TNA, PRO, SP1/78 fo. 7 (*LP* VI, 843); SP1/78 fo. 19 (*LP* VI, 860).

270. TNA, PRO, SP1/78 fo. 30 (*LP* VI, 893).

271. TNA, PRO, SP1/80 fo. 49 (*LP* VI, 1367).

272. TNA, PRO, SP1/78 fo. 7 (*LP* VI, 843); BL, Cotton MS, Titus B I fo. 462v (*LP* VII, 108).

273. TNA, PRO, SP1/44 fos 211v and 246v (*LP* IV, ii, 3536).

274. TNA, PRO, SP1/52 fos 146–147 (Merriman, *Life and Letters of Thomas Cromwell*, i. 323–325; *LP* IV, iii, 5186). Cromwell's agent at Lesnes, Edward Boughton, was a contact he had made in the 1520s when overseeing this. See TNA, PRO, SP1/56 fo. 144 (*LP* IV, iii, 6118).

275. TNA, PRO, E40/13578 (*LP* V, 1537); E40/13579 (*LP* V, 1571); E40/13500 (*LP* V, 1580); E40/13580 (*LP* V, 1581); E40/13581 (*LP* V, 1606); E40/13582 (*LP* V, 1607); E40/13583 (*LP* V, 1611), not E40/13582 as listed in TNA, PRO, *List and Index* guide to *Letters and Papers*; E40/13584 (*LP* V, 1615).

276. TNA, PRO, SP1/73 fo. 61 (*LP* V, 1705 [2]).

277. TNA, PRO, SP1/73 fo. 59 (*LP* V, 1705 [1]).

278. BL, Cotton MS, Faustina E. VII fos 33–38 (*LP* V, 1495); printed in full in J. G. Nichols, ed., *The Chronicle of Calais, in the Reigns of Henry VII. and Henry VIII., to the year 1540* (London, 1846), pp. 125–130.

279. Colvin, *History of the King's Works*, iii. 347.

280. The work, which was commenced in late 1533, was carried out in response to an argument made by Lisle and others for the 'sure defence' of Calais. See *LP* VI, 930; Colvin, *History of the King's Works*, iii. 348.

281. TNA, PRO, SP1/239 fo. 36v (*LP* Add. I, i, 924).

282. TNA, PRO, SP1/82 fo. 227 (*LP* VII 293).

283. Hall, *Chronicle*, p. 775.

Chapter Four Cromwell and the English Church

1. G. W. Bernard, *The Late Medieval Church: Vitality and Vulnerability before the Break with Rome* (London, 2012), pp. 17–49.

2. G. Harriss, *Shaping the Nation: England, 1360–1461* (Oxford, 2005), p. 310.

3. W. A. Pantin, *The English Church in the Fourteenth Century* (Cambridge, 1955), pp. 30–31.

4. W. A. Pantin, 'The Fourteenth Century', in C. H. Lawrence, ed., *The English Church and the Papacy in the Middle Ages* (New York, 1965), p. 188.

5. Gwyn, *King's Cardinal*, pp. 43–50; Gunn, 'Edmund Dudley and the Church', pp. 516–518; Bernard, *Late Medieval Church*, pp. 17–49.

6. Gwyn, *King's Cardinal*, pp. 309–310.

7. TNA, PRO, SP1/47 fo. 222 (*LP* IV, ii, 4201); SP 1/49 fo. 216 (*LP* IV, ii, 4634); SP2/J fos 17–26 (*LP* IV, iii, 6094 [ii]); SP1/52 fos 18–19 (*LP* IV, ii, 5111 [3]); SP1/52 fo. 19 (*LP* IV, ii, 5111 [iv]); SP1/236 fo. 74 (*LP* Add. I, i, 637); SP1/65 fo. 175 (*LP* V, 160), erroneously placed in 1531 in *Letters and Papers*: it is of 1528.

8. *CSP, Spanish*, IV, ii, 796.

9. *LP* V, 418; TNA, PRO, SC7/64/63; TNA, PRO, SP1/67 fo. 79 (*State Papers*, vii. 319; *LP* V, 419); TNA, PRO, C82/649 and C66/659 m. 15 (*LP* V, 627 [3]); C82/649 and C66/658 m. 21 (*LP* V, 627 [8] and [8/ii]).

10. TNA, PRO, C82/649 and C66/659 m. 15 (*LP* V, 627 [3]); TNA, PRO, SP1/68 fos 143, 143v (*LP* V, 657).

11. TNA, PRO, SP1/69 fo. 111 (*LP* V, 802).

12. TNA, PRO, SP1/69 fo. 209 (*LP* V, 918). A pardon for intrusions was indeed granted to the archbishop in July 1532. See TNA, PRO, C82/656 and C66/661 m. 35 (*LP* V, 1139 [7]). A draft of this pardon, prepared by Cromwell's office, is TNA, PRO, SP2/M fos 5–7 (*LP* V, 1139 [7/ii]).

13. BL, Cotton MS, Titus B I fo. 378 (*LP* V, 1138).

14. Ibid.; my italics for emphasis.

15. TNA, PRO, SP1/69 fo. 209 (*LP* V, 918); SP1/69 fos 111–111v (*LP* V, 802).

16. During the thirteenth and fourteenth centuries, these revenues were accounted before the barons of the Exchequer. See M. Howell, *Regalian Right in Medieval England* (London, 1962), pp. 98–102. By the sixteenth century, however, as a 'memoriall for the Kings highnes' makes clear, these were now 'accompted before the general surueyours'. See TNA, PRO, SP1/67 fo. 29 (*LP* V, 397).

17. TNA, PRO, SP1/65 fo. 129 (*LP* V, 95). This was placed in 1531 in *Letters and Papers*, but belongs to 1532; see the dating of his account of the money sent to Cromwell, below n. 18. Also see SP1/65 fo. 130 (*LP* V, 96), which should be similarly redated.

18. TNA, PRO, SC6/HenVIII/412 (*LP* V, 822); TNA, PRO, E36/143 fo. 26 (*LP* VI, 299 [ix]).

19. TNA, PRO, SC6/HenVIII/412 fo. 11 (*LP* V, 822). Cromwell's warrant recording his receipt of this is dated 25 February; see TNA, PRO, E101/421/5 (*LP* V, 825).

20. TNA, PRO, SP1/65 fos 31–32 (*LP* V, 13). Exactly when the bishop died is unclear, but the generally accepted date appears to be sometime in late 1530. See A. A. Chibi, 'Blyth, Geoffrey (*c.*1470–1530)', *ODNB*, which states that his will was proved on 1 March 1531. Curiously, however, Blythe was still listed as a commissioner of the peace in several locations as late as March 1531. See TNA, PRO, C66/656 m. 17d (*LP* V, 119 [56] and *LP* V, 166 [60]); C66/656 m. 14d (*LP* V, 119 [70]); C66/656 m. 18d (*LP* V, 166 [44]). Moreover, Strete's account of the money he handled as receiver runs from 19 January 1532 to 19 January 1533, suggesting Blythe's death may actually have occurred a little later than 1530. See TNA, PRO, SC6/HenVIII/7156 (*LP* VI, 52).

21. TNA, PRO, SP1/66 fos 33–33v (Merriman, *Life and Letters of Thomas Cromwell,* i, 339–340; *LP* V, 277); SP1/66 fo. 155 (*LP* V, 332); SP1/237 fo. 31 (*LP* Add. I, i, 736). These three letters were erroneously placed in 1531 in *Letters and Papers* but date to 1532, during the suppression of Calwich Priory, Staffordshire, see above pp. 124–125 and below n. 27. Also see SP1/70 fo. 54 (*LP* V, 1045); SP1/75 fos 174–175 (*LP* VI, 389).

22. TNA, PRO, SP2/N fo. 108 (*LP* VI, 228).

23. Starkey, 'Court and Government', p. 44; F. Heal, *Of Prelates and Princes: A Study of the Economic and Social Position of the Tudor Episcopate* (Cambridge, 1980), pp. 107, 108.

24. TNA, PRO, SP1/69 fo. 141 (*LP* V, 848).

25. Howell, *Regalian Right*, pp. 60–63; Heal, *Of Prelates and Princes*, p. 107.

26. TNA, PRO, SP1/69 fo. 141 (*LP* V, 848). See also Randall Wodnut's letters to Strete on the difficulties in gathering the Cheshire rents; TNA, PRO, SP1/75 fo. 159 (*LP* VI, 373); SP1/76 fo. 42 (*LP* VI, 479). Both belong to 1532, not 1533 as in *Letters and Papers*. For the redating, see below, n. 27 and above pp. 124–125.

27. TNA, PRO, SP1/66 fo. 33 (Merriman, *Life and Letters of Thomas Cromwell*, i. 339–340; *LP* V, 277); my italics for emphasis. This letter was placed in 1531 by the editors of *Letters and Papers*, and this dating was also accepted by Professor Elton, *Tudor Revolution in Government*, pp. 90 and 144. Other instructions in Cromwell's letter to Strete, however, relate to the suppression of Calwich Priory, Staffordshire, which did not occur until 1532; see above, pp. 124–125.

28. TNA, PRO, SP1/69 fo. 141 (*LP* V, 848).

29. TNA, PRO, SP1/82 fo. 200v (*LP* VII, 257).

30. BL, Cotton MS, Titus B I fo. 493v (*LP* VI, 1194); TNA, PRO, E36/143 fo. 69 (*LP* VI, 1589).

31. TNA, PRO, SP1/83 fo. 169 (*LP* VII, 563).

32. TNA, PRO, SP1/77 fo. 68 (*LP* VI, 689).

33. TNA, PRO, SP1/80 fo. 174 (*LP* VI, 1507). Hornyold's account as receiver-general is TNA, PRO, SC6/HenVIII/4035.

34. TNA, PRO, SP1/79 fo. 155 (*LP* VI, 1244). One of Cromwell's remembrances was to write 'a lettre to the prior and conuent of Ely to permitte suche persons as the kinges highnes shall appoynte to Be receyuors of the reuenues of the Bisshopriche of Elye without any their impechement or lette'; TNA, PRO, E36/143 fo. 70 (*LP* VI, 1589).

35. TNA, PRO, SP1/79 fo. 155 (*LP* VI, 1244). The summary of this letter given in *Letters and Papers* has transcribed 'escheter' as 'Exchequer', which does make more sense in the context of the sentence. The original letter to Cromwell is written in a hand that is difficult to read but it does look like the prior has written 'escheter'.

36. TNA, PRO, SP1/78 fo. 110v (*LP* VI, 977 [ii]); SP1/79 fo. 192 (*LP* VI, 1310).

37. TNA, PRO, SP1/80 fos 165–165v (*LP* VI, 1494).

38. *LP* II, ii, 472; *LP* III, ii, 1408.

39. Heal, *Of Prelates and Princes*, p. 107.

40. TNA, PRO, SP1/75 fo. 68 (*LP* VI, 304).

41. TNA, PRO, SP2/O fo. 26 (*LP* VI, 717).

42. TNA, PRO, SP2/N fo. 107 (*LP* VI, 228).

43. TNA, PRO, SP2/N fo. 108 (*LP* VI, 228).

44. B. P. Wolffe, 'The Management of English Royal Estates under the Yorkist Kings', *English Historical Review*, lxxi (1956), pp. 17, 19; F. C. Dietz, *English Government Finance, 1485–1558* (second edn, London, 1964), p. 31; B. P. Wolffe, *The Crown Lands, 1461 to 1536: An Aspect of Yorkist and Early Tudor Government* (London, 1970), pp. 113, 120.

45. TNA, PRO, E101/421/5 (*LP* V, 825).

46. TNA, PRO, SP1/77 fo. 68 (*LP* VI, 689); SP1/76 fo. 99 (*LP* VI, 533).

47. TNA, PRO, SP1/76 fo. 99 (*LP* VI, 533). For Cromwell's handling of these matters, see also TNA, PRO, SP1/79 fo. 169 (*LP* VI, 1274); SP1/80 fo. 174 (*LP* VI, 1507).

48. TNA, PRO, E36/141 fo. 39 (*LP* V, 1285 [ix]). There is a slight discrepancy concerning this. A list of fines drawn up after February records this, but only £200 is recorded as being paid, with £466 13s 4d outstanding. See TNA, PRO, SP1/68 fo. 142 (*LP* V, 657). The confusion is not helped by the fact that Cromwell's warrant for this payment has not survived.

49. TNA, PRO, SP2/N fo. 108 (*LP* V, 228).

50. TNA, PRO, E101/421/5 (*LP* V, 825). The list of warrants made by one of Cromwell's clerks describes this erroneously as being dated 15 February; see TNA, PRO, E36/141 fo. 41 (*LP* V, 1285 [ix]). The pardon was granted in February 1532; see TNA, PRO, C66/658 m. 32 and C82/652 (*LP* V, 909 [7]).

51. TNA, PRO, SP2/N fo. 108 (*LP* VI, 228). Longland's fine was £666 13s 4d for the breach at his gaol, but he consistently looked to Cromwell for respite from payments, evidently with some success. See TNA, PRO, SP1/68 fo. 107 (*LP* V, 623); SP1/70 fo.

123 (*LP* V, 1107); SP1/70 fo. 143 (*LP* V, 1144). Longland's pardon was finally granted in March 1534; see TNA, PRO, C82/679 and C66/663 m. 6 (*LP* VII, 419 [10]); TNA, PRO, SP1/82 fo. 249 (*LP* VII, 322).

52. For an excellent overview of these events, see J. Guy, 'Henry VIII and the *Praemunire* Manoeuvres', pp. 481–503.

53. W. T. Waugh, 'The Great Statute of Praemunire', *English Historical Review*, xxxvii (1922), pp. 173–205; R. N. Swanson, *Church and Society in Late Medieval England* (Oxford, 1989), p. 186.

54. G. W. Bernard, 'The Pardon of the Clergy Reconsidered', *Journal of Ecclesiastical History*, 37 (1986), p. 262.

55. TNA, PRO, E135/8/37.

56. TNA, PRO, SP2/N fo. 108 (*LP* VI, 228).

57. TNA, PRO, SP1/71 fo. 39 (*LP* V, 1326).

58. For the names of those involved and the details surrounding this, see Guy, 'Henry VIII and the *Praemunire* Manoeuvres', pp. 482–487 and 500–502.

59. TNA, PRO, SP1/68 fo. 142 (*LP* V, 657). Of the fifteen original clerics, only Skeffington and Robert Fuller, abbot of Waltham and prior of St Bartholomew's, Smithfield, were required to pay individual fines in excess of their contributions to the subsidy of £100,000. See Guy, 'Henry VIII and the *Praemunire* Manoeuvres', p. 501.

60. TNA, PRO, SP1/68 fo. 82 (*LP* V, 577).

61. The list of Cromwell's warrants compiled by one of his clerks describes this 100 marks as being paid to Cromwell on 27 May, 'in the xxiii yere' of Henry VIII, i.e. May 1531. This appears to be an error. Cromwell's warrant for this payment is dated 27 May 'in the xxiiiith yere', i.e. 1532. See and compare TNA, PRO, E36/141 fo. 39 (*LP* V, 1285 [ix]) and E101/421/5 (*LP* V, 1052). See also John Mille's letter to Cromwell, which informs him that the bringer of his letter 'shall delyuer vnto you C markes for my lord of Bangor'. Curiously this letter is dated 10 June; TNA, PRO, SP1/70 fo. 97 (*LP* V, 1084).

62. For the names of those involved and the details surrounding this, see Guy, 'Henry VIII and the *Praemunire* Manoeuvres', pp. 482–487 and 500–502.

63. TNA, PRO, SP60/1 fo. 148 (*State Papers*, ii. 158; *LP* V, 878).

64. TNA, PRO, C82/652 and C66/658 m. 16 (*LP* V, 838 [10]).

65. TNA, PRO, E36/141 fo. 39 (*LP* V, 1285 [ix]); TNA, PRO, SP1/68 fo. 42 (*LP* V, 657).

66. TNA, PRO, SP2/N fo. 108 (*LP* VI, 228). Alen was killed in 1534, with £200 still owing to the king. See TNA, PRO, SP60/2 fos 57–57v (*LP* VII, 1109); SP60/2 fos 62–62v (*LP* VII, 1404); SP60/2 fo. 49 (Merriman, *Life and Letters of Thomas Cromwell*, i. 357–358; *LP* VI, 791), mistakenly placed in 1533: it is of 1534.

67. TNA, PRO, C82/656 and C66/661 m. 19 (*LP* V, 1139 [10/i]); TNA, PRO, SP2/M fos 8–10 (*LP* V, 1139 [10/ii]) is a draft of this grant prepared by Cromwell's office.

68. TNA, PRO, E36/141 fo. 42 (*LP* V, 1285 [ix]). The summary of this in *Letters and Papers* mistakenly describes the payment as £100.

69. TNA, PRO, SP2/N fo. 108 (*LP* VI, 228).

70. TNA, PRO, SP1/68 fo. 82 (*LP* V, 577).

71. TNA, PRO, SP1/68 fo. 142 (*LP* V, 657).

72. TNA, PRO, SP1/69 fo. 143 (*LP* V, 849).

73. TNA, PRO, SP1/72 fo. 8 (*LP* V, 1506).

74. TNA, PRO, SP1/71 fo. 58 (*LP* V, 1356).

75. I. J. Churchill, *Canterbury Administration* (2 vols, London, 1933), i. 551.

76. TNA, PRO, SP1/74 fo. 24 (*LP* VI, 34).

77. TNA, PRO, SP1/74 fo. 123 (*LP* VI, 108).

78. TNA, PRO, SP1/79 fo. 5 (*LP* VI, 1067); SP3/12 fo. 145 (*LP* VI, 1433).

79. TNA, PRO, SP1/80 fo. 85 (*LP* VI, 1396).

80. On the concept of sovereignty embodied in the act, see G. R. Elton, 'The Evolution of a Reformation Statute', *English Historical Review*, lxiv (1949), p. 195; G. Nicholson, 'The Act of Appeals and the English Reformation', in C. Cross, D. Loades and J. Scarisbrick, eds, *Law and Government under the Tudors: Essays Presented to Sir Geoffrey Elton* (Cambridge, 1988), p. 30.

81. *Statutes of the Realm*, iii. 24 Henry VIII c. 12.
82. For the new appeal procedures put in place by Cromwell, see Elton, 'Evolution of a Reformation Statute', pp. 187–194.
83. TNA, PRO, SP1/80 fos 18–18v (*LP* VI, 1335).
84. TNA, PRO, SP1/80 fo. 85 (*LP* VI, 1396).
85. *CSP, Spanish*, V, i, 45.
86. TNA, SP1/69 fo. 210 (*LP* V 920); SP1/73 fo. 153 (*LP* V 1784).
87. TNA, PRO, SP1/80 fos 103–103v (*LP* VI, 1440); SP1/79 fo. 71 (*LP* V, 1158); SP1/80 fo. 105 (*LP* VI, 1441); SP1/80 fo. 108 (*LP* VI, 1451); SP1/80 fo. 109 (*LP* VI, 1452).
88. TNA, PRO, SP1/80 fo. 108 (*LP* VI, 1451).
89. TNA, PRO, SP1/81 fo. 139 (*LP* VI, 1692).
90. TNA, PRO, SP1/81 fo. 140 (*LP* VI, 1693).
91. Gwyn, *King's Cardinal*, pp. 309–312.
92. D. Knowles and R. N. Hadcock, *Medieval Religious Houses: England and Wales* (London, 1971), p. 494.
93. The following is based on F. A. Gasquet, *English Monastic Life* (London, 1904), pp. 42–48, 183; A. Hamilton Thompson, *The Abbey of St. Mary of the Meadows, Leicester* (Leicester, 1949), pp. 17–19; D. Knowles, *Religious Orders in England*, ii. 250.
94. M. Heale, '"Not a Thing for a Stranger to Enter Upon": The Selection of Monastic Superiors in Late Medieval and Early Tudor England', in J. Burton and K. Stöber, eds, *Monasteries and Society in the British Isles in the Later Middle Ages* (Woodbridge, 2008), p. 53.
95. Gwyn, *King's Cardinal*, p. 317.
96. These were: the priory of St Giles of Barnewell, Cambridgeshire, TNA, PRO, C82/637 (*LP* V, 80 [27]) and C82/639 (*LP* V, 166 [27]); St Mary's, York, TNA, PRO, C82/638 and C66/656 m. 32 (*LP* V, 119 [19]); C82/640 and C66/657 m. 25 (*LP* V, 220 [9]); Burton-on-Trent, Staffordshire, TNA, PRO, C82/638; C66/656 m. 33 (*LP* V, 119 [21]) and C82/639; C66/657 m. 28 (*LP* V, 166 [53]); St Albans, Hertfordshire, TNA, PRO, C82/638 (*LP* V, 119 [44]) and C82/639 (*LP* V, 166 [28]); Athelney, Somerset, TNA, PRO, C82/638, C66/656 m. 33 (*LP* V, 119 [66]), C82/639 and C66/657 m. 28 (*LP* V, 166 [55]); Elstow, Bedfordshire, TNA, PRO, C82/640 and C66/659 m. 14 (*LP* V, 278 [1]).
97. This was the priory of St Andrew, Northampton, whose abbot resigned in August 1532. See TNA, PRO, C82/659 (*LP* V, 1270 [15]) and C82/660 (*LP* V, 1499 [2]). Given the overwhelming statistics quoted above, it would seem highly likely that Cromwell was also involved with this one, but there is no evidence that can link him with it.
98. Cromwell was involved in the election of Dan Matthew Dyvers as abbot of Holmcultram, Cumberland, which probably occurred in early 1532. Exactly when this occurred, however, is unclear. No *congé d'élire* has survived for this appointment, and the editors of the *VCH, Cumberland*, ii, believed that Dyvers was elected in 1531 (pp. 170 and 178). This was based on the dating of several documents in *Letters and Papers*, which have been redated in this study. See also D. M. Smith, ed., *The Heads of Religious Houses: England and Wales* (3 vols, Cambridge, 2008), iii. 300.
99. TNA, PRO, C82/654 (*LP* V, 978 [23]).
100. TNA, PRO, SP1/70 fo. 53 (*LP* V, 1044).
101. TNA, PRO, C82/658 (*LP* V, 1207 [24]); C82/658 and C66/661 m. 21 (*LP* V, 1207 [35]). See also TNA, PRO, C82/658 and C66/661 m. 35 (*LP* V, 1207 [25]), which is a licence for Fuller to obtain papal bulls allowing him to hold the priory of St Bartholomew's and Waltham Abbey, for life, *in commendam*.
102. TNA, PRO, SP1/82 fo. 200 (*LP* VII, 257); BL, Cotton MS, Titus B I fo. 463 (*LP* VII, 408).
103. TNA, PRO, C82/656 (*LP* V, 1065 [30]); C82/657 (*LP* V, 1139 [23]).
104. TNA, PRO, SP1/68 fo. 143v (*LP* V, 657). The fine was £33 6s 8d, with £10 recorded as having already been paid.
105. TNA, PRO, SP2/N fo. 107 (*LP* VI, 228); TNA, PRO, C82/656 and C66/661 m. 6 (*LP* V, 1139 [4]); C82/658 (*LP* V, 1207 [43]).

106.   TNA, PRO, SP2/N fo. 108 (*LP* VI, 228); TNA, PRO, C82/666 and C66/660 m. 15 (*LP* VI, 300 [15]). A memorandum in Cromwell's hand reminded him 'To send to the abbott of Westminster for his end', and was concerned with the completion of this appointment. See TNA, PRO, SP1/78 fos 215–215v (*LP* VI, 1056 [2]). William Boston succeeded at St Peter's in early 1533, and several letters to Cromwell do indeed hint at his involvement; see TNA, PRO, SP1/72 fo. 163 (*LP* V, 1665); SP1/73 fo. 99 (*LP* V, 1725). Boston did not receive his temporalities until April 1533; see TNA, PRO, C82/667 and C66/661 m. 21 (*LP* VI, 417 [21]).

107.   TNA, PRO, SP1/78 fo. 217v (*LP* VI, 1057). The abbots and sums are as follows: Westminster, £1,000; Malmesbury, £1,000; Colchester, £200; Burton, £100; Athelney, £100.

108.   TNA, PRO, C82/670 (*LP* VI, 578 [19]); TNA, PRO, SP1/78 fo. 215 (*LP* VI, 1056 [2]).

109.   TNA, PRO, SP1/76 fo. 173 (*LP* VI, 621). Marshall's temporalities were not in fact restored until January 1534; see TNA, PRO, C82/680 and C66/663 m. 10 (*LP* VII, 147 [16]). It is also interesting to note that the abbot asked for Cromwell's 'favor and ayd in recoueryng such rentes and de[wties] as be withdrawen frome the monastery'.

110.   TNA, PRO, C82/658 and C66/661 m. 17 (*LP* V, 1207 [27]); TNA, PRO, SP1/70 fo. 154 (*LP* V, 1163).

111.   TNA, PRO, SP1/70 fo. 185 (*LP* V, 1213).

112.   TNA, PRO, C82/659 and C66/661 m. 17 (*LP* V, 1270 [18]).

113.   TNA, PRO, SP1/71 fo. 23 (*LP* V, 1304).

114.   TNA, PRO, SP1/76 fo. 48 (*LP* VI, 489).

115.   On this point, see also the note among Cromwell's remembrances 'to speke with the king that he grante no elecyon for bewlay [Beaulieu] without desire of congye'; see TNA, PRO, SP1/78 fo. 215 (*LP* VI, 1056 [2]).

116.   TNA, PRO, SP1/66 fo. 46 (*LP* V, 300). Erroneously placed in 1531 in *Letters and Papers*, it is of 1533; see n. 141 for its redating. See also Smith, *Heads of Religious Houses*, iii. 51, who was unsure whether this episode occurred in 1531 or 1533.

117.   In a letter to the king on this matter, signed by Bristow, he is described as 'coffurer'; TNA, PRO, SP1/66 fo. 133 (*LP* V, 322). This was mistakenly placed in 1531 by the editors of *Letters and Papers,* but clearly relates to this episode of 1533.

118.   This was despite one of his associates, William Popley, urging him to act on Bristow's behalf. See TNA, PRO, SP1/76 fo. 50 (*LP* VI, 492).

119.   BL, Cotton MS, Cleopatra E IV fos 28–28v (*LP* VI, 674); TNA, PRO, SP1/77 fo. 56 (*LP* VI, 676).

120.   BL, Cotton MS, Cleopatra E IV fo. 28 (*LP* VI, 674).

121.   Ibid., fos 28, 29r.

122.   Ibid., fo. 28.

123.   TNA, PRO, SP1/66 fo. 133 (*LP* V, 322), misdated in *Letters and Papers*, it is off 1533; TNA, PRO, SP1/77 fo. 196 (*LP* VI, 816)

124.   TNA, PRO, SP1/238 fo. 87 (*LP* Add. I, i, 858), SP1/66 fo. 133 (*LP* V, 322), incorrectly placed in 1531 in *Letters and Papers*.

125.   TNA, PRO, SP1/77 fo. 196 (*LP* VI, 816); SP1/77 fo. 197 (*LP* VI, 817).

126.   TNA, PRO, SP1/77 fo. 196 (*LP* VI, 816).

127.   BL, Cotton MS, Cleopatra E IV fos 28–28v (*LP* VI, 674); TNA, PRO, SP1/77 fo. 56 (*LP* VI, 676); *VCH, Wiltshire*, iii. 226.

128.   TNA, PRO, SP1/77 fo. 56 (*LP* VI, 676); *VCH, Wiltshire*, iii. 226.

129.   TNA, PRO, SP1/78 fo. 9 (*LP* VI, 847).

130.   TNA, PRO, C82/672 (*LP* VI, 929 [51]). Restitution of temporalities was granted in December: TNA, PRO, C82/677 and C66/662 m. 38 (*LP* VI, 1595 [15]). See also TNA, PRO, SP1/73 fo. 121 (*LP* V, 1746), which is a letter asking for Cromwell to excuse the abbot of Malmesbury for being behind in the money he owed Cromwell for his temporalities. It is undated, and placed in 1532 in *Letters and Papers*, but surely dates to 1533. Three other letters concerning Cromwell's influence at Malmesbury were also erroneously placed in 1531 and 1533 by the editors of *Letters and Papers*, see

TNA, PRO, SP1/70 fo. 10 (*LP* V, 990); SP1/76 fo. 196 (*LP* VI, 629); SP1/76 fo. 195 (*LP* VI, 628). They are of the year 1534.

131. TNA, PRO, C82/659 and C66/661 m. 18 (*LP* V, 1270 [7]).
132. TNA, PRO, SP1/70 fo. 106 (*LP* V, 1088); SP1/237 fo. 211 (*LP* Add. I, i, 785).
133. TNA, PRO, SP1/70 fo. 107 (*LP* V, 1089).
134. TNA, PRO, SP1/70 fo. 156 (*LP* V, 1167).
135. TNA, PRO, SP1/237 fo. 210 (*LP* Add. I, i, 784).
136. TNA, PRO, SP1/70 fo. 192 (*LP* V, 1225); SP1/70 fo. 197 (*LP* V, 1230).
137. TNA, PRO, SP1/70 fo. 196 (*LP* V, 1229).
138. TNA, PRO, SP1/70 fo. 196 (*LP* V, 1229).
139. TNA, PRO, C82/660 (*LP* V, 1370 [11]); C82/661 (*LP* V, 1499 [16]). A note among Cromwell's papers reminded him to obtain the warrant for the restitution of these temporalities, see TNA, PRO, E36/143 fo. 9 (*LP* VI, 299 [ii]).
140. TNA, PRO, SP1/66 fo. 45 (*LP* V, 294). Mistakenly placed in 1531 in *Letters and Papers*. For its redating to 1533, see n. 141, below.
141. TNA, PRO, SP1/66 fo. 46 (*LP* V, 300); mistakenly placed in 1531 in *Letters and Papers*. This, and the previous letter cited immediately above, along with a letter to Cromwell from the newly elected abbot, Robert Hamlyn, informing Cromwell that he had sealed the obligations he had requested (TNA, PRO, SP1/68 fo. 34 [*LP* V, 501]) were all actually sent in 1533. A grant of March 1531 confirms the assent of John Major as abbot of Athelney, which is chronologically incompatible with Courtenay's request; TNA, PRO, C82/639 and C66/657 m. 28 (*LP* V, 166 [55]). Major died in February 1533, and the next abbot was Robert Hamlyn. Royal assent to his appointment was given on 22 June 1533, which correlates with Lee and Courtenay's remarks. See C82/671 (*LP* VI, 737 [18]). In his letter to Cromwell on 17 June, Lee also informed him that 'thys day . . . I intende towards malmeysbury and thayre to doo after your commandment . . . the eleccion thayre shalbe apon Wedynesday'. See TNA, PRO, SP1/66 fo. 46 (*LP* V, 300). As outlined earlier (pp. 112–115), the election at Malmesbury occurred in mid-1533, not 1531. *Cf.* Smith, *Heads of Religious Houses*, iii. 51.
142. BL, Cotton MS, Vespasian F XIII fo. 178 (*LP* VI, 446).
143. TNA, PRO, SP1/74 fo. 168 (*LP* VI, 169).
144. TNA, PRO, SP1/79 fo. 167 (*LP* VI, 1270).
145. TNA, PRO, SP1/80 fo. 167 (*LP* VI, 1495); SP1/80 fo. 169 (*LP* VI, 1499). The editors of *Letters and Papers* also placed a letter from Sir Edward Chamberlain to Cromwell regarding the election of a new prior at Ixworth, Suffolk, in 1534. See BL, Cotton MS, Cleopatra E IV fo. 64 (*LP* VII, 43). This letter actually belongs to January 1536. See *LP* X, 89 and Smith, *Heads of Religious Houses*, iii. 450.
146. TNA, PRO, SP1/78 fo. 140 (*LP* VI, 1007).
147. TNA, PRO, SP1/78 fo. 138 (*LP* VI, 1006). Cromwell himself was also written to in support of the abbot of Waverley to succeed at Beaulieu. See TNA, PRO, SP1/78 fo. 137 (*LP* VI, 1001); SP1/79 fo. 14 (*LP* VI, 1074).
148. TNA, PRO, SP1/75 fo. 58 (*LP* VI, 285). This was placed in 1533 in *Letters and Papers*, but it might more reasonably be placed in 1534, when Cromwell began making notes for the position there to be filled. A *congé d'élire* was granted for Wilton in March 1534; see TNA, PRO, C82/680 and C66/662 m. 15 (*LP* VII, 419 [14]).
149. TNA, PRO, SP1/75 fo. 68 (*LP* VI, 304); undated, but placed in 1533 in *Letters and Papers*. It would be more reasonable to date this to 1534, when Cromwell began making notes to have this position filled. TNA, PRO, SP1/75 fo. 69 (*LP* VI, 305) also dates to 1534;.
150. BL, Cotton MS, Titus B I fo. 428 (*LP* VII, 48); TNA, PRO, E36/143 fo. 43 (*LP* VII, 50); TNA, PRO, SP1/82 fo. 113 (*LP* VII, 107).
151. TNA, PRO, C82/681 and C66/665 m. 7 (*LP* VII, 589 [3]); C82/684 and C66/665 m. 8 (*LP* VII, 761 [41]). She was previously the prioress at Kington St Michael, Wiltshire, and had borrowed money to procure her position as abbess there. See TNA, PRO, C1/902/34 and Smith, *Heads of Religious Houses*, iii. 660 and 706.

152. TNA, PRO, SP1/83 fo. 9 (*LP* VII, 376). See also TNA, PRO, SP1/82 fo. 231 (*LP* VII, 297); SP1/238 fo. 69 (*LP* Add. I, i, 843).
153. TNA, PRO, SP1/77 fo. 137 (*LP* VI, 756); SP1/77 fo. 80 (*LP* VI, 700); SP1/77 fo. 89 (*LP* VI, 715); SP1/77 fo. 90 (*LP* VI, 716).
154. TNA, PRO, C82/672 and C66/663 m. 13. He did not receive his temporalities until April the following year, see TNA, PRO, C82/681 and C66/662 m. 23 (*LP* VII, 587).
155. TNA, PRO, SP1/83 fo. 43v (*LP* VII, 360); TNA, PRO, C82/680 and C66/662 m. 15 (*LP* VII, 419 [23]); SP1/82 fo. 270 (*LP* VII, 346).
156. TNA, PRO, SP1/75 fo. 82 (*LP* VI, 328); this is of 1534, not 1533 as in *Letters and Papers*. John Wyche, the prior at St Mary's, was elected abbot there. See TNA, PRO, SP1/83 fo. 77 (*LP* VII, 460); TNA, PRO, C82/683 (*LP* VII, 761 [22]); C82/685 and C66/665 m. 7 (*LP* VII, 922 [5]).
157. Heale, '"Not a thing for a stranger to enter upon"', p. 65.
158. TNA, PRO, SP1/72 fo. 119 (*LP* V, 1618).
159. On the contrary, the bequest was actually increased from 13s 4d to 20s. See TNA, PRO, SP1/54 fo. 242v (Merriman, *Life and Letters of Thomas Cromwell*, i. 62; *LP* IV, iii, 5772).
160. TNA, PRO, E36/140 fos 29r–62v.
161. TNA, PRO, SP1/70 fo. 53 (*LP* V, 1044).
162. TNA, PRO, E36/140 fo. 43r.
163. TNA, PRO, SP2/M fos 46–52 (*LP* V, 1339).
164. TNA, PRO, SP1/78 fo. 138 (*LP* VI, 1006). Cromwell himself was also written to in support of the abbot of Waverley to succeed at Beaulieu; see TNA, PRO, SP1/78 fo. 137 (*LP* VI, 1001); SP1/79 fo. 14 (*LP* VI, 1074).
165. TNA, PRO, SP1/78 fo. 138 (*LP* VI, 1006).
166. TNA, PRO, SP1/71 fos 23–23v (*LP* V, 1304). The abbot was resigning because he was old and sick.
167. TNA, PRO, SP1/71 fos 23–23v (*LP* V, 1304); my italics for emphasis.
168. TNA, PRO, SP1/71 fo. 50 (Merriman, *Life and Letters of Thomas Cromwell*, i. 347–348; *LP* V, 1340).
169. Admittedly, there is some discrepancy over when the next head was appointed, but John Elye was apparently elected abbot in July 1533, with Fitzjames taking his oath of fealty. See TNA, PRO, C66/663 m. 28 (*LP* VI, 929 [38]). For the discrepancy, see Smith, *Heads of Religious Houses*, iii. 397.
170. Heale, '"Not a thing for a stranger to enter upon"', p. 65.
171. The *congé d'élire* there was granted in January 1534, following Pexall's resignation; see TNA, PRO, C82/678 (*LP* VII, 147 [10]). A memorandum of Cromwell's, 'Item the Restytucyons for leycester', was also a reminder to attend to this; see BL, Cotton MS, Caligula B I fo. 463 (*LP* VII, 108).
172. G. G. Peery, 'Episcopal Visitation of the Austin Canons of Leicestershire and Dorchester', *English Historical Review*, iv (1889), pp. 304–309; A. Hamilton Thompson, ed., *Visitations of Religious Houses in the Diocese of Lincoln* (3 vols, London, 1940–1947), ii. 206–217; Hamilton Thompson, *Abbey of St Mary of the Meadows*, pp. 77–79.
173. A letter from the abbot to Cromwell reveals that Longland had previously installed several of his own canons in an attempt to resolve matters. See TNA, PRO, SP1/80 fo. 168 (*LP* VI, 1496); SP1/70 fo. 161 (*LP* V, 1175).
174. TNA, PRO, SP1/70 fo. 200 (*LP* V, 1233).
175. TNA, PRO, C82/679; C66/663 m. 14 (*LP* VII, 262 [9 and 28]). Thompson states Bourchier had been Cromwell's choice, but offers no evidence in support of this; see Hamilton Thompson, *Abbey of St Mary of the Meadows*, p. 85. Cromwell also received the fee for Bourchier's temporalities; TNA, PRO, SP1/82 fo. 234 (*LP* VII, 301).
176. TNA, PRO, SP1/83 fo. 174 (*LP* VII, 579); *VCH, Leicestershire*, ii. 17; Hamilton Thompson, *Abbey of St Mary of the Meadows*, p. 89.
177. TNA, PRO, SP1/70 fo. 152 (*LP* V, 1158).
178. TNA, PRO, SP1/71 fo. 101 (*LP* V, 1426).
179. TNA, PRO, SP1/77 fo. 136 (*LP* V, 755).

180. It should be noted that Leonard Grey also asked Cromwell to be Pexall's 'frend at my desyre', which may also have contributed to his acting in the abbot's interests. See TNA, PRO, SP1/70 fo. 200 (*LP* V, 1233).

181. A memorandum reminded him 'for pexsalles pardon to be assignyd', and Cromwell received his thanks in December 1533 'for your most tendir kyndenesse in all my busyness trusting . . . suche order to be takyn for my pension'. See TNA, PRO, SP1/83 fo. 43v (*LP* VII, 414); SP1/81 fo. 25 (*LP* VI, 1565); SP1/82 fo. 15 (*LP* VII, 18).

182. *VCH, Leicestershire*, ii. 16; TNA, PRO, SP1/83 fo. 93 (*LP* VII, 513); SP1/83 fo. 174 (*LP* VII, 579).

183. TNA, PRO, SP1/82 fo. 145 (*LP* VII, 169). Notes among Cromwell's remembrances reminded him to obtain a 'conge de lyre for thurgarton', which was granted in March, and to attend to 'the elleccyon of the pryor of thurgarton'. See BL, Cotton MS, Titus B I fo. 463 (*LP* VII, 108); TNA, PRO, C82/679 and C66/662 m. 29 (*LP* VII, 419 [2]); TNA, PRO, SP1/83 fo. 43v (*LP* VII, 414).

184. TNA, PRO, C82/681 and C66/662 m. 29 (*LP* VII, 587 [11]); restitution of temporalities was granted in May, C82/684 and C66/664 m. 15 (*LP* VII, 761 [28]); TNA, PRO, SP1/75 fo. 25 (*LP* VI, 236).

185. TNA, PRO, SP1/79 fo. 186 (*LP* VI, 1304). This letter was placed in 1533 in *Letters and Papers*, but it is of 1532. The abbot deposed must have been Edmund Emery, who resigned and had a pension awarded to him on 13 March 1533. See *VCH, Essex*, ii. 136 n. 34; Smith, *Heads of Religious Houses*, iii. 340.

186. TNA, PRO, SP1/72 fo. 42 (*LP* V, 1557).

187. *Cartularium Abbatthiae de Rievalle*, ed. J. C. Atkinson (London, lxxxiii, 1889), p. cvi.

188. TNA, PRO, SP1/80 fo. 91 (Merriman, *Life and Letters of Thomas Cromwell*, i. 366; *LP* VI, 1408).

189. TNA, PRO, SP1/80 fo. 176 (*LP* VI, 1513); Smith, *Heads of Religious Houses*, iii. 325. See also TNA, PRO, SP1/84 fo. 84 (*LP* VII, 724) and *VCH, York*, iii. 152, for Cromwell's involvement with the pension granted to Abbot Kirkby in May 1534.

190. TNA, PRO, SP1/71 fo. 34 (*LP* V, 1317); SP1/78 fo. 118 (*LP* VI, 987); SP1/78 fo. 117 (*LP* VI, 986).

191. TNA, PRO, SP1/78 fos 115–115v (*LP* VI, 985), SP1/81 fo. 18 (*LP* VI, 1557). That he would become the last abbot of Holmcultram in September 1538 suggests that he was not convicted. See *VCH, Cumberland*, ii. 173.

192. Boradalle wrote to Cromwell complaining he had been kept 'outt of my awn hows the space of xx weikkes', and had been moved from Byland to Furness Abbey. See TNA, PRO, SP1/78 fo. 117 (*LP* VI, 986), SP1/78 fo. 118 (*LP* VI, 987), this is probably of 1532, not 1533 as in *Letters and Papers*; SP1/81 fo. 18 (*LP* VI, 1557). For the dispositions and examination taken in regards to this crime, see *LP* Add. I, i, 866; *LP* VI, 988.

193. TNA, PRO, SP1/77 fo. 175 (Merriman, *Life and Letters of Thomas Cromwell*, i. 362–363; *LP* VI, 778).

194. TNA, PRO, SP1/71 fo. 152 (*LP* V, 1477).

195. TNA, SP1/77 fo. 175 (Merriman, *Life and Letters of Thomas Cromwell*, i. 362–363; *LP* VI, 778). The abbot of Vaudey had sent Cromwell his account detailing the state of the monastery to illustrate this, SP1/71 fo. 152 (*LP* V, 1477).

196. TNA, PRO, SP1/77 fo. 175 (Merriman, *Life and Letters of Thomas Cromwell*, i. 362–363; *LP* VI, 778).

197. TNA, PRO, SP1/77 fo. 176 (*LP* VI, 779). Saxton was indeed replaced in late 1532 by William Stile; see *VCH, Lincoln*, ii. 144–145.

198. *VCH, Lincoln*, ii. 144; *VCH, Bedfordshire*, i. 367–370; TNA, PRO, SP1/77 fo. 176 (*LP* VI, 779).

199. TNA, PRO, SP1/102 fo. 5v (*LP* X, 254 [i]); SP1/102 fo. 8v (*LP* X, 254 [ii]).

200. *Cf.* A. N. Shaw, 'The *Compendium Compertorum* and the Making of the Suppression Act of 1536' (University of Warwick PhD thesis, 2003), p. 410.

201. J. H. Bettey, *Suppression of the Monasteries in the West Country* (Stroud, 1989), p. 20. Bettey's subject was of course the condition of the monasteries in the West Country, but I believe his comments are reflective of a much wider vulnerability.

202. C. Harper-Bill, 'Dean Colet's Convocation Sermon and the Pre-Reformation Church in England', *History*, 73 (1988), pp. 194–196; G. W. Bernard, 'The Dissolution of the Monasteries', *History*, 96 (2011), pp. 393–394.

203. *LP* III, i, 1124, 1216; *LP* IV, i, 585.

204. *LP* IV, ii, 4921 [2]; *LP* IV, ii, 4900; *LP* IV, iii, 5638, 5639.

205. Bernard, *Late Medieval Church*, p. 195.

206. Knowles, *Religious Orders in England*, iii. 157–164.

207. R. W. Hoyle, 'The Origins of the Dissolution of the Monasteries', *Historical Journal*, 38 (1995), pp. 284–290; Bernard, 'Dissolution of the Monasteries', pp. 393–394.

208. See *VCH, Wiltshire*, iii. 302. The royal assent for Longleat's suppression is *LP* IV, iii, 5664. Its property was appropriated to the Carthusian house of Hinton, Somerset. Mountjoy Priory, Norfolk, was also dissolved in April 1529, and had been intended for the endowment of Wolsey's Ipswich college. The monastery's patron, however, William Hales, lord of Heveringland, seized the opportunity to claim the lands by right of escheat. Wolsey's fall prevented the matter from being resolved. See B. Thompson, 'Monasteries and their Patrons at Foundation and Dissolution', *Transactions of the Royal Historical Society*, Sixth Series, 4 (1994), pp. 115–116.

209. E. Jeffries Davis, 'The Beginning of the Dissolution: Christchurch, Aldgate, 1532', *Transactions of the Royal Historical Society*, Fourth Series, viii (1925), pp. 127–150; Knowles, *Religious Orders in England*, iii. 200–201.

210. TNA, C54/400 m. 35d (*LP* V, 823).

211. Jeffries Davis, 'Beginning of the Dissolution', p. 135. Certainly, one of the late canons wrote to Cromwell in distress following the suppression, having believed the monastery to have been in a peaceful condition and devoted to religion. See TNA, PRO, SP1/73 fo. 119 (*LP* V, 1744).

212. 'Two London Chronicles from the Collections of John Stow', ed. C. L. Kingsford, *Camden Society*, xii (London, 1910), p. 6.

213. TNA, PRO, SP 1/73 fo. 96 (*LP* V, 1722).

214. TNA, PRO, E36/108; E36/162; E315/279/1; TNA, PRO, SC12/11/12; TNA, PRO SP1/74 fo. 3 (*LP* VI, 4); SP2/N fo. 107 (*LP* VI, 228). A number of letters from Nicholas Hancock, the former prior, also underlines Cromwell's oversight of the suppression. He frequently requested that Cromwell 'discharge me' from the debts of the house. See TNA, PRO, SP1/73 fo. 106 (*LP* V, 1731); SP1/73 fo. 107 (*LP* V, 1732); SP1/73 fo. 108 (*LP* V, 1733); SP1/73 fo. 109 (*LP* V, 1734); SP1/73 fo. 110 (*LP* V, 1735); SP2/M fo. 87 (*LP* V, 1362).

215. TNA, PRO, C82/680 and C66/663 m. 37 (*LP* VII, 419 [28]); C66/663 m. 37 (*LP* VII, 587 [10]); Stow, *Survey of London*, i. 141–142.

216. F. A. Gasquet, *Henry VIII and the English Monasteries* (London, 1906), p. 194; G. H. Cook, *Letters to Cromwell and Others on the Suppression of the Monasteries* (London, 1965), pp. 105–107. This has not been helped by the fact that documents relating to it have been calendared sporadically in *Letters and Papers*.

217. TNA, PRO, SP1/57 fo. 55 (*LP* IV, iii, 6313). This letter was placed in 1530 in *Letters and Papers*, but it belongs to 1532.

218. Ibid.

219. TNA, PRO, SP1/69 fos 260–261 (*LP* V, 969).

220. The 'valor' of the house, cattle and church apparel alone amounted to £117 8s 10d. See BL, Cotton MS, Cleopatra E IV fos 283–283v (*LP* X, 857), incorrectly placed in 1536, it is of 1532. G. H. Cook also mistakenly included this letter in 1536 in his *Letters to Cromwell*, pp. 105–107.

221. TNA, PRO, SP1/77 fo. 41 (*LP* VI, 645) placed in 1533 by the editors of *Letters and Papers*, it is of 1532. So too is TNA, PRO, SP1/66 fo. 33 (*LP* V, 277), which was erroneously placed in 1531 in *Letters and Papers*. TNA, PRO, 1/70 fo. 54 (*LP* V, 1045); SP1/71 fo. 131 (*LP* V, 1456).

222. TNA, PRO, SP1/70 fo. 54 (*LP* V, 1045).

223. In August Cromwell was required to send his servant William Brabazon to assist with the finding of the office. Brabazon reported concern over the partiality of the jury empanelled, and the claims of the earl of Shrewsbury to some of the monastery's

lands. He added, however, that 'Maister Strete & I perswaded my lord [of Shrewsbury] his counseill ... that they shuld suffer the office to be Founden withowte eny Interupcion'. See TNA, PRO, SP1/70 fo. 201 (*LP* V, 1234).

224. TNA, PRO, SP1/75 fo. 174 (*LP* VI, 389).

225. *VCH, Staffordshire*, iii. 238.

226. TNA, PRO, SP1/69 fo. 260 (*LP* V, 969).

227. BL, Cotton MS, Cleopatra E IV fo. 31 (*LP* VI, 115); BL, Cotton MS, Cleopatra E IV fo. 34 (*LP* VI, 116).

228. TNA, PRO, SC12/11/15 fos 7–7v; Jeffries Davis, 'Beginning of the Dissolution', pp. 134, 147.

229. TNA, SP1/75 fo. 65 (*LP* VI 295).

230. TNA, PRO, SP1/73 fo. 138 (*LP* V, 1762); SP1/73 fo. 139 (*LP* V, 1763).

231. A. W. Pollard and G. R. Redgrave, eds, [*The*] *S*[*hort*] *T*[*itle*] *C*[*atalogue*] *of Books Printed in England, Scotland, and Ireland, 1475–1640*], second edn, revised and enlarged by W. A. Jackson, F. S. Ferguson and K. F. Pantzer (London, 1976), 10492.

232. J. McConica, *English Humanists and Reformation Politics under Henry VIII and Edward VI* (Oxford, 1965), p. 118.

233. Knowles, *Religious Orders in England*, iii. 201; Jeffries Davis, 'Beginning of the Dissolution', p. 128.

234. TNA, PRO, SP1/78 fo. 109 (*LP* VI, 976); *Statutes of the Realm*, iii. 25 Henry VIII c. 33; Jeffries Davis, 'Beginning of the Dissolution', pp. 141–143.

235. Knowles, *Religious Orders in England*, iii. 289–290.

236. *The Papers of George Wyatt Esquire*, ed. D. M. Loades, *Camden Fourth Series*, v (London, 1968), p. 159; my italics for emphasis.

237. See, for example, the many requests that Cromwell received from suitors wanting positions or patronage from him. TNA, PRO, SP1/69 fo. 114 (*LP* V, 812); SP1/69 fo. 159 (*LP* V, 861); SP1/81 fo. 109 (*LP* VI, 1654) and SP1/72 fo. 125 (*LP* V, 1624); SP1/79 fo. 55 (*LP* VI, 1132); SP1/71 fo. 22 (*LP* V, 1302); SP1/71 fo. 103 (*LP* V, 1428); SP1/73 fo. 16 (*LP* V, 1691); SP1/71 fo. 116 (*LP* V, 1443) and SP1/71 fo. 137 (*LP* V, 1462); SP1/72 fo. 147 (*LP* V, 1563); SP1/73 fo. 120 (*LP* V, 1745); *LP* V, 1672; TNA, PRO, SP1/69 fo. 14 (*LP* V, 716); SP1/74 fo. 178 (*LP* VI, 179); SP1/77 fo. 69 (*LP* VI, 690); SP1/80 fo. 153 (*LP* VI, 1484); SP1/75 fo. 166 (*LP* VI, 380). This list could be considerably lengthened.

238. J. A. F. Thomson, *The Early Tudor Church and Society, 1485–1529* (London, 1993), pp. 85–86; TNA, PRO, C82/659 and C66/660 m. 28 (*LP* V, 1270 [8]); C82/664 and C66/662 m. 44 (*LP* VI, 105 [13]).

239. Gywn, *King's Cardinal*, p. 300; M. Kelly, 'Canterbury Jurisdiction and Influence during the Episcopate of William Warham, 1503–1532' (Cambridge University PhD thesis, 1963), p. 10.

240. Kelly, 'Canterbury Jurisdiction', p. 14.

241. TNA, PRO, SP1/82 fo. 123 (*LP* VII, 122); SP1/82 fo. 176 (*LP* VII, 222).

242. TNA, PRO, SP2/P fo. 148 (*LP* VII, 416 [2]); SP2/P fo. 147 (*LP* VII, 416 [1]).

243. TNA, PRO, SP2/O fos 114–115 (*LP* V, 1622); SP1/82 fo. 234 (*LP* VII, 301).

244. TNA, PRO, SP1/72 fo. 19 (*LP* V, 1528); SP1/72 fo. 23 (*LP* V, 1540); SP1/74 fo. 21 (*LP* VI, 30); SP1/74 fo. 71 (*LP* VI, 77); SP1/75 fo. 31 (*LP* VI, 250); SP1/72 fo. 21 (*LP* V, 1530); SP1/74 fo. 151 (*LP* VI, 153); SP1/74 fo. 152 (*LP* VI, 154); SP1/75 fo. 185 (*LP* VI, 404); TNA, PRO, C82/656 and C66/660 mm. 19 and 20 (*LP* VI, 196 [31, 32, 33]). Cromwell also obtained 'the office of the commyssaryship within the towne & marches of Calice' for Benolt and one William Peterson in October 1532, see TNA, PRO, SP1/71 fo. 140 (*LP* V, 1465).

245. TNA, PRO, SP1/70 fo. 19 (*LP* V, 1006), placed in 1532 in *Letters and Papers*, but it might be more reasonable to place this in 1533 alongside the rest of the correspondence on this matter; TNA, PRO, SP1/79 fos 36–36v (*LP* VI, 1105); SP1/79 fo. 38 (*LP* V, 1106). For the benefice, see *VCH, Yorkshire, North Riding*, ii. 200–202.

246. TNA, PRO, SP1/73 fos 115–116 (*LP* V, 1740); SP1/73 fos 116–117 (*LP* V, 1741); SP1/73 fo. 117 (*LP* V, 1742); SP1/50 fo. 207 (*LP* IV, ii, 4877); SP1/50 fo. 213 (*LP*

IV, ii, 4888). See also TNA, PRO, SP1/50 fo. 207 (*LP* IV, ii, 4877); SP1/59 fo. 91 (*LP* IV, iii, 3103); SP1/59 fo. 90 (*LP* IV, iii, App. 83); SP1/55 fo. 105 (*LP* IV, ii, 5946).

247. TNA, PRO, SP1/70 fo. 19 (*LP* V, 1006); SP1/79 fo. 38 (*LP* V, 1106).

248. TNA, PRO, SP1/79 fo. 39 (*LP* VI, 1107); SP1/79 fo. 71 (*LP* VI, 1158)

249. TNA, PRO, SP1/79 fo. 145 (*LP* VI, 1226).

250. TNA, PRO, SP1/72 fo. 45 (*LP* V, 1563); SP1/74 fo. 10 (*LP* VI, 14). A draft letter on behalf of the absentee bishop Ghinucci appointing Bagarde to this office is corrected by Cromwell, testifying to his personal involvement in the selection. See TNA, PRO, SP1/237 fo. 264 (*LP* Add. I, i, 800). Bagarde himself attributed his possession of the office to Cromwell on several occasions; see TNA, PRO, SP1/72 fo. 45 (*LP* V, 1563); SP1/74 fo. 10 (*LP* VI, 14).

251. TNA, PRO, SP1/76 fo. 14 (*State Papers*, vii. 454; *LP* VI, 438); SP1/72 fo. 45 (*LP* V, 1563).

252. C. R. Chapman, *Ecclesiastical Courts, Officials and Records: Sin, Sex and Probate* (second edn, Dursley, 1997), pp. 33–34.

253. TNA, PRO, SP1/74 fo. 10 (*LP* VI, 14).

254. TNA, PRO, SP1/75 fo. 197 (*LP* VI, 411).

255. TNA, PRO, SP1/70 fo. 141 (*LP* V, 1141); TNA, PRO, C82/658 and C66/661 m. 35 (*LP* V, 1207 [23]).

256. TNA, PRO, SP1/81 fo. 128 (*LP* VI, 1674).

257. TNA, PRO, SP1/75 fo. 166 (*LP* VI, 380); SP1/75 fo. 174v (*LP* VI, 389); TNA, PRO, C82/667 (*LP* VI, 417 [26]).

258. TNA, PRO, SP1/71 fo. 102 (*LP* V, 1427); SP1/71 fos 110–110v (*LP* V, 1435); SP1/71 fo. 132 (*LP* V, 1457).

259. TNA, PRO, SP1/78 fo. 46 (*LP* VI, 912); SP1/78 fo. 47 (*LP* VI, 913); SP1/78 fo. 143 (*LP* VI, 1011); SP1/78 fo. 170 (*LP* VI, 1043).

260. TNA, PRO, SP1/80 fo. 198 (*LP* VI, 1534).

261. TNA, PRO, SP1/74 fo. 213 (*LP* VI, 218).

262. See p. 139.

263. *CSP, Spanish*, IV, ii, 796.

264. D. MacCulloch, *Thomas Cranmer: A Life* (London, 1996), pp. 75, 83–84.

265. *Liber Monasterii De Hyda*, ed. E. Edwards (London: Rolls Series, 1866), pp. lxvi–lxviii; A. J. Louisa, 'Capon, John (d. 1557)', *ODNB*; F. Heal, 'Goodrich, Thomas (1494–1554)', *ODNB*.

266. *Cf.* Gwyn, *King's Cardinal*, pp. 298–299.

267. TNA, PRO, SP1/81 fo. 27 (*LP* VI, 1567).

268. TNA, PRO, SP1/79 fo. 140 (*LP* VI, 504); SP1/80 fo. 108 (*LP* VI, 1451).

269. TNA, PRO, SP1/79 fo. 42 (*LP* VI, 1109); SP1/79 fo. 98 (*LP* VI, 1182); SP1/79 fo. 145 (*LP* VI, 1226); SP1/80 fo. 177 (*LP* VI, 1514). Cromwell was also similarly looked to for the benefices of Thomas Goodrich, when he was promoted to the bishopric of Ely. See TNA, PRO, SP1/83 fo. 32 (*LP* VII, 403).

270. BL, Cotton MS, Titus B I fo. 456r (*LP* VII, 143 [ii]); TNA, PRO, SP1/82 fo. 200v (*LP* VII, 257).

271. TNA, PRO, SP1/81 fos 63–63v (*LP* VI, 1594).

272. TNA, PRO, SP1/77 fo. 135 (*LP* VI, 754); SP1/82 fo. 250 (*LP* VII, 323).

273. A. J. Slavin, *Thomas Cromwell on Church and Commonwealth: Selected Letters, 1523–1540* (New York, 1969), pp. 184–188; Slavin, 'Cromwell, Cranmer and Lord Lisle', pp. 316–336; Loades, *Thomas Cromwell*, pp. 168, 185. See also Block, 'Thomas Cromwell's Patronage of Preaching', pp. 37–50, for a similar view of Cromwell's patronage of preachers.

274. Underwood, 'Thomas Cromwell and William Marshall', pp. 536, 539. Cromwell had been acquainted with Marshall since the late 1520s, when the two men had come into contact through Cromwell's work for Wolsey. In 1533 Marshall also wrote to Cromwell on behalf of Nicholas Statham, who had purchased a lease from Cromwell. See TNA, PRO, SP1/57 fo. 17 (*LP* IV, iii, 6222); SP1/59 fo. 113 (*LP* IV, iii, App. 133); SP1/81 fo. 119 (*LP* VI, 1665).

275. TNA, PRO, SP1/83 fo. 51 (*LP* VII, 422); SP1/83 fo. 52 (*LP* VII, 423); *STC*, 5641, 17817, 10504. *Cf.* Underwood, 'Thomas Cromwell and William Marshall', p. 522.

276. TNA, PRO, SP1/83 fo. 51 (*LP* VII, 422).

277. *CSP, Spanish*, V, i, 1. My italics for emphasis.

278. *CSP, Spanish*, V, i, 1.

279. Foxe, *Acts and Monuments* (1563 edn), p. 654; Foxe, *Acts and Monuments* (1570 edn), p. 1392.

280. Dickens, *Thomas Cromwell*, p. 51.

281. Beckingsale, *Thomas Cromwell*, pp. 75–77, 120, 129, 145.

282. R. McEntegart, *Henry VIII, the League of Schmalkalden and the English Reformation* (Woodbridge, 2002), p. 136; Schofield, *Rise and Fall*, pp. 33–44; Loades, *Thomas Cromwell*, p. 237.

283. The term Protestant did not become familiar in England until *circa* 1553. As Diarmaid MacCulloch has noted, 'evangelical' is a more suitable term to describe the religious reformist attitudes among many in Henry VIII's England during the 1530s, and denotes 'a religious outlook which makes the primary point of Christian reference the Good News of the *Evangelion*, or the text of scripture generally'. See MacCulloch, *Thomas Cranmer*, p. 2; D. MacCulloch, 'Henry VIII and the Reform of the Church', in MacCulloch, ed., *The Reign of Henry VIII: Politics, Policy and Piety* (Basingstoke, 1995), pp. 168–169.

284. D. MacCulloch, *Reformation*, p. 199; MacCulloch, *Thomas Cranmer*, pp. 114, 135; Brigden, 'Thomas Cromwell and the "Brethren"', pp. 31–50.

285. Guy, *Tudor England*, p. 178. See also Guy, 'Reassessing Thomas Cromwell', pp. 4–5.

286. L. Wooding, *Henry VIII* (London, 2009), pp. 242–243.

287. For Elton's fluctuating views on Cromwell's religion, see and compare *England under the Tudors*, p. 151; 'Thomas Cromwell', *History Today*, p. 531; *Policy and Police*, p. 424; *Reform and Reformation*, p. 172; *Thomas Cromwell*, pp. 35–36.

288. P. O'Grady, *Henry VIII and the Conforming Catholics* (Collegeville, MN, 1994), p. 9; F. E. Hutchinson, *Cranmer and the English Reformation* (London, 1961), pp. 85–86; B. Bradshaw, 'The Tudor Commonwealth: Reform and Revision', *Historical Journal*, 22 (1979), p. 469; Bernard, *King's Reformation*, pp. 514–521.

289. Williams, *Cardinal and the Secretary*, pp. 261–263; Davies, *Peace, Print and Protestantism*, p. 190; Guy, *Tudor England*, pp. 178, 181, 183, 188.

290. McEntegart, *League of Schmalkalden*, p. 223. For similar views, see Guy, *Tudor England*, pp. 181, 183; Brigden, 'Cromwell and the "Brethren"', p. 32; R. Rex, *Henry VIII and the English Reformation* (Basingstoke, 1993), p. 144.

291. *Cf.* Bernard, *King's Reformation*, p. 518; O'Grady, *Henry VIII and the Conforming Catholics*, p. 9.

292. For Cromwell and the vicegerency, see Lehmberg, 'Supremacy and Vicegerency', pp. 225–236; Logan, 'Thomas Cromwell and the Vicegerency', pp. 658–668.

293. *LP* XII, i, 790.

294. McEntegart, *League of Schmalkalden*, pp. 104–105.

295. Ibid., p. 105. *Cf.* MacCulloch, who takes a different view, and suggests that Cromwell was absent from the meetings with the envoys because he was dealing with the so-called 'Exeter conspiracy'. See MacCulloch, *Thomas Cranmer*, pp. 215–216.

296. TNA, PRO, SP1/54 fo. 235 (Merriman, *Life and Letters of Thomas Cromwell*, i. 56; *LP* IV, iii, 5772).

297. Ibid., fo. 242.

298. Ibid., fo. 242v.

299. Ibid.

300. Merriman vaguely suggested that the revisions were made at 'a later date', while Mary Robertson noted that the increase in wealth between the original and revised versions seemed 'relatively modest and [suggested] that the revision was made not long after the original'. S. E. Lehmberg pointed out that 'all one can safely say is that the revision occurred before 1536, when Cromwell was made a baron and would no longer have referred to himself merely as a gentleman of London'. See Merriman,

Life and Letters of Thomas Cromwell, i. 56 n.1; M. L. Robertson, 'Profit and Purpose', p. 320; S. E. Lehmberg, 'The Religious Beliefs of Thomas Cromwell' in R. L. DeMolen, ed., *Leaders of the Reformation* (London, 1984), pp. 135–136.

301. Rompney in South Wales was acquired in May 1532, while Canonbury House was bought by Cromwell in September 1532 (see Chapter Five). Both of these properties feature in the revised will, and therefore help to date it. Robertson, in her study of Cromwell's landed estates, mistakenly thought they were bought in 1529 or possibly 1530 because they are listed on the will. See Robertson, 'Profit and Purpose', p. 321 n. 7.

302. In a letter now lost. Merriman, *Life and Letters of Thomas Cromwell,* i. 327.

303. Cited in Brigden, 'Thomas Cromwell and the "Brethren"', p. 37, from Bodleian Library, Jesus College MS 74, fo. 192, which is a seventeenth-century note from a lost original.

304. TNA, PRO, SP1/42 fos 108v, 109 (*LP* IV, ii, 3197); see also fos 104, 106, 106v, 108 and SP1/162 fos 83–92v (*LP* XV, 1029 [6]).

305. TNA, PRO, SP1/73 fo. 133 (*LP* V, 1757).

306. MacCulloch, *Thomas Cranmer,* p. 86; G.W. Bernard, 'Anne Boleyn's Religion', *Historical Journal,* 36 (1993), p. 5; *LP* V, 850, 1013; *LP* VI, 232; *LP* VIII, 666.

307. In 1533 Chapuys reported that a German had arrived in England offering an alliance in case of war. The ambassador's comment – 'I hear that Cremvel [Cromwell] is the man appointed to treat with him, not the Duke, which circumstance makes me believe that he has been sent here by Melanchton himself' – is frustratingly cryptic. This might be read as an endorsement that Cromwell had Lutheran sympathies. Alternatively, it might merely show that the German was thought to be of considerable importance and that the king's chief minister should deal with him. See *CSP, Spanish,* IV, ii, 1055.

308. McEntegart, *League of Schmalkalden,* pp. 14–25, 200.

309. BL, Cotton MS, Titus B I fo. 430 (*LP* VII, 52); TNA, PRO, SP1/82 fo. 128 (*LP* VII, 137); McEntegart, *League of Schmalkalden,* p. 22.

310. McEntegart, *League of Schmalkalden,* pp. 15–16. The two men were Stephen Vaughan and Christopher Mont. For their careers, see Richardson, *Stephen Vaughan;* E. Hilderbrandt, 'Christopher Mont, Anglo-German Diplomat', *Sixteenth Century Journal,* 15 (1984), pp. 281–292.

311. BL, Cotton MS, Cleopatra E VI fos 327v–328 (*LP* VI, 1487); McEntegart, *League of Schmalkalden,* pp. 17–18.

312. Merriman, *Life and Letters of Thomas Cromwell,* i. 279.

313. Hall, *Chronicle,* pp. 838–839.

314. TNA, PRO, E36/120 fo. 101 (*LP* VI, 87).

315. Cavendish, *Life and Death of Cardinal Wolsey,* p. 106.

316. For details on these men, see M. R. J. Everett, 'Qualities of a Royal Minister: Studies in the Rise of Thomas Cromwell, *c.*1520–1534' (University of Southampton PhD thesis, 2012), pp. 185–188.

317. TNA, PRO, SP1/48 fo. 79 (*LP* IV, ii, 4314).

318. TNA, PRO, SP1/85 fos 168–169 (*LP* VII, 1135).

319. Foxe, *Acts and Monuments* (1570 edn), p. 1385.

320. TNA, PRO, SP1/83 fo. 51 (*LP* VII, 422); SP1/83 fo. 52 (*LP* VII, 423).

321. TNA, PRO, SP1/78 fo. 49 (*LP* VI, 916); A. B. Emden, *A Biographical Register of the University of Oxford, A. D. 1501 to 1540* (Oxford, 1974), p. 49.

322. TNA, PRO, E36/104 fo. 7v.

323. TNA, PRO, SP1/89 fo. 39 (*LP* VIII, 68). The benefice Biseley referred to was Staplehurst, Kent, where he is recorded as rector in 1535. See *Valor Ecclesiasticus,* ed. J. Caley and J. Hunter (6 vols, London, 1810–1834), i. 95. Biseley originally came from York. A 'Suppplication of Richard Biseley scoler of yorke' is among Cromwell's remembrances, and in his letter to Cromwell, Biseley also mentioned that Cromwell had been good to his father. See TNA, PRO, E36/139 fo. 103 (*LP* VII, 923); SP1/89 fo. 39 (*LP* VIII, 68).

324. TNA, PRO, SP1/241 fo. 264 (*LP* Add. I, i, 1284); *Calendar of State Papers, Domestic, Edward VI – Elizabeth I, 1547–1580,* ed. R. Lemon (London, 1856), p. 287.

325. TNA, PRO, SP1/89 fo. 39 (*LP* VIII, 68).

326. C. H. Garrett, *The Marian Exiles: A Study in the Origins of Elizabethan Puritanism* (Cambridge, 1966), pp. 85–86.

327. See, for example, Brigden, 'Thomas Cromwell and the "Brethren"', pp. 31–57.

328. TNA, PRO, SP1/30 fos 240–241v (*LP* IV, i, 166); Vaughan was one of the three intended executors of Cromwell's will, and he was also bequeathed a sum of 100 marks in this. See also TNA, PRO, SP1/41 fos 158–158v (*LP* IV, ii, 3053); SP1/235 fo. 78 (*LP* Add. I, i, 498).

329. TNA, PRO, SP1/39 fo. 192 (*LP* IV, ii, 2358 [8]); SP1/52 fo. 38 (*LP* IV, ii, 5115); TNA, PRO, E101/518/14 fos 9r, 8v (*LP* IV, ii, 5117); TNA, PRO, SP1/53 fo. 128 (*LP* IV, iii, 5398); TNA, PRO, E37/117 fos 19, 20 (*LP* IV, iii, 5787).

330. TNA, PRO, SP1/58 fo. 147 (*LP* IV, iii, 6744); SP1/58 fo. 173 (*LP* IV, iii, 6754); BL, Cotton MS, Galba B X fo. 47 (*LP* V, 65); BL, Cotton MS, Galba B X fos 354–355 (*LP* V, 248; Merriman, *Life and Letters of Thomas Cromwell*, i. 336–337); TNA, PRO, SP1/70 fo. 59 (Merriman, *Life and Letters of Thomas Cromwell*, i. 344; *LP* V, 1055); SP1/70 fo. 189 (*LP* V, 1220); SP1/71 fo. 17v (Merriman, *Life and Letters of Thomas Cromwell*, i. 348–349; *LP* V, 1298); SP1/78 fos 50–50v (*LP* VI, 917); SP1/78 fos 75–77r (*LP* VI, 934); SP1/78 fos 167–168v (*LP* VI, 1040); SP1/79 fos 22–22v (*LP* VI, 1082).

331. TNA, PRO, SP1/68 fos 51–52 (*LP* V, 533); BL, Cotton MS, Galba B X fos 23–25v (*LP* V, 574); BL, Cotton MS, Galba B X fos 26–26v (*LP* V, 618).

332. BL, Cotton MS, Galba B X fo. 23 (*LP* V, 574).

333. See pp. 235–236, 237.

334. BL, Cotton MS, Galba B X fo. 23–25v (*LP* V, 574).

335. TNA, PRO, SP1/44 fo. 34 (*LP* IV, ii, 3388); SP1/65 fo. 238 (*State Papers*, i. 383–384; *LP* V, 221). This was placed in 1531 in *Letters and Papers*, with a note from the editors that it had been mistakenly printed in that year and belongs to the period before 1527.

336. J. F. Mozley, *Coverdale and his Bibles* (London, 1953), pp. 2–3.

337. TNA, PRO, SP1/65 fo. 238 (*State Papers*, i. 383–384; *LP* V, 221). Cromwell would employ Coverdale to work on the production of the English Bible. See McConica, *English Humanists*, pp. 163–166.

338. TNA, PRO, SP1/141 fos 126–127 (*LP* XIII, ii, 1223). *Cf.* Elton, *Reform and Renewal*, pp. 26–28.

339. Elton, *Reform and Renewal*, p. 28.

340. J. Ridley, *Thomas Cranmer* (Oxford, 1962), pp. 144–145; MacCulloch, *Thomas Cranmer*, p. 84; McEntegart, *League of Schmalkalden*, pp. 23, 93, 107.

341. BL, Cotton MS, Vespasian F XIII fo. 145 (*LP* VI, 137); *CSP, Spanish*, IV, ii, 1048 (p. 601); TNA, PRO, SP1/78 fo. 25 (Merriman, *Life and Letters of Thomas Cromwell*, i. 361; *LP* VI, 861).

342. Dickens, *Thomas Cromwell*, p. 51; McEntegart, *League of Schmalkalden*, pp. 23, 93, 107.

343. MacCulloch, *Thomas Cranmer*, p. 135.

344. BL, Cotton MS, Vespasian F XIII fo. 145 (*LP* VI, 137).

345. MacCulloch, *Thomas Cranmer*, p. 135; MacCulloch, 'Henry VIII and the Reform of the Church', p. 170.

346. BL, Cotton MS, Otho C X fo. 165 (*LP* VI, 496); TNA, PRO, SP1/76 fo. 171 (*LP* VI, 616); *The Works of Thomas Cranmer*, ed. J. E. Cox (2 vols, Cambridge, 1846), ii. 252 (*LP* VI, 868); TNA, PRO, SP1/77 fo. 79 (*LP* VI, 698); SP1/79 fo. 59 (*LP* VI, 1143); SP1/80 fo. 196 (*LP* VI, 1531); BL, Cotton MS, Vespasian F XIII fo. 145 (*LP* VI, 137); TNA, PRO, SP1/82 fo. 14 (*LP* VII, 17); BL, Harley MS 6148 fo. 81 (Merriman, *Life and Letters of Thomas Cromwell*, i. 372; *LP* VII, 19); TNA, PRO, SP1/82 fo. 16 (*LP* VII, 20); BL, Cotton MS, Cleopatra E VI fo. 175 (*LP* VII, 499).

347. The phrase is MacCulloch's; see *Thomas Cranmer*, p. 135.

348. TNA, PRO, SP1/75 fo. 57v (*LP* VI, 501).

349. BL, Cotton MS, Vespasian F XIII fo. 145 (*LP* VI, 137); TNA, PRO, SP1/75 fo. 149 (*LP* VI, 360); SP1/79 fo. 187 (*LP* VI, 1305); SP 1/80 fo. 134 (*LP* VI, 1473).

350. TNA, PRO, SP1/76 fo. 19 (*LP* VI, 447).

351. Ibid., fo. 19; TNA, PRO, SP1/80 fo. 167 (*LP* VI, 1495).

352. TNA, PRO, E101/421/9 (*LP* VI, 31). This was a portion of £2,000 that was delivered to Cromwell by Thomas Alvard. The remaining £1,000 was paid into the Privy Coffers.

353. TNA, PRO, SP1/80 fo. 135 (*LP* VI, 1474).

354. See above, p. 101.

355. TNA, PRO, SP1/235 fo. 74 (*LP* Add. I, i, 494); SP1/235 fo. 75 (*LP* Add. I, i, 495); SP1/235 fo. 216 (*LP* Add. I, i, 539).

356. Foxe, *Acts and Monuments* (1570 edn), pp. 1386–1387.

357. TNA, PRO, SP 1/72 fo. 19 (*LP* V, 1528); SP 1/72 fo. 23 (*LP* V, 1540); SP 1/74 fo. 21 (*LP* VI, 30); SP 1/74 fo. 71 (*LP* VI, 77); SP 1/75 fo. 31 (*LP* VI, 250); SP 1/72 fo. 21 (*LP* V, 1530); SP 1/74 fo. 151 (*LP* VI, 153); SP 1/74 fo. 152 (*LP* VI, 154); SP 1/75 fo. 185 (*LP* VI, 404); TNA, PRO, C82/656 and C66/660 mm. 19 and 20 (*LP* VI, 196 [31, 32, 33]). Cromwell also obtained 'the office of the commyssaryship within the towne & marches of Calice' for Benolt and one William Peterson in October 1532; see TNA, PRO, SP 1/71 fo. 140 (*LP* V, 1465).

358. Davies, *Peace, Print and Protestantism*, pp. 190, 212; Block, 'Thomas Cromwell's Patronage of Preaching', pp. 37–50; Slavin, 'Cromwell, Cranmer and Lord Lisle', pp. 316–336; Guy, 'Reassessing Thomas Cromwell', pp. 4–5.

359. P. J. Ward, 'The Politics of Religion: Thomas Cromwell and the Reformation in Calais, 1534–1540', *Journal of Religious History*, 17 (1992), p. 160.

360. *LP* IV, i, 2321 [i]; TNA, PRO, SP1/238 fos 233–236 (*LP* IV, i, 2321 [ii]); *LP* IV, ii, 3216; TNA, PRO, SP1/46 fos 27–28 (*LP* IV, ii, 3737); TNA, PRO, E24/5/4 (*LP* IV, ii, 4461); TNA, PRO, SP1/51 fo. 101 (*LP* IV, ii, 5024); SP1/59 fo. 127 (*LP* IV, iii, App. 233). For Gostwick's career, see H. P. R. Finberg, 'The Gostwicks of Willington', *Publications of the Bedfordshire Historical Record Society*, xxxvi (1955), pp. 46–75.

361. TNA, PRO, SP1/73 fo. 117 (*LP* V, 1742); SP2/O fos 20–22 (*LP* VI, 664); Elton, *Tudor Revolution in Government*, pp. 192–203.

362. Foxe, *Acts and Monuments* (1570 edn), p. 2080; MacCulloch, *Thomas Cranmer*, p. 252. For Gostwick's religious outlook, see Finberg, 'Gostwicks of Willington', p. 72.

363. TNA, PRO, SP1/57 fo. 75 (*LP* IV, iii, 6346); SP1/74 fo. 157 (*LP* VI, 158); SP1/69 fo. 69 (*LP* V, 743); SP1/57 fo. 130v (*LP* IV, iii, 6411); SP1/236 fo. 71 (*LP* Add. I, i, 634).

364. TNA, PRO, SP1/82 fo. 200v (*LP* VII, 257); SP1/79 fo. 183 (*LP* VI, 1299).

365. Foxe, *Acts and Monuments* (1583 edn), p. 1112.

366. Ibid.; K. Carelton, 'Bonner, Edmund (d. 1569)', *ODNB*; D. Loades, *Mary Tudor: A Life* (Oxford, 1989), p. 284.

367. TNA, PRO, SP1/47 fo. 292v (*LP* IV, ii, 4229 [x]); SP1/50 fo. 69 (*LP* IV, ii, 4696); SP1/50 fo. 101 (*LP* IV, ii, 4755); BL, Cotton MS, Titus B I fos 281–282 (*LP* IV, ii, 4778); TNA, PRO, SP1/53 fos 141–141v (*LP* IV, iii, 5411); SP1/52 fo. 253 (*LP* IV, iii, 5533); TNA, PRO, C66/655 m. 1 (*LP* IV, iii, 5805); TNA, PRO, SP1/57 fo. 1 (*LP* IV, iii, 6212); SP1/236 fo. 71 (*LP* Add. I, i, 634); TNA, PRO, E41/290.

368. TNA, PRO, SP1/237 fo. 5 (*LP* Add. I, i, 724); SP1/75 fo. 85 (*LP* V, 337); SP1/68 fo. 22 (*LP* V, 479); SP1/78 fo. 143 (*LP* VI, 1011); SP1/78 fo. 111 (*LP* VI, 981); SP1/78 fo. 145 (*LP* VI, 1014).

369. TNA, PRO, SP1/85 fo. 44 (*LP* VII, 967).

370. TNA, PRO, SP1/70 fo. 194 (*LP* V, 1227).

371. TNA, PRO, C82/659 and C66/660 m. 28 (*LP* V, 1270 [8]).

372. TNA, PRO, SP1/79 fo. 42 (*LP* VI, 1109); SP1/81 fo. 50 (*LP* VI, 1579); TNA, PRO, C82/677 and C66/662 m. 37 (*LP* VI, 1695 [20]).

373. TNA, PRO, SP1/79 fo. 145 (*LP* VI, 1226).

374. TNA, PRO, SP1/80 fos 75v–76r (*LP* VI, 1385).

375. Gunn, 'Edmund Dudley and the Church', p. 526.

376. Foxe, *Acts and Monuments* (1570 edn), p. 1392.

377. TNA, PRO, SP1/123 fo. 197 (*LP* XII, ii, 434).

378. *Works of Thomas Cranmer*, ii. 346.

379. *LP* XIII, ii, 1163. See also Cromwell's involvement in the 'Rochepot affair' in A. J. Slavin, 'The Rochepot Affair', *Sixteenth Century Journal*, 10 (1979), pp. 3–19.

380. Bernard, *King's Reformation*, p. 523.
381. For the careers of these men, see Lehmberg, 'Religious Beliefs of Thomas Cromwell', pp. 139–148; T. Sowerby, *Renaissance and Reform in Tudor England: The Careers of Sir Richard Morison c.1513–1556* (Oxford, 2010), especially pp. 155–187 for Morison's religious views.
382. Lehmberg, 'Religious Beliefs of Thomas Cromwell', p. 139.
383. TNA, PRO, E36/122/ fo. 26 (*LP* XII, i, 853); TNA, PRO, SP1/118 fo. 284 (*LP* XII, i, 1021 [3]); SP1/118 fos 292–293 (*LP* XII, i, 1021 [5]).
384. *LP* XIV, ii, 423.
385. BL, Additional Manuscript 48028 fos 161v–162. This is not printed in *Statutes of the Realm*, but it can be found printed in Burnet's *History of the Reformation*, iv. 105–109.
386. E. W. Dormer, *Gray of Reading* (Reading, 1923), p. 80.
387. Burnet, *History of the Reformation*, p. 107.
388. G. R. Elton, 'Thomas Cromwell's Decline and Fall', in Elton, *Studies*, i. 225.
389. Merriman, *Life and Letters of Thomas Cromwell*, ii. 264–267. *Cf.* Redworth, *In Defence of the Church Catholic*, pp. 122–126.
390. Hall, *Chronicle*, p. 839; Foxe, *Acts and Monuments* (1570 edn), pp. 1400–1401.
391. Foxe, *Acts and Monuments* (1570 edn), pp. 1400–1401; Hall, *Chronicle*, p. 839.
392. Lehmberg, 'Religious Beliefs of Thomas Cromwell', p. 138.
393. Foxe, *Acts and Monuments* (1570 edn), p. 1385.

Chapter Five Royal Government

1. Elton, *Tudor Revolution in Government, passim*.
2. Ibid.
3. R. B. Wernham, 'Review', pp. 92–95; Harriss and Williams, 'A Revolution in Tudor History?', pp. 3–59; J. P. Cooper, 'A Revolution in Tudor History?', pp. 110–113; Elton, 'The Tudor Revolution: A Reply', pp. 26–50; Harriss and Williams, 'A Revolution in Tudor History?', pp. 87–97; Elton, 'A Revolution in Tudor History?', pp. 103–110; C. Coleman and D. Starkey, eds, *Revolution Reassessed: Revisions in the History of Tudor Government and Administration* (Oxford, 1986); Bernard, 'Politics and Government', pp. 159–182; McFarlane, *Letters to Friends*, pp. 97–98; Bernard, 'Elton's Cromwell', in Bernard, *Power and Politics*, pp. 108–129. The most recent discussion on this question has examined the originality of Elton's claims; see Harris, 'Some Origins of a Tudor Revolution', pp. 1355–1385.
4. *CSP, Venetian*, IV, 694.
5. Gwyn, *King's Cardinal*, p. 204.
6. G. R. Elton, *The Tudor Constitution: Documents and Commentary* (Cambridge, 1962), p. 101.
7. TNA, PRO, SP1/70 fos 181–181v (*LP* V, 1209).
8. *LP* V, 1421.
9. *CSP, Venetian*, IV, 694 (p. 297).
10. Elton, *Tudor Revolution in Government*, pp. 316–352.
11. J. A. Guy, 'The Privy Council: Revolution or Evolution?', in Coleman and Starkey, eds, *Revolution Reassessed*, pp. 59–86.
12. Gywn, *King's Cardinal*, p. 204–205.
13. A. P. Newton, 'The King's Chamber under the Early Tudors, *English Historical Review*, xxxii (1917), pp. 348–372; A. F. Pollard, 'Council, Star Chamber, and Privy Council under the Tudors: 1. The Council', *English Historical Review*, xxxvii (1922), pp. 337–360; A. F. Pollard, 'Council, Star Chamber, and Privy Council under the Tudors: 2. The Star Chamber', *English Historical Review*, xxxvii (1922), pp. 516–539; A. F. Pollard, 'Council, Star Chamber, and Privy Council under the Tudors: 3. The Privy Council', *English Historical Review*, xxxviii (1923), pp. 42–60; T. F. Tout, *Chapters in the Administrative History of Mediaeval England* (6 vols, Manchester, 1920–1933); Dietz, *English Government Finance*; F. M. G. Evans, *The Principal Secretary of State. A Survey of the Office from 1558 to 1680* (Manchester, 1923); K. Pickthorn, *Early Tudor Government* (2 vols, Cambridge, 1934).

14. Starkey, 'King's Privy Chamber', *passim*; Starkey, 'Representation Through Intimacy', pp. 187–224; Starkey, 'Intimacy and Innovation', pp. 71–118.
15. Starkey, *Reign of Henry VIII*, pp. 105–107; Starkey, 'Intimacy and Innovation', pp. 108–110.
16. E. Ives, *The Life and Death of Anne Boleyn* (Oxford, 2004), pp. 207–209; Starkey, *Reign of Henry VIII*, pp. 105–106.
17. Mears, 'Courts, Courtiers and Culture', p. 704.
18. Ives, who has argued that they were close allies, concedes this point in a footnote, but claimed that Anne 'normally communicated by messenger'. See Ives, *Life and Death of Anne Boleyn*, p. 396 n. 19.
19. TNA, PRO, SP1/71 fo. 121v (*LP* V, 1450); see pp. 229–230.
20. C. Haigh, 'Review', *English Historical Review*, cxxi (2006), pp. 1456–1457.
21. Ives, *Life and Death of Anne Boleyn*, pp. 207–208.
22. For the debate regarding just how separate administrative government was from the royal court, see G. R. Elton, 'Tudor Government', *Historical Journal*, 31 (1988), pp. 425–434; D. Starkey, 'Communications, A Reply: Tudor Government: the Facts?', *Historical Journal*, 31 (1988), pp. 921–931; G. W. Bernard, 'Court and government', in G. W. Bernard, *Power and Politics in Tudor England* (Aldershot, 2000), pp. 129–134.
23. S. J. Gunn, 'The Courtiers of Henry VII', *English Historical Review*, cviii (1993), p. 28.
24. Ibid.
25. An itinerary of Henry VIII's movements can be found in TNA, PRO, OBS, 1/1418. A readily available, although not entirely accurate, itinerary for Cromwell can be found in Merriman, *Life and Letters of Thomas Cromwell*, ii. 279–282. A more accurate record of Cromwell's whereabouts can be found in Everett, 'Qualities of a Royal Minister', pp. 322–324.
26. BL, Cotton MS, Titus B I fos 483–484 (*State Papers*, i. 380; *LP* V, 394).
27. BL, Cotton MS, Cleopatra E VI fos 325–328 (*LP* VI, 1487 [1]); TNA, PRO, SP6/3 fos 85–88 (*LP* VI, 1487 [2]); *LP* VII, 149; *CSP, Spanish*, IV, ii, 1165.
28. BL, Cotton MS, Cleopatra E VI fos 325–328 (*LP* VI, 1487 [1]); TNA, PRO, SP 6/3 fo. 87 (*LP* VI, 1487 [2]).
29. BL, Cotton MS, Cleopatra E VI fos 329–329v (*State Papers*, i. 414; *LP* VI, 1486).
30. BL, Cotton MS, Cleopatra E VI fo. 327v (*LP* VI, 1487 [1]).
31. TNA, PRO, SP1/81 fos 1–2 (*LP* VI, 1542); SP1/81 fos 3–3v (*LP* VI, 1543); SP1/103 fo. 221 (*LP* X, 1231); BL, Cotton MS, Titus B I fo. 478 (*LP* VI, 1381 [2]).
32. Guy, *Cardinal's Court*, p. 138.
33. TNA, PRO, SP1/70 fo. 122 (Merriman, *Life and Letters of Thomas Cromwell*, i. 345; *LP* V, 1106).
34. TNA, PRO, SP1/80 fo. 14 (Merriman, *Life and Letters of Thomas Cromwell*, i. 366; *LP* VI, 1332).
35. BL, Cotton MS, Titus B I fo. 161v (*LP* VI, 1381 [3]).
36. Ibid.
37. Elton, *Tudor Revolution in Government*, p. 344.
38. D. E. Hoak, *The King's Council in the Reign of Edward VI* (Cambridge, 1976), p. 223.
39. TNA, PRO, SP1/73 fo. 90 (*LP* V, 1718); SP1/75 fo. 53 (*LP* VI, 271).
40. TNA, PRO, SP1/68 fo. 37 (*LP* V, 507); SP1/68 fo. 120 (*LP* V, 636); SP1/68 fo. 140 (*LP* V, 655); SP1/71 fo. 2 (*LP* V, 1271); SP1/73 fo. 11 (*LP* V, 1686); SP1/73 fo. 12 (*LP* V, 1687); SP1/70 fo. 140 (*LP* V, 1140); SP1/73 fo. 24 (*LP* V, 1697); SP1/73 fo. 100 (*LP* V, 1726); SP1/73 fo. 105 (*LP* V, 1729); SP2/M fo. 202 (*LP* V, 1793); SP2/M fos 208–209 (*LP* V, 1797); SP2/O fo. 105 (*LP* VI, 1606).
41. TNA, PRO, SP1/76 fo. 156 (*LP* VI, 595); SP1/80 fo. 2 (*LP* VI, 1320); SP1/76 fo. 164 (*LP* VI, 607); SP1/80 fo. 2 (*LP* VI, 1320); SP1/238 fo. 82 (*LP* Add. I, i, 855).
42. TNA, PRO, E36/142 fos 1–8 (*LP* VI, 480 [i]).
43. TNA, PRO, E36/120 fos 63–63v (*LP* V, 759).
44. TNA, PRO, SP1/70 fos 181–181v (*LP* V, 1209); SP1/71 fo. 29 (*LP* V, 1312).
45. Elton, *Reform and Renewal, passim*.

46. P. L. Hughes and J. F. Larkin, eds, *Tudor Royal Proclamations* (3 vols, London, 1964), i. 201–203.
47. TNA, PRO, E36/142 fos 13–26v (*LP* VI, 480 [ii]).
48. TNA, PRO, SP1/72 fo. 137 (*LP* V, 1639).
49. TNA, PRO, SP1/74 fo. 157 (*LP* VI, 158).
50. Williams, *Tudor Regime*, p. 190.
51. Ibid., pp. 185–190.
52. BL, Cotton MS, Titus B I fos 483–484 (*State Papers*, i. 380; *LP* V, 394).
53. Cromwell's amended version is TNA, PRO, SP 6/3 fos 85–88 (*LP* VI, 1487 [2]); the final set of instructions produced by Sadler is BL, Cotton MS, Cleopatra E VI fos 325–328 (*LP* VI, 1487 [1]).
54. Elton, *Tudor Revolution in Government*, p. 363.
55. Bernard, 'Elton's Cromwell', in Bernard, *Power and Politics*, p. 113.
56. Graves, 'Management of the Elizabethan House of Commons', pp. 11–38.
57. *Journals of the House of Lords, Volume 1: 1509–1577* (London, 1836), p. 58.
58. TNA, PRO, SP1/68 fo. 79 (*LP* V, 571); SP1/68 fo. 83 (*LP* V, 578); SP1/68 fo. 102 (*LP* V, 612); SP1/68 fo. 106 (*LP* V, 621); BL, Cotton MS, Titus B I fo. 371 (*LP* V, 625); TNA, PRO, SP1/68 fo. 128 (*LP* V, 644); SP1/69 fo. 10 (*LP* V, 708); *LP* V, 709; TNA, PRO, SP1/69 fo. 66 (*LP* V, 734); SP1/69 fo. 66 (*LP* V, 741).
59. BL, Cotton MS, Cleopatra E VI fos 156–158 (*LP* VII, 239).
60. TNA, PRO, SP1/83 fo. 62 (*LP* VII, 438).
61. Graves, 'Management of the Elizabethan House of Commons', pp. 16–17.
62. TNA, PRO, E36/143 fo. 27 (*LP* VI, 299); TNA, PRO, SP1/99 fo. 202 (*LP* IX, 1077); and for its redating to 1533, see A. F. Pollard, 'Thomas Cromwell's Parliamentary Lists', *Bulletin of the Institute of Historical Research*, 9 (1931–1932), pp. 32–43.
63. BL, Cotton MS, Titus B I fo. 437 (*LP* V, 1548). This book is mentioned in *Statutes of the Realm*, iii. 6 Henry VIII c. 16.
64. BL, Cotton MS, Titus B I fo. 464v (*LP* VI, 1382).
65. TNA, PRO, SP1/74 fo. 22 (*LP* VI, 31).
66. BL, Cotton MS, Titus B I fo. 266 (Merriman, *Life and Letters of Thomas Cromwell*, ii. 199; *LP* XIV, i, 538).
67. TNA, PRO, SP1/69 fo. 75 (*LP* V, 753).
68. BL, Cotton MS, Galba B X fo. 6v (*LP* V, 870).
69. Hall, *Chronicle*, p. 788.
70. Ibid., p. 765.
71. C. Haigh, 'Anticlericalism and the English Reformation' in C. Haigh, ed., *The English Reformation Revised* (Cambridge, 1987), pp. 56–74.
72. For the problem of sources, see P. R. Cavill, 'Debate and Dissent in Henry VII's Parliaments', *Parliamentary History*, 25 (2006), pp. 160–175; P. R. Cavill, *The English Parliaments of Henry VII, 1485–1504* (Oxford, 2009), pp. 8–12. I am also grateful to Dr Cavill for discussing this topic with me.
73. S. Payling, 'The House of Commons, 1307–1529', in C. Jones, ed., *A Short History of Parliament* (Woodbridge, 2012), pp. 75–86, at p. 79.
74. *CSP, Spanish*, IV, ii, 907, 922, 926.
75. R. Rex, 'Jasper Fyloll and the Enormities of the Clergy: Two Tracts written during the Reformation Parliament', *Sixteenth Century Journal*, 31 (2000), pp. 1043–1062.
76. J. A. Guy, 'Wolsey and the Parliament of 1523', in C. Cross, D. Loades and J. J. Scarisbrick, eds, *Law and Government under the Tudors* (Cambridge, 1988), pp. 15–16.
77. Merriman, *Life and Letters of Thomas Cromwell*, pp. 37–38.
78. TNA, PRO, SP1/68 fo. 105 (*LP* V, 620); SP1/71 fo. 56v (*LP* V, 1354).
79. TNA, PRO, SP1/72 fo. 15 (*LP* V, 1514); SP1/71 fo. 150 (*LP* V, 1476); BL, Cotton MS, Titus B I fo. 89 (*LP* V, 1518).
80. TNA, PRO, SP1/71 fo. 121 (*State Papers*, i. 385; *LP* V, 1450); SP1/71 fo. 121 (*State Papers*, i. 385; *LP* V, 1450); BL, Cotton MS, Titus B I fo. 89 (*LP* V, 1518).
81. Hall, *Chronicle*, p. 784.
82. TNA, PRO, SP1/71 fo. 121 (*State Papers*, i. 385; *LP* V, 1450).

83. BL, Cotton MS, Titus B I fo. 89 (*LP* V, 1518).

84. TNA, PRO, SP1/74 fo. 129 (*LP* VI, 120); TNA, PRO, E36/143 fo. 20 (*LP* VI, 299); TNA, PRO, SP1/72 fo. 15 (*LP* V, 1514).

85. TNA, PRO, E36/143 fos 22, 31 (*LP* VI, 299).

86. TNA, PRO, SP1/69 fos 17–18 (*LP* V 721 [12]); SP2/L fos 100–105 (*LP* V 721 [8]); *Statutes of the Realm*, iii. 23 Henry VIII c. 8.

87. *CSP, Spanish*, IV, ii, 899; Hall, *Chronicle*, pp. 784–785; BL, Cotton MS, Titus B I fo. 483v (*LP* V, 394); E. W. Ives, 'The Genesis of the Statute of Uses', *English Historical Review*, cxxxii (1967), pp. 682–686.

88. TNA, PRO, SP2/N fos 22–25 (*LP* VI, 120 [4]); *Statutes of the Realm*, iii. 24 Henry VIII c. 10; TNA, PRO, SP2/L fos 91–99 (*LP* V, 721 [7]); *Statutes of the Realm*, iii. 23 Henry VIII c. 7.

89. The act as finally passed is *Statutes of the Realm*, iii. 25 Henry VIII c. 13. For the details of the probable passage of this bill, see Elton, *Reform and Renewal*, pp. 90–92.

90. TNA, PRO, SP1/82 fos 82–82v (Merriman, *Life and Letters of Thomas Cromwell*, i. 373; *LP* VII, 73).

91. Williams, *Tudor Regime*, pp. 180–182; Gwyn, *King's Cardinal*, pp. 412–435.

92. TNA, PRO, SP1/69 fo. 114 (*LP* V, 812).

93. TNA, PRO, SP1/238 fos 33v–34r (*LP* Add. I, i, 824).

94. TNA, PRO, E101/58/13 (*LP* VII, 66 [1]); TNA, PRO, SP2/P fos 131–135 (*LP* VII, 66 [2]).

95. Elton, *England under the Tudors*, p. 167; Elton, 'Political Creed of Thomas Cromwell', in Elton, *Studies*, ii. 224–227.

96. BL, Cotton MS, Titus B I fos 318v–319 (Merriman, *Life and Letters of Thomas Cromwell*, i. 410; *LP* VIII 1062); my italics for emphasis.

97. *Cf.* Elton, 'Political Creed of Thomas Cromwell', in Elton, *Studies*, ii. 226, which presents the opposite view.

98. TNA, PRO, SP1/71 fo. 20 (*LP* V, 1300). Audeley has not received a great deal of attention from historians, but there is a useful article by S. E. Lehmberg, 'Sir Thomas Audley: A Soul as Black as Marble?', in A. J. Slavin, ed., *Tudor Men and Institutions: Studies in English Law and Government* (Baton Rouge, LA, 1972), pp. 3–32. See also L. L. Ford, 'Audley, Thomas (1487/8-1544)', *ODNB*; Bindoff, *House of Commons*, i, pp. 350–353.

99. Bindoff, *House of Commons*, i. 350; TNA, PRO, E179/69/10 (*LP* IV, ii, 2972 [8]); TNA, PRO, SP1/56 fo. 124 (*LP* IV, iii, 6110).

100. TNA, PRO, SP2/C fos. 8–9 (*LP* IV, ii, 2375); SP1/44 fo. 119 (*LP* IV, ii, 3460); SP1/55 fo. 197 (*LP* IV, iii, 6034); TNA, PRO, C1/587/13.

101. BL, Cotton MS, Vespasian CXIV fos 166–166v (*LP* V, 1430).

102. Jeffries Davis, 'Beginning of the Dissolution', pp. 142–143.

103. *Statutes of the Realm*, ii. 8 Henry VI c. 16; 18 Henry VI c. 6.

104. *Statutes of the Realm*, iii. 25 Henry VIII c. 33; Jeffries Davis, 'Beginning of the Dissolution', pp. 141, 143.

105. Elton, 'Political Creed of Thomas Cromwell', in Elton, *Studies*, ii. 226.

106. J. A. Guy, *Christopher St German on Chancery and Statute* (London, 1985), pp. 21–33.

107. J. Fortescue, *The Governance of England*, ed. C. Plummer (Oxford, 1885), pp. 109–110.

108. G. W. O. Woodward, 'The Role of Parliament in the Henrician Reformation', in H. Cohn, ed., *Government in Reformation Europe, 1520–1560* (London, 1971), p. 120; *Statutes of the Realm*, iii. 25 Henry VIII c. 19; 26 Henry VIII c. 1.

109. Davies, 'Cromwellian Decade: Authority and Consent", p. 178.

110. Cavill, *English Parliaments of Henry VII*, p. 8.

111. TNA, PRO, C82/654 and C66/659 m. 36 (*LP* V, 978 [13]); C82/658 and C66/660 m. 33 (*LP* V, 1207 [36]); C82/667 and C66/661 m. 27 (*LP* VI, 417 [22]).

112. Elton, *Tudor Revolution in Government*, pp. 158–159.

113. Ibid., p. 98.

114. Later biographers of Cromwell have naturally commented on his work in these offices, but when doing so they have relied on Elton's findings.

115. Elton, *Tudor Revolution in Government*, p. 99.
116. Ibid., pp. 98–117.
117. Ibid., pp. 98, 109, 120.
118. Ibid., p. 117.
119. The profits that could be accumulated through holding office are discussed in the next chapter.
120. Elton, *Tudor Revolution in Government*, pp. 109–110.
121. TNA, PRO, SP1/70 fo. 186 (*LP* V, 1214); SP1/71 fo. 109 (*LP* V, 1434).
122. TNA, PRO, SP2/O fo. 41 (*LP* VI, 861).
123. TNA, PRO, SP2/M fos 183–185 (*LP* V, 1730); SP2/N fo. 108 (*LP* VI, 228).
124. TNA, PRO, SP2/O fos 52–52a (*LP* VI, 970 [1]), SP2/O fo. 53 (*LP* VI, 970 [2]). See also TNA, PRO, E212/102 (*LP* VI, 970 [1/ii]), which is a bond connected with this.
125. Lee later heard, however, that Cromwell had since 'commaunded that they shalbe levied', and was shocked considering this earlier promise. See TNA, PRO, SP1/79 fo. 71 (*LP* VI, 1158).
126. TNA, PRO, SP2/O fo. 149 (*LP* VI, 1668). *Cf.* Elton, *Tudor Revolution in Government*, pp. 114–115. See also TNA, PRO, SP2/O fo. 150 (*LP* VI, 1680).
127. TNA, PRO, E101/421/5 (*LP* V, 1237); BL, Royal MS 7 CXVI fos 40–46v (*LP* V, 1376); BL, Cotton MS, Appendix XXVIII fos 39–39v (*LP* V, 1385); *LP* V, 1399; TNA, PRO, SP1/82 fo. 128 (*LP* VII, 137); TNA, PRO, E101/421/6 (*LP* VI, 6); TNA, PRO, SP1/76 fo. 122 (*LP* VI, 566); SP1/80 fo. 49 (*LP* VI, 1367); TNA, PRO, E36/143 fo. 69 (*LP* VI, 1589); TNA, PRO, SP1/71 fos 117–118 (Merriman, *Life and Letters of Thomas Cromwell,* i. 348–349; *LP* V, 1298); SP1/71 fo. 19 (*LP* V, 1299); TNA, PRO, C36/85 (*LP* V, 1799); TNA, PRO, SP1/78 fo. 169 (*LP* VI, 1041); SP1/80 fos 165–165v (*LP* VI, 1494); SP2/P fo. 9 (*LP* VII, 10); BL, Cotton MS, Titus B I fo. 493 (*LP* VI, 1194); BL, Cotton MS, Titus B I fo. 465 (*LP* VI, 1382); TNA, PRO, E36/143 fo. 69 (*LP* VI, 1589); TNA, PRO, SP1/82 fo. 165 (*LP* VII, 213).
128. Elton, *Tudor Revolution in Government*, p. 111.
129. TNA, PRO, SP1/70 fos 61–63 (*LP* V, 1060); SP1/69 fo. 239 (*LP* V, 957); *LP* V, 1065 [14 and 32], TNA, PRO, SP1/70 fo. 147 (*LP* V, 1152); TNA, PRO, E101/421/5 (*LP* V, 1314); TNA, PRO, SP2/M fos 31–34 (*LP* V, 1205); SP1/68 fo. 102 (*LP* V, 612); SP1/69 fo. 70 (*LP* V, 874); SP1/69 fos 236–237 (*LP* V, 955); SP1/71 fo. 58 (*LP* V, 1356); SP1/81 fos 94–94v (*LP* VI, 1641); SP1/83 fo. 2 (*LP* VII, 356).
130. TNA, PRO, SP1/80 fo. 175 (*LP* VI, 1508); TNA, PRO, E101/421/8 (*LP* V, 1264 [1]); TNA, PRO, SP2/M fos 38–42 (*LP* V, 1264[2]); TNA, PRO, E101/421/9 (*LP* VI, 283); TNA, PRO, SP1/75 fo. 83 (*LP* VI, 330).
131. TNA, PRO, SP1/68 fo. 82 (*LP* V, 577); TNA, PRO, E101/421/5 (*LP* V, 825; *LP* V, 1052); *LP* V, 1314; *LP* V, 1346; TNA, PRO, SP1/70 fo. 49 (*LP* V, 1040); SP1/70 fo. 128 (*LP* V, 1119); SP2/M fos 13–16 (*LP* V, 1169); SP1/70 fo. 204 (*LP* V, 1244); SP1/72 fo. 6v (*LP* V, 1504); SP1/72 fo. 8 (*LP* V, 1506).
132. Hall, *Chronicle*, p. 795; TNA, PRO, SP1/72 fo. 137 (*LP* V, 1639); SP2/O fo. 26 (*LP* VI, 717); SP1/66 fo. 157 (*LP* V, 334), which was probably misdated in *Letters and Papers* and belongs to at least 1532, when this policy was initiated, SP1/72 fo. 98 (*LP* V, 1608); SP1/76 fo. 33 (*LP* VI, 468); SP1/76 fo. 43 (*LP* VI, 481); SP1/76 fo. 67 (*LP* VI, 509); SP1/76 fo. 70 (*LP* VI, 514); SP1/76 fo. 77 (*LP* VI, 516); SP1/76 fo. 81v (*LP* VI, 521), SP1/76 fo. 2 (*LP* VI, 421); BL, Cotton MS, Vespasian F XIII fo. 282 (*LP* VI, 550).
133. TNA, PRO, SP1/72 fo. 137 (*LP* V, 1639).
134. TNA, PRO, SP2/M fo. 194 (*LP* V, 1785).
135. TNA, PRO, SP1/80 fo. 49 (*LP* VI, 1367); BL, Cotton MS, Otho E IX fos 58–61 (*LP* VII, 1564).
136. TNA, PRO, SP1/68 fo. 53 (*LP* V, 538); SP1/68 fo. 123 (*LP* V, 639); SP1/71 fo. 58 (*LP* V, 1356); SP1/81 fos 94–94v (*LP* VI, 1641); SP1/83 fo. 2 (*LP* VII, 356).
137. It is interesting to note here that Elton believed one of the accounts was written in Cromwell's own hand, while he thought another contained additions by him. See *Tudor Revolution in Government*, pp. 141–142. In actual fact, none of the accounts is in Cromwell's hand. The hand Elton mistook for Cromwell's is that of his clerk and

early household treasurer, William Body, although, in fairness to Elton, the hand is remarkably similar to that of Cromwell. There can be no doubt, however, that it was Body who drew these accounts up. The handwriting on TNA, PRO, SP2/O fos 25–30 (*LP* VI, 717), which Elton thought was drawn up by Cromwell, and that on TNA, PRO, SP2/N fo. 110 (*LP* VI, 228), which was thought to contain Cromwell's additions, should be contrasted with that on Body's account of Cromwell's private income and expenditure between January and July 1533, TNA, PRO, SP2/O fos 34–40 (*LP* VI, 841). In case there remains any doubt, the account which Elton thought was wholly in Cromwell's hand is also endorsed on the reverse of the first folio as being 'Bodies declarac[i]on'. See TNA, PRO, SP2/O fo. 25v (*LP* VI, 717).

138. TNA, PRO, SP1/72 fos 136–137 (*LP* V, 1639). According to the 'Arrerages' on this account, there was an earlier account which was begun on 2 April.

139. TNA, PRO, SP2/N fos 107–110 (*LP* VI, 228).

140. TNA, PRO, SP2/O fos 25–30 (*LP* VI, 717).

141. TNA, PRO, SP1/83 fo. 55 (*LP* VII, 430).

142. TNA, PRO, SP2/N fos 109–110 (*LP* VI, 228); SP2/O fo. 29 (*LP* VI, 717).

143. For convenience these have been given in pounds only.

144. At the end of this account is a list of incomes due but not yet collected. These included 'Fynes for knyghtes sessid by the said Thomas Cromwell ... and nat paid', £2,180, and fines negotiated by him with 'sondry persons spirituall and temporall', £7,200. See TNA, PRO, SP1/72 fo. 137 (*LP* V, 1639).

145. Although this account runs from 22 November 1532 to 11 March 1533, at the bottom of the account there is a list of additional receipts and payments made by Cromwell since 11 March. According to the summary, Cromwell received £4,000 during this period, and paid out £6,374. See TNA, PRO, SP2/N fos 110–110v (*LP* VI, 228).

146. Elton, *Tudor Revolution in Government*, pp. 139, 154, 155.

147. TNA, PRO, SP2/N fo. 108 (*LP* VI, 228).

148. TNA, PRO, SP2/O fo. 26 (*LP* VI, 717).

149. Elton, *Tudor Revolution in Government*, p. 147.

150. Starkey, 'King's Privy Chamber', pp. 401–402; Starkey, 'Court and Government', pp. 44–45 and n. 64.

151. BL, Royal MS 7 CXVI fo. 75 (*LP* V, 1388).

152. Starkey argued that this document shows that the royal treasuries were arranged a bit like modern bank accounts, with a deposit account (the Privy Coffers) and a current account (the Privy Purse, and later Cromwell's Jewel House), each topping the other up when one was flush with money. I am not wholly convinced by this claim.

153. For an account of the war, see R. W. Hoyle, 'The Anglo-Scottish War of 1532–3', *Camden Society*, xxxi, Fourth Series, 44 (London, 1992), pp. 23–29.

154. Troops had been ordered to muster at Newcastle on 18 September, and by the beginning of October Chapuys was reporting that a number of small raids had been conducted on both sides. See Devonshire Manuscripts, Chatsworth, Bolton Abbey MSS 14a, fo. 10r; *CSP, Spanish*, IV, ii, 802. A truce was agreed in May 1533, and was continually extended until a formal peace treaty was signed in London in 1534.

155. TNA, PRO, SP2/N fo. 109 (*LP* VI, 228). This is similar to the total sum recorded on Lawson's own account detailing the money received from Cromwell. See TNA, PRO, SP2/O fos 20–22 (*LP* VI, 664). Lawson's account shows that between September and June he received a total of £20,034 13s 4d from Cromwell. This leaves a discrepancy in Cromwell's own accounts, suggesting he paid out around £50 more than Lawson recorded receiving.

156. See and compare TNA, PRO, SP2/O fo. 26 (*LP* VI, 717) and SP2/O fo. 20 (*LP* VI, 664).

157. BL, Royal MS 7 CXVI fo. 75 (*LP* V, 1388).

158. See and compare TNA, PRO, SP2/O fo. 26 (*LP* VI, 717) and SP2/O fo. 20 (*LP* VI, 664).

159. Elton, *Tudor Revolution in Government*, p. 147; Starkey, 'Court and Government', p. 45.

160. BL, Royal MS 7 CXVI fo. 75 (*LP* V, 1388).

161. TNA, PRO, E36/141 fos 39–46 (*LP* V, 1.285 [ix]). The warrants can be found in three bundles in TNA, PRO, E101/421/5 (*LP* V, 825, 1052, 1237, 1314, 1346, 1392, 1590,

1646, 1668, 1671); E101/421/6, which contains 33 warrants not calandered in *Letters and Papers*; and E101/421/9 (*LP* VI, 6, 130, 131, 149, 170, 220, 229, 283, 326). Several of Cromwell's warrants can also be found among the State Papers and records of the Exchequer. See: TNA, PRO, E101/420/1 (*LP* V, 341); E101/420/5 (*LP* V, 1215); TNA, PRO, SP1/70 fo. 128 (*LP* V, 1119); SP1/78 fos 216–217 (*LP* VI, 1057); SP1/80 fo. 49 (*LP* V, 1367); SP1/82 fo. 128 (*LP* VII, 137); SP1/80 fo. 175 (*LP* VI, 1508).

162. TNA, PRO, E36/141 fo. 42 (*LP* V, 1285 [ix]).
163. TNA, PRO, E101/421/5 (*LP* V, 1052).
164. TNA, PRO, E36/141 fo. 42 (*LP* V, 1285 [ix]).
165. TNA, PRO, SP1/70 fo. 128 (*LP* V, 1119); TNA, PRO, E101/141 fo. 43 (*LP* V, 1285 [ix]).
166. TNA, PRO, SP2/N fos 108–109 (*LP* VI, 228); TNA, PRO, E101/421/9 (*LP* VI, 131).
167. TNA, PRO, SP2/N fos 108–109 (*LP* VI, 228). This was probably the revenues of the vacant see of Canterbury, and the £100 received from the archbishop's executors for a 'mounte'.
168. Ibid., fo. 110.
169. Although the sums recorded as being paid out since 11 March are very similar to some of the payments made in account C (which overlaps the period covered by B), those which can be identified appear to be different payments. Compare, for instance, the payments made to the king's tombmaker on TNA, PRO, SP2/N fo. 110 (B) with those recorded on SP2/O fo. 28 (C); and the £1,000 paid to Sir George Lawson on B, which does not correspond to the breakdown given of the £5,000 paid to him for the Anglo-Scottish war on C.
170. TNA, PRO, SP2/O fo. 27 (*LP* VI, 717); E101/421/9 (*LP* VI, 326).
171. TNA, PRO, SP1/72 fos 136–137 (*LP* V, 1639).
172. TNA, SP2/N fo. 110 (*LP* VI, 228).
173. Elton, *Tudor Revolution in Government*, p. 148 n.1.
174. D. Hoak, 'The Secret History of the Tudor Court: The King's Coffers and the King's Purse, 1542–1553', *Journal of British Studies*, 26 (1987), pp. 212–213.
175. TNA, PRO, SP2/N fo. 107 (*LP* VI, 228); SP2/O fo. 25 (*LP* VI, 717).
176. TNA, PRO, SP2/N fo. 10 (*LP* VI, 228); SP2/O fo. 28 (*LP* VI, 717).
177. TNA, PRO, SP2/N fo. 10 (*LP* VI, 228); SP2/O fos 28–30 (*LP* VI, 717).
178. TNA, PRO, SP1/83 fo. 55 (*LP* VII, 430).
179. TNA, PRO, SP1/72 fo. 137 (*LP* V, 1639).
180. 'The purpose behind his treasurership was, it seems, a desire to be independent of all other agencies in the covering of that expenditure. He wished to be free to employ ambassadors, to build the king's palaces, to fortify the realm and supply the navy, and to fulfil all the other tasks of government which he attended without having to go to others for the necessary money.' Elton, *Tudor Revolution in Government*, p. 156; see also Starkey, 'King's Privy Chamber', pp. 403–404.
181. Starkey, 'King's Privy Chamber', pp. 393–410; Starkey, 'Court and Government', p. 44; Guy, 'Henry VIII and the *Praemunire* Manoeuvres', pp. 44–45; Hoyle, 'Origins of the Dissolution', p. 290; R. W. Hoyle, 'War and Public Finance', in D. MacCulloch, ed., *The Reign of Henry VIII: Politics, Policy and Piety* (Basingstoke, 1995), pp. 78–79. Not all, however, have been convinced by this. See Bernard, 'Pardon of the Clergy Reconsidered', pp. 259–262.
182. Hall, *Chronicle*, pp. 785–786. See also Lehmberg, *Reformation Parliament*, pp. 133, 147–148, 157–158. *CSP, Spanish*, IV, ii, 948, 952.
183. *Statutes of the Realm*, iii. 26 Henry VIII c. 19.
184. Elton, 'Taxation for War and Peace', pp. 33–48. R. Schofield seemingly concurred with this assessment; see Schofield, *Taxation*, p. 13.
185. *Statutes of the Realm*, iii. 26 Henry VIII c. 19.
186. G. L. Harriss, 'Thomas Cromwell's "New Principle" of Taxation', *English Historical Review*, xciii (1978), pp. 721–738.
187. Starkey, 'Court and Government', p. 45.
188. TNA, PRO, E135/8/37. For the details of the northern convocation's fine see p. 324 n. 98.

189. Ibid.
190. TNA, PRO, SP1/69 fo. 235 (*LP* V, 953).
191. The £1,602 14s for 'Chaynes molten', the £21 8s received from Robert Draper and John Halalie 'of the Juell howse', and the payment to a goldsmith of £300, clearly related to his responsibilities as master of the king's jewels. See TNA, PRO, SP2/N fo. 108 (*LP* VI 228); SP2/O fo. 30 (*LP* VI 717). £300 is also recorded as 'Reuenewes of the hanaper'. See TNA, PRO, SP2/N fo. 108 (*LP* VI 228).
192. Elton, *Tudor Revolution in Government*, p. 156; Starkey, 'King's Privy Chamber', p. 404; Starkey, 'Court and Government', p. 45.
193. Although Cromwell continued to hold this position, he shared it from late 1535 or early 1536 with John Williams, who was previously one of the clerks in the Jewel House. See Elton, *Tudor Revolution in Government*, p. 100.
194. Ibid., p. 101.
195. Richardson, *Tudor Chamber Administration*, pp. 94–95.
196. According to an act of parliament, all revenues from forfeited lands were directed to be paid into the Chamber. See *Statutes of the Realm*, iii. 14 & 15 Henry VIII c. 15.
197. TNA, PRO, SP1/69 fo. 54 (*LP* V, 730); SP1/74 fos 45–45v (*LP* VI, 51); SP1/74 fos. 211–211v (*LP* VI, 217); SP1/75 fo. 27 (*LP* VI, 241); SP1/75 fo. 133 (*LP* VI, 343); SP1/76 fo. 55 (*LP* VI, 498); SP1/78 fo. 7 (*LP* VI, 843); SP1/78 fo. 128v (*State Papers*, i. 404; *LP* VI, 992); SP1/78 fo. 133 (*LP* VI, 995); SP1/79 fo. 102 (*LP* VI, 1185); BL, Cotton MS, Titus B I fo. 493v (*LP* VI, 1194); TNA, PRO, SP1/82 fo. 102 (*LP* VII, 91); SP1/82 fo. 199 (*LP* VII, 255); TNA, PRO, E101/421/14 (*LP* VII, 372); TNA, PRO, SP1/239 fo. 46 (*LP* Add. I, i, 932).
198. *LP* V, p. 321.
199. Elton, *Tudor Revolution in Government*, p. 111.
200. TNA, PRO, SP1/70 fo. 37 (*LP* V, 1026); SP1/70 fo. 147 (*LP* V, 1152); SP1/70 fo. 171 (*LP* V, 1189).
201. TNA, PRO, SP1/70 fo. 195 (*LP* V, 1228); SP1/76 fo. 98 (*LP* VI, 532).
202. TNA, PRO, SP1/78 fo. 128v (*State Papers*, i. 404; *LP* VI, 992).
203. TNA, PRO, SP1/70 fo. 195 (*LP* V, 1228). This letter was wrongly placed in 1532 in *Letters and Papers*. It was written in 1533.
204. TNA, PRO, SP1/80 fo. 49 (*LP* VI, 1367).
205. BL, Cotton MS, Otho E IX fos 58–61 (*LP* VII, 1564).
206. TNA, PRO, SP1/82 fo. 102 (*LP* VI, 91).
207. TNA, PRO, E101/421/5 (*LP* V, 1646); TNA, PRO, SP2/N fo. 109 (*LP* VI, 228 [ii]); SP2/O fos 27–28 (*LP* VI, 717); SP1/75 fo. 57v (*LP* VI, 284); SP1/78 fo. 216v (*LP* VI, 1057); BL, Cotton MS, Titus B I fo. 493 (*LP* VI, 1194); TNA, PRO, E36/143 fo. 69 (*LP* VI, 1589); TNA, PRO, SP1/82 fo. 128 (*LP* VII, 137); BL, Cotton MS, Galba B X fo. 48 (*LP* VII, 167); TNA, PRO, E101/421/5 (*LP* V, 1668); TNA, PRO, SP2/36 fo. 60 (*LP* VII, 501); TNA, PRO, E101/421/9 (*LP* VI, 149, 229); TNA, PRO, SP1/74 fo. 149 (*LP* VI, 150); SP1/75 fos 156–157 (*LP* VI, 372); BL, Cotton MS, Titus B I fo. 493v (*LP* V, 1194); TNA, PRO, SP1/82 fo. 179 (*LP* VII, 227); SP1/80 fo. 175 (*LP* VI, 1508); SP1/78 fos 216–217 (*LP* VI, 1057); TNA, PRO, E36/143 fo. 77 (*LP* VI, 1371).
208. TNA, PRO, SP1/79 fos 68–70 (*LP* VI, 1156); SP1/75 fos 156–157 (*LP* VI, 372 [1]); SP1/78 fo. 158 (*LP* VI, 372 [2]); SP1/78 fo. 215 (*LP* VI, 1056 [2]); BL, Cotton MS, Titus B I fo. 493v (*LP* VI, 1194); BL, Cotton MS, Galba IX fo. 163 (*LP* VII, 253).
209. TNA, PRO, SP1/78 fo. 133 (*LP* VI, 995); BL, Cotton MS, Titus B I fo. 493v (*LP* VI, 1194).
210. TNA, PRO, SP1/82 fo. 179 (*LP* VII, 227); BL, Cotton MS, Galba B IX fo. 163 (*LP* VII, 253).
211. BL, Cotton MS, Titus B IV fos 117v–118 (*LP* VII, 254).
212. TNA, PRO, SP1/78 fo. 215 (*LP* VI 1056 [2]); SP1/82 fo. 207 (*LP* VII 263); BL, Cotton MS, Titus B I fo. 419 (*LP* VII 48); SP1/82 fo. 200 (*LP* VII 257).
213. TNA, PRO, SP1/74 fo. 149 (*LP* VI, 150). The eventual warrant Cromwell obtained is TNA, PRO, E101/421/9 (*LP* VI, 149).

214. TNA, PRO, SP1/74 fo. 149 (*LP* VI, 150). The eventual warrant Cromwell obtained is TNA, PRO, E101/421/9 (*LP* VI, 131).

215. BL, Cotton MS, Otho E IX fos 58–61 (*LP* VII 1564).

216. TNA, PRO, SP1/74 fos 121–122 (*LP* VI, 107).

217. TNA, PRO, E101/421/9 (*LP* VI 130).

218. Elton, *Tudor Revolution in Government*, p. 155.

219. TNA, PRO, SP1/237 fo. 266 (*LP* Add. I, i, 801).

220. TNA, PRO, SP1/74 fo. 127 (*LP* VI, 117). For a broader attempt to redress the king's interest in financial administration, see S. M. Jack, 'Henry VIII's Attitude towards Royal Finance: Penny Wise and Pound Foolish?', in C. Giry-Deloison, ed., *Francois Ier et Henri VIII. Deux princes de la Renaissance (1515–1547)*, (Arras, 1997), pp. 145–163.

221. TNA, PRO, SP1/77 fos 92–92v (*LP* VI, 724); SP1/79 fos 24–25 (*State Papers*, vii. 505; *LP* VI, 1084); SP1/80 fos 187–188v (*LP* VI, 1524); SP1/81 fos 20–22 (*LP* VI, 1559).

222. BL, Cotton MS, Titus B I fo. 493v (*LP* VI, 1194); BL, Cotton MS, Titus B I fo. 456 (*LP* VII, 143 [2]). See also TNA, PRO, E36/143 fos 55 (*LP* VI, 1370); E36/143 fo. 77 (*LP* VI, 1371); BL, Cotton MS, Titus B I fo. 427v (*LP* VII, 48); BL, Cotton MS, Titus B I fo. 463 (*LP* VII, 108); TNA, PRO, SP1/82 fo. 207 (*LP* VII, 263); SP1/83 fo. 23 (*LP* VII, 397).

223. TNA, PRO, SP1/78 fo. 133 (*LP* VI, 995); SP1/78 fo. 215 (*LP* VI, 1056 [2]); BL, Cotton MS, Titus B I fo. 493v (*LP* VI, 1194).

224. TNA, PRO, SP1/78 fo. 6 (*LP* VI, 842).

225. *Cf.* C. Etty, 'Tudor Revolution? Royal Control of the Anglo-Scottish Border, 1483–1530' (University of Durham PhD thesis, 2005), pp. 95–96, on which I have drawn for this paragraph. Gwyn has attempted some general comments regarding Wolsey and financial administration; see *King's Cardinal*, pp. 362–365.

226. Elton, *Tudor Revolution in Government*, p. 44.

227. *LP* IV, iii, 5749, 5750.

228. TNA, PRO, C82/478 (*LP* III, 361 [13]).

229. TNA, PRO, E101/57/4.

230. TNA, PRO, SP1/27 fos 78–79; TNA, PRO, E36/221; E101/61/31/88; E101/61/31/85; E101/61/31/87. Cited in Etty, 'Tudor Revolution?', pp. 95–96.

231. TNA, PRO, E101/58/7.

232. TNA, PRO, E36/254. My italics for emphasis.

233. Elton, *Tudor Revolution in Government*, p. 45.

Chapter Six The Minister and his Household

1. *CSP, Spanish*, V, i, 228.

2. One exception to the focus on Cromwell's 'public' career has been the work of Mary Robertson. She wrote a prosopographical thesis on Cromwell's servants, and an article on his landed estates. See Robertson, 'Thomas Cromwell's Servants'; Robertson, 'Profit and Purpose', pp. 317–346.

3. Williams, *Tudor Regime*; D. Starkey, 'The Age of the Household: Politics, Society and the Arts *c.*1350–*c.*1550', in S. Medcalf, ed., *The Later Middle Ages* (New York, 1981), pp. 225–290; B. J. Harris, 'Women and Politics, pp. 259–281'. For a good summary of this 'New Tudor political history' and the historians associated with it, see Mears, 'Courts, Courtiers, and Culture', pp. 703–722.

4. Harris, 'Women and Politics', pp. 260, 281.

5. S. Gunn, 'The Structures of Politics in Early Tudor England', *Transactions of the Royal Historical Society*, Sixth Series, 5 (1995), p. 71.

6. Starkey, 'Age of the Household', p. 230.

7. TNA, PRO, SP1/51 fo. 105 (*LP* IV, ii, 5034); SP1/53 fo. 128 (*LP* IV, iii, 5398); SP1/56 fo. 227 (*LP* IV, iii, 6196); SP1/57 fo. 23 (*LP* IV, iii, 6223); SP1/57 fo. 145 (*LP* IV, iii, 6429); SP1/59 fo. 133 (*LP* IV, iii, App. 237); SP1/71 fo. 106 (*LP* V, 1432); SP1/71 fo. 110v (*LP* V, 1435); SP1/71 fo. 139 (*LP* V, 1464); SP1/71 fo. 143 (*LP* V, 1467); SP1/71 fo. 146 (*LP* V, 1472); SP1/71 fo. 155 (*LP* V, 1483).

8. Bindoff, *House of Commons*, i. 733–734.
9. TNA, PRO, SP1/71 fo. 101 (*LP* V, 1426); SP1/75 fo. 56 (*LP* VI, 275); SP1/75 fo. 59 (*LP* VI, 286); SP1/75 fo. 178 (*LP* VI, 394); SP1/79 fo. 96 (*LP* VI, 1177); SP1/80 fo. 84 (*LP* VI, 1395); SP1/81 fo. 107 (*LP* VI, 1653).
10. TNA, PRO, SP2/O fo. 97 (*LP* VI, 1591 [2]); SP1/74 fo. 16 (*LP* VI, 25); SP1/74 fo. 121 (*LP* VI, 107); SP2/O fos 20–22 (*LP* VI, 664); William Roper, *Lyfe of Sir Thomas Moore*, p. 74.
11. TNA, PRO, SP1/77 fo. 211 (*LP* VI, 837).
12. Bindoff, *House of Commons*, i. 734.
13. M. Girouard, *Life in the English Country House* (London, 1978), pp. 14–21; Starkey, 'Age of the Household', pp. 243–250.
14. TNA, PRO, SP1/72 fo. 10 (*LP* V, 1509).
15. Robertson, 'Thomas Cromwell's Servants', pp. 84–129.
16. TNA, PRO, SP1/72 fo. 10 (*LP* V, 1509); Robertson, 'Thomas Cromwell's Servants', pp. 84–129.
17. TNA, PRO, SP1/71 fo. 110–110v (*LP* V, 1435); SP1/72 fo. 10 (*LP* V, 1509); SP1/71 fo. 139 (*LP* V, 1464); SP1/71 fo. 114v (*LP* V, 1442); SP1/71 fo. 128 (*LP* V, 1454); SP1/71 fo. 146 (*LP* V, 1472); SP1/72 fo. 13 (*LP* V, 1512).
18. TNA, PRO, E36/141 fos 148 (*LP* V, 1285).
19. G. R. Batho, 'The Household Papers of Henry Percy, Ninth Earl of Northumberland (1564–1632)', *Camden Society*, Third Series, xciii (London, 1962), pp. xxi–xxxiv; Girouard, *English Country House*, p. 18; Robertson, 'Thomas Cromwell's Servants', pp. 81–82.
20. TNA, PRO, SP1/54 fo. 244 (Merriman, *Life and Letters of Thomas Cromwell*, i. 56–63; *LP* IV, iii, 5772); TNA, PRO, SP1/71 fo. 114 (*LP* V, 1442); SP1/71 fo. 149 (*LP* V, 1475).
21. TNA, PRO, SP1/72 fo. 136v (*LP* V, 1639); SP2/O fo. 25v (*LP* VI, 717); SP2/O fos 36–40 (*LP* VI, 841); SP1/83 fo. 55 (*LP* VII, 430 [1]); SP1/83 fo. 56 (*LP* VII, 430 [2]).
22. TNA, PRO, SP1/71 fo. 128 (*LP* V, 1454).
23. *LP* XIII, ii, 1184.
24. Robertson, 'Thomas Cromwell's Servants', p. 9.
25. Cavendish, *Life and Death of Cardinal Wolsey*, p. 21. For a description of Wolsey's household, see pp. 18–21.
26. Dickens, *Thomas Cromwell*, p. 8; Williams, *Cardinal and the Secretary*, p. 173; Beckingsale, *Thomas Cromwell*, p. 5; Robertson, 'Thomas Cromwell's Servants', p. 9; Wilding, *Thomas Cromwell*, p. 55.
27. Stow, *Survey of London*, i. 88.
28. Pollard, *Wolsey*, p. 327.
29. Stow, *Survey of London*, i. 88–89.
30. Ibid., i. 89.
31. Girouard, *Life in the English Country House*, p. 23.
32. TNA, PRO, SP1/72 fo. 10 (*LP* V, 1509).
33. Foxe, *Acts and Monuments* (1570 edn), p. 1400.
34. J. Stevens, *Music and Poetry in the Early Tudor Court* (Cambridge, 1979), p. 296.
35. TNA, PRO, SP1/76 fo. 15 (*LP* VI, 441).
36. TNA, PRO, SP1/54 fo. 244 (Merriman, *Life and Letters of Thomas Cromwell*, i. 56–63; *LP* IV, iii, 5772). The earliest dateable reference to Body being in Cromwell's service is not found until October 1532. See TNA, PRO, SP1/71 fo. 114 (*LP* V, 1442); SP1/71 fo. 149 (*LP* V, 1475).
37. TNA, PRO, SP1/71 fo. 149 (*LP* V, 1475); SP1/72 fos 136–137 (*LP* V, 1639); SP2/O fos 36–40 (*LP* VI, 841); SP1/83 fo. 55 (*LP* VII, 430 [1]); SP1/83 fo. 56 (*LP* VII, 430 [2]).
38. TNA, PRO, SP1/65 fo. 119 (*LP* V, 84) and for its redating to 1527, see p. 272 n. 238, SP1/39 fo. 192 (*LP* IV, ii, 2358 [8]); SP1/42 fo. 143 (*LP* IV, ii, 3212 [10]); SP1/44 fo. 219 (*LP* IV, iii, 3536); SP1/59 fo. 133 (*LP* IV, iii, App. 237); SP1/52 fo. 38 (*LP* IV, iii, 5115); SP1/57 fo. 2 (*LP* IV, iii, 6217); SP1/57 fo. 16 (*LP* IV, iii, 6221); SP1/235 fo. 78

(*LP* Add. I, i, 498); SP1/80 fo. 49 (*LP* VI, 1367). Swift was bequeathed £6 13s 4d by Cromwell in his will (Merriman, *Life and Letters of Thomas Cromwell*, i. 62).

39. TNA, PRO, SP1/59 fo. 133 (*LP* IV, iii, App. 237); SP1/80 fo. 49 (*LP* VI, 1367).

40. BL, Cotton MS, Titus B I fo. 163v (*LP* V, 584).

41. Compare TNA, PRO, SP1/238 fos 90–91 (*LP* Add. I, i, 860) and SP1/78 fos 25–25v (Merriman, *Life and Letters of Thomas Cromwell*, i. 360–362; *LP* VI, 887).

42. TNA, PRO, SP1/79 fo. 96 (*LP* VI, 1177); SP3/7 fo. 160 (*LP* Add. I, i, 886).

43. TNA, PRO, SP1/69 fo. 87 (*LP* V, 789). See also TNA, PRO, SP1/57 fo. 145 (*LP* IV, ii, 6429); BL, Cotton MS, Galba B X fos 7–7v (*LP* V, 247); BL, Cotton MS, Galba B X fo. 3 (*LP* V, 804).

44. Robertson, 'Thomas Cromwell's Servants', p. 441.

45. TNA, PRO, SP1/80 fo. 175 (*LP* VI, 1508).

46. TNA, PRO, SP2/O fos 114–115 (*LP* V, 1622); SP2/O fos 118a–118av (*LP* V, 1624); SP1/82 fo. 123 (*LP* VII, 122); SP1/82 fo. 176 (*LP* VII, 222); SP1/82 fo. 234 (*LP* VII, 301); SP2/P fo. 148 (*LP* VII, 416 [2]); SP1/78 fo. 31 (Merriman, *Life and Letters of Thomas Cromwell*, i. 362; *LP* VI, 894).

47. *LP* VII, 122, 1122 [12]; *LP* XIV, ii, 5, 8, 24; M. A. Lyons, 'Brabazon, Sir William (d. 1552)', *ODNB*; Robertson, 'Thomas Cromwell's Servants', pp. 451–452.

48. Slavin, *Politics and Profit*, pp. 46–47; G. Gibbons, *The Political Career of Sir Thomas Wriothesley, First Earl of Southampton, 1505–1550, Henry VIII's Last Chancellor* (Lampeter, 2001), p. 61; Elton, *Tudor Revolution in Government*, pp. 312–313.

49. TNA, PRO, SP1/73 fo. 136 (*LP* V, 1760).

50. TNA, PRO, SP1/71 fo. 100 (*LP* V, 1424).

51. TNA, PRO, SP1/73 fo. 1 (*LP* V, 1680). For further examples, see also SP1/66 fo. 43 (*LP* V, 292); SP1/74 fo. 68 (*LP* VI, 72).

52. TNA, PRO, SP1/83 fo. 92 (*LP* VII, 508).

53. Harris, 'Women and Politics', p. 264.

54. TNA, PRO, SP1/68 fo. 90 (*LP* V, 588); SP1/68 fo. 136 (*LP* V, 651).

55. TNA, PRO, SP1/71 fo. 100 (*LP* V, 1424); SP1/82 fo. 121 (*LP* VII, 117).

56. TNA, PRO, SP1/81 fo. 155 (*LP* VI, 1705). See the endorsement on the reverse by one of Cromwell's clerks, 'a copy or forme of ons writing that sheweth to be in my master his seruice' (fo. 155v).

57. Letters to Cromwell were often addressed to him as 'dwellynge at the freare Awstene gaytte', 'by the Freyers awstyns' or 'at the frer Augustens'. See TNA, PRO, SP1/65 fo. 185v (*LP* V, 174); SP1/235 fo. 360v (*LP* Add. I, i, 602); SP1/235 fo. 70v (*LP* Add. I, i, 490); SP1/45 fo. 217v (*LP* IV, ii, 3675); SP1/58 fo. 173v (*LP* IV, iii, 6754); SP1/235 fo. 74v (*LP* Add. I, i, 494). For a thorough architectural reconstruction of Cromwell's house, see N. Holder, 'The Medieval Friaries of London: A Topographic and Archaeological History, before and after the Dissolution' (University of London PhD thesis, 2011), pp. 160–170.

58. TNA, PRO, SP1/42 fos 101–116 (*LP* IV, ii, 3197).

59. D[rapers'] C[ompany] R[ecords], A I, 61. Cromwell paid £12 a year for these properties. A draft of this lease written in Cromwell's hand, and dated 26 May, can be found in TNA, PRO, SP2/L fos 183–188 (*LP* V, 1028).

60. TNA, PRO, SP1/71 fo. 106 (*LP* V, 1432); SP1/71 fos 110–110v (*LP* V, 1435); SP1/71 fo. 114v (*LP* V, 1442); SP1/71 fo. 128 (*LP* V, 1454); SP1/71 fo. 136 (*LP* V, 1461); SP1/71 fo. 139 (*LP* V, 1464); SP1/71 fo. 143 (*LP* V, 1467); SP1/71 fo. 146 (*LP* V, 1472); SP1/71 fo. 156 (*LP* V, 1487); SP1/72 fo. 10 (*LP* V, 1509); SP1/72 fo. 13 (*LP* V, 1512); SP1/73 fo. 97 (*LP* V, 1723).

61. TNA, PRO, SP1/71 fo. 144 (*LP* V, 1469).

62. TNA, PRO, SP1/71 fo. 143 (*LP* V, 1467).

63. Stow, *Survey of London*, ii. 179.

64. The property was forfeited to the Crown on Cromwell's fall in 1540. Sir Thomas Wriothesley rented the house from the Crown shortly after this, but it was finally sold to the Drapers in 1543 for £666 13s 4d. See *LP* XV, 942 [113]; *LP* XVIII, ii, 231 [2]; DCR, Charter X.

65. DCR, MB/ I C, pp. 761–762 (Court of Assistants Minutes, 1543–1553); DCR, A XII, 121.

66. DCR: A I, 64, 65, 66; A I 67, 68, 69; A I 70; A I 71 [1–2]; A I 75; TNA, PRO, E36/153 fo. 41 (*LP* VII, 1617). See also Stow, *Survey of London*, ii. 179. For the building works from 1535 onwards, see: TNA, PRO, SP1/95 fo. 90 (*LP* IX, 106); SP1/95 fo. 114 (*LP* IX, 131); SP1/95 fo. 159 (*LP* IX, 172); SP1/96 fo. 129 (*LP* IX, 340); SP1/96 fo. 200 (*LP* IX, 414); SP1/105 fo. 144 (*LP* XI, 159); SP1/106 fo. 30 (*LP* XI, 335); SP1/106 fo. 172 (*LP* XI, 455).

67. TNA, PRO, E36/153 fo. 41 (*LP* VII, 1617); *LP* VIII, 1105.

68. DCR, MB/ I C, p. 762.

69. TNA, PRO, SP1/44 fo. 219 (*LP* IV, ii, 3536).

70. TNA, PRO, SP1/53 fo. 128 (*LP* IV, iii, 5398).

71. TNA, PRO, E36/143 fos 18, 23 (*LP* VI, 299 [iv and vii]).

72. TNA, PRO, E36/140 fos 19r, 12v. This document, which is badly water damaged, is not calendared in *Letters and Papers*. It appears to be a list of papers in Cromwell's possession relating to his career as a lawyer as well as to work for Wolsey.

73. See, for example, TNA, PRO, SP1/58 fo. 124v (*LP* IV, iii, 6698); SP1/235 fo. 360v (*LP* Add. I, i, 602); SP1/65 fo. 122v (*LP* V, 86); SP1/53 fo. 250v (*LP* IV, iii, 5526); SP1/67 fo. 89v (*LP* V, 442); SP1/65 fo. 244v (*LP* V, 237); SP1/65 fo. 45v (*LP* V, 23).

74. *LP* V, p. v.

75. *LP* VIII, 516, 556; *LP* XIII, i, 756; *LP* XIII, ii, 232; Elton, *Tudor Revolution in Government*, p. 327.

76. TNA, PRO, SP1/54 fos 235–248 (Merriman, *Life and Letters of Thomas Cromwell*, i. 56–64; *LP* IV, iii, 5772).

77. TNA, PRO, SP1/81 fo. 29 (*LP* VI, 1574).

78. TNA, PRO, 60/6 fo. 48v (*State Papers*, ii. 551; *LP* XIII, i, 471 [1]).

79. BL, Additional Manuscript 48028 fo. 164.

80. Merriman, *Life and Letters of Thomas Cromwell*, i. 50.

81. Williams, *Cardinal and the Secretary*, p. 149.

82. M. St Clare Byrne, *The Lisle Letters* (6 vols, Chicago, IL, 1981), i. 11 and ii. 560.

83. G. R. Elton, 'How Corrupt was Thomas Cromwell?', *Historical Journal*, 36 (1993), pp. 907–908.

84. Ibid., pp. 905–907.

85. Slavin, *Politics and Profit*, pp. 177–178; J. S. Block, 'Political Corruption in Henrician England', in C. Charlton, R. L. Woods, M. L. Robertson and J. S. Block, eds, *State, Sovereigns and Society in Early Modern England* (Stroud, 1998), pp. 45–57; J. Hurstfield, 'Political Corruption in Modern England: The Historian's Problem', in J. Hurstfield, *Freedom, Corruption and Government in Elizabethan England* (London, 1973), pp. 137–163.

86. TNA, PRO, SP1/69 fo. 9 (*LP* V, 701).

87. TNA, PRO, E36/140 fo. 33r.

88. TNA, PRO, C82/654 and C66/659 m. 36 (*LP* V, 978 [13]); C82/658 and C66/660 m. 33 (*LP* V, 1207 [36]).

89. TNA, PRO, E36/140 fo. 52v; Elton, *Tudor Revolution in Government*, p. 101; TNA, PRO, SP2/O fo. 34 (*LP* VI, 841).

90. TNA, PRO, C82/667 and C66/661 m. 27 (*LP* VI 417 [22]); TNA, PRO, E36/140 fo. 52v.

91. TNA, PRO, SP1/68 fo. 92 (*LP* V, 591).

92. TNA, PRO, SP1/68 fo. 105 (*LP* V, 620).

93. TNA, PRO, SP1/77 fo. 149 (*LP* VI, 792).

94. TNA, PRO, SP1/72 fo. 123 (*LP* V, 1621).

95. TNA, PRO, SP1/72 fo. 146 (*LP* V, 1651).

96. For further examples of food given as gifts and rewards, see: TNA, PRO, SP1/65 fo. 111 (*LP* V, 79); SP1/65 fo. 187 (*LP* V, 181); SP1/68 fo. 40 (*LP* V, 514); SP1/68 fo. 79 (*LP* V, 571); SP1/68 fo. 93 (*LP* V, 596); SP1/68 fo. 119 (*LP* V, 635); SP1/68 fo. 130 (*LP* V, 646).

97. TNA, PRO, SP1/70 fo. 135 (*LP* V, 1129).

98. TNA, PRO, SP1/80 fo. 23 (*LP* VI, 1346).

99. TNA, PRO, SP1/70 fo. 157 (*LP* V, 1168).

100. TNA, PRO, SP1/71 fo. 120 (*LP* V, 1447); SP1/74 fo. 21 (*LP* VI, 30).
101. TNA, PRO, SP1/77 fo. 40 (*LP* VI, 644).
102. TNA, PRO, SP1/237 fo. 169 (*LP* Add. I, i, 779).
103. TNA, PRO, SP1/57 fo. 265 (*LP* IV, iii, 6556); SP1/68 fo. 116 (*LP* V, 632); SP1/69 fo. 240 (*LP* V, 960); SP1/71 fo. 85 (*LP* V, 1398); SP1/69 fo. 14 (*LP* V, 716); SP1/70 fo. 56 (*LP* V, 1049); SP1/70 fo. 116 (*LP* V, 1100); SP1/70 fo. 132 (*LP* V, 1123); SP1/70 fo. 136 (*LP* V, 1132).
104. *CSP, Spanish*, IV, ii, 1107; TNA, PRO, SP1/69 fos 223–224 (*LP* V, 944); SP1/71 fo. 145 (*LP* V, 1470).
105. TNA, PRO, SP1/73 fo. 4 (*LP* V, 1682).
106. Elton, 'How Corrupt was Thomas Cromwell?', p. 907.
107. Slavin, *Politics and Profit*, p. 180; Elton, *Tudor Revolution in Government*, pp. 101–102.
108. Elton, *Tudor Revolution in Government*, p. 126.
109. TNA, PRO, E315/96 fo. 122. This grant is printed and translated in Youings, *Dissolution of the Monasteries*, p. 144.
110. TNA, PRO, SP1/75 fo. 144 (*LP* VI, 354).
111. TNA, PRO, SP1/74 fo. 55 (*LP* VI, 59); SP1/76 fo. 167 (*LP* VI, 612); BL, Cotton MS, Cleopatra E IV fo. 178 (*LP* VI, 632); TNA, PRO, SP1/80 fo. 153 (*LP* VI, 1484).
112. TNA, PRO, SP1/70 fo. 184 (*LP* V, 1212); SP1/81 fo. 26 (*LP* VI, 1566). The grant was not formalised until October 1533. See TNA, PRO, E36/140 fo. 58v.
113. TNA, PRO, E36/140 fo. 62v. For the details of the exchange, see Miller, *Henry VIII and the English Nobility*, pp. 219–220.
114. TNA, PRO, SP1/82 fo. 150 (*LP* VII, 180); SP1/77 fo. 128 (*LP* VI, 746).
115. TNA, PRO, SP1/75 fo. 141 (*LP* VI, 349).
116. BL, Cotton MS, Titus B I fo. 371 (*LP* V, 625). Richard Master was another who sent Cromwell 'ii gold royalls' in return for a pardon. In 1533 Rowland Lee also sent Cromwell 'the rewarde I Resaueyd for my Intrecession to you' for an unnamed man's 'fauorable delyuerans' from punishment. See TNA, PRO, SP1/81 fo. 120v (*LP* VI, 1666); SP1/81 fo. 23 (*LP* VI, 1560).
117. Evans, *Principal Secretary of State*, p. 211.
118. TNA, PRO, SP3/11 fo. 10 (*LP* V, 961).
119. MacCaffrey, 'Place and Patronage in Elizabethan Politics', pp. 95–127.
120. TNA, PRO, E101/420/15 (*LP* V, 686); TNA, PRO, SP2/N fos 1–10 (*LP* VI, 32); TNA, PRO, E101/421/13 (*LP* VII, 9); TNA, PRO, SP1/65 fo. 111 (*LP* V, 79).
121. TNA, PRO, E36/140 fo. 60v; R. Somerville, *History of the Duchy of Lancaster* (2 vols, London, 1953), ii. 604.
122. TNA, PRO, C82/656 and C66/660 m. 19 (*LP* V, 1065 [33]); TNA, PRO, SP1/72 fo. 44 (*LP* V, 1562).
123. TNA, PRO, SP1/88 fo. 21 (*LP* VII, 1610). This abstract was placed in 1534 in *Letters and Papers*, but dates to mid-1535 at the earliest. One of the lands mentioned in it, the manor of Donton, Bedfordshire, was not acquired by Cromwell until June 1535. See *LP* VIII, 962 [22].
124. TNA, PRO, SP1/71 fo. 52 (*LP* V, 1342).
125. TNA, PRO, SP2/O fos 68–72 (*LP* VI, 1176). The formal grant of this is TNA, PRO, E41/219. See also SP2/O fos 73–74 (*LP* VI, 1176 [2]).
126. See pp. 88–89, 115.
127. Block, 'Political Corruption', p. 52.
128. TNA, PRO, SP1/75 fo. 68 (*LP* VI, 304). For its redating, see, p. 295 n. 148.
129. TNA, PRO, SP1/237 fo. 261 (*LP* Add. I, i, 798).
130. TNA, PRO, SP1/68 fo. 118 (*LP* V, 634); placed in 1531 in *Letters and Papers*, but considering that Bowes and Ralph Rowlett were appointed as joint master workers in April 1533, this request to Cromwell surely dates to late 1532 at the earliest. See TNA, PRO, C54/402 m. 36d–38d (*LP* V, 919), which is misdated to 1532 in *Letters and Papers*; TNA, PRO, C82/667 and C66/661 m. 28 (*LP* VI, 417 [7]); Challis, *Tudor Coinage*, pp. 80–81, 311–312.
131. TNA, PRO, SP1/74 fo. 178 (*LP* VI, 179).

132. Williams, *Tudor Regime*, pp. 102–107; J. Hurstfield, *The Queen's Wards: Wardship and Marriage under Elizabeth I* (London, 1958), pp. 267–268, 279; L. Stone, 'The Fruits of Office: The Case of Robert Cecil, First Earl of Salisbury, 1596–1612', in F. J. Fisher, ed., *Essays in the Economic and Social History of Tudor and Stuart England* (Cambridge, 1961), pp. 89–117.

133. Williams, *Tudor Regime*, p. 103.

134. Ibid., p. 106.

135. Although several studies of particular ministers and courtiers have made attempts at assessing their wealth, a breakdown of how the sums were accumulated is often lacking. The most detailed studies for the period include Slavin, *Politics and Profit*, pp. 158–211; G. W. Bernard, 'The Rise of Sir William Compton, Early Tudor Courtier', *English Historical Review*, xcvi (1981), pp. 754–777; S. Doran, 'The Finances of an Elizabethan Nobleman and Royal Servant: A Case Study of Thomas Radcliffe, Third Earl of Sussex', *Historical Review*, 61 (1988), pp. 286–300.

136. TNA, PRO, E36/140 fos 29r–62v. A similar list of Cromwell's annuities is to be found in *Letters and Papers*, but the uncalendared version offers a more complete account. Those recorded on the calendared list appear on it, along with several others. See and compare TNA, PRO, E36/143 fos 29r–34v (*LP* V, 1285 [vi]).

137. TNA, PRO, E36/140 fo. 29r.

138. TNA, PRO, E36/140 fo. 36v.

139. Pollard, *Wolsey*, p. 321.

140. Bernard, 'Rise of Sir William Compton', p. 772.

141. Ibid., p. 774 n. 4.

142. Slavin, *Politics and Profit*, pp. 173–175.

143. *LP* XIV, ii, 792.

144. Elton, 'How Corrupt was Thomas Cromwell?', p. 908. Although in this article Elton mistakenly cited Avery's account book as being *LP* XIV, ii, 758; it is actually *LP* XIV, ii, 792.

145. H. E. Bell, *An Introduction to the History and Records of the Court of Wards and Liveries* (Cambridge, 1953), pp. 1–16.

146. TNA, PRO, SP1/70 fo. 164 (*LP* V, 1178); SP1/74 fo. 56 (*LP* VI, 60).

147. TNA, PRO, SP2/O fo. 34 (*LP* VI, 841).

148. TNA, PRO, SP1/78 fo. 20 (Merriman, *Life and Letters of Thomas Cromwell*, i. 359; *LP* VI, 872).

149. TNA, PRO, SP2/O fos 119–131 (*LP* VI, 1625 [5]).

150. *Cf.* Robertson, 'Profit and Purpose', p. 322.

151. TNA, PRO, SP2/M fos 46–52 (*LP* V, 1339). These were leased from the monastery of St Bartholomew's, West Smithfield, to which Cromwell paid £26 8s 4d yearly. Robertson mistakenly believed that Cromwell acquired these properties before 1529, because they are mentioned in his will from that year. In fact, the inclusion of Canonbury and Cutlers (as well as Rompney) was made to the will when Cromwell amended it sometime after September 1532.

152. TNA, PRO, SP2/M fos 47–38 (*LP* V, 1339). For a history of the manor, see W. Thornbury, *Old and New London* (6 vols, London, 1828–1876), ii. 269–273.

153. E. A. Webb, *The Records of St. Bartholomew's Priory, West Smithfield* (2 vols, London, 1921), i. 343.

154. TNA, PRO, SP1/78 fo. 52 (*LP* VI, 919); SP1/84 fo. 156 (*LP* VII, 813); SP2/5 fo. 127 (*LP* VII, 1182); SP1/84 fo. 141 (Merriman, *Life and Letters of Thomas Cromwell*, i. 384; *LP* VII, 790); SP1/85 fo. 143 (Merriman, *Life and Letters of Thomas Cromwell*, i. 387–388; *LP* VII, 1134); SP1/85 fo. 172 (Merriman, *Life and Letters of Thomas Cromwell*, i. 388; *LP* VII, 1179).

155. TNA, PRO, SP2/N fo. 115 (*LP* VI, 263). One of Cromwell's accounts records a slightly larger amount of £72 paid to the same workmen for the same period.

156. TNA, PRO, SP1/81 fo. 136 (*LP* VI, 1687).

157. TNA, PRO, SP1/78 fo. 215 (*LP* VI, 1056 [2]); SP1/79 fo. 40 (*LP* VI, 1108); SP1/80 fos 21–21v (*LP* VI, 1337); SP1/74 fo. 86 (*LP* VI, 93). This final letter is dated January

and was placed in 1533 in *Letters and Papers*. It would make more sense to place it in 1534, following on from Cromwell's requests in September 1533.

158. TNA, PRO, SP1/80 fo. 10 (*LP* VI, 1329); SP1/80 fo. 15v (*LP* VI, 1333); *LP* VI, 1128; SP 3/2 fo. 163 (Merriman, *Life and Letters of Thomas Cromwell*, i. 365; *LP* VI, 1141); SP1/83 fo. 180 (*LP* VII, 593); SP1/238 fo. 155 (*LP* Add. I, i, 879). See also Elton, *Reform and Renewal*, p. 27 n. 63.

159. Robertson, 'Profit and Purpose', p. 324.

160. TNA, PRO, SP1/71 fo. 6 (*LP* V, 1274 [6]); TNA, PRO, C82/660 and C66/660 m. 25 (*LP* V, 1370 [3/i]), C66/662 mm. 44–47 (*LP* V, 1499 [23/i]). See and compare with Robertson, 'Profit and Purpose', p. 322.

161. TNA, PRO, SP1/75 fo. 32 (*LP* VI, 251), incorrectly placed in 1533 in *Letters and Papers*: it is of 1531. Compare with Robertson, 'Profit and Purpose', p. 322.

162. TNA, PRO, SP1/88 fo. 21 (*LP* VII, 1610).

163. H. Miller, 'Subsidy Assessments of the Peerage in the Sixteenth Century', *Bulletin of the Institute of Historical Research*, 28 (1955), p. 18.

164. *The Lay Subsidy Rolls for the County of Sussex, 1524–1525* ed. J. Cornwall, Sussex Record Society, 56 (1956), pp. 8, 12, 26, 146, cited in Robertson, 'Profit and Purpose', p. 324.

165. For a more detailed treatment of Cromwell's later acquisitions, see Robertson, 'Profit and Purpose', pp. 324–329.

166. *LP* XII, ii, 1008 [3].

167. *LP* XII, ii, 1101; *LP* XIII, i, 384 [74].

168. Robertson, 'Profit and Purpose', pp. 324–329.

169. *LP* XV, 611 [8, 37]; Robertson, 'Profit and Purpose', p. 328.

170. Robertson, 'Profit and Purpose', pp. 332–337.

171. *LP* XII, i, 1101, 1191, 1030, 1154, 1311 [30].

172. *LP* XII, i, 216, 252.

173. Robertson, 'Profit and Purpose', p. 330.

174. TNA, PRO, SP1/69 fo. 69 (*LP* V, 743); SP1/70 fo. 86 (*LP* V, 1066); SP1/74 fo. 157 (*LP* VI, 158).

175. Stow, *Survey of London*, ii. 179.

176. E. Hasted, *The History and Topographical Survey of the County of Kent* (12 vols, Canterbury, 1797), xii. 461 n. 51.

177. *CSP, Spanish*, IV, ii, 1107; *LP* VI, 975; TNA, PRO, SP1/77 fo. 149v (*LP* VI, 762).

178. TNA, PRO, SP1/71 fo. 9 (*LP* V, 1281); SP1/76 fo. 111 (*LP* VI, 547); SP1/78 fo. 79 (*LP* VI, 938); SP1/78 fo. 125 (*LP* VI, 989).

179. TNA, PRO, SP1/77 fo. 111 (*LP* VI, 741); SP1/42 fos 108v, 110 (*LP* IV, ii, 3197); SP1/58 fo. 147 (*LP* IV, iii, 6744).

180. TNA, PRO, SP1/57 fo. 145 (*LP* IV, iii, 6429). Florence Voluzence also sent Cromwell a 'treaty of hystoire'; TNA, PRO, SP1/237 fo. 24 (*LP* Add. I, i, 731).

181. TNA, PRO, SP1/68 fo. 85 (*LP* V, 585).

182. Merriman, *Life and Letters of Thomas Cromwell*, i. 314 (*LP* IV, iii, App. 57); the document is not to be found in TNA.

183. *LP* XIV, ii, 782.

184. G. W. Bernard, 'The Fall of Anne Boleyn', *English Historical Review*, cvi (1991), p. 598; G. W. Bernard, *Anne Boleyn: Fatal Attractions* (London, 2010), pp. 155–156.

185. TNA, PRO, SP1/129 fo. 174 (*LP* XIII, i, 450).

186. TNA, PRO, SP1/121 fo. 55 (*LP* XII, ii, 35).

187. BL, Additional Manuscript 20706 fo. 22v.

188. TNA, PRO, SP1/24 fo. 73 (*LP* XII, ii, 549).

189. The National Portrait Gallery, London, 6310, 6311.

190. A. W. Franks and H. A. Grueber, eds, *Medallic Illustrations of the History of Great Britain and Ireland* (19 vols, London, 1904), i, plate II, no. 10; E. Hawkins, A. W. Franks and H. A. Grueber, eds, *Medallic Illustrations of the History of Great Britain and Ireland to the Death of George II* (2 vols, London, 1885), i. 39–40.

191. A good copy, probably dating to the early seventeenth century, can be found in the National Portrait Gallery, London. See NPG 1727

192. TNA, PRO, SP1/71 fo. 9 (*LP* V, 1281).

193. *CSP, Spanish*, IV, ii, 1107.

194. *CSP, Spanish*, V, i, 228.

195. Foxe, *Acts and Monuments* (1570 edn), pp. 1395–1397; *Novels of Matteo Bandello*, pp. 110–116.

196. *LP* XIV, i, 200 (p. 82); *LP* XVI, 404.

197. *In Defence of the Unity of the Church* was first published in 1539 against Pole's wishes. The *Apologia Reginaldi Poli ad Carolum V. Caesarem super quatuor Libris a se Scriptis de Unitate Ecclesice*, which is its first preface, and contains the account of Pole's meeting with Cromwell, was not published until much later. Although it was written in 1539, it was originally a polemical letter sent to Charles V to persuade him to launch a crusade against England. See Van Dyke, 'Reginald Pole and Thomas Cromwell', pp. 696–724.

198. T. F. Mayer, *Reginald Pole: Prince and Prophet* (Cambridge, 2000), p. 97; *LP* XIV, i, 200 (esp. p. 82); Van Dyke, 'Reginald Pole and Thomas Cromwell', pp. 707–708.

199. Merriman, *Life and Letters of Thomas Cromwell*, i, 85; see also pp. 86–87.

200. Innes, *Ten Tudor Statesmen*, p. 123. See also P. Hughes, *The Reformation in England* (fifth edn, London, 1962), p. 225; Wilding, *Thomas Cromwell*, pp. 62–66.

201. Van Dyke, 'Reginald Pole and Thomas Cromwell', p. 709.

202. Ibid., pp. 712–713.

203. TNA, PRO, SP1/57 fo. 75 (*LP* IV, iii, 6346); SP1/143 fos 74–74v (*LP* XIV, i, 285).

204. Bernard, *Anne Boleyn*, p. 195.

205. Merriman, *Life and Letters of Thomas Cromwell*, i. 314 (*LP* IV, iii, App. 57). The document is not to be found in TNA.

206. T. M. Parker, 'Was Thomas Cromwell a Machiavellian?', *Journal of Ecclesiastical History*, 1 (1950), pp. 63–75.

207. Elton, 'Political Creed of Thomas Cromwell', in Elton, *Studies*, ii. 215–235.

208. Ibid., 227–230; Elton, *Reform and Renewal*, p. 65; Williams, *Cardinal and the Secretary*, p. 173; Beckingsale, *Thomas Cromwell*, p. 7.

209. TNA, PRO, SP1/83 fo. 52 (*LP* VII, 423); SP1/83 fo. 51 (*LP* VII, 422); Underwood, 'Thomas Cromwell and William Marshall', pp. 517–539; See pp. 130–131.

210. TNA, PRO, E36/143 fo. 55 (*LP* VI, 1371); BL, Cotton MS, Titus B I fo. 422 (*LP* VII, 52); BL, Cotton MS, Titus B I fo. 428v (*LP* VII, 48 [2]).

211. Bernard, 'Elton's Cromwell', in Bernard, *Power and Politics*, p. 119.

212. I owe this formulation to Dr Paul Cavill, and I am grateful to him for discussing these matters with me.

213. J. Watts, *Henry VI and the Politics of Kingship* (Cambridge, 1996), pp. 13–51.

214. Elton, *Tudor Revolution in Government*, pp. 3–9.

215. Loades, *Thomas Cromwell*, pp. 241, 265.

216. Starkey, *Reign of Henry VIII*, pp. 103–105.

217. Gywn, *King's Cardinal*, pp. 6–16.

218. Cavendish, *Life and Death of Cardinal Wolsey*, pp. 13–14.

219. Scarisbrick, *Henry VIII*, p. 41.

220. For the only account of this war, see Hoyle, 'Anglo-Scottish War', pp. 23–29.

221. TNA, PRO, SP1/72 fo. 165 (*LP* V, 1670); SP2/O fo. 20 (*LP* VI, 664).

222. TNA, PRO, E101/421/5 (*LP* V, 1671).

223. TNA, PRO, SP1/72 fo. 149 (*LP* V, 1655). The difficulty in calculating the speed of royal posts in late medieval and early modern England is a familiar one. Travel times, where they are calculable, appear to have varied depending on the efficiency of the system in operation, distance covered, weather conditions and the importance of the news itself. See C. A. J. Armstrong, 'Some Examples of the Distribution and Speed of News in England at the Time of the Wars of the Roses', in R. W. Hunt, W. A. Pantin and R. W. Southern, eds, *Studies in Medieval History Presented to Fredrick Maurice Powicke* (Oxford, 1948), pp. 445 and 439; M. Brayshay, P. Harrison and B. Chalkley, 'Knowledge, Nationhood and Governance: The Speed of the Royal Post in

Early-Modern England', *Journal of Historical Geography*, 24 (1998), p. 281. For the Anglo-Scottish conflict of 1532–1533, however, several letters concerning the war indicate when they were written and received, and it is from these that the above average figure has been calculated.See TNA, PRO, SP1/237 fo. 266 (*LP* Add. I, i, 801); SP1/72 fo. 165 (*LP* V, 1670); SP1/74 fo. 16 (*LP* VI, 25); SP1/74 fo. 45 (*LP* VI, 51); SP1/74 fo. 127 (*LP* VI, 117); SP1/74 fo. 194 (*LP* VI, 199); SP1/74 fo. 211 (*LP* VI, 217).

224. TNA, PRO, SP1/74 fos 121–122 (*LP* VI, 107).
225. TNA, PRO, E101/421/9 (*LP* VI, 130).
226. TNA, PRO, SP1/74 fos 121–121v (*LP* VI, 107).
227. TNA, PRO, SP1/74 fo. 173 (*LP* VI, 174).
228. C. S. L. Davies, 'Provisions for Armies, 1509–50: A Study in the Effectiveness of Early Tudor Government', *Economic History Review*, Second Series, 17 (1964), pp. 243–248.
229. *CSP, Spanish*, IV, ii, 1061.

Chapter Seven The Break with Rome

1. *LP* XIV, i, 200 (p. 82); Van Dyke, 'Reginald Pole and Thomas Cromwell', p. 706; Foxe, *Acts and Monuments* (1570 edn), p. 1387.
2. Merriman, *Life and Letters of Thomas Cromwell*, i. 89–92.
3. Elton, *England under the Tudors*, p. 122.
4. Elton, 'King or Minister', in Elton, *Studies*, i. 177, 186.
5. Elton, *Tudor Revolution in Government*, pp. 89–90, 97.
6. Elton, *England under the Tudors*, pp. 128, 129; Elton, *Reform and Reformation*, pp. 152–156; Elton, *Thomas Cromwell*, p. 11.
7. Nicholson, 'Act of Appeals and the English Reformation', pp. 19–31; Guy, 'Thomas Cromwell and the Intellectual Origins', pp. 151–178; Bernard, 'Pardon of the Clergy Reconsidered', pp. 262–275; Bernard, *King's Reformation*, pp. 30–68.
8. Haigh, *English Reformations*, pp. 111–116; Guy, *Public Career*, pp. 130–138 and 175–201; Guy, *Tudor England*, pp. 124–134; Brigden, *New Worlds*, pp. 117–118; Leithead, 'Cromwell, Thomas (*c*.1485–1540)', *ODNB*; Hutchinson, *Thomas Cromwell*, pp. 47–70; Schofield, *Rise and Fall*, pp. 45–57; Loades, *Thomas Cromwell*, pp. 57–84; Borman, *Thomas Cromwell*, pp. 123–171.
9. John Guy, for instance, initially followed Elton's interpretation that the change in royal policy regarding the praemunire attack on the Church in 1530–1531 was Cromwell's doing, before later changing his mind. See Guy, *Public Career*, pp. 136–138; Guy, 'Henry VIII and the *Praemunire* Manoeuvres', pp. 481–503. Similarly, Elton himself, although resolute in his belief that Cromwell conceived the idea of schism, was forced to modify drastically his chronology of Cromwell's strategy, in order to suit the findings of one of his own research students (Graham Nicholson). In his later writings, Elton presented Cromwell as providing the solution to the king's 'great matter' as early as 1530. See Elton, *Reform and Reformation*, pp. 136–138.
10. Elton, 'King or Minister?', in Elton, *Studies*, i. 184.
11. Haigh, *English Reformations*, p. 105; Guy, 'Henry VIII and the *Praemunire* Manoeuvres', p. 494.
12. Elton, 'King or Minister?', in Elton, *Studies*, i. 173–230.
13. Nicholson, 'Act of Appeals and the English Reformation', pp. 19–31; Guy, 'Thomas Cromwell and the Intellectual Origins', pp. 151–178.
14. D. Hoak, 'The Iconography of the Crown Imperial', in D. Hoak, ed., *Tudor Political Culture* (Cambridge, 1995), pp. 54–104; R. Koebner, 'The Imperial Crown of this Realm: Henry VIII, Constantine the Great, and Polydore Vergil', *Bulletin of the Institute of Historical Research*, 26 (1953), pp. 29–52.
15. P. Grierson, 'The Origins of the English Sovereign and the Symbolism of the Closed Crown', *British Numismatic Journal*, 33 (1964), p. 127.
16. *LP* I, ii, 1661, 2305; *LP* I, iii, 2686, 2842.
17. TNA, PRO, SP1/36 fo. 224 (*LP* IV, i, 1859).

18. BL, Cotton MS, Galba B V fo. 82v (*LP* II, ii, 2911).
19. W. Ullmann, 'This Realm of England is an Empire', *Journal of Ecclesiastical History*, 30 (1979), pp. 175–203.
20. *Miscellaneous Writings of Henry the Eighth, King of England, France and Ireland*, ed. F. Macnamara (London, 1924), pp. 48–49. It is interesting to note, however, that 'Henry's own pronouncements on the papacy [in the *Assertio*] were not nearly as sweeping as they have usually been said to be. If we recall that Henry wrote his book to win a title from the pope, we may be prepared for some regal syrup to be sloshed on the pope's head'. See R. C. Marius, 'Henry VIII, Thomas More, and the Bishop of Rome', in M. J. Moore, ed., *Quincentennial Essays on St Thomas More* (Boone, NC, 1978), pp. 95–96.
21. Roper, *Lyfe of Sir Thomas Moore*, p. 68.
22. J. Canning, *A History of Medieval Political Thought, 300–1450* (London, 1996), pp. 91–96.
23. Elton, *England under the Tudors*, p. 171.
24. *Statutes of the Realm*, iii. 24 Henry VIII c. 12; my italics for emphasis.
25. Elton, 'Evolution of a Reformation Statute', p. 183.
26. *Statutes of the Realm*, iii. 26 Henry VIII c. 1.
27. Cited in M. Bloch, *The Royal Touch: Sacred Monarchy and Scrofula in England and France* (London, 1973), p. 22.
28. L. W. Legg, ed., *English Coronation Records* (London, 1901), p. 240. Henry VIII substantially revised the coronation oath, which had been unchanged since the reign of Edward II, by stipulating that the monarch should maintain the rights and liberties of the Church 'nott preiudyciall to hys Jurysdiccion and dignite royall'. See Legg, *Coronation Records*, p. 240. Walter Ullmann believed that Henry made this alteration before his own coronation in 1509. But the 1530s seem a much more likely date for this amendment. See Ullmann, 'Realm of England', p. 183; P. Tudor-Craig, 'Henry VIII and King David', in D. Williams, ed., *Early Tudor England: Proceedings of the 1987 Harlaxton Symposium* (Woodbridge, 1989), p. 187.
29. A. Hudson, *The Premature Reformation: Wycliffite Texts and Lollard History* (Oxford, 1988), pp. 328–340.
30. Edmund Dudley, *The Tree of Commonwealth*, ed. D. M. Brodie (Cambridge, 1988), p. 32–33.
31. Gwyn, *King's Cardinal*, p. 44.
32. Dudley, *Tree of Commonwealth*, p. 41; Gunn, 'Edmund Dudley and the Church', pp. 509–526, esp. p. 514.
33. Baker, *Reports of John Spelman*, ii. 66–68; Gunn, *Early Tudor Government*, p. 16; P. Cavill, '"The Enemy of God and His Church": James Hobart, Praemunire and the Clergy of Norwich Diocese', *Journal of Legal History*, 32 (2011), pp. 127–150.
34. R. Houlbrooke, 'The Decline of Ecclesiastical Jurisdiction under the Tudors', in R. O'Day and F. Heal, eds, *Continuity and Change: Personnel and Administration of the Church in England, 1500–1642* (Leicester, 1976), pp. 239–259.
35. *Statutes of the Realm*, iii. 4 Henry VIII c. 2. But this act only lasted until the next parliament in 1515, when – after much controversy – it was not renewed. See P. R. Cavill, 'A Perspective on the Church–State Confrontation of 1515: The Passage of 4 Henry VIII, c. 2', *Journal of Ecclesiastical History*, 63 (2012), pp. 655–670.
36. We do not possess Henry's exact words. A summary of what was said can be found in J. H. Baker, ed., *Reports of Cases by John Caryll* (2 vols, London, 2000), ii. 691. The best detailed discussion of the conferences held at Blackfriars and Baynard's Castle, where Henry made these remarks, is Gwyn, *King's Cardinal*, pp. 46–50.
37. T. F. Mayer, 'On the Road to 1534: The Occupation of Tournai and Henry VIII's Theory of Sovereignty', in D. Hoak, ed., *Tudor Political Culture* (Cambridge, 1995), pp. 13, 21; Gywn, *King's Cardinal*, p. 50.
38. R. Rex, 'The Religion of Henry VIII', *Historical Journal*, 57 (2014), p. 28.
39. Baker, *Reports of Cases by John Caryll*, pp. 690, 691.
40. Swanson, *Church and Society*, pp. 142–144; Bernard, *Late Medieval Church*, pp. 37–40; I. D. Thornley, 'The Destruction of Sanctuary', in R. W. Seton-Watson, ed., *Tudor Studies* (London, 1924), pp. 182–208.

41. Hudson, *Star Chamber Extracts*, fos 44v–45, cited in Baker, *Reports of John Spelman*, ii. 343.
42. Baker, *Laws of England*, vi. 547–550.
43. Rex, 'Religion of Henry VIII', p. 29.
44. *LP* I, i, 2310.
45. Henry VIII, *Assertio septem sacramentorum*, ed. Fraenkel, pp. 128, 130, cited and translated in Rex, 'Religion of Henry VIII', p. 29.
46. *LP* II, i, 780; my italics for emphasis.
47. *CSP, Venetian*, II, 633.
48. *LP* III, i, 791.
49. There has been a good deal of discussion about Tournai. See Mayer, 'On the Road to 1534', pp. 11–30; T. F. Mayer, 'Tournai and Tyranny: Imperial Kingship and Critical Humanism', *Historical Journal*, 34 (1994), pp. 257–277; C. S. L. Davies, 'Tournai and the English Crown, 1513–1519', *Historical Journal*, 41 (1998), pp. 1–26; G. W. Bernard, 'The Piety of Henry VIII' in N. S. Amos, A. Pettegree and H. Van Nierop, eds, *The Education of a Christian Society: Humanism and the Reformation in Britain and the Netherlands* (Aldershot, 1999), pp. 63–65; Bernard, *Late Medieval Church*, pp. 41–43; Rex, 'Religion of Henry VIII', p. 27.
50. Henry's letter survives in three forms: TNA, PRO, SP1/14 fos 255–258; BL, Harleian MS, 297 fos 69–73; BL, Cotton MS, Vitellius B III fos 107v–108v. It is summarised poorly in *LP* II, i, 2871.
51. Davies, 'Tournai and the English Crown', p. 259; Bernard, *Late Medieval Church*, pp. 42–43; Rex, 'Religion of Henry VIII', p. 27.
52. TNA, PRO, SP1/14 fo. 256–257 (*LP* II, i, 2871).
53. *LP* IV, ii, 3913, 4897.
54. Bernard, 'Piety of Henry VIII', p. 64.
55. BL, Harleian MS, 297 fo. 72v.
56. *LP* II, ii, 2895; BL, Cotton MS, Vitellius B III fo. 130 (*LP* II, ii, 2886).
57. Bernard, *Late Medieval Church*, p. 43.
58. *Cf.* ibid.
59. For a fuller discussion of Henry's earliest threats of independent action, see Bernard, *King's Reformation*, pp. 30ff.
60. *LP* IV, ii, 3644.
61. TNA, PRO, SP1/47 fo. 182 (*LP* IV, ii, 4167).
62. *LP* IV, iii, 5210.
63. Haigh, *English Reformations*, p. 102.
64. BL, Cotton MS, Vitellius B XI fo. 169v (*LP* IV, iii, 5703).
65. *LP* IV, ii, 4980.
66. V. Murphy, 'The Literature and Propaganda of Henry VIII's First Divorce', in D. MacCulloch, ed., *The Reign of Henry VIII: Politics, Policy and Piety* (Basingstoke, 1995), pp. 146–154, esp. pp. 150–151.
67. Bernard, *King's Reformation*, pp. 36ff.
68. *Statutes of the Realm*, iii. 21 Henry VIII c. 13.
69. Hughes and Larkin, eds, *Tudor Royal Proclamations*, i. 197–198.
70. *CSP, Spanish*, III, ii, 160.
71. *LP* IV, iii, 6307.
72. *CSP, Spanish*, IV, i, 460.
73. Elton, *Reform and Reformation*, p. 132.
74. Guy, *Tudor England*, p. 117.
75. *CSP*, Spanish, IV, i, 290.
76. *LP* VI, 142.
77. *Cf.* Bernard, *King's Reformation*, p. 52–53.
78. Haigh, *English Reformations*, p. 101.
79. For a detailed narrative and analysis of these events, see J. Scarisbrick, 'The Pardon of the Clergy, 1531', *Historical Journal*, 12 (1956), pp. 22–39; Scarisbrick, *Henry VIII*, pp. 273–276; Guy, 'Henry VIII and the *Praemunire* Manoeuvres', pp. 481–503; Bernard, 'Pardon of the Clergy Reconsidered', pp. 258–287.

80. For these interpretations, see and compare Guy, 'Henry VIII and the *Praemunire* Manoeuvres', p. 491, and Bernard, 'Pardon of the Clergy Reconsidered', pp. 258–287.

81. The best account of these events is Guy, 'Henry VIII and the *Praemunire* Manoeuvres', pp. 481–503, although I do not agree with his analysis of what lay behind them.

82. Guy, 'Henry VIII and the *Praemunire* Manoeuvres', pp. 489–490; *cf.* Scarisbrick, 'Pardon of the Clergy', pp. 27–28.

83. TNA, PRO, E135/8/36; *Statutes of the Realm*, iii. 22 Henry VIII c. 15. See also TNA, PRO, SP1/56 fos 57–84v (*LP* IV, iii, 6047 [3]), incorrectly placed in 1529 in *Letters and Papers*.

84. Elton, *Reform and Reformation*, pp. 140–144. See also the earlier comments in Hughes, *Reformation in England*, p. 227, who similarly believed that Cromwell was behind the plan.

85. BL, Cotton MS, Appendix L fo. 81 (Merriman, *Life and Letters of Thomas Cromwell*, i. 334; *LP* IV, iii, 6699).

86. Guy has argued that the change occurred after January 1531. See Guy, 'Henry VIII and the *Praemunire* Manoeuvres', pp. 488–492. It should be noted that this argument hinges on the reliability of Edward Hall as an eyewitness to these events. For Hall's comments, see Hall, *Chronicle*, p. 774.

87. In contrast to Guy, Scarisbrick believed that the change must have come in late 1530, and cited Cromwell's comments as evidence for this. See Scarisbrick, 'Pardon of the Clergy', pp. 27–28. He appears to contradict himself somewhat, however, with his remarks on p. 29.

88. Guy, 'Henry VIII and the *Praemunire* Manoeuvres', p. 502.

89. Scarisbrick, 'Pardon of the Clergy', p. 29.

90. *Cf.* Gwyn, *King's Cardinal*, p. 630.

91. For these events, see M. Kelly, 'The Submission of the Clergy', *Transactions of the Royal Historical Society*, Fifth Series, 15 (1965), pp. 97–121.

92. Oxford, Christ Church Library, MS 306 fos 33–36; D. Wilkins, *Concilia Magnae Britanniae et Hiberniae* (4 vols, London, 1737) iii. 725.

93. Oxford, Christ Church Library, MS 306 fo. 34.

94. Elton, *Reform and Reformation*, pp. 143–144.

95. Oxford, Christ Church Library, MS 306 fos 34–36; Wilkins, *Concilia*, iii. 725; Scarisbrick, 'Pardon of the Clergy', p. 33.

96. F. Atterbury, *The Rights, Powers, and Privileges of an English Convocation* (London, 1701), pp. 82–83.

97. Lehmberg, *Reformation Parliament*, p. 114. John Fisher, bishop of Rochester, is the generally accepted figure, as Lehmberg acknowledged.

98. Scarisbrick, 'Pardon of the Clergy', p. 29; Kelly, 'Submission of the Clergy', p. 119 n. 1. The York convocation had agreed to follow its southern counterpart and granted the king a subsidy of £ 18,840 on 4 May 1531. See A. G. Dickens, 'The Northern Convocation and Henry VIII', *Church History Quarterly*, cxxvii (1938), p. 86; *Statutes of the Realm*, iii. 23 Henry VIII c. 19.

99. 'We recall the decisive appearance of Cromwell in Convocation. We conclude that we know who stood behind the policy of subduing the clergy by forcing them to buy a pardon and make sweeping concessions. Cromwell really proved the point in May when he managed the parallel surrender of the northern Convocation'. Elton, *Reform and Reformation*, pp. 143–144.

100. TNA, PRO, SP1/65 fo. 239 (*LP* V, 224). For its redating, see and compare it with Rowland Lee's letter to Cromwell; TNA, PRO, SP1/75 fo. 179 (*LP* VI, 398). Evidently, the editors of *Letters and Papers* realised their mistake because it was later placed in its proper chronological position, in *LP* VI, 431. Nevertheless, it was cited incorrectly by Scarisbrick ('Pardon of the Clergy', p. 29 n. 35); and by Kelly ('Submission of the Clergy', p. 119 n. 1). Kelly also cited *LP* V, 225 alongside this letter. This was correctly dated to 1531, but does not refer to Cromwell, being a summary of the meeting of the northern convocation.

101. TNA, PRO, SP1/65 fo. 244 (*LP* V, 327).

102. TNA, PRO, SP1/66 fos 13–17 (*LP* V, 264).

103. TNA, PRO, SP1/237 fo. 25 (*LP* Add. I, i, 732).

104. BL, Cotton MS, Titus B I fos 483–484 (*State Papers*, i. 380; *LP* V, 394).

105. See above pp. 106–107. For examples of Cromwell dealing with problems associated with the collection of this fine from 1532 onwards, see also TNA, PRO, SP1/69 fo. 143 (*LP* V, 849); SP1/72 fo. 8 (*LP* V, 1506); SP1/178 fo. 100 (*LP* VI, 960).

106. Hall, *Chronicle*, p. 785; *Statutes of the Realm*, iii. 23 Henry VIII c. 20.

107. J. J. Scarisbrick, 'Clerical Taxation in England, 1485 to 1547', *Journal of Ecclesiastical History*, 11 (1960), pp. 44–49; Elton, *Reform and Reformation*, pp. 148–149.

108. BL, Cotton MS, Cleopatra E VI fos 274–275 (Wilkins, *Concilia*, iii. 760–761; *LP* V, 721 [5]).

109. *CSP, Spanish*, IV, i, 224.

110. TNA, PRO, E175/7 fos 1–12 (*LP* VI, 721 [6]). Cromwell's corrections, which are not noted in *Letters and Papers* or by Elton, can be found on fos 11 and 12.

111. BL, Harley MS 6849 fos 60–61; G. R. Elton, 'A Note on the First Act of Annates', *Bulletin of the Institute of Historical Research*, 23 (1950), pp. 203–204.

112. TNA, PRO, SP1/69 fo. 40v (Merriman, *Life and Letters of Thomas Cromwell*, i. 343; *LP* V, 723).

113. *CSP, Spanish*, IV, ii, 907, 922, 926.

114. Ibid., 926.

115. Hall, *Chronicle*, p. 784.

116. TNA, PRO, SP1/69 fo. 121 (*State Papers*, vii. 349; *LP* V, 831).

117. *CSP, Spanish*, IV, ii, 907. Bernard has noted that the original manuscript housed in Vienna is slightly different to the summary given above, and reads, 'nothing had been settled in their Parliament'. See Bernard, *King's Reformation*, p. 61. See also similar remarks about little occurring in parliament in *CSP, Spanish*, IV, ii, 899.

118. G. R. Elton, 'The Commons' Supplication of 1532: Parliamentary Manoeuvres in the Reign of Henry VIII', *English Historical Review*, lxvi (1951), pp. 507–534; reprinted in Elton, *Studies*, ii. 107–137. For Elton's later comments on these events, see also *Reform and Reformation*, pp. 150–156.

119. *CSP, Spanish*, IV, ii, 922.

120. These are all in TNA, PRO: A = SP2/L fos 181–182 (*LP* V, 1016 [3]); B = SP1/56 fos 39–42 (*LP* IV, iii, 6043 [7]); C_1 = SP6/7 fos 93–101 (*LP* V, 1016 [4]); C_2 = SP6/7 fos 102v–105 (*LP* V, 1016 [4]); D = SP2/L fos 171–180 (*LP* V, 1016 [2]); E = SP6/1 fos 86–95 (*LP* V, 1016 [1]).

121. Elton, 'Commons' Supplication', p. 520.

122. Ibid., pp. 511 and 520.

123. Ibid., pp. 521 and 523.

124. J. P. Cooper, 'The Supplication against the Ordinaries Reconsidered', *English Historical Review*, lxxii (1957), pp. 621 and 629. Certainly, the reference in C_1 to Henry as 'the onely hed souereigne lorde protectour' (TNA, PRO, SP6/7 fo. 100v; *LP* V, 1016 [4]) makes it highly unlikely that this was composed before 1531 when the king had extracted the title 'supreme head'. Elton argued that A was of 1529 because of its reference to an act 'lately devised' limiting the number of proctors in the Court of Arches to ten. See TNA, PRO, SP2/L fo. 181 (*LP* V, 1016 [3]). An ordinance to this effect was made by Archbishop Warham in March 1528, and Elton thought the phrase 'lately devised' made more sense if it had been written in 1529 rather than 1532 (Elton, 'Commons' Supplication', p. 518). Although this would seem a reasonable conclusion, C_1 and D, both of which were drawn up in 1532, also refer to Warham's ordinance devised 'now of late'. See TNA, PRO, SP6/7 fo. 94v (*LP* V, 1016 [4]); SP2/L fo. 75 (*LP* V, 1016 [2]).

125. TNA, PRO, SP1/56 fos 39–42 (*LP* IV, iii, 6043 [7]); Hall, *Chronicle*, p. 766.

126. TNA, PRO, SP6/7 fos 102v–105 (*LP* V, 1016 [4]). It is printed in Merriman, *Life and Letters of Thomas Cromwell*, i. 109–111.

127. *Statutes of the Realm*, iii. 21 Henry VIII c. 4 and 21 Henry VIII c. 5.

128. Haigh, *English Reformations*, pp. 111–115; Redworth, *In Defence of the Church Catholic*, p. 35; Ives, *Life and Death of Anne Boleyn*, p. 153. So too did Beckingsale, *Thomas Cromwell*, pp. 33–36 and Williams, *Cardinal and the Secretary*, pp. 11–115.

129. Guy, *Public Career*, pp. 175–201.
130. Hall, *Chronicle*, p. 784; my italics for emphasis.
131. TNA, PRO, SP2/L fos 171–180 (*LP* V, 1016 [2]); Hall, *Chronicle*, p. 784.
132. Bernard, *King's Reformation*, p. 60.
133. TNA, PRO, SP1/56 fo. 39v (*LP* IV, iii, 6043 [7]); italics signify additions in Cromwell's hand.
134. TNA, PRO, SP2/L fo. 181 (*LP* V, 1016 [3]).
135. Ibid.
136. Bernard, *King's Reformation*, pp. 60–61; Kelly, 'Submission of the Clergy', p. 105. The Supplication in its final form is: TNA, PRO, SP6/1 fos 85–95 (*LP* V, 1016 [1]). It is printed in A. Ogle, *The Tragedy of the Lollards' Tower: Its Place in History, 1514–1533* (Oxford, 1949), pp. 324–330.
137. Hall, *Chronicle*, pp. 784–785.
138. Ives, 'Genesis of the Statute of Uses', pp. 676–697.
139. Bernard, *King's Reformation*, p. 62.
140. Hall, *Chronicle*, pp. 784–785.
141. Ibid., p. 788.
142. Wilkins, *Concilia*, iii. 750–752.
143. TNA, PRO, SP6/9 fos 104–104v (*LP* VI, 276 [2]).
144. Hall, *Chronicle*, p. 788.
145. *CSP, Venetian*, IV, 761.
146. Foxe, *Acts and Monuments* (1570 edn), p. 1387.
147. TNA, PRO, E36/143 fos 28, 35 (*LP* VI, 299).
148. Hall, *Chronicle*, p. 788.
149. TNA, PRO, SP2/L fos 72–74 (*LP* V, 721 [1]). This draft also contains additions by Audeley, see TNA, PRO, SP2/P fos 10–12 (*LP* VII, 57 [2]), which was misdated in *Letters and Papers:* it is of 1532. Also note the similarity in passages of these drafts with the wording of the famous preamble to the appeals act: 'the said prelatis rulers and mynistres and other spirituall subiecttes to gethers with the nobelles nobylyte and lay comens of this realme ... make and contayne but one body poletik lyving vnder the alegyauns obediens tuycion and defens of the kinges Roiall maiestie being ther only supreme Emperiall hede and souerayn ...'. See TNA, PRO, SP2/P fo. 10 (*LP* VII, 57 [2]).
150. TNA, PRO, SP2/P fo. 12 (*LP* VII, 57 [2]); SP2/L fo. 74 (*LP* V, 721 [1]).
151. Kelly, 'Submission of the Clergy', p. 113, esp. n. 3.
152. TNA, PRO, SP1/70 fos 29–31v (*LP* V, 1023).
153. Elton, 'Commons' Supplication', p. 533.
154. Guy, *Public Career*, pp. 201–202.
155. Ibid.
156. *Letters of Stephen Gardiner*, pp. 48–49.
157. TNA, PRO, SP1/70 fo. 35 (*State Papers*, vi. 370; *LP* V, 1025).
158. TNA, PRO, SP1/69 fos 67–67v (*LP* V, 742).
159. TNA, PRO, SP1/69 fo. 41 (Merriman, *Life and Letters of Thomas Cromwell*, i. 344; *LP* V, 723).
160. *CSP, Spanish*, IV, ii, 1047.
161. Ibid.
162. H. A. Kelly, *The Matrimonial Trials of Henry VIII* (Stanford, CA, 1976), pp. 198–200. These questions included whether it was lawful for a man to marry his deceased brother's wife; whether Catherine's marriage to Prince Arthur had been consummated; and whether the pope had any dispensing powers in these matters.
163. BL, Cotton MS, Cleopatra E VI fo. 257 (*LP* VI, 361).
164. BL, Cotton MS, Caligula B III fo. 169 (*LP* VI, 486).
165. TNA, PRO, SP1/75 fo. 179 (*LP* VI, 398); SP1/65 fo. 239 (*LP* VI, 431); SP1/76 fo. 25 (*LP* VI, 452); SP1/76 fo. 46 (*LP* VI, 487).
166. TNA, PRO, SP1/76 fo. 46 (*LP* VI, 487).
167. TNA, PRO, SP1/76 fo. 25 (*LP* VI, 452); SP1/76 fo. 46 (*LP* VI, 487).
168. TNA, PRO, SP1/76 fo. 49 (*LP* VI, 491).
169. TNA, PRO, SP1/78 fo. 46 (*LP* VI, 912); SP1/78 fo. 47 (*LP* VI, 913).

170. *CSP, Spanish*, IV, ii, 1056.

171. Elton, 'Evolution of a Reformation Statute', pp. 195, 197; reprinted in Elton, *Studies*, ii. 82–107.

172. The drafts corrected by Cromwell are as follows: TNA, PRO, SP2/N fos 48–58 (*LP* VI, 120 [7]) – Elton's draft C; SP2/N fos 59–67, 69 (*LP* VI, 120 [7]) – Elton's draft D; SP2/N fos 70–82 (*LP* VI, 120 [7]) – Elton's draft E; SP2/N fos 83–95 (*LP* VI, 120 [7]) – Elton's draft F; SP2/N fos 96–101 (*LP* VI, 120[8]) – Elton's draft G; SP2/Q fo. 115 (*LP* VII, 1611 [2]) – Elton's figure 3. The remaining drafts are: TNA, PRO, SP2/N fos 28–38 (*LP* VI, 120 [7]) – Elton's draft A; SP2/N fos 39–47 (*LP* VI, 120 [7]) – Elton's draft B; BL, Cotton MS, Cleopatra E VI fos 185–200 (*LP* VI, 120 [6]) – Elton's draft H; TNA, PRO, SP2/N fos 102–104 (*LP* VI, 120 [9]) – Elton's figure 1; SP2/N fos 105–106 (*LP* VI, 120 [9]) – Elton's figure 2; SP2/N fos 67a–68 (*LP* VI, 120 [7]) – Elton's figure 4.

173. Bernard, 'Elton's Cromwell', in Bernard, *Power and Politics*, pp. 111–113; Guy, 'Thomas Cromwell and the Intellectual Origins', p. 161.

174. See also Guy, 'Thomas Cromwell and the Intellectual Origins', pp. 151–178.

175. TNA, PRO, SP2/N fo. 84 (*LP* VI, 120 [7]) – Elton's draft F; BL, Cotton MS, Cleopatra E VI fo. 185 (*LP* VI, 120 [6]) – Elton's draft H. *Cf.* Elton, 'Evolution of a Reformation Statute', p. 183.

176. TNA, PRO, SP2/N fo. 60 (*LP* VI, 120 [7]) – Elton's draft D; *Cf.* Elton, 'Evolution of a Reformation Statute', p. 184.

177. For Elton's comments, see 'Evolution of a Reformation Statute', pp. 177–178.

178. Ibid., p. 177.

179. TNA, PRO, SP2/N fos 148–154v (*LP* VI, 311 [4]). The editors of *Letters and Papers* wrongly describe this draft, and that which follows it, SP2/N fos 155–156v (*LP* VI, 311 [5]), as being in Cromwell's hand. They were both written by Audeley.

180. TNA, PRO, SP2/N fo. 149 (*LP* VI, 311 [4]).

181. Audeley, it will be recalled, also amended the bill introduced in parliament following the clergy's oath to the pope being read there (see above, p. 225 n. 149). In August 1533 he was also instructed to make the 'ratificacions' to the act of annates, and in that year he drafted a parliamentary bill declaring that the clergy in convocation had declared Henry's first marriage invalid. See TNA, PRO, SP2/L fos 171–180 (*LP* V, 1016 [2]); Hall, *Chronicle*, p. 784; TNA, PRO, SP2/L fos 72–74 (*LP* V, 721 [1]); SP1/78 fo. 174 (*LP* VI, 1049); SP2/N fos 155–156v (*LP* VI, 311 [5]), this final bill is written entirely in Audeley's hand, not Cromwell's as specified in *Letters and Papers*.

182. *Statutes of the Realm*, iii. 24 Henry VIII c. 12.

183. There are only three drafts containing the famous preamble, which also have corrections somewhere on the draft by Cromwell. Only on one of these drafts did Cromwell amend the preamble itself. In Elton's draft E, Cromwell corrected the spelling of the word 'storyes' [stories] thus: 'Wher by dyuers sundry old autentike stores *storyes* and cronicles it is manifestlie declared . . .'. He also inserted the two words – 'or provocacion' – into the phrase 'without restraynt apeale *or provocacion* to any foreyn prynces' (italics signify Cromwell's additions); see TNA, PRO, SP2/N fo. 70 (*LP* VI, 120 [7]). These were hardly notable inclusions or changes. Moreover, in the other two drafts which contain amendments by Cromwell, none were made by him to the preamble that supposedly embodied his political beliefs; see SP2/N fo. 48 (*LP* VI, 120 [7]) – Elton's draft C; SP2/N fo. 59 (*LP* VI, 120 [7]) – Elton's draft D. The only detailed amendment Cromwell made to the beginning of the act was in Elton's draft C, where he inserted a fairly lengthy piece of rhetoric justifying it; see SP2/N fo. 51 (*LP* VI, 120 [7]) – Elton's draft C.

184. TNA, PRO, SP2/N fos 91, 92, 93 (*LP* VI, 120 [7]) – Elton's draft F; SP2/N fo. 54 (*LP* VI, 120 [7]) – Elton's draft C; SP2/N fo. 67 (*LP* VI, 120[7]) – Elton's draft D.

185. TNA, PRO, SP2/N fo. 93 (*LP* VI, 120 [7]).

186. Elton, 'Evolution of a Reformation Statute', p. 186.

187. Ibid., pp. 186–189.

188. TNA, PRO, SP1/75 fo. 84 (*LP* VI, 333); BL, Cotton MS, Otho CX fo. 165 (*LP* VI, 496); TNA, PRO, SP1/76 fo. 57 (*LP* VI, 501); BL, Cotton MS, Otho CX fo. 163v

(*LP* VI, 461); BL, Cotton MS, Otho CX fo. 164 (*LP* VI, 497); BL, Cotton MS, Otho CX fo. 165v (*LP* VI, 527); TNA, PRO, SP1/76 fo. 82 (*LP* VI, 525); SP1/76 fo. 4v (*LP* VI, 423); SP1/75 fo. 153 (*LP* VI, 368). See also the note among Cromwell's memoranda, which reminded him to have 'the judgement ... preparyd ... In the Kynges gret matyr'. See TNA, PRO, SP1/76 fo. 4v (*LP* VI, 423).

189. Hall, *Chronicle*, pp. 798–805; Ives, *Life and Death of Anne Boleyn*, pp. 172–183; Bernard, *Anne Boleyn*, pp. 67–71; T. Sowerby, 'Anne Boleyn's Coronation', in T. Betteridge and G. Walker, eds, *The Oxford Handbook to Tudor Drama* (Oxford, 2012), pp. 386–402.

190. Hall, *Chronicle*, p. 798.

191. TNA, PRO, SP1/76 fo. 4v (*LP* VI, 423).

192. TNA, PRO, SP1/76 fo. 62 (*LP* VI, 505); SP1/76 fo. 81v (*LP* VI, 521); SP1/76 fo. 119 (*LP* VI, 554).

193. Colvin, *History of the King's Works*, iii. 266–267.

194. TNA, PRO, SP1/103 fos 220v–221 (*LP* X, 1231).

195. Hall, *Chronicle*, p. 798.

196. TNA, PRO, SP1/76 fo. 198 (*LP* VI, 631).

197. Murphy, 'Literature and Propaganda', pp. 135–158; Guy, 'Thomas Cromwell and the Intellectual Origins', pp. 151–178.

198. TNA, PRO, SP1/75 fo. 151 (*LP* VI, 366).

199. BL, Cotton MS, Otho CX fo. 167v (*LP* VI, 1062).

200. *Works of Thomas Cranmer*, ii. 255, 256.

201. TNA, PRO, SP1/78 fo. 174 (*LP* VI, 1049).

202. Murphy, 'Literature and Propaganda', pp. 135–158.

203. TNA, PRO, SP1/83 fo. 35 (*LP* VII, 406).

204. BL, Cotton MS, Cleopatra E VI fo. 326v (*LP* VI, 1486).

205. BL, Cotton MS, Titus B I fo. 420v (*LP* VII, 418 [2]); TNA, PRO, SP6/3 fos 85v, 86v (*LP* VI, 1487 [2]).

206. BL, Cotton MS, Otho C X fo. 167v (*LP* VI, 1062).

207. TNA, PRO, SP1/75 fo. 25 (*LP* VI, 1305). Henry VIII also sent an anti-papal book to Francis I, while Cromwell showed a similar pamphlet to the Scottish ambassador. See *CSP, Spanish*, V, i, 1, 19.

208. T. Sowerby, '"All our Books do be Sent into Other Countreys and Translated": Henrician Polemic in its International Context', *English Historical Review*, cxxi (2006), pp. 1271–1299, at p. 1278; *STC*, 9177.

209. *CSP, Spanish*, IV, ii, 1165; TNA, PRO, SP1/82 fo. 117 (*State Papers*, vii. 534; *LP* VII, 115).

210. W. G. Zeeveld, *Foundations of Tudor Policy* (London, 1948); Elton, *Policy and Police*; Sowerby, '"All our Books"', pp. 1271–1299.

211. See above, pp. 72–73.

212. BL, Cotton MS, Galba B X fo. 46v (*LP* V, 65 [ii]).

213. TNA, PRO, SP1/65 fo. 253v (*LP* V, 246).

214. TNA, PRO, SP1/66 fo. 47 (*LP* V, 303).

215. TNA, PRO, SP1/66 fo. 121 (*LP* V, 311).

216. BL, Cotton MS, Titus B I fo. 373 (*LP* V, 532); TNA, PRO, SP1/68 fo. 51 (*LP* V, 533); *STC*, 24443.

217. TNA, PRO, SP1/68 fo. 52 (*LP* V, 533).

218. Ibid., fo. 51.

219. *Works of Thomas Cranmer*, ii. 246; TNA, PRO, 3/3 fo. 126 (*LP* VI, 682); *LP* VI, 761.

220. G. Walker, *Writing under Tyranny: English Literature and the Henrician Reformation* (Oxford, 2005), p. 47; *STC*, 11394.

221. TNA, PRO, SP1/65 fo. 252v (*LP* V, 246).

222. BL, Cotton MS, Galba B X fos 355v–356 (Merriman, *Life and Letters of Thomas Cromwell*, i. 338; *LP* V, 248); italics signify additions in Cromwell's hand.

223. Ibid., fo. 356.

224. TNA, PRO, SP1/66 fo. 121 (*LP* V, 311).

225. *STC*, 11386.5; *LP* V, App. 18.

226. TNA, PRO, SP1/71 fo. 106 (*LP* V, 1432); SP1/71 fo. 133 (*LP* V, 1458); SP1/71 fo. 143 (*LP* V, 1467).
227. TNA, PRO, SP1/71 fo. 133 (*LP* V, 1458); my italics for emphasis.
228. TNA, PRO, SP1/68 fo. 96 (*LP* V, 605).
229. TNA, PRO, SP1/72 fo. 57 (*LP* V, 1575).
230. TNA, PRO, SP1/83 fo. 51 (*LP* VII, 422); SP1/83 fo. 52 (*LP* VII, 423); *STC*, 5641, 17817. *Cf.* Underwood, 'Thomas Cromwell and William Marshall', p. 522.
231. S. W. Haas, 'Martin Luther's "Divine Right" Kingship and the Royal Supremacy: Two Tracts from the 1531 Parliament and Convocation of the Clergy', *Journal of Ecclesiastical History*, 31 (1980), pp. 317–325, at p. 319. The *Document* is printed in N. Pocock, *Records of the Reformation: The Divorce, 1527–1533* (2 vols, Oxford, 1870), ii. 100–103.
232. TNA, PRO, SP6/2 fos 81–83 (*LP* V, 1022), misdated to 1532 in *Letters and Papers*. See Lehmberg, *Reformation Parliament*, p. 114.
233. Haas, 'Martin Luther's "Divine Right" Kingship', p. 318.
234. *STC*, 12510; S. W. Haas, 'The *Disputatio Inter Clericum Et Militem*: Was Berthelet's 1531 Edition the first Henrician Polemic of Thomas Cromwell?', *Moreana*, xiv (1977), pp. 65–72.
235. Haas, 'The *Disputatio*', p. 66.
236. BL, Cotton MS, Galba B X fo. 46v (*LP* V, 65 [ii]).
237. *CSP, Spanish*, IV, ii, 753.
238. Haas, 'The *Disputatio*', p. 67.
239. *STC*, 11919; Pocock, *Records of the Reformation*, ii. 385–421.
240. *STC*, 14286.
241. Pocock, *Records of the Reformation*, ii. 385–421.
242. For disagreements over the dating of the *Glasse*, see: S. W. Haas, 'Henry VIII's *Glasse of Truthe*', *History*, 64 (1979), pp. 353–362; R. Rex, 'Redating Henry VIII's A Glasse of the Truthe', *The Library*, Seventh Series, 4 (2003), pp. 16–27.
243. TNA, PRO, SP1/71 fo. 36 (*LP* V, 1320).
244. Ibid.
245. TNA, PRO, SP1/27 fo. 286 (*LP* III, ii, 3015). See also TNA, PRO, SP1/69 fos 134–135v (*LP* III, ii, 3680 [1]); SP1/53 fo. 176 (*LP* IV, iii, 5459).
246. TNA, PRO, SP1/71 fos 48–48v (*LP* V, 1338).
247. TNA, PRO, SP1/72 fo. 48v (*State Papers*, vii. 386; *LP* V, 1564).
248. TNA, PRO, SP1/72 fo. 154 (*LP* V, 1660); *State Papers*, vii. 487; *LP* VI, 903.
249. TNA, PRO, SP1/70 fo. 41 (*LP* V, 1032).
250. TNA, PRO, SP1/74 fo. 68 (*LP* VI, 72).
251. TNA, PRO, E36/143 fos 2, 22 (*LP* VI, 299). By 1533 other papers in Cromwell's possession on these matters included: 'ii little bokes concerning the [kin]ges high matter'; 'a mynute drawne by my master concernyng the kynges gret cause'; 'a paper of articles resityng what power the pope hath'; 'a paper of de potestate pape'; 'a boke made with figures concernyng the kynges power Royall'; 'a boke concernyng the popes power and whether one may applie from hym'; 'the reason of sence of the bishop of winton concernyng the kynges cause'; 'a boke written de potestate ecclias-tica'; 'a paper concernyng the kynges high matter'; 'a paper of Remembraunces concernyng the kynges gret cause'; and 'the opyneons and sayinges of Bisshopes written with there owne hands concernyng the kynges high matter'. See TNA, PRO, E36/143 fos 2, 3, 15, 16, 17, 18, 19, 22, 23 (*LP* VI, 299).
252. TNA, PRO, SP1/88 fo. 142 (*LP* VII, App. 23).
253. TNA, PRO, SP1/72 fo. 48v (*State Papers*, vii. 386; *LP* V, 1564).
254. TNA, PRO, SP1/80 fo. 106 (*LP* VI, 1448).
255. TNA, PRO, SP2/O fo. 28 (*LP* VI, 717); *cf.* Schofield, *Rise and Fall*, p. 40.
256. TNA, PRO, SP1/76 fos 48–48v (*LP* V, 1338).
257. *CSP, Spanish*, V, i, 1.
258. BL, Cotton MS, Titus B I fo. 420v (*LP* VII, 418 [2]); TNA, PRO, SP6/3 fo. 85v, 86v (*LP* VI, 1487 [2]).
259. TNA, PRO, SP1/76 fo. 46 (*LP* VI, 487).

260. C. S. L. Davies, 'Review: Representation, Repute, Reality', *English Historical Review*, cxxiv (2009), p. 1444.

261. Merriman, *Life and Letters of Thomas Cromwell*, i. 99, 116.

262. Innes, *Ten Tudor Statesmen*, p. 140; Wilding, *Thomas Cromwell*, pp. 59, 89.

263. Elton, *Policy and Police*, p. 424.

264. BL, Lansdowne MS 116 fo. 53 (*LP* V, 1142); TNA, PRO, SP1/70 fo. 142 (*LP* V, 1143); SP1/70 fo. 180 (*LP* V, 1208); SP1/70 fo. 220 (*LP* V, 1259); SP1/70 fo. 221 (*LP* V, 1260); BL, Cotton MS, Cleopatra E IV fo. 12 (*LP* V, 1371); BL, Cotton MS, Otho C X fos 214–215 (*LP* VI, 1253); BL, Cotton MS, Cleopatra E IV fo. 34 (*LP* VI, 116); TNA, PRO, SP1/79 fo. 51 (*LP* VI, 1122); SP1/81 fo. 118 (*LP* VI, 1664); SP1/81 fo. 131 (*LP* VI, 1677); SP1/82 fo. 131 (*LP* VII, 140); SP1/83 fo. 83 (*LP* VII, 480); SP1/83 fo. 87 (*LP* VII, 497); SP1/77 fo. 94 (*LP* VI, 726); SP1/78 fo. 75 (*State Papers*, vii. 489; *LP* VI, 934); SP1/78 fos 34–35 (*LP* VI, 899); SP1/78 fo. 36 (*LP* VI, 900); SP1/69 fo. 77 (*LP* V, 757); *LP* VI, 1385.

265. *CSP, Spanish*, IV, ii, 984, 986; TNA, PRO, SP1/71 fo. 133 (*LP* V, 1458); SP1/71 fo. 106 (*LP* V, 1432); SP1/71 fo. 143 (*LP* V, 1467).

266. TNA, PRO, SP1/78 fo. 25 (Merriman, *Life and Letters of Thomas Cromwell*, i. 360–361; *LP* VI, 887); BL, Cotton MS, Cleopatra E VI fo. 327v (*LP* VI, 1487 [1]).

267. TNA, PRO, SP1/66 fo. 171 (*LP* V, 360).

268. TNA, PRO, SP1/80 fo. 10 (*LP* VI, 1329).

269. TNA, PRO, SP1/238 fo. 125 (*LP* Add. I, i, 871); TNA, PRO, SP1/238 fo. 155 (*LP* Add. I, i, 879).

270. TNA, PRO, SP1/83 fo. 83 (*LP* VII, 480).

271. TNA, PRO, SP1/80 fo. 171 (*LP* VI, 1503).

272. Robertson, '"The Art of the Possible"', pp. 793–816; Speight, '"The Politics of Good Governance"', pp. 623–638; Robertson, 'A Reply to Helen Speight', pp. 639–641.

273. P. Williams, 'Review', *English Historical Review*, lxxxviii (1973), pp. 594–595.

274. See, for example, TNA, PRO, SP1/81 fo. 131 (*LP* VI, 1677); SP1/82 fo. 131 (*LP* VII, 140); SP1/83 fo. 83 (*LP* VII, 480); SP1/238 fo. 125 (*LP* Add. I, i, 871); SP1/80 fos 10–10v (*LP* VI, 1329); BL, Lansdowne MS 116 fo. 53 (*LP* V, 1142); BL, Cotton MS, Cleopatra E IV fo. 34 (*LP* VI, 116).

275. TNA, PRO, SP1/80 fo. 10 (*LP* VI, 1329); SP1/80 fo. 171 (*LP* VI, 1503).

276. TNA, PRO, SP1/83 fo. 70 (*LP* VII, 448); SP1/83 fo. 71 (*LP* VII, 450); SP1/83 fo. 81 (*LP* VII, 472); SP1/83 fo. 82 (*LP* VII, 473).

277. TNA, PRO, SP1/79 fo. 80 (*LP* VI, 1169); BL, Cotton MS, Titus B I fo. 494 (*LP* VI, 1194); SP1/78 fo. 25 (Merriman *Life and Letters of Thomas Cromwell*, i. 360–361; *LP* VI, 887); SP1/79 fo. 62 (*LP* VI, 1149); SP1/82 fo. 14 (*LP* VII, 17).

278. TNA, PRO, SP1/78 fos 25–25v (Merriman, *Life and Letters of Thomas Cromwell*, i. 360–361; *LP* VI, 887); SP1/78 fos 106–106v (*LP* VI, 967); SP1/79 fo. 61v (*LP* VI, 1148); BL, Cotton MS, Titus B I fos 493v, 494 (*LP* VI, 1194); TNA, PRO, SP1/79 fo. 161 (*LP* VI, 1256); SP1/80 fo. 15 (*LP* VI, 1333); BL, Cotton MS, Titus B I fos 464, 464v (*LP* VI, 1382); TNA, PRO, SP1/80 fo. 97 (*LP* VI, 1422); BL, Cotton MS, Cleopatra E VI fos 154–154v (*LP* VI, 1467); BL, Cotton MS, Cleopatra E IV fo. 96 (*LP* VI, 1512); TNA, PRO, SP1/82 fo. 14 (*LP* VII, 17).

279. *Works of Thomas Cranmer*, ii. 252.

280. TNA, PRO, SP1/75 fo. 197 (*LP* VI, 411).

281. Ibid.

282. *LP* VI, 247.

283. BL, Cotton MS, Cleopatra E V fo. 365 (*LP* VI, 246).

284. BL, Cotton MS, Cleopatra E IV fo. 73 (*LP* VI, 799); TNA, PRO, SP2/O fo. 32 (*LP* VI, 799 [ii]); SP6/3 fo. 55 (*LP* VI, 572); SP1/78 fo. 21 (*LP* VI, 873).

285. BL, Cotton MS, Cleopatra E IV fo. 73 (*LP* VI, 799); TNA, PRO, SP1/77 fo. 186 (*LP* VI, 796); my italics for emphasis.

286. TNA, PRO, SP1/78 fo. 21 (*LP* VI, 873); M. C. Skeeters, *Community and Clergy: Bristol and the Reformation, c.1530–c.1570* (Oxford, 1993), p. 42.

287. The mayor, who had appointed Latimer to preach, wrote to Cromwell petitioning against the 'lewed demener of hubberdyn'. See TNA, PRO, SP1/77 fo. 186 (*LP* VI,

796). Cromwell's friend Stephen Vaughan also requested that Cromwell be a 'solycitour' on Latimer's behalf to the king. See TNA, PRO, SP1/69 fo. 239 (*LP* VI, 957).

288.　*Cf.* Skeeters, *Community and Clergy*, p. 38. Latimer ceased to preach at Bristol, but would later preach before the king. See *LP* VII, 30; TNA, PRO, SP1/82 fos 42–42v (*LP* VII, 32); SP3/6 fo. 25 (*LP* VII, 228).

289.　TNA, PRO, SP1/78 fo. 88 (*LP* VI, 951).

290.　TNA, PRO, SP1/78 fo. 106 (*LP* VI, 967).

291.　TNA, PRO, SP1/79 fo. 80 (*LP* VI, 1169).

292.　TNA, PRO, SP1/78 fo. 25 (Merriman, *Life and Letters of Thomas Cromwell*, i. 361; *LP* VI, 887).

293.　TNA, PRO, SP1/80 fo. 50 (Merriman, *Life and Letters of Thomas Cromwell*, i. 370–371; *LP* VI, 1369).

294.　Ibid., fos 50–50v.

295.　Elton, *Policy and Police*, pp. 383–400; Williams, *Tudor Regime*, pp. 386–387.

296.　TNA, PRO, SP1/82 fo. 67v (*LP* VII, 71); SP1/81 fo. 121 (*LP* VI, 1666); *LP* VII, 1026 [10].

297.　BL, Cotton MS, Cleopatra E IV fos 101–104 (Merriman, *Life and Letters of Thomas Cromwell*, i. 377; *LP* VII, 238).

298.　*Statutes of the Realm*, iii. 26 Henry VIII c. 13.

299.　J. G. Bellamy, *The Law of Treason in England in the Middle Ages* (Cambridge, 1970), pp. 116–121.

300.　S. Rezneck, 'Constructive Treason by Words in the Fifteenth Century', *American Historical Review*, 33 (1928), pp. 544–552.

301.　*LP* VIII, 856 [7], 858.

302.　Elton, *Policy and Police*, p. 287.

303.　Thornley, 'Treason Legislation', p. 90.

304.　TNA, PRO, SP1/65 fos 82–86 (*LP* V, 52 [1]); SP1/65 fos 87–90 (*LP* V, 52 [2]); BL, Cotton MS, Titus B I fo. 484 (*State Papers*, i. 380–383; *LP* V, 394). *Cf.* Elton, *Tudor Revolution in Government*, p. 95; Elton, *Policy and Police*, p. 265 n. 2.

305.　For these earlier alterations, see Elton, *Policy and Police*, pp. 266–272. Elton's suggestion that in 1532 the government's parliamentary agenda was monopolised by other concerns is highly plausible (p. 273).

306.　BL, Cotton MS, Titus B I fo. 425 (*LP* VII, 51).

307.　*Statutes of the Realm*, iii. 25 Henry VIII c. 22.

308.　*Statutes of the Realm*, iii. 26 Henry VIII c. 13.

309.　Elton, *Policy and Police*, p. 276.

310.　Elton thought that 'Cromwell was guilty of a significant slip' when he first wrote 'woord' and had to substitute 'deed' in his memorandum, regarding the 'woord wrytyng or dede' cited above; BL, Cotton MS, Titus B I fo. 425 (*LP* VII, 51). See Elton, *Policy and Police*, pp. 276, 291.

311.　TNA, PRO, SP1/65 fos 87–90 (*LP* V, 52 [2]); SP2/Q fos 81a–87 (*LP* VII, 1381 [5]), this was prepared in 1532, not 1534 as in *Letters and Papers*; SP2/Q fos 76, 77 (*LP* VII, 1381 [4]).

312.　TNA, PRO, SP2/Q fos 69–75 (*LP* VII, 1381 [3]); SP2/Q fos 76–81a (*LP* VII, 1381 [4]).

313.　TNA, PRO, SP2/Q fo. 77 (*LP* VII, 1381 [4]).

314.　TNA, PRO, SP2/Q fos 81–81v (*LP* VII, 1381 [5]); Elton, *Policy and Police*, pp. 285–286.

315.　TNA, PRO, SP2/Q fos 76, 77 (*LP* VII, 1381 [4]).

316.　TNA, PRO, SP1/65 fos 87–90 (*LP* V, 52 [2]); *LP* Add. I, i, 1480 (p. 287); TNA, PRO, SP2/Q fos 81a–87 (*LP* VII, 1381 [5]).

317.　TNA, PRO, SP2/Q fos 86–87 (*LP* VII, 1381 [5]).

318.　BL, Cotton MS, Titus B I fo. 484 (*State Papers*, i. 380–383; *LP* V, 394). *Cf.* Elton, *Policy and Police*, p. 272.

319.　*CSP, Spanish*, V, ii, 43.

Conclusion

1. Dickens, *Thomas Cromwell*, pp. 47, 48, 52–59; Beckingsale, *Thomas Cromwell*, pp. 29–41; Williams, *Cardinal and the Secretary*, pp. 162–169; H. Leithead, 'Cromwell, Thomas (*c*.1485–1540)', *ODNB*.
2. Guy, *Public Career*, pp. 175–201; Haigh, *English Reformations*, pp. 111–116.
3. Merriman, *Life and Letters of Thomas Cromwell*, i. 91, 112; Robertson, 'Thomas Cromwell's Servants', p. 66.
4. Guy, 'Thomas Wolsey, Thomas Cromwell and the Reform of Henrician Government', pp. 42–43.
5. Elton, 'Evolution of a Reformation Statute', p. 197.
6. Elton, *Tudor Revolution in Government*, pp. 96–97.
7. Elton, 'King or Minister?', in Elton, *Studies*, i. 185.
8. Elton, *Reform and Reformation*, pp. 135–137, esp. p. 136.
9. Elton, *Thomas Cromwell*, p. 11.
10. TNA, PRO, SP1/70 fo. 176 (*LP* V, 1199).
11. TNA, PRO, SP1/70 fo. 59 (Merriman, *Life and Letters of Thomas Cromwell*, i. 344; *LP* V, 1055); SP1/70 fo. 112 (Merriman, *Life and Letters of Thomas Cromwell*, i. 344–345; *LP* V, 1092).
12. TNA, PRO, SP1/71 fos 17–18 (Merriman, *Life and Letters of Thomas Cromwell*, i. 348–349; *LP* V 1298).
13. TNA, PRO, SP1/78 fos 25–25v (Merriman, *Life and Letters of Thomas Cromwell*, i. 360–361; *LP* VI, 887); SP1/80 fos 50–50v (Merriman, *Life and Letters of Thomas Cromwell*, i. 370–371; *LP* VI, 1369); SP1/82 fos 82–82v (Merriman, *Life and Letters of Thomas Cromwell*, i. 373; *LP* VII, 73).
14. *LP* V, App. 33.
15. TNA, PRO, SP 2/M fo. 43 (*LP* V, 1297 [2]); the final warrant is TNA, PRO, C82/660 (*LP* V, 1297 [1]).
16. TNA, PRO, SP1/71 fo. 85 (*LP* V, 1398); my italics for emphasis.
17. TNA, PRO, SP1/71 fo. 91 (*LP* V, 1408).
18. TNA, PRO, SP1/71 fo. 124 (*LP* V, 1452).
19. TNA, PRO, SP1/72 fo. 10 (*LP* V, 1509).
20. TNA, PRO, SP1/72 fo. 32 (*LP* V, 1554).
21. BL, Cotton MS, Vitellius B XIII fo. 227 (*LP* V, 1657).
22. TNA, PRO, SP1/73 fo. 126 (*LP* V, 1751).
23. TNA, PRO, SP1/74 fo. 44v (*LP* VI, 50); SP1/74 fo. 199 (*LP* VI, 104); SP1/75 fo. 31v (*LP* VI, 250); SP1/75 fo. 54 (*LP* VI, 272); SP1/75 fo. 61v (*LP* VI, 288); SP1/75 fo. 157v (*LP* VI, 372); SP1/79 fo. 195v (*LP* VI, 1312); SP1/80 fo. 92v (*LP* VI, 1410); SP1/78 fo. 131v (*LP* VI, 994); SP1/79 fo. 53v (*LP* VI, 1124); SP1/238 fo. 61v (*LP* Add. I, i, 839); BL, Cotton MS, Titus B I fo. 426v (*LP* VII, 51); SP1/82 fo. 125v (*LP* VII, 124). The large number of people who believed Cromwell had been made a knight might suggest that he had in fact become one. Though as the editors of *Letters and Papers* recognised, he continued to sign himself merely as Thomas Cromwell in all the government documents he worked on in 1533 and 1534. He was not made a knight until 1536. See W. A. Shaw, *The Knights of England* (2 vols, London, 1906), ii. 50.
24. *CSP, Spanish*, IV, ii, 1048.
25. *CSP, Spanish*, IV, ii, 1061.
26. BL, Cotton MS, Vespasian F XIII fo. 218 (*LP* VI, 484).
27. *CSP, Spanish*, IV, ii, 1144.
28. TNA, PRO, SP1/81 fo. 116 (*LP* VI, 1661); SP1/79 fo. 96 (*LP* VI, 1177); SP 3/7 fo. 160 (*LP* Add. I, i, 886).
29. It is not clear exactly when Cromwell became the king's secretary, as the office was not one confirmed by patent. On 7 April the appellation 'Good Master Secretarie' was used when addressing Cromwell, however, and the first warrant he signed as secretary is dated 19 April 1534. See BL, Cotton MS, Vespasian F XIII fos 178–178v (*LP* VII, 446); BL, Cotton MS, Vespasian F XIII fos 266–266v (*LP* VII, 451); TNA, PRO, SP 3/6 fo. 102 (*LP* VII, 483); TNA, PRO, C82/681 (*LP* VII, 587 [26]).

30. Elton, *Tudor Revolution in Government*, p. 127.
31. TNA, PRO, E36/143 fo. 55 (*LP* VI, 1371); BL, Cotton MS, Titus B I fo. 422 (*LP* VII, 52); BL, Cotton MS, Titus B I fo. 428v (*LP* VII, 48 [2]); BL, Cotton MS, Titus B I fo. 430 (*LP* VII, 52); BL, Cotton MS, Titus B I fo. 456 (*LP* VII, 143 [2]).
32. I owe this point to Dr Paul Cavill.
33. TNA, PRO, SP1/74 fo. 5 (*State Papers*, iv. 631; *LP* VI, 8).
34. TNA, PRO, SP1/74 fo. 12 (*LP* VI, 16).
35. Hall, *Chronicle*, p. 785.
36. TNA, PRO, SP1/237 fo. 266 (*LP* Add. I, i, 801). In a letter sent to Cromwell in February 1533, Lawson highlighted to Cromwell the 'gret costes and charges' that he was put to by the war, and asked Cromwell to get the king to clarify the position on Lawson's wages. He had also written to Norfolk on this matter. See TNA, PRO, SP1/74 fo. 144v (*LP* VI, 145).
37. TNA, PRO, SP 2/M fos 123–124 (*LP* V, 1670 [ii]).
38. TNA, PRO, SP1/72 fo. 129 (*LP* V, 1630).
39. TNA, PRO, SP1/74 fo. 212 (*LP* VI, 217); SP1/75 fo. 133 (*LP* VI, 343).
40. TNA, PRO, SP1/75 fo. 133 (*LP* VI, 343).
41. BL, Cotton MS, Titus B I fo. 427v (*LP* VII, 48); BL, Cotton MS, Titus B I fo. 493v (*LP* VI, 1194).
42. BL, Cotton MS, Titus B I fo. 463 (*LP* VII, 108). See also TNA, PRO, E36/143 fo. 55 (*LP* VI, 1370); BL, Cotton MS, Caligula B I fos 453–454v (*LP* VI, 1381); BL, Cotton MS, Titus B I fo. 427v (*LP* VII, 48).
43. TNA, PRO, SP1/74 fo. 173 (*LP* VI, 174). See and compare BL, Cotton MS, Caligula B III fos 164–165v (*State Papers*, iv. 648; *LP* VI, 802) and BL, Cotton MS, Caligula B III fo. 167 (*LP* VI, 801); TNA, PRO, SP1/74 fo. 200 (*LP* VI, 205); BL, Cotton MS, Caligula B III fo. 168 (*LP* VI, 744).
44. See, for example, TNA, PRO, SP1/237 fo. 266 (*LP* Add. I, i, 801); SP1/74 fo. 130 (*LP* VI, 124), SP1/74 fo. 20 (*LP* VI, 29); SP1/74 fo. 127 (*LP* VI, 117). This list could be considerably lengthened.
45. BL, Cotton MS, Caligula B III fo. 167 (*LP* VI, 801).
46. BL, Cotton MS, Caligula B III fo. 168 (*LP* VI, 803).
47. TNA, PRO, SP1/78 fo. 43 (*LP* VI, 908). See also TNA, PRO, SP1/78 fo. 44 (*State Papers* IV, 657; *LP* VI, 909); SP1/78 fo. 142 (*LP* VI, 1010).
48. TNA, PRO, SP1/78 fo. 25 (Merriman, *Life and Letters of Thomas Cromwell*, i. 360; *LP* VI, 887). Cromwell's letter was dated 23 July and written from London; Henry was at Windsor on 22 July, and presumably remained so on the 23 July. See TNA, PRO, OBS 1/1418, p. 42.
49. TNA, PRO, SP1/78 fo. 110 (*LP* VI, 977).
50. TNA, PRO, C82/689 and C66/665 m. 1 (*LP* VII, 1352 [3]).
51. *LP* XV, 540, 541.
52. *LP* XV, 766, 767, 805.
53. *Cf.* Elton, 'Decline and Fall', in Elton, *Studies*, i. 225.
54. *LP* XVI, 590.

BIBLIOGRAPHY

Manuscript Sources

British Library (BL)

Additional MS 20706, 48028
Cotton MSS   Appendix L
                Appendix XXVIII
                Caligula B III
                Caligula B VI
                Cleopatra E IV
                Cleopatra E VI
                Faustina C III
                Faustina E VII
                Galba B IX
                Galba B X
                Otho C X
                Otho E IX
                Titus B I
                Titus B IV
                Vespasian F XIII
                Vespasian C XIV
                Vitellius B X
                Vitellius B XIII
Egerton MS   2886
Harley MS   368, 442, 6148, 6849, 6989
Harleian MS   297
Lansdowne MS 116
Royal MS   7 CXVI

Bodleian Library, Oxford

Christ Church MS 306

College of Arms, London

MS 2 G4, fo. 35v

Devonshire Manuscripts, Chatsworth

Bolton Abbey MSS 14a

Drapers' Company Records (DCR), London

A I, 61, 64, 65, 66, 67, 68, 69, 70, 71 [1–2], 75
A XII, 121
Charter X
MB/ I C (Court of Assistants Minutes, 1543–1553)

The National Archives, Public Record Office (TNA, PRO), Kew

C1	Court of Chancery: Early Proceedings: Richard II to Philip and Mary
C36	Chancery: Ordinary and Appeal Petitions
C131	Chancery: Extents for Debts, Series I
C142	Chancery: Inquisitions Post Mortem, Series II and other Inquisitions, Henry VII to Charles I
C244	Chancery: Petty Bag Office: Files, Tower and Rolls Chapel Series, Corpus Cum Causa
C66	Chancery, Patent Rolls
C82	Chancery, Warrants for the Great Seal: Series II
E24	Exchequer: Treasury of Receipt: Deeds relating to Cardinal Wolsey's Colleges in Oxford and Ipswich
E30	Exchequer, Treasury of Receipt: Diplomatic Documents
E36	Exchequer: Treasury of Receipt: Miscellaneous Books
E40	Exchequer, Treasury of Receipt: Ancient Deeds, Series A
E41	Exchequer, Treasury of Receipt: Ancient Deeds, Series AA
E101	Exchequer, King's Remembrancer: Accounts Various
E135	Exchequer: Miscellaneous Ecclesiastical Documents
E175	Exchequer: King's Remembrancer and Treasury of Receipt: Parliament and Council Proceedings, Series II
E179	Exchequer: King's Remembrancer: Particulars of Account and other Records Relating to Lay and Clerical Taxation
E407	Exchequer of Receipt: Miscellaneous Rolls, Books and Papers
OBS 1/1418	State Paper Office: Itinerary of Henry VIII
PROB 11	Prerogative Court of Canterbury and related Probate Jurisdictions: Will Registers
REQ2	Court of Requests: Pleadings
SC6	Special Collections: Ministers' and Receivers' Accounts
SC7	Special Collections: Papal Bulls
SC12	Special Collections: Rentals and Surveys, Portfolios
SP1	State Papers, Henry VIII: General Series
SP2	State Papers, Henry VIII: Folios
SP3	State Papers, Lisle Papers
SP6	Theological Tracts, Henry VIII
SP60	State Papers, Henry VIII: Ireland Series
STAC2	Court of Star Chamber: Proceedings, Henry VIII

Westminster Abbey Muniments (WAM), London

3231
18048
18049a
18049b
18049c
32335
32345

Printed Primary Sources

Calendar of Close Rolls, Henry VII, ed. K. H. Ledward and R. A. Latham (2 vols, London, 1955–1963).

Calendar of Letters, Despatches, and State Papers, Spanish, Henry VIII, ed. G. A. Bergenroth and P. de Gayangos (15 vols in 20 parts, London, 1862–1954).

Calendar of State Papers, Domestic, Edward VI–Elizabeth I, 1547–1580, ed., R. Lemon (London, 1856).

Calendar of State Papers, Venetian, Volume IV: 1527–1533, ed. R. Brown (London, 1871).

Cartularium Abbatthiae de Rievalle, Volume LXXXIII (London, 1889).

Cavendish, G., *The Life and Death of Cardinal Wolsey*, ed. R. S. Sylvester (London, 1959).

The Complete Works of St Thomas More, ed. E. Surtz and J. H. Hexter (15 vols, New Haven, CT, and London, 1965).

Court Rolls of the Manor of Tottenham, 2 Henry VIII to 22 Henry VIII, ed. F. H. Fenton (London, 1960).

Dudley, E., *The Tree of Commonwealth*, ed. D. M. Brodie (Cambridge, 1988).

Ellis, H., *Original Letters Illustrative of English History* (11 vols in three series, London, 1824–1846).

Extracts from the Court Rolls of the Manor of Wimbledon, Extending from 1 Edward IV to A.D. 1864, ed. P. H. Lawrence (London, 1866).

Feet of Fines for Essex, Volume IV: 1423–1457, ed. P. H. Reaney and M. Fitch (Colchester, 1964).

Fortescue, J., *The Governance of England*, ed. C. Plummer (Oxford, 1885).

Hall, E., *The Union of the Two Noble and Illustre Famelies of Lancastre and Yorke* (Hall's *Chronicle*), ed. H. Ellis (London, 1809).

Holinshed, R., *Chronicles of England, Scotland and Ireland* (6 vols, London, 1807–1808).

Hughes, P. L. and Larkin, J. F., eds, *Tudor Royal Proclamations* (3 vols, New Haven, CT, and London, 1964).

Jacobs, G. and Tomlins, T. E., *The Law Dictionary* (6 vols, Philadelphia, PA, and New York, 1811).

Journals of the House of Lords, Volume 1: 1509–1577 (London, 1836).

Le Neve, J., *Fasti Ecclesiae Anglicanae, 1300–1541* (12 vols, London, 1963).

Letters and Papers, Foreign and Domestic, of the Reign of Henry VIII, 1509–1547 (LP), ed. J. S. Brewer, J. Gairdner and R. H. Brodie (21 vols and addenda, London, 1862–1932).

The Letters of Stephen Gardiner, ed. J. A. Muller (Cambridge, 1933).

Liber monasterii de Hyda, ed. E. Edwards (London, 1866).

Miscellaneous Writings of Henry the Eighth, King of England, France and Ireland, ed. F. Macnamara (London, 1924).

Nichols, J. G., ed., *The Chronicle of Calais, in the Reigns of Henry VII and Henry VIII, to the Year 1540* (London, 1846).

Nicolas, N. H., *The Privy Purse Expenses of Henry the Eighth, 1529–1532* (London, 1827).

The Novels of Matteo Bandello, trans. J. Payne (6 vols, London, 1890).

The Papers of George Wyatt Esquire, ed. D. M. Loades, *Camden Fourth Series*, v (London, 1968).

The Register of Admissions to Gray's Inn, 1521–1889, ed. J. Foster (London, 1889).

Roper, W., *The Lyfe of Sir Thomas Moore, Knighte*, ed. E. V. Hitchcock (London, 1935).

State Papers Published Under the Authority of His Majesty's Commission, King Henry VIII (State Papers) (11 vols, London, 1830–1852).

Statutes of the Realm, ed. A. E. Luders *et al.* (11 vols, London, 1810–1828).

Stow, J., *A Survey of London*, ed. C. L. Kingsford (2 vols, Oxford, 1908).

'Two London Chronicles from the Collections of John Stow', ed. C. L. Kingsford, *Camden Miscellany*, xii (1910).

Valor Ecclesiasticus, ed. J. Caley and J. Hunter (London, 1810–1834).

Wilkins, D., *Concilia Magnae Britanniae et Hiberniae* (4 vols, London, 1737).

The Works of Thomas Cranmer, ed. J. E. Cox (2 vols, Cambridge, 1846).

Online Primary Sources

Foxe, J. *Acts and Monuments* (The Unabridged Acts and Monuments Online, Humanities Research Institute, University of Sheffield. Sheffield: HRI Online Publications, 2011). Available from www.johnfoxe.org.

Secondary Works

Alford, S., 'Politics and Political History in the Tudor Century', *Historical Journal*, 42 (1999), pp. 535–548.

Archer, I., 'The London Lobbies in the Later Sixteenth Century', *Historical Journal*, 31 (1988), pp. 17–44.

Armstrong, C. A. J., 'Some Examples of the Distribution and Speed of News in England at the Time of the Wars of the Roses', in R. W. Hunt, W. A. Pantin and R. W. Southern, eds, *Studies in Medieval History Presented to Fredrick Maurice Powicke* (Oxford, 1948), pp. 429–454.

Alsop, J. D., 'Cromwell and the Church in 1531: The Case of Waltham Abbey', *Journal of Ecclesiastical History*, 31 (1980), pp. 327–330.

Atterbury, F., *The Rights, Powers, and Privileges of an English Convocation* (London, 1701).

Baker, J. H., *The Reports of John Spelman* (2 vols, London, 1978).

—, *The Order of Serjeants at Law* (London, 1984).

—, 'The English Legal Profession, 1450–1550', in J. H. Baker, *The Legal Profession and the Common Law: Historical Essays* (London, 1986), pp. 75–99.

—, 'Oral Instruction in Land Law and Conveyancing, 1250–1500', in J. A. Bush and A. Wijffels, eds, *Learning the Law: Teaching and the Transmission of English Law, 1150–1900* (London, 1999), pp. 157–175.

—, *Reports of Cases by John Caryll* (2 vols, London, 2000).

—, *The Oxford History of the Laws of England, Volume VI: 1483–1558* (Oxford, 2003).

—, *Legal Education in London, 1250–1850* (London, 2005).

Ban, J. D., 'English Reformation: Product of King or Minister?', *Church History*, 41 (1972), pp. 186–197.

Batho, G. R., 'The Household Papers of Henry Percy, Ninth Earl of Northumberland (1564–1632)', *Camden Society*, Third Series, xciii (1962).

Beckingsale, B. W., *Thomas Cromwell: Tudor Minister* (London, 1978).

Bell, H. E., *An Introduction to the History and Records of the Court of Wards and Liveries* (Cambridge, 1953).

Bellamy, J. G., *The Law of Treason in England in the Middle Ages* (Cambridge, 1970).

Bernard, G. W., 'The Rise of Sir William Compton, Early Tudor Courtier', *English Historical Review*, xcvi (1981), pp. 754–777.

—, *The Power of the Early Tudor Nobility: A Study of the Fourth and Fifth Earls of Shrewsbury* (Brighton, 1985).

—, 'The Pardon of the Clergy Reconsidered', *Journal of Ecclesiastical History*, 37 (1986), pp. 262–275.

—, 'Politics and Government in Tudor England', *Historical Journal*, 31 (1988), pp. 159–182.

—, 'The Fall of Anne Boleyn', *English Historical Review*, cvi (1991), pp. 584–610.

—, 'Anne Boleyn's Religion', *Historical Journal*, 36 (1993), pp. 1–20.

—, 'The Fall of Wolsey Reconsidered', *Journal of British Studies*, 35 (1996), pp. 277–310.

—, 'Elton's Cromwell', *History*, 83 (1998), pp. 587–607.

—, 'The Piety of Henry VIII', in N. S. Amos, A. Pettegree and H. Van Nierop, eds, *The Education of a Christian Society: Humanism and the Reformation in Britain and the Netherlands* (Aldershot, 1999), pp. 62–88.

—, 'Court and Government', in G. W. Bernard, *Power and Politics in Tudor England* (Aldershot, 2000), pp. 129–134.

—, 'Elton's Cromwell', in G. W. Bernard, *Power and Politics in Tudor England* (Aldershot, 2000).

—, *Power and Politics in Tudor England* (Aldershot, 2000).

—, *The King's Reformation: Henry VIII and the Remaking of the English Church* (New Haven, CT and London, 2005).

—, *Anne Boleyn: Fatal Attractions* (New Haven, CT and London, 2010).

—, 'The Dissolution of the Monasteries', *History*, 96 (2011), pp. 390–409.

—, *The Late Medieval Church: Vitality and Vulnerability before the Break with Rome* (New Haven, CT and London, 2012).

Bettey, J. H., *Suppression of the Monasteries in the West Country* (Stroud, 1989).

Biddle, M., L. Barfield and A. Millard, 'The Excavation of the Manor of the More, Rickmansworth, Hertfordshire', *Archaeological Journal*, 116 (1959), pp. 136–199.

Bindoff, S. T., ed., *History of Parliament: The House of Commons, 1509–1558* (3 vols, London, 1982).

Bloch, M., *The Royal Touch: Sacred Monarchy and Scrofula in England and France* (London, 1973).

Block, J., 'Thomas Cromwell's Patronage of Preaching', *Sixteenth Century Journal*, 8 (1977), pp. 37–50.

—, *Factional Politics and the English Reformation, 1520–1540* (Woodbridge, 1993).

—, 'Political Corruption in Henrician England', in C. Charlton, R. L. Woods, M. L. Robertson and J. S. Block, eds, *State, Sovereigns and Society in Early Modern England* (Stroud, 1998), pp. 45–57.

Borman, T., *Thomas Cromwell: The Untold Story of Henry VIII's Most Faithful Servant* (London, 2014).

Bowker, M., 'The Supremacy and the Episcopate: The Struggle for Control, 1534–1540', *Historical Journal*, 18 (1975), pp. 227–243.

Bradshaw, B., 'Cromwellian Reform and the Origins of the Kildare Rebellion, 1533–34', *Transactions of the Royal Historical Society*, Fifth Series, 27 (1977), pp. 69–93.

—, 'The Tudor Commonwealth: Reform and Revision', *Historical Journal*, 22 (1979), pp. 455–476.

Brand, P., *The Origins of the English Legal Profession* (Oxford, 1992).

Brayshay, M., P. Harrison and B. Chalkley, 'Knowledge, Nationhood and Governance: The Speed of the Royal Post in Early-Modern England', *Journal of Historical Geography*, 24 (1998), pp. 265–288.

Brigden, S., 'Popular Disturbances and the Fall of Thomas Cromwell and the Reformers, 1539–1540', *Historical Journal*, 24 (1981), pp. 257–278.

—, 'Thomas Cromwell and the "Brethren"', in C. C. Cross, D. Loades and J. J. Scarisbrick, eds, *Law and Government under the Tudors: Essays Presented to Sir Geoffrey Elton* (Cambridge, 1988), pp. 31–50.

—, *New Worlds, Lost Worlds* (London, 2000).

Brooks, C. W., *Pettyfoggers and Vipers of the Commonwealth: The Lower Branches of the Legal Profession in Early Modern England* (Cambridge, 1986).

Burnet, G., *The History of the Reformation of the Church of England* (4 vols, London, 1837).

Canning, J., *A History of Medieval Political Thought, 300–1450* (London and New York, 1996).

Carlton, C., 'Thomas Cromwell: A Study in Interrogation', *Albion*, 5 (1973), pp. 116–127.

Cavill, P. R., 'Debate and Dissent in Henry VII's Parliaments', *Parliamentary History*, 25 (2006), pp. 160–175.

—, *The English Parliaments of Henry VII, 1485–1504* (Oxford, 2009).

—, '"The Enemy of God and His Church": James Hobart, Praemunire and the Clergy of Norwich Diocese', *Journal of Legal History*, 32 (2011), pp. 127–150.

—, 'A Perspective on the Church-State Confrontation of 1515: The Passage of 4 Henry VIII, c. 2.', *Journal of Ecclesiastical History*, 63 (2012), pp. 655–670.

Challis, C. E., *The Tudor Coinage* (Manchester, 1978).

Chambers, D. S., *Cardinal Bainbridge in the Court of Rome* (Oxford, 1965).

Chapman, C. R., *Ecclesiastical Courts, Officials and Records: Sin, Sex and Probate* (second edn, Dursley, 1997).

Chibi, A. A., *Henry VIII's Bishops: Diplomats, Administrators, Scholars and Shepherds* (Cambridge, 2003)

Chrimes, S. B., *English Constitutional Ideas in the Fifteenth Century* (Cambridge, 1936).

Churchill, I. J., *Canterbury Administration* (2 vols, London, 1933).

Coby, J. P., *Thomas Cromwell: Henry VIII's Henchman* (London, 2012).

Cohn, H. J., ed., *Government in Reformation Europe, 1520–1560* (Basingstoke, 1971).

Coleman, C. and D. Starkey, eds, *Revolution Reassessed: Revisions in the History of Tudor Government and Administration* (Oxford, 1986).

Collier, J., *An Ecclesiastical History of Great Britain* (9 vols, London, 1840–1841).

Collinson, P., 'The Monarchical Republic of Queen Elizabeth I', *Bulletin of the John Rylands University Library of Manchester*, 69 (1987), pp. 394–424.

—, 'Geoffrey Rudolph Elton, 1921–1994', *Proceedings of the British Academy*, 94 (1997), pp. 429–455.

Colvin, H. M., ed., *History of the King's Works* (6 vols, London, 1963–1982).

Cook, G. H., *Letters to Cromwell and Others on the Suppression of the Monasteries* (London, 1965).

Cooper, J. P., 'The Supplication against the Ordinaries Reconsidered', *English Historical Review*, lxxii (1957), pp. 616–641.

—, 'A Revolution in Tudor History?', *Past and Present*, 26 (1963), pp. 110–113.

Cox, M. H. and P. Norman, *Survey of London, Volume XIII: The Parish of St Margaret, Westminster, Part II* (London, 1930).

Croft, P., 'Political Biography: A Defence', *Contemporary British History*, 10 (1996), pp. 67–75.

Davies, C. S. L., 'Provisions for Armies, 1509–50: A Study in the Effectiveness of Early Tudor Government', *Economic History Review*, 17 (1964), pp. 243–248.

—, *Peace, Print and Protestantism* (London, 1976).

—, 'The Cromwellian Decade: Authority and Consent', *Transactions of the Royal Historical Society*, Sixth Series, vii (1996), pp. 177–195.

—, 'Tournai and the English Crown, 1513–1519', *Historical Journal*, 41 (1998), pp. 1–26.

—, 'Review: Representation, Repute, Reality', *English Historical Review*, cxxiv (2009), pp. 1432–1447.

Derry, J., 'Political Biography: A Defence (2)', *Contemporary British History*, 10 (1996), pp. 75–81.

Dickens, A. G., 'The Northern Convocation and Henry VIII', *Church History Quarterly*, cxxvii (1938), pp. 84–102.

—, *Thomas Cromwell and the English Reformation* (London, 1959).

—, *The English Reformation* (London, 1964).

Dietz, F. C., *English Government Finance, 1485–1558* (second edn, London, 1964).

Doran, S., 'The Finances of an Elizabethan Nobleman and Royal Servant: A Case Study of Thomas Radcliffe, Third Earl of Sussex', *Historical Review*, 61 (1988), pp. 286–300.

Dormer, E. W., *Gray of Reading* (Reading, 1923).

Douthwaite, W. R., *Gray's Inn, its History and Associations* (London, 1886).

Edwards, A. S. G., 'Thomas Cromwell and Cavendish's Life of Wolsey: The Uses of a Tudor Biography', *Revue de l'Université d'Ottawa*, 43 (1972), pp. 292–296.

Ellis, J. J., *Thomas Cromwell* (London, 1891).

Ellis, S. G., 'Thomas Cromwell and Ireland, 1532–1540', *Historical Journal*, 23 (1980), pp. 497–519.

Elton, G. R., 'The Evolution of a Reformation Statute', *English Historical Review*, lxiv (1949), pp. 174–197.

—, 'A Note on the First Act of Annates', *Bulletin of the Institute of Historical Research*, 23 (1950), pp. 203–204.

—, 'The Commons' Supplication of 1532: Parliamentary Manoeuvres in the Reign of Henry VIII', *English Historical Review*, lxvi (1951), pp. 507–534.

—, *The Tudor Revolution in Government: Administrative Changes in the Reign of Henry VIII* (Cambridge, 1953).

—, 'King or Minister? The Man behind the Henrician Reformation', *History*, 39 (1954), pp. 216–232.

—, 'Thomas Cromwell', *History Today*, 6 (1956), pp. 528–536.

—, *The Tudor Constitution: Documents and Commentary* (Cambridge, 1962).

—, 'The Tudor Revolution: A Reply', *Past and Present*, 29 (1964), pp. 26–50.

—, 'A Revolution in Tudor History?', *Past and Present*, 32 (1965), pp. 103–110.

—, *Policy and Police: The Enforcement of the Reformation in the Age of Thomas Cromwell* (Cambridge, 1972).

—, *Reform and Renewal: Thomas Cromwell and the Common Weal* (Cambridge, 1973).

—, 'Thomas Cromwell's Decline and Fall', in G. R. Elton, *Studies in Tudor and Stuart Politics and Government, Papers and Reviews, 1946–1972*, Volume I, *Tudor Politics/Tudor Government* (Cambridge, 1974), pp. 189–231.

—, 'The Political Creed of Thomas Cromwell', in G. R. Elton, *Studies in Tudor and Stuart Politics and Government, Papers and Reviews, 1946–1972* Volume II, *Parliament/Political Thought* (Cambridge, 1974), pp. 215–236.

—, *Studies in Tudor and Stuart Politics and Government, Papers and Reviews, 1946–1990* (4 vols, Cambridge, 1974–1992).

—, 'Taxation for War and Peace in Early-Tudor England', in J. M. Winter, ed., *War and Economic Development: Essays in Memory of David Joslin* (Cambridge, 1975).

—, *Reform and Reformation, England 1509–1558* (London, 1977).

—, 'Thomas Cromwell Redivivus', in G. R. Elton, *Studies in Tudor and Stuart Politics and Government*, Volume III, *Papers and Reviews, 1973–1981* (Cambridge, 1983), pp. 373–390.

—, 'Tudor Government', *Historical Journal*, 31 (1988), pp. 425–434.

—, 'Thomas More and Thomas Cromwell', in G. J. Schochet, ed., *Reformation, Humanism, and 'Revolution'* (Washington, DC, 1990), pp. 95–111.

—, *England under the Tudors* (third edn, London, 1991).

—, *Thomas Cromwell* (Bangor, 1991).

—, 'How Corrupt was Thomas Cromwell?', *Historical Journal*, 36 (1993), pp. 905–908.

—, *The Practice of History* (second edn, Oxford, 2002).

Emden, A. B., *A Biographical Register of the University of Oxford, A. D. 1500 to 1540* (Oxford, 1974).

Evans, F. M. G., *The Principal Secretary of State. A Survey of the Office from 1558 to 1680* (Manchester, 1923).

Finberg, H. P. R., 'The Gostwicks of Willington', *Publications of the Bedfordshire Historical Records Society*, xxxvi (1955), pp. 46–75.

Fisher, H. A. L., *The Political History of England, Volume V: From the Accession of Henry VII to the Death of Henry VIII, 1485–1547* (London, 1906).

Fisher, R. M., 'Thomas Cromwell, the Dissolution of the Monasteries, and the Inns of Court, 1534–1540', *Journal of the Society of Public Teachers of Law*, 14 (1977), pp. 103–118.

—, 'Thomas Cromwell, Humanism and Educational Reform, 1530–40', *Bulletin of the Institute of Historical Research*, 50 (1977), pp. 151–163.

Foster, J., ed., *Alumni Oxonienses: The Members of the University of Oxford, 1500–1714* (4 vols in 2, Nendeln and Lichtenstein, 1968).

Franks, A. W. and H. A. Grueber, eds, *Medallic Illustrations of the History of Great Britain and Ireland* (19 vols, London, 1904).

Freeman, T., 'Text, Lies and Microfilm: Reading and Misreading Foxe's "Book of Martyrs"', *Sixteenth Century Journal*, 30 (1999), pp. 23–46.

Froude, J. A., *History of England from the Fall of Wolsey to the Death of Elizabeth* (12 vols, London, 1856–1870).

Gairdner, J., 'Review: Life and Letters of Thomas Cromwell by Roger Bigelow Merriman', *English Historical Review*, xvii (1902), pp. 787–790.

Galton, A., *The Character and Times of Thomas Cromwell: A Sixteenth-Century Criticism* (Birmingham, 1887).

Garrett, C. H., *The Marian Exiles: A Study in the Origins of Elizabethan Puritanism* (Cambridge, 1966).

Gasquet, F. A., *English Monastic Life* (London, 1904).

—, *Henry VIII and the English Monasteries* (London, 1906).

Gibbons, G., *The Political Career of Thomas Wriothesley, First Earl of Southampton, 1505–1550, Henry VIII's Last Chancellor* (Lampeter, 2001).

Girouard, M., *Life in the English Country House* (London, 1978).

Graves, M. A. R., 'The Management of the Elizabethan House of Commons: The Council's "Men of Business"', *Parliamentary History*, 2 (1983), pp. 11–38.

Grierson, P., 'The Origins of the English Sovereign and the Symbolism of the Closed Crown', *British Numismatic Journal*, 33 (1964), pp. 118–135.

Griffiths, R. A., *Sir Rhys ap Thomas and his Family: A Study of the Wars of the Roses and Early Tudor Politics* (Cardiff, 1993).

Gunn, S. J., *Charles Brandon, Duke of Suffolk, c.1484–1545* (Oxford, 1988).

—, 'The Courtiers of Henry VIII', *English Historical Review*, cviii (1993), pp. 23–49.

—, *Early Tudor Government, 1485–1558* (Basingstoke, 1995).

—, 'The Structures of Politics in Early Tudor England', *Transactions of the Royal Historical Society*, Sixth Series, 5 (1995), pp. 59–90.

—, 'Sir Thomas Lovell (*c*.1449–1524): A New Man in a New Monarchy?', in J. L. Watts, ed., *The End of the Middle Ages? England in the Fifteenth and Sixteenth Centuries* (Stroud, 1998), pp. 117–153.

—, 'Edmund Dudley and the Church', *Journal of Ecclesiastical History*, 51 (2000), pp. 509–526.

Guy, J. A., *The Cardinal's Court: The Impact of Thomas Wolsey in Star Chamber* (Hassocks, 1977).

—, *The Public Career of Sir Thomas More* (Brighton, 1980).

—, 'The Tudor Commonwealth: Revising Thomas Cromwell', *Historical Journal*, 23 (1980), pp. 681–687.

—, 'Henry VIII and the *Praemunire* Manoeuvres of 1530–1531', *English Historical Review*, xcvii (1982), pp. 481–503.

—, *Christopher St German on Chancery and Statute* (London, 1985).

—, *The Court of Star Chamber and its Records to the Reign of Elizabeth I* (London, 1985).

—, 'Law, Faction and Parliament in the Sixteenth Century', *Historical Journal*, 28 (1985), pp. 441–453.

—, 'The Privy Council: Revolution or Evolution?', in C. Coleman and D. Starkey, eds, *Revolution Reassessed: Revisions in the History of Tudor Government and Administration* (Oxford, 1986), pp. 59–86.

—, 'Thomas Cromwell and the Intellectual Origins of the Henrician Reformation', in A. Fox and J. Guy, eds, *Reassessing the Henrician Age: Humanism, Politics and Reform, 1500–1550* (Oxford, 1986), pp. 151–178.

—, 'Wolsey and the Parliament of 1523', in C. Cross, D. Loades and J. J. Scarisbrick, eds, *Law and Government under the Tudors* (Cambridge, 1988), pp. 1–19.

—, 'Reassessing Thomas Cromwell', *History Sixth*, 6 (1990), pp. 2–6.

—, *Tudor England* (Oxford, 1990).

—, 'Thomas Wolsey, Thomas Cromwell and the Reform of Henrician Government', in D. MacCulloch, ed., *The Reign of Henry VIII: Politics, Policy and Piety* (Basingstoke, 1995), pp. 35–57.

—, 'Tudor Monarchy and Political Culture', in J. Morrill, ed., *The Oxford Illustrated History of Tudor and Stuart Britain* (Oxford, 1996), pp. 219–238.

—, *Thomas More* (London, 2000).

—, ed., *The Tudor Monarchy* (London, 1997).

Gwyn, P., *The King's Cardinal: The Rise and Fall of Thomas Wolsey* (London, 1990).

Haas, S. W., 'The *Disputatio inter Clericum et Militem*: Was Berthelet's 1531 Edition the First Henrician Polemic of Thomas Cromwell?', *Moreana*, xiv (1977), pp. 65–72.

—, 'Henry VIII's Glasse of Truthe', *History*, 64 (1979), pp. 353–362.

—, 'Martin Luther's "Divine Right" Kingship and the Royal Supremacy: Two Tracts from the 1531 Parliament and Convocation of the Clergy', *Journal of Ecclesiastical History*, 31 (1980), pp. 317–325.

Haigh, C., 'Anticlericalism and the English Reformation', in C. Haigh, ed., *The English Reformation Revised* (Cambridge, 1987), pp. 56–75.

—, *English Reformations: Religion, Politics, and Society under the Tudors* (Oxford, 1993).

—, 'Review', *English Historical Review*, cxxi (2006), pp. 1456–1457.

Hamilton, N., 'In Defence of the Practice of Biography', *Contemporary British History*, 10 (1996), pp. 81–97.

Hamilton Thompson, A., *Visitations of Religious Houses in the Diocese of Lincoln, Volume II, Part I* (London, 1919).

—, *The Abbey of St Mary of the Meadows, Leicester* (Leicester, 1949).

Harper-Bill, C., 'Dean Colet's Convocation Sermon and the Pre-Reformation Church in England', *History*, 73 (1988), pp. 191–210.

Harris, B. J., 'Women and Politics in Early Tudor England', *Historical Journal*, 33 (1990), pp. 259–281.

Harris, I., 'Some Origins of a Tudor Revolution', *English Historical Review*, cxxvi (2011), pp. 1355–1385.

Harriss, G. L., 'Thomas Cromwell's "New Principle" of Taxation', *English Historical Review*, xciii (1978), pp. 721–738.

—, *Shaping the Nation: England, 1360–1461* (Oxford, 2005).

—, 'Medieval Government and Statecraft', *Past and Present*, 25 (1963), pp. 8–39.

—, and P. Williams, 'A Revolution in Tudor History?', *Past and Present*, 25 (1963), pp. 3–59.

—, 'A Revolution in Tudor History?', *Past and Present*, 31 (1965), pp. 87–97.

Harvey, P. D. A., *Manorial Records* (London, 1977).

Hasted, E., *The History and Topographical Survey of the County of Kent* (12 vols, Canterbury, 1797).

Hawkins, E., A. W. Franks and H. A. Grueber, eds, *Medallic Illustrations of the History of Great Britain and Ireland to the Death of George II* (2 vols, London, 1885).

Headrick, T. E., *The Town Clerk in English Local Government* (London, 1982).

Heal, F., *Of Prelates and Princes: A Study of the Economic and Social Position of the Tudor Episcopate* (Cambridge, 1980).

Heale, M., '"Not a Thing for a Stranger to Enter Upon": The Selection of Monastic Superiors in Late Medieval and Early Tudor England', in J. Burton and K. Stöber, eds, *Monasteries and Society in the British Isles in the Later Middle Ages* (Woodbridge, 2008), pp. 51–68.

Higham, C. S. S., *Wimbledon Manor House under the Cecils* (London, 1962).

Higham, F. M. G., 'A Note on the Pre-Tudor Secretary', in A. G. Little and F. M. Powicke, eds, *Essays in Medieval History Presented to Thomas Fredrick Tout* (Manchester, 1925), pp. 361–367.

Hilderbrandt, E., 'Christopher Mont, Anglo-German Diplomat', *Sixteenth Century Journal*, 15 (1984), pp. 281–292.

Hoak, D. E., *The King's Council in the Reign of Edward VI* (Cambridge, 1976).

—, 'The Secret History of the Tudor Court: The King's Coffers and the King's Purse, 1542–1553', *Journal of British Studies*, 26 (1987), pp. 208–231.

—, 'The Iconography of the Crown Imperial', in D. Hoak, ed., *Tudor Political Culture* (Cambridge, 1995), pp. 54–104.

Holdsworth, W. S., *A History of English Law*, Volume VI (second edn, London, 1937).

Houlbrooke, R., 'The Decline of Ecclesiastical Jurisdiction under the Tudors', in R. O'Day and F. Heal, eds, *Continuity and Change: Personnel and Administration of the Church in England, 1500–1642* (Leicester, 1976), pp. 239–259.

Howell, M., *Regalian Right in Medieval England* (London, 1962).

Hoyle, R. W., 'The Anglo-Scottish War of 1532–3', *Camden Miscellany*, xxxi, Fourth Series, 44 (1992), pp. 23–24.

—, 'Henry Percy, Sixth Earl of Northumberland, and the Fall of the House of Percy', in G. W. Bernard, ed., *The Tudor Nobility* (Manchester, 1992), pp. 180–211.

—, 'The Origins of the Dissolution of the Monasteries', *Historical Journal*, 38 (1995), pp. 275–305.

—, 'War and Public Finance', in D. MacCulloch, ed., *The Reign of Henry VIII: Politics, Policy and Piety* (Basingstoke, 1995), pp. 78–79.

Hudson, A., *The Premature Reformation: Wycliffite Texts and Lollard History* (Oxford, 1988).

Hughes, P., *The Reformation in England* (London, 1984).

Hurstfield, J., *The Queen's Wards: Wardship and Marriage under Elizabeth I* (London, 1958).

—, 'Political Corruption in Modern England: The Historian's Problem', in J. Hurstfield, *Freedom, Corruption and Government in Elizabethan England* (London, 1973), pp. 137–163.

Hutchinson, F. E., *Cranmer and the English Reformation* (London, 1961).

Hutchinson, R., *Thomas Cromwell: The Rise and Fall of Henry VIII's Most Notorious Minister* (London, 2007).

Innes, A. D., *Ten Tudor Statesmen* (London, 1906).

Ives, E. W., 'The Genesis of the Statute of Uses', *English Historical Review*, lxxxii (1967), pp. 673–697.

—, 'The Common Lawyers in Pre-Reformation England', *Transactions of the Royal Historical Society*, Fifth Series, 18 (1968), pp. 145–173.

—, *The Common Lawyers of Pre-Reformation England, Thomas Kebell: A Case, Study* (Cambridge, 1983).

—, 'The Fall of Wolsey', in S. J. Gunn and P. G. Lindley, eds, *Cardinal Wolsey: Church, State and Art* (Cambridge, 1991), pp. 286–316.

—, *The Life and Death of Anne Boleyn* (Oxford, 2004).

Jack, S. M., 'Henry VIII's Attitude towards Royal Finance: Penny Wise and Pound Foolish?', in C. Giry-Deloison, ed., *Francois Ier et Henri VIII. Deux princes de la Renaissance (1515–1547)* (Arras, 1997), pp. 145–163.

Jeffries Davis, E., 'The Beginning of the Dissolution: Christchurch, Aldgate, 1532', *Transactions of the Royal Historical Society*, Fourth Series, 8 (1925), pp. 127–150.

Kelly, H. A., *The Matrimonial Trials of Henry VIII* (Stanford, CA, 1976).

Kelly, M., 'The Submission of the Clergy', *Transactions of the Royal Historical Society*, Fifth Series, 15 (1965), pp. 97–119.

Kitching, C. J., 'The Probate Jurisdiction of Thomas Cromwell as Vicegerent', *Bulletin of the Institute of Historical Research*, 46 (1973), pp. 102–106.

Knowles, D., *The Religious Orders in England* (3 vols, Cambridge, 1955).

—, 'The Eltonian Revolution in Early Tudor History', *Historical Journal*, 17 (1974), pp. 867–872.

—, and R. N. Hadcock, *Medieval Religious Houses: England and Wales* (London, 1971).

Koebner, R., 'The Imperial Crown of this Realm: Henry VIII, Constantine the Great and Polydore Vergil', *Bulletin of the Institute of Historical Research*, 26 (1953), pp. 29–52.

Lander, J. R., *Government and Community: England, 1450–1509* (London, 1980).

Legg, L. W., *English Coronation Records* (London, 1901).

Lehmberg, S. E., 'Supremacy and Vicegerency: A Re-examination', *English Historical Review*, lxxxi (1966), pp. 225–236.

—, *The Reformation Parliament, 1529–1536* (Cambridge, 1970).

—, 'Sir Thomas Audeley: A Soul as Black as Marble?', in A. J. Slavin, ed., *Tudor Men and Institutions: Studies in English Law and Government* (Baton Rouge, LA, 1972), pp. 3–32.

—, 'The Religious Beliefs of Thomas Cromwell', in R. L. DeMolen, ed., *Leaders of the Reformation* (London, 1984), pp. 134–152.

List and Index Society, Volume 316, Key to The National Archives Documents in Letters and Papers, Foreign and Domestic, Henry VIII, Volume IV, ed. J. M. Crawford and A. R. Hanson (Wiltshire, 2006).

List and Index Society, Volume 325, Key to The National Archives Documents in Letters and Papers, Foreign and Domestic, Henry VIII, Volumes V–IX, ed. J. M. Crawford and A. R. Hanson (Wiltshire, 2008).

Loades, D., *Mary Tudor: A Life* (Oxford, 1989).

—, *Thomas Cromwell: Servant to Henry VIII* (Stroud, 2013).

Logan, F. D., 'Thomas Cromwell and the Vicegerency in Spirituals: A Revisitation', *English Historical Review*, ciii (1988), pp. 658–668.

Lunt, W. E., *Financial Relations of the Papacy with England, 1327–1534*, (Cambridge, MA, 1962).

Lyson, D., ed., *The Environs of London* (4 vols, London, 1792).

MacCaffrey, W. T., 'Place and Patronage in Elizabethan Politics', in S. T. Bindoff, J. Hurstfield and C. H. Williams, eds, *Elizabethan Government and Society: Essays Presented to Sir John Neale* (London, 1961), pp. 95–127.

McCampbell, A. E., 'The London Parish and the London Precinct, 1640–1660', *Guildhall Studies in London History*, 2 (1976), pp. 107–124.

McConica, J. K., *English Humanists and Reformation Politics under Henry VIII and Edward VI* (Oxford, 1965).

—, ed., *The History of the University of Oxford*, Volume III, *The Collegiate University* (Oxford, 1986).

MacCulloch, D., 'Henry VIII and the Reform of the Church', in D. MacCulloch, ed., *The Reign of Henry VIII: Politics, Policy and Piety* (Basingstoke, 1995), pp. 159–181.

—, *Thomas Cranmer: A Life* (New Haven, CT, and London, 1996).

—, *Reformation: Europe's House Divided* (London, 2003).

McEntegart, R., *Henry VIII, the League of Schmalkalden and the English Reformation* (Woodbridge, 2002).

McFarlane, K. B., *Letters to Friends, 1940–1966*, ed. G. L. Harriss (Oxford, 1997).

Malden, H. E., ed., *A History of the County of Surrey* (4 vols, London, 1912).

Mantel, H., *Wolf Hall* (London, 2009).

—, *Bring up the Bodies* (London, 2012).

Marius, R., 'Henry VIII, Thomas More, and the Bishop of Rome', in M. J. Moore, ed., *Quincentennial Essays on St Thomas More* (Boone, NC, 1978), pp. 89–108.

—, *Thomas More* (London, 1993).

Matthew, H. C. G. and B. Harrison, *Oxford Dictionary of National Biography* (*ODNB*) (Oxford, 2004).

Mayer, T. F., 'Tournai and Tyranny: Imperial Kingship and Critical Humanism', *Historical Journal*, 34 (1994), pp. 257–277.

—, 'On the Road to 1534: The Occupation of Tournai and Henry VIII's Theory of Sovereignty', in D. Hoak, ed., *Tudor Political Culture* (Cambridge, 1995), pp. 11–31.

—, *Reginald Pole: Prince and Prophet* (Cambridge, 2000).

Mears, N., 'Courts, Courtiers, and Culture in Tudor England', *Historical Journal*, 46 (2003), pp. 703–722.

Merriman, R. B., *Life and Letters of Thomas Cromwell* (2 vols, Oxford, 1902).

Metzger, F., 'The Last Phase of the Medieval Chancery', in A. Harding, ed., *Law-Making and Law-Makers in British History* (London, 1980), pp. 79–90.

Miller, H., 'Subsidy Assessments of the Peerage in the Sixteenth Century', *Bulletin of the Institute of Historical Research*, 28 (1955), pp. 15–34.

—, 'London and Parliament in the Reign of Henry VIII', *Bulletin of the Institute of Historical Research*, 35 (1962), pp. 128–149.

—, *Henry VIII and the English Nobility* (Oxford, 1986).

Morgan, D. A. L., 'The Individual Style of the English Gentleman', in M. Jones, ed., *Gentry and the Lesser Nobility in Later Medieval England* (Stroud, 1986), pp. 15–36.

Mozley, J. F., *Coverdale and his Bibles* (London, 1953).

Murphy, V., 'The Literature and Propaganda of Henry VIII's First Divorce', in D. MacCulloch, ed., *The Reign of Henry VIII: Politics, Policy and Piety* (Basingstoke, 1995), pp. 135–158.

Newman, J., 'Cardinal Wolsey's Collegiate Foundations', in S. J. Gunn and P. G. Lindley, eds, *Cardinal Wolsey: Church, State and Art* (Cambridge, 1991), pp. 103–116.

Newton, A. P., 'The King's Chamber under the Early Tudors', *English Historical Review*, xxxii (1917), pp. 348–372.

Nicholson, G., 'The Act of Appeals and the English Reformation', in C. Cross, D. Loades and J. Scarisbrick, eds, *Law and Government under the Tudors: Essays Presented to Sir Geoffrey Elton* (Cambridge, 1988), pp. 19–30.

O'Brien, P., 'Is Political Biography a Good Thing?', *Contemporary British History*, 10 (1996), pp. 60–67.

O'Grady, P., *Henry VIII and the Conforming Catholics* (Collegeville, MN, 1994).

Ogle, A., *The Tragedy of Lollards' Tower: Its Place in History, 1514–1533* (Oxford, 1949).

Pantin, W. A., *The English Church in the Fourteenth Century* (Cambridge, 1955).

—, 'The Fourteenth Century', in C. H. Lawrence, ed., *The English Church and the Papacy in the Middle Ages* (New York, 1965), pp. 157–194.

Parker, T. M., 'Was Thomas Cromwell a Machiavellian?', *Journal of Ecclesiastical History*, 1 (1950), pp. 63–75.

Parks, G., *The English Traveller to Italy* (Rome, 1954).

Payling, S. J., 'The Rise of Lawyers in the Lower House, 1395–1536', *Parliamentary History*, 23 (2004), pp. 103–120.

—, 'The House of Commons, 1307–1529', in C. Jones, ed., *A Short History of Parliament* (Woodbridge, 2012), pp. 75–86.

Peery, G. G., 'Episcopal Visitations of the Austin Canons of Leicestershire and Dorchester', *English Historical Review*, iv (1889), pp. 304–312.

Phillips, J., 'The Cromwells of Putney', *Antiquarian Magazine*, ii (1882), pp. 56–62 and 178–186.

Pickthorn, K., *Early Tudor Government* (2 vols, Cambridge, 1923).

Pocock, N., *Records of the Reformation: the Divorce, 1527–1533* (2 vols, Oxford, 1870).

Pollard, A. F., *Henry VIII* (London, 1913).

—, 'Council, Star Chamber, and Privy Council under the Tudors: 1. The Council', *English Historical Review*, xxxvii (1922), pp. 337–360.

—, 'Council, Star Chamber, and Privy Council under the Tudors: 2. The Star Chamber', *English Historical Review*, xxxvii (1922), pp. 516–539.

—, 'Council, Star Chamber, and Privy Council under the Tudors: 3. The Privy Council', *English Historical Review*, xxxviii (1923), pp. 42–60.

—, *Wolsey* (London, 1929).

—, 'Thomas Cromwell's Parliamentary Lists', *Bulletin of the Institute of Historical Research*, 9 (1931–32), pp. 32–43.

Pollard, A. W. and G. R. Redgrave, eds, *The Short Title Catalogue of Books Printed in England, Scotland and Ireland, 1475–1640* (second edn, revised and enlarged by W. A. Jackson, F. S. Ferguson and K. F. Pantzer, London, 1976).

Potter, D., 'Sir John Gage, Tudor Courtier and Soldier (1479–1556)', *English Historical Review*, cxvii (2002), pp. 1109–1147.

Prestwich, M., 'Medieval Biography', *Journal of Interdisciplinary History*, 40 (2010), pp. 325–346.

Pronay, N., 'The Chancellor, the Chancery, and the Council at the End of the Fifteenth Century', in H. Hearder and H. R. Loyn, eds, *British Government and Administration: Studies Presented to S. B. Chrimes* (Cardiff, 1974), pp. 87–103.

Pugh, T. B., *The Marcher Lordships of South Wales, 1415–1536* (Cardiff, 1963).

Rail, L. W., 'The Shallow End of History? The Substance and Future of Political Biography', *Journal of Interdisciplinary History*, 40 (2010), pp. 375–397.

Ramsay, N., 'What was the Legal Profession?', in M. A. Hicks, ed., *Profit, Piety and the Professions in Later Medieval England* (Stroud, 1990), pp. 62–71.

Redworth, G., *In Defence of the Church Catholic: The Life of Stephen Gardiner* (Oxford, 1990).

Rex, R., *Henry VIII and the English Reformation* (Basingstoke, 1993).

—, 'Jasper Fyloll and the Enormities of the Clergy: Two Tracts written during the Reformation Parliament', *Sixteenth Century Journal*, 31 (2000), pp. 1043–1062.

—, 'Redating Henry VIII's *A Glasse of the Truthe*', *The Library*, Seventh Series, iv (2003), pp. 16–27.

—, 'The Religion of Henry VIII', *Historical Journal*, 57 (2014), pp. 1–32.

Rezneck, S., 'Constructive Treason by Words in the Fifteenth Century', *American Historical Review*, 33 (1928), pp. 544–552.

Richardson, G., 'Eternal Peace, Occasional War: Anglo-French Relations under Henry VIII', in S. Doran and G. Richardson, eds, *Tudor England and its Neighbours* (Basingstoke, 2005).

Richardson, W. C., *Tudor Chamber Administration, 1485–1547* (Baton Rouge, LA, 1952).

—, *Stephen Vaughan: Financial Agent of Henry VIII* (Baton Rouge, LA, 1953).

—, *History of the Court of Augmentations, 1536–1554* (Baton Rouge, LA, 1961).

Ridley, J., *Thomas Cranmer* (Oxford, 1962).

Robertson, M. L., '"The Art of the Possible": Thomas Cromwell's Management of West Country Government', *Historical Journal*, 32 (1989), pp. 793–816.

—, 'Profit and Purpose in the Development of Thomas Cromwell's Landed Estates', *Journal of British Studies*, 29 (1990), pp. 317–346.

—, 'A Reply to Helen Speight', *Historical Journal*, 37 (1994), pp. 639–641.

Rosser, G. and S. Thurley, 'Whitehall Palace and King's Street, Westminster: The Urban Cost of Princely Magnificence', *London Topographical Record*, 26 (1990), pp. 57–78.

Russell, C., 'Thomas Cromwell's Doctrine of Parliamentary Sovereignty', *Transactions of the Royal Historical Society*, Sixth Series, 5 (1996), pp. 235–247.

St Clare Byrne, M., *The Lisle Letters* (6 vols, Chicago, 1981).

Sainty, J., *A List of English Law Officers, King's Counsel and Holders of Patents of Precedence* (London, 1987).

Scarisbrick, J. J., 'The Pardon of the Clergy, 1531', *Historical Journal*, 12 (1956), pp. 22–39.

—, 'Clerical Taxation in England, 1485 to 1547', *Journal of Ecclesiastical History*, 11 (1960), pp. 41–54.

—, *Henry VIII* (New Haven, CT and London, 1997).

Schochet, G.J., ed., *Reformation, Humanism, and Revolution* (Washington, D.C., 1990).

Schofield, J., *The Rise and Fall of Thomas Cromwell: Henry VIII's Most Faithful Servant* (Stroud, 2008).

Schofield, R., *Taxation under the Early Tudors, 1485–1547* (Oxford, 2004).

Sharkey, J., 'Between king and pope: Thomas Wolsey and the Knight Mission', *Historical Research*, 84 (2011), pp. 236–248.

Shaw, W. A., *The Knights of England* (2 vols, London, 1906).

Skeeters, M. C., *Community and Clergy: Bristol and the Reformation, c.1530–c.1570* (Oxford, 1993).

Slavin, A. J., *Politics and Profit: A Study of Sir Ralph Sadler* (Cambridge, 1966).

—, *Thomas Cromwell on Church and Commonwealth: Selected Letters, 1523–1540* (New York, 1969).

—, 'Cromwell, Cranmer and Lord Lisle: A Study in the Politics of Reform', *Albion*, 9 (1977), pp. 316–336.

—, 'The Rochepot Affair', *Sixteenth Century Journal*, 10 (1979), pp. 3–19.

—, 'The Gutenberg Galaxy and the Tudor Revolution', in G. P. Tyson and S. S. Wagonheim, eds, *Print and Culture in the Renaissance: Essays on the Advent of Printing in Europe* (Newark, NJ, 1986), pp. 90–109.

—, 'Thomas Cromwell and the Printers: The Boston Pardons', in G. J. Schochet, ed., *Reformation, Humanism, and 'Revolution'* (Washington, DC, 1990), pp. 235–247.

Smith, D. M., ed., *The Heads of Religious Houses: England and Wales* (3 vols, Cambridge, 2008).

Somerville, R., *History of the Duchy of Lancaster* (2 vols, London, 1953).

Sowerby, T., '"All *Our* Books Do Be Sent into other Countreys and Translated": Henrician Polemic in its International Context', *English Historical Review*, cxxi (2006), pp. 1271–1299.

—, *Renaissance and Reform in Tudor England: The Careers of Sir Richard Morison c.1513–1556* (Oxford, 2010).

—, 'Anne Boleyn's Coronation', in T. Betteridge and G. Walker, eds, *The Oxford Handbook to Tudor Drama* (Oxford, 2012), pp. 386–402.

Speight, H. M., '"The Politics of Good Governance": Thomas Cromwell and the Government of Southwest England', *Historical Journal*, 37 (1994), pp. 623–638.

Starkey, D., 'Representation through Intimacy: A Study of the Symbolism of Monarchy and Court Office in Early Modern England', in I. Lewis, ed., *Symbols and Sentiments: Cross-Cultural Studies in Symbolism* (London, 1977), pp. 187–224.

—, 'The Age of the Household: Politics, Society and the Arts c.1350–c.1550', in S. Medcalf, ed., *The Later Middle Ages* (New York, 1981), pp. 225–290.

—, *The Reign of Henry VIII: Personalities and Politics* (London, 1985).

—, 'Court and Government', in C. Coleman and D. Starkey, eds, *Revolution Reassessed: Revisions in the History of Tudor Government and Administration* (Oxford, 1986), pp. 29–58.

—, 'Intimacy and Innovation: The Rise of the Privy Chamber, 1485–1547', in D. R. Starkey, ed., *The English Court from the Wars of the Roses to the Civil War* (London, 1987), pp. 71–118.

—, 'Communications: A Reply: Tudor Government: the Facts', *Historical Journal*, 31 (1988), pp. 921–931.

Stevens, J., *Music and Poetry in the Early Tudor Court* (Cambridge, 1979).

Stone, L., 'The Political Programme of Thomas Cromwell', *Bulletin of the Institute of Historical Research*, 24 (1951), pp. 1–18.

—, 'The Fruits of Office: The Case of Robert Cecil, First Earl of Salisbury, 1596–1612', in F. J. Fisher, ed., *Essays in the Economic and Social History of Tudor and Stuart England* (Cambridge, 1961), pp. 89–117.

Storey, R. L., 'Gentleman-Bureaucrats', in C. H. Clough, ed., *Profession, Vocation and Culture in Later Medieval England* (Liverpool, 1982), pp. 90–129.

Swanson, R. N., *Church and Society in Late Medieval England* (Oxford, 1989).

—, *Indulgences in Late Medieval England: Passports to Paradise?* (Cambridge, 2009).

Thomas, W., *The Pilgrim*, ed. J. A. Froude (London, 1861).

Thompson, B., 'Monasteries and their Patrons at Foundation and Dissolution', *Transactions of the Royal Historical Society*, Sixth Series, 4 (1994) pp. 115–116.

Thomson, J. A. F., *The Early Tudor Church and Society, 1485–1529* (London, 1993).

Thornbury, W., *Old and New London* (6 vols, London, 1828–1876).

Thornley, I. D., 'The Treason Legislation of Henry VIII (1531–1534)', *Transactions of the Royal Historical Society*, Third Series, 11 (1917), pp. 87–123.

—, 'The Destruction of Sanctuary', in R. W. Seton-Watson, ed., *Tudor Studies* (London, 1924), pp. 182–208.

Thurley, S., 'The Domestic Building Works of Cardinal Wolsey', in S. J. Gunn and P. G. Lindley, eds, *Cardinal Wolsey: Church, State and Art* (Cambridge, 1991), pp. 76–102.

—, *The Royal Palaces of Tudor England: Architecture and Court Life, 1460–1547* (New Haven, CT and London, 1993).

—, *Whitehall Palace: An Architectural History of the Royal Apartments, 1240–1690* (New Haven, CT and London, 1999).

Tout, T. F., *Chapters in the Administrative History of Mediaeval England* (6 vols, Manchester, 1920–1933).

Tudor-Craig, P., 'Henry VIII and King David', in D. Williams, ed., *Early Tudor England: Proceedings of the 1987 Harlaxton Symposium* (Woodbridge, 1989), pp. 183–205.

Ullmann, W., 'This Realm of England is an Empire', *Journal of Ecclesiastical History*, 30 (1979), pp. 175–203.

Underwood, W., 'Thomas Cromwell and William Marshall's Protestant Books', *Historical Journal*, 47 (2004), pp. 517–539.

Van Dyke, P., 'Reginald Pole and Thomas Cromwell: An Examination of the Apologia Ad Carolum Quintum', *American Historical Review*, 9 (1904), pp. 696–724.

—, *Renaissance Portraits* (New York, 1905).

Venn, J., and J. A. Venn, *Alumni Cantabrigienses* (2 vols, Cambridge, 1924).

Victoria History of the Counties of England, ed. H. A. Doubleday and W. Page (London):
A History of the County of Bedfordshire, i, ed. H. A. Doubleday and W. Page (1904).
A History of the County of Cumberland, ii, ed. W. Page (1907).
A History of the County of Hertfordshire, ii, ed. W. Page (1908).
A History of the County of Kent, ii, ed. W. Page (1926).
A History of the County of Leicestershire, ii, ed. W. G. Hoskins (1954).
A History of the County of Lincolnshire, ii, ed. W. Page (1906).
A History of the County of Middlesex, ii, ed. W. Page (1911).
A History of the County of Oxfordshire, iii, ed. R. B. Pugh (1907).
A History of the County of Staffordshire, iii, ed. M. W. Greenslade (1970).
A History of the County of Suffolk, ii, ed. W. Page (1907).
A History of the County of York, iii, ed. W. Page (1913).

Walker, G., *Writing under Tyranny: English Literature and the Henrician Reformation* (Oxford, 2005).

Ward, P. J., 'The Politics of Religion: Thomas Cromwell and the Reformation in Calais, 1534–1540', *Journal of Religious History*, 17 (1992), pp. 152–171.

Watts, J., *Henry VI and the Politics of Kingship* (Cambridge, 1996).

Watts, L., ed., *The End of the Middle Age? England in the Fifteenth and Sixteenth Centuries* (Stroud, 1998.)

Waugh, W. T., 'The Great Statute of Praemunire', *English Historical Review*, xxxvii (1922), pp. 173–205.

Webb, E. A., ed., *The Records of St Bartholomew's Priory, West Smithfield* (2 vols, London, 1921).

Wernham, R. B., 'Review: The Tudor Revolution in Government', *English Historical Review*, lxxi (1956), pp. 92–95.

Wilding, P., *Thomas Cromwell* (London, 1935).

Williams, N., *The Cardinal and the Secretary* (London, 1975).

Williams, P., 'Review', *English Historical Review*, lxxxviii (1973), pp. 594–595.

—, *The Tudor Regime* (Oxford, 1979).

Wolffe, B. P., 'The Management of English Royal Finances under the Yorkist Kings', *English Historical Review*, lxxi (1956), pp. 1–27.

—, *The Crown Lands, 1461 to 1536: An Aspect of Yorkist and Early Tudor Government* (London, 1970).

Wooding, L., *Henry VIII* (London and New York, 2009).

Woodward, G. W. O., 'The Role of Parliament in the Henrician Reformation', in H. Cohn, ed., *Government in Reformation Europe, 1520–1560* (London, 1971), pp. 113–125.

Youings, J., *The Dissolution of the Monasteries* (London, 1971).

Youngs, D., *Humphrey Newton (1466–1536): An Early Tudor Gentleman* (Woodbridge, 2008).

Zeeveld, W. G., *Foundations of Tudor Policy* (London, 1948).

Unpublished Dissertations

Elton, G. R., 'Thomas Cromwell: Aspects of his Administrative Work' (University of London PhD thesis, 1948).

Etty, C., 'Tudor Revolution? Royal Control of the Anglo-Scottish Border, 1483–1530' (University of Durham PhD thesis, 2005).

Everett, M. R. J., '"Without Recognisione of any Superior": Henry VIII and Imperial Kingship, 1509–1533' (University of Southampton MA thesis, 2009).

—, 'Qualities of a Royal Minister: Studies in the Rise of Thomas Cromwell, *c*.1520–1534' (University of Southampton PhD thesis, 2012).

Holder, N., 'The Medieval Friaries of London: A Topographic and Archaeological History, before and after the Dissolution' (University of London PhD thesis, 2011).

Kelly, M., 'Canterbury Jurisdiction and Influence during the Episcopate of William Warham, 1503–1532' (Cambridge University PhD thesis, 1963).

Robertson, M. L., 'Thomas Cromwell's Servants: The Ministerial Household in Early Tudor Government and Society' (University of California, Los Angeles, PhD thesis, 1975).

Shaw, A. N., 'The *Compendium Compertorum* and the Making of the Suppression Act of 1536' (University of Warwick PhD thesis, 2003).

Starkey, D. R., 'The King's Privy Chamber, 1485–1547' (University of Cambridge PhD thesis, 1973).

Ward, P. J., 'The Origins of Thomas Cromwell's Public Career: Service under Cardinal Wolsey and Henry VIII, 1524–1530' (University of London PhD thesis, 1999).

INDEX